MW01595490

RERUM BRITANNICARUM MEDII ÆVI
SCRIPTORES,

OR

CHRONICLES AND MEMORIALS OF GREAT BRITAIN
AND IRELAND

DURING

THE MIDDLE AGES.

# THE CHRONICLES AND MEMORIALS

OF

# GREAT BRITAIN AND IRELAND
## DURING THE MIDDLE AGES.

PUBLISHED BY THE AUTHORITY OF HER MAJESTY'S TREASURY, UNDER THE
DIRECTION OF THE MASTER OF THE ROLLS.

ON the 26th of January 1857, the Master of the Rolls submitted to the Treasury a proposal for the publication of materials for the History of this Country from the Invasion of the Romans to the Reign of Henry VIII.

The Master of the Rolls suggested that these materials should be selected for publication under competent editors without reference to periodical or chronological arrangement, without mutilation or abridgment, preference being given, in the first instance, to such materials as were most scarce and valuable.

He proposed that each chronicle or historical document to be edited should be treated in the same way as if the editor were engaged on an Editio Princeps; and for this purpose the most correct text should be formed from an accurate collation of the best MSS..

To render the work more generally useful, the Master of the Rolls suggested that the editor should give an account of the MSS. employed by him, of their age and their peculiarities; that he should add to the work a brief account of the life and times of the author, and any remarks necessary to explain the chronology; but no other note or comment was to be allowed, except what might be necessary to establish the correctness of the text.

a 2

The works to be published in octavo, separately, as they were finished; the whole responsibility of the task resting upon the editors, who were to be chosen by the Master of the Rolls with the sanction of the Treasury.

The Lords of Her Majesty's Treasury, after a careful consideration of the subject, expressed their opinion in a Treasury Minute, dated February 9, 1857, that the plan recommended by the Master of the Rolls "was well calculated for the accomplishment of this important national object, in an effectual and satisfactory manner, within a reasonable time, and provided proper attention be paid to economy, in making the detailed arrangements, without unnecessary expense."

They expressed their approbation of the proposal that each chronicle and historical document should be edited in such a manner as to represent with all possible correctness the text of each writer, derived from a collation of the best MSS., and that no notes should be added, except such as were illustrative of the various readings. They suggested, however, that the preface to each work should contain, in addition to the particulars proposed by the Master of the Rolls, a biographical account of the author, so far as authentic materials existed for that purpose, and an estimate of his historical credibility and value.

*Rolls House,*
*December* 1857.

# ROYAL AND HISTORICAL LETTERS

DURING THE REIGN OF

# HENRY THE FOURTH,

KING OF ENGLAND AND OF FRANCE,

AND LORD OF IRELAND.

EDITED BY THE

## REV. F. C. HINGESTON, M.A.,

OF EXETER COLLEGE, OXFORD, INCUMBENT OF
HAMPTON GAY, AND DOMESTIC CHAPLAIN TO VISCOUNTESS FALMOUTH,
BARONESS LE DESPENCER.

PUBLISHED BY THE AUTHORITY OF THE LORDS COMMISSIONERS OF HER MAJESTY'S
TREASURY, UNDER THE DIRECTION OF THE MASTER OF THE ROLLS.

VOL. I.

A.D. 1399—1404.

LONDON:

LONGMAN, GREEN, LONGMAN, AND ROBERTS.

1860.

# CONTENTS OF VOL. I.

a 3

# PREFACE.

# PREFACE.

AMONG the numerous Materials available for the History of Great Britain during the Middle Ages, widely differing as they do both in their nature and their importance, a high position must be assigned to the Letters of Sovereigns and other persons eminent in Church and State. "History," writes Sir Henry Ellis, "confined to the greater events which it " records, is usually certain and true; but in the co- " louring which writers give it, and which they are " proud to call the philosophy of History, it is too " frequently erroneous. Characters are drawn by those " who could not know the persons they describe; facts " are imperceptibly perverted to the uses of party; and " events which owe their origin to the simplest are " often traced back to the remotest causes. Thus cir- " cumstanced, History, however comprehensive in its " view, partakes too much of the embellished nature " of Romance."[1]

<sup></sup>*The value of Letters for historical purposes.*

How applicable all this is to the English Histories which have been written in recent years need scarcely be pointed out. Old materials have been worked up over and over again in new forms; while for additional facts, and the evidence of those contemporaneous and authentic documents which can alone supply the new, or reflect the light of truth upon the old, have been

---

[1] *See* "Original Letters," (First Series,) vol. i., page vii.

*The value of Letters for Historical purposes.* substituted the wild and unprofitable conjectures of the indifferent, or the deliberate perversions of the partizan.

The same charge is applicable, though probably in a far less degree, to the Mediæval Chronicles also. It was a common temptation in those times to flatter great men to an extent which would be simply ridiculous in our own day ; and it is, perhaps, hardly reasonable to expect from monks a really impartial account of the proceedings of detested heretics or the misdeeds of Popes and Prelates.

But Letters are the Key to History ; they unlock difficulties, detect false interpretations, and expose erroneous deductions. Written to convey the knowledge of facts, we gather simple and unvarnished facts from them ; and, if it were possible to discover a full and unbroken chronological series of them, most of the obstacles which the Historian now finds in his way would be removed. For, again to quote Sir Henry Ellis, they " bear the " impress of their respective times ; and, whilst many of " them regard affairs in which the writers were actively " engaged, all afford a closer and more familiar view of " characters, manners, and events, than the pen of the " most accomplished compiler of regular History, even if " he might be trusted, could supply. They unravel " causes of action which without their aid would be " impenetrable ; and even throw new light upon parts " of History which superficial readers suppose to be " exhausted." [1] It remains for us, accordingly, to estimate at their true value those which the destroying hand of time and of man may have spared to us, and to make the best use we can of them.

*Period comprised in this Series.* The series of Letters, the first instalment of which is presented to the public in this volume, is designed to illustrate that period of our History which embraces

---

[1] See " Original Letters," (First Series,) vol. i. p. viii.

the Reign of Henry the Fourth, from his accession on the 30th of September 1399, to his death on the 20th of March 1413.

There is, perhaps, no period of our more recent History of which we know less, certainly, than of the reigns of this King and his two immediate successors. The reign of Henry the Sixth especially, and the bloody Wars of the Roses which disturbed England for so many years and resulted in the overthrow of the House of Lancaster, may be said, with but little exaggeration, to be shrouded in mystery. The desolation which defiled the face of the land, covering it with the bodies of its own slain, extended to peaceful libraries and muniment rooms, and thousands of priceless documents, which can never be replaced, were swept away in the general destruction. Of those which have been preserved too many are still permitted to rest in an obscurity as dark as that which broods over the events which their careful study would bring to light, and from which only partial efforts have hitherto been made to rescue them. And this is especially true of the Historical Letters of the period, comparatively few of which have been published, notwithstanding their acknowledged importance.

*Necessity for its additional illustration.*

For the only systematic Collections of the Royal and Historical Letters of the Lancastrian period which have been made hitherto we are indebted to Thomas Rymer, Sir Henry Ellis, and Sir Harris Nicolas.[1]

---

[1] To these may be added the curious and useful Collection of the letters of a private family known as the " Paston Letters ;" and, perhaps, the Collections of Mrs. Green (Letters of Royal and Illustrious Ladies of Great Britain), and Mr. J. O. Halliwell (Letters of the Kings of England) ; but of these the two last consist of English translations only.

a 6

Existing Collections by Sir Henry Ellis, — Of these Collections, however, only one[1].—that of Sir Henry Ellis—consists entirely of Letters ; and of these but a very few indeed belong to our period, the majority having been written in the time of Henry the Eighth, and during subsequent reigns.

Rymer, — The "Fœdera" again, as its title imports, consists mainly of Treaties, Conventions, Instructions, and the like: a few documents, however, which may be strictly called Letters, are scattered here and there throughout its pages.

And scarcely less miscellaneous are the contents of the Sir Harris Nicolas. "Proceedings and Ordinances of the Privy Council of England,"[2] though a large number of most interesting and important Letters, gathered chiefly from the Cottonian MSS. Cleopatra, F. III., IV., and V., are embodied in it.

Many single Letters of this period are also to be found scattered about in miscellaneous works, and consequently of diminished value, as available Material, to the Historian, who may easily overlook them altogether.

Scope of the present work. — The present Collection will consist of all Letters of general or particular interest, which the Editor has been able to discover, and which have not been already published in one or other of the above works.

Letters, temp. Hen. IV. — The Letters of the Reign of Henry the Fourth, with which we are at present more immediately concerned, are derived almost entirely from MSS. in the Cottonian Collection, some from the Harleian MSS., others from MSS. preserved in the Public Record Office, and in the Bodleian Library, and a few from the Registers of English Bishops.

---

[1] Original Letters, illustrative of English History, including numerous Royal Letters. 1st series, 3 vols., London, 1824 ; 2nd series, 4 vols., 1827 ; 3rd series, 4 vols., 1846.

[2] From 10 Rich. II. to 39 Hen. VI., in seven volumes. Edited by Sir Harris Nicolas. London, 1834-7.

They are of three descriptions :— *The MSS.*

1. The Original Letters.

2. Contemporaneous copies of the Originals, including in many instances, the Original draughts.

3. Recent transcripts, made by Rymer for the "Fœdera," but never published.

The Letters are, for the most part, written in Latin and French. Some, however, are written in English; and a few in Portuguese and Spanish. *Their character.*

Of these last, and of all the French Letters, translations have been given.[1] *Translations.*

Of the MSS. themselves it is impossible to give a particular description in this place; they are of all shapes and sizes, and written some on vellum, some on paper. A foot-note is, however, appended to every Letter, with a reference to the MS. Collection in which it occurs, and stating the material on which it is written, and, as far as could be ascertained, whether it is original or merely a transcript. *Their present condition and arrangement.*

The MS. Cotton. Nero B. II., from which many of the Letters are taken, is a paper folio, consisting of 318 leaves. The contents, so far as they relate to this period, are written continuously in an early handwriting, and are probably nearly contemporaneous transcripts of the originals. *Cotton. MSS.*

MS. Brit. Mus. Addit., No. 14,820, consists of a collection of Original Letters, on paper, preserved in a case.[2]

The others are pasted into separate volumes, some carefully—others very carelessly; the endorsements being frequently pasted down, so as to be no longer

---

[1] The Editor has endeavoured to make his translations as literal as the idioms of the languages would permit; as well as to overcome the numerous difficulties which are always encountered in dealing with old French, especially with documents written in rude Flemish *patois*, such as the Duchess of Burgundy's Letters, and the still ruder French of the letters from Wales.

[2] They were bought of Payne and Foss in 1844. The seals are very perfect and of great interest.

*The MSS.* legible, or deliberately cut through in the attempt to reduce the Letter itself to a neat and uniform shape. The seals of the Original Letters have been occasionally preserved, but have more frequently been destroyed : traces of the wax, however, occur continually, and these instances are carefully recorded: in some cases they are the only certain proofs that a Letter is the Original.

*The Text.* The Text has been made with all possible care from the MSS. ; missing words, or parts of words, being supplied within brackets in all cases where it is obvious what had perished.[1] Thus, while an intelligible and readable text has been provided, the brackets indicate precisely the present state of the MSS. themselves.

*Chronological arrangement.* The Letters will be arranged in chronological order throughout ; and a Chronological Catalogue, drawn up for purposes of ready reference with all possible conciseness, will be prefixed to each volume.

This arrangement has been by far the most difficult part of the Editor's task : most of the Letters have no date except the day of the month, while in some cases even that has perished; and the dates assigned in the respective Catalogues of MSS. are so frequently erroneous, as to be calculated to mislead rather than to be of any service. This difficulty was very deeply felt by the learned Editor of the " Proceedings of the Privy Council," while he was engaged in preparing that work for the press ; and the present Editor, having carefully weighed the internal evidence in the case of every Letter, and done his best to secure perfect accuracy, and feeling, with Sir Harris Nicolas, that the uncertainty as to the result can only be equalled by the necessity for certainty,—desires to adopt as his own the free confession of that careful and painstaking man. " It is not " without much hesitation," he tells us in the Preface to his First Volume, " that he has in some cases ventured

---

[1] A few conjectural restorations, which occurred to the Editor after the sheets were printed, are given among the *Addenda.*

" to attribute a positive date to documents. This remark " more particularly applies to part of the Minutes and " Letters of the early years of the reign of Henry the " Fourth; for, as that monarch was engaged for two or " three consecutive years in subduing the rebels in Wales " and in the North, it not unfrequently happens that " nearly the same facts are mentioned in Letters written " in each of those years. Though the greatest trouble " has been taken to ensure accuracy in fixing the dates " of the articles alluded to—and the Editor trusts he has " seldom been wrong in the period to which he has " assigned them—he, nevertheless, suggests that no date " should be *implicitly relied upon* which does not occur " in the Letter or article itself."[1]

It remains to give a brief abstract of the contents of the Letters comprised in the present volume, so far, at least, as to enable the reader to connect them with similar Letters and other documents of the same period already published, and to appreciate in some degree the light which they throw upon contemporaneous history. To deal, however, as fully as might be desired with so large and varied a mass of materials within the limits of a Preface, is out of the question : the Editor can only hope to be able to afford such a clue to his volumes as may be necessary to assist the historical student in his practical use of them ; and to give the more general reader an intelligible analysis of their contents.

With this view, it has been considered desirable to group the Letters together according to a topographical arrangement, rather than in the chronological order in which they stand in the text of the work.

Letters of a miscellaneous character, which do not properly belong to any of these groups, will be briefly noticed in a separate article, at the end of the Preface.

---

[1] Proceedings and Ordinances of the Privy Council, vol. 1., page xii.

Scotland.   And, first, of the Letters which refer to the History of
A.D. 1398. our intercourse with SCOTLAND at this period.

The times, it is hardly necessary to remark, were most
eventful.   Since the reign of the first Edward there had
been no real peace ; truce after truce had been made, only
to be broken, and the pretensions of the English Kings
were such as to preclude the possibility of any lasting
reconciliation being effected between the rival kingdoms.
Richard was engaged with his expedition into Ireland,
and Henry, Duke of Lancaster, furious at the wrongs
which had been inflicted on him, was hastening to assert
his claim to the English crown.   Towards the close
of the year 1398, John, Duke of Lancaster, and the
Duke of Rothsay had met, and arranged that the truce
which expired at Michaelmas in that year, should be
prolonged till Michaelmas 1399.[1]

A.D. 1399.   That day proved to be the last of the reign of the ill-
fated English King ; and on its morrow, when Henry of
Lancaster usurped the throne, he found it necessary at
once to direct his attention to his northern neighbours,
who began without delay to ravage the border counties.
At the end of the month a March-day had been held
at Haddenstank, when the preliminaries of a truce[2] were
arranged ; and Henry wrote a Letter to Robert, the
Scottish King, (which reached him on the 3rd of October,)
reminding him of the fact, and requesting that immediate
steps might be taken for the declaration and confirmation
of the truce.   Robert replied, on the 6th, that he would
send an answer as soon as he had had an opportunity of
consulting with his Council.   Accordingly, on the 2nd
of November,[3] he again wrote to the English King,
agreeing to his proposal, and promising to take steps for

---

[1] See Rymer, viii. 65.                    [3] See p. 8.
[2] From Michaelmas 1399 to
Michaelmas 1400.   See p. 5.

pacifying his own people during the deliberations of the Scotland.
commissaries, if Henry would do the same. It appears, A.D. 1399.
however, that he was not successful in this, and that he
had been also guilty of some evasion, for Henry, in his
reply [1] (which is without a date), complains that his
first Letter had only been partially answered, that
Robert had not expressed his readiness to maintain
the truce according to its terms, and that since the
promise to pacify his subjects "very great and horrible
" outrages" had been perpetrated within the kingdom
of England [2] by the eldest sons of the wardens of the
Marches of Scotland, and by others of that realm. [3] Notwithstanding this, the English King gave orders to the
wardens of his Marches that they should meet at Kelso
on the 5th of January next ensuing to settle when
the commissaries should assemble to treat for peace,
and to make order for the pacifying of the people on
either side. [4]

This Letter was received by Robert, at Perth, as late A.D. 1400.
as the 4th of January, that is, the very day before
that appointed for the meeting. No reply was sent till

---

[1] Two draughts of this reply are
preserved. The first, which contains little more than an acknowledgment of Robert's letter, and a
promise to appoint commissaries,
is printed at page 12, note (2).
This appears to .have been considered too mild, or, perhaps, the
news of the outrages in the north
arrived after it was written; so the
strongly-worded letter given in the
text was substituted for it.

[2] " Scoti per tempus Parliamenti
. . . . quia partes Angliæ Boreales
per illud tempus premebantur
grandi pestilentia, partes illas hostiliter intraverunt, et Castrum de
Werk, quod deputatum fuerat custodiæ Domini Thomæ Gray, Militis . . . . ceperunt, et per tempus
aliquod tenuerunt . . . . aliaque

multa mala fecerunt in terra." Camd.
Walsingh. p. 362, 20.

[3] See p. 11.—It should be observed
that Robert addresses the English
King throughout simply as "Duke
of Lancaster," which Henry notices
in his reply (p. 11), " voz lettres a
nous come Duc de Lancastre, Comte
de Derby, et Seneschal d'Engleterre
darreinement envoiees." Later he
styles him " nostre treschier cousin
d'Engleterre."

[4] Letter VI., (p. 14,) which has
no date, either of the year or month,
relates to certain conferences which
were held at the close of the year
1400. It was probably written early
in the following year. Fulthorp,
Heron, Newerk, and Mitford were
commissioned on the 18th of March
1401. (Rymer viii., 185.)

b

Scotland. the 14th of March, when Robert wrote from Linlithgow
A.D. 1400. and again requested that there might be a meeting at
Haddenstank. But it was now too late. The English
were enraged by the continued acts of hostility committed by the Scottish borderers, and were also encouraged through the internal troubles which distracted
Scotland at that time, to undertake active measures for
their prevention. On the 9th of February a great
Council was held at Westminster, to take into consideration the dangers to which the kingdom was exposed,
and to provide a remedy. Among other matters it was
shown "coment les Escotz avoient ore tard fait grauntz
" invasions, arsures, chivachees, et attemptatz encountre
" les trieves, et purposent de faire ce mesme, par l'aide
" de ceux de France, sur les marches vers Escoce, si
" hastive resistence n'y soit purveu." [1] The greatest
enthusiasm prevailed, and the Lords spiritual and temporal taxed themselves that they might not endanger
the King's popularity by taxing his subjects. About
this time also, George Dunbar, Earl of March, who
had been " gretly wrangit be the Duc of Rothesay,
" the quhilk, he wrote to Henry, spousit my douchter,
" and now . . . spouses ane other wife, as it ys said,"
claimed relationship with the English King, and
offered to go over to his side, that he might have
his revenge on his enemies and "gete amendes of the
" wrangis and the defowle" that had been done him.[2]
Thus encouraged and strengthened Henry made preparations for the invasion of Scotland. On the 14th
of March, a letter was despatched to the Earl of
Westmoreland,[3] commanding him to meet the Earl
of March without delay,[4] and it was further determined, at the same time, to pay certain stipends and
sums of money to him for his allegiance.[5]

---

[1] *See* Nicolas, i. p. 103.
[2] *See* p. 23.
[3] The original draught of the
" Instructions issued on the 13th of
March, 1400, to Ralph Neville,

Earl of Westmoreland, and Christopher, Abbot of Alnwick," are
printed in Nicolas, i. 114.
[4] *See* p. 28.
[5] *See* p. 30, note (¹).

Numerous documents relating to the invasion (which Scotland. took place on the 14th of August) are printed by Rymer A.D. 1400. and Nicolas. The latter gives, among others, the King's Letter to the mayor, sheriffs, and aldermen of London, being one of the Letters sent at this time to the principal ports on the east coast of England, thanking the inhabitants for their faithful services and liberal contributions in time past, and requiring them to provide victuals for the King and his army, who were on their way to invade Scotland. The Letter to the authorities and people of Lynn, given in the present work, was of similar import.[1]

Allusion is also made to this invasion in a Letter from Peter Holt, written from London, on the 11th of July (shortly after Henry's departure), to the Emperor Manuel II., who was then at Paris on his way from the East to the English Court. Holt informs the Emperor that, "from the day on which his Lord, the "King " of England, took in hand the helm of his kingdom, the " Scots had inflicted not a few evils upon the realm, " in warlike manner, openly ; and that the King, for " the defence of his kingdom, was making the best of " his way towards the North with his army, that, God " helping him, he might resist their malice and their " inroads." He adds that, " the undertaking being so " arduous, no one can tell with certainty when he will " return ;" and he recommends the Emperor not to come to England till he has received some more definite information.[2]

The next Letter in our Collection relating to the A.D. affairs of Scotland is from the Earl of Douglas and 1401-2. Galloway to Henry the Fourth,[3] and was written on the 1st of February in a subsequent year. Its date is somewhat uncertain. In the Catalogue it is assigned to the year 1400, which is manifestly incorrect, as it contains allusions to a truce, to which the King was

---

[1] See p. 40.
[2] See p. 39.

[3] See p. 52.

b 2

Scotland.
A.D. 1402.
a party through the Earl of Northumberland, made in the spring of the year preceding that in which it was written, and therefore before his accession. It appears that a truce was arranged by the Earl of Northumberland in the year 1400,[1] which would fix the date of this letter in 1401, and to this year it has been assigned.[2] The writer accuses the Earl of Northumberland to the King, charging him with being the cause of the rupture of the truce between the two kingdoms, and .praying that the matter may be investigated and redress made. Henry, in his reply,[3] acquits the Earl, and shows that the fault lay on the other side. He also promises to send certain commissaries to Kelso in April, to discuss the treaty once more.

A.D. 1404.
Allusion is made, in a Postscript[4] to a Letter written to Henry IV., by Hugh Luttrell from Calais, on the 10th of January, 1404, to the Embassy which had been sent by the Council at Paris into Scotland, " ad con- " trahendum parentelam ex parte Gallicorum cum filio " Comitis de Dougleys, qui prætenditur heres apparens " in regno Scotiæ successurus."

The title of " Novelx des Marches d'Escoce" is given in the MS. to a Letter[5], written on the 13th of January, apparently in 1404, to Henry IV. by John Coppyll, Constable of Bamborough Castle, telling him that it was still safe, but in danger; for the Castles of Berwick, Alnwick, and Werkworth were kept by main force by William de Clifford and the Percies, who were prepared to hold these Castles against the King if possible. He adds that the said knights had " procured to themselves " a great multitude of men, and given them the livery " of the crescents" (le lyveray des cressauntz).[6] Clifford

---

[1] Rymer, viii. 166.

[2] Or it may, perhaps, be assigned to 1402.

[3] See p. 58.

[4] See p. 205.

[5] See p. 206.

[6] The badge of the House of Percy. See Nicolas i. 210,—" Et pluseurs chivachent devers lui leur cressans as braas."

and the Percies were publicly reconciled to the King on the 24th of June: the Earl of Northumberland had been pardoned in January.[1] Scotland. A.D. 1404.

In a letter from Richard Aston, written to the Duke of Burgundy, on the 18th of March in this year, a curious allusion is made to an advantage taken by the French of the disputes between England and Scotland.[2] He enumerates the injuries inflicted from time to time upon the English, and, among them, complains that " the men of Harfleur and others from divers parts of " the realm of France, under the pretence and colour- " able pretext of one or two Scotchmen domiciled and " inheriting among them, put to sea, and seized and " plundered from the servants and subjects of the King " of England more than 100,000l. sterling, over and " above the allowances of the merchants and mariners " . . . and all this " as in the name, and serving in the " war of the King of Scotland, paying no regard to the " article in the truce to the contrary."

- Our next Letter is dated the 26th of August, and is from Robert III. to the English King.[3] It simply refers to some intercourse which had been carried on between the two sovereigns through the medium of David Fleming, and is remarkable only for some words in the opening sentence indicative of the writer's desire for peace: he wishes for his cousin of England—"Salutem et quietis desiderium."[4]

The Letter from the Countess of March to Henry IV. has been placed next in the series, merely because it relates to the affairs of Scotland, and—there is internal evidence to prove—must have been written in this year. It contains, however, no mention of the time

---

[1] See Camd Walsingh, pp. 369, 371.

[2] See p. 218.

[3] See p. 298.

[4] An interesting Letter from " David Flemyng de Bygar" to Henry the Fourth will be found in Volume II. (10th Jan., 1405).

Scotland.
A.D. 1404. when it was written, or the place. It is not necessary to repeat in this place the oft narrated story of the Earl of March's sufferings and poverty after his defection from the Scottish cause. Since the death of Hotspur at Shrewsbury, it appears from this Letter, his English quarters had become most uncomfortable: his enemies, he feared, would ingratiate themselves with the King to his undoing; his debts were ruinous, and his very life was in danger from a plague, in the midst of which he was compelled to remain. Under these circumstances he prevailed upon his wife to write this piteous appeal to the King, for whose sake he had involved himself in so many perils.[1]

Wales. The Letters relating to the rebellion in WALES are numerous and of considerable interest. They should be read in connexion with the Letters on the same subject printed by Ellis and Nicolas, together with which they form a tolerably continuous series.

A.D. 1400. The first, written apparently in 1400, is from Lord Grey de Ruthyn to Griffith ap David ap Griffith. The Letter to which it is an answer is printed in Ellis (p. 5), as well as a Letter from Lord Grey to the Prince of Wales, enclosing both for his inspection (p. 3). All three are written in English, and are very striking examples of the almost savage character of the struggle in Wales, even at its very commencement. Griffith's Letter, in which he complains that he is the victim of treachery, and prays Lord Grey that he "wold her how the fals John Wele served" him, is not less fierce and barbarous in its menaces than rude and rugged in its language. Lord Grey might well call him "the strengest thiefe of Wales." But his own letter has not the advantage in point of courtesy; and the contrast is strong, certainly, between the

---

[1] *See* Appendix II.

formal civility of Griffith's concluding prayer, "Gode Wales.
"kepe your worschipfull astate in prosperite," and A.D. 1400.
the more honest but vindictive imprecations of the Lord
of Ruthyn, written, too, in mocking verse,—

> "But we hoope we shalle do the a pryve thyng ;
> A roope, a ladder, and a ring,
> Heigh on gallowes for to henge,
> And thus shalle be your endyng.
> And He that made the be ther to helpyng,
> And we on our behalfe shalle be welle willyng.
> For thy lettre is knowlechyng."

Sir Henry Ellis is, undoubtedly, right in assigning these
letters to the year 1400, in which the rising of the Welsh
commenced.[1] Lord Grey, it will be remembered, was,
by his unjust invasion of the lands and rights of Owen
Glyndwr, the immediate cause of the rebellion. He
contrived, however, by an unworthy stratagem, to
transfer the blame from himself to the man whom he
had injured, and he was commissioned by the English
King to put down the revolt. Arriving at Ruthyn, he
received and answered the menacing letter of Griffith ap
David ap Griffith, and wrote a report of the matter to
the Prince of Wales on the 23rd of June. In this letter
he begged him, among other matters, "to witte that I
"have resceyved our liege Lordes pryve seal, with your
"oun worshipfull lettres to me sent, commaundyng me
"unto see, and to appees the misgovernance and the
"riote *wich ye heiren that is begunnen* heer in the
"Marches of North Wales;" and he further asked,
"Plese hit you to . . . . giffe me a moore pleyner com-
"myssioun then I have yit."[2] This may be regarded as
definitely fixing the date. The three letters speak for
themselves and need no explanation.

---

[1] *See* Ellis (2nd Series) i. 2.  |  [2] Ibid., p. 3.

Our next Letter has no date, even of the day of the month. It contains, however, internal evidence sufficient to prove that it was written in the year 1401, and most probably in or about the months of May or June. It is addressed by Henry the Fourth to the Prince of Wales, and acknowledges the receipt of the Prince's Letter announcing that certain treaties had been carried on between his Council and the rebels in respect of the Castle of Conway. Sir Henry Percy had written to the Council from Carnarvon on the 3d of May 1401, informing them that North Wales was obedient in all points to the laws, except the rebels in the Castle of Conway, and Rees who was in the mountains, who (he expected) would shortly have to yield to the force which the Prince of Wales was preparing to send against them.[1] His anticipations appear to have been speedily fulfilled, and, accordingly, we find in the Minutes of the English Privy Council, 5 July, 2 Hen. IV. (1401), the following entry: — "Aucuns du Conseil de Monsieur " le Prince apporterent ovesques eux devant le Conseil " nostre Seigneur le Roy l'endenture fait parentre " Monsieur le Prince susdit et Monsieur Henri Percy " le filz, d'une part, et ceux qui pristrent et entrerent le " Chastel de Conewey d'autre part, au temps de la " deliverance et restitucion de mesme le Chastell."[2]

The Indenture here referred to, says Sir Harris Nicolas in a note on this passage, "does not appear " to be preserved, but the conditions may be presumed " from the annexed petition to Sir Henry Percy from " William ap Tudor and his brother, two of the prin- " cipal persons who defended that fortress ; which peti- " tion was, there can be little doubt, submitted by " Hotspur to the Council." The petition is printed in vol. i. p. 147. That this conjecture was right, is proved by the present Letter, which Sir Harris appears not to

---

[1] See Nicolas, i. 150.     |     [2] See Nicolas, i. 145.

have seen, for the King, in mentioning the fact that to himself and to his Council had been communicated, " to " what result the said William, Howel Vaughan,[1] and " all other companions and persons who are rebels with " him in the Castle of Conway, have finally arrived " by their *offer and supplication*," adds " of which " we have seen the copy."

The petition in question, in which William ap Tudor and Rees, his brother, offered to surrender Conway, " provided that a pardon were granted them and their " followers . . . and that a guarantee were given that " no ulterior proceedings should be instituted against " them for the burning of the town of Conway, or " any other offence by them or their followers pre- " viously committed," was unsatisfactory to the Prince, and to the King, his father, who, in the Letter under consideration, confirms the Prince's plans, and praises " the good arrangement of men-of-arms and archers, " and works made for the siege of the said Castle ;" promising to send a sufficient force to punish the rebels " according to their deserts," or at least to procure from them some treaty more agreeable and more ho- nourable than the offer contained in their petition. This determination resulted in the surrender of the Castle[2] to the royal forces before the 5th of July, on

Wales.
A.D. 1401.

---

[1] *See* Rymer, viii. 209.

[2] The surrender, however, was not altogether free from conditions, and recompense was ordered to be made to those who, for having trea- cherously seized it, were deprived of their lands. This appears by the Minutes of Council already quoted above : — " Item, come en la dite endenture soit entre autres choses contenuz que ceux qui traiterouse- ment pristrent le susdit Chastel ave- roient recompense pur les terres et tenemenz, rentz et possessions par eux forfaitz pour la dicte cause,— l'avis des ditz Seignurs du dit Con- seil est que, en cas que le Roy ave- roit les dites forfaitures a son oeps, adonques le Roy ferroit avoir as dites persones recompensacion pur mesmes les forfaitures [come lui plerroit], et si Monsieur le Prince averoit les dites forfaitures qadonqes recompensacion en serroit fait as ditz persones par mon dit Seigneur le Prince."

*Wales.*
*A.D. 1401.* which day, as we have seen above, the news of the event and the indenture that had been made on the surrender were submitted to the English Council.

Thus is the date of the King's Letter fixed by assigning to it its place among these documents, which mutually illustrate it and one another. It must have been written after Hotspur's Letter of the 3d of May, probably immediately after the petition of the rebels in Conway Castle, and before the surrender of the Castle was announced to the Council on the 5th of July.

The remainder of the Letter is interesting. The King's pleasure was, that all due precaution being taken, the Castle should be captured by a strong hand; and further, that pecuniary assistance should be forthcoming out of the Treasury, if it were needed; although, the Castle being the Prince's in fee, the expense ought properly to fall on him, and the sages of the English Council were of that opinion.

*A.D. 1402.* From a Letter of the Prince of Wales to John Spenser, his Receiver-general, dated the 6th of April, 1402, we find that Nicholas Burdon and William Spridlington were appointed to audit the accounts of his ministers in the Counties of Chester and Flint, from the 7th of April to the 2d July, 1401.[1]

*A.D. 1403.* The Letters of the year 1403 are numerous and valuable.

The first was written by John Faireford, Receiver of Brecon, on the 4th of July.[2] The endorsement has been destroyed, so that it is doubtful who were the "Honures Sires" to whom it was addressed. It is, however, almost certain that the Sheriff and other authorities of the County of Hereford were intended, as in a Letter from them to the King, dated the 7th of July,[3] allusion

---

[1] *See* p. 95.
[2] *See* p. 138.

[3] *See* p. 146.

is made to such a Letter as this having been just received by them.

Faireford's object in writing was to obtain immediate assistance, as the rebellion was making rapid progress in his neighbourhood. The Warden of Dynevor had, that same morning, written thus to him,—"Oweyn Glyndour, " Henri Don, Res Duy, Res ap Grff ap Llewellyn, and " Res Gethin, hau y won the town of Kermerdyn, and " Wygmor, Constable of the Castell, hadd y ȝeld op the " Castell of Kermerdyn to Oweyn, and hau y brend the " town,[1] and y slay of men of town mor than l. men; " and thei budd yn purpos to Kedweli, and a seche ys " y ordeynyd at the Castell that I kepe, and that ys " gret peril for me, and all that buth wydde me."[2] This letter contained other news of an equally alarming character, and was evidently written under the influence of a panic : they were failing in "vitels and men, and " namlich men," and the writer suggested that they should "come bi niȝt and stele away to Brechnoc," abandoning their Castle to its fate. Moreover, while Faireford was writing, information was brought to him that Glyndwr was at Llandovery, and that his power was rapidly increasing. Brecon itself was threatened; the danger was imminent ; the need of aid pressing.

On the 7th of July, the crisis becoming still more serious, Faireford wrote to the King,[3] and enclosed a Letter which he had received from John Skidmore, informing him that "al Kermerdyn schire, Kedewely, " Carnwaltham, and Yskenyn ben sworyn to Oweyn

---

[1] Caermarthen was not burned immediately on its being taken, but after an interval of a day or two, as we learn from another Letter : if this be borne in mind, some apparent discrepancies in these Letters will be easily explained. It is not to be expected that men in such danger, and writing in such a condition of excitement, should always state minute facts with literal accuracy ; not unfrequently traces of evident, but doubtless unintentional, exaggeration will be observed.

[2] *See* Ellis (2nd Series), i. 14.

[3] *See* p. 141.

" yesterday, and he lay to nyȝt was yn the Castel of " Drosselan with Rees ap Gruffuth ; and ther y was and " spake with hym upon truys, and prayed of a sauf- " conduyt under his seal to send home my wif and " hir moder, and thair mayne, but he wold none graunte " me."[1] Skidmore further stated that Pembrokeshire was threatened, and that Glyndwr " halt hym siker of " al the Castell and Townes in Kedewelly, Gowerslond, " and Glamorgan, for the same cuntries hade under- " take[2] the seges of hem til thei ben wonnen."[3] His Letter was " written at the Castel of Carreckennen[4] " the v. day of Juil."

Faireford also states that Brecon is threatened, and that the enemy are doing all the mischief they can in its immediate neighbourhood, and especially in the Manor of Bryn-Llys ; and he declares that ruin can be averted no longer unless he be reinforced.

The same night Faireford again wrote to the King,[5] reiterating his urgent appeal for immediate assistance. A second Letter from Jenkin Hanard, written on the 4th of July, had just reached him, and contained most alarming intelligence. Glyndwr " logged hym at Seint Cler, " and destruid al the contre about," and as for Caermarthen, it was not then decided whether "the Castell and " Town shall be brend or no." The enemy were in great strength around Dynevor Castle, for " Oweyn ys moster

---

[1] *See* Ellis (2nd Series), i. 19.

[2] Hence the strong language of Faireford in this and his previous Letter,—" All the Welsh nation is " adhering to this evil purpose of " rebellion, and they are assured " thereto, how fully from one day " to another, by the support they " give to it, clearly appears more " openly." . . . "The whole Welsh " nation are by all these said " parties confirmed in this rebellion, " and with good will consent to-

" gether, as openly appears from " day to day, by their governance, " and also by their support against " you and all your faithful ones ; " may it please your royal Majesty " to ordain a final destruction of " all the false nation aforesaid, or " otherwise all your faithful ones " in these parts are in great peril."

[3] *See* Ellis (2nd Series), i. 20.

[4] Carreg Cennen.

[5] *See* p. 144.

" a Monday was, as they seyyn hem selvyn, viij. mill. Wales.<br>A.D. 1403. " and xij$^x$ spers, such as they wer."[1]

On this same 7th of July was written the Letter from the Authorities of the County of Hereford to Henry IV.[2], to which allusion has already been made. They report that, in compliance with the commands of the King, they had proceeded to Brecon and had removed the siege; but that while they were yet waiting to announce this, two letters had arrived, informing them that the rebels were rising again, and purposed " to come " in haste, with a great multitude to Brecon, and to " take the town, and to invade the marches and coun- " ties adjoining, to their destruction." One of these undoubtedly was from Faireford,[3] as his words are quoted very closely.

The writers conclude by asking for speedy assistance, and they add that it will be of little use unless the King can come *in person*, and support by his presence

---

[1] *See* Ellis (2nd Series), i. 15, 16.—To this year and month must be assigned the original Letter from the Mayor and Burgesses of Caerleon to those of Monmouth, preserved in Cleopatra F. III. fol. 116, and printed in Ellis (2nd Series) i. 21. Caermarthen had been taken, and Glyndwr from thence had sent " after Hopkyn ap Thomas of Gower " to come and speke with hym upon " trewes. And when Hopkyn come " to Owein he priede hym, in as " meche as he huld hym Maister of " Brut, that he schuld do hym to " understonde how and what maner " hit schold be falle of hym." The Letter, further, contained tidings " that ther was a day of batell " y take by twyxt the worthy Baron " of Carewe and Owein Glyndor " . . . . that thys day of bataill " schulde have be do the xij. day of

" Jule; and the ny$\mathfrak{z}$t be fore that " thys bataill schulde be do, Oweyne " wes y purpos to have yvoidede " ym to the Hull azeinward; and " for he wold y wete whar his " way wer clere y nowe to passe. " $\mathfrak{z}$yf he hede nede, to the Hull, he " send vij. C. of his meine to serche " the weyes, and thes vij. C. menne " went to serche thys weyes, and " ther thys vij. C. menne were y " mette with the Baron's menne of " Carew, and islay up everychone, " that ther was no$\mathfrak{z}$t on that sc . . . " . . . . . . alyve."—It is satisfactory to be able to assign to this important and most curious Letter its proper place in the Welsh series, which no writer who has used it has attempted hitherto.

[2] *See* p. 146.

[3] *See* p. 139.

those who had already for his sake sustained "grievous costs and labours," and had the same prospect still before them. The desire that the King should endeavour to suppress the rebellion in person became at this time all-engrossing, and the general impression seems to have been that nothing less would be of the slightest avail. This is very strongly put in two Letters, written to the King somewhat later in the year, from Hereford, by Richard Kingeston, Dean of Windsor, to which we shall have occasion to recur presently.

Our next Letter is from Hugh de Waterton to the King. It is dated at London, and appears[1] to have been written on the 13th of July.

Skidmore, in his Letter to Faireford on the 5th of July, had charged him thus,—"Wherfore wryteth to "Sir Hugh Waterton, and to all thilke that ye suppose "wol take this mater to hert, that thei exite the Kyng "hederwardes in al hast to vengen hym on summe of "his false traytors, the wheche he hath overmeche "chereyschid."[2] And Waterton, in this Letter, informs the King that "a servant of the Receiver of Brecon had brought to him a letter of news from those parts, directed to his Master by the Lieutenant of the Lord Audley at Llandovery. Waterton was in ill health at the time, and afraid to go out for fear of "taking cold." He could not, therefore, follow Henry, who had set out for the North, and this Letter was written because it was necessary that the alarming news which he had received should be communicated at once to the King, and his Majesty urged to send into Wales without delay a sufficient number of knights and others, or otherwise, on his arrival there, he would "find all in confusion."

On the 10th of July Henry was at Higham-Ferrers,[3] on his way to join the Percies, and on the 16th at

---

[1] *See* p. 151, note (¹).

[2] *See* Ellis (2nd Series), i. 20.

[3] *See* Nicolas, i. 206.

Burton-on-Trent, where he first heard of their revolt.[1] Wales. A.D. 1404. On the 23d he defeated them at Shrewsbury, and at once departed for the North to restore tranquillity in the Border Counties. On the 25th he was at Stafford;[2] at Pontefract on the 4th of August;[3] at Doncaster on the 17th;[4] on the 18th at Worksop.[5]

On the 23d William de Beauchamp, of Abergavenny, wrote to the King some particulars of the rebellion, and especially what had befallen one John Assheby, a soldier in his service at Abergavenny.[6] He takes occasion, at the same time, to tell the King what danger he is in for want of succour, and that, if it does not arrive soon, he "holds himself for destroyed." This Letter was written at Hereford.[7]

Henry was now on his way to Wales, and reached Worcester on the 8th of September.

On the 3d, Kingeston, Dean of Windsor, and Archdeacon of Hereford, wrote to him from Hereford in very urgent terms,[8] giving a most alarming account of the proceedings of the rebels,—"they have captured and " slain, within your county of Hereford, many men, " and beasts in great number." . . . . . "Send me this " night, or early to-morrow morning at the latest, " Master Beaufort, or some other valiant person, who " is willing and able to labour, with one hundred " lances and six hundred archers, until your most " gracious arrival to the salvation of us all, for other- " wise, I hold all the country to be destroyed." This Letter is written partly in French and partly in English,

---

[1] *See* Nicolas, i. 206-8.
[2] *See* Rymer, viii. 320.
[3] Ibid., p. 321.
[4] Ibid., p. 324.
[5] Ibid.
[6] *See* p. 152.
[7] On the 8th of September the King, at Worcester, issued an order " De Castris in partibus Walliæ " custodiendis." One of these was

directed " Willielmo Beauchamp, " Chivaler, pro custodia Castrorum " de Bergeveney et Harald Ewyas." (*See* Rymer, viii. 328, 9.) On the 14th, at Hereford, he gave power to receive unto his grace rebels pertaining to these Castles " Carissimo Consanguineo suo, Willielmo " Beauchamp."
[8] *See* p. 155.

the two languages being mingled in a wonderful manner, as though the writer thought French the proper thing, but at times was so led away by his eagerness in begging the King to come as to be unable to endure the trammels of the less familiar language, and so resorted to his native tongue. " Jeo prie," he ends his epistle, " la Benoit Trinite que vous ottroie bone vie " ove tresentier sauntee a treslonge durre, *and sende* " *ʒowe sone to ows in help and prosperitee; for in* " *good fey, I hope to Al Mighty God that ʒef ʒe come* " *ʒoure owne persone, ye schulle have the victorie of all* " *ʒoure enemyes. And for salvation of ʒoure Schire* " *and Marches al aboute, treste ye nought to no* " *Leutenant.*"[1]

---

[1] *See* p. 158.—Kingeston had written a somewhat similar letter, in the same excited strain, and with the same curious mixture of English and French, some two months earlier. This letter [printed in Ellis (2nd series), i. 17.] is dated the 8th of July. He writes thus to the King, "de jour en " autre y vienent Lettres de Gales, " contenantz lettre illeoques par " queles vous pourrez entendre " qe toute la pais est perdu *sy* " *vous ne venez le plus hastif-* " *ment.* Sur quoy vous plese vous " taillor devers noz parties ave " toute le poer qe vous poez, " en chivachant si bien de noet " come de jour, pour salvation " des parties. Et vous plese asavoir " qe il est graunt vergoigne, si " bien come per de qe vous per- " derez ou suffrez estre perduz le " pais en vostre comencement, " qe voz nobles auncestres ount " gaignez, et pour sy longe temps " peisiblement tenuz, car les gentz " parlont tresmalvaisement. Et " j'envoie a vostre noblesse la " copie d'une Lettre q'est venuz " de John Skydmore y cest matin. " . . . . . Escrit en haste [and " above the line 'grant haste'], a " Herford." The allusion to the letter from John Skidmore is curious : without doubt it was written on the 5th, and was a duplicate of that sent to Faireford on the same day, portions of which have been quoted above. The English postscript to Kingeston's Letter is as follows : — " And for Gode's " love, my lyge Lord, thinkith on " ʒour self and ʒour astat, or be " my trowthe all is lost elles ; " but and ʒe come ʒoure self all " other wolle followin aftir. And " ot, on Fryday last [6 July] " Kermerdyn town is taken and " brent, and the Castell ʒolden be " Ro. Wygmore, and the Castell " Emelyn is y ʒoldin; and slayn " of the toune of Kermerdyn mo " thanne 1. persones. Writen in " ryght gret haste on Sunday; " and Y crye ʒow mercy, and " putte me in ʒoure hye grace " that Y write so schortly ; for be " my trowthe that Y owe to ʒow, " it is needfull."

Henry reached Worcester on the 8th, and remained Wales.<br>A.D. 1403. there till the 10th, or perhaps later (see Rymer viii. 330). On the 14th we find him at Hereford, and thus the good Archdeacon had his wish; but the results of the royal presence must have sadly disappointed his too sanguine expectations. Glyndwr was not to be crushed so easily.

Our next Letter is from the Constable of Kidwelly to Henry IV., and was written on the 3d of October. " Henry Don, and all the rebels of South Wales, with " the men from France and Bretagne,[1] were coming " towards Kidwelly," and had "destroyed all the grain " on every side around the town." The castle and all within it[2] were "destroyed and undone for ever," unless immediate succours could be sent. Allusion has been made in previous Letters to the dangers threatening Kidwelly; but it does not appear what was the result of this appeal to the King.

Allusion is made, incidentally, to the absence of the King in Wales at this time, in a Letter from the Privy Council to Conrad de Jungingen,[3] who had demanded the restitution of certain ships and merchandise captured from his subjects by the English. The Council replied that the King had just before, " with his warlike army " girded himself for a journey towards the remote parts " of Wales subject to his sway, to do justice upon his

---

[1] The main army of the French, long preparing for invasion, did not land in Wales till 1405. Smaller bodies of auxiliaries were, however, sent to Glyndwr earlier. In a Letter from the inhabitants of Shropshire to the King, dated 1 April 1403, allusion is made to "Voz "rebelles avanditz, et lez Fraunces ore de novel a eux venuz." (*See* Nicolas, i. 77). And later, in July, a body of French land-

ed in South Wales and burned Tenby.

[2] In the "Ordinances of the Council respecting the fortresses of Wales, 3 or 4 Hen. IV." occur the following entries :—
" ✚ Kedwelly—Mons. Johan " Oldecastelle.—xl. lanc., cxx. ar- " chiers.
"✚ Item—le Constable illeoques. " —xij. lanc., xxiiij. archiers."

[3] *See* p. 162.

c

*Wales.*
*A.D. 1403.*

" subjects in those parts, who, led away by rash daring,
" had ventured to assume a spirit of rebellion against
" him and against their own allegiance." They consented to the immediate restoration of so much of the property as had been found in English ports, but declared that restitution of the scattered property could not be made until "their Lord's return in peace." This Letter was written on the 5th of October.

*On the
Chronology of
Letters
LVI. to
LXII.*

A few words are necessary in explanation of the Chronology of the seven Letters, LVI. to LXII. inclusive, and the reasons for assigning them all to the year 1403.

The MS. Cleopatra, F. III., from which they are taken, is simply mentioned in the Cottonian Catalogue, and no Calendar of its contents is given. Consequently no dates are assigned to any of the Letters or Articles it contains. The Letters are themselves without dates, and, with two exceptions, the endorsements have been cut away and destroyed.

Other Letters preserved in the same MS. (viz. those printed by Sir Henry Ellis), which are clearly alluded to in these Letters and manifestly belong to the same year with them (as we have shown above), have been used by various writers in a confused manner, and evidently without a knowledge of their true date. This has arisen from mistaking one expedition of Henry IV. into Wales for another; and, also, from confounding the ravages made by Glyndwr in certain places in one particular year with those committed by him in the same places in other years. Indeed, the similarity of events, really quite distinct, at this period, is very puzzling, and the Letters can scarcely be said to contain sufficient internal evidence of a historical character to enable us to fix with certainty the year in which they were written. Since, however, it is manifest, from the evident connexion between them already pointed out, that all were written in the same year, the discovery of the date of one would

decide that of the whole : and this is afforded by two of those in the present series, and by one in Ellis, though it has hitherto, apparently, escaped observation. Wales. A.D. 1403.

Faireford's two Letters to Henry IV., written on the same day, are dated "le vij. jour de Juyllet." In both Letters the date is also given at the commencement as well as at the end, and, in addition, *the day of the week ;* thus,--(1.) "mesme ceste y *Samady,* al houre de none, le vij. jour de Juyllet ;" (2.) "yceste *Samady,* a noet, le vij. jour de Juyllet." Now the 7th of July fell on a Saturday during the reign of Henry IV. twice only, viz., in the year 1403 and in 1408. The most cursory reader of these Letters will see at a glance that they could not have been written in the latter year ; of that there is abundant proof. The evidence, therefore, that they were written in 1403 may be considered complete.

Corroborative proof of this is afforded by the third Letter (No. VI. in Sir Henry Ellis's Collection), being the first of the two from Richard Kingeston to the King. It is dated "le viij. jour de Juyll," and in the Postscript we find that it was "writen in ryght gret haste on *Sunday.*" It is moreover stated in this Postscript that "on *Fryday last* Kermerdyn town is taken and brent." This, then, was July the 6th ; and it will be remembered that Jenkin Hanard had informed Faireford, that, as to Carmarthen, it was not decided whether "the Castele and Town schale be brend or no" at the time when he wrote, viz., on Wednesday (July the 4th), two days before the calamity took place.

The interest and value of these remarkable Letters, and the circumstance that their true date has been misapprehended hitherto, will, it is hoped, afford sufficient apology for the length at which the subject has been discussed in this place.

---

[1] *See* above, and Ellis (2nd Series), i. 16.

c 2

Wales.    To return to the movements of the King.  On the
A.D. 1403. 15th of September we find him at Devennok (Devynock,
in the County of Brecon), where he appears to have
had an interview with Faireford.[1]

On the 29th he was at Carmarthen.[2]

On the 8th of October at Gloucester.[3]

On the 25th at Bristol; and here was written the
Letter to the Privy Council, printed at page 167.

The latter portion only of this Letter relates to the
affairs of Wales.  First, he thanks them for " the brave
" exploit of the Earl of Warwick and the Lord Audley,"
" of which they had made mention in their Letters.

Richard Beauchamp, Earl of Warwick, was (according
to Dugdale), in 1403, "retained to serve the King for
" one whole year with one hundred men at arms, and
" three hundred archers, John Lord Audley being then
" of his retinue."[4]  In the same year, as we learn from
a curious life of this Earl,[5] written by John Rouse, who
died on the 14th of January, 1491, he distinguished
himself against Glyndwr, and against the Percies at
Shrewsbury.  Rouse gives pictures of both events,
with the following explanations :—

" Here shewes howe at theis daies appeared a blasyng
" sterre called *Stella Comata*,[6] which after the seiyng of

---

[1] *See* Rymer, viii. 331, 332.

[2] *See* Nicolas, i. 217.

[3] *See* Rymer, viii. 334.

[4] The following entries occur in
the Minutes of the Council, Nov.,
2 Hen. IV. 1401 :—

" Item seront demorantz par icel·
" temps au Chastiel de Llanandevrry
" dys hommes d'armes et vingt
" archiers as coustages du Sire
" d' Audeley.

" Item seront par icel temps
" demourantz au Paynescastille en
" Elvel dousze hommes d'armes
" et vingt et quatre archiers as

" constages du Counte de Warre-
" wyk." (Nicolas i. 174.)

[5] MS. Cotton. Julius E. iv.,
fol. 201.

[6] " Anno gratiæ M.CCCC.II. co-
" meta apparuit mense Martio, primo
" inter chorum et septentrionem,
" videlicet in circio flammas emit-
" tens, postremo comas in boream
" transferens; præsignans fortassis
" effusionem humani sanguinis circa
" partes Walliæ et Northumbriæ ex
" post futuram." Camd. Walsingh.
p. 364.

" Clerkys, signyfied great deth and blodeshede. And
" soue upon beganne the warre of Wales by Owen of
" Glendour, their chief capteyn, whom amonges other
" Erle Richard so sore sewed, that he hadde nere hande
" taken hym, and put hym to flyght, and toke his
" baner, and moche of his people, and his banerer."

Wales.<br>A.D. 1403.

" Here shewes how at the battell of Shrewsbury,
" between Kyng Henry the Fourth and Sir Henry
" Percy ; Earl Richard then beyng in the Kynges party,
" ful notably and manly behaved hymself, to his great
" laude and worship ; in which batell was slayne the said
" Sir Henry Percy, and many others with hym ; and on
" the Kynges party there was slayne in the Kynges cote
" armoure, chef of al other, the Erle of Stafford, Erle
" Richards auntes son, wyth many other in gret nombre;
" on whoes sowles God have mercy. Amen."[1]

The former event is probably that to which the
King here alludes as " le bon exploit."

" L'exploit de Monsieur le Duc d'Everwyk " is evidently connected with the allusion made in the title of
this Letter to " le paiement pur le garnison a Kermerdin." On the 8th of October the Earl of Somerset,
the Bishop of Bath, Lord Grey, and Sir Thomas Beaufort, having custody of Caermarthen, had written to
the Council, and desired that they would send thither
" le Duc d'Everwyk, ou autre Seignieur, ou capitain
" . . . . ovecque une certayne nombre de gens d'armes
" et archiers . . . pour la save garde du dicte ville et
" du pais environ, sicomme il estoit accorde et apoynte
" au departir de nostre Seigneur le Roy de deca." This
arrangement was consented to, and the King had
written[2] " to cause payment to be sent to him, at

---

[1] *See* Strutt's Donba 'Anẓel-cynnau, (vol. ii., page 122) in which the whole of these remarkable illus-trations, fifty-nine in number, are engraved.

[2] *See* Nicolas i. 217.

Wales.
A.D. 1403.
" Bristol, by Saturday next (after the date of this " second Letter[1]), for the Duke's more speedy expe- " dition."

" Henry remained in or near Wales until November, " when he returned to London, leaving the Prince of " Wales to oppose the rebels."[2]

A.D. 1404. The next Letter relating to Welsh affairs is that from Richard, Bishop of Bangor (whom Glyndwr had de- prived) to the King: it is dated at London, the 2nd of August. Angelus Cristofore, he says, and other mer- chants, had received letters from their friends in Bruges, which contained information to the effect that the Count de la Marche of France was ordained against Wales " cum quingentis bassinettis et ij$^c$ balisteriis." This in- formation was shortly after laid before the Council assembled at Lichfield on the 29th of August, as ap- pears from Nicolas, i. 233,—" En primes considerees les " novelles a nostre Soverein Seignur le Roy reportees " que le Conte de la Marche de France a fait assembler " en le haven de Harfleur lx. niefs, et les a fait estu- " fer de gens d'armes et balestiers prest pour passer en " pays de Gales en toute haste possible; et considerez " aussi que nostre dit Seigneur le Roy ne poet tantost " estre accompaignez a son honeur d'aler as dictes " parties de Gales." It was recommended, in conse- quence of this intelligence, that the King should remain at or near Tutbury until the assembling of Parliament.

Numerous allusions to this threatened invasion occur in the later Letters written by the Ambassadors to Flanders from Calais. These will, however, be more conveniently described hereafter in their proper place.

---

[1] Saturday, October the 27th, 1403.
[2] See Nicolas, i., page liv.

The Lettersillustrative of Irish History[1] comprised in the present Volume, though only two in number, are of considerable interest. Ireland.<br>A.D. 1401.

The first[2] was written on the 20th of August 1401, to Henry IV., by Thomas Cranley, Archbishop of Dublin,[3] and Chancellor of Ireland, Laurence Merbury, the Treasurer, Janico Dartasso, the Admiral, and others, who complain that their poverty is such that the government of the country is with difficulty carried on; that Thomas of Lancaster, the Lieutenant of Ireland, is " so destitute of money that he has not a penny " in the world nor can borrow a single penny, be- " cause all his jewels and plate are spent and sunk in " wages." They add, that " his soldiers are departing " from him, and the very people of his household " on the point of departing;" and they earnestly beg that relief may be sent to them, for, by reason of the danger of their position, they cannot go in person to the King, none of them daring to leave the Lieutenant alone.

The next Letter[5] is from Thomas of Lancaster himself, and it tells the same tale. It was written to the King, his father, from Drogheda, on the 18th of February in the following year. Stephen le Scrope had occasion to go to the King's presence " to plead before him con- " cerning the charge of Roxburgh Castle;"[6] and he A.D. 1402.

---

[1] The more remarkable Irish Letters that have been found belong to the period comprised in the Second Volume.

[2] See p. 73.

[3] See Rymer, viii. 208.

[4] Want of money was Henry's great difficulty, especially in the commencement of his reign. See page lxxxviii.

[5] See p. 85.

[6] Minutes of the Council; November, 1401 :—Quant au Chastiel " de Rokesburgh soient lettres du " prive seel a Monsieur Ric. Le " Scrope, piere, et Monsieur Ro- " ger Le Scrope, frere de Monsieur " Estiphienne Le Scrope, Capitain " du Chastiel, pour venir devant le " Conseil, et y trouver seurte de bien " garder le dit Chastiel, *ou autre-* " *ment soit traictie avec autres qi icel* " *Chastiel vueillent garder.*" This was, probably. the difficulty which required, shortly after, the presence of Le Scrope in London.—Mention

Ireland. appears to have been the bearer of this Letter. The
A.D. 1402. Prince had done his best, but all was going wrong, and
the soldiers had finally refused to serve any longer
unless their wages were paid : he craves assistance, and
requests that Scrope may be sent back to him speedily,
as he could not do without him, no other knowing so
well the circumstances of the people.

Denmark, The Letters relating to our intercourse with Den-
Sweden, mark, Sweden, and Norway (at that time united under
and
Norway. the joint rule of Eric IX. and Margaret his mother),
A.D. 1401. are numerous, and not devoid of interest, though illustrative of delays and procrastination in international
business rather than of any work done. They tell,
indeed, one long tale of postponements, and excuses
from Ambassadors for delay in going or in coming ;
and though the series commences as early as the year
1401, it proceeds *re infecta* till the middle of 1406,—
beyond the limits of the present Volume, -- when
Philippa, second daughter of Henry the Fourth, left
England for the court of her husband Eric, to whom
she had been contracted in May 1402.

On the 3rd of May Henry the Fourth, at Westminster,
granted Letters of safe-conduct to Peter Lucke,[1] Archdeacon of Roeskilde, and Ambassador of the Queen of
Denmark, extending from that date to Christmas in the
same year, on account of " certain matters, affecting
" himself and his kingdom, as well as the said Queen
" and her kingdom."[2] Somewhere about the same
time, it would appear, Richard Yonge, Bishop of
Bangor, and John Perant, were appointed by the English

---

is made in a letter of the 28th of
February in this year, from the
King to the Treasurer, of " an
" indenture made between our
" dear and faithful knight, Ste-
" phen Le Scrope, Warder of our
" Castle of Roxburgh, and the

" Collectors [of Customs at South-
" ampton], for five hundred and
" sixty pounds." (*See* p. 91.)

[1] The name is variously spelt,
*Lucke, Lukke,* and *Lykke,* in the
MSS.

[2] *See* Rymer, viii. 192.

King to go into Denmark on the same business. On the 5th of April the King wrote to them instructing them to return,[1] and in their reply, dated at Roeskilde, the 18th of June, they state the reasons for their necessary delay, and promise to avail themselves of the first opportunity that shall offer. They add, that they distrust the "navigia linguæ Theutonicorum," and must obtain, before starting, Letters commendatory from the King and Queen, or at least from the Bishop of Roes-kilde.[2] The Bishop of Bangor contrived, however, to effect his return before the 5th of July, on which day he attended a Meeting of the Privy Council in England.[3]

Our next Letter is from Eric IX. to Henry IV.[4] It is dated the 15th of October. John Parant, who had remained behind in Denmark, was the bearer of this Letter, excusing his delay: the Letter contained no particulars of the business in hand, as Parant, and Peter Lucke (who accompanied him), had been fully instructed, and were ordered to inform the King, as to the object of their mission, by word of mouth. They did not leave for England, however, till on or after the 25th, on which day Lucke's two credentials, one from Eric,[5] the other from the Queen his mother,[6] were written.

These negotiations had reference to two proposals of marriage, (1), of Henry, Prince of Wales, with Katherine of Denmark, the sister of Eric, which was never brought about ; (2), of the Princess Philippa, daughter of Henry the Fourth, with Eric himself.

On the 18th of April 1402, the King, at Windsor, wrote to the Council in reference to the latter of these schemes, announcing to them that, since he had last met them, he had received at the hands of the Bishop of Bangor and John Parant, a Letter from the King of

*[margin note]* Denmark, &c. A.D. 1401.

*[margin note]* A.D. 1402.

---

See p. 67.
[2] See p. 68.
See Nicolas, i. 145.

[4] See p. 77.
[5] See p. 80.
[6] See p. 81.

Denmark, and that, after well considering its contents, " and especially an article touching the desire which he " and the people of his realm had, that the marriage " should come to pass between the said King and his " daughter Philippa," he was decidedly of opinion that unless a more suitable answer were devised than had been yet determined on, the other party would have good cause for refusing the marriage altogether. Accordingly the King, who was clearly anxious for the match, sent to them for their approval a copy of a Letter, such as, in his opinion, it was right to send, and requested their advice on the matter.[1]

The Bishop of Bangor was despatched to Denmark again shortly after this; for, as he tells us himself, he landed " in the parts of Dacia, on the feast of Saint James," *i.e.*, on the 25th of July.[2]

On the 2nd of October Peter Lucke wrote to Henry IV. from Copenhagen,[3] excusing the delay that had occurred in the departure for England of the Danish Ambassadors; assuring him that they would shortly leave, and hoped, if the wind served, to reach England before winter. He mentions, also, that peace had been re-established in the kingdom, and gives some interesting particulars of the termination of the struggle which had been raging in Gothland, and of the truce between the Prussians and his own sovereign, to which it had led.

Our next letter is from the Bishop of Bangor, William Burchier, Richard Dereham, and John Parant, to the Privy Council. It is dated the 2nd of November.[4] They had been appointed ambassadors, for the purpose of negotiating the two royal marriages, on the 28th of June, and landed in Denmark, as we have already seen, on the 25th of the following month. They were not able, however, to proceed at once to business. The

---

[1] *See p.* 97.
[2] *See* p. 117.
[3] *See* p. 114.
[4] *See* p. 117.

war in Gothland had ended, indeed, as early as March, Denmark,
but it was not till October the 2nd that Peter Lucke &c.
was able to write of his King and Queen,—"Optata A.D. 1402.
" gaudent sospitate in tribus regnis suis, pacificeque
" gubernant."[1] The Ambassadors found that the Queen
was absent holding a treaty with the Prussians in a
distant part of her kingdom; as well as engaged in
burning " the man who falsely and feignedly asserted
" that he was the King of Denmark, Norway, etc.,"
and in other state concerns of importance. It was
not till the 10th of October that an interview was
granted to them; and " then," as they tell us in
the present Letter, " having inspected the person of
" the Lady Katherine, according to the full intent
" of their instructions, they began, all of them toge-
" ther, to treat with the said King and Queen in
" person on the business which had been committed to
" their management, in the Castle of Helsingborg,
" which is situated on a narrow strait of the sea."
The establishing of an alliance between the kingdoms
formed one part of the object of their mission, and on
this point a disagreement appears to have arisen at the
very outset, on the question of including or excluding
certain other sovereigns, and especially the King of
France. The consequence was that Burchier and Dereham returned to England for further instructions, while
their colleagues remained behind awaiting their return.[2]

---

[1] See p. 114.
[2] The time allowed was till the
2nd of July, the Feast of the Visi-
tation of the Blessed Virgin, chosen
by Eric, as he says in his Letter to
Henry IV., "ex eo quod factum
" istud Beatæ Mariæ Virgini, et
" Filio Suo committimus, confi-
" dentes et sperantes quod taliter
" inde disponant quatinus Eis sit
" placabile, nobisque et regnis nos-

" tris ex utraque parte proficuum
" et honestum." They appear not
to have started earlier than the
25th, on which day the Bishop of
Bangor and Parant, writing to the
Council, say, that their messengers,
" vivæ vocis oraculo vos noverint
" plenius informare; idcirco hic
" sistendo ratem, calamum dictis
" Reverentiis vestris ulterius non
" duximus extendendum."

Denmark, &c. A.D. 1402. The letter concludes with an article on the succession to the throne, which they deem it expedient to add to the proposed articles of marriage.

On the following day, November the 3rd, Eric wrote to Henry the Fourth,[1] thanking him for his kindness to the Archdeacon of Roeskilde, and for the gifts which he had sent. He enclosed a copy of the Articles of Marriage, and expressed an earnest wish that all might go on favourably, and be brought to a successful issue. The Queen, his mother, wrote to Henry the Fourth at the same time and to the same effect.[2]

That the English Ambassadors, however, were by no means satisfied with the progress of affairs, is plain from the Bishop of Bangor's letter of the 25th of November, addressed to the Council.[3] The schedule which was enclosed has, unfortunately, not been preserved, but the nature of its contents may be partly inferred from the letter itself. It had reference to the question of succession, and gave an account of certain " perils," which the additional article mentioned in their previous Letter was intended to obviate.

A.D. 1404. The next Letters were written, apparently at the close of the year 1404.

It appears from the Minutes of Council, of the 25th of April, 1404, that the discussion of the proposed marriage of Eric and Philippa was postponed from that time till Michaelmas in the same year. The minute referred to is as follows:—" En primes, touchant la ma-" riage de ma dame Philippe, coment on doit respondre " al ambassiatour de Denmark, et s'il plest au Roy, que " icelle matire puisse estre mys en suspense jusques a la " feste de Saint Michel, ou la entour, et ce par cer-" teines causes et colours que pourrons estre communez " ovec le dit ambassiatour."[4] The first Letter is from

---

Augustine, Bishop of Christiania, and certain other Am- Denmark, &c. A.D. 1404.
bassadors, to Henry the Fourth, and was written on the
18th of November.[1] Since Michaelmas Day they had
been prepared to embark for England, but an unfavourable wind, which still prevailed, detained them. They
promise, if the wind changes soon, to lose no time in
starting, and, if otherwise, to embark immediately after
the ensuing February. They entreat the King to consider all the points of the matter in hand carefully,
that, if possible, all may be arranged some time during
the next May.

On the same day, Peter Lucke (one of those who
signed the above) wrote a letter to the King of England
on his own account, in which he enters somewhat
more minutely into particulars, and expresses his
anxiety for the prosperous and speedy issue of the
negotiations.[2]

King Eric, also, himself wrote on the same day to the
King of England. He explained the reason of the delay
of the Ambassadors, and says, that if they are prevented
from coming now, they shall come as soon after
February as the ice may be broken up. And he looks
forward to receiving his Queen in the month of May
following.[3]

On the next day Eric wrote to King Henry again,
on a very different matter. Two townsmen of Aalborg
had been robbed of their goods by English sailors
on the open sea, restitution of which was earnestly
sought.[4]

The month of May, 1406, was finally fixed for sending
over the Princess; and she went in August of that
year.[5]

---

[1] *See* p. 406.
[2] *See* p. 407.
[3] *See* p. 409.

[4] *See* p. 412.
[5] *See* Nicolas, i. 291, 294.

Spain.
A.D. 1403.
The Letters relating to Spain are valuable and of much interest; the more remarkable, however, belong to the period comprised in our Second Volume.

A.D. 1402.
At page 108 is printed a very curious Letter from Henry III. of Castile to the King of England, in Spanish, original, and signed by the King himself. It relates, however, to matters of no particular historical interest, and, therefore, need not be minutely described. It is dated at Segovia, the 18th of July, and is supposed to have been written in 1402.

At page 132 is given the substance of a Letter to be written by Henry the Fourth to Henry of Castile, as decided upon at a Council held at Eltham. It has reference to the restitution of certain goods which was demanded on either side, and was in all probability written in the year 1403. Mention of such a treaty being in hand is made in a writ issued to the sheriffs of Devon and ten other counties on the sixth of July in that year;[1] and from a similar document addressed to the sheriffs of Cornwall and seven other counties on the 28th of January, 1404,[2] we find that the time had been prolonged for the purpose of allowing such restitution to be made.

Spain, and
Portugal.
A.D. 1403.
On the 9th of September, 1403, the King, at Worcester, issued a command to all the admirals of his kingdom, that they should give free passage from any port he might choose, to "Johannes Gomecii de Silva," the Ambassador of the King of Portugal, who had lately come into England, and was about to return.[3] The object of his embassy was to secure the admission of the King of England into the alliance between the King of Portugal and the King of Castile,

---

[1] *See* Rymer, viii. 312.
[2] Ibid., p. 345.
[3] Ibid., p. 329.

which had been agreed to originally on "the 15th of Spain and
" August, 1440, according to the era of Spain," (A.D. Portugal.
1402), to last till the 1st of March, 1441 (A.D. 1403), A.D. 1403.
and had then been renewed for ten years—viz., till
the 1st of March, 1451 (A.D. 1413). The interesting
letter from John I. to the English King (printed at
p. 191), was written at Lisbon on the 30th of December, 1403, to inform Henry that this treaty for ten
years had been arranged, and that he was included
in it, in case he should send a written expression
of his wish to be so. The writer acknowledges that
two such documents had been already sent, but
says that the King of Castile had rejected one of them
on account of certain informalities in the way of sending it and drawing it up. He, therefore, begs the
King of England, "since it pleased him to consent to
" the said treaties, and to agree with them, and he
" had written to tell him so by the aforesaid docu-
" ments, that it would please him to send one such
" paper in addition," according to a form which he
would transmit for the purpose. This request was
complied with, and the document was given under the
great seal at Westminster on the 27th of February,
1404.[1] On the 22nd of March orders were issued for
the proclamation of the truce in England. The letter
from King John to the English Privy Council,[2] dated
at Coimbra, the 1st of April, appears to have been
written to announce the final completion of the arrangements for including the King of England in the
said treaty; unless, indeed, which is possible, it were
written in the previous year, and intended simply to
announce the settlement of the treaty on the 1st of
March, before it was known whether the King of
England had decided on becoming a party to it.

---

[1] *See* Rymer, viii. 352. | [2] *See* p. 228.

France and Flanders A.D. 1399 —1404. The Letters illustrative of our dealings with FLANDERS and with FRANCE during this period are very numerous; they are also of considerable importance and interest, not only because they form a nearly unbroken series, at least during the earlier years of the reign of Henry the Fourth, and especially in the year 1404, but for the continual allusions which they contain to facts of contemporaneous History more or less connected with their subject matter.

On the usurpation of Henry the Fourth, not the King of Scotland only but the King of France, Charles VI., refused to acknowledge him and threatened to invade the country. This, they alleged, would involve no violation of truces made when Richard the Second was on the throne, and which were broken by those who had deposed him. The joint invasion was never accomplished; but, as we have seen in the case of Scotland, the peace—such as it was—had been effectually broken, and all attempts to establish it again were more or less fruitless. It was the same in the case of France: continual outrages were committed upon the English by French subjects, and especially by the Count of Saint Pol. Nor were the English slow in retaliating; at first, perhaps, by way of reprisal; but it appears that, after a short time, acts of piracy and rapine became so common that the seas were no longer safe,[1] and the carrying out of legitimate commerce became an impossibility.

---

[1] An incidental illustration of this is found in the Letter, already alluded to, from the English Ambassadors in Norway and Sweden, written to Henry IV. on the 16th of June, 1401. They excuse their delay in returning to England, and say, that they will return, under God's guidance, as soon as they can; but they add,—"to the ships "of the Teutonic tongue, on ac- "count of those things which in "these parts are publicly and gene- "rally related about them, as "having happened to them and to "their friends in these days, in

Such a state of things could not, of course, continue France and long without some attempt being made by the rival Flanders. A.D. 1399 nations to provide a remedy, or, at least, without —1404. great and continual complaints being made to those in authority by the injured individuals on either side. The present correspondence is founded upon such complaints, and relates to the consequent negotiations.

The King of France, it has been well remarked,[1] was a "mere puppet in the hands of his unprincipled relations, the Dukes of Orleans and Burgundy." The latter (Philip the Hardy) was, by marriage, Count of Flanders. Flanders, accordingly, became a mere *apanage* of France, and thoroughly subject to French influence, though attempts were made at various times to dissemble the fact. Hence the English Ambassadors, sending copies of some correspondence which they had held with the Flemish Authorities early in 1404, to Henry the Fourth, inform him that he may gather from it " the intentions of the French, though " set forth in, and veiled under, the Letters of the " Flemings ; as well as that the intentions of the " Flemings were conformed to, and accessory to the " will, conclusion, and determination of the French," though " declared in their letters with subtilty of " words."[2] And, later in the same year, the same Ambassadors again writing to Henry the Fourth, with news of the active preparations which were being made by both French and Flemings for the invasion of Wales,

---

" various parts of your English sea, " we dare not commit ourselves, " unless first by the King and " Queen themselves, or by the " Lord Bishop of Roeskilde, . . . . " we be specially and strenuously " recommended to them. Never- " theless, the aforesaid Bishop, even " though he has been most press-

" ingly asked by us, does not dare " to attempt this, as he said, with- " out first ascertaining the will of " the said King and Queen." *See* p. 68.

[1] *See* " Annals of England" (Parkers, 1856), ii. 13, *note* (x).

[2] *See* p. 212.

d

or, perhaps, of " the northern parts of his kingdom, or " some other part," add that they " verily and indeed " believe that, taking into consideration that the " country of Flanders is with one mind, and alto- " gether, as much subject to his adversary of France " as any portion of England is to himself; having " regard also to the fact that, as it were, all the officials " of Flanders are Frenchmen; on those accounts it is " to be feared that the treaty with Flanders (i. e. with " the Duchess of Burgundy [1]) will avail little apart " from the treaty with France;" [2] which, therefore, ought to be pushed forwards with all speed, the fidelity of the Flemings being well known of old. Hence also the language employed by the Lieutenant of Calais, Richard Aston, in his Letter to the Duke of Burgundy of the 18th of March 1404, in which he complains of the outrages committed by the Duke of Orleans and the Count of Saint Pol, and others, and requires him to provide therein as he knows that the matter requires, " calling to his remembrance that of ancient time the " rightful Kings of France, who bore the reputation of " excellence, among all other Kings, as Lords of an " abundant fountain of equity and justice, were not " accustomed at all to be disobeyed, or frustrated, or " oppressed by their subjects." [3] Bearing in mind, therefore, that Flanders was at this time practically a part of France, and that this fact was, for obvious political reasons, continuously dissembled by both French and Flemings in their dealings with England, we will proceed to consider, together, the entire correspondence relating to the two countries.

---

[1] Philip II. died on the 27th of April, 1404; his wife, Margaret, Duchess of Burgundy and Countess of Flanders, on the 16th of March in the following year.

[2] See p. 379.

[3] See p. 224.

Our first Letter,[1] written to the Council, from Calais, on the 18th of July 1402, by John, Bishop of Rochester, and three others who had been appointed with him to take cognizance of such matters, states a complaint which had been made to them by the authorities of Bruges, to the effect that in the month of June, in the previous year, John Hauley, of Dartmouth,[2] and his accomplices, had plundered a ship of Abbeville, and carried off a quantity of goods belonging to the inhabitants of Bruges. This was only one among many similar outrages committed about that time. The same Letter contains mention of certain ships having been captured by men of Fowey;[3] and of one ship, laden with nine casks of wine, which had been taken by Richard and John Spicer.[4] No attempt is made by the writers to deny the truth of these charges or to palliate the guilt of their countrymen, but they entreat the Council to take the matter up, and see that restitution is duly made.

Early in this year proceedings with a view to negotiations had been commenced, and a meeting was held on the 2nd of May, at Westminster,[5] which was prorogued to the 1st of July[5]; then to the 29th of August,[6] and the 10th of November,[6] successively. Nothing, however, was settled; according

*France and Flanders. A.D. 1402.*

---

[1] *See* p. 111.

[2] *See* Rymer, viii. 303; *see also* Letter XCVIII.

[3] Some twenty years before, the Flemings had been guilty of a similar offence against these Cornish mariners, when "the fals Flemyngis," to use the quaint words of John Capgrave, "took a barge "of Fowey, which is in Cornwayle;

"and the men that were within "schip they killid, save o boy that "fled to on of the Flemysch "shippis, and hid him in the "horrok." *See* "The Chronicle of England," p. 234.

[4] They were of Portsmouth. *See* Rymer, viii. 304.

[5] Ibid., p. 374.

[6] Ibid., p. 375.

d 2

France and Flanders. to English accounts through the obstinacy of the Flemings.

A.D. 1403. Similar negotiations were held in 1403.[1] Hugh Luttrell, John Croft, Nicholas de Ryssheton, John Urban, and others, proceeded to Calais as Ambassadors, and deputies were at the same time appointed by the Duke of Burgundy.[2] On the 4th of December the English Ambassadors addressed a Letter[3] to the Duke of Burgundy and to the Great Council of France, and sent a copy of it to the Flemish Deputies.[4] They complained that the truce which had been agreed to, pending the negotiations, had been grievously broken. On the 17th of November they had entered Calais; their credentials and other papers had been forwarded on the very next day, and no reply had been vouchsafed to them.[5] On the contrary, they had heard " by the " relation of reliable persons that the Duke of Orleans " and the Count of Saint Pol had written to their " Lord, the King of England and of France, a certain " disgraceful epistle; whose malice and false abuse," they added, " would be repressed by the grace of God, " and published to future ages, and exposed throughout " the whole world." They then proceed to complain of the offensive attitude of the French fleet, the countless number of their ships, and the fact that they were filled with armed men; and they express their

---

[1] See Rymer, viii. pp. 312, 327.

[2] For Flanders—The Bishop of Chartres, Reginald de Trya, John de Poupaincourt, John de Hangesto, and John de Sanctis, had been previously appointed for 14 Aug. 1402 to 1 May 1403, for France (Rymer viii. 274.) See also, *infra*, p. 171, for the names of the French Ambassadors in the autumn of 1403.

[3] See p. 170.

[4] See p. 185.

[5] In the Letter to Langley, written on the 18th of December (given in the Appendix), De Ryssheton mentions this, and states further, that he expected no answer, for that the road to Gravelines and also that towards S. Omer and the parts of Boulogne, were blockaded by the command of the King of the French.

inability to believe that such a state of things can be connived at by the Duke of Burgundy and the Council, seeing that they are bound to respect and guard the oath of their Lord all the more "in the time of his infirmity." They accordingly demand an explanation to be sent back by the bearer of their Letter, and to be informed whether a meeting in the ensuing March is still contemplated, or whether the outrages really have proceeded from the authority and orders of the Duke and the Council; in which case they were of opinion that it would be expedient to give up the negotiations altogether, and not to vex themselves any longer, at a great expense, to no purpose. Their concluding remonstrance is dignified and worthy of Englishmen : "Of a truth," they say, " many men wonder that the aforesaid Lords (Orleans " and Saint Pol) have so much power within the realm " of France, taking into consideration their youthful " frailty and impetuosity, as to be able to kindle " afresh the coals of hatred between the two realms ; " and, as far as in them lies, infringe the truce ; and " so greatly offend against the Majesty of God ; and " irreparably overturn the common profit of both " realms ; and bring about conflagrations—even of " churches, and shedding of Christian blood, and many " other evils which cannot be numbered, lamentably " and detestably,—alas ! the shame !—to the great " peril of their own souls, and the impeding and dis- " turbing of Christianity itself, to say nothing of " injury and mischief not a little inflicted upon both " kingdoms. For it is absurd, as well as troublesome " and shameful; improper also, contrary to all reason, " and intolerably unjust—wonderful in the realm of " France—that the aforesaid Duke and Count are " able (on account of their own private and parti- " cular grievances and pretences), to wage universal " war against the King and his kingdom, by land and

France and Flanders. A.D. 1403.

" by sea, and to stir up so great a scandal : to take, too,
" for their own defence and place of refuge, the entire
" kingdom of France, and its resources in money and
" in men; and after the manner of a castle and a
" fortified town, for their own shield and buckler, to
" fortify the kingdom of France round about them-
" selves, without thereby (as they pretend) manifestly
" infringing the truce and violating their own oaths.
" Which things, in defect of justice being done, God
" of His Goodness regard and appoint a remedy ! since
" their private complaint and allegations, which they
" have made against the King of England, will not
" be able to exempt them from the charge of infring-
" ing the truce, nor worthily excuse them for the
" violation of their own oath."

Meanwhile the treaty of Flanders was standing still,
while the two parties were disputing about the place
for holding their meetings; the English insisting upon
Calais, to which the Flemings objected. On the
1st of December De Ryssheton wrote to Langley, the
Lord Privy Seal,[1] acquainting him with the state of
the case, and, while recapitulating the advantages
possessed by Calais, recommending that the point
should be yielded to the Flemings.

It is clear that the English were very averse to this
demand of the Flemings that the meeting should be
held on neutral ground ; for, notwithstanding the con-
cession suggested in the Letter to Langley, we find
them writing some twelve days later[2] to the Flemish
Deputies, bidding them come to Calais as they re-
spected their oaths, and not to seek a change of place.
The Flemish Deputies received this Letter on the 18th,
but did not reply to it till the 24th, when they repeated their request that some neutral place on the

---

[1] *See* Appendix II.  |  [2] *See* p. 173.

borders should be selected. Their letter was received France and
by the English Ambassadors on the 26th,[1] who, on the $\begin{array}{l}\text{Flanders.}\\\text{A.D. 1403.}\end{array}$
29th answered it at length : the Flemings, they pro-
tested, had broken their oaths and all their most solemn
engagements of every kind; they had offended against
the truce, and the privilege granted by their Lord, the
Duke of Burgundy; they were making delays only
with a view to postponing the restitution they were
bound to render of goods seized by them and kept at
Sluys; they had even condescended to pervert the
Letters of the English from their true and obvious
meaning; their sudden desire for a change of place
was an evidence of inconstancy and love of change,
and was founded on no right whatever; on the contrary,
the proposed change would be an invasion of the King
of England's just rights, and a departure, without any
reason, from the original programme. Nevertheless, in
spite of all, the English Ambassadors were ready, for
the sake of peace, to give up the point. But the
goods taken from English merchants must be at once
restored.[2]

At the same time, probably on the same day,[3] they
wrote to the King, giving him an account of their
proceedings, and acknowledging the receipt of a letter
from the Council, in which permission was given for
the change of place. But they ask for more particular
directions,—is the place to be within or beyond the
jurisdiction of Calais, as at Lulyngham or Gravelines? or within, one day and beyond, the next? They
also ask for a safe-conduct for French and Flemish
fishermen; announce that their Letter to the Duke

---

[1] *See* p. 177.

[2] At the end of the Letter is a
curious Postscript, in the shape of
a hint to the Four Members of
Flanders that they should in future
take more care how they write
letters, and how they read those
which they receive, "absque sinistra
" informatione clericorum."

[3] *See* p. 186.

France and of Burgundy and the French Council still remained
Flanders. unanswered; and say that they have no news to com-
A.D. 1403. municate, except that the Count of Saint Pol, whose
movements at that time were matter of no small
interest to the English Government, had just, according
to common report, returned to Paris.

This was only one of several Letters to the King
on the same subject.[1] One of the earlier Letters
appears to have reached him at Abingdon; at least
he wrote from that place on the 29th of December,
to the Council, directing them to fix on any spot
they, in their wisdom, thought best for the meeting
of the commissaries on either .side, and to renew the
safe-conduct for the fishermen, if, on inquiry, they
found that it could be done without prejudice to his
own subjects.

Meanwhile piracy on the open seas went on un-
checked. On this same 29th of December the magistrates of Bruges wrote to the English Ambassadors,
complaining that a vessel of Schiedam, coming from
la Rochelle, laden with wine, had been chased by a
war-galley from Calais, and had been seized with
its cargo. The Ambassadors in their reply justify the
act, on the ground that the Calais sailors thought
that the wine was French, taking refuge under the
Flemish flag. They promise, however, to retain the
cargo, and investigate the matter, and remind the
writers that this was but a solitary case of wrong
compared with the innumerable occasions on which
the Flemings had injured the English. They also
earnestly request an answer to their previous Letters.

A.D. 1404.   On the 4th of January Luttrell and the others
again wrote[2] to the King, sending him copies of the
correspondence, that he might understand "the manifest

---

[1] *See* p. 189, *note*.          |   [2] *See* p. 197.

" chicanery of the Flemings and their inexcusable love France and
" of change, as well as that they themselves had $\begin{array}{l}\text{Flanders.}\\ \text{A.D. 1404.}\end{array}$
" shown some little diligence in prosecuting their
" work." They mention a report that shortly there
would be held a Great Council in Paris, and tell the
story of the capture of the wine, and the reply which
they had sent to the Letter of complaint from
Bruges.

At last, on the 6th of January, the Flemish Deputies wrote,[1] but only to cause further delays ; they
had sent deputies to ask counsel of the Duke of
Burgundy, and begged that nothing might be done till
their return.

The English Ambassadors replied angrily on the
12th.[2] "It does not become," they argue, "the Am-
" bassadors of any Kings and Princes whatsoever,
" and specially those of so mighty a Prince as our
" King, that your Ambassadors of the Four Members
" of Flanders, at such a time, without a seeming
" response should pretend to reply satisfactorily to our
" letters." Contrary to all custom and to everything
that was ever heard of before, we have changed the
place of meeting to please you, and yet after all we
have waited for your arrival in vain. They also state
that on the 14th Parliament will meet, when they
are required by the King to be present; that one
of their co-ambassadors must be sent to be present
on the first day of the session, to give an account
of the delay that had already occurred ; but that they
will remain, awaiting a definite answer, till the 20th
and no later.

On the same day they wrote to the King,[3] sending
their Letter by the hands of William Lysle, reporting

---

[1] See p. 200.
[2] See p. 202.

[3] See p. 204.

France and Flanders. A.D. 1404. progress, and asking whether they were to return to England to the Parliament, or whether they were to await at Calais the final answer of the French and the Flemings.[1]

January passed, and part of February, but no tidings were heard of the Flemings, except that a report reached the English Ambassadors that the deputies who had been sent to the Duke of Burgundy, at Paris, had returned. Accordingly on the 14th of February they wrote[2] to inquire whether the report were true, and to express their surprise that the promised communication had not been made. The Flemings replied on the 23rd, stating that not all the deputies returned at the time alluded to, but only part of them, and that as the negotiation between France and England would shortly commence at Lulingham, the treaty of Flanders must be postponed.

At this crisis Luttrell and Urban were despatched to England, the bearers of a letter from Croft and De Ryssheton to the King,[3] setting forth how the Flemings were but playing into the hands of the French, and requesting that further directions might be sent to them. Their want of money also now began to be a grievance; to what a height it grew shortly after we shall see presently; on this occasion they only give a hint, as it were, incidentally, and, while asking for something else, add quietly, "*una cum stipendiis nostris.*"

---

[1] The Postscript to this Letter contains a few curious items of news, relating to some of the results of the Council which was then being held in Paris.

[2] *See* p. 210.

[3] *See* p. 112.

[4] At the end of the Letter they beg the King to " turn his eyes to " the town of Gravelines for the " defence of his subjects, and to " provide a remedy opportunely, as " the Governours of his Castles in " Picardy, and the Lieutenant of " Calais have too much on their " hands already to allow them to " attend to anything else."

Meanwhile the outrages on English subjects, both France and by French and Flemings, were continued ceaselessly, Flanders. A.D. 1404. and threatened to put a stop to the negotiations which were pending.

The Letter of Sir Richard Aston, Deputy-Governour and Lieutenant of Calais (written to the Duke of Burgundy on the 18th of March in this year, and sent to him, as the writer mentions, by a certain Scotchman, "prisoner of John Molton, the master porter of Calais"), is a document of remarkable interest and value, for the succinct and clear account it gives of the principal of these events.[1] The French Ambassadors had written to those of England complaining that the English were the more worthy of blame;[2] that they had "ravaged, pillaged, and robbed at Boulogne, " and elsewhere in Picardy, and withal had killed and " taken prisoners even women and young children." This, he says, was an exaggeration,[3] and proceeds to compare it with the more grievous outrages committed by the other side. While yet the Ambassadors of the two realms were assembled together at Lulingham, the isle of L'Orne was attacked, the houses fired, and as many of the inhabitants made prisoners as they could carry away. The injustice of this act had been admitted, but no manner of restitution had been made from that time to the present. Shortly after the men of Harfleur had put to sea, under the pretence of the Scotch flag, and had robbed English merchants of considerably more than one hundred thousand pounds sterling. What wonder, then, that the English should make some attempt at reprisal? Nevertheless, it was

---

[1] See p. 214.
[2] See p. 213.
[3] Yet Croft and De Ryssheton had written to Henry IV. on the 27th of February, "pro excusatione

" equitaturæ per stipendiarios ves-
" træ villæ Calisii nuper factæ;
" quam non credimus vestram Ma-
" jestatem ignorare." (See p. 213.)

France and
Flanders.
A.D.1404.
" against the will of their King, and without his leave, knowledge, or licence" that they did so. Again, the men of Brittany, very shortly afterwards, had, "with " a great force of armed vessels, passed into England, and " burned, pillaged, and plundered the town of Plymouth," murdering or taking prisoners many of the inhabitants. And, not content with this, they had invaded the islands of Jersey and Guernsey, " where they set fire " to the houses, took prisoners and booty, and laid the " islands under an intolerable contribution." The Count of Saint Pol, also, though sworn to maintain the truce, had long kept a powerful fleet in the Duke of Burgundy's own harbour of Gravelines, and had acted as a very pirate and a robber. In short, the whole seaboard of Flanders had become an armed arsenal against English merchants, through the hostile practices of the men of Dunkirk, Newport, Ostend, Bieruliet, and other Flemish ports. Finally, the Count of Saint Pol, no longer content with plundering on the high seas, had openly defied the King of England, and invaded his territory. With a party of his followers he had descended suddenly upon the Isle of Wight, and had overpowered, "and taken prisoners certain poor fishermen, with their nets and implements," and had " seized on certain sheepfolds," greatly to the grief of the unfortunate owners. Aston justly complains that such violations of a solemn oath are intolerable, and reminds the Duke of Burgundy that the Count is not only a rightful subject and liegeman of the King of France, but also of himself by right of his heritages situated in Flanders. He had, accordingly, on the suggestion of Nicholas De Ryssheton, who was then at Calais, written thus fully in detail, praying for redress, and reminding the Duke that there was a time when " the rightful Kings of France bore the reputation of " excellence among all other Christian Kings, as lords " of an abundant fountain of equity and justice."

He also asks for a safe-conduct to the presence of the France and King and Council at France for Sir John Cheyney, Flanders. for which he had previously written to the Duke. A.D. 1404.

On the same day Aston wrote to Henry IV.,[1] informing him that he had written for the safe-conduct in question, and that there had been some difficulty about the transmission of his previous letter, to which as yet he had received no reply.

Shortly after this, viz. on the 27th of April, the Duke of Burgundy died.

On the 30th the authorities of Bruges announced the fact[2] to the English Ambassadors, who had returned from Calais to London. They stated, further, that Flanders thereby had reverted to Margaret, the late Duke's widow, who was daughter and heiress of Louis II., late Count of Flanders. And, while lamenting the troubles which had arisen between England and France and Flanders, " by the means of certain free- " booters and pirates of the sea, Belial's own sowers of " tares, and sons of iniquity," they declare that their Countess desires to promote the restoration of peace so far as her own dominions are concerned.

The English Ambassadors replied, on the 7th of May,[3] that the King of England and his Council, earnestly desiring peace with the Four Members of Flanders, and, to avoid for the future the shedding of Christian blood, notwithstanding all the horrors which the Flemings had inflicted on Englishmen, were prepared to treat forthwith.

It would appear that the Duchess of Burgundy was sincere in her desire to re-establish friendly relations with England. On the 14th of May, (probably almost immediately after the receipt of the English Letter at Bruges,) she issued a Letter to the High Bailiffs of

[1] *See* p. 225.
[2] *See* p. 230.
[3] Ibid.

Flanders, the Bailiffs of Bruges and other places, in which, (after stating that her own subjects of Ghent, Bruges and Ypres had complained to her against certain of their fellow townsmen, who, by their piratical deeds, had nearly put a stop to that commerce on which the prosperity of Flanders mainly depended.) she proceeded to order that a proclamation should be at once made in every part of Flanders and wherever else necessary, that no subject of hers should attack or rob the merchants of England or of any country whatsoever. A saving clause, however, of which some use was made hereafter, was added at the end—" provided, that those " of the part of England do, and cause to do, the like."

Two days later the Duchess gave notice of these proceedings to Sir Richard Aston.[1] In this Letter the " saving clause " is repeated, with the additional proviso " that on the part of England they hold to it better " than has been done in time past."

This Letter, or another to the same effect, was answered shortly after by John Urban, Lieutenant of the Staple at Calais,[2] who informed the Duchess that he had notified her proclamation to his King, together with the proviso that a similar proclamation should be made in England ; and that he had received a favourable answer. She replied, on the 7th of June, that immediately on the death[3] of her late Lord, she had sent to the King of France for powers to treat, which had been granted to her, and to her son the Duke of Burgundy ; that the Letters were drawn up, and that she daily expected to receive them. She required, also, a full account of the King of England's message as to his intentions in the matter of the proclamation against piracy.

---

*See* p. 235.
*See* p. 245.

[3] *See* p. 247.

Meanwhile, the English Ambassadors had again France and written, on the 18th of June,[1] repeating and confirming Flanders. A.D. 1404. the declarations made in their previous Letter of the 7th of May, to the Flemish Deputies; who replied, on the 13th, that their Countess was favourable to the treaty. But suspicions and doubts were still rife,—as is clear from a Letter written by the Flemish Deputies to the Mayor of the Staple at Calais on the 17th of the same month, in which they allege that " sundry mar- " vellous reports had reached them, within the past " four or five days, concerning certain enterprises which " were to be undertaken in England against the land " of Flanders," and pray that, if it be indeed so, it may be stopped at once, for the sake of the treaty, and the honour of both parties.

They wrote on the same day to the English Am- bassadors, and to the same effect.[2] In this Letter, however, they state specifically from whom the danger was apprehended, viz. Henry Le Spenser, Bishop of Norwich,[3] a prelate, who (it will be remembered) distin- guished himself in quelling the riots in Norfolk during the rebellion in the reign of Richard II., and was, generally, so much fonder of martial than of pastoral work, that he had earned the title of " The Warlike."

The Ambassadors were still in London when this Letter reached them, and De Ryssheton wrote at once to the King, inquiring whether the report was true. He also enclosed the Letters which had passed in reference to this matter and the negotiations, and

---

[1] *See* p. 249.

[2] *See* p. 256.

[3] They had cause to remember him of old. In 1383 he had been sent by the Pope into Flanders " contra schismaticos in Flandria " Crucesignatus;" and though his expedition was unsuccessful, so that he was censured in Parliament on his return to England, he undoubt- edly contrived to effect a great deal of mischief. *See* his Life in Capgrave's " Liber de Illustribus Henricis," Ed. 1858 ; pp. 170-174.

France and requested an explicit answer. This Letter is dated the
Flanders. 25th of June.[1]
A.D. 1404.

On the 6th of July, the Duchess of Burgundy wrote
to Urban,[2] announcing that she had received Letters
Patent from the King of France; naming her Deputies;
and requesting that the English Ambassadors might be
ready, as hers would be, on the 20th of the month. This
Letter was forwarded at once to De Ryssheton and
Urban, in London,[3] who, in reply to it, wrote to the
Four Members of Flanders on the 20th, stating that
Ambassadors had been appointed on the English part,
but that they could not reach Calais before the
15th of August. They requested that the Four
Members, as well as their Countess, should send
Deputies, and that a safe-conduct should be provided
for themselves from the Count of Saint Pol, as well
as from the King of France.

Before starting, De Ryssheton wrote a pitiful appeal
to the King for the payment of the arrears of his
stipend.[4]

At this time the dread of a French invasion, hitherto
undefined and depending upon little more than rumour,
began to assume a definite shape. The Letter from
the Bishop of Bangor to the King, printed at
page 280, is a curious and remarkable document. It
was written in London on the 2nd of August. The
news which it contained came by an indirect channel,
but, as the event proved, it was authentic as well as
important. One Angelus Cristofore, or Christopher,
a merchant, and other his fellow-merchants, had received a letter from some friends of theirs at Bruges,
the contents of which the said Angelus requested the
Bishop to communicate to the King, as he was himself

---

[1] See p. 264.
[2] See p. 266.
[3] See p. 277.
[4] See p. 279.

about to go abroad. The pieces of intelligence were France and
two in number : 1st, Isabella, late Queen of England, $\underset{\text{A.D. 1404.}}{\text{Flanders.}}$
was to be married to the youthful Duke of Orleans,
" who would receive with her for a dowry the whole
" of the subsidy lately granted to the pretended King
" of France ;" 2nd, The High Constable of France was
preparing an expedition against Aquitaine, and the
Count de la Marche, at the head of a powerful armament, was about to invade Wales.

Shortly after, on the 10th of the same month, we find
Henry writing to the Doge of Venice for cables, ropes,
and hawsers : the cables and hawsers were to be of
somewhat stronger make than those commonly employed
for Venetian carracks; and, if it were impossible to
send all that was required at once,[1] they were to
send as much as they could first, and the remainder
at the earliest opportunity.

At this critical juncture a Letter was received by
the King,[2] and another to the same effect by the
Council,[3] from Sir Richard Aston, written, both of
them, on the 17th of August. They set forth, in
piteous strains, the miseries endured by the King's
subjects in Calais; the garrison was nearly starved
out for want of money, and the good people of the
town, who had supplied the necessary means of
subsistence hitherto, were afraid to lend anything
more "for fear of losing the whole ; and, indeed,
" had it not in their power to lend more." The arrears
would amount at the ensuing Michaelmas to more
than two years. In case money were not quickly
sent from home it was even possible that it might
be necessary to abandon the place altogether.

---

[1] The quantity ordered was considerable,—Sixty thousand pounds
of hemp made up into cables, and
twenty thousand in hawsers; eighty
thousand pounds' weight in all.
[2] *See* p. 284.
[3] *See* p. 289.

e

France and Flanders. A.D. 1404. Shortly after these Letters had been received, Croft and De Ryssheton and the other Ambassadors left England.

They landed at Calais on the 20th,[1] and proceeded at once to inform the Duchess of Burgundy, of their arrival.

On the 23d they wrote to the Four Members of Flanders, requiring an answer to their previous Letters, and demanding immediate restitution of those goods which had been openly stolen from English merchants, or their value in full. They name the 6th of the then ensuing month of September for the day of meeting; and, the substitution for Calais of some neutral spot between the two countries having been previously conceded, they choose Santingfield, where the Ambassadors of one party might stand on their own territory, and also those of the other "on a place where the borders " and limits of either realm are notoriously marked " out by border stones." They object to Eynes, which had been named for the purpose, because " the borders and extreme limits are not clearly " distinguished there at present, so that they could " not assemble on an equal footing without disturbing " the boundary line." After complaining that the forbearance of the English in repressing their navy had been rewarded by treachery on the part of the Flemings, they conclude with the following significant request: "Take " care that your Ambassadors be *legales et tractabiles*, " for it may happen that the French intend to throw " hindrances in the way of our present mutual treaty, " if they are able to obtain from your Mistress and " from you the power of treating, a point which " well deserves your attention, and affords a good

---

[1] *See* p. 294.

" reason for your using more diligence in our pre- France and
" sent negotiations than has been your wont hitherto." Flanders.
They ask, in a Postscript, for safe-conducts for the A.D. 1404
appointed Ambassadors,[1] some of whom were in England, but would be present with the rest on the appointed day.

A Letter to the same effect, and nearly in the
same words, was written to the Duchess of Burgundy,
probably on the same day.[2]

The former of these Letters was answered, on the
31st, in the briefest manner.[3] The will of the Duchess
had not been ascertained; when it was known it
should be communicated.

Meanwhile the negotiations seemed likely to be
brought prematurely to a stand-still by the absence
or illness of the English Ambassadors. We have a
Letter from Swinborn, Croft, and De Ryssheton to
the Privy Council,[4] dated on this same 31st of
August, announcing that they were carrying on
communications, both with the Flemings and with the
French. But De Ryssheton was in danger of being
left alone ; for Swinborn was about to leave for
England ; Croft was so ill that he could not ride on
horseback, or even leave his abode. Lysle and Urban
were in England already. They pray accordingly
that other Ambassadors might be appointed. The
Postcript, written with quite another ink, is curious,
inasmuch as it proves that this Letter was not
sent for several days after the 31st, on which it
was written; for it is added to announce the arrival

---

[1] Thomas Swinborn; John Croft; William Lysle, the younger ; Tho-mas Swinford; Ralph Bottreaux; Nicholas De Ryssheton, and John Urban.

[2] *See* p. 297.

[3] *See* p. 302.

[4] *See* p. 303.

France and of the Letter from the Four Members of Flanders
Flanders. which was also written on that day.
A.D. 1404.

Our next Letter is from Swinford and De Ryssheton
to the French Council,[1] and has reference to the
mission of Sir John Cheyney. It was written from
Calais on the 13th of September, and states that, no
safe-conduct having been afforded to him, he had been
obliged to give his Letters into the hands of the Ambassadors instead of delivering them to the French King and
Council. They earnestly entreat that the negotiations
may be speedily proceeded with, having evidently in
their minds the dread of treachery, and not forgetting
the rumours which had reached Henry, while De
Ryssheton was yet in England, of the meditated
invasion of that country by the French.

On the 13th,[2] the French Ambassadors wrote an
ambiguous and evasive answer to the contents of
this Letter, in a reply to a previous Letter from the
English Ambassadors, dated the 23rd of August;
they declined to write particularly; reminded the
English that the armistice, within certain limits,
would not end till the 1st of November; that there
was time enough, therefore, for all purposes, and that
meanwhile, "the Lord granting it, whatever things
" ought to be done on their own part would be
" accomplished."

These concluding words, though capable of a harmless
interpretation, were, doubtless, intended to convey a
threat. At least, it is certain that Swinford and his
colleagues thought so. In a Letter written by them to
the Privy Council, on the 19th of September,[3] they
complain that their Letter to the French Council still
remained unanswered, and end their Letter thus,—

[1] See p. 306.
[2] See p. 312.
[3] See p. 331.

" Also, because a notable and mighty naval armament France and Flanders.
" has been prepared in France, which in the present A.D. 1404.
" month, as is professed, is to effect a landing in the
" parts of Wales, or in some other parts of England;
" therefore, for full security, it is expedient that the
" sea should be strongly guarded with all possible
" speed, and defended in every port, because the French
" dispose themselves rather to the sword than to the
" observance of a truce." This was the result of their
anticipations founded on common report; but when they
received the apparently not unfavourable and mildly
worded reply of the French Ambassadors, they opened
their Letter, and added the following Postscript:—
" After the writing and sealing of the present Letter,
" certain Letters on the part of the Ambassadors of
" France were presented to us, by which, in our judg-
" ment, it will be sufficiently apparent that the French
" are making arrangements against the feast of All
" Saints (1 Nov.) for preparing for us and bringing
" upon us all manner of evils." And they went on to
state that great dangers were certainly at hand, unless
due measures were taken, and with more precautions
*than usual*, against the power of the enemy, or God
should save the English nation by a miracle.

They wrote also at the same time, and to the same
effect, to the King,[1] telling him that the French demon-
stration was to be in favour of his Welsh rebels, and
that they hoped to invade England, destroy the English
fleets, and inflict all possible evils, meanwhile, upon the
realm. They, moreover, point out the true remedy for
this state of suspense, and the results which would
surely follow its being adopted,—" if the sea in the
" meantime, especially in the parts of Wales, be both
" powerfully guarded and also put into a state of

---

[1] *See* p. 329.

" defence, we take it that we shall very shortly receive
" a peaceable answer from the French, *otherwise* they
" will do their worst, in conjunction with their allies,
" to the no small injury and depression of your
" kingdom."

This advice appears to have been taken at once, or
rather, the preparations which had been previously
determined on, were hastened in consequence of it.
Accordingly, we find the French at once throwing all
the blame of the prevailing suspicion upon the English, and stating that *they* were the breakers of the
truce. This was communicated to the King by Swinford and De Ryssheton in a Letter written on the 26th
of September;[1] in which they also remind him of the
threatening Letter which had been lately forwarded to
him, and interpret it further to imply that the French
do not intend to answer his royal Letters after the 18th
of November, but to attack the English in conjunction
with their allies of Spain.[2]

Meanwhile Swinford and his colleagues were busied
also with the prosecution of the Flemish negotiations,
into which a new element of difficulty and disagreement
had entered towards the end of August. After the
partial lull, acts of hostility and reprisal had been
renewed by the Flemings, who continued " lying in
" ambush along the sea coast, with a view to commit-
" ting all the evil that they could upon the English
" King's lieges."[3] " Just recently," Henry writes to

---

[1] *See* p. 338.

[2] A curious allusion is made in
this Letter to the late King of
England and his Queen Isabella;
they had written to the French
Ambassadors " quoad ampliorem
" vestram excusationem et declara-
" tionem, sub prætextu resignationis
" per Dominum Regem Ricardum

" nuper factæ vestræ Celsitudini,
" ac vestro regno per Ducem Au-
" relianum ac Comitem Sancti
" Pauli nequiter et malitiose im-
" positæ; necnon quoad ducenta
" millia francorum, ratione dotis
" ex parte Dominæ Isabellæ nuper
" Reginæ Angliæ petita indebite."
[3] *See* p. 309.

the Duchess of Burgundy, on the 10th of September, "your subjects of Flanders [1] have captured a ship, in "which our dearly beloved in God, Robert Mascall, "lately our confessor, was proceeding from Middle-"burgh towards our realm ; and, after they had thrust "all hands out of the ship into the sea, they sent away "the said Robert to Dunkirk, and there they detain "him a prisoner, and will not deliver him out of their "custody without his paying them a sum of money and "a ransom." The King expresses his astonishment at these proceedings, and demands the release of the Bishop without ransom, declaring that he "cannot and will not "endure such horrible proceedings any longer." But worse remained behind. The "robbers and pirates of "Dunkirk, Newport, Bieruliet, and Sluys," had not only committed this outrage, in defiance of oaths and treaties, but they they had also, off the north coasts of England, attacked a little fleet of fishing vessels, and "captured one hundred and sixty-eight, or, according "to the more reliable accounts, about six hundred "poor English fishermen with seven-and-twenty or "eight-and-twenty vessels." [2]

<aside>France and Flanders. A.D. 1404.</aside>

The Duchess of Burgundy had written on the 12th of September to the English Ambassadors, sending them a safe conduct, and promising to send her deputies to meet them at Santingfield on the 25th. They answered her on the 16th, and stated that they were ready to meet her Deputies, but required her to compel the Four Members of Flanders to make restitution of the properties seized at Sluys, and not to countenance their wrongdoing. They, moreover, entered a protest against the capture of the Bishop of Hereford and the fishermen, and returned her safe-conduct for correction. The original of this very curious document has been preserved,

---

[1] "Of Dunkirk, and other parts "of Flanders."—*See* p. 316.

[2] *See* p. 353.

[3] *See* p. 314.

with the suggestions of the English Ambassadors written upon it, as it was sent back to the Duchess.[1]

On the 19th Croft and De Ryssheton addressed a Letter to the Privy Council,[2] giving an account of their progress, and stating that the proposed meeting at Santingfield on the 25th would be held, notwithstanding the defects in the safe-conduct, which they had returned. This Letter, though signed by Croft and De Ryssheton, was clearly indited by the latter. In one place the words " Ego Nicholaus " have been, on revision, prefixed above the line, to a personal complaint of the writer's : he had received no stipend for some time, and was in danger of being left alone, for Swinborn and Urban were in England; Lysle would join them before the proposed day of meeting, and Croft, through illness, was entirely laid by. The difficulties of his position and his despair are curiously brought out in the Postscript to this Letter :—" Though I alone, with two " clerks writing unceasingly, by reason of the absence " of the other commissaries, am willing, for the pleasure " of our Lord the King and his kingdom, as far as in " me lies, to undertake labours, and to meet the or- " dinary expenses which have been incurred to no " small extent, yet I shall not be able to supply the " place or number of four persons in the negotiations, " or in any manner to represent them." [3]

In their last Letter to the Duchess, the English Ambassadors (it will be remembered) had insisted on the Four Members being compelled to do justice to those whom they had wronged, as a preliminary condition to the prosecution of the negotiations; and they had called upon her not to give the sanction of her authority to their delinquencies. The result was that

---

[1] See pp. 318–329 : also pp. 322, 3, where the suggested corrections are given in the notes.

[2] See p. 331.

[3] See p. 334.

the Duchess refused to proceed in conjunction with the France and Flanders. A.D. 1404. Four Members, and would treat with the English by her own Deputies only. Proceedings were, therefore, stayed; the proposed meeting on the 25th was abandoned; and the commission was returned, through the English Ambassadors on the 26th to the Privy Council, for the necessary alterations.[1] Swinford and De Ryssheton wrote on the same day to the King,[2] giving him an account of these changes[3] and requesting that the commission might be returned to them without delay.

Meanwhile, they had found abundant occupation in pleading the cause of the unfortunate Bishop of Hereford and the six hundred poor fishermen, as well as in watching the Flemings, and providing, as far as possible, against other similar outrages. On the 28th of September, they wrote again[4] on these points to the Duchess; and complained that, whereas their King had kept his Admirals and his subjects in check, and had constantly repressed every attempt to violate the truce, her subjects, especially those of Newport and Dunkirk, were still acting as pirates, and "anew congregated, and were at " that moment congregating together, a certain fleet " for the purpose of spoiling the English, and taking " them captive, and plundering them."

On the 30th, they wrote another similar Letter,[5] in a more indignant strain,—"We wonder, more than " we are capable of expressing in writing, that you " tolerate " such deeds being committed by your subjects: "moreover, as is asserted, you cause the spoils " thus acquired to be brought into your presence, and

---

[1] See p. 335.
[2] See p. 338.
[3] They appear to have caused considerable discontent in England; the reformed commission was long detained, and the English Ambassadors sent for it by special messengers on nine several occasions without success. (See p. 398.)
[4] See p. 345.
[5] See p. 348.

" you make distribution of them according to your
" pleasure, which is not honest, considering the purport
" of several Letters of yours sent to Calais, nor can it
" be long endured, neither does it lead the way to peace,
" but it is rather a signal for battle on the part of your
" Excellency."

On the day following, they wrote also [1] to the Four
Members of Flanders, on the proposed arrangements
for treating separately with them.   In this Letter
they renew their protest against the shameful detention
of the Bishop of Hereford, and the fishermen ; and
make mention of the report that the Duchess of
Burgundy was privy to these robberies, and even
superintended the distribution of the spoil.

On the 3rd of October,[2] they wrote once more to the
Duchess herself on the same subjects.   Entreaties having
failed, they now resort to threats,—" We require of your
" Excellency that it please you with speed to remit the
" fine [inflicted on the Bishop of Hereford], and to set
" free the captives and the prisoners, and to make
" restitution of them, moreover, in full, with their ships
" and goods . . . . . For such wrongs as these, so
" notorious, unless they be speedily corrected, will easily
" avail to subvert the treaty and altogether to put a
" stop to it,—which God forbid ! For on Tuesday next
" the English Parliament will assemble, and, unless a
" speedy answer as to the above matters shall have
" been made with due deliberation, there will be reason
" to fear that the Commons of the realm will appoint
" a remedy (which God forbid !) exceedingly severe." [3]

No doubt, this strongly worded language was amply
justified by the occasion, but it was not exactly calculated to secure the desired result.   Harassed by troubles

---

[1] *See* p. 350.          [3] *See* p. 359.
[2] *See* p. 356.

in the north of his kingdom, by active rebellion in France and Wales, by the anxieties arising from an impoverished Flanders. A.D. 1404. exchequer, and by the continual dread of a French invasion, the King of England had too much upon his hands already to permit of his engaging in an open quarrel with Flanders, a country under the protection, and practically subject to the rule, of his chief foe. Accordingly, this Letter appears to have had no more effect upon the Duchess than had their previous Letter of the 28th, in which they had held out a threat of the "*majus malum*"—war. She wrote to the English Ambassadors on the 6th of October,[1] all but justifying the misdeeds of her subjects, on the ground that the English had brought these troubles upon themselves by their own fault, especially by their descent, on the 14th of August, upon an island near Sluys, where they had " dismantled a church, set many " of the houses on fire, and robbed and plundered her " subjects of their cattle and other property :" for they, " grieving and irritated at this damage done against " herself and them, were forced to commit some assault " upon the other side, and in doing so have taken " prisoner the said Bishop."[2] As to the charge of complicity brought against her, in their previous Letter of the 3rd, she would have them know "that neither " her predecessors nor herself had at all been accustomed " to live by plundering or robberies, or to mix them- " selves up with such affairs, or with other dishonest " proceedings," and she expressed herself "greatly

---

[1] *See* p. 361.

[2] The contrast between the offence and the retribution is marked: —The seizure of a bishop and six hundred fishermen is justified on the ground that Flemish islanders had been plundered of their cattle. The damage done to the latter, as the Ambassadors observe in their reply to this Letter, was a mere trifle in comparison, *ad modicum valorem seu damnum respective non centum nobilium*, " whereof, by God's grace," they added, " satisfaction " shall be made even to the utter- " most penny." (*See* p. 389.)

" surprised that they should write to her in such a " strain." And, as to the second charge, that her councillors and collaterals, giving her their support, defended the pirates who plundered the English, or participated in their robberies, she was " not in the least aware that she " had such people in her Council, or such collaterals ; " she would not at all have people of such a description ; " and, if she were to find any, she would punish them " in such a manner as would be an example for all " others." [1]

The altered commission had not yet arrived. De Ryssheton, accordingly, wrote on the 6th of October [2] to the Archbishop of Canterbury to entreat that it might be sent. This was already the fifth time he had written in vain ; and, waxing somewhat warm with vexation at such procrastination, he ventures to express some surprise that the Council had been for so long a time, " so wandering, and weak, and divided," as not to have been able to answer his Letters, " considering " the tempests, which, as it were, from every quarter, " daily rage more and more against the King and his " realm." " A fleet was assembled at Harfleur, and in " other ports of Normandy, for the invasion of Wales, " or Orwell, or some other part of England." " Some " of the French soldiers," he writes, " amounting " even to a noteworthy number, who had not been " able to enter the aforesaid fleet at Harfleur, have " set off to-day for Sluys, to embark there, and ac- " complish, as is reported, some noteworthy undertaking. " And even the Flemings have collected a fleet of seven- " and-thirty ships, taking the small with the large, " and are embarking, either for the purpose of spoiling " our fishermen in the north, or else to attack the " Duke of Holland, or in favour of the French, " whose intention is at present unknown to us."

---

[1] *See* p. 366.                    |       [2] *See* p. 367.

The situation was indeed critical;[1] but negotiations France and were not yet broken off. The French Ambassadors wrote on the 27th of September,[2] but their Letter did not reach the English Ambassadors till the 6th of October ; it contained a proposal that a meeting should be held on the 15th. Swinford and De Ryssheton replied, on the 8th, that they could not comply with their request on so short a notice. They wrote, also, three days later, to the King,[3] sending him copies of the Letter, and of their reply.[4] They told him that the term of the armistice had nearly arrived, that both French and Flemings were in arms, as a messenger just arrived had told them ; that all negotiations were at a stand-still for lack of the commission for which they had so often applied ; and that the peace would certainly be broken. After this Letter was sealed, another messenger arrived from Sluys, with alarming intelligence of most extensive preparations being made there ; a fleet of ships had just arrived there, full of men, and of provisions, including a quantity of hay chopped very fine, and other food for horses. Indeed, there was provision made for

France and Flanders. A.D. 1404.

---

[1] A Postscript was added to this Letter reflecting upon the conduct of Sir Richard Aston, the Lieutenant of Calais. The armistice, which had been arranged until the 18th of November, as to the tract of country lying between the Somme and Gravelines, would shortly expire ; he had expressed his intention not to seek its renewal ; and the Ambassadors begged the Archbishop to suggest to the King that he should be compelled to do so. They added that, " as to the " state and government of the " town of Calais, William Lysle " and Richard Guest would give " him oral information ; for they " feared that the said Lieutenant,

" with his stipendiaries, would be " able easily to hinder the treaty, " unless a remedy were speedily " applied and in good time."—See also p. 213,—" pro excusatione equi- " taturæ per stipendiarios vestræ " villæ Calisii nuper factæ." This then was not the first occasion upon which the indiscreet zeal of the Lieutenant of Calais had been near bringing the Ambassadors of peace into trouble.

[2] See p. 374.

[3] See p. 376.

[4] Informing him, also, that they were still doing their best to procure from the Duchess of Burgundy the release of the Bishop of Hereford and the captive fishermen.

France and Flanders. A.D. 1404. no less than three thousand horses at Sluys, and for as many at Harfleur ; and this great armament was intended for Wales or some other part of England.

On the 14th of October De Ryssheton wrote again ; this time to William Askham, Mayor of London.[1] " The French and Spaniards, recently incensed afresh " against us, with their powerful fleet at Harfleur to " the number of fifteen thousand armed men and " cavalry, or thereabout, provisioned for half a year " both for themselves and for their horses, are now on " the sea, prepared to attack Bordeaux, or else to enter " into Wales and seize and rebuild the castles in Wales " which had been destroyed, and to inflict upon us all " manner of evils and losses possible ; the Flemish fleet, " also, with as many French infantry and cavalry, as- " sembled in Sluys, is prepared, together with the aid of " them of Prussia, to attack Sandwich, or other parts " of England. And, finally, they intend, it is reported, " to decline towards Calais, and lay siege thereto." And " the Governour of Calais is absent, and a large number " of his stipendiaries, as well as the merchants of the " Staple ; and, if all were present, the town of Calais " would not be sufficiently provided with soldiers and " victuals and many other requisites, even in the matter " of artillery." He, therefore, begged for aid, and that vessels laden with wool or corn should not attempt to sail for Bordeaux.

On the 17th Swinborn and his colleagues replied to the Letter of the Duchess of Burgundy,[2] recapitulated again all their grievances as for the last time, excused the foray of the English upon the island of Wulpen, and informed her that, if they did not receive a favourable answer by the 1st of November, it was their intention to remain no longer at Calais, " vexing themselves with

---

useless labour and expenses," to no profit. Her town France and of Gravelines, they moreover tell her, has become " a  Flanders. A.D. 1404. den of robbers."

Several Letters, also, passed at this time between the English and French Ambassadors, but with no result; first, they could not agree on a day for meeting, and, when the day was fixed, they could not agree on a place. The corrected commission for Flanders had not arrived, though Swinford and De Ryssheton had applied for it nine several times.[1] Utterly wearied, they wrote plainly to the King on the 22nd :—"unless it be sent " immediately, since without it for various reasons " we labour in vain for the treaty of Flanders, we will " return without delay after the feast of All Saints " (1 November) to the feet of your royal Majesty." And they kept their word. Our next Letter from De Ryssheton, addressed to the Bishop of Chartres, is dated at Coventry on the 2nd of November.[2] He wrote at the same time and place to the Duchess of Burgundy :[3] but both these Letters pertain to the continuation of this series in the Second Volume.

Thus ended, for 1404, with no appreciable results the long and arduous endeavours of the King of England to establish friendly relations between his kingdom and France and Flanders, on terms which would secure that justice should be done to both parties, and a full restitution made of the properties which had been seized by either. Doubtless, there was grievous fault on both sides; but it is impossible to read and study this lengthy and almost unbroken series of Letters without coming to the conclusion that the English were by far the least to blame, and were certainly actuated by a sincere desire to make peace on equitable terms; a desire for which

[1] *See* pp. 398, 399, 400.
[2] *See* p. 402.
[3] *See* p. 404.

France and very little credit can be given to the other side.
Flanders.
A.D. 1404. The English Ambassadors remained in Calais to the
very last, prepared to adopt conciliatory measures,
even while they were surrounded on every side by
hostile fleets and amply provisioned armaments,
obviously intended for long foreign service, and that
against their fatherland. English subjects were kept
as far as possible from acts of reprisal, though the
provocations they had to endure were neither few
nor insignificant; and the other side continued their
hostilities after the Duchess of Burgundy's proclamation against them, and rather added to them than
otherwise. The whole correspondence, taken together
and considered in all its details, exhibits a new and
striking illustration of one of those numerous perils and
distractions which rendered uneasy indeed the early
years of the reign of the first Monarch of the House
of Lancaster; affording yet another proof of the
vigour of the mind of the man who could pass safely
through so many troubles, and, at last, obtain success;
and, certainly, not exhibiting his character in an unfavourable light beside that of neighbouring Princes
in his day. The year 1404 closed in darkness and
in doubt; rebellion was successful in Wales, and the
great armament of the French was on the sea: the
threatened invasion came with the new year; but the
firmness and personal courage and, activity of Henry
encouraged and strengthened all for the contest, and
the end, as we shall see, was that he was victorious
finally, and able to establish himself and his family
more firmly than ever on the throne.

Illustra-        Of the Letters of the reign of Henry IV., preserved
tions of the in the Public Record Office, the greater number relate to
"Monasti-
con Angli- Monastic affairs, and chiefly to the election of Heads
canum."   of Monastic Houses. These are both interesting and
A.D. 1399
—1404.    useful documents; but, being nearly all of a formal character, they are unsuitable to a Collection such as the
present.

A few, however, are of more general interest as illustrative of Monastic life, or of the public acts of the Abbats. Such are the Letter from a Prioress of Rowney (whose name is unknown), to Henry the Fourth, entreating him to correct and send back Johanna Adeleshey, a refractory nun, who had fled from the Monastery; and a similar Letter from the Abbat of Welbeck, given at p. 79. A translation of the former Letter was printed in 1846 by Mrs. Green in her " Letters of Royal and Illustrious Ladies."[1]

More important are the Letters from various English Abbats, naming the proxies who were to represent them in Parliament. It is much to be regretted that only a few of these have been preserved; a complete list would have been of great value. The following is a summary of the information on this head afforded by the Letters printed in the present Volume, which are all, belonging to the period (A.D. 1399–1404), that the Editor has been able to discover.

### EVESHAM.

Proxies of Robert Zatton, Abbat,—

Thomas Stowe,[2]
William Stewkeley, Knight, } 6 Oct. 1399.[3]

Thomas Stowe,[2]. . . . . . . . . .
Robert Farington,[3] . . . . . . . } 20 Jan 1401.[4]
John Barel, . . . . . . . . . . . .

### WYNCHCOMBE.

Proxies of William Bradeley, Abbat,—

Nicholas Bubbewyth, and
John Rome, } 20 Jan. 1401.[5]

---

[1] *See* vol. 1. p. 73.
[2] Doctor of Laws, Archdeacon of London and Bedford.
[3] *See* p. 50. *note.*
[4] *See* pp. 50, 51.
[5] *See* p. 49.

These are small results of a long search. But they have their value, as has been said, nevertheless. It is at least something to learn that Nicholas Bubbewith, who was afterwards successively, Bishop of London, of Salisbury, and of Bath and Wells, Master of the Rolls, Keeper of the Privy Seal, and Lord High Treasurer, was in 1401, while Archdeacon of Dorset, one of the Proxies in Parliament for the Abbat of Wynchcombe.

A few similar Letters, belonging to the second half of the reign of Henry the Fourth, will be found in the Second Volume.

Henry the Fourth's "Eastern Correspondence."

The curious collection of Letters preserved in MS. Cotton, Nero B. XI., and aptly styled by Sir Henry Ellis " Specimens of Henry the Fourth's Eastern Correspondence," have been placed in the Appendix [1] on account of the uncertainty of their dates. They are there sufficiently described ; and it is only necessary to mention, in this place, that they afford good evidence of the English King's anxious desire to establish relations of familiar and amicable intercourse with those Eastern Potentates to whom they are addressed, as well as with the sovereigns nearer home who were less willing to acknowledge his pretensions.

Three other Letters, of kindred character, occur in the body of the work. Two of these have reference to the visit of the Emperor Manuel the Second to England in the year 1400. The former was written to the Emperor on the 11th of June in that year, from London, by Peter Holt, Prior of the Hospital of St. John of Jerusalem in Ireland, in reply to a Letter from the Emperor dated at Paris on the 25th of June.[2] He advises the Emperor not to come into England yet, as

---

[1] *See* Appendix I., p. 419.      |      [2] *See* p. 39.

the King is absent on the invasion of Scotland. The latter was written by the Emperor himself, in London, on the 3rd of February 1401. It is in the form of an acknowledgment for a sum of money given up to him by the English King. He mentions that he received the said sum by the hand of Peter Holt, mentioned above.

The third Letter[1] is from John Palæologus to Henry the Fourth, praising the brave deeds of the English, and entreating aid against the Infidels in the dire extremity of the Imperial city. It was written on the 1st of June, 1402.

The first Letter in the present Collection, and several others which occur later, are inserted as illustrative of the King's desire to be recognized by neighbouring Princes, some of whom were from the first disposed to treat him as an usurper, rather than as a rightful sovereign. This Letter announces the fact of his accession to William Duke of Juliers: "seeing," he tells him, "that Divine Providence had given to his rule the "kingdom of England, he directed the far-seeing eyes "of his mind to those inhabitants of foreign parts who "are friendly and well-disposed towards his realm." This produced a Letter of congratulation from the Duke of Juliers, in which he proposed to visit the English court. Henry replied,[2] on the 20th of May 1400, and expressed great delight at the prospect of seeing him. Of a similar description are Henry's Letters to Albert, Count of Hainault; and the Letter of Coentzo de Visschenich to Henry, announcing the death of the Duke of Juliers, and the accession of Duke Reynald.[3]

*Letters on the accession of Henry IV*

---

[1] *See* p. 56.

[2] *See* p. 33.

[3] This Letter contains also some curious information about the proceedings of the Emperor, and a Postscript recommending Gerhard, the writer's servant, as the bearer of other news.

*Miscellaneous Letters.*

The miscellaneous detached Letters comprised in the present Volume, though many of them interesting, and all of them (it is hoped) useful either for historical or genealogical purposes, for the most part speak for themselves. A few, however, seem to require particular description.

*Bishop Merks, A.D. 1401.*

The Letter from Thomas Merks, the unfortunate Bishop of Carlisle, to Robert de Faringdon,[1] acquaints us with the fact that he held the Prebend of Masham in the Cathedral Church of York, though his name does not occur in Le Neve's List. It is dated at Oxford, the 7th of June 1401, and signed "Episcopus Samastanensis."[2]

*Sir Philip Courtenay, A.D. 1402.*

It appears from a Letter of Philip de Courtenay to the Council,[3] that the King had commanded him to provide and man two ships of war at Southampton early in 1402, to proceed "to the parts of Brittany." After he had accomplished this commission, and had remained some time at Southampton, "at heavy charges to himself," he received another Letter from the King ordering him to go to Southampton on the 22d of June for the same purpose. He writes, on the 26th of June, to complain of this uncertainty, and to beg that a day for his departure may be fixed, or, otherwise, he must be ruined.

*John Hauley, Dartmouth, A.D. 1401 —1404.*

John Hauley (or Hawley), of Dartmouth, is mentioned at page 112 as being implicated, with others of that place, in an act of piracy, committed against some merchants of Bruges in June 1401. He was a person of some importance in his time.[4] At page 270 will be found an interesting Letter, written

---

[1] *See* p. 66.

[2] Bishop of Samothrace, a title conferred on him by the Pope, after his deposition from the See of Carlisle for defending the cause of Richard the Second.

[3] He was brother of Peter de Courtenay, who was appointed Governour of Calais on the 2nd of November, 1399 (*See* p. 7).

[4] His monument, a fine brass, still remains before the High Altar of the Parish Church, the Chancel of which he built.

by him on the 14th of July 1404, to Henry the Fourth, excusing himself from appearing personally before the King, as he had been commanded to do, because of a disorder in one of his legs, which prevented him from riding, and almost from walking. This Letter contains particulars about some Breton prisoners, among others " Tange Castell, brother to the Lord of Castell," who had been captured at the time of the then recent descent of the Bretons· upon the south coast of Devon.

Several Letters[1] occur from the authorities of the Hanseatic Towns, all written in 1404, and all containing complaints of robberies committed on their fellow-citizens by English mariners upon the high seas. In addition to the numerous details which they furnish of these frequent and harassing depredations, these Letters are of interest as serving to show how great were the dangers to which merchants and their property were exposed at this period, and how difficult, nay impossible, it was for the sovereigns of the maritime countries in North Europe to restrain their subjects from piracy. Similar complaints were made, about this time, by the Magistrates of Stralsund,[2] especially against John Brandon of Lynn,[3] whose offences appear to have been very numerous, and of an aggravated description. Hanseatic Towns,&c. A.D. 1404.

The last two Letters[4] in this Volume relate to Ecclesiastical affairs, and are of much interest. The second of them is stated in the Catalogue to have been written by the Archbishop of Canterbury, but this is not at all certain. Fitz-Alan was averse to the election of Langley, and probably, therefore, would not write to recommend it. It was, perhaps, written by Beaufort, Bishop of Lincoln, the Chancellor, or by some other person of high position and influence. Ecclesiastical Affairs. A.D. 1404.

---

[1] *See* pp. 208, 238, 240, 251, 371, 372.

[2] *See* pp. 258, 382, 401.

[3] *See* p. 34.

[4] *See* pp. 413, 415.

English Provinces in France. A.D. 1402. The Letters in the Fourth Appendix must, unfortunately, be ranked among the "detached Letters," the greater part of the valuable correspondence which would have illustrated their contents, having been destroyed by the fire. They are valuable as affording a proof of the unsettled state of the English provinces in the south of France during the early years of Henry's reign, and as giving numerous interesting details; as well as for the insight which they give into the character and acts of some of the leading men of the day in those parts.

Prussia. A.D. 1404. The Letters relating to our intercourse with Prussia at this period will be more appropriately considered in the Preface to the Second Volume, in which the series will be continued and the more important Letters comprised.

Incidental Allusions in the Letters. A large Collection of Miscellaneous Letters, such as the present, may naturally be expected to be full of interesting incidental allusions to matters more or less connected with their main subject. This is so in the case of the present Volume; but it is unnecessary to particularise such matters minutely in a Preface, as the reader may fairly be left to discover them for himself.

There are two points, however, which are of sufficient prominence to demand a special notice: these are, first, the light thrown by their own admissions upon the education and knowledge of men entrusted with such an embassy as that of De Ryssheton and his colleagues into France and Flanders; and, secondly, the confirmation which this work affords, in every part, of the historical truth of the conclusion that one of the greatest, if not the very greatest difficulty of Henry the Fourth's reign was his want of money.

In one of their Letters to the King,[1] Swynford and De Ryssheton apologise for "a certain inelegance and

---

[1] *See* Letter CXIX., p. 340.

" rudeness of style, devoid perchance of due digestion," the " correction, filling up, and determination of the " meaning" of which they beg the King to undertake, excusing their "simplicity and ignorance." No doubt, there is a little of the usual voluntary humility in this ; and their Latin composition is, on the whole, far from being so bad as they seemed to think it. But it is strange to find a man like De Ryssheton, " a Doctor of both Laws," and selected to negotiate a difficult and important matter with French and Flemish rulers, utterly ignorant of the French tongue. Yet so he was, and so were all his colleagues. As long as the other side wrote in Latin they were content : but when they began occasionally to receive Letters written in the French tongue, they at once complained of it. "Be " pleased," they wrote to the French Council in September 1404,[1] " to declare fully concerning the said " points 'in Latin, and not in French.' " And again, on the 3d of October, writing to the Duchess of Burgundy, they make a similar complaint, and employ a curious argument in support of their petition. French, it seems, was all very well for princes and great men ; more in their way, indeed, than Latin,—" Although the " general truces between England and France arranged " by temporal Lords and Princes, as the Dukes of " Lancaster and York, of Berry and Burgundy, of " excellent memory, who did not perfectly understand " Latin as they did French, have been (by their express " agreement) taken and confirmed in French ; never- " theless, letters missive, sent to and fro in treaty " between England and France, had continuously up to " this time been drawn up in Latin, as being the " common and vulgar idiom ; all which we have ready " to show, by the example of the Blessed Jerome, who

*Incidental Allusions in the Letters.*

---

[1] *See p. 307.*

Incidental Allusions in the Letters.
" turned and translated all the Books of the Hebrews " in the Old Testament into the Latin tongue, as being " the more easily understood and common,—by which " translation he merited exceeding well of the Church, " both Triumphant and Militant."[1] Their arguments appear to have had no effect whatever; at least, the French Ambassadors took no notice of their request, and Swynford, evidently piqued and annoyed as well as inconvenienced, on the 21st of October acknowledges the receipt of their " Letters written in French, to " us unlearned ones just as if in the idiom of the " Hebrews !"

The second of the allusions spoken of is to a matter of more importance.

Sir Harris Nicolas has directed attention (in his Preface to the "Proceedings and Ordinances of the Privy Council") to the great difficulties entailed upon Henry the Fourth by the low state of the royal exchequer; several proofs of which are contained in that work.

Of these, the most notable is the fact that the rebellion of the Percies in 1403 is, undoubtedly, to be attributed to this cause.

The Earl of Northumberland wrote to the King on the 26th of June in that year (signing himself " Vostre Matathias"), complaining grievously that he had not been paid great part of the large sum expended by him and his son Hotspur on the King's behalf, and adding " that if payment were not soon ordered, it was " very probable that the fair renown of the chivalry " of the realm would not be maintained, to the utter " dishonour and grief of him and his son, who were " the King's loyal subjects."[2]

---

[1] See p. 357.      [2] See Nicolas, i. xlviii.

" This Letter," continues Sir Harris Nicolas, " pre- Incidental
" ceded the rebellion of the Percies by less than four Allusions in the
" weeks, and that event may, it is presumed, be Letters.
" mainly attributed to the inattention shown to their
" request of payment of the large sums which they
" had expended in the King's service. They were
" not only harassed by debts, and destitute of means to
" pay their followers, but their honour, as the Earl
" expressly told the King, was involved in the fulfilment
" of their engagements; a breach of which not only
" exposed them to the greatest difficulties, but, in the
" opinion of their chivalrous contemporaries, perhaps
" affected their reputation. That under these circum-
" stances, and goaded by a sense of injuries and in-
" justice, the fiery Hotspur should throw off his
" allegiance and revolt is not surprising; but it is a
" matter of astonishment that Henry should have
" hazarded such a result. To the house of Percy he
" was chiefly indebted for his crown ; and it is scarcely
" credible that, at the moment of their defection, it
" could have been his policy to offend them . . . . .
" Instead of refusing to pay to the Percies the money
" which they claimed, from the desire to lessen their
" power or to inflict upon them any species of mor-
" tification, all which is known of the state of this
" country justifies the inference that Henry had the
" strongest motives for conciliating that family. The
" neglect of their repeated demands seems, therefore, to
" have arisen solely from his being unable to comply
" with them ; and the King's pecuniary embarrassments
" are shown by the documents in this work[1] to have

---

[1] Among others, may be mentioned " a Letter from the Bishop
of Lincoln, the Earl of Somerset,
and the Earl of Worcester, who
were sent to bring the Duchess
[of Bretagne, Henry's second wife]
to this country."—" This Letter,"
says Sir Harris Nicolas, " proves
" the low state of the Royal Ex-
" chequer, the difficulty of obtain-

" been of so pressing and so permanent a nature that
" there is no difficulty in believing such to have been
" the case." [1]

This conclusion, as we have said already, is fully
borne out by many of the documents contained in the
present work also.

It will be sufficient to notice the case of De Ryssheton and his fellow Ambassadors, who were left for
months, without any supplies from England, and without their stipends, to conduct an arduous and expensive
business. It is curious to note how at first they
modestly ask in four words (as we have seen) for the
moneys due to them, and gradually lose all patience, as
their just demands continue to be disregarded ; till they
are reduced to beggary, and write to declare their
intention of throwing up the negotiations altogether,
and returning to England, unless they are paid at
once.

On the 24th of July De Ryssheton wrote to the
King on this subject, detailing the work and the
reward : "from the 14th day of November [1403] even
" to the day of writing this Letter for my arrears of
" stipend, I have been able to obtain not a single
" penny."[2]

Again, on the 19th of September, growing bolder, he
wrote to the Council,—"the Commissaries named in
" your Commissions, being without stipends or remu-

---

" ing the wages of mariners and
" soldiers ; the mutinous manner in
" which they insisted upon pay-
" ment ; and the impediments to
" the King's service which arose
" therefrom." See also, at p. 99 of
the present work, a Letter from
Esturmy and Kington, who had
been employed to conduct the
Princess Blanche into Germany.
They complain bitterly of the non-

payment of their stipends, and
state it to be their intention to
return to England at once unless
they are paid, as they cannot go on
incurring further debts.

[1] See Nicolas, pp. xlix, l.

[2] See p. 280.—He adds, that he
would go with speed to visit the
King if he could provide himself
with horses and other necessaries
of which he was then in need.

" neration, justifiably refuse to undertake labours, for- Incidental
" asmuch as no one is compelled to go to war at his Allusions in the
" own cost; and from the 14th day of November to Letters.
" the present time, for arrears of stipend and future
" pay, I, Nicholas, have received only sixty pounds
" sterling." Two hundred pounds had been promised
him by the Council, and the balance which was then
due he begged might be paid at once, "for otherwise,
" through lack thereof, I shall not be able any longer
" to continue my labours ; but, leaving the negotiations
" incomplete, shall return into England, to offer my
" excuses before our Lord the King and the Par-
" liament." [1]

Again, in a Postscript to his Letter of the 26th of
September, also addressed to the Council, he wrote,—
" Unless I am paid the balance of the two hundred
" pounds over and above the sixty pounds already
" paid, *you must ordain for yourselves some other*
" *clerk in my place* to carry on these negotiations ;
" for by reason of poverty and want I shall not be
" able to sustain any further labour. Therefore, other-
" wise, I shall return into England to the Parliament."[2]

This is, without doubt, plain language ; but the
position of the writer was a most distressing and per-
plexing one ; and he seems to have had no alternative.
Aston's Letters to the King and to the Council, of the
17th of August in the same year, show clearly that the
garrison of Calais, where the Ambassadors' head-quarters
were, was equally badly off for funds, and much in debt :
relief, therefore, they could give none ; it could only
be sent from England, and for months none was forthcoming for either party. The conclusion is inevitable,
that Henry had no available funds, or he would not
have hazarded the success of these important negotiations

---

[1] *See* pp. 332, 333.     |     [2] *See* p. 337.

Incidental Allusions in the Letters.

at such a dangerous crisis especially, for the sake of a sum so comparatively paltry as one hundred and forty pounds. The debt to the Percies was of many thousands, a heavier drain upon his exchequer, and more difficult to raise at a short notice. That he should have imperilled his relations with France and Flanders by withholding month after month for more than a year —while civil war was raging at home, and the danger of a French war imminent—so small a trifle, if he could have contrived to pay it conveniently, is incredible indeed ; and gives us a far more vivid idea of the terribly "low state of the royal exchequer" than any other case that we have met with.

Many of the subjects comprised in the present Volume are incomplete without the continuations which, according to true chronological arrangement, have been necessarily reserved for the Second Volume, and which include the more interesting of the Welsh, Scottish, and Spanish Letters. The Index to the entire reign will then be given, and thus the repetition of a great many articles common to the two Volumes will be avoided, and easier means of reference afforded to the events of that period, and to the names of persons and places mentioned in their pages.

The Editor cannot conclude his labours without expressing his anxious hope that they have not been in vain : of the great value of the materials to the historical student he has no doubt; and it is his earnest trust, that he has been able to set them forth so as to increase and not to diminish that value.

He does not imagine that his Book is faultless ; but he has used his best exertions to insure accuracy, and has spared neither time nor trouble in his endeavours to overcome the difficulties—not a few nor far between— with which he has been obliged to grapple. It must be

obvious, even to a cursory reader of his Book, that there is scarcely a page of it in which it has not been necessary to use a nice discretion on some point or other; scarcely a Letter in the whole Series which has not been fruitful of doubtful questions, arising either from the serious mutilation of the MSS., or from difficulties of translation, irreconcileable chronology, and the like.

Neither can he omit to thank the many kind friends who have readily assisted him whenever he has had occasion to consult them, and to whom he is indebted for numerous most valuable suggestions. His thanks are especially due to the Rev. H. R. Luard, M.A., Fellow and Assistant-Tutor of Trinity College, Cambridge; the Rev. T. B. Wilkinson, M.A., Fellow and Tutor of Corpus Christi College, Cambridge; R. Barnes, Esq., Secretary to the Bishop of Exeter; R. Swan, Esq., Secretary to the Bishop of Lincoln; and J. Kitson, Esq., Secretary to the Bishop of Norwich: also to the Secretary of the Bishop of Worcester, and to G. W. Leitner, Esq., of King's College, London; the latter of whom rendered him the greatest service in preparing the Spanish Letters for the Press.

EXETER COLLEGE, OXFORD.
December 26th, 1859.

# CHRONOLOGICAL CATALOGUE.

# CHRONOLOGICAL CATALOGUE.

## 1 HENRY IV.. 1399—1400.

Page

g 2

Page

Page

## APPENDIX I.

These Letters are of uncertain date; they are catalogued at pp. 419, 420.

## APPENDIX II.

See above, 1 *December*, 1403.

## APPENDIX III.

See above, 18 *August*, 1404.

## APPENDIX IV.

# A COLLECTION OF

# ROYAL AND HISTORICAL LETTERS

### DURING THE REIGN OF

# HENRY IV.

# A COLLECTION, &c.

## 1 HENRY IV.

### 30 September, 1399, to 29 September, 1400.

### I.

#### HENRY IV. TO WILLIAM, DUKE OF JULIERS.

*Henricus, Dei gratia Rex Angliœ et Franciœ, et* A.D. 1399.
*Dominus Hiberniœ, Magnifico Principi Willelmo,*
*Juliacensi et Gelriœ Duci, consanguineo nostro*
*carissimo, salutem et sincerœ dilectionis continuum*
*incrementum.*

Postquam enim Divina Providentia[1] regnum Angliæ On his ac-
nostro regimini tradiderit gubernandum, ad amicos the English
atque benevolos dicti regni, partium incolas exterarum, throne.
dirigimus nostræ mentis oculos perspicaces ; de quorum
quidem amicorum numero vestram personam fuisse et
esse benevolentissimam satis a diu cognovimus ab
experto. Cujus rei gratia volumus deinceps, scitote
veraciter, votis vestris existere proniores. Et, quum
pridie dilectus armiger vester, Hermannus Mekeren,
nostro referebat auditui fidissimæ dilectionis claritatem
quam nostram erga personam geritis, vestris affectibus
perintime gratulamur.

---

I.] MS. Cott. Galba, B. 1. fol. 126.   [1] *Providentia*] Corrected from
—On vellum.   " Clementia."

A 2

A.D. 1399. Quod si, secundum suggestionem prædicti Hermanni, vos, qui præcessori nostro alligati fuistis, ad quodvis alligantiæ fœdus nobiscum ineundum, nuncios vestros penes nostram præsentiam censueritis delegare, hoc utique nostro desiderio complacebit.

Et quantum ad alia, litteras vestras homagii et fidelitatis, quæ præcessori nostro dudum fecistis, præfato Hermanno secundum postulationem vestram sponte tradidimus, confidentes indubie quod litterarum deliberatione prædictarum in aliquo non obstante vos eatenus velle nobis in omnibus adhærere, quatenus præcessori nostro prædicto, cui immediate riteque succedimus, primitus adhæsistis.

Et vestram personam, de cujus incolumitate nos, qui (Deo laudes) ad præsens sumus incolumes, certificari gestimus, Divinæ Custodiæ commendamus.

Datum etc. tertio[1] Octobris, anno etc. primo.

## II.

### ROBERT III., KING OF SCOTLAND, TO HENRY IV.

*Robert, par la grace de Dieu Roy d'Escoce, a nostre treschier et tresame cousin le Duc de Lencastre, Count de Derby, et Seneschale d'Engleter, salus et dilection.*

---

### [TRANSLATION.]

*Robert, by the grace of God King of Scotland, to our very dear and well-beloved cousin the Duke of Lancaster, Earl of Derby, and Constable of England greeting and love.*

---

[1] *tertio*] Corrected from "primo die."

II.] MS. Cotton. Vespas. F. VII. fol. 77.—On vellum ; original.

Treschiers et tresame cousin.

A.D. 1399.

Voillies savoir que nous avons receu vos lettres a Lythkw le tiers jour d'Octobre, contenantes comment un jour de Marche estoit tenus a Haudenstank, a quel jour fut accordes et jures par les commissairs d'une part et d'autre certeines trieves, a continuer par un an entier, de le Saint Michiel[1] darreine passe jusques a Saint Michiel[1] prochein avenir; seur queles trieves il vous semble expedient que nous envoissemes par de la auchunes de nostre Conseil, tels comme nous affions, pour la declaration et confirmation des dictes trieves.

To the Duke of Lancaster [Henry IV.]

As queles choses, treschiers et tresame cousin, vous plaise a savoir que, quant nous receumes vos dictes lettres, nostre Conseil tel comme apertient a si haute et tele matere n'estoit pas ou nous present, et nient-moins ceo est nostre entente de assembler nostre parlement vers nous; par nostre Conseil tiel comme a

He promises to send Commissioners to ratify the late truce.

---

Very dear and well-beloved cousin.—May it please you to know that we have received your letters at Linlithgow the third day of October, relating how that a March-day had been held at Haddenstank, on which was agreed and sworn by the commissaries of one part and of the other a certain truce, to continue for one entire year, from Michaelmas last past until Michaelmas next to come; concerning which truce it seems to you expedient that we should thither send certain of our Council, such as we might trust, for the · declaration and confirmation of the said truce.— Concerning which things, very dear and well-beloved cousin, may it please you to know that, when we received your said letters, our Council such as pertains to so high and such a matter was not present with us, but notwithstanding it is our intention to assemble our parliament before us, and by our Council such as in this matter is

---

[1] September 29.

A.D. 1399. ceo matere afiert ferons response, la quele nous vous envoirons par auchunes des nostres ou plus tost que boinement fair ce porra.

Treschier cousin, le Saint Esprit vous ait en Sa seinte garde !

Escript a Lythkw susdicte, le sisme jour d'Octobre susdit.

*Endorsed :*—" A nostre treschier et tresame [cousin, le Duc de][1] Lencastre, Count de Derby, [et Seneschale] d'Engleter."[2]

---

becoming we will make answer, the which we will send you by certain of ours as soon as can conveniently be done. —Very dear cousin, the Holy Ghost have you in His holy keeping !—Written at Linlithgow aforesaid, the sixth day of October aforesaid.

*Endorsed :*—" To our very dear and well-beloved cousin, the Duke of Lancaster, Earl of Derby, and Constable of England."

---

[1] The letters which constitute the present volume, being generally written on small pieces of vellum or paper, and therefore liable to injury, are not unfrequently imperfect. When words are cut away, or effaced by damp or other causes, their place will be supplied in the text by dots, the length of the dotted space indicating, as nearly as possible, the number or length of the lost words. In all cases when it is quite evident what words have perished, as in the present instance, they will be supplied within brackets.

[2] Other letters and documents relating to the affairs of Scotland at this time are printed in the Fœdera, viii. pp. 113, 125, 144, 146, 147, 149, 150, 154, 155, 156, 157, 162, 166, 167, 185, 190, 251. See also Nicolas, i. 123, 124 ; ii. 52, 57.

## III.

HENRY IV. TO PETER DE COURTENAY.

*Rex dilecto et fideli consanguineo suo, Petro de Courteney, salutem.*

Sciatis quod nos, de circumspecta fidelitate vestra plenius confidentes, constituimus vos capitaneum villæ nostræ Calesii in regno nostro Franciæ, ita quod vos villam prædictam ad opus nostrum custodiatis, et custodiri faciatis, a primo die Octobris proxime præterito usque ad finem sex annorum ex tunc proxime sequentium, plenarie completorum, juxta formam indenturæ inde inter nos et vos confectæ. *(margin: Appointing him to be Governor of Calais.)*

Majori etenim, ballivis, et omnibus aliis ministris villæ prædictæ, necnon universis et singulis habitatoribus ejusdem villæ, ac in ea existentibus et accedentibus ad eandem, damus tenore præsentium in mandatis, eis nihilominus sub forisfactura omnium quæ nobis forisfacere poterunt, firmiter injungentes quod vobis, ac locum vestrum tenenti ibidem, et deputatis a vobis in absentia vestra, cum ad nos in Anglia seu alibi extra villam prædictam ad mandatum nostrum, seu aliis causis necessariis, accedere vos contingat, in omnibus quæ ad salvam et securam custodiam villæ prædictæ, tam de nocte quam de die pertinent, intendentes sint consulentes et auxiliantes, quotiens et quando per vos seu dictum locum vestrum tenentem ac deputatos a vobis ex parte nostra fuerint præmuniti.

Damus insuper vobis ac dicto locum vestrum tenenti, et deputatis a vobis in absentia vestra, sicut prædictum est, potestatem puniendi et casti-

---

III.] MS. Brit. Mus. Sloane, 4596, fol. 81.—Copied by Rymer for the Fœdera, but never published. The marginal reference is "Franc. 1 H. 4. m. 22."

A.D. 1399. gandi omnes vobis contrarios seu rebelles in iis quæ ad villæ prædictæ pertinent salutionem, prout de jure et rationabiliter fuerit faciendum, et etiam amovendi omnes et singulos qui in munitione dictæ villæ indebite se habebunt, et alios idoneos loco eorum ponendi. Ita quod munitio prædicta prout vobis melius videbitur firmiter teneatur.

In cujus etc.

Teste Rege apud Westmonasterium, secundo die Novembris. Per ipsum Regem.

## IV.

### ROBERT III., KING OF SCOTLAND, TO HENRY IV.

*Robart, par la grace de Dieu Roi d'Escoce, a nostre tresame et treschier cousyn, le Duk de Lancastre, Counte de Derby, et Seneschal d'Engleterre, salutz et dilection.*

To the Duke of Lancaster [Henry IV.]

Treschier et tresame cousyn.

Nagairs que vous avoms escript par Cornewayle haraut, que, sur voz lettres par luy a nous envoyez, vous renvoieroms la responce, si tost come bonement

---

### [TRANSLATION.]

*Robert, by the grace of God King of Scotland, to our well-beloved and very dear cousin, the Duke of Lancaster, Earl of Derby, and Constable of England, greeting and love.*

Very dear and well-beloved cousin.—Lately we wrote to you by Cornwall herald, that, concerning your letters sent to us by him, we would send you the answer as

---

purroms estre conseilliez. Es queles voz lettres il vous A.D. 1399.
sembla expedient que nous envoissemez ascuns de
nostre Conseille perdevers vous.

Sur quoi, treschier et tresame cosyn, come nous He pro-
desiroms toutz jours pays et tranquillite de noz sub- poses that the depu-
gies, il nous semble moult expedient et necessaire, que ties should
de vostre partie feussent envoiez as Marches a Hauden- meet at Haddenstank, ou il est acustume de traitier sur Marches, stank.
commissairs et deputez, de tiel estate que bone vous
semblerra, aiantz poair suffisant de vostre partie pur
traitier et acorder sur triewes, ou plus avant, s'il
plust a vostre partie. Et nous envoieroms tresvo-
lenters commissaires de semblable estate pur le mesme
cause, mes que nous fuissoms certifiez del estate de voz
commissaires, et del temps qu'ils puissent assembler;
le quel nous semblerroit covenable d'estre ensi tost
come bonement faire ceo purroit. Et que les commissairs de vostre partie aient puissance de refourmer
et redresser toutz attemptatz contre les triewes, so-

----

soon as we might conveniently be advised; in which
letters of yours it seemed expedient unto you that we
should send some of our Council unto you.—Concerning
which, very dear and well-beloved cousin, as we always
desire the peace and the tranquillity of our subjects, it
seems to us very expedient and necessary that on your
part there should be sent to the Marches at Haddenstank,
where it is customary to treat concerning the Marches,
commissaries and deputies of such rank as may seem good
to you, having sufficient power on your behalf to treat
and agree on a truce, or still further, if it be agreeable
on your part. And we will very willingly send commissaries of like rank for the same cause, provided we be
certified of the rank of your commissaries, and of the time
when they can assemble; which it seems to us desirable
should be as early as conveniently may be. And that the
commissaries on your part should have power to reform
and redress all attempts contrary to the truce, according to

A.D. 1399. lonc ceo que les endentes faitz par bone memoire le Duc de Lancastre, vostre pier (que Dieu assoille), et nostre aisne filz le Duc de Rothesaye proportient; et nous donoroms a noz commissaires semblable pouair pur faire semblablement pur nostre partie. Et que de vostre partie, si tost come bonement faire purroit, soit commande as gardeins de voz Marches, pur convenir et assemblier ovesque noz gardeyns, pur purvoier et ordeyner coment les subgiez de toutes les deux parties purrount estre paisiez jusques al venir des commissairs desusditz. Et nous donoroms semblable commandement as gardeyns de noz Marches d'ensy faire, si tost come de vostre partie serroms certifiez.

Et sur toutz les choses avauntditz voillez, treschier cosyn, nous faire certifier par le porteur de ces presentes, si tost come vous plest.

Treschier et tresame cousyn, le Seint Esprite vous ait en Sa seinte garde!

Done soulz nostre seal secre a Lynlythen, le secounde jour de Novembre.

---

that which is provided in the indentures made by the Duke of Lancaster, your father, of virtuous memory (whom God assoil), and our eldest son the Duke of Rothsay; and we will give to our commissaries like power to act in like manner on our behalf. And that on your part, as soon as it may conveniently be done, it be commanded to the wardens of your Marches to convene and assemble with our wardens, to provide and ordain how the subjects on both sides may be pacified until the arrival of the commissaries aforesaid. And we will give like commandment to the wardens of our Marches to do so, as soon as we shall be certified on your part.—And, touching all things aforesaid, be pleased, very dear cousin, to cause us to be certified by the bearer of these presents as soon as it may please you. — Very dear and well-beloved cousin, the Holy Ghost have you in His holy keeping.—Given under our privy seal, at Linlithgow, the second day of November.

## V.

### HENRY IV. TO ROBERT III., KING OF SCOTLAND.

*A haut et puissant Prince, R., par la grace de Dieu nostre chier cousin d'Escoce, H., par ycelle mesme grace Roy d'Engleterre et de France, et Seignur d'Irlande, salut.*[1]

Chier cousin.

Nous avons receu voz lettres a nous come Duc de Lancastre, Conte de Derby, et Seneschal d'Engleterre darreinement envoiees, par les queles nous avons conceuz que, pur le bien de pees et tranquillites de noz subgiz, il vous semble moult expedient et necessaire que de nostre partie feussent envoiez as Marches a Haudenstank, quel vous ditez estre lieu acustumez de treter sur Marches, commissaires et deputez, de

He acknowledges the receipt of the Scotch King's letter.

---

### [TRANSLATION.]

*To the high and mighty Prince, Robert, by the grace of God our dear cousin of Scotland, Henry, by that same grace King of England and of France, and Lord of Ireland, greeting.*

Dear cousin.—We have received your letters last sent to us as Duke of Lancaster, Earl of Derby, and Constable of England, by which we have learned that, for the benefit of the peace and tranquillity of our subjects, it seems to you very expedient and necessary that of our part there should be sent to the Marches at Haddenstank (which you say is an accustomed place to treat concerning the Marches) commissaries and deputies, of such rank as

---

V.] MS. Cotton. Vespas. F. vii. fol. 96.—On paper.

[1] This letter is without a date, but is clearly in answer to No. IV., from which it contains several quotations.

A.D. 1399. tieux estatz que bon nous semblera; et que mande soit as gardeins de noz Marches pour convenir et assembler ovesque voz gardeins, pur purvoier et ordenir coment les subgitz d'une coustee et d'autre purront estre peisez, jusqes a la venue des commissaires susditz, et coment pur vostre partie vous vous offrez de faire yce mesme, sicome en voz dites lettres entre autres pleinement est contenuz.

Si veullez savoir, chier[1] cousin,[2] que en vostre susdite lettre ne fumes pleinement responduz a noz lettres par Cornewayl heraud darrein a vous envoiees, a savoir si vous veullez tenir les trieves en lour nature: et

---

shall seem good to us; and that it be commanded to the wardens of our Marches to convene and assemble with your wardens, to provide and ordain how the subjects of the one side and of the other may be pacified, until the arrival of the above-named commissaries, and how on your part you offer yourself to do the same, as in your said letters among other things is fully contained.—May it also please you to know, dear cousin, that in your above-named letter we were not fully answered as to our letters last sent to you by Cornwall herald, that is to say, whether you are willing to maintain the truce according to its terms; and since

---

[1] *chier*] This word has been substituted above the line for "honoure," which has been struck out with a pen.

[2] There is a draught of another letter at fol. 80. in the same MS. volume with the present, and corresponding with it from the beginning thus far. The remainder, which is different, is as follows:—"Si veullez savoir, chier cousin, que nous avons donez en mandement as gardeins de noz Marches devers Escoce d'envoier lour deputez, pur con- venir et assembler ovesques les deputez des gardeins de voz Marches, pur purvoier et ordener pur peiser noz subjiz come desus, et de treter et accorder d'aucun lieu sur les Marches d'auncien temps accustumez, et de nous certifier du lieu, si d'aucun ils purront accorder ovesques les deputez des gardeins de vostre partie sur les Marches susdites. Sur quele certification nous vous ferrons savoir nostre entention et voluntee. — Donne, etc."

depuis celles lettres et voz primeres lettres de re- A.D. 1399.
sponse a nous envoiees, tresgrandz et horribles mes- Complains
prisions ont este perpetrez dedeinz nostre roiaume, a of the outrages
faire de guerre par les eisnez filz de voz gardeins et which had
autres de vostre roialme, sanz notice a nous faire de been committed by
vostre cause. the sons
of the
Nientmeins, al honur de Dieu, et pur le bien de Scottish
pees, nous avons done en mandement[1] as gardeins de wardens;
but con-
noz Marches d'envoier lour deputez[2] pur convenir et sents to
assembler ove tieux come vous semble envoier de lour arrange a
truce.
degree a[3] l'abbatie de Kelcowe, Lundy le quint jour de
Janver prochein venant,[4] ove poaire de treter et d'accorder d'ascun lieu sur les Marches d'auncien temps
acustumez, ou noz commissaires d'ambe part puissent[5]
assembler, et d'ordeigner pur peiser[6] noz subgiz en

---

those letters and your first letters of reply sent unto us,
very great and horrible outrages have been perpetrated
within our kingdom, through the making of war by the
elder sons of your wardens and others of your realm,
without notice given to us of your complaint.—Nevertheless,
for the honour of God, and for the benefit of peace, we
have given in commandment to the wardens of our Marches
to send their deputies to convene and assemble with such
of their rank as you may think good to send to the
abbey of Kelso, on Monday the 5th day of January
next coming, with power to treat and to agree on some
place upon the Marches of ancient time accustomed, where
our commissaries on both sides can assemble, and make
order for the pacifying our subjects in the meanwhile, as

---

[1] mandement] After this word
the following have been struck out
with a pen :—" a noz chiers et foialx
A. B. C."

[2] deputez] After this word " de "
has been struck out.

[3] a l'abbatie] Altered from "a
Dalketh."

[4] venant] After this word have
been struck out " de Kelsowe le
. . . jour, etc."

[5] puissent] After this word has
been struck out the word "encontrer."

[6] peiser] Altered from "peiser
en."

A.D. 1399. le moien temps come desus. Et sur ce nous certifier si bien du lieu come de vostre entention, sur queles matires et pourpos voz ditz commissaires deussent assembler; et apres la certification de vostre entention a nous faite, nous vous ferrons assavoir dedeinz brief nostre pleine voluntee de les matires susdites. Et avons donez en mandement a noz gardeins de tenir repos sur les Marches parensi que ce soit tenuz semblablement de vostre partie.

## VI.

A.D. 1400.

HENRY IV. TO ROBERT III., KING OF SCOTLAND.

Chier cousin,

On the confirmation of the truce.

Sur ce que, par l'information a nous donee par noz commissairs et deputes, assemblez darreinement ovesques voz commissairs et deputes sur la Marche d'Escoce, a cause du tretee de pees, nous fumes certifiez, que voz

---

above. And upon this, to certify us as well of the place as of your intent, on what matters and purposes your said commissaries should assemble; and after the certification of your intention made to us we will speedily cause you to be informed of our full intention concerning the aforesaid matters. And we have given in commandment to our wardens to preserve tranquillity on the Marches in like manner as it may be similarly preserved on your part.

---

Dear cousin.—Touching the matter of which, by the information given to us by our commissaries and deputies, lately assembled with your commissaries and deputies on the March of Scotland, in order to treat for peace, we were certified,

---

VI.] MS. Cotton. Vespas. F. vii. fol. 84.—On vellum; a corrected draught.

ditz commissairs desiroient que noz deux persones et A.D. 1400. les Seigneurs et Marchiers d'ambe partz serrient jurez pour loialement affermer, tenir, et garder les trieves prises parentre noz ditz commissairs et les vostres a Kelkowe, le xxj. jour de Decembre darrein; veullez savoir, chier cousin, q'il nous plest bien de ce faire pour nous et les nostres, et vous requerons que as certeins jour et lieu ore apres Pasques[1] prochein avenir, fatez assembler les Seigneurs de vostre partie pour ceste cause en vostre presence, et envoiez par de cea voz lettres de saufconduyt pur noz chers et foialx Chivaler William Fulthorp, et Gerard Heron, et pur noz amez Clerc et Esquier, Mestre Alein Newerk, et Johan de Mitford, ou pur trois ou deux de eux,[2] les queux nous envoierons pardevers vous pour vous veoir et les vostres jurer les dites trieves. Et certefiez a nostre treschier et

that your said commissaries desired that we two in person and the Lords and Marchers on both parts should be sworn loyally to affirm, keep, and maintain the truce agreed on between our said commissaries and yours at Kelso, the 21st day of December last; may it please you to know, dear cousin, that it is well pleasing to us to do so for ourselves and our subjects, and we request you that on a certain day and place after the next ensuing Easter you cause the Lords on your part to assemble for this purpose in your presence, and send hither your letters of safe-conduct for our dear and faithful Knight, William Fulthorp, and Gerard Heron, and for our beloved Clerk and Esquire, Master Alein Newerk, and John de Mitford, or for three or two of them, whom we will send unto you to witness you and yours swear to the said truce. And certify to our very dear and faithful cousin, the Earl

---

[1] Easter Day fell on April 18 in the year 1400.

[2] The words "Noz chers . . . . eux" are written along the bottom in another hand, and referred by a mark to this place in the text, where the words "A. B., etc." have been scratched out.

A.D. 1400. foial cousin, le Conte de Northumbre, les nonns [1] ceux de vostre partie pur queux vous desirez avoir semblable saufconduit ; au quel nostre cousin nous avons, pour brieftee de temps, donez plein poair pur lour doner suffissant saufconduit pur venir devers nostre presence, pur nous veoir et les nostres semblement jurer les trieves susdites.[2] Entendantz que si tost que nous soions pleinement certifiez que vous eiez en vostre persone jurez, et fait jurer par les vostres mesmes les trieves, nous les jurerons, et les ferrons semblablement estre jurez par les nostres, sanz fraude ou mal engyn.

---

of Northumberland, the names of those of your part for whom you desire to have like safe-conduct ; to the which our cousin we have, on account of the shortness of time, granted full power to give them sufficient safe-conduct to come into our presence, to witness the swearing of us and ours in like manner to the above-named truce. It being understood that as soon as we may be fully certified that you in your person have sworn, and have caused yours also to swear to the truce, we will swear to it, and in like manner will cause it to be sworn to by ours, without fraud or evil design.

---

[1] *les nonns*] Altered from "les nonns des persones."

[2] *Et certefiez . . . . susdites.*] The whole of this passage is written in another hand at the bottom of the letter, and marked for insertion in this place; the following having been struck out :—"Et nous veullez certifier auxi par voz lettres les nonns des persones as queux nous ferrons noz lettres de saufconduyt pour venir devers nous, a recevire le serement de nous et de noz en semblable manere."

A.D. 1400.

## VII.

HENRY, PRINCE OF WALES, TO JOHN GREYNDORE.

*Henry, aisnez filz du Roy d'Engleterre et de France, Prince de Gales, Duc de Guyenne, de Lancaster, et de Cornewaille, et Conte de Cestre, a notre treschier et bien ame Chivaler, Johan Greindore, Visconte de Glomorgan, salut.*

Comme notre tresredoubte Seignur et pere par ses Lettres Patentes ait donne et ottroie a son treschier Escuier, Pierres Crulle, la garde de tous les terres et tenements, ove les appurtenans, queux feurent a Johan Norreys, Chivaler, qui mort est, dedeins la seigneurie de Glomorgan, qui nagairs tenoit en chief de Thomas jadis Sire le Despenser, et les queux terres et tenements, tant par la mort du dit Johan, et par en-

For Peter Crulle.

[TRANSLATION.]

*Henry, eldest son of the King of England and of France, Prince of Wales, Duke of Guienne, of Lancaster, and of Cornwall, and Earl of Chester, to our very dear and well-beloved Knight, John Greindore, Sheriff of Glamorgan, greeting.*

As our dread Lord and father, by his Letters Patent, hath given and granted unto his very dear Esquire, Peter Crulle, the custody of all the lands and tenements, with the appurtenances, which belonged to John Norreys, Knight, now deceased, within the lordship of Glamorgan, who recently held in chief of Thomas late Lord le Despenser, and the which lands and tenements, as well by the death of the said John, and by reason of the

VII.] MS. Brit. Mus. Sloane, 4596, fol. 168.

B

A.D. 1400. cheson de la maniere age de Margarete, fille et heire du dit Johan Norreys, come par la forfacture d'icellui Thomas, sont devenuz as maynes de notre dit Seignur et Pere; a ce q'est dit, a avoir au dit Pierres la garde de tous les ditz terrez et tenemens, ove les appurtenans tanque a la pleine age de la dite heire, avec la mariage d'icelle, sanz desparagement, si come en les dites Lettres pleinement est contenuz. Vous mandons enchargeantz que veues ces presentes vous fatez mettre le dit Pierres, ou son attorne en son nom, en possession des terres et tenemens avantditz, ove lez appurtenances, selonc l'effect et teneur des Lettres Patentes de notre dit Seignur et Pere dessusdites. Et ce ne lessez.

Donne soubz notre seal a Westmonaster, le vj jour de Fevrier, l'an du regne de notre dit tresredoubte Seignur pere primer.

---

minority of Margaret, daughter and heiress of the said John Norreys, as by the forfeiture of that Thomas, are fallen into the hands of our said Lord and father; to the said Peter, as hath been said, to have the custody of all the said lands and tenements, with the appurtenances, until the full age of the said heiress, and also her marriage, without disparagement, as in the said letters is fully set forth. We command and charge you that, on sight of these presents, you cause to put the said Peter, or his attorney, in his name, in possession of the aforesaid lands and tenements, with the appurtenances, according to the effect and tenour of the Letters Patent of our said Lord and father above mentioned. And in this fail not.—Given under our seal at Westminster, the 6th day of February, the first year of the reign of our said dread Lord and father.

## VIII.

### THE DUCHESS OF BRETAGNE TO HENRY IV.

Mon trescher et treshonore Seigneur et cousin. *A letter of credence for Johanna of Bavalen.*
Pour ce que ge suy desirante d'ouir vostre bon
estat,—lequel nostre Seigneur vuille qu'il soit tousdiz
si bon comme vostre noble cuer la sauroit mieulx
souhaiter, et einfin comme ge vouldraie pour moy,—
ge vous prie, mon trescher et treshonore Seigneur et
cousin, que bien souvent vous plaise m'en faire assavoir la certainete, pour tresgrant aise et loece de mon
cuer; car toutesfoiz que g'en puis ouir en bien ce me
resjiouist le cuer moult grandement.

Et si de vostre courtaisie de celuy de pardeca
voudriez ouir—vostre merci—a la faisance de cestes
je et mes enfans estions ensemblement en bonne saute
de noz persoines, (graces a Dieu, Quy ce vous ottroit!)

---

[TRANSLATION.]

My most dear and most honoured Lord and cousin.—
Forasmuch as I am desirous to hear of your good estate,
—the which may our Lord will that it may at all times
be as good as your noble heart knows best to desire, and in
fact as I for my part could wish for you,—I pray you, my most
dear and most honoured Lord and cousin, that it may very
often please you to let me know the certainty, for the very
great comfort and gladness of my heart; for whenever I
am able to hear a good account of you it rejoices my heart
most exceedingly.—And if of your courtesy you would hear
of the same from over here—my thanks to you—at the
writing of these presents I and my children were altogether
in good health of our persons, (thanks be to God, and may

---

VIII.] MS. Cotton. Jul. B. VI. fol. 25 (a).—On paper; original.

A.D. 1400. comme plus a plain Jahanne de Bavalen, quelle vait pardela, vous pourra dire; la quelle vous plaise avoir pour recommande en ce quelle aura a faire pardela.

Et s'aucune chouse vous plaist pardeca que je puisse, je vous prie de le me faire assavoir, et je l'acompliroy de tresbon cuer a mon pouair.

Mon trescher et treshonore Seigneur et cousin, je prie le Saint Esprit qu'Il vous ait en Sa saincte garde.

Escript a Vennes, le xv<sup>e</sup> jour de Fevrier.

LA DUCHESSE DE BRETAIGNE.[1]

---

He grant the same to you!) as Johanna of Bavalen, who is going thither, can tell you more plainly : whom may it please you to have recommended in the matter which she is going over to transact.—And if any thing will please you that I am able to do over here, I pray you to let me know ; and I will accomplish it with a very good heart according to my power.—My most dear and most honoured Lord and cousin, I pray the Holy Ghost that He will have you in His holy keeping.—Written at Vannes, the 15th day of February.

THE DUCHESS OF BRETAGNE.

---

[1] This and another letter are described together in the Catalogue as from "the Dutchess of Britanny to Richard II." It is clear, however, that this letter was written after the death of her husband, the Duke of Bretagne, as she makes no mention of him in enumerating her family, and it has therefore been rightly assigned by Mrs. Green (in her collection of translations of the Letters of Illustrious Ladies) to this year. The date of the other letter alluded to is 16 March, 1399.

A.D. 1400.

## IX.

### HENRY IV. TO ALBERT, COUNT OF HAINAULT.

*Henri, par la grace de Dieu Roy d'Engleterre et de France, et Seignur d'Irlande, a nostre treschier et tresame Cousin, le Duc Aubers de Bayune, Conte de Hayune, Holande, Zeelle, et Sire de Frize, saluz et entier dilection.*

Treschier cousin.

De vostre leesse en coer de ce que a estat roial de tout nostre poeple d'Engleterre sumes receuz, come voz bones lettres a nous par vostre conseiller et de vostre houstel, William, Seignur de Dynsedore, Chivaler, a nous presentees, purportant, et de ce aussi que par la grande affection que a nostre persone avez, vostre dit Chivaler avez pardevers nous envoiez

*In answer to congratulations on his accession.*

---

[TRANSLATION.]

*Henry, by the grace of God King of England and of France, and Lord of Ireland, to our very dear and much beloved Cousin, the Duke Albert of Bayonne, Count of Hainault, Holland, and Zealand, and Lord of Friesland, greeting and undiminished love.*

Very dear cousin.—For your gladness of heart that we are received to the royal estate of all our people of England, as your good letters to us, presented to us by your counsellor and one of your household, William, Lord of Dynsedore, Knight, purport ; and for this also, that for the great affection which you have towards our person, you have sent your said Knight unto us to know our

---

IX.] MS. Cotton. Galba, B. I. fol. 127.— On vellum.

A.D. 1400. pur nostre estat savoir, et vous ent la certeinetee reporter ; vous mercions de tresentier coer tant come plus savons ou poons.

Si veullez savoir, treschier cousin, que a la faisance de cestes feusmes, Dieu merciez, tout sains et en bon point, esteantz tresjoious de vostre bon estat et sauntee, dount par voz dictes lettres nous avetz signifiez. Vous empriantz que d'icel nous veullez certifier le plus souvent que bonement puvez, pur leese et confort de nous, et vostre bone voluntee et affection tout dys envers nous continuer, sur la grande affiance que en vous avons. Et si nous troverez par tant prestz de faire, si Dieu plest, ce que a vous et lez voz tournir purra a honur et plaisir, sicome le dit William, vostre chivaler et le nostre, vous declarera pluis pleine- ment de bouche ; a qui veullez adjouster ferme foy et creance de ce q'il vous en dirra depar nous.[1]

---

conditions and to report to you the certainty thereof, we thank you with all our heart as much as we possibly can. —Be pleased to learn, very dear Cousin, that at the writing of this letter we were, thank God, quite well and in good spirits, being very joyous at your good estate and health, of which you have signified to us by your said letters. Beseeching you that you vouchsafe to assure us of the same as often as you conveniently may, for our satisfaction and comfort, and to continue your good will and affection towards us ever, according to the great trust we have in you. And you will find us, also, in like degree ready to do, God willing, all that may turn to the honour and pleasure of you and yours, as the said William, your knight and ours, will more fully declare unto you by word of mouth ; to whom be pleased to give firm faith and credence as to all that he may say to you on our behalf.—

---

[1] *sicome . . . . . nous.*] This passage has been added in the bottom margin.

Treschier et tresame cousin, la Benoite Trinitee A.D. 1400. vous veulle tout dys ottroier joie et sauntee et treslong duree!

Donne souz nostre prive seal, a nostre Paleys de Westmonstier, le xvj. jour de Feverer.

Very dear and much beloved cousin, the Blessed Trinity vouchsafe to grant you joy and health always, and very long life!—Given under our privy seal, at our Palace of Westminster, the 16th day of February.

---

## X.

### THE EARL OF MARCH TO HENRY IV.

Excellent, mychty, and noble Prince.

Likit yhour Realte to wit that I am gretly wrangit be the Duc of Rothesay, the quhilk spousit my douchter, and now, ageyn his oblisyng to me, made be hys lettre and his seal, and agaynes the law of Halikirc, spouses ane other wife, as it ys said. *Complains of his daughter's rejection by the Duke of Rothsay, and offers to espouse Henry's cause.*

Of the quhilk wrang and defowle to me and my douchter in swilk maner done, I, as ane of yhour poer kyn, gif it like yhow, requere yhow of holp and suppowall fore swilk honest service as I may do efter my power to yhour noble lordship, and to yhour lande: fore tretee of the quhilk matere will yhe dedoy[ne] to charge the Lord the Foarnivalle, ore the Erle of Westmerland, at yhour likyng to the Marche, with swilk gudely haste as yhow like, qware

---

X.] MS. Cotton. Vespas. F. vii. fol. 22.—On paper; original, with traces of a seal. See also Letter XII.; Rymer, viii. 133, 149, 154, 205, 212, 245; Nicolas, i. 114, 171, 172, 177, 182, 187.

A.D. 1400. that I may have spekyng with quhilk of thaim that yhe will sond, and schew hym clerly myne entent; the quhilk I darre nocht discover to nane other bot tyll ane of thaim, be cause of kyn, and the grete lewtee that I traist in thaim, and as I suppose yhe traist in thaim on the tother part.

*Asks for a safe-conduct.*

Alsa, noble Prince, will yhe dedeyne to graunt and to send me yhour saufconduyt,[1] endurand quhill the fest of the Nativite of Seint John the Baptist,[2] fore a hundreth knichtis and squiers, and servantz. gudes, hors, and harnais, als wele within wallit town, as with owt, ore in qwat other resonable manere that yhow like, fore travaillyng and dwellyng within yhour land gif I hafe myster.

*Explains his relationship to Henry IV.,*

And, excellent Prince, syn that I clayme to be of kyn tyll yhow, and it peraventour nocht knawen on yhour parte, I schew it to yhour Lordschip be this my lettre, that gif Dame Alice the Bowmount was yhour gud-dame, Dame Marjory Comyne, hyrre full sister, was my gud-dame on the tother syde, sa that I am bot of the feirde degre of kyn tyll yhow, the quhilk in alde tyme was callit neir.

*and entreats his help.*

And syn I am in swilk degre tyll yhow, I requere yhow as be way of tendirness thareof, and fore my service in manere as I hafe before writyn, that yhe will vouchesauf tyll help me, and suppowell me, tyll gete amendes of the wrangis and the defowle that ys done me; sendand tyll me gif yhow like yhour answer of this with all gudely haste.

And, noble Prince, mervaile yhe nocht that I write my lettres in Englishe, fore that ys mare clere to myne understandyng than Latyne or Fraunche.

Excellent, mychty, and noble Prince, the Haly Trinite hafe yhow evermare in kepyng!

---

[1] See Rymer, viii. 131.      [2] June 24.

Writyn at my castell of Dunbarr, the xviij. day of A.D. 1400. Feverer.

LE COUNT DE LA MARCHE D'ESCOCE.[1]

Endorsed :—"Au tresexcellent trespuissant et tres- noble Prince, le Roy d'Engleterre."

## XI.

ROBERT III., KING OF SCOTLAND, TO HENRY IV.

Robert, par la grace de Dieu Roi [d'Escoce, a nostre tres]chier cousin d'Engleterre salutz.

Sachies nous avoir recu le Dimanche le iiij$^{me}$ jour de Janver, a Perth, vos lettres[2] a nous envoies par Douglas, nostre heraut en province de Cornuwaille vostre heraut, contenantz entre autres choses qu'il vous plust a envoier a Kelcow [Lundy] le v. jour du meisme mois vos commissairz.

Sur quoy, chier cousin, vous faisons asavoir

*Relating to the marches of Scotland.*

---

[TRANSLATION.]

Robert, by the grace of God, King of Scotland, to our very dear cousin of England, greeting.

Know that we have received, on Sunday the 4th day of January at Perth, your letters sent to us by Douglas our herald in the province of Cornwall your herald, containing among other things that it had pleased you to send to Kelso, on Monday the 5th day of the same month, your commissaries. —Concerning which, dear cousin, we bid you know that

---

[1] George Dunbar, eleventh Earl.
XI.] MS. Cotton.Vespas. F. VII. fol. 81 (*B*).—On vellum.

[2] See Letter V.

A.D. 1400. que nous n'estiemes point pres des Marches, et le temps contenu es vos lettres estoit si brief, que ce n'estoit pas possible d'envoier commissairz de nostre partie au dit lieu le jour devantdit. Et pour ce il nous semble que ce n'estoit point omis en nostre defaut; mais, chier cousin, par vos devantditz lettres n'estoit mie respondu [a nos] derreines lettres a vous envoies,[1] en les queles desirames d'estre certefies s'il vous plust d'envoier commissair[z] a Haudenstank, lequel est lieu accustume pour traitier parentre nous sur nos Marches, aiantz suffisant pooir a redresser et refourmer les attemptatz contre les triewes autrefois prises, selonc le teneur des endentures faites parentre nostre treschier fils, le Duc de Rothesay, pour nostre partie, et de bonne memoire vostre pere, (que Diex assoille) de vostre partie. Car il nous semble se vous fussies en bonne volente de refourmer et redresser les attemptatz contre les devantditz triewes, nous

---

we were not near the Marches, and the time mentioned in your letters was so brief that it was not possible to send commissaries on our behalf to the said place on the aforesaid day. And for this it seems to us that this was not an omission by our default ; but, dear cousin, by your aforesaid letters there was no answer to our recent letters sent to you, in the which we desired to be certified if it pleased you to send commissaries to Haddenstank (which is an accustomed place to treat as between us concerning our Marches), having power to redress and reform the attempts against the truce formerly established, according to the tenour of the indentures made between our very dear son, the Duke of Rothsay, on our part, and your father of good memory (whom God assoil) of your part. For it seems to us if you were of good will to reform and redress the attempts against the aforesaid truce,

---

[1] See Letter IV.

pouissiemes en temps a venir affier que triewes a A.D. 1400. prendre deussent miex estre gardes et tenus. Et pour ce, chier cousin, il nous semble convenable et nous plaist, s'il vous plust, d'envoier commissairs de nostre partie, a convenir au lieu desusdit acustume avoec vos commissairs, aiant povoir d'ambedex parties pour refourmer et redresser les attemptatz contre les avantdit triewes ; selonc le teneur des endentures devantdites, et outre ce a traitier sur triewes, ou plus avant s'il vous sembloit expedient.

Sur quoy, chier cousin, nous veullies certefier par lettre, si tost comme bonement pouees, en si bien de l'estate de vos commissairs comme del temps qu'ilz deussent assembler.

E chier cousin, le Tout-puissant vous ait en Sa sainte garde !

Escript a Lythqw, le xiiij$^{me}$ jour de Mars.

*Endorsed :*—"A nostre chier cousin d'Engleterre."

---

we might in time to come feel assured that any truce to be undertaken would be better guarded and kept. And for this purpose, dear cousin, it seems to us convenient, and it pleaseth us, if it please you, to send commissaries on our part to meet with your commissaries at the above-mentioned accustomed place, having power on both sides to reform and redress the attempts against the aforesaid truce ; and besides this to treat concerning a truce, or still further if it seemed to you expedient.—Concerning which, dear cousin, be pleased to certify us by letter, as soon as you conveniently can, as well of the rank of your commissaries, as of the time when they should assemble.—And dear cousin, the Almighty have you in His holy keeping !—Written at Linlithgow, the 14th day of March.

*Endorsed:*—"To our dear cousin of England."

A.D. 1400.

## XII.

### HENRY IV. TO THE EARL OF WESTMORELAND.

On behalf
of George
Dunbar,
Earl of
March.

Trescher et tresame frere.

Puis[1] le temps que nous vous escrivasmes darreinement par noz lettres, en queles feut enclosee la copie
d'une lettre[2] a nous envoiee par le Conte de la Marche
d'Escoce et la response d'icelle,[3] ovesques certeine charge
a vous donee par noz dites lettres, nous avons receuz
certeins autres lettres a nous envoieze par le dit Conte,[4]
contenantes en substance l'effect de ses primeres lettres,
ensemblement ovesque certeine credence a nous mon-
stree et declaree de par lui par l'Abbe de Alnewyk,
la quele credence ycelui Abbe,[5] portour de cestes, vous

---

### [TRANSLATION.]

Very dear and much-beloved brother.—Since the time
that we last wrote to you by our letters, in which was
enclosed the copy of a letter sent to us by the Earl of the
March of Scotland, and the answer thereto, with a certain
charge given to you by our said letters, we have received certain other letters sent unto us by the said Earl, containing in
substance the effect of his first letters, together with a certain
credential shown and explained to us on his behalf by the
Abbat of Alnwick, the which credential this Abbat, bearer of
these presents, will be able fully to explain to you by word of

---

XII.] MS. Cotton. Vespas. F. VII.
fol. 68.—On vellum. A corrected
draft.

[1] This letter originally began
with the words " Nous avons,"
which have been struck out.

[2] See Letter X.

[3] *et la response d'icelle*] Added
above the line.

[4] *Conte*] After this word " ovesque certein " have been struck out.

[5] *Abbe*] After this word the
following have been struck out :---
" qui va presentement par devers."

sauvra par bouche pleinement declarer. Si volons et A.D. 1406.
vous mandons que oiee et entendue la dite credence,
vous vous trehez devers la Marche d'Escoce si has-
cunement come faire le purrez bonement, pur treter
ovesques le dit Conte de la Marche sur la matire de
la dite credence, selonc le purport de les commission et
enstruction queles nous vous envoions par celle cause.

Et si vous envoions une saufconduit [pu]r le dit
Conte, et pur a tantz de gentz come il ad demande, a
durer tanque a la Nativitee de Seint Johan le
Baptiste [1] prochein avenir, liquel saufconduit nous
volons que selonc le tretee affaire parentre vous et
l'avantdit Conte, si vous semble expedient et necessaire, vous lui fatez deliverer; [2] nous certifians clerement per voz lettres l'entention du dit Conte et ce
que vous ferriez en celle partie. Et ce ne vuillez

---

mouth. Therefore, we will and we command you that, after
having heard and understood the said credential, you proceed
towards the March of Scotland as speedily as you conveniently
can, to treat with the said Earl of the March on the matter of
the said credential according to the purport of the commission
and instruction that we send you for this cause. And we also
send you a safe-conduct for the said Earl, and for as many persons
as he has required, to continue in force until the Nativity of
S. John the Baptist next ensuing, the which safe-conduct we
will that, according to the treaty to be made between you and
the aforesaid Earl, if it seem to you expedient and necessary,
you cause to be delivered to him ; certifying to us clearly by
your letters the intention of the said Earl, and what you shall

---

[1] June 24.
[2] deliverer] After this word have     been struck out "le saufconduit susdit."

A.D. 1400. en nulle manere lesser, pur amour de nous, et sicome nous nous fions de vous.

Donne, etc. le xiiij. jour de Marz.[1]

*Endorsed :*—" A nostre treschier et tresame frere, le Conte de Westmerland." [2]

do on this behalf. And in this be pleased in no manner to fail, for love of us, and as we have confidence in you.

Given, etc. the 14th day of March.

*Endorsed :*—" To our very dear and well-beloved brother, the Earl of Westmoreland."

[1] At fol. 39. of the same MS. is the following deed (on vellum), whereby King Henry allows certain sums of money and stipends to the Earl of March for his allegiance :— " Fait remembrer que le Roy ad veu et entendu l'informatioun et instructioun baillez a le Sire de Furnevale, et a Thomas Stanley, clerc, messages envoiez a le Conte de la Marche d'Escoce, ensemblement ovec la response du dit Conte endente et delivere as ditz messages. Sur quoy y semble au Roy que si le dit Conte se voet descharger del homage fait au Roy d'Escoce, et faire homage lige au Roy, et devenir son homme, le Roy lui ferra deliverer sis mille marcz en mayn pur regarde de sis anz perignant pur chescun an mille marcz, et si Dieu face pardon du dit Conte deinz les ditz sis anz, q'alors ce que remaint aderer de la dicte somme outre mille marcz par an soit repaie au dit Roy, et apres les vj. anz finz vivant le dit Conte, le Roy lui donrra cynk centz marcz par an a terme de sa vie, ou tanque lui soit purveu par le Roy de terre ou de rent a la value ; et q'en le meen temps le dit Conte, ne nulle des gentz du dit Conte, ne nulle autre q'il port a son loial poair sanz fraude ou mal engyn cesser ou impedier, ne serra ne serront armez encontre le Roy, ne nulle de ses liges, et q'ils ne ferront ne nulle de eux ferra aucun damage, riot, attemptat, n'autre male ne grief qiconque au dit Roy, na nulle de ses subgitz, na lour chastelx, seigneuries, biens, et possessions qiconqes."

[2] Ralph Neville, first Earl.

A.D. 1400.

## XIII.

### HENRY IV. TO JOHN DE SCARLE.

*Henri, par la grace de Dieu Roy d'Engleterre et de France, et Seignur d'Irlande, a nostre treschier Clerc, Johan de Scarle, nostre Chanceller, saluz.*

Come a ce que nous sumes enformez Florimont, jadis Sire de Lesparre, feusse tenuz et obligez a William le Scrop, nadgairs Conte de Wilteshire, qui mort est, en une certeine somme, la quele feut du tresor de Sire Richard, nadgairs Roy d'Engleterre, nostre darrein predecessour (qui Dieux assoille), baillee a l'avantdit William le Scrop pur ses gages, quant il feut seneschal de Guyene pur nostre dit predecessour: de la quele

*Releases William Amanien from the payment of a debt.*

---

[TRANSLATION.]

*Henry, by the grace of God King of England and of France, and Lord of Ireland, to our very dear Clerk, John de Scarle, our Chancellor, greeting.*

As we are informed, Florimont, formerly Lord of Lesparre, was held and bound unto William le Scrope, late Earl of Wiltshire, now deceased, in a certain sum, the which from the treasury of Lord Richard, recently King of England, our late predecessor (whom God assoil), was assigned to the aforesaid William le Scrope for his wages, when he was constable of Guienne for our said predecessor ; of the which sum, as it is

---

XIII.] From the Volume of Autographs preserved in the Public Record Office.—On vellum. See Rymer, viii. 181.

A.D. 1400. somme sicome l'en dit ad este paiee la greindre partie, et de la quele y remeint uncore nient paiee la somme de mille livres d'esterlings, a nous due par Guilliem Amanien, ore Sire de Lesparre et de Roasan[1]; la quele somme il ne nous poet paier saunz grand amentissement de son estat, sicome il nous ad donez a entendre. Et nous de nostre grace especiale, et pur les bones et greables services que le dit Guilliem Amanien nous ad fait et ferra en temps avenir, lui eons pardonez la dite somme de mille livres esteant aderere come avant est dit, veuillantz qu'il et ses heirs ent soient quitz et deschargez envers nous pur touz jours.

Vous mandons que sur ce fatez faire lettres souz nostre Grant Seal en due fourme.

Donne souz nostre prive seal a Westmonaster, le xvij. jour de Mars, l'an de nostre regne primer.

---

said, there has been paid the greater part, and of the which there remains still unpaid the sum of one thousand pounds sterling, to us due from William Amanien, now Lord of Lesparre and of Roasan ; the which sum he is unable to pay us without great minishing of his estate, as he has given us to understand. And we, of our especial grace, and for the good and pleasant services that the said William Amanien has done for us and will do in time to come, have forgiven him the said sum of one thousand pounds, being in arrear as is aforesaid ; willing that he and his heirs be quit and discharged of it towards us for ever.—We command you that concerning this you cause letters to be written under our Great Seal in due form.—Given under our privy seal at Westminster, the 17th day of March, the first year of our reign.

---

[1] See Rymer, viii. 445.

A.D. 1400.

## XIV.

### HENRY IV. TO WILLIAM, DUKE OF JULIERS.

*Henricus, Dei gratia Rex Angliæ et Franciæ, et Dominus Hiberniæ, magnifico ac potenti Principi Willielmo de Juliaco, Duci Gelriæ et Juliacensi ac Comiti Zutphaniæ, consanguineo nostro carissimo, salutem et votivorum successuum continuam ubertatem.*

Magnifice Princeps, consanguinee noster carissime. Litteras vestras, nostris jam tarde manibus præsentatas, recepimus, ac contenta in eisdem ad plenum intelleximus, inter alia memorialiter retinentes qualiter de nobis ac statu nostro prospero vestra cupit Nobilitas audire sæpius bona nova. Unde eidem regratiamur. Significamus igitur Nobilitati præfatæ quod in præsentium consectione litterarum perfecta mentis et corporis sanitate gaudemus, cunctaque nobis succedunt prospere juxta vota,—laudes Christo, Qui vobis quamvis id concedat ! de status vestri incolumitate votiva nova audire corditer affectantes. *In answer to a letter of congratulation.*

Magnifice Princeps, consanguinee noster carissime, quoad hoc quod nobis alias vestra patefecit Nobilitas antedicta eandem pro ipsius aliquali solatio nostræ Majestatis velle præsentiam visitare ; de quo noster non renuit animus consolari. Verum est, consanguinee carissime, quod, si absque incommodo vestro tempus vobis congruum ad ea captare poteritis, nostræ placebit voluntati vestra intentio prælibata, adventusque vester ad regni nostri partes, nostram etiam et personam, erit placidus et acceptus. Et si qua penes *The King will be glad to receive the Duke's visit.*

---

XIV.] MS. Cotton. Galba, B. i. fol. 128.—On paper ; original, with traces of a seal. See Nicolas, i. 128, 129.

C

A.D. 1400. nos fuerint in quibus votis vestris poterimus complacere, nobis inde significare velitis ; nam ea libentissime
faciemus.

Magnifice Princeps, consanguinee noster carissime,
Altissimus vos conservet prospere et longæve !

Datum sub signeto nostro, in Palatio nostro Westmonasterii, mensis Maii die xx.

*Endorsed :*—" Magnifico ac potenti Pr[incipi], Duci
Gelriæ et Juliacensi, [ac Comiti Zutphaniæ, con]sanguineo nostro carissimo."

## XV.

### HENRY IV. TO THE MAYOR OF LYNN AND OTHERS.

*Henricus, Dei gratia Rex Angliæ et Franciæ, et
Dominus Hiberniæ, Majori villæ Lenn, Johanni de
Brandoun, Thomæ Trosbut, Thomæ Waterden, et
Roberto de Burnham, et eorum cuilibet, salutem.*

For the
restoration
of a barge
to a mer-
chant of
Dieppe.

Præcipimus vobis firmiter injungentes quod statim
visis præsentibus, Johanni Doulle, mercatori de Dyeppe
in Normannia, quandam bargeam suam, per vos, seu
per alios ex parte vestra, nuper supra mare captam,
cum bonis suis quibuscumque intra dictam bargeam
tempore quo ipsa sic, ut præmittitur, capta fuit
existentibus, deliberetis, et eidem Johanni Doulle
plenam et integram restitutionem inde habere faciatis,
aliquo mandato nostro vobis prius in contrarium
directo non obstante ; proviso semper quod idem
Johannes Doulle custumas nobis pro bonis suis, quæ
intra regnum nostrum Angliæ vendet, debitas solvat,
ut est justum.

Teste me ipso apud Westmonasterium, vj. die Junii,
anno regni nostri primo.

XV.] MS. Brit. Mus. Sloane, 4596, fol. 187.

## XVI.

LORD GREY DE RUTHYN TO GRIFFITH AP DAVID AP GRIFFITH.

Gruffuth ap David ap Gruffuth.

We send the greting welle, but no thyng with goode hert.

And we have welle understande thy lettre to us sent by Deykus Vaghan, our tenaunt, which maken mention and seist that the fals John Weele hath disseyved the.[1] And seist that alle men knowne welle

*In answer to a letter complaining of treachery. Lord Grey recapitulates the points of this letter, and answers them.*

XVI.] MS. Cotton. Cleop. F. III. fol. 70 b.—On paper ; a contemporaneous MS.

[1] The following is a reprint from Ellis of the letter here referred to, so far as it is quoted in this answer :—

"I wold pray ȝou hertli that ȝe wold her how the fals John Wele served me, as al men knoyn wel.

"I was under the protexion of Mered ap Owein; he sende to me be trety of my cosynes Maester Edward and Edward ap David, and askyt ȝif I wold cum in, and he wold gete me the King's charter, and I schuld be Maester Forster, and Keyshat in Chirke is lond; and other thinges he behiȝt me, the qwich he fulfullyt not.

"Afterward he askyt me qwether I would go over see with hym, and he wold gete me my charter of the Kynge, and bringe me to hym sounde and saff, and I schuld have wages as muche as any gentilman schuld have that went with hym. And over thys he seide befor the Byschop of Seint Assaph, and befor my forsaede cosynes, that, rather then I schuld fael, he wold spene of his own godde xx marke.

"Her apon I trust, and gete me ij men, and boȝt armery at all pees,

and horses, and other araement, and come to Oswestre a nyȝt befor or thei went. And on the morw ther after I send Piers Cambr̄, the Resevor of Chirke is lond, thryes to him, for to tel him that I was redy. He saed that I schuld speke no word with him ; and at the last he saed that he hade no wages for me ; and that he hade al his retenev ; but bade me go to Sᵣ Ric. Lakin [MS. Kakin] to loke qwether he hade nede of me. With the qwych I had never ado nor no covenande made, for I wold a gon for no wages with hym over see, but for to have my charter of the Kyng, and sum levyng that I myȝt dwel in pees and in rest. And this, as a wytnes of Sᵣ Ric. Lakyn and of Straunge, I was redy and wylly for to a gon with hym, hedde he be truw.

"He come and saed prively to Sᵣ Ric. and to Straunge (qᵈ he) her is Gruffuth ap David ap Gruffuth in this town, and has no savecondyt but in Chirke is lond, and ȝe mown take hym and ȝe wolle ; and a gode frende come and told me this ; and I hert this and trust me thens in al the haste that I myȝt. And so I was begyllyd and deseyved of that fals Wele, as al men knoyn welle."

A.D. 1400. that thu was under the protectioun of Mered ap Owyn, and sent to the as thu seist by trete of thy cousynes, Maester Edward, and Edwarde ap David, and asked the if thu woldest come inne, and he wolde gette the thy chartere of the Kyng, and that thu sholdest be Keyshate in Chirklond ; and other thyngis he beheght the, which he fullfylled noght, as thu seiste ; and after warde asked the whether thu woldest go over the see with him, and he wolde gette the thy chartere of the King, and bryng the to hym sounde and saufe, and thu sholdest have wages as moche as any gentelle man that went with hym. And overe thus thu seideist that John Welle seide befor the Bishope of Seint Assaph,[1] and befor thy cousynes, that, rather than thu sholdest faile, he wolde spenne of his oun goode xx marcis.

Heer up on thu trusted, as thu seiste, and duddest gete the two men, and boght the armoure for alle peces, horsen, and other araie, and comest to Oswaldestree a nyght befor that thei went ; and on the morowe after thu sendest Piers Cambr̄, the receyvour of Chirklonde, thries to hym, to telle hym that thu was redy, and he seide that thu sholdest speke no worde with him. And at the last he saide he hadde no wages for the, as thu seiste, and he hadde fully his retenue, and bade the goo to Sir Richarde Laken to loke whether he hadde nede of the other noo, with the which thu, as thu seiste, haddest nevere ado, ne nevere madest covenaunt with. For thu woldest, as thu seiste, have goon for no wages with hym over see, but for to have thy chartere of the Kyng, and sume lyvyng that thu myghtest dwelle in pees.

And, as thu seist, Sir Richard Laken and Straunge wolle berre wittenesse that thu was redy and wylly for to goon with hym giffe he hadde be trewe. And

---

[1] John Trevaur.

also thu seiste he cam to Laken and to Straunge and A.D. 1400. wolde have made hem to take the, and thu haddest wittyng ther of, as thu seiste, and trussed the fro thennes, and knowelechest[1] that thy men cam and breeke our parke by nyght, and tooke out of hyt two of our horses, and of our menis.

And, as hit is tolde the, thu seiste, that we ben in pourpose to make our men brenne and slee in what so ever cuntree thu be inne, and wilt withouten doute, as thu seiste, as many men as we slee and as many housen that we brenne for thy sake, as many brenne and slee for our sake. And, as thu seiste, thu wilt have bothe breede and ale of the best[2] that is in our lordshipe; and heer of thu biddest us have no doute, the whiche is agayn our wylle, gife any thu have breede other ale so, and ther as thu berrest up on us that we sholde ben in pourpose to brenne and sleen men and housen for thy sake, or for any of thyn enclinant to the, or any of hem that ben the Kinges trewe liege men, we was nevere so mys avised to worch agayn the Kyng no his lawes, whiche giffe we dudde, were heigh tresoun; but thu hast hadde fals messageres and fals reportoures of us touchyng this matere; and that shalle be welle knowen un to the King and alle his Counsaile.

---

[1] "And as I herd ther been taken ij horses of ȝour men that wern pyte in ȝour parke, thoo horsys I wod qwer thei ben; but for no hatered that I hade to ȝou or ȝour Lordschip thei wern taken, but my men toke ham, and boȝt ham of hem.

"And hit was told me that ȝe ben in purpos for to make ȝour men bran and sle in qwade soever cuntre that I be and am sesened in. With owten doute as mony men that ȝe sleu, and as mony howsin that ȝe bran for my sake, as mony wol I bran and sle for ȝour sake; and doute not I wolle have both bredde and ale of the best that is in ȝour lordschip."

The letter concludes thus:—"I can no more, but Gode kepe ȝour worschipfull astate in prosperite.

"I wrettin in grete haste at the parke of Brinkiffe, the xj day of June.—From GRUFFUTH AP DAVID AP GRUFFUTH."

[2] of the best.] Added above the line.

A.D. 1400.

Ferthermore, ther as thu knowlechest by thyn oun lettre that thy men hath stolle our horsen out of our parke, and thu recettour of hem, we hoope that thu and thy men shalle have that ye have deserved. For us thynketh, thegh John Welle hath doon as thu aboven has certefied, us thynketh that that sholde noght be wroken towarde us. But we hoope we shalle do the a pryve thyng; a roope, a ladder, and a ring, heigh on gallowes for to henge. And thus shalle be your endyng. And he that made the be ther to helpyng, and we on our behalfe shalle be welle willyng. For thy lettre is knowlechyng. Written, etc.[1]

---

[1] This remarkable letter is one of a series of three preserved in MS. Cotton. Cleop. F. III., two of which are printed in Sir Henry Ellis's "Original Letters" (2nd Series, i. 3—7).

It is there suggested, in a note at page 5, that this is the letter alluded to in that printed as No. I., in which Reginald Lord Grey de Ruthin, writing to the Prince of Wales, says,—"the strengest thiefe of Wales sent me a lettre, which lettre I send to you." It is clear, however, that the letter here alluded to is that printed as No. II. in Ellis's collection, to which the letter in the text is an answer, being from Lord Grey de Ruthyn himself, and addressed to, not written by, Griffith ap David ap Griffith. The true order is, therefore, as follows :—

I. From Griffith ap David ap Griffith to Lord Grey de Ruthyn, MS. Cotton. Cleopat. F. III. fol. 72; (Ellis, p. 5), June 11, 1400.

II. Lord Grey's answer, printed above, and dated on or before the 23rd of June, 1400.

III. Lord Grey's letter to the Prince of Wales (Ellis, p. 3), informing him of the receipt of Letter I., and that he had written an answer to it (Letter II.), of which he enclosed a copy. There can be little doubt that the MS. from which the text is printed, and which is pasted on the back of Lord Grey's letter to the Prince, is the "copy" here alluded to. The passage in full is as follows : "And, gracious Lorde, please hit you to witte that the day that the Kynges messager cam with the Kynges lettres, and with youres to me, the strengest thiefe of Wales sent me a lettre, which lettre I send to you, that ye mowe knowen his goode wyll and gouvernance, with a copie of an other letter that I have send to him agayn of an answere."

## XVII.

### PETER HOLT TO THE EMPEROR MANUEL II.

Excellentissime et serenissime Princeps.

Vestræ Sublimitatis litteras, xxjᵃ die Junii scriptas Parisius, litteris meis nuper vestræ Serenitati transmissis inter cetera cordi vobis inhærentia responsivas, cum reverentia debita et honore recepi, cupiens vestris desideriis ex affectu pro meæ parvitatis modulo complacere.

Cum, itaque, serenissime Princeps, a tempore quo Dominus meus Rex Angliæ gubernacula regni sui suscepit, durantibus treugis inter ipsum et adversarium suum Franciæ, pro ipsis et eorum alligatis hinc inde firmatis, Scoti non nulla damna regno Angliæ modo guerrino patenter intulerint, ac idem Dominus meus Rex, pro defensione regni sui, versus partes Boreales cum ipsius exercitu transitum suum acceleret, ut Scotorum illorum malitiæ atque invasioni, Divina sibi assistente Potentia, resistere valeat; nec de tempore reditus ejus quisquam certus esse poterit, tam arduo causante negotio; non videtur mihi, serenissime Princeps, quod vestro statui congruat aut honori, præfato Domino meo Rege in tam remotis agente, huc in regnum vestram accelerare præsentiam. Sed hoc juxta meæ parvitatis consilium velitis in suspenso relinquere, donec Excellentiæ vestræ scripsero plenius quid circa præmissa facere debeatis, habituri pro certo, serenissime Princeps, quod ad præsentiam ejusdem Domini mei Regis præsentialiter me diverto, ut, supra

*On the Emperor's proposed visit to the English Court.*

---

XVII.] MS. Cotton. Vesp. F. I. fol. 118.—On vellum; original, with marks of the seal. See Letter XXV.

A.D. 1400. præmissis ejus intentione concepta, voluntatem suam litteratorie vestræ Serenitati valeam citius declarare.

In Illo Qui Principibus dat salutem et gratiam Excellentia vestra valeat feliciter et votive !

Scriptum Londoniæ, undecimo die Julii.

Majestatis vestræ excellentissimæ humilis servitor, Frater PETRUS HOLT, Tricoplerius de Rood, Prior Hospitalis Sancti Johannis Jerusalem in Hibernia.

*Endorsed :*—" Excellentissimo Principi, Manuelo, [in Christo Deo] fideli Imperatori, et moderatori Romæorum semper Aug[usto]."

## XVIII.

### HENRY IV. TO THE MAYOR, &c. OF LYNN.

*Henri, etc. a noz bien amez les Maire, Baillife, et bones gentz de nostre ville de Lenne, saluz.*

Requiring supplies for carrying on the war in Scotland.

Nous vous remercions sovent de voz[1] foialx services travaux et coustages, queux fait[2] avez et sustenuz en

[TRANSLATION.]

*Henry, etc. to our well-beloved the Mayor, Bailiff, and good people of our town of Lynn, greeting.*

We thank you often for your faithful services, labours, and expenses which you have performed and sustained in

XVIII.] MS. Cotton. Vespas. F. VII. fol. 68.—A corrected draft on vellum. See Nicolas, i. 122.

[1] *voz*] Altered from "vostre."

[2] *fait*] "Vous" (written under "fait,") and "fait" (repeated after "avez,") have been struck out.

alantz ore tard sur la mer,[1] et vous mettantz en A.D. 1400. aventure pur l'onur[2] et bien de nostre roiaume, et pur resister a la malice de noz enemys d'Escoce, qui s'afforcent de jour en autre de faire invasion, et tout le mal qu'ils purront a nostre roiaume susdit. Et[3] certes fumes[4] bien leez de la bone emprise[5] que Dieux de Sa grace ottreiez vous ad[6] en vostre dit journee, a grant comfort de tout[7] nostre roialme. Si vous prions enchargeantz que en continuance ce que vous avez ensi bien commencez, si bien a l'onur de nous come a vostre profit, fatez envoier par meer a la havene de Tynemouthe Shelles a toute la haste que vous purrez, a tantz de vitailles come vous purrez bonement si bien de vins, flour, frument,[8] et aveins,

---

proceeding now lately to sea, and placing yourselves in peril for the honour and welfare of our realm, and to resist the malice of our enemies of Scotland who from day to day strive to effect invasion, and all the evil they can possibly do to our said kingdom. And certainly we were right glad of the good success which God of His grace vouchsafed you in your said voyage, to the great comfort of all our realm. Therefore we pray and charge you that, in continuance of what you have thus so well begun, as well for our honour as for your profit, you cause to be sent by sea to the haven of Tynemouth Shields, with all possible speed, as much victuals as you conveniently can, as well of wines, flour, wheat,

---

[1] Here the words "pur resister a" have been scratched out.

[2] l'onur] Altered from "le bien et honour."

[3] susdit. Et] Added above the line.

[4] Et certes fumes] Written at first, "et fumes."

[5] de, etc.] Altered from "de l'emprise la bone et graciouse."

[6] Dieux de, etc.] Originally Dieux vous ad, etc."

[7] de tout, etc.] Written at first "de nous et de tout, etc."

[8] frument] Originally "frument foyn."

A.D. 1400. come d'autres vitailles que soient busoignables pur le refresshement de nous et de nostre host, et qui fumes ore[1] en alantz vers les Marches d'Escoce pur la defense de nostre dit roialme, et socour de nostre poeple en celles parties. Et ce[2] en nulle manere ne lessez, sur la grande affiance que nous portons de vous, et come vous desirez la sauvatioun de l'estat et honur de mesme nostre roialme. Entendantz que nous volons que pur mesmes les vitailles vous eiez suffisant assignement d'estre paiiez de noz custumes en port de nostre dite ville. Vuillantz outre que vous purrez faire[3] vostre profit a mesme de ce que vous gaignerez sur nos enemys desusditz.[4]

Et fatez auxi proclamer en nostre dite ville, et parmy le paiis, ou vous semblera expedient, que

---

and oats, as of other victuals that may be needful for the refreshment of us and of our army, who are now proceeding towards the Marches of Scotland for the defence of our said realm, and the help of our people in those parts. And this in no manner fail to do for the great confidence that we bear towards you, and as you desire the salvation of the state and the honour of our said realm. It being understood that our will is that for the same victuals you have sufficient security for payment from the port customs of our said town. And that we are further desirous that you may be able to make your profit also from what you may gain from our enemies aforesaid. And, further, cause it to be proclaimed in our said town and in the country around, wherever it may seem to you expedient, that all other persons who

---

[1] ore] Added above the line.
[2] Et ce] Originally "entendant."
[3] faire] Added above the line.
[4] The letter originally ended here with the sentence commencing, "Donne, etc.," as below. This has been scratched out, and so has the old commencement of the next sentence, which was "Fezantz outre."

touz [1] autres qui veullent [2] amesner vitailles par A.D. 1400.
meer [3] pur le refresshement de nostre dit host serront
paiez [4] d'atant come mesmes les vitailles vaudrons en
nostre host susdit.

Donne etc. a Westmonaster, le xij. jour de Juil,
l'an etc. primer. [5]

On the back of this draft occurs the following :—

*Henri, etc. au Conestable de nostre [6] Chastel de
Dovorre, et Gardein de noz Cynk Portz, ou a son
[Depute] saluz.*

Nous vous mandons form . . . . enchargeant que sur [7]

---

are willing to send victuals by sea for the refreshment of
our said army shall be paid as much as the same victuals
may be worth in our army aforesaid. — Given, etc. at
Westminster, the 12th day of July, the first year, &c.

*Henry, etc. to the Constable of our Castle of Dover,
and Warden of our Cinque Ports, or to his Deputy,
greeting.*

We send to you . . . . . . charging that concerning

---

[1] The word "ceux" has been twice scratched out, after "que" and after "touz."

[2] *qui veullent*] Written at first "qui de lour bon grace veuillent."

[3] *par meer*] Originally "par meer ou autrement."

[4] *paiez a*] Originally "prestement paiez a louz venue."

[5] See Nicolas, i. 122, where is printed a letter from the King to the Council, dated at York, 4 July, 1400, ordering the letter in the text to be sent to Lynn, and similar letters to certain other ports ; viz., "noz lettres en due forme as Maire,

Vicontes, et Aldermans de nostre cite de Londres, et as Maire et Bailliefs de Cynk Portz, et de noz villes de Orwelle, Yernemuthe, Lynne, de Saint Botulphe, Grymmesby, Bartoun sur Humbre, Kyngestoun sur Hulle, Whitby, et Scardeburgh, et d'autres noz villes." The letter to the Mayor, &c. of London is printed by Nicolas at p. 123. It differs in many respects from the letter to Lynn given above.

[6] *Conestable*] Altered from "Gardein."

[7] *sur*] Originally "de."

A.D. 1400. noz autres lettres desouz nostre prive seal, a vous ou tard directes pur Gar[deins], les Barons de noz ditz portz,. pur estaiffer vynt noefes ou barges de gentz d'armes, et de vitailles pur le refresshe[ment] de nous et de nostre host; et, sicome en noz ditez lettres pleniement est contenuz, fatez envoier a nostre Conseil pleine [1] res[ponse] a toute la haste que vous purrez en aucune manere, et especialement [2] combien de vitailles les dit Barons —— [3] Et ce en nulle manere ne lessez sur la foi que vous n[ous en] devez.

Donne, etc.

———

our other letters under our privy seal to you now lately directed for the Wardens, the Barons of our said ports, to furnish twenty vessels or barges with men at arms, and with victuals for the refreshment of us and of our army; and, as is fully expressed in our said letters, you cause to be sent to our Council a full answer with all your possible speed, in any manner, and especially how much victuals the said Barons . . . . . . . . And in this in no manner fail, by the fidelity that you owe to us.— Given, etc.

———

[1] *pleine*] Added above the line.
[2] *et especialement*] Added above the line.
[3] *Barons.*] Here the following words have been struck out in the original: "nous veuillent et nostre host a ceste fois refressher."

A.D. 1400.

## XIX.

### COSMATUS, A CARDINAL, TO JOHN ARLAM.

*Cosmatus, miseratione Divina titulo Sanctæ Crucis in Jerusalem, sacrosanctæ Romanæ Ecclesiæ Presbyter Cardinalis, dilecto nobis in Christo Johanni Arlam, laico Dunelmensis Diœcesis, salutem in Domino sempiternam.*

Affluens devotionis sinceritas, quibus nostris obsequiis inhæsisti et de die in diem ferventer inhæres, sic erga personam tuam affectum excitat mentis nostræ quod ad ea libenter intendimus, per quæ tui honoris et commodi proveniat incrementum. *Admitting him into his household.*

Hinc est quod nos devotionem tuam diligentius intendentes, ac volentes te propterea prærogativa nostræ benevolentiæ pervenire, te in familiarem nostrum domesticum continuum recepimus, et aliorum familiarum nostrorum domesticorum continuorum numero et consortio aggregamus, volentes ut deinceps privilegiis libertatibus honoribus et favoribus, quibus alii familiares nostri domestici continui potiuntur, ubilibet gaudeas et utaris, et ad nos in agendis tuis recursum habeas specialem. Idcirco universos amicos et benevolos nostros affectuose rogamus, subditos autem sacrosanctæ Romanæ Ecclesiæ requirimus et rogamus, quatinus te, una cum tribus sociis equitibus vel peditibus, valisiis, rebus, armis, arnesiis, litteris, et bonis tuis quibuscumque, quandocumque, et quotienscumque, per civitates, terras, fortilitia, castra, oppida, districtus, portus, et loca alia ipsorum transitu

A.D. 1400. feceris, eundo, stando, morando, aut redeundo, absque alicujus Gabellæ, Pedagii, Dacii, Mutæ, Theolonei, aut alterius impositionis exactione, libere et pacifice transire permittant ac suscipiant nostri intuitu favorabiliter recommissum; ita quod eis et eorum cuilibet exinde teneamur ad merita gratiarum; has nostras patentes litteras, sigilli nostri appensione munitas, in fidem et testimonium præmissorum concedentes.

Datum Romæ, in domo habitationis nostræ, sub anno Nativitatis Domini Millesimo quadringentesimo, indictione octava, die vero octava mensis Augusti, Pontificatus sanctissimi in Christo Patris ac Domini nostri, Domini Bonifacii, divina Providentia Papæ VIIII., anno undecimo.

## XX.

### OTHO ROIMAR, GOVERNOR OF BERGHEN, TO HENRY IV.

On the privileges of certain merchants.

Præmissa in Domino mei recommendatione servitii cum salute, Majestati vestræ regiæ significo per præsentes quod Domina mea carissima, Domina Margareta, Dei gratia Sweciæ, Daciæ, Norvegiæque regnorum Regina dignissima, mihi demandando scripserat quod compositionem amicabilem et finalem facerem inter Anglicos et Almanos mercatores Borgæ constitutos, de querelis quas Anglici mercatores conquesti fuerant coram vobis super mercatores Almanos supradictos.

Ea propter volo vos scire quod tres ab utraque parte cautionem sufficientem præstiterant de treugis et pace servandis immobiliter inter eos, quousque prænominata venerabilissima Domina mea, Margareta Regina,

---

XX.] MS. Cotton. Nero. B. III. fol. 18 (β).—On paper; original.

seu Dominus meus illustrissimus, Dominus Ericus, A.D. 1400.
Ejusdem gratia prædictorum regnorum Rex, præfatam civitatem intraverit, et deinceps per mensem
proximum continuo tunc sequentem. Quia vero Domina He denies
mea Regina memorata, coram Majestate vestra quo- that the
English at
dammodo delata, dicatur mercatoribus Almanis huc- Berghen
usque plus favisse quam Anglicis, et quod de voluntate had been
unfairly
Dominæ meæ sæpedictæ dictant esse quod Almani treated.
mercatores cum Anglicis nec emere nec vendere quid-
quid deberent, hoc ad credulitatis januam, si sic est,
vestræ Celsitudinis apex humiliter supplico non ad-
mittat, et ut strenuus miles ex parte Dominæ falsum
esse probabo; quia de mandatis supradictæ illustrissimæ Dominæ meæ Reginæ habeo magis Anglicos
præ ceteris quosque honorandos, cum id solum erga
præfatos vestros homines dicta Domina mea Regina
egerat, pro quo a vobis et vestratibus magis est merito
commendanda.

In Domino valete, mihi super vestris beneplacitis
præcepturi.

Scriptum Bergæ, xxii. die Septembris.

OTTO ROIMAR,
Miles, et Capitaneus loci Bergensis
supradicti.

*Endorsed:* —" Excellentissimo Principi Dominoque gloriosissimo, Domino Henrico, Dei gratia
regnorum Angliæ et Franciæ Regi,
Domino Hiberniæ, ac Duci Aquitaniæ,
cum reverentia præmittetur."

A.D. 1400.

## 2 HENRY IV.

From 30 September, 1400, to 29 September, 1401.

### XXI.

#### THE PRIORESS OF ROWNEY TO HENRY IV.

*Excellentissimo in Christo Principi et Domino, Domino Henrico, Dei gratia Regi Angliae et Franciae, et Domino Hiberniae illustri, sua humilis et devota oratrix Priorissa de Roweney divina precum suffragia cum omnimodis reverentia et honore.*

On the misconduct of a Nun.
Vestræ Celsitudini regiæ tenore præsentium certifico, quod soror Johanna Adeleshey, monialis in Ordine Sancti Benedicti, et Domo prædicta, notorie professa, de patria in patriam in habitu seculari, spreto voto obedientiæ suæ, vagatur et discurrit in animæ suæ grave periculum, ac Ordinis sui scandalum manifestum, et perniciosum exemplum aliorum. Placeat igitur Excellentiæ vestræ regiæ, pro captione prædictæ Johannæ secundum regulam Ordinis sui castigandam, de clementia vestra regia, in casu hujusmodi hactenus satis grata, brachium extendere seculare, ne pro defectu castigationis debitæ taliter pereat plantatio divino cultui mancipata.

Et regiam Majestatem vestram in prosperis conservet Qui cunctis regibus dat regnare!

Datum apud Roweney, duodecimo die Novembris, anno Domini Millesimo quadringentesimo.

XXI.] MS. Publ. Rec. Off., portf. 1.—On vellum.

A.D. 1401.

## XXII.

### The Abbat of Wynchcombe to Henry IV.

*Excellentissimo Principi et Domino nostro, Domino Henrico, Dei gratia Regi Angliæ et Franciæ, et Domino Hiberniæ, vester (si libeat) capellanus humilis et devotus, Frater Willelmus,[1] Abbas vestri Monasterii Wynchecombiæ, orationum obsequia devota in Eo per Quem reges regnant et principes dominantur.*

Ad comparendum pro nobis et nomine nostro in parliamento vestro instanti apud Westmonasterium, in octavis Sancti Hillarii[2] proxime futuris, cum continuatione et prorogatione dierum sequentium celebrando, necnon. ad tractandum cum ceteris dominis proceribus et prælatis super ibidem tractandum et consentiendum quatinus in nobis est salubriter ordinandum, causasque et excusationes absentiæ nostræ proponendum et allegandum, fidemque faciendum in forma debita super ipsis ac omnia alia exercenda et expedienda, quæ nos, si personaliter interessemus, ibidem possemus et deberemus exercere, dilectos nobis in Christo Magistrum Nicholaum Bubbewyth,[3] et Magistrum Johannem Rome, clericos, procuratores nostros et nuncios speciales, conjunctim et divisim ac utrumque eorum in solidum ita quod non sit melior

*Naming his Proxies in Parliament.*

---

XXII.] MS. R., portf. 1.—On vellum.

[1] William Bradeley.— Dugd. ii. 298.

[2] January 20.

[3] Archdeacon of Dorset. He was made Bishop of London on May 14, 1406 ; was Master of the Rolls, Keeper of the Privy Seal, and Lord Treasurer. In 1407 he was translated to Salisbury, and at the end of the same year to Bath and Wells, where he died on Oct. 27, 1424.

D

A.D. 1401. conditio occupantis, sed quod unus eorum inceperit alter confirmare valeat, et finire, ordinamus facimus et constituimus per præsentes; ratum et gratum nos promittentes sub hypotheca omnium rerum nostrarum perpetuo habituros quicquid iidem procuratores nostri fecerint, seu alter ipsorum fecerit, in præmissis.

In cujus rei testimonium sigillum nostrum præsentibus est appensum.

Datum apud Wynchecombe, primo die mensis Januarii, anno regni Regis Henrici Quarti post Conquæstum secundo.

## XXIII.

### FROM THE ABBAT OF EVESHAM.

Naming his Proxies in Parliament.

Pateat universis per præsentes quod nos, Rogerus,[1] permissione divina Abbas monasterii Eveshamiæ, Or-

---

XXIII.] MS. Publ. Record Off., portf. 1;—on vellum.—A similar letter from this Abbat of Evesham is preserved in the same portfolio, but too much mutilated to admit of its being printed. The beginning and ending, however, which are the essential parts, as they contain the names of the Proxies and the date of the letter, are nearly perfect. They are as follows:—"Noverint universi quod nos Rogerus, permissione divina Abbas Monasterii Eveshamensis, ordinis Sancti Benedicti, Wigornensis Diœcesis, ad Romanam Ecclesiam nullo pertinentis, ad comparendum pro nobis et nomine nostro in instanti parliamento apud Westmonasterium, die

Lunæ proximo post festum Sancti Ieronimi Confessoris proxime futurum, (i. e. the Monday after September 30, in the year 1399, viz. Oct. 6,) dilectos nobis in Christo [Magistrum] Thomam de Stowe, Archidiaconum Londoniensem ac Bedefordensem, Legum Doctorem, et Magistrum Willelmum Stewkeley, Militem . . . . . . conjunctim et divisim, facimus etc. . . . . . . [Datum] Eveshamiæ, quinto die mensis Octobris, anno Domini Millesimo tricentesimo nonagesimo nono; regni vero Regis Henrici Quarti post Conquæstum primo."

[1] Roger Zatton, Abbat from Nov. 20, 1379, till Nov. 26, 1418.—*Dugd. Monast.* ii. 7.

dinis Sancti Benedicti, Wygornensis Diœcesis, ordi- namus, facimus, et constituimus venerabiles viros Magistrum Thomam Stowe, Legum Doctorem, Dominum Robertum Faryngton, Magistrum Johannem Barel, Clericos, conjunctim et quemlibet per se divisim et in solidum, ita quod non sit melior conditio occupantis, sed quod unus eorum incepit quilibet eorundem prosequi valeat mediare et finire, procuratores nostros ad comparendum pro nobis et nomine nostro in instanti parliamento Domini nostri, Domini Henrici, Dei gratia Regis Angliæ et Franciæ illustris, in Octavis Sancti Hillarii[1] proxime futuris apud Westmonasterium tenendo, cum continuatione et prorogatione dierum sequentium, ad excusandam absentiam nostram necessariam, et causas legitimas atque veras hujusmodi excusationis nostræ allegandas et probandas, prout opus fuerit in debita forma; necnon ad tractandum et consentiendum iis quæ tunc ibidem de communi consilio ipsius regni Angliæ, Divina favente clementia, contigerit ordinari : ratum habentes et habituri quicquid dicti procuratores nostri, vel aliquis eorum nomine nostro, fecerint vel fecerit in præmissis.

In cujus rei testimonium sigillum nostrum præsentibus apposuimus.

Datum in monasterio nostro Eveshamiæ, die Martis proxima[2] post Epiphaniam Domini. Anno Domini Millesimo CCCC$^{mo}$,[3] regni vero Regis Henrici Quarti post Conquæstum secundo.

---

[1] January 20.
[2] Tuesday, January 11.

[3] i. e. 1401, according to the computation of the Historical year.

A.D. 1401.

## XXIV.

### THE EARL OF DOUGLAS TO HENRY IV.

Accusing the Earl of Northumberland of breaking the truce.

Excellent et trespuissant Prince.

Plaise vostre tresnoble Haultesse a savoir que a Kemlyspeth, le xvj$^e$ jour de Maii darrein passe, estoit accorde parentre le Conte de Northumbre et moy que certaines treves endureroient et devroient tenir par terre et per mer, parentre vous, vostre realme, voz subgies et allies de l'une part, et mon souverain Seignour le Roy, son realme, ses subgits et allies de l'autre part, a comencer a le feste de Saint Martin[1] en yver darrein passe, et endurer pour un an delors prochein ensuant, s'il pleust a vous et [vostre Cons]eil d'une coste, et a mon souverain Seignour le Roy de l'autre coste, et son Conseil ; sur certification sur ce a y estre faite

---

### [TRANSLATION.]

Excellent and most mighty Prince.—May it please your most noble Highness to know that at Kemlyspeth, the 16th day of May last past, it was agreed between the Earl of Northumberland and me that a certain truce should endure and ought to be maintained by land and by sea between you, your realm, your subjects and allies on the one part, and my sovereign Lord the King, his realm, his subjects and allies on the other part, to commence on the feast of S. Martin in the winter just past, and to continue for one year thence next ensuing if it should be agreeable to you and your Council on the one side, and to my sovereign Lord the King and his Council on the other side ; on certification of which there was to be made interchange

---

XXIV.] MS. Cott. Vespas. F. VII. fol. 120.—On paper ; original, with some traces of the seal.—The answer to this letter will be found at page 58.

[1] November 11.

entrechange [de foi] parentre le dit Conte et moy A.D. 1401.
en le feste de la Nativite de Saint John le Baptiste[1]
prochein delors ensuant, la quelle certification . . . . .
eust este de nonplesance a aucune des parties susdites:
le jour d'encontrer des grants commissairs devoit
avoir este a [le] Lundy en trois semaines apres la
Nativite de Saint John le Baptiste[1] darrein passe, ou
les dits commissairs puissient en beaute [du temps]
et des longs jours avoir tretie sur pais ou longes treves.
Et en cas que bonne accorde eust faillie, que les
seignours et les commissairs d'ambedeux parties se
puissient avoir ordenes pour la guerre en tele maniere qu'ils n'eust pas este soudainment deceus comment ils [feu]rent. Et si la dite certification eust
este de plesance as ambedeux parties, quadonques le
jour d'encontrer des grants commissairs seroit pro-
roge pour estre tenu a Yhectam Kyrke Lundy en
quinsze jours apres le feste de Saint Michel[2] darrein

---

of faith between the said Earl and me, on the feast of the
Nativity of S. John the Baptist then next ensuing, the which
certification . . . . . would have been unpleasing to either
of the aforesaid parties : the day for the meeting of the grand
commissaries ought to have been on the Monday, in three
weeks after the Nativity of S. John the Baptist lately past, when
the said commissaries might in fineness of the time of the year
and of long days have treated concerning peace or a long truce.
And in case there had been failure of good accord, that the
lords and the commissaries of both parties might have made
order for war in such manner that they should not have been
suddenly deceived, as they were. And if the said certification
had been agreeable to both parties, that then the day for the
meeting of the grand commissaries might be prorogued, to be
held at Yhectam-Kirke on the Monday fortnight after the feast
of S. Michael last past, as more plainly appears by the inden-

---

[1] June 24.  [2] September 29.

A.D. 1401. passe, comme plus a plein appert es endenturez entre le dit Conte de Northumbre et moy sur ce factes.

Sur quoy le dit Conte de Northumbre . . . feit certification par sa lettre desoubs son seal en le feste de la Nativite de Saint John le Baptiste [1] susdit, qu'il plaisoit bien a [vous] et vostre Conseil que les dites treves dureroient del feste de Saint Martin [2] en yver darrein passe pour un an delors prochein [ensuan]t. Et sur ce le jour d'encontrer des grants commissairs se tenoit Lundy en quynsze jours apres le feste de Saint Michel [darre]in passe a Yhectam Kirke. A quel jour je disoy au dit Conte de Northumbre, en la presence des commissairs d'ambedeux [dites parties], que les treves furent prinses pour un an en la maniere susdit, comme sa lettre de certification sur ce tesmoigneit, les quelles [treves] de faire tenir garder et parfournir en tous points, et de faire redres estre fait de tous attemptatez faitez par terre et par

---

tures made between the said Earl of Northumberland and me on this matter.—Concerning which the said Earl of Northumberland . . . . made certification by his letter under his seal, on the feast of the Nativity of S. John the Baptist aforesaid, that it was well-pleasing to you and your Council that the said truce should continue from the feast of S. Martin in the winter last past for one year thence next ensuing. And on this, the day for the meeting of the grand commissaries was held on Monday fortnight after the feast of S. Michael last past at Yhectam-Kirke. On which day I said to the said Earl of Northumberland, in the presence of the commissaries of both the said parties that the truce was settled for one year in the manner aforesaid, as his letter of certification on this subject witnesseth, the which truce he was to cause to be kept, maintained, and performed in all points, and to cause redress to be made of all attempts made by land and by sea for all the realm

---

[1] June 24.        [2] November 11.

mer pour tout le realme d'Escoce, ainsy que nul A.D. 1401.
default devroit par raison estre impute a mon Seignour
souverain ne a moy; le quelles sont empeschez et
faillies entierment, comme j'entend en la defaulte de
dit Conte de Northumbre.

Pour quoy, excellent et puissant Prince, vostre tres-
grande noblesse je requere qu'il vous plaise a envoier
certains commissairs de grant estat a[s Marches], aiants
de vous pouvaire pour oir, declarer, et amender teulx
defaultis comme susdits, et je procureroi a mon Seignour
sov[erain le Roy] d'envoier as Marchez commissairs de
semblable estat pour semblablement faire. Devant les
quelx, a l'aide de Dieu, je ferai clerement estre cognu
que le dit Conte de Northumbre n'ay pas fait comme
sa lettre de certification contenit [et prop]ortit; et
que les dites treves de cest an et le redres de tous
attemptatez audevant faitez sont plainement empeschez
[et fai]llies en son default.

Et, excellent et trespuissant Prince, ce que sur ceste
matiere vous plaist a faire vostre tres noble [Haul]tesse
le moy veulle certifier par le porteur d'ycestes.

---

of Scotland, so that no default might rightly be imputed to my
sovereign lord nor to me ; the which have been hindered and
have entirely failed, as I understand, by the default of the said
Earl of Northumberland.—Wherefore, excellent and mighty
Prince, I beseech you, of your most great nobility, that it may
please you to send certain commissaries of high rank to the
Marches, having from you power to hear, declare, and amend all
such defaults as the aforesaid, and I will procure from my sovereign Lord the King to send to the Marches commissaries of
like rank to do the like. Before whom, by God's help, I will
cause it to be clearly known that the said Earl of Northumberland hath not done as his letter of certification contains,
and provides ; and that the said truce of this year and the redress of all attempts heretofore made have plainly been hindered
and have failed by his default.—And, excellent and most
mighty Prince, deign to certify to me by the bearer of these
presents what it may please your most noble Highness to do in

A.D. 1400. Si prie nostre Seignour. excellent et trespuissant Prince, qu'Il vous ait [en Sa] sainte garde.

Escript a Edybredschellis, le primier jour de Fevrier.

LE CONTE DE DOUGLAS, Seignour de Galway et de Dunbar.[1]

*Endorsed :—* " A excellent et trespuissant Prince, le Roy d'Angleterre."

this matter.—I pray our Lord, excellent and most mighty Prince, that He may have you in His holy-keeping.—Written at Edinburgh, the 1st day of February.

THE EARL OF DOUGLAS, Lord of Galway and of Dunbar.[1]

*Endorsed:—*"To the excellent and most mighty Prince, the King of England."

## XXV.

### FROM THE EMPEROR MANUEL II.

*Universis Christi fidelibus ad quos præsentes litteræ pervenerint Manuelus, Deo devotus, Imperator et moderator Romæorum Paleologus et semper Augustus, salutem in omnium Salvatore.*

In acknowledgment of the receipt of a sum of money given to him by Henry IV.

Noverit Universitas vestra quod, cum tria millia marcarum, tempore claræ memoriæ Domini Ricardi, nuper Regis Angliæ post Conquæstum Secundi, a clero et populo regni sui Angliæ pro defensione partium Romæorum contra invasionem inimicorum Fidei Chris-

---

[1] Archibald, fourth Earl.

XXV.] MS. Cotton. Nero, B. xi. fol. 174.—On vellum ; original. See

Rymer, viii. 174. See also Letter XVII.

tianæ collectæ fuerint et levatæ, et per Reginaldum A.D. 1401. Grille, mercatorem de Janua, de dicti Regis voluntate receptæ; idemque Reginaldus, et alii, ad solvendum dicta tria millia marcarum nobis, Imperatori prædicto, infra certum terminum jamdiu effluxum, per suas litteras dicto Domino Ricardo Regi et heredibus suis fuerint obligati, ac hujusmodi solutio infra dictum terminum facta non fuerit; et quamquam eo prætextu vigore dictæ obligationis, prædicta tria millia marcarum excellentissimo et illustrissimo Principi, Domino Henrico, Dei gratia nunc Regi Angliæ, debeantur; idem tamen nunc Rex, attendens et considerans immensos labores ac onera expensarum per nos circa persecutionem præfati negotii penes quoscumque Catholicos Principes et alios Christi fideles hactenus supportata, summam trium millium marcarum auri de Thesauro ejusdem Regis, in recompensationem tantæ summæ, per præfatum Reginaldum modo quo supra receptæ, nobis de gratia sua speciali donavit.

Quam quidem summam per manus honorabilis et religiosi viri, Fratris Petri de Holt, Prioris Hospitalis Sancti Johannis de Jerusalem in Hibernia, ex hujusmodi generoso dono recepimus, cum immensis actionibus gratiarum. Et ideo præfatum Reginaldum ac alios quoscumque quorum in hac parte interesse versatur inde quietos facimus per præsentes, quas nostri sigilli appensione[1] fecimus communiri.

Datum Londoniæ in crastino Purificationis Beatæ Mariæ,[2] Anno Domini (secundum cursum et computationem Ecclesiæ Anglicanæ) millesimo quadringentesimo,[3] et regni dicti Regis Henrici secundo.

---

[1] The mutilated remains of the seal are still attached to the letter.

[2] February 3.

[3] *Secundum cursum, etc.*] The year of the Anglican Church commenced on March 25. This date is therefore 1401 according to the computation of the Historical year.

A.D. 1401.

## XXVI.

### HENRY IV. TO THE EARL OF DOUGLAS.

Honure Sire.

On the affairs of the Borders.

Nous avons receuz voz lettres, escrites a Edebredesheles le primer jour de cest present mois de Feverer,[1] par les queles signifiez nous avez entre autres, coment le seszisme jour de May darein [passe] a Kemelespeth estoit acordez parentre nostre treschier cousin, le Conte de Northumbre, et vous, que certeines trieves se rendroient par terre et par meer parentre les deux roiaumes et leur alliez, a comencer a la feste de Seint [Martin[2]] darein passez en yverne, et a durer par un an lors prochein ensuant, s'il plerroit a nous et a nostre Conseil d'une part, et a nostre adversaire d'Escoce et a son Conseil d'autre part,

---

[TRANSLATION.]

Honoured Sir.—We have received your letter written at Edinburgh the first day of this present month of February, by the which you have signified unto us, among other things, that on the 16th day of May last past, at Kemelespeth, it was agreed between our very dear cousin, the Earl of Northumberland, and you, that a certain truce should be established by land and by sea between the two kingdoms and their allies, to commence at the feast of S. Martin, in the winter last past, and to continue for one year then next ensuing, if it should so please us and our Council on the one part, and our adversary of Scotland and his Council on the other part, on certifications

---

XXVI.] MS. Cotton. Vespas. F. VII. fol. 88.—On vellum.
[1] See Letter XXIV., to which this letter is a reply; also Rymer, viii. 166.
[2] November 11.

sur certifications ent affaire parentre le dit Conte A.D. 1401.
et vous, en la feste de la Nativitee de Seint Johan
le Baptiste[1] darein passez, au fin que grandz commissairs deussent avoir assemblez pur treter sur pees
ou longes trieves parentre les deux roiaumes. Et
coment nostre dit cousin, en la dite feste de Seint
Johan,[1] vous certifia par ses lettres desouz son seal,
q'il plust bien a nous et a nostre Conseil que les dites
trieves se tiendroient et durerent par le dit an, de la
dite feste de Saint Martin. Pourquoi le jour de
l'assent des grandz commissairs se tenoit Lundy en
quinsze jours apres la feste de Seint Michel[3] darein
passez. Au quel jour, a ce que voz dites lettres pur-
portent par la ou vous disoites au dit Conte en
reherceant coment les dites trieves feurent prises pur
un an, en la manere susdite, come sa lettre de certification sur ce faite tesmoigna. Et combien que vous
vous offristes de faire tenir et garder et parfornir

---

thereof to be made between the said Earl and you, on the feast
of the Nativity of S. John the Baptist last past, to the
end that grand commissaries might have assembled to treat
concerning peace, or a long truce, between the two kingdoms;
and how our said cousin, on the said feast of S. John,
certified you by his letters under his seal that it was well-
pleasing to us and to our Council that the said truce should be
established, and should continue for the said year from the said
feast of S. Martin. Accordingly the day for the session
of the grand commissaries was held on Monday fortnight after
the feast of S. Michael last past. On which day, according
to the purport of your said letters, you spake to the said Earl
rehearsing how the said truce was established for one year in
the manner aforesaid, as his letter of certification written on
this matter testified. And how you offered yourself to cause

---

[1] June 24.
[2] November 11.
[3] September 29.

A.D. 1401. mesmes les trieves en touz pointz, et de faire redresse estre fait des attemptatz par terre et par meer pur tout le roiaume d'Escoce, si que nulle defaute ne serroit trovez de vostre coustee, come en voz dites lettres est contenuz. Nientmains vous vous compleigner grandement de nostre dit cousin, en surmettant a lui que les dites trieves sont empeschez et faillez entierement en son defaute, et contre l'effect de ses dites lettres de certification. Sur quoi requys nous avez que nous vorriens envoier certeins noz commissairs de grand estat as Marches, eiantz de nous poair d'oier declarer et amender tielx defautes; et vous procurerez que nostre dit adversaire envoiera as Marches commissairs de parail estat pur faire semblablement, dont vous desirez estre certifiez par le portour de voz dites lettres.

Si vuillez savoir que veues et entendues mesmes voz lettres nous fismes venir a nostre presence l'onurable piere en Dieu l'Evesque de Bangor, et le dit Conte, et auxi noz treschiers et foiaux cousins, le Conte de

---

the same truce to be kept and maintained and performed in all points, and to cause redress to be made of attempts by land and by sea, for the whole kingdom of Scotland, so that no default should be found on your side, as is stated in your said letters. Nevertheless you greatly complain of our said cousin, imputing to him that the said truce was hindered and entirely failed by his default, and contrary to the purport of his said letters of certification. Touching which you have requested us that we would send certain our commissaries of high rank to the Marches, having from us power to hear, to declare, and to amend such defaults; and you will procure that our said adversary shall send to the Marches commissaries of equal rank to do likewise; of which you desire to be certified by the bearer of your said letters.—Be pleased to know that, having seen and considered your said letters, we caused to come into our presence the honourable Father in God the Bishop of Bangor, and the said Earl, and also our very dear and faithful

Westmerland, et le Sire de Grey, Gerard Heron, Chi- A.D. 1401.
valer, et Johan Cursoun, Esquier, pur nous ent pleinement enformer. Si que par bone examination par
nous faite en celle partie nous fumes certainement
apris que nostre dit cousin, le Conte de Northumbre,
a le dit darein assemblee apres la Seint Michel, riens
ne fesoit sinon de comun avys et assent des dites
persones a lui associez come noz commissairs, lour
conformantz a l'instruction pur nous a eux ent donez.

Et quant a ce que vous affermez que le dit Conte The King
ad fait contre l'effect de ses dites lettres de certifica- acquits the
Earl of
tion a vous envoiees, come desus, sachez que nous Northum-
avons veue la copie de celles lettres de certification de berland of
the charge
nostre voloir et entention, touchant les dites trieves of having
broken the
a estre tenuz par un an, come avant est dit ovec truce,
tiele clause, parensi que mesmes les trieves feussent
affermez tenuz et gardez selonc la forme nature et
effect d'icelles. De la quele condition ou clause, ad-
joustee en les dites lettres de nostre cousin susdit,

---

cousins, the Earl of Westmoreland and the Lord de Grey,
Gerard Heron, Knight, and John Curson, Esquire, to inform
us fully on the matter. So that, by good examination made by
us on this behalf, we were with certainty apprized that our
said cousin, the Earl of Northumberland, at the said late meet-
after Michaelmas, did nothing without the common advice and
consent of the said persons with him associated as our commissaries, conforming themselves to the instruction given
to them by us in the matter.—And as to your assertion that
the said Earl has done contrary to the purport of his said
letters of certification sent to you as above, know that we have
seen the copies of those letters of certification of our will and
intention concerning the said truce being maintained for one
year, as is aforesaid, with such a clause as this,—That the same
truce should be affirmed, maintained, and preserved according to its form, nature, and effect. Of the which condition
or clause, inserted in the said letters of our aforesaid cousin,

A.D. 1401. vous n'avez fait nulle mention en voz dites lettres a nous envoiees; dont nous esmerveillons. Et voirs est, a ce que aucuns de noz ditz messages nous ont certainement enformez, que, qant ils furent rehercer a vous et as autres grandz commissairs de vostre costee certeins pointz comprises en les trieves prises et accordes parentre nostre treschier cousin, Sire Richard, nadgaires Roy d'Engleterre, et son adversaire de France, pur eux et pur lour alliez, et par especial touchant les metes et boundes des chastelx et les jurisdictions d'icelx a estre declarez pur meillour conservation de mesmes les trieves; as queux trieves les dites endentures faites a Kelsowe fesoient relation: et quant ils demanderent de vous si celles pointz entre autres comprises en mesmes les trieves deussent estre tenuz et gardez, et auxi si vous voudriez proceder a la declaration de mesmes les pointz, tantost il feust responduz de vostre part a chescun point en refusant de ce faire que purroit avoir este la seure conservation

---

you have made no mention in your said letters sent to us; at which we marvel. And it is to be observed, according to what certain of our said messengers have with certainty informed us, that, when they were rehearsing to you and to the other grand commissaries on your side certain points comprised in the said truce, and agreed to between our very dear cousin, Lord Richard, late King of England, and his adversary of France, for them and for their allies, and especially touching the declaration of the metes and bounds of the castles and their jurisdictions, for better conservation of the same truce; to the which truce the said indentures made at Kelso bore relation: and when they asked of you whether these points among others comprised in the same truce ought to be held and maintained, and also whether you would proceed to the declaration of the said points, you quickly made answer on your part to each point, refusing to do that which might have been the sure conservation of this

de celles trieves. Et par la, ou ce nonobstant noz A.D. 1401. dits commissairs vous offrirent d'avoir accordez sur certeines trieves pur avoir este tenuz simplement, et sanz aucune condition ou declaration, tanque au certein temps apres la Noel lors prochein avenir, au fin que les commissairs d'une part et d'autre purroient avoir fait report a lour Seignurs si lour plerroit acorder a aucun autre jour, ou a plus longes trieves. Nepurquant vous ne vousistis a ce en nulle manere accorder, et [final]ement depuy cestes fayz plus traiter avec nos commissairs desusditz, come par inspection d'un publik instrument ent fait nous estiens aussi clerement enformez. Et deinz brief temps apres ils feurent en retournant pardevers nous, vous chiv[aucher] . . . . en vostre propre persone, forciblement, arraiez a feure de guerre ove baner ou penon desplaie, a nostre ville de Bamburgh, et grande partie de mesme la ville et autres lieux la environ[nants] arder, come dit est. Si que vous commenceastes en vostre persone la

---

truce. And besides or notwithstanding this, our said commissaries offered you to agree to a certain truce, to be maintained simply, and without any condition or declaration, until a certain time after Christmas then next ensuing, to the end that the commissaries on the one side and on the other might report to their Lords whether it might please them to agree to some other day, or to a longer truce. Nevertheless you were not willing to agree to this in any manner, and finally after these facts to treat with our abovenamed commissaries, as by inspection of a public instrument made in the matter we were very clearly informed. And in a short time after their return to our presence, you rode in your own person, with force, arrayed in manner of war, with banner and pennon displayed, to our town of Bamborough, and burned great part of the said town and other places in its neighbourhood as it is said. So that you began the war, personally, as one of the wardens

A.D. 1401. guerre, come un des gardeins des Marches d'Escoce,

and lays the blame on the Earl of Douglas.
avant que nostre dit cousin ou aucun autre des gardeins de noz Marches vers Escoce en leur propre persones firent a voz Marches aucun damage, a ce que nous est reportez ; si que il semble que le defaute ne serra trovez en mesme nostre cousin, si toutes choses soient bien considerees.

He expresses his readiness to come to a new arrangement.
Nientmains, pur ce mettre en bone voie, selonc vostre [requisition], nous pensons d'envoier a Kelsowe[1] aucuns noz messages de meindres estatz, c'est assavoir le dit Gerard Heron, et William Fulthorp, Chivalers, Johan Mitford, et Mestre Aleyn Newerk, eux quatre, trois, ou [deux] de eux, de y estre le disme jour d'Avrill prochein venant, pur treter et accorder ovec autres de parail estat, des jour, manere, forme, et lieu, as queux l'en purra purvoier par voie de bone traitee de covenable [forme af]fin sur les matires avantdites.

Parquoi, s'il vous semble expedient que celle journee

---

of the Marches of Scotland, before that our said cousin, or any other of the wardens of our Marches towards Scotland, in their proper persons, did any damage to your Marches, according to the reports made to us ; so that it appears that the fault will not be found in our same cousin, if all things be well considered.—Nevertheless, to put this in right course, according to your request, we think of sending to Kelso some of our messengers of lower rank ; that is to say, the said Gerard Heron and William Fulthorp, Knights, John Mitford and Master Aleyn Newerk ; these four, three, or two of them, to be there on the 10th day of April next ensuing, to treat and agree with others of like rank concerning the day, manner, form, and place in which they may finally provide, by way of good treaty of suitable form, upon the matters aforesaid.—Wherefore, if it seem to you expedient

---

[1] a Kelsowe] "as dites Marches" had been written, and afterwards struck out.

se tiegne, facez envoier a les avantditz Gerard, William, A.D. 1401.
Aleyn, et Johan, lettres de seure et sauf conduyt,
bones et suffisantes, si par temps que celle journee
ne soit empeschez pur defaut de mesme le saufconduit; entendantz que nous avons donez en charge
as gardeins de noz Marches vers Escoce, pur doner
semblables lettres et saufconduit a ceux qui serront
envoiez de vostre coustee as jour et lieu desusditz.[1]

Donne souz nostre prive seal, a nostre Palois de
Westmonster, le xxvij. jour de Feverer.

Savoir vous fesons en outre que noz messages desus-
nomez serront a Kelsowe Marsdy prochein apres la
Dymenge.[2]

*Endorsed:*—"A honure Seigneur, le Conte de Douglas."

---

that this day hold good, cause to be sent to the aforesaid
Gerard, William, Aleyn, and John, letters of sure and safe
conduct, good and sufficient, and in such good time that this
day may not be hindered for want of such safe-conduct;
understanding that we have given in charge to the wardens of
our Marches towards Scotland to give like letters and safe
conduct to those who shall be sent on your part, at the above-
named day and place.—Given under our privy seal, at our
Palace of Westminster, the 27th day of February. — We
give you to know, farther, that our above-named messengers
will be at Kelsowe the Thursday next after the Sunday.

*Endorsed:*—" To the honoured Lord, the Earl of Douglas."

---

[1] *desusditz.*] Added above the
line. After this word the following
have been struck out:—" que serra
entre acordez par celle cause."

[2] Here the words "des Palmes
prochein avenir, pur y assembler
ovec les messages de vostre coustee.
Donne come desus," have been
struck out, and the following added
in another hand:—" Parensi que

mesmes noz messages a lour venus
as jour et lieu desusditz puissent
savoir que escrit nous avez ensi de
la volontee et assent de nostre
adversaire d'Escoce, et outre ce que
la volontee de luy et des . . . . .
de . . . . . . . . . bones et aima-
bles tretees se pringnent d'entre les
deux roiaumes, sanz fraude ou mal
engin."

E

A.D. 1401.

## XXVII.

### THOMAS MERKS TO ROBERT DE FARINGDON.

Reverende Domine et amice carissime.

Quia in nostro ultimo colloquio, in magna Aula Westmonasterii, vobis tetigi de materia tangente pre-bendam meam de Massam in Ecclesia Cathedrali Eboraci, pro attornatis pro me in hac parte faciendis, et quia difficile mihi foret de Oxonia venire, prout tunc vobis retuli, pro ordinatione eorumdem, vos de vestra gratuita affectione dixistis quod ego nomina attornatorum meorum vobis transmitterem in scriptis, et promisistis quod vos eos pro attornatis meis recordare velletis.

Quocirca, reverende amice, nomina attornatorum meorum hujusmodi sunt hæc, videlicet Johannes Mapelby, senior in Cancellario, Thomas Holmes in Banco Regis, et Willelmus Wakefield in Communi Banco, quos volo, ordino, et facio attornatos meos conjunctim et divisim in forma meliori qua potero, vestræ Discretioni, in qua summe confido, cordialiter supplicans quatinus ipsos attornatos meos, ubi et prout vobis melius videbitur expedire, recordare velitis totiens quotiens fuerit opportunum. Et si qua vobis complacentia facere valeo mihi certificare velit vestra Discretio reverenda.

Quam conservet in prosperis clementia Salvatoris! Scriptum Oxoniæ, vij° die Junii.

THOMAS MERKS,
Episcopus Samastanensis.

*Endorsed :*—" Reverendæ discretionis viro, Domino Roberto de Faryngdon, amico nostro spirituali."

---

XXVII.] MS. Public Record Office.—On vellum. See Rymer, viii. 150, 165; Nicolas, i. 116.

## XXVIII.

### RICHARD OF BANGOR AND JOHN PERANT TO HENRY IV.

Invictissime atque metuendissime Princeps.

Nos, humiles et devoti orator et servitor vestræ Majestatis, commendamus nos ejusdem Majestatis gloriæ attentius quo possumus et valemus, postquam noscat Serenitas vestra nos litteras vestras magnificas de redeundo ad partes, nobis directas, feria tertia hebdomadæ Paschæ[1] cum omni reverentia nobis possibili læto animo recepisse. Unde statissime per nuncium nostrum proprium Dominis Regi et Reginæ Daciæ Sweciæ et Norwegiæ scripsimus, pro licentia ad partes recedendi, una cum nuncio eorundem, qui tunc venerat de Anglia cum litteris vestris magnificis eisdem directis; in quibus ad partem in quadam copia de hujusmodi licentia danda, immo de revertendo nos ad partes intelleximus plenius contineri.

De quibus, propter locorum distantiam, in festo Corporis Christi[2] et non ante responsum reportavimus, et tale prout ex quadam copia præsentibus interclusa, ad quod incontinenti eisdem rescripsimus, et taliter prout in alia copia, etiam præsentibus inclusa, Majestati vestræ antedictæ luculentius poterit apparere.

Ea propter, affectu quo valemus humiliori, eidem Majestati vestræ supplicamus, quatinus Serenitas vestra discretissima pro mora nostra hujusmodi, per nos

*Excusing themselves for delay in returning to England.*

---

XXVIII.] MS. Cotton. Nero, B. III. fol. 19 (δ). — On paper ; original.

[1] April 5, being the Tuesday after Easter Day, which fell on April 3 in the year 1401.

[2] June 2, being the Thursday after Trinity Sunday, which fell on May 29 in the year 1401.

A.D. 1401. nullo modo affectata, dignetur nos habere excusatos ; et citius quo poterimus cum proximo secuto navigio, Deo duce, intendimus remeare.

Sed ad navigia linguæ Theutonicorum, propter ea quæ in partibus istis publice et famose referuntur de iis, quæ eis et eorum amicis his diebus circa mare vestrum Anglicanum contingebant, ponere nos ausi non sumus, nisi prius per ipsos Regem et Reginam, vel Dominum Episcopum Roskeldensem, quem, propter eximios honores intuitu dictæ vestræ Serenitatis nobis impensos, ipsa Serenitas dignetur habere merito recommissum, specialiter et obnixe eis essemus commendati. Præfatus tamen Episcopus etiam per nos instantissime rogatus, nisi audita voluntate dictorum Regis et Reginæ, hoc non audet, ut dixit, attemptare.

Alia non occurrunt his scriptis digna, nisi quod Majestatem vestram ad regimen populorum sibi commissorum diu conservet Altissimus feliciter, ut optamus.

Scriptum in Civitate Roskeldensi, xvi. die mensis Junii.

Vestri humiles { RICARDUS,[1] Minister Ecclesiæ Bangorensis, continuus orator ; ac
JOHANNES PERANT, serviens ad arma servitor,—
Ad imperia et mandata semper promptissimi.

Endorsed: — " Invictissimo ac strenuissimo Principi, Henrico, Dei gratia Regi Angliæ et Franciæ, Domino suo præcipuo."

Also :—" Litteræ Ambassiatorum pro parte Angliæ in partibus Norwegiæ et Sweciæ existentium."

---

[1] Richard Yonge, elected 21 Oct. 1399.

A.D. 1401.

## XXIX.

### HENRY IV. TO THE PRINCE OF WALES.

Treschier et tresame fiz, nous vous salvons souvent, ovec la benison de Dieu, et la nostre.

Treschier et tresame fiz.

Sur noz darreines lettres desouz nostre signet, a vous ore tarde envoiees, nous avons receuz voz lettres responsives ; par les queles, entre autres, signifiez nous avez coment parentre nostre treschier et foial Cousin, Henri de Percy, et nostre chier et foial Arnaud Savage, et autres de vostre Conseil, sur le fet touchant Rez et William ap Tudour, et autre noz rebelx, lour adherentz, certeines tretees ont este pris ; et coment, et a quele issue le dit William, Howel Waghan, et

*On the submission of Rees and Wm. ap Tudor.*

------

### [TRANSLATION.]

Most dear and most beloved son, we greet you often, with the blessing of God, and our own.—Most dear and most beloved son.—In reference to our last letter under our signet, now lately sent to you, we have received your letter in answer ; by the which, among other things, you have signified to us how that between our most dear and faithful cousin, Henry de Percy, and our dear and faithful Arnald Savage, and others of your Council, on the matter touching Rees and William ap Tudor, and other our rebels, their adherents, certain treaties had been settled ; and how, and to what result the said William, Howel Vaughan, and all

------

XXIX.] MS. Cotton. Cleopatra, F. III., fol. 122 b.—On vellum ; a contemporaneous draught.

A.D. 1401. touz autres compaignons et gentz rebelx esteantz ovec lui deinz le Chastel de Conewey, sont finalement condescenduz par lour offre et supplicatioun, (dont nous avons veue la copie[1],) et entenduz en outre la bone ordenance quele vous et nostre dit Cousin avez fait de gentz d'armes, et d'archiers, et des bastiles, pur le siege du dit Chastel, en nous donant vostre avys que $VI^{xx}$ hommes d'armes et CCC archiers serroient demorantz sur le dit siege, tanque a la Seint Michel,[2] ou la Touz Seintz[3] prochein venantz, au fin que les ditz rebelx puissent estre puniz, selonc lour desert, ou que nous eussens au meyne aucune autre tretee que nous serroit pleisante et plus honurable que n'estoit aucun de les offres de noz rebelz susditz ; queles a ce que semble a le sage avys de vous, et de nostre dit Cousin, ne sont pas honurables

---

other companions and persons who are rebels with him in the Castle of Conway, have finally arrived by their offer and supplication, (of which we have seen the copy,) and considering moreover the good arrangement of men of arms and archers, and works, which you and our said cousin have made, for the siege of the said Castle, giving us your advice that one hundred and twenty armed men and three hundred archers should remain employed upon the said siege, until the feast of S. Michael, or the feast of All Saints next coming, to the end that the said rebels might be punished according to their deserts, or that we should have at least some other treaty which should be agreeable to us and more honourable than was any one of the offers of our aforesaid rebels ; the which, as seems to your sage counsel, and that of our said cousin, are not at all honourable to us, but a matter of most evil

---

[1] Printed in Nicolas, i., 147.
[2] September 29.

[3] November 1.

a nous, maiz chose de tresmal ensample, come en les A.D. 1401.
lettres de vous et de mesme nostre Cousin, a nous
envoiees de present, est plus pleinement contenuz.

Sur toutes lesqueles matieres desus escritent vous
desirez de savoir nostre ententioun et voloir.

Si vuillez savoir, treschier et tresame fiz, que, de
vostre grande peine et dilligence queles vous y mys
avez pur le temps nous vous savons moult espiciau-
ment bon gree ; vuillantz et vous priantz que de
sicome le dit Chastel estoit pris en defaute de vostre
Conestable d'icelle, puis le temps que vous aviez la
Principalitee de Gales de nostre donn,[1] par le sage avys
de nostre dit Cousin et ceux de vostre Conseil, ne
puissez mieulz faire a plus hastive exploit en celle partie, sauvant nostre honour et le vostre, fatez ordenier
que par fort main le dit Chastel puisse estre restituez

---

precedent, as in the letters from you and from the same our
cousin, sent to us at the present time, is more fully contained.—Concerning all which matters above written, you
desire to know our intention and will.—You will therefore
know, most dear and most beloved son, that for your great
pain and diligence that you have bestowed upon us for
the time we very specially render you good thanks ; willing and praying you that, as the said Castle was taken
through the negligence of your Constable thereof, after
the time that you had received the Principality of Wales
by our gift, by the sage advice of our said cousin, and those
of your Council,—not to undertake a premature exploit in
this behalf, saving our honour and your own,—you cause to
ordain that by a strong hand the said Castle may be restored
into your hand. And forasmuch as it seems good to the

---

[1] *Que de sicome . . . donn.*]    end, with a mark of reference to
This passage, omitted in the body    this place.
of the letter, has been added at the

A.D. 1401. en vostre main. Et combien q'il semble as sages de nostre Conseil que celle charge ne doit appartenir sinon a vous, qi avez le dit Chastel, et la Seignurie d'ycelle en fee; nientmains nous, considerantz les grandz charges queux vous avez supportez puis la comencement de vostre estat en cea, et que pour tant vous ne purrez bien sustenir le dit grande charge saunz autre aide,—si volons de l'assent de nostre dit Conseil que de nostre tresor vous serrez relevez, c'est assavoir de la moyte des custaiges queux sur ce vous ferrez, et en averez paiement a plustost que du grant a nous fait en nostre darrein parlement nous faire le purrons bonement autres plus grandz charges primerement supportez.[1]

sages of our Council that this charge ought not to appertain to any one but to you, who have the said Castle and the Lordship thereof in fee; nevertheless we, considering the great charges which you have sustained since the commencement of your settlement therein, and that on this account you cannot well sustain the said great charge without other aid,—we will, therefore, by the assent of our said Council, that you should be relieved out of our treasure, that is to say of the moiety of the costs that you shall bear thereon, and shall have payment in anticipation of the grant made to us in our last parliament to enable us to bear other far greater charges previously incurred.

[1] This letter is without a date. But see Nicholas i., p. 145.

## XXX.

### THE ARCHBISHOP OF DUBLIN AND OTHERS TO HENRY IV.

Tresexcellent, tresredoute, et nostre tressoverain Seigneur.

Le pluis humblement et tresobeissantement que nous savons, ou pluis puissons, nous, voz treshumblez lieges, nous recomandons a vostre treshaute et roiale Magestee.

A la quelle please assavoir que nous pensons bien que vous avez en sovenance, s'il vous plest, comment nous nadgairs escrevames a vostre haulte Noblesse de le grande disease et peril que nostre treshonoure Seigneur, vostre fitz, et tous ses gens et soldiours alors avoient, pour nounpaiement hors d'Angleterre ; et de le grande meschief qe de legier en purroit avoir aucunz. Le quel

*Complaining of the want of money for carrying on the government in Ireland.*

---

[TRANSLATION.]

Most excellent, most dread, and most sovereign Lord.

With the greatest humility, and with all the obeissance that we know how, or have power to render, we, your most humble lieges, commend ourselves to your most high and royal Majesty.—Whereupon please you to know that we are well assured that you have in remembrance, if it please you, how we not long since wrote to your high Nobleness concerning the great inconvenience and danger which our most honoured Lord, your son, and all his people and soldiers at that time were under, through nonpayment out of England ; and of the great mischief which any of them might easily incur. The which

---

XXX.] MS. Cotton. Titus, B. IX. fol. 19.—On paper ; original.

A.D. 1401. desease, peril, et meschief, au point encrescez si grandement, nous compellent et constreignent unqore de
certifier a vostre dicte Hautesse la verite des ditz disease
et meschiefs, pour nous loialement acquiter devers vous,
nostre tressoverain Seigneur, et nostre dit Seigneur,
vostre fitz.

Sur quoy de poisant cuer nous certifions de rechief
a meisme vostre Hautesse, que nostre dit Seigneur,
vostre fitz, est si destituit de monoy qu'il n'ad un
denier en monde, ne nul denier poet creancer, qar
tous ses joialx et ses vesselx que poy queux de necessite lui faut avoir, sont mys et demergent en gage.
Et sont ses souldiours departiez de lui, et les gens. de
son hostiel en point de departier, et, combien qu'ils
voloient attendre nostre dit Seigneur, n'est pas de poar
de eux tenir ensemble a vis de soicourer ovec vynt
ou dusze personnes, ovec moy, vostre humble oratour
de Dyvelyn, ou ovec moy, vostre humble liege Janico,
qi a trestout vostre paier : et outre ferrons nostre

---

inconvenience, danger, and mischief, on the point of increasing
so greatly, compel and constrain us again to certify to your
said Highness the truth of the said inconvenience and mischiefs, in order to acquit ourselves loyally towards you, our
most sovereign Lord, and our said Lord, your son.—Upon
which with heavy heart we testify anew to the same your
Highness, that our said Lord, your son, is so destitute of
money that he has not . a penny in the world, nor can
borrow a single penny, because all his jewels, and his
plate, that he can spare of those which he must of necessity keep, are spent and sunk in wages. And, also, his
soldiers are departed from him, and the people of his household are on the point of departing, and, however much they
might wish to attend upon our said Lord, it is not in their
power to keep together with a view to helping, with twenty
or a dozen persons, with me, your humble orator of Dublin,
or with me your humble liege, Janico, who has paid you his

entier devoir envers lui, et tant comme nous vivrons A.D.1401. [ . . . . . . . a] vous suymes soverain[ment] obligez. Et est la pays si enfieblez et empoverez pour la longe nounpaicment, si bien en temps nostre dit Seigneur, vostre fitz, comme en temps des autres lieutenantz devant lui, que mesme la pays ne poet pluis tiele charge porter, come ils dient, et pour lour faitz m'en priroyt. Et en bon foy, nostre tressoverain Seigneur, merveille est comment ils ont tiele charge si longement portez.

Pourqoy vous supplions, nostre tresexcellent et tressoverain Seigneur, le pluis humblement et tres-entierement que nous pluis puissons, que vous plese ordenner hastive remede des ditz perils et diseases, et nous tenir pour excusez et si aucun peril ou disease (que Dieux ne veuille) aveigne a nostre dit Seigneur, vostre fitz, par les ditz causes; pour lesquelles pluis pleinement declairer a vostre Hautesse, troys ou deux de nous deussient avoir venuz devers vostre haulte personne.

---

very all : and besides we will render our entire duty towards him, and so long as we shall live, we are . . . . . bound by sovereign obligation to you. And the country is so weakened and impoverished by the long nonpayment, as well in the time of our said Lord, your son, as in the time of the other lieu-tenants before him, that the same country can no longer bear such charge, as they affirm, and on this account have besought me. And in good faith, our most sovereign Lord, it is a wonder that they have borne such a charge so long.—Where-fore we entreat you, our most excellent and most sovereign Lord, with all the humility and fulness that we may, that you please to ordain speedy remedy of these said dangers and inconveniences, and to hold us excused also if any danger or inconvenience (which may God avert) befal our said Lord, your son, by the said causes ; for the more full declaring of which to your Highness, three or two of us ought to have come before your high presence. But such is the great danger on

A.D. 1401. Mais tant est le peril grande pardeca, que nul de nous ose departier de la personne nostre dit Seigneur.

Tresexcellent, tresredoute, et nostre tressoverain Seigneur, nous prions a le Benoit Fitz de Dieu[1] qu'Il vous sauve et garde, en honoure et prosperitee, et qu'Il vous ottroie la victorie de touz voz enmys.

Escript a La Naas, le xx jour d'Augst.

Vos tres humbles et foialx lieges,

L'Ercevesque de Dyvelyn, vostre Chanceller d'Irland,

Laurence Merbury, vostre Tresorer illoeques,

Esmon Noon,

Antoyn Seint Quintyn, et

Janico . . .

this side, that no one of us dares depart from the person of our said Lord.—Most excellent, most dread, and our most sovereign Lord, we pray the Blessed Son of God that He save and defend you in honour and prosperity, and that He grant you the victory over all your enemies.—Written at La Naas, the 20th day of August.

Your most humble and faithful lieges,

The Archbishop of Dublin, your Chancellor of Ireland,

Lawrence Merbury, your Treasurer there,

Esmond Noon,

Anthony St. Quintyn, and

Janico . . . . .

[1] de Dieu] Added above the line.

## 3 HENRY IV.

From 30 September, 1401, to 29 September, 1402.

## XXXI.

### ERIC X. TO HENRY IV.

*Invictissimo Principi, Domino Henrico, Dei gratia Regi Angliæ illustrissimo, fratri nostro præcarissimo, Ericus eadem gratia Daciæ, Sueciæ, Norvegiæ, Slavorum Gothorumque Rex, ac Dux Pomeraniæ, salutem et prosperos ad vota successus.*

Princeps et frater præcarissime.

Vestræ regiæ Fraternitatis negotia, tam serenissimæ Dominæ et matri nostræ, quam nobis, et per ejusdem et nostrum dilectum Clericum, Magistrum Petrum Lykke, Archidiaconum Roskildensem, ac per vestræ regiæ Fraternitatis servitorem ad arma, Johannem Parant, ac Henricum de Odem, tam litteris quam verbis per vestram regiam Fraternitatem intimata, læto animo suscepimus intellecta. Pro quibus Omnipotenti Deo laudum præconia, ac tam Ipsi quam vestræ regiæ Fraternitati referimus correquisita gratiarum vota, cum instantia, ut tanta ambaxiatorum ipsorum ac negotiorum mora regiam vestram mentem ingrate non moveat,

*Excusing the delay of the Ambassadors, and commending them to the King.*

---

XXXI.] MS. Cotton. Nero, B. III. fol. 19 (α).—On paper; original. The Royal seal is still attached, and is in a tolerably perfect state.

A.D. 1401. ex certis causis superveniens, de quibus ipse Johannes Parant vestræ regiæ Serenitati novit his litteris nostris expressius informare.

Nosque [eti]am vestram regiam Fraternitatem et affective rogamus patienter tolerandum quod hæo- scripta nostra pro hac vice de ipso negotio, ut bene decern[itur], plene non continent; præcipue quia præfatum Johannem Parant, servitorem vestrum, in præsentia tam memoratæ serenissimæ Dominæ ma- tris nostræ quam nostrorum consiliarium, his scriptis amplius duximus instruendum. Cui speramus per ves- tram regiam Fraternitatem firmam fidem adhiberi in iis quæ a nobis in commisso obtinuit a vestra regia Fraternitate non celare.

In mente et gerimus proprium nostrum certum nun- cium, prout ipsi Johanni etiam diximus, ad vestræ Fraternitatis præsentiam in brevi dirigere, ad aperien- dum ipsi vestræ Fraternitati quam hæ litteræ continent plenius de præmissis.

Et, Princeps et frater præcarissime, si quid speciale vestra regia Fraternitas per nos dilexerit faciendum, læto vultu [sus]cepimus id nobis intimatum.

Excellentissimam vestram regiam Fraternitatem con- servet Altissimus prosperam et illæsam!

Scriptum in Castro nostro Gorghe, anno Domini MᵒCDᵒ primo, xv. die mensis Octobris. Nostro sub secreto, etc.

*Endorsed :*—" Illustrissimo Principi, Domino Hen[rico, Regi Angliæ] illustrissimo, Fratri nostro præca[rissimo]."

A.D. 1401.

## XXXII.

THE ABBAT OF WELBECK TO HENRY IV.

*Excellentissimo Principi et Domino, Domino Henrico, Dei gratia Regi Angliæ et Franciæ illustri, et Domino Hiberniæ, suus orator humilis et devotus, Johannes, Abbas Monasterii de Welbek, Ordinis Præmonstratensium, divina orationum suffragia cum omnimodis reverentiis et honore.*

Excellentiæ vestræ regiæ notum facimus per præsentes, quod Frater Simon de Casteltoun, Concanonicus noster, in Ordine et Domo nostra prædictis notorie expresse professus, rejectoque freno obedientiæ suæ de patria in patriam vagatur et discurrit, insolentiis variis nequiter et vitiose utendo, in [animæ] suæ grave periculum, et Ordinis prædicti scandalum manifestum, ac aliorum perniciosum exemplum. Quocirca vestram regiam Majestatem precibus aggredimur humilibus et devotis, quatinus pro ipso Fratre Simone de Casteltoun capiendo, et Domui nostræ prædictæ juxta regulam Ordinis illius resurgenda consueta misericordia extendere dignemini brachium seculare, ne (quod absit!) pro defectu vel negligentia coertionis debitæ et refrenationis insolentiæ hujusmodi taliter pereat plantatio divino cultui mancipata.

On the misconduct of a Friar.

Valeat vestra Celsitudo in Eo Qui regibus dat regnare !

In cujus rei testimonium sigillum nostrum præsentibus duximus apponendum.

Datum in Monasterio prædicto, vicesimo die mensis Octobris, anno Domini Millesimo CCCC$^{mo}$ primo.

XXXII.] MS. Publ. Rec. Off., portf. 1.—On vellum original.

A.D. 1401.

## XXXIII.

### ERIC X. TO HENRY IV.

*Invictissimo Principi, Domino Henrico, Dei gratia Regi Angliæ illustrissimo, fratri nostro præcarissimo, Ericus, eadem gratia regnorum Daciæ, Sueciæ, Norvegiæ, Slavorum Gothorumque Rex, ac Dux Pomeraniæ, salutem et prosperos ad vota successus.*

A Credential for Peter Lucke.

Princeps et frater præcarissime.

Prout alias vestræ scripsimus regiæ Fraternitati de certo nostro nuncio, ad ipsam vestræ regiæ Fraternitatis præsentiam in brevi dirigendo, hinc est quod [nos seren]issimæ Dominæ et matris nostræ et nostrum dilectum Clericum, Magistrum Petrum Lykke, Archidiaconum Roskildensem, ad ipsam vestram Fraternitatem . . . . . transmittimus. Cui in ipsius Dominæ et matris nostræ, et consiliarium nostrorum præsentia, nostra pro hac vice ad ipsam vestram Fraternitatem commisimus negotia ; affective instantes quatinus ipsa vestra regia Fraternitas eidem in negotiis quæ nuncii tam vestræ Fraternitatis quam [persona]liter nos ex utraque parte tractaverant, hac vice fidem velit adhibere creditivam, ac si nos ipsi vestræ Fraternitati de his [in perso]na loqueremur, nullam ambiguitatem, auxiliante Domino, in hoc admittendo.

De viarum etenim periculis, violentæ captionis [litterar]um timore, ac aliis, propter quæ expressius scribere ad præsens omittimus, novit præfatus Petrus [Lykke vestram] regiam Fraternitatem vivæ vocis oraculo facere contentatam.

---

XXXIII.]    MS. Cotton. Nero, B. III. fol. 19 (β).—On paper ; original.

Et, frater ac Princeps præcarissime, si quid speciale A.D. 1401
vestra regia Fraternitas per nos dilexerit faciendum
læto vultu suscepimus id nobis intimatum.

Vestram regiam Fraternitatem conservet Altissimus
prosperam et illæsam!

Scriptum in Castro Syoburgh, anno Domini M°CD°
primo, xxv. die mensis Octobris. Nostro sub secreto.

*Endorsed :*—" Invictissimo Principi, Domino Henrico,
Dei gratia regi Angliæ et Franciæ, et
Domino Hiberniæ illustrissimo, fratri
nostro præcarissimo."

## XXXIV.

MARGARET, QUEEN OF DENMARK, ETC., TO HENRY IV.

*Illustrissimo Principi, Domino Henrico, Dei gratia
[Regi Angliæ] illustrissimo, [fratri nostro] carissimo,
Margareta, eadem gratia Waldemari, Danorum Regis,
filia, salutem et felicitatis continuum incrementum.*

Princeps et frater præcarissime.

A Creden-
tial for
Peter
Lucke.

Prout alias amantissimus filius noster et nos vestræ
regiæ Serenitati de suo certo nuncio ad vestræ regiæ
Fraternitatis præsentiam in brevi scripsimus dirigendo,
hinc est quod ipse filius noster, jam in nostra et
suorum consiliarium præsentia, suo et nostro dilecto
servitori et Clerico, Magistro Petro Lykke, Archidiacono
Roskildensi, de illis negotiis exposuerat ; cui Magistro
Petro nos, una cum præfato nostro filio, petimus a vestra regia Fraternitate in sibi commissis, ut p[rædic]itur,

XXXIV.] MS. Cotton. Nero, B. III. fol. 19 (γ).—On paper ; original.

F

A.D. 1401. negotiis hac vice fidem adhiberi, ac si ipse filius et nos vestræ regiæ Fraternitate jam in persona loqueremur, nullam ambiguitatem in hoc, auxiliante Domino, admittendo.

De viarum etenim periculis, violentæ captionis litterarum timore, et aliis, propter quæ expressius scribere ad præsens omittimus, novit præfatus Magister Petrus Lykke vestram regiam Fraternitatem vivæ vocis oraculo facere contentatam. Et, Princeps et frater præcarissime, si quid speciale vestra regia Fraternitas per nos dilexerit faciendum, læto vultu suscipimus id nobis intimatum.

Excellentissimam vestram regiam Fraternitatem conservet Altissimus prosperam et illæsam!

Scriptum in Castro nostro Syeburgh, anno Domini M°CD° primo, xxv. die mensis Octobris. Nostro sub secreto.

## XXXV.

### HENRY IV. TO THE TREASURER.

*Henricus, Dei gratia etc., as Tresorer, Baronz, et Chamberleyns de nostre Escheker salutz.*

On behalf of Thomas Stanley and Hugh Lyllebourne.

Come nous, le xix. jour de Feverer, l'an de nostre regne seconde, par nostre brief mandasmes as gardeynes

---

[TRANSLATION.]

*Henry, by the grace of God, etc., to the Treasurer, Barons, and Chamberlains of our Exchequer, greeting.*

As we, on the 19th day of February, the second year of our reign, by our brief commanded the wardens of

---

XXXV.] MS. Cotton. Cleop. E. ii. fol. 243.—On vellum; a contemporaneous MS.

dil passage en le ports de Londres, Dovorre, Orwelle, A.D. 140
et Sandwycz, que ils suffrerent Thomas Stanley, Frere
d'Ordre dez Prechours, ove un compaynoun ovesque lui,
de nostre licence aler en pilgrimage devers la Court
de Rome, en ascun dez portez avauntditz, ascun mandement a eux devaunt direct nientobstant, come en
le dit brief pluis pleynement assiert, le quel brief fuist
delivere a Thomaus Leycestre, depute a Thomaus
Prendregeste, sercheour en le port de Londres en
l'ewe de Themese, le septisme jour de June darrein ; et
nientobstant le dit depute, par vertue d'une estatut
fait a Westminster l'an de nostre regne suisdit,—en
quel estatut parentre altres choses est contenuz que si
desore en avaunt ascun de noz sercheours purroit trover
or ou argent, en soyne ou en masse, en la garde d'acuny
qi serroit en passant, ou sur son passage en ascun
nief ou vesselle, pour aler hors d'aucun port, haviene,
ou cryke du roialme, saunz especial conge de nous,
tut cel or ou argent soit forffait a nous forpris ses

---

passage in the ports of London, Dover, Orwell, and Sandwich, that they should permit Thomas Stanley, a Friar
of the Order of Preachers, and one companion with him,
by our licence to go on pilgrimage to the court of Rome
from any of the aforesaid ports, any command previously
addressed to them notwithstanding, as in the said brief
is more fully expressed, the which brief was delivered to
Thomas Leicester, deputy to Thomas Prendergast, searcher
in the port of London, in the harbour of Thames, the 7th
day of June last ; and, notwithstanding, the said deputy,
by virtue of a statute made at Westminster, in the aforesaid
year of our reign, in which statute, among other things, is
contained that, if from that time forward any of our searchers
could find gold or silver, in coin or in mass, in the custody of any one who should be passing, or should be on
his passage in any ship or vessel, to go out of any port,
haven, or creek of the realm, without especial leave from us,
all this gold or silver should be forfeit to us, except his

F 2

A.D. 1401. resonables dispenses, quelx il serroit tenuz confesser et discoverer meintenant apres que a ce faire il serroit garniz et chargez par mesme le sercheour, ou autrement tut celle monee ensi concele serroit forffait a nous ;—

Et sur ce Hugh Lyllebourne, compaignoun le dit Thomaus Stanley, conist se aver x. marcz sur lui pour ces expenses, et sur ce le dit depute lui sercha et ensi trova et les aresta le septisme jour de June avauntdit, supposant que le dit Hughe ne fuist compaignoun au dit Thomas Stanley, lez quels dys marcz le dit depute delivera a nostre Tresorer, et puis apres le dit Thomaus Stanley vient devaunt nostre Conseil, c'est assavoir le xj$^{me}$ jour de June darrein, et fuist serement devaunt nostre dit Conseil que l'entent du dit Thomaus Stanley fuist le jour du dit brief pourchace, que le dit Hugh serroit son compaynoun d'aler en le pilgrimage suisdicte : sera q'en tutes choses considerez par nostre Con-

---

reasonable expenses, which he should be bound to confess and discover immediately after that he should be warned and charged to do so by the said searcher, or otherwise all this money so concealed should be forfeit to us ;—And upon this, Hugh Lyllebourne, companion of the said Thomas Stanley, acknowledged that he had with him ten marks for his expenses, and thereupon the said deputy searched him, and so found and seized them the 7th day of June aforesaid, supposing that the said Hugh was not a companion of the said Thomas Stanley,—the which ten marks the said deputy delivered to our Treasurer,—and then afterwards the said Thomas Stanley came before our Council, that is to say, on the 11th day of June last, and made oath before our said Council that the purpose of the said Thomas Stanley was, on the day when he obtained the said brief, that the said Hugh should be his companion to go on the aforesaid pilgrimage : therefore, all things being considered by our Council aforesaid, we com

seil avauntdit, vous mandons noz ditz Tresorer et Chamberleyns[1] que vous fatez repaier au dit Hugh Lillebourne lez x. marcz avauntditz; et vous, Tresorer et Baronz, que vous discharger si bien le dit sercheour et son dit depute, come le dit Hugh Lillebourne, de lez x. marcz avauntditz, et ent estre quite envers nous pour tous jours.

Donne etc.[2]

A.D. 1401.

---

mand our said Treasurer and Chamberlains that you cause the aforesaid ten marks to be repaid to the said Hugh Lyllebourne; and you, Treasurer and Barons, that you discharge as well the said searcher and his deputy as the said Hugh Lyllebourne, of the ten marks aforesaid, and that they be quit of the same towards us for ever.

Given, &c.

## XXXVI.

### THOMAS OF LANCASTER TO HENRY IV.

Tresexcellent, trespuissant, et mon tressouvereigne Seigneur et piere.

Je me recommaunt a vostre Hautesse aussi tres-

A.D. 1402.
On the state of Ireland, and his want of money.

---

[TRANSLATION.]

Most excellent, most mighty, and my most sovereign Lord and father.—I commend myself to your Highness as very

---

[1] *Chamberleyns*] Altered from "Baronz."

[2] The month is uncertain. The letter, however, is properly placed here, as it refers to events which took place in the year 1401.

XXXVI.] MS. Cotton. Titus, B. XI., fol. 22.—On paper; original. The MS. is very much mutilated.

A.D. 1402. humblement come je scey, ou en aucun manere obeissantement pluis puisse, en vous suppliant treshumblement s'il vous plest vostre gracieuse [Majeste, et]
empriant a Dieu Tout-puissant, q'il me doiant tousjours d'oier et savoir d[e vous et] vostre treshaut et
treshonnorable estat si vrayment bones et joieuses
novelles comme vous, mon tressoverain Seigneur et
piere, savez mieux pour vous penser ou souzhaider.

Et qant de moy, vostre treshumble fitz, et de
mon petit estat, plese assavoir vostre Hautesse que,
a l'escrivre d'icestes, j'estoy en bonne sauntee (Dieu
merciez), et ay tenuz mon Nowel a le Chastiel de
. . . . . . . . . . en fesant as Chivaliers, Esquiers,
et autres Gentils de la paiis le meilleur chere que
je poay.

Depuis quelle fest de Nowel, par avis de mon
Conseil, j'ay chivache sur les joioys voz (?) . . . . . . .
en fesant le mieux que je pourroy pour eux grever,
et suy retornez moy et mes gens sauvement (merciez
ent soit Dieu) . . . . . . . . . . . . . . . . . . . . . . . . . .

---

humbly as I know, or in any manner possibly can, with all
obeisance, beseeching you most humbly, if it may please
your gracious Majesty, and praying to God Almighty that
He will grant to me ever to hear and know of you and
your most high and most honourable estate as truly good
and joyous news as you, my most sovereign lord and father,
may best know how to imagine or desire for yourself.—
And as for me, your most humble son, and my low estate,
may it please your Highness to know that, at the writing of
these presents, I am in good health (thank God), and have
kept my Christmas at the Castle of . . . . . . . . . making to
the Knights, Esquires, and other Gentry of the country the
best cheer that I possibly could. Since which feast of
Christmas, by the advice of my Council, I have taken a journey
on horseback . . . . . . . . . . . doing the best that I could
to crush them, and am returned, I and my people, in safety,
(thanked be God for it) . . . . . . . . . . . came the soldiers

. . . . . . . viendrent les soudeours pardecea, la pluis A.D. 1402.
grande partie a mez treschiers et bien amez Monsieur
Estiephen Le Scrop, Monsieur . . . . . . . . . . . . . .

. . . . . . . dartus, lur chevitayns, come ils me ont
rapportez, lour demandantz congie et licence pour
departire et passer . . . . . . . . . . . . . . . . . . . . . . . .
[en di]santz q'ils ne pouvroient pluis outre ser-
vier sanz ce q'ils avoient paiement de leur gages, et
unquore . . . . . . . . . . . . . . . . . . . . . . . . . . . . .
plusieurs sont departiez; pour quelles matires si hastivement remede ne soit ordeignez par vous . . . . . . .
. . . . . je me doubte que graunt mal en purra avenir
a moy et a vostre dit paiis, comme le susdit Monsieur
Estiephen vous sait . . . . . . . . . . . . . pluis plaine-
ment declarer par bouche, que je ne scey escrire par
lettre ; liquel lequel Monsieur Estiephen m'a enformez
que force en . . . . . . . . . . . en sauvation de son
estat passer devers vostre haulte presence, pour poursuer
devers vous touchant le charge [de vostre Chastiel de]
Rokesburgh.

Pourqoy je vous supplie, mon tressouverain Sei-

---

hither, the greater part to my very dear and well-beloved
Master Stephen Le Scrope, Master . . . . . . . . . . . their
captains, as they have informed me, demanding their leave
and licence to depart, and proceed . . . . . . . . . saying
that they could no longer serve, unless they had payment
of their wages, and still . . . . . . . . . . . . many have
departed ; concerning which matters, if some remedy be not
speedily ordained by you . . . . . . . . . . . . . I fear that
great damage may accrue to me and to your said country,
as the aforesaid Master Stephen knows . . . . . . . . . more
plainly to declare by mouth than I can write by letter ; the
which Master Stephen has informed me that it was necessary
. . . . . . . . for the preservation of his estate to proceed
unto your high presence, there to plead before you concerning
the charge of your Castle of Roxburgh.—Wherefore, I beseech
you, my most sovereign Lord and father, that the aforesaid

A.D. 1402. gneur et piere, que le susdit Monsieur Estiephen et mez ditz soudeours . . . . . besoignes propres, vous plese gracieusement avoir pour recommandez, et lui esploiter et deliverer si en[1] . . . . . . retornir devers moy, qar je ne lui puisse leintement desportier, s'il vous plest, tant est . . . . . . . . . . . . . . . [et l]a grande conissance q'il ad de la governance de les guerres, et de les conditions des gens pardeca; a quel vous pleise [donner foy] et creance en ce q'il vous exposera, si vous plest, de ma parte, si bien touchant les dites matires, come d'autres choses [tout] l'estat de ceste paiis grandement touchantz. Moy commandantz tousjours vos treshonourables pleasirs et comendemantz, come a vostre treshumble obeissant subjit fitz, toutdis prest de les perfaire et accompler a trestout mon poair.

Tresexcellent, trespuissant, et mon tressoverain Seigneur et piere, je prie a Dieu qu'll vous sauve et

---

Master Stephen and my said soldiers . . . . . . . . . own necessities, it may please you graciously accept as recommended, and to expedite and send him on if . . . . . . . . to return to me, for I have not been able . . . . . . . . . ., if it may please you, so great is . . . . . . . . . . and the great knowledge he has of war, and of the circumstances of the people here; to whom may it please you to give faith and credence in that which he shall declare unto you, if it so please you, in my behalf, as well concerning the said matters, as of other things . . . . . . . . . . . greatly affecting the condition of this country. Commending to me ever your most honourable will and commands, as to your most humble obedient subject son, always ready to perform and accomplish them to the very utmost of my power.—Most excellent, most mighty, and my most sovereign Lord and father, I pray God to preserve and keep you in health and

---

[1] The MS. is torn into two pieces at this place.

garde en sauntee et prosperitee, et vous doigne attant A.D. 1402. de joi et lesce a cuer, comme vous desirez, a treslong durer.

Escript a Drogheda, le xviij jour de Feverer.

T. . . . . . . .[1]

prosperity, and that he may vouchsafe to give you as much joy and gladness of heart as you may desire, for very long to endure. — Written at Drogheda, the 18th day of February.

THOMAS OF LANCASTER.

## XXXVII.

### HENRY IV. TO THE TREASURER.

*Henri, par la grace de Dieu Roy d'Engleterre et de France, et Seignur d'Irlande, a notre Tresorer d'Engleterre, q'or'est, et qui pur le temps serra, saluz.*

Come pur la grande busoigne et necessitee que nous avons d'estre purveuz de monnie pur pleuseurs grantz et chargeantes busoignes touchantz nous et

On behalf of William Parker and John Dyghster.

[TRANSLATION.]

*Henry, by the grace of God King of England and of France and Lord of Ireland, to our Treasurer of England that now is, and for the time shall be, greeting.*

Since for the great need and necessity that we have to be provided with money for many great and pressing affairs concerning ourselves and our kingdom ; and amongst others,

---

[1] The signature is nearly cut away.

XXXVII.] MS. Brit. Mus., Sloane, 4596, fol. 350.

A.D. 1402. notre roiaume, et entre autres pur le passage de notre tresame fille, Blaunche, vers les parties d'Allmaigne, fait avons, de l'avis de notre Conseil, examiner les coillours de nos custumes et subsides des leyns, quirs, et peaux lanuz de pluseurs noz portz de notre roiaume, s'ils avoient en lour mains aucuns noz deniers, pur paier a nous et a noz ministres a notre oeps en ceste notre necessitee ; et entre autres William Parker, et Johan Dyghster, coillours de noz ditz custumes et subsides en port de notre ville de Southampton, par tiele manere examinez ne vorroient confesser qu'ils avoient en lour mains aucuns noz deniers : mais grante nous ount de nous faire chevance de noef centz livres dount ils desiront estre repaiez par lour mains propres, de noz custumes et subsides susditz. Si nous, considerantz lour bone affection et corage, vuillantz par tant lour faire seur de repaiement des dites noef centz livres, volons de l'assent de notre Grant Conseil, et vous mandons, que receves

---

for the journey of our much beloved daughter, Blanche, unto the parts of Germany, we have, with the advice of our Council, caused to be examined the collectors of our customs and subsidies of wool, hides, and woolly skins, of many our ports of our kingdom, whether they had in their hands any of our moneys, to pay to us and our ministers for our help in this our necessity ; and among others, William Parker and John Dyghster, collectors of our said customs and subsidies in the port of our town of Southampton, in such manner examined, would not confess that they had in their hands any of our moneys, but have promised us to make us a loan of nine hundred pounds, of which they desire repayment, by their own hands, out of our aforesaid customs and subsidies. Now we, considering their good affection and purpose, and willing accordingly to assure them of the repayment of the said nine hundred pounds, do, with the assent of our Council, will and command you, that, having received

des ditz William et Johan noef centz livre de che- A.D. 1402
vance a notre oeps, leur en fatez assignement par
lour mains propres, et aussi veues les endentures
severales lettres desouz expressees, c'est assavoir,—

Une endenture faite parentre notre chier et foial
Chivaler, Estiephne Le Scrope, Gardein de notre Chastel
de Rokesburgh, et les ditz coillours, de cynk centz
et sessante livres.

Une autre endenture faite parentre notre ame Clerc,
John Legburn, Receivour de notre Chambre, et les
ditz coillours, de sys centz et sessante livres.

Une autre endenture faite d'entre notre ame
Esquier, William Loveneye, Gardein de notre Grande
Garderobe, et mesmes les coillours, de noef centz et
quatorze livres et un denier.

Et certeins lettres desouz le seal de notre treschier
et foial cousin le Conte de Wircestre,[1] contenantes
la some de cent et cynquante livres.

---

from the said William and John nine hundred pounds on
loan for our help, you make them an assignment by their
own hands, and also having seen the several written indentures hereunder expressed, that is to say,—An indenture
made between our dear and faithful knight, Stephen
Le Scrope, warden of our Castle of Roxburgh, and the said
collectors, of five hundred and sixty pounds.—Another
indenture made between our beloved Clerk John Legburn,
Receiver of our chamber, and the said collectors, of six
hundred and sixty pounds.—Another indenture made between
our beloved Esquire, William Loveneye, warden of our great
wardrobe, and the same collectors, of nine hundred and
fourteen pounds and one denier.—And certain letters under
the seal of our very dear and faithful cousin the Earl of
Worcester, comprising the sum of a hundred and fifty

---

[1] Thomas Percy, younger brother of Henry, Earl of Northumberland.

A.D. 1402. Les queles sommes par tailles livres a la receite de notre Eschequier, fait aviens nadgairs assigner as dites persones, d'estre paiez de nos custumes et subsides en port susdit, par les mains des couillours susditz ; soeffrez mesmes les couillours demorer en lour ditz offices tanque ils soient primierement repaiez par lour mains propres do les susdites noef centz livres, par eux a nous apprestees, et que delors ils averont pleinement paiez les autres assignementz dessusditz ; aucuns autres assignementz sur les ditz coillours faitz avant ces heures forsque celles que dessus ou autres assignementz sur eux affaire desore en avant nient contre esteantes.

Donne souz notre prive seal a Westminster, le xxviij jour de Feverer, l'an de notre regne tierz.

─────────────

pounds.—The which sums duly delivered at the receipt of our Exchequer, we have recently caused to be assigned to the said persons, to be paid from our customs and subsidies in the aforesaid port by the hands of the aforesaid collectors ; suffer the said collectors to remain in their said offices until they are in the first place repaid by their own hands the aforesaid nine hundred pounds by them lent to us, and that then they shall have fully paid the other aforesaid assignments ; any other assignments upon the said collectors previous to this time, except those afore-mentioned, or other assignments to be made on them henceforth notwithstanding.—Given under our privy seal at Westminster, the 28th day of February, the third year of our reign.

A.D. 1402.

## XXXVIII.

### COENTZO DE VISSCHENICH TO HENRY IV.

Subjectionem debitam, et regalibus mandatis humiliter, ut teneor, semper obedire.

Illustrissime ac magnifice Princeps, dominorum maxime gratiose.

De vestræ regiæ clementiæ gratioso homagio per Gerardum de Mutroit, meum servitorem, mihi transmisso, reverenter ut decuit recepto, serenæ vestræ Majestati, cum humili genuflectionis et cervicis inclinatione, quantas valeo gratiarum refero actiones.

Præterea, dominorum gratiosissime, ad vestræ Serenitatis devotæ exoro devenire notitiam, illustrem Dominum, Wilhelmum, Gelrensem et Juliacensem olim Ducem, post longam suam in qua decubuit ægritudinem, xvᵃ. mensis Februarii die proxime præterita, debito universæ carnis persoluto, Deo jubente, ab hoc seculo emigrasse; fratre suo germano illustri Domino Reynoldo[1] relicto superstite, universali ad cuncta per mortem suam derelicta successore.

Qui jam a notabilioribus utrorumque ipsorum ducatuum oppidis ac militaribus, palmitatione subjectivæ fidelitatis ipsi præstita, reverenter (uti debebant) est receptus, ac per ceteros continue recipitur subditos; ita quod in ipsis suis ducatibus, nullo sibi obstante obstaculo, solum et in solidum dominantem gerit principatum. In casu ergo quo vestræ regali Magnificentiæ quicquid vestræ voluntatis ipsum jam Dominum Du-

*Announcing the death of William Duke of Juliers,*

*and the accession of Duke Reynald.*

---

XXXVIII.] MS. Cotton. Galba, B. I. fol. 133.—On paper; original with marks of the seal.

[1] *Reynoldo*] Sic MS. (See note, p. 94.)

A.D. 1402. cem Reynaldum [1] indaganter volueritis per me attemptari, id vestra gratiosa Majestas mihi, vestro humili ac, ut decet, obedienti quantocius dignetur rescriptare.

*News of the Emperor.*

Insuper, præclarissime Domine, de serenissimorum Romanorum Regis et Reginæ, suorumque illustrissimorum filiorum in Venetiis residentium corporum Dei dono incolumitate, congrua prosperitate sanctissimi in Christo Patris ac Domini, Domini Bonifacii, eidem Domino Regi fideli assistentis ac coronæ suæ imperialis assequendæ proposito, necnon ipsius concepta voluntate salubris sui principii ad salubriorem finem pro universali Ecclesia et sacro Romano Imperio Dei adjutorio, ut speratur, ante suum ad Almaniæ partes reditum illic in Italia exequendi, veridicorum relatibus, et ex ipsius Domini Regis Romanorum emissis litteris, intellexi.

Magnificentissime Princeps, vestra regia Majestas pro vobis, vestrisque illustribus filiis et filiabus, Dominis et Domicillabus meis, quorum et quarum sanitatem et prosperitatem summopere desidere in cunctis meæ declivitati possibilibus percipere dignetur mihi, vestro humillimo et parvo servulo, vestrum omnium felicitatem ardenter, sicut decet, sitienti, Deo omnium cordium Scrutatore Teste.

Qui vestram regalem Serenitatem conservare dignetur feliciter et longæve!

Datum meo sub sigillo, iiij[a] die mensis Martii.

Vestræ regiæ serenæ Majestatis
    COENTZO DE VISSCHENICH, Miles,
        fidelis servitor humilis et devotus.

Præterea, serenissime Domine mi Rex, in casu quo vestræ regali Majestati placeret de aliis novitatibus, seu partium Almaniæ circa Rhenum statibus, singularius percontari, de his Gerhardus, servitor meus, præ-

---

[1] *Reynaldum*] Sic MS. (See note, p. 93.)

sentium exhibitor, vestram dominantem gratiam requi- A.D. 1402.
situs poterit informare; cui in hujusmodi exquirendis,
et per ipsum videndis, vestra regalis Serenitas fidem
velit exhibere, sicuti in negotiis meis apud vestram
Magnificentiam peragendis creditivam.[1]

*Endorsed :—*" Illustrissimo et magnificentissimo Principi, [Henrico], Angliæ et Franciæ
Regi, ac Domino Hiberniæ, D[omino]
maxime gratioso."

*Also :—*" Littera Coentzo de Vissenich, Militis."

## XXXIX.

### HENRY, PRINCE OF WALES, TO JOHN SPENSER.

*Henry, eisne filz au noble Roy d'Engleterre et de
France, Prince de Gales, Duc de Guyenne, de Lancastre, et de Cornewayle, Counte de Cestre, a notre
bien ame Esquier, Johan Spenser, notre Receyvour
General, saluz.*

Come noz bien amez, Nicholas Burdon et William On behalf
Spridlyngton, par vertue de notre Commission a eux of Nicholas
Burdon, &
William
Spridlyng-
ton.

-------

### [TRANSLATION.]

*Henry, eldest son of the noble King of England and
of France, Prince of Wales, Duke of Guienne, of Lancaster,
and of Cornwall, Earl of Chester, to our well-beloved
Esquire, John Spenser, our Receiver-General, greeting.*

As our well-beloved, Nicholas Burdon and William
Spridlyngton, by virtue of our Commission to them directed,

-------

[1] This post-script has been detached from the letter, and has
been pasted on folio 134 of the MS.

XXXIX.] MS. Brit. Mus. Sloane,
4596, fol. 336.

A.D. 1402. faite, aient travaillez necessarement en notre service entour l'audit dez accomptez de noz ministrez, si bien en countees de Cestre et Flynt, come es parties de Northgales et Southgales, de l'an du reigne notre dit Seignur et pier primer, lour viage par celle cause comenceant le vij$^{me}$ jour d'April, l'an du reigne notre dit Seignur et pier seconde, et durant jusques al seconde jour de Juyl lors prochein ensuant, preignant chescun de eaux par mesme le temps quarant deniers le jour pour leur gages, par avis de notre Conseil dount la somme amount a vyngt et neof livres; volons et vous mandons, que des deniers de votre receipte fatez paier as ditz Nicholas et William les vyngt et neof livres avantditz; et volons que par garrant d'icestez mesmes lez deniers soient a vous allouez en votre prochein acompte.

Donne soubz notre seal, a notre Manour de Kenyngton, le vj$^{me}$ jour d'Averyl, l'an du regne nostre tresredoute Seignur et pier le Roy suisdit tierce.

---

have laboured necessarily in our service concerning the audit of the accounts of our ministers, as well in the counties of Chester and Flint, as in the parts of North Wales and South Wales, in the first year of our said Lord and Father, their journey on this account commencing the 7th day of April, the second year of the reign of our said Lord and father, and continuing until the second day of July then next ensuing, each of them taking for the same time forty deniers a day for their wages, by the advice of our Council, the sum of which amounts to twenty and nine pounds: we will and command you that from the deniers of your receipt you cause to be paid to the said Nicholas and William the twenty and nine pounds aforesaid; and we will that for your security these same deniers be allowed to you in your next account.—Given under our seal, at our Manor of Kennington, the 7th day of April, the third year of the reign of our most dread Lord and father, the King above-mentioned.

A. D. 1402.

## XL.

### HENRY IV. TO THE PRIVY COUNCIL.

Depar le Roy.

Tresreverentz Peres en Dieu, et noz treschiers et foiaulx.

Nous vous salvons souvent, et savoir vous faisons que puis nostre departir de vous nous avions inspection des lettres du Roy de Denmarke, ja tarde a nous apportees par l'onnourable Pere en Dieu l'Evesque de Bangore,[1] et nostre ame Escuier Johan Paraunt, noz messages, ore a leur retour pardevers nous; et ycelles lettres bien entendues, et par especial un article touchant le desir que nous et les grandz et le peuple de nostre royaume avions, que le mariage se prendroit d'entre le dit Roy et nostre treschiere et tresamee fille Phelippe, quel article mesme le Roy fait

*On the proposed marriage of the Princess Philippa.*

---

[TRANSLATION.]

Most Reverend Fathers in God, and our very dear and trusty.—We greet you often, and cause you to know that, after our departure from you, we have had inspection of the letters of the King of Denmark, lately brought unto us by the honourable Father in God the Bishop of Bangor, and our beloved Esquire John Parant, our messengers, now recently returned to us; and these letters being well considered, and more especially an article touching the desire which we and the great men and the people of our realm had, that the marriage should come to pass between the said King and our most dear and well-beloved daughter Philippa, of which article the same king hath made mention

---

XL.] MS. Cotton. Nero, B. III., fol. 23.

[1] Richard Yonge.

G

A.D. 1402. rehercer en ses dictes lettres : certes il nous semble de nostre advis que la response que nous ferions au dit Roy, selon ce que vous et nous en avions communication, ne pourra honestement passer ne resounablement, sanz luy donner bonne cause de refuser tout outrement cel mariage.

Et pensons bien que, si vous eussiez bien veue les susdictes lettres, vous eussiez este moevez de lui avoir fait donner autre response plus convenable et accepte a luy que n'est encore appointie, sanz enfreindre la besoingne, et sanz venir au contraire de ce que promis luy avons expressement par noz autres lettres passees de l'advis et deliberation de nostre Conseil. Si avons par tant fait faire une copie d'une lettre, quelle il nous semble estre raisonable et correspondent a les siens; la quelle copie nous vous envoions par l'onneurable Pere en Dieu l'Evesque de Bath,[1] ovec les dictes lettres du dit Roy, et pour

---

in his said letter ; it certainly seemeth to us in our opinion, that the answer which we should make to the said King, according to that on which you and we have had mutual communication, could not honourably or reasonably pass over without giving them good cause for refusing this marriage altogether.—And we are well assured that, if you had well inspected the aforesaid letters, you would have been moved to have made him another answer more suitable and acceptable to him than is yet determined on, without infringing the business, and without going contrary to that which we had expressly promised him by our other letters, sent by the advice and deliberation of our Council. Wherefore we have caused to be made a copy of a letter, the which seemeth to us to be reasonable and corresponding to his own ; and this copy we send to you by the honourable Father in God the Bishop of Bath, together with the said letters of the said King, for your

---

[1] Henry Bowet.

les veoir. Vous prians treschierement que sur ce A.D. 1402. donner nous vuilliez vostre sage advis a la conservation de l'estat de nous et de tout nostre royaume. Et ce ne vuilliez lesser, come nous nous fions de vous.

Donne soubz nostre signet, a nostre Chastel de Wyndesore, le xxviij^me jour d'Avril.[2]

*Endorsed :* — " Littera regia, suo directa Concilio, super transmissione quarundam litterarum Regi Daciæ, Norwegiæ, et Sweciæ, etc."

---

perusal. And we pray you very affectionately that you will be pleased to give us your sage advice on this matter, to the preservation of our estate and of our whole realm. And in this fail ye not, as we trust in you.—Given under our signet, at our Castle of Windsor, the 28th day of April.

## XLI.

### ESTURMY AND KINGTON TO J. FRY.

Socie et amice merito prædilecte.

Pridem cum eramus in regno, ministrata nobis erant, Requiring prout credimus novistis, stipendia, pro quinquaginta the payment of the duntaxat diebus, xvi. diem mensis Februarii, quo balance of their ex-

---

[2] See also Nicolas, i., 291. 222, 294 ; and Rymer, viii., 443, 447, 448 ; also Halliwell's " Letters of the Kings of England," i. 61.

XLI.] MS. Cotton. Galba, B. 1. fol. 149.—On paper ; original, with traces of the seal. See Rymer VIII. 176 et seqq., 242, 245 ; Nicolas I. 184.

A.D. 1402. navem Londoniæ ascendimus, immediate sequentibus.

penses, incurred in conducting the Princess Blanche into Germany. Cum igitur quinquaginta dies hujusmodi a diu elapsi existunt, aliique quadraginta septem dies etiam die datæ præsentium evanuerunt, nosque præter expensas nostras personales, tam pro salvorum-conductuum impetratione, necnon navium pro ascensu Dominæ nostræ Blanchiæ a partibus superioribus Reni et aliis adductarum provisione, nautarumque in navibus ipsis constitutorum sumptuum erogatione, non mediocres per dies plurimos sustinuimus et in dies sustinemus expensas, adeo quod nobiscum apportata per multorum dierum jam lapsorum transcursum consumpta sunt et exhausta, ita quod, nisi celerius nobis de opportunis provideatur expensis, urgente necessitate, quod utique nollemus, cogimur repatriare, cum mutuum aliud, præter id quod contraximus[1] de cetero contrahere non valemus.

Vos igitur rogamus quatinus præmissa Dominis nostris de Concilio simul coadunatis, ac etiam divisim, cum se ad hoc obtulerit facultas opportuna, et prout vobis videbitur expedire, seriosius intimare curetis, harum nostrarum precum interventu.

Socium nostrum prædilectum conservet Altissimus in continuum incrementum!

Scriptum Dordraci, die Mercurii ante festum Corporis Christi.[2]

W. ESTURMY, Chivalier;
J. KYNGTOUN, Clericus.

News of the Emperor. Scripsissemus et Dominis nostris de Concilio nova de reditu Domini Regis Romanorum de Italia et Alemannia, et aliis, si non fuissemus opinati eos de novis ipsis tam per Dominum J. Colvyle, Militem, etc., et alios, plenius fuisse informatos. Unum tamen certum est, quod, die Lunæ proxime præterito, idem Dominus

---

[1] There is here a long erasure.　|　[2] May 24, 1402.

Rex venit ad civitatem suam Maguntinam, tam cum A.D. 1402. Dominis Principibus Electoribus quam aliis etc., pro prosperitate Romani imperii parliamentum celebraturus, etc.

*Endorsed :*—"Socio nostro et amico prædilecto, J. Fry, Clerico, cum honorabili viro, Domino Custode Sigilli privati Domini nostri Regis, commoranti.

W. ESTURMY, J. KYNGTOUN."

## XLII.

### JOHN PALÆOLOGUS TO HENRY IV.

*Serenissimo Principi et potentissimo Domino, Henrico, Dei gratia, Regi Angliæ, consanguineo nostro præcarissimo, Johannes, in Christo Deo fidelis Imperator et Moderator Romæorum, Palæologus, salutem in Eo per Quem reges regnant.*

Magnis instantibus nobis periculis, necessariis indi- Entreating gemus auxiliis; ideoque inclitam regiam Majestatem against the vestram rogamus et requirimus quatinus ipsa dignetur, Infidels. propter nomen Salvatoris Jhesu Christi, et ob famam quam ipsa Excellentia regia habet in toto orbe terrarum, conferre ad auxilium et subsidium huic civitati nostræ Constantinopolitanæ, quæ quidem ex longissima tempestate, et angustia guerrarum habitarum, quas præsentialiter habet cum Turchis infidelibus, persecutoribus nominis Christiani, tandem extenuata viribus et potentia ac facultatibus quibuscumque, jacet prostrata, non

XLII.] MS. Brit. Mus., Harl. 431, fol. 10.

A.D. 1402. valens ulterius hostes offendere, immo nec ab ipsis se defendere; pereclitatur subire jugum ipsorum infidelium Saracenorum, nisi a vestra, et aliorum Regum et Principum Christianorum potentia, mediante Divina Gratia, sublevetur a periculo tantæ cladis.

Et si forte regia Celsitudo vestra in præsenti non valet tantum quantum gliscit subsidium et auxilium conferre, prout nobis scripsit serenissimus et excellentissimus Dominus et Pater meus, Dominus Imperator, saltem dignetur regia clementia vestra subsidium et succursum impendere ac conferre de gentibus-armorum et pecunia, in tanta parte quod dicta civitas valeat a prædictis periculis et hostium incursibus præservari, usque ad majorem et magis ordinatam provisionem auxilii et succursus fiendam a vestra Majestate, una cum ceteris Regibus et Principibus Christianis, eo quod quia si (quod absit!) amitteretur dicta civitas de manibus Christianorum, quæ civitas potest Domus Dei nuncupari, cederet ad damnum et dedecus omnium fidelium Christianorum, et timendum est quod deleretur et amitteretur nomen Jhesu Christi de istis partibus Orientis.

Ceterum, inclite Rex, quia rectos decet collaudatio, non debemus nec possumus sub silentio[1] præterire illos qui virtutum operibus illustrantur, et actus laudabiles non desinunt quotidie exercere; sane cum nobiles nonnulli ex vestratibus in hujus urbis defensione commorantes, sint per eorum opera dignis laudibus merito excolendi. Ideo, intervenientibus eorum bonis operibus, adsurgimus vobis ad gratiarum actiones refererendas valde dignas, quoniam ipsi ad omnem defensionem hujus civitatis ab hostibus, et ad nostrum commodum et honorem, solertem et intrepidam curam contulerunt, velut optimi operantes, nihil de contingentibus omittendo quod respiceret bonum et securum statum nostrum

---

[1] silentio] scilencio, MS.

et dictæ nostræ Civitatis, et civium ejusdem. Nec enim A.D. 1402. clarissimæ Angliæ novum est producere tales fructus.

Valeat et augeat inclita regia Celsitudo vestra præ-libata in optatis feliciter per tempora longiora!

Datum in urbe Constantinopolitana,[1] Anno a Nativi-tate Domini Millesimo CCCCmo secundo, die prima Junii.

## XLIII.

### THE BISHOP OF WINCHESTER AND THE EARL OF SOMERSET TO THE COUNCIL.

Reverendi Patres, et Domini.

Clamore plus quam valido non solum nobis, immo Domini nostri Regis officiatis apud Dordracum consti-tutis, exposuerunt ii quorum nomina in cedula præsen-tibus interclusa continentur, de spoliis et gravaminibus in eadem contentis, emendam a nobis competentem cum instantia fieri postulantes. Cumque iidem exponentes verbis pacificis, non sine difficultate ad mansuetudi-nem fuissent reducti, demum extitit condictum quod vobis nostra scripta opportuna dirigeremus in hac parte.

On behalf of certain citizens of Dort, who had been injured by the Eng-lish.

Vos igitur consulendo rogamus quatinus in dicta cedula nominatis justitiam, de qua confidimus, super conquestis non postponatis ministrare, eoque celerius quo in reditu nostro reprisalias Domini nostri Regis

---

[1] Constantinopolitana] "Consti-nopolitana." MS.

XLIII.] MS. Cotton. Galba, B. i. fol. 157.—On paper ; original, with marks of the seal.—See Rymer, viii. 253.

A.D. 1402. ligeis comminatas quas non eminus conspicimus immi-
nere, valeamus et valeant evitare.

In successus prosperos vos[1] ad votum dirigat[2] nostri
clementia Salvatoris.

Scripta apud Dordracum, xviij die Junii.

R., WYGORNENSIS EPISCOPUS[3];

J., COMES SOMERSET, Angliæ
Camerarius.[4]

*Endorsed*:—"Reverendis in Christo Patribus, Dominis
Edmundo,[5] Cancellario, Henrico[6] Ba-
thoniæ, Angliæ Thesaurario, Episcopis,
ceterisque Dominis de Concilio Domini
nostri Regis, Londoniæ existentibus."

## XLIV.

### PHILIP DE COURTENAY TO THE COUNCIL.

*Complaining that the ships which he had prepared at Southampton, by the King's command, were lying idle there.*

Tresreverentz Piers en Dieu, et mes tresnobles
Seignurs.

Je me recommaunt a vous a taunt com je say

---

[TRANSLATION.]

Most reverend Fathers in God, and my most noble Lords.—
I commend me to you as much as I know or am able,

---

[1] *vos*] Added above the line.
[2] There is an erasure in this place.
[3] Richard Clifford.
[4] John Beaufort.
[5] Edmund Stafford, Bishop of Exeter.

[6] Henry Bowet.

XLIV.] MS. Cotton. Julius,
B. VI., fol. 28.—On paper; original,
with traces of the seal.

ou puisse, humblement requeraunt vos gracieus A.D. 1402. benisons.

Et vous plese entendre, mes tresnobles Seignurs, coment nostre tresredoute Seignur le Roy m'ad comaunde par ces treshonourables lettres d'estre ad ville de Southamptoun a certein jour assigne, ovesque deux niefs bien et suffisamment armes, arraies, et estouffes de gentz armes, et archiers, prestz d'alir ovesque autres en son message outre la meer envers les parties de Briteigne. Les quels comaundementz je parforna a tout le hast que je purroy ; et al ville de Southamptoun estoy ovesque deux niefs, arraies com devaunt est dit, prest d'alir, sicom j'estoy comaundez, a grauntz costages de moy.

Et puys nostre dit tresredoute Seignur le Roy m'ad comaunde par ces treshonourables lettres autreforth d'estre a dit ville, pour la matiere avaundit, le xxij jour de Juyn ; a quel jour j'envoia un de mes servauntz a dit ville de Southamptoun, pur savoir la

---

humbly beseeching your gracious benisons.—And may it please you to know, my most noble Lords, how that our most dread Lord the King hath commanded me by his most honourable letters to be at the town of Southampton at a certain appointed day, with two ships well and sufficiently armed, arrayed, and furnished with men at arms, and archers, ready to depart with others on his errand beyond the sea towards the parts of Brittany. The which commands I performed with all the speed that I could ; and at the town of Southampton I was with two ships, arrayed as is aforesaid, ready to depart, as I was commanded, at heavy charges to myself.—And then our said most dread Lord the King hath commanded me by his most honourable letters another time to be at the said town, for the aforesaid purpose, the 22nd day of June ; on which day I sent one of my servants to the said town of Southampton, to know the truth of the said matter. And

A.D. 1402. verite du dit matiere. Et nul homme fuist la prest d'alir, com j'estoy enformez. Parqoi je fu en nouncertein a quels temps je serra illoeques pur accomplier la volentee nostre dit tresredoute Seignur le Roy, et son service. Et vous plese assavoir que je ne say coment je gardera mes compaignouns longement encemble, si n'avera brevement jour assigne en certein de nostre alir, ou autrement que nous ferromps en icels. Si vous supplie effectuelment de tout mon cuer que vous me plese certifier par lettre la volentee nostre dit tresredoute Seignur le Roy, et jour en certein de nostre alir, si le jour susdit soit aloignez, en salvatioun de mon povre estat, et pour eschuer les grauntz costages que je porte de jour en autre pur icels. Cest ma priere vous plese bonement prendre a cuer. et parforner a present, com ma graunt affiaunce est toudis envers vous ; requeraunt nostre Seignur Tout-

---

no man was there ready to depart, as I was informed. Wherefore I was in uncertainty at what time I should be there to accomplish the will of our said most dread Lord the King, and his service. And may it please you to know that I know not how I shall long keep my companions together, if I have not shortly a day fixed, with certainty, for our departure, or otherwise what we shall do in these circumstances. Therefore I beseech you earnestly with all my heart that it may please you to certify me by letter of the will of our said most dread Lord the King, and of a fixed day for our departure, if the above-mentioned day be postponed, for the preservation of my poor estate, and to avoid the heavy expenses that I bear from one day to another in present circumstances. This my prayer may it please you to take kindly to heart, and presently to perform it, as my great confidence is ever towards you ; beseeching our Almighty

Puissaunt q'Il vous eit tous jours en Sa tresseint sive A.D. 1402. garde, et encresce vos honours.

Escript le xxvj jour de Juyn.

PHILIP DE COURTENAY.

*Endorsed :* — " A tresreverentz Piers en Dieu, et mes [tresnobles Seignurs] l'Evesque d'Excestre,[1] Chaunceller d'Eng[leterre, l'Evesque de] Bath,[2] Tresourer d'Engleterre, et a le[s Seignurs] del tresage Councel nostre tresredoute [Seignur le Roy.]"

*Also ;*—" Littera Philippi Courteney."

---

Lord that He may have you ever in His most holy safe-keeping, and may increase your honours.—Written the 26th day of June.

PHILIP DE COURTENAY.

*Endorsed.*—" To the most reverend Fathers in God, and my most noble Lords, the Bishop of Exeter, Chancellor of England, the Bishop of Bath, Treasurer of England, and to the Lords of the most learned Council of our most dread Lord the King."

---

[1] Edmund Stafford.     [2] Henry Bowet.

A.D. 1402.

## XLV.

### HENRY III., KING OF CASTILE, TO HENRY IV.

*Al muy poderoso Principe, Don Enrique, por la gracia de Dios Rey de Inglaterra, Señor de Yrlanda, mi muy caro e muy amado [herman]o, Don Enrique, por esa mesma gracia Rey de Castiella e de Leon, salud, e agrecentamiento de toda buena audanca como [vos me]des deseiades.*

In answer to his letter requesting that justice might be done to Moses Mahieu.

Muy caro e muy amado hermano.

Fago vos saber que vy vuestras cartas que me enviastes con John Hull, Escu[dero, e John Es]trumestre, e entendi todo lo en ellas contenido, e alo que

---

### [TRANSLATION.]

*To the most powerful Prince, the Lord Henry, by the grace of God King of England and Lord of Ireland, my dearest and most beloved brother, Don Henrique, by this same grace King of Castile and of Leon, health, and increase of all good fortune, as you yourself may desire it.*

Most dear and most beloved brother.—I cause you to know that I have seen your letters which you sent me with John Hull the Knight, and with John Estrumestre, and that I understand all that is contained in them, and

---

XLV.] MS. Cotton. Vespas., F. III., fol. 39 (a). On paper; original, with marks of the seal. This letter has suffered very severely | from damp; it is more or less obscure and difficult to read throughout, and in some places the ink is quite obliterated.

me enviastes desir en fecho del oficio del . . . . .
e as mill florines annales que desides que el Rey,
Don Enrique, mi avuelo (que Dios perdone), diera
a Mosen Mahieu, [e otr]osi de honze mill florines de
Florencia, que el dicho Mosen Mahieu aiya prestado
al dicho Rey, mi avuelo, que [deseia]des que me
ploguyese de le fazer cumplimiento de justicia.

Muy caro e muy amado hermano, 'como las [cartas
prese]ntadas a mi sobresto por los dichos John
Hull e John Estrumestre, en nonbre del dicho
Mosen Mahieu, sean . . . . . . fe ; por lo qual
yo no puedo seer ben enformado, ni saber el fecho
de la verdad, mayormente en fecho [tanto], por
ende yo non vos puedo complidamente a ello re-
sponder ; mas quando los originales parecieren, yo—
Dios . . . sabre la verdad del fecho—e mandare
faser al dicho Mosen Mahieu cumplimiento de justicia.

---

as to what you sent to tell me in the affair of the court
of justice of . . . . . . ., and the thousand annual
florins which you said that the King Henrique, my grandfather (on whom God have mercy), had to give to Moses
Mahieu ; and moreover, as to the eleven thousand florins
which the said Moses Mahieu had lent to the said King
my grandfather, as to which you desired that it might
please me to cause full justice to be done to him.—Most
dear and most beloved brother, as the letters presented
to me on this behalf by the said John Hull and John
Estrumestre, in the name of the said Moses Mahieu, are
such as . . . require credence, since by them I cannot be
well informed, nor know the truth of the affair ; the more
so in an affair of such importance, therefore I am not able
to give you a full answer about this : but when the originals
shall appear, I—God knows the truth of the matter—will
order full justice to be done to the said Moses Mahieu.
And immediately in the very moment I answered to the

A.D. 1402. E luego de presente respondi alos dichõs John Hull e John Estrumestre a sy como a per curadores del dichõ Mosen Mahieu, que si yo en alguna [cosa[1]] le so tenudo e obligado que lo demande da lante de los mis oydores,[2] los quales son jueses principales para los tales fechõs, los [qua]les faran cumplimiento de derechõ.

Otrosi, muy caro e muy amado hermano, a lo que mi escriviestes en el fechõ de casa d'Ujos de Monte, ya sobresto esta pleito pendiente en la mi audiencia entre Donna Ynes de Ayala, sa avuela, e otros que . . . . . ran quales preneste [?] los quales seguen sa pleito. E yo no puedo negar justicia a quellos que la demandan; e por ende siguan derecho por la dicha audiencia, que enteramente les sara guardado.

E, muy caro e muy amado hermano, si algunas cosas aia vos plazen, que yo por onnrra vuestra pueda

said John Hull and John Estrumestre, as to curators of the said Moses Mahieu, that if I in any thing am bound and obliged to him, he should require it in the presence of my hearers, who are the principal judges for the like matters; and these will see him fully righted.—Also, most dear and most beloved brother, as to that which you wrote about the affair of the house of Ujos de Monte, this lawsuit is already pending on its account in my court of justice between Dona Ynes de Ayala, her grandmother, and others, who . . . . . . . . follow her law-suit. And I cannot deny justice to those who demand it; and therefore let it be according to the regular course through the said court of law, which will entirely be kept for them.—And, dearest and most beloved brother, if there are any things pleasing you, which I, for your honour's sake, could do, send to tell them to me,

---

[1] Or perhaps " maniera."
[2] mis oydores.] " My hearers,"

 i.e., judges appointed to hear the pleading in law-suits.

faser, enviad me las desir que yo las fare muy de A.D. 1402. buen talante.

Dada en Segovia, dies e ocho dias de Jullio.

*Endorsed :*—" Al muy alto, muy poderoso Principe, Don Enrrique, por la gracia de Dios Rey de Inglaterra, Senõr de Irlanda, mi muy caro e muy amado hermano."

that I may do them with the greatest readiness.—Given in Segovia, the 18th day of July.

I THE KING.

*Endorsed :*—" To the most high and most powerful Prince the Lord Henry, by the grace of God King of England, Lord of Ireland, my very dear and very beloved brother."

## XLVI.

THE BISHOP OF ROCHESTER, ETC., TO THE PRIVY COUNCIL.

Reverendissimi Patres et Domini præcipui, humillima recommendatione præmissa ; cum ferventi desiderio justitiam exequendi.

On the seizure of certain ships by John Hawley and others, of Dartmouth.

---

<sup>1</sup> *i.e.* " YO EL REY," an exact fac-simile of the original signature of the King. It will be observed that the signature is enclosed between two flourishes or ornamental brackets of similar form.

XLVI.] MS. Cotton. Galba, B. I., fol. 134.—On paper ; original, with traces of the seal.

A.D. 1402.  Ad nostram Calesius accedentes præsentiam, nonnulli sagaces viri, pro parte communitatis et burgensium villæ de Brugges ad nos destinati, inter cetera proposuerunt quod, de mense Junii, Anno Domini Millesimo quadringentesimo primo, Johannes Hawle, et sui complices de Dertemouthe, quandam navem Johannis de la Chapelle Jovene d'Abbevill magistri ejusdem navis per mare ceperunt; in qua quidem navi octingenti et xvj. mensuræ de frumento, quatuor lestæ de farina, et ducentæ et tres ulnæ de cannacio apud Sclusam fuerunt oneratæ, quorum bonorum quarta pars frumenti et farinæ ac totum cannacium pertinebant ad Franciscum Davesnes et Walterum Foyti, burgenses villæ de Brugges, prout per litteras Scabinorum et Burgensium villæ de Brugges prædictæ, ipsorum communi sigillo sigillatas, nobis exhibitas manifeste liquebat. Pleniusque in negotio prædicto informati, litteras suscepimus a nobili viro, Domino Thoma de Remyston, admirallo versus Occidentem, sub sigillo officii sui, continentes qualiter Dominus noster Rex eidem mandavit quod restitutio ejusdem quartæ partis cum toto cannacio præfatis Francisco et Waltero fieret per officium suum, seu aliter quod præfatus Johannes Hawle, Edmundus Arnald, et Johannes Willyam, citarentur ad diem jam effluxum coram nobis de et super captione bonorum hujusmodi hic responsuri, et facturi quod esset justum. Quarum copiam vobis transmittimus cum præsentibus. Et reportato ad nos certificatorio citationis hujusmodi de præfato Johanne Hawle ac Edmundo Arnald dumtaxat factæ, ac habita informatione ulteriori de et super veritate suggestorum, videtur nobis unanimiter in pœnam contumaciæ ipsorum citatorum non comparentium restitutionem ejusdem quartæ partis cum toto cannacio debere fieri Francisco et Waltero memoratis.

Quocirca, ob amorem inter nostros mercatores et Flandrenses hinc inde alliciendum, et dispendia quæ verisimiliter occasione præmissorum et aliorum inter eosdem

oriri poterint in futurum submovenda, vos attentius A.D. 1402.
rogamus quatinus contra præfatos Johannem et Edmundum, quatinus ad ipsos attinet, executionem de ipsa quarta parte cum toto cannacio,[1] si bona hujusmodi extiterint, alioquin ad ipsorum verum valorem, facere velitis, itaque bona hujusmodi, videlicet quarta pars frumenti et farinæ et cannacii prædicti præfatis Francisco et Waltero, seu attornato eorundem, plenarie, cum ipsorum damnis et expensis, restituatur.

Insuper præfati viri communitatis prædictæ nobis alias by the men billas monstrarunt de quibusdam navibus eorundem of Fowey, captis per homines de Fowy ; quibus respondebamus quod negotia illa jam sunt in executione in regno Angliæ, et propterea illa non oportét refricare nobiscum : ipsa tamen pro justitia habeatis cordi.

Item conqueruntur de Ricardo Spicer, et Johanne, and by fratre ejusdem, quod cepissent unam navem ipsorum Richard and John cum novem doliis vini oneratam ; et ad istud responde- Spicer. bamus quod super hæc inquiretur in partibus, et, vocatis quorum interest, fiet justitiæ complementum. In his quoque nostræ inbecillitati addat vestra discretio, et prout viderint opportunum mandent nobis vestræ Discretiones solidæ et circumspectæ.

Quas semper in prosperis conservet Clementia Omnium Conditoris !

Scriptum Calesius, xviij$^{mo}$ die mensis Julii.

Vestri ad vota, $\left\{\begin{array}{l} \text{J., EPISCOPUS ROFFENSIS.}^2 \\ \text{W. HERON.} \\ \text{R DE HOLM.} \\ \text{J. URBAN.} \end{array}\right.$

*Endorsed :*—"Reverendissimis Patribus, Dominis Cancellario et Thesaurario Angliæ, [Custodi] privati sigilli, et aliis magnificis Dominis de Concilio D[omini Regis], Londoniæ exi[stentibus]."

---

[1] *cannacio*] conacio, MS.     |     [2] John de Bottlesham.

H

# 4 HENRY IV.

## 30 September, 1402, to 29 September, 1403.

### XLVII.

#### PETER LUCKE TO HENRY IV.

Reporting that the Ambassadors will shortly leave for England ;

Inclitissime Princeps, Regum præclarissime.

Propter certas causas eos hactenus retardantes, ambassiatores illustrissimi Regis Daciæ, Sweciæ, et Norwegiæ, ad vestram regiam Celsitudinem transituri, ante hæc tempora congregari nullatenus potuerunt ; sed, favente Domino, in brevi parati erunt, sic quod ante immediate futuram hyemem, si prospere velis eorum ventus servierit, ad Angliam venire proponunt pro incepti per me negotii votivo complemento.

and that peace had been re-established.

Ceterum vestram regiam Majestatem scire desidero, quod inclitissimi Rex Daciæ, etc. præfatus, et consanguinea sua carissima Domina, Regina Margareta, optata gaudent sospitate in tribus regnis suis, pacificeque gubernant, Illo præstante per Quem reges regnant.

Of the struggle in Gothland,

De guerris equidem Prucenorum in Gotlandia scire dignetur ipsa vestra regia Celsitudo quod Pruceni

---

XLVII.] MS. Cotton. Nero, B. III., fol. 26 (a).—On paper ; original.

Gotlandiam, in septimana Palmarum[1] jam proximo A.D. 1402. præterita, navigio intrantes, bastutam quandam ligneam ibidem de novo per nostros ædificatam, cum decem millibus armatorum obsidione cingebant; et, in tribus aggressibus ad [ip]sam bastutam, centum quinquaginta de nostris in ea existentes, ultra septingentos Prucenos cum eorum capitaneo, occiderunt. Videntes autem residui se contra nostros cum tanta multitudine in nul[lo modo] posse proficere, inde recesserunt, pro ampliore armatorum numero versus Pruciam transmittentes; et sic demum ex abrupto reversi, ad bastutam præfatam sedecim millia armatorum cum [ma]chinis et maximis gunnis, iterum interfecta per nostros magna eorum multitudine, nondum per vim eam habere potuerunt; tandem tractatum erat inter eos utrobique quod nostri bastutam illam cum duabus aliis in Gotlandia, per nostros de novo ædificatis, igni succendere debebant, et cum rebus harnesiisque suis ad propria remeare.

Consequenter per illos de Hensa tractatum est de and the treugis inter inclitissimum Regem Daciæ, etc. et truce between the ipsos Prucenos, usque ad proximo futurum festum Prussians Sancti Johannis Baptistæ[2] observandis, necnon de and the King of termino in quo ipsi Pruceni ad inclitissimi Regis Denmark. Daciæ, etc. præsentiam se conferant, ad tractandum de restitutione prædictæ terræ Gotlandiæ memoratæ regiæ Celsitudini per ipsos Prucenos facienda; nec ipsi Pruceni minimum pedem terræ infra aliquod regnorum Daciæ, Sweciæ, vel Norwegiæ in istis guerris conquæsti sunt, nec tenent, excepto dumtaxat illo quod ante ipsas guerras in Gotlandia occupabant.

Altissimus vestram regiam Majestatem dignetur incolumem conservare !

---

[1] Palm Sunday fell on March 19 in the year 1402.  |  [2] June 24.

H 2

A.D. 1402. Scriptum in Castro Hasnensi, mensis Octobris die secunda, meo sub sigillo.

Vestrorum humillimus,

PETRUS LUCKE,
Archidiaconus Roskildensis,
vestræ regiæ Celsitudini
seipsum recommendans.

*Endorsed :*—"Invictissimo Principi, ac Domino suo gratioso, Domino Henrico, Dei gratia Regi Angliæ et Franciæ, et Domino Hiberniæ, cum omni reverentia præsentetur."

## XLVIII.

### FROM THE DUKE OF JULIERS, FOR ADOLPHUS COUNT OF CLEVES.

*Promising allegiance.* Nos Reynaldus, Dei gratia Dux Juliacensis et Gelrensis, ac Comes Sutphaniensis, omnibus hominibus facimus manifestum publice cognoscentes quod nos nunquam faciemus consilio, opere, verbis, neque factis, occulte seu manifeste, quovismodo adversus et contra dilectum nostrum consanguineum, Adolphum, Comitem Clevensem et de Marka, heredes suos et successores, Comites Clevenses et de Marka, nec eorum territoria, homines, et subditos, quos nunc habet aut inposterum acquirere potest seu poterint, nec adversus et contra omnes et singulos quos dilectus noster consanguineus jam dictus, heredes, aut successores sui verbis defendere aut nobis voluerit seu voluerint inhibere, omnes articulos

---

XLVIII.] MS. Cotton. Galba, B. i., fol. 114.—On paper ; original.

et quemlibet eorum specialiter bona fide promisimus et A.D. 1402. erectis digitis ac præstitis corporaliter ad Sacrosancta juramentis assecuravimus firmiter, continue, et inviolabiliter observare absque ulla contradictionum, fictionum, atque factionum redargutione quarumcumque, et absque omni dolo, in testimonium sigilli nostri præsentibus appensi.

Datum Anno Domini M$^{mo}$ CCCC secundo, crastino[1] Gereonis et Victoris, etc.

## XLIX.

### THE BISHOP OF BANGOR AND OTHERS TO THE PRIVY COUNCIL.

Reverendi Patres ac magnifici Domini; sincera recommendatione præmissa.

Scire dignemini quod, licet in festo Sancti Jacobi[2] feliciter, laudato Deo, partibus Daciæ applicuimus, tamen propter absentiam Reginæ, quæ in finibus ultimis regni Sweciæ cum Prucenis tractatum habuit, tam circa præsentationem personæ illius qui falso et ficte asseruit se Regem Daciæ et Norwegiæ, etc., et ejus combustionem, de quibus aliquando vobis scripsimus, quam alia negotia, statum regnorum, etc., concernentia, cum rege Daciæ, etc., seu cum ipsa vel eorum Conciliis usque ad decimum[3] diem mensis Octobris proximo præteritum loqui non potuimus. Et tunc visa persona Dominæ Katerinæ, prout nostra instructio omnino

*On the proposed marriage of King Eric with the Princess Philippa of England.*

---

[1] October 11.

XLIX.] MS. Cotton. Nero, B. III., fol. 20.—On paper; original.

[2] *July* 25, A.D. 1402. — See Rymer, viii. 267.

[3] *decimum.*] There has been an erasure here. The word appears to have been originally " duodecimum."

A.D. 1402. voluit, etiam per nos omnes incepimus tractare cum dictis Rege et Regina personaliter, in castro de Helsyngburgh super stricto maris transitu situato, super negotiis et articulis nobis commissis.

Et, quia in eisdem nostris articulis super liga conceptis, adempta fuit nobis expresse potestas excipiendi personas Dominorum quorumcumque præterquam de præsenti alligatos, et reservabatur potestas Domino nostro Regi, et ambassiatoribus Regis Daciæ, cum in Angliam venirent cum Domina Katerina, hujusmodi personas excipiendi et eas exprimendi; tum quia consimiliter reservabatur potestas usque in Angliam de succursu in specie hinc inde ipsis Regibus ministranda, videlicet tam de numero personarum, quam expensis et vadiis earundem, tam etiam propter certos novos articulos, ex parte ipsius Regis Daciæ nobis ministratos, super quibus partem in vim instructionis nobis traditæ tractandi et eos terminandi non habuimus; igitur ligam, in forma nobis tradita ante hujusmodi expressionem et responsionem ad ipsorum novos articulos, facere nolunt; quam tamen ligam et ipsa matrimonia omnia habere volunt et desiderant, hujusmodi expressionibus et responsionibus sibi factis;—intendunt enim omnimodo, si poterunt, excipere Regem Franciæ, et plures alios,—ad quas expressiones et responsiones habendas, et pro finali conclusione ipsorum omnium negotiorum, omnimodo voluerunt dicti Rex et Regina, quod duo ex nobis, videlicet [1] nos Willelmus Burcher, Miles, et Magister Ricardus de Derham, per nos tamen ad hoc prius electi, et ex causa una cum aliquibus vel aliquo plene instructis ex parte eorum, transiremus ad Dominum nostrum, Regem Angliæ; et quod interim alii duo, videlicet nos, Episcopus Bangorensis, et Johannes Péraunt, usque ad expressas declarationem ac responsionem prædictas interim in Dacia omnino remaneremus.

---

[1] *videlicet.*] Added above the line.

De quibus inter nos hinc inde ne negotia frustrarentur A.D. 1402.
effectum extat concordatum, præmisso ultro citroque
sollemniter per stipulationem, quod, usque ad Festum
Visitationis Beatæ Mariæ Virginis[1] proxime futurum,
ipsa omnia negotia tam circa ligam, quam etiam circa
ipsa matrimonia, in eisdem terminis prout nunc stant,
nulla interim variatione facta, firmiter stabunt ac sus-
pendentur. Ad quorum executionem et aliorum occur-
rentium, nos, Dominus Willelmus Burchier, Miles, et
Magister Ricardus præfatus, cum omni festinatione per
terram versus Dominum nostrum Regem ac Reverentias
et Magnificentias vestras iter sumus arrepturi.

Insuper, quia ex informationibus nonnullorum, veri- They deem
dicarum personarum et religiosarum, ac aliorum, plene it expedient to
intelleximus quod regna Daciæ et Sweciæ non per add to the
successionem sed per electionem transeunt, intellex- articles of
marriage
imusque insuper, quod ex causis supradictis, ac etiam another on
the succes-
ex difficultate quam fac . . . . . . . . . . . . . . . . . . sion to the
in ætatem Dominæ Philippæ, secundo-genitam Domini throne.
nostri Regis,[2] negotia, ut supradictum est, deberet sus-
pendi, pro securitate eventualiter in ea parte obtinenda,
ultra nostram instructionem, ad conditionem partis
nostræ meliorandam, dedimus articulum continentem
hunc tenorem :—

" Item, in eundem eventum petitur, quod, cum adeo The sug-
" vel plus interest Domini Regis Daciæ, et etiam Reginæ, gested
article.
" quam partis nostræ, etc., quod successio regnorum
" prædictorum devolvatur et deveniat ad eorum prox-
" imos consanguineos quam ad alios, et per conditiones
" ad dictam Dominam Katerinam et ejus heredes, petitur
" pro parte nostra quod quatinus efficacius et firmius
" poterit esse de jure promittatur sollemniter per illos ad
" quos hæc res pertinet, quod in casum et eventum quo

---

[1] July 2.
[2] ac etiam . . . nostri Regis.]
The whole of this passage is written upon an erasure, which is of
much larger extent than the substituted passage.

A.D. 1402. " Dominus Ericus, Rex præfatus, decedat sine liberis,
" (quod absit, et Deus avertat!) quod eligere debeant,
" et cum effectu eligant, unum de liberis (quod Deus
" concedat!) inter serenissimum Dominum, Dominum
" Henricum, Principem Walliæ, et dictam Dominam
" Katerinam procreatis. Et primo per omnes Dominos,
" tam spirituales quam temporales, hic modo præsentes
" et deinde in proximo parliamento per omnes Dominos
" et status qui in ipso parliamento intererunt, cum
" roboratione ipsorum sigillorum, in meliori juris forma,
" cum de jure et etiam in Anglia habetur de consuetu-
" dine quod, deficientibus masculis, feminæ succedant in
" regno, etc."

Et licet,[1] Patres reverendi ac Domini præscripti, iste articulus videatur illicita pactio,[2] quia de successionis futura continuatione; tamen pacisci quod ille succedat qui aliquando de jure est successurus non videtur illicitum, quia, in eventum in quem datur articulus, illi pro quibus paciscitur tam de jure communi quia proximiores i sanguine, quam de consuetudine ibidem, quæ est ut eligere consueverant unum de regalibus proximiorem, vel unum de liberis—ut continet articulus. Nam cessante jure eligendi ibidem Dominus Rex Daciæ modernus, et post eum (si sine liberis decedat) dicta Domina Katerina, proximiores sunt ad succedendum in regno Daciæ, prout de hoc et de jure dicti Domini Regis in regnis prædictis patet in cedula præsentibus interclusa; et etiam datur ex[emplum], ad omnem juris effectum efficaciorem, qu exinde sequi poterit vel debebit; et etiam plenius patebit tam de iis quam de aliis in adventu præfatorum Willelmi Burchier et Ricardi Derham, qui Reverentias ac Dominationes vestras plenius informabunt.

Quas in adjumentum Regis et reipublicæ conservet Altissimus tempora per longæva!

---

[1] A word has been erased here.    [2] *illicita pactio*] illicitam pactionem, MS

Scriptum in Dacia apud Elsingburgh, secundo die A.D. 1402. mensis Novembris, etc.

. . . . . scripturæ propter festinum recessum navis.

Vestri semper { RICARDUS,[1] Episcopus Bangorensis ; WILLELMUS BURCHIER, Miles ; RICARDUS DE DERHAM, inclitissimi Regis nostri capellanus; ac JOHANNES PERAUNT, dicti Domini Regis serviens ad arma ; } ad vota parati.

*Endorsed :*—" Reverendis in Christo Patribus, ac Magnificis Dominis, Dominis de Concilio Domini Regis, Londoniæ existentibus, Dominis præcipuis."

## L.

ERIC X. TO HENRY IV.

*Serenissimo Principi ac Domino⸱potentissimo, Domino Henrico, Dei gratia Regi Angliæ illustrissimo, fratri nostro carissimo, Ericus, eadem gratia Regnorum Daciæ, Sweciæ, Norwegiæ, Slavorum, Gothorumque, Rex, et Dux Pomeranorum, salutem, et prosperos ad vota successus.*

Vestræ sinceræ Dilectioni, pro multiplicibus favoris intimi ostensionibus nobis, vasallis, et servitoribus

On his proposed marriage

[1] Richard Yonge.
L.] MS. Cotton. Nero, B. III., fol. 26 (β.)—On paper; original.

This letter has been very much injured by damp.

nostris, per fraternam vestram Celsitudinem quam-
pluries exhibitis, et præcipue in gratuita exceptione
Clerici nostri, Magistri Petri, Archidiaconi Roskildensis, nuperrime cum in Anglia moram traxit, quem
vestra Serenitas . . . . . . . . . . . . . . . ditatu nobis
remittere non omisit; necnon de litteris et donatis
vestris nobis per ambassiatores vestros in non modici
amoris intersignium transmissis, ad eas quas valemus
assurgimus gratiarum actiones, in desiderio habendi id
cum se tempus obtulerit grata vicissitudine remerceri.

Et in casu quo aliqua in regnis nostris pro votis
vestræ Sinceritatis forent, arbitraremur nobis magnam
exhiberi sinceri amoris oblationem, si per vestræ
Magnificentiæ litteras id nobis intimaretur.

Ceterum, Princeps nobilissime, de factis ex utraque
parte nos et regna nostra concernentibus, de quibus,
prout bene novit vestra regia Sagacitas, per nuncios
nostros intermedios sæpius tractatum est, scire vos
desideramus quod, quemadmodum nobis nuperrime
scripsistis quod vestri, de plena vestra voluntate informati super præmissis, ad nostram præsentiam trans-
mitterentur, sic post adventum eorundem vestrorum,
jam nuper accercitis ad nos propter hoc politis
potioribus trium regnorum nostrorum de Concilio
nostro, in præsentia honorabilium vestrorum ambassiatorum, nos paratos offerebamus ad tractandum et
concludendum de omnibus quæ inter nos super hujusmodi materia utrobique per nuncios nostros intermedios huc usque tractata fuerant, et, ut speramus, in
præmissis nec ex parte nostra, neque ex parte nostrorum nunciorum, erat repertus defectus, prout pro-
babile fore nullatenus hæsitamus: nihilominus tamen
speramus quod tam intentio vestræ Celsitudinis, quam
etiam ambassiatorum vestrorum certa negotia prætacta sint bona et sincera, non obstante quod vestri
ad præsens nec volebant nec audebant se fortes reddere ad concordandum nobiscum super quibusvis

articulis, [juxta] id quod eisdem commiserat vestra A.D. 1402. regia Celsitudo, sed articulos aliquos vestræ Majestati asserebant reservatos.

Speramus tamen quod nullos eis articulos proposuimus nisi eos quos arbitramur consonos fore rationi, et æqualiter honestos et profituos parte pro utraque ; quos quidem articulos vestræ regiæ Excellentiæ, manu eadem scriptos qua sunt præsentes, et eisdem inclusos transmittimus, ad finem quod, ipsis articulis coram vestra Celsitudine et sagaci suo Concilio lectis et intellectis, præfata negotia hinc inde desiderata optatum finem, Domino largiente, sortiantur.

Et, si Deo, vobis, et Concilio vestro placuerit, omnes prædictos articulos eo modo quo positi sunt admittere, ex tunc nobis, infra hinc et proximum festum Visitationis Beatæ Mariæ Virginis,[1] quod occurrit in crastino Octavarum Natalis Beati Johannis Baptistæ ;—quod quidem festum pro termino limitavimus ex eo quod factum istud Beatæ Mariæ Virgini et Filio Suo committimus, confidentes et sperantes quod taliter inde disponant quatinus Eis sit placabile, nobisque et regnis nostris ex utraque parte profituum et honestum ;—rescribere dignemini omnes ipsos articulos vestræ fore plenariæ voluntatis ; quod si feceritis, ex tunc, quanto citius poterimus, ad vestram Celsitudinem ambassiatores [nostros], comites vestrorum, quos penes nos retinemus, cum plena potestate ad concludendum de singulis præmissis articulis, transmittemus.

Si autem de voluntate vestra, ut præmissum est, infra prædictum tempus super præmissis rescriptum non sit, ex tunc vestra regia Sagacitas considerare poterit rem ipsam, de qua sermo, ex parte nostra seu nostrorum non deficere. Perpendere etenim dignetur

---

[1] July 2.

A.D. 1402. vestra Magnificentia in hujusmodi facto moram non partium nostrarum . . . . . . . . . . . . . . . . . . . . . fore fructuosam. Ceterum, regum præclarissime, si per nos[1] vel sororem nostram fœdera matrimonialia iniisse voluissemus, contra vos et regna vestra ligam faciendo . . . . . . . . . . . . . . . est, sine dubio contigisset, antequam ad notitiam nostram devenit quod aliquam habuissetis filiam ; ex quo considerare poteritis, quod regio nostro nomini non convenit contra amicos nostros, vel . . . . . . . . . . . . . . . . . ligam facere, qui nobis et regnis nostris consimilem qualem vestra Caritas exhibuerat amorem fraternalem. Et, si, quod non speramus, vobis non placuerit, ut præmissum est, nihilominus . . . . . . . . . . . . . . . . . ob amorem Dei, et vestræ inclitissimæ Celsitudinis, necnon ob spem utilitatis, et honoris regnorum nostrorum, utrobique huc usque cum maritagiis nostri et sororis nostræ supersederamus et adhuc . . . . . . . . . . usque ad Festum Visitationis[1] libita . . . . . . . . . . . supersedere velimus. Et, si alicubi post hoc alias per nos vel sororem nostram fœdera matrimonialia[2] contraxerimus, vel contrahi fecerimus, nihilominus tamen de vestris et regnorum vestrorum amicitiam . . . . sperantes, desideramus corde sincero amicitiam et servitium vestræ regiæ Majestati ubicumque poterimus exhibere, nobis et regnis nostris per vestram inclitam Dilectionem et sua regna gratam reddi vicissitudinem nullatenus hæsitantes. Ceterum ambassiatores vestri nobis promiserant quod de liberis vestris, Domino Principe et Domina Philippa, non disponatur aliter, quantum ad sponsalia, infra hinc et Festum Visitationis Beatæ Mariæ Virginis[3] sæpedictum ; et quod duo eorum ad præsentiam vestræ Celsitudinis

---

[1] *si per nos.*] Repeated in the MS.
[2] *fœdera matrimonialia*] Added above the line.
[3] July 2.

se transferant, præscripta tamen articula eidem inti- A.D. 1402.
mando : alii vero duo hic in regno nostro remaneant,
quousque [intellexeri]mus utrum præfata vestra Excellentia nobis infra præscriptum tempus super præmissis
quidque dignum duxerit remandare.

Altissimus vestram regiam spiritualem Celsitudinem
dignetur conservare !

Datum in castro nostro Helsingberg, anno Domini
MCD. secundo, crastino Commemorationis Animarum,[1]
nostro sub [secreto.]

*Endorsed :*—" Serenissimo Principi ac Domino, Domino
Henrico, Dei gratia Regi Angliæ, et
Domino Hiberniæ, fratri suo carissimo,
præsententur."

*The following document (MS. Cotton. Nero. B. III.,
fol. 25, on vellum), referred to in the above letter, was
enclosed in it :—*

" Articuli super tractatu de matrimonio contrahendo
inter illustrissimum Principem, Dominum Ericum,
Regem Daciæ, Sweciæ, et Norvegiæ, ac Ducem Pomeranorum, ex parte una, et nobilem Dominam, Dominam Philippam serenissimi ac illustrissimi Principis,
Domini Henrici, Regis Angliæ et Franciæ, filiam
legitimam ; necnon inclitum Principem, Dominum
Henricum, filium primogenitum illustrissimi Principis,
Henrici, Regis Angliæ, etc., prædicti, et nobilem Dominam, Dominam Katerinam, sororem legitimam præfati
regnorum Daciæ, Sweciæ, et Norvegiæ prædictorum
Regis, sequuntur in hoc modo :—

" In primis, quod serenissimus Princeps, Dominus
Ericus, Daciæ, Sweciæ, et Norvegiæ Rex, ad honorem

---

[1] November 3. — *All Saints' Day* is Nov. 1 ; the " *Commemoratio
Animarum*" on Nov. 2.

A.D. 1402. Dei, et pro bono pacis perpetuo stabiliendæ inter ipsum et regna sua et præfatum illustrissimum Principem, Henricum, Regem Angliæ, etc., et regnum prædictum Angliæ, et alia sua dominia; necnon propter affectionem quam idem Dominus Rex Daciæ, etc., gerit ad nobilitatem domus et sanguinis regalis Anglicanæ, toto corde affectat et petit instanter præfatam Dominam Philippam in uxorem. Ad quam petendum, et consentiendum in eandem pro parte sua, venerabilem et discretum virum, Magistrum Petrum Lukke, Archidiaconum Roskildensem, suum fecit nuncium et ambassiatorem, absque tamen mandato in [re tali] fieri consueto. Præfatus tamen Magister Petrus asserit quod præfatus Dominus Rex Daciæ, etc., promisit tractata in hac parte per præfatum Petrum inviolabiliter observare. Cujus rei testis est Johannes Paraunt, serviens armorum Domini Regis Angliæ, etc., supradicti.

" Item, ut inter præfatos illustrissimos Principes, et Dominos Reges prædictos, et sua regna et dominia prædicta, fortius vinculum[1] et majoris confœderationis et alligantiæ causa indissolubili contrahantur, ad satisfaciendum in illo requisitioni et voluntati antedicti invictissimi Regis Angliæ, affectat idem Dominus Rex Daciæ, etc., ut præfatus inclitus Princeps, Dominus Henricus, Princeps Valliæ, etc., Henrici Regis prædicti ligamine matrimoniali in uxorem legitimam habeat sororem suam legitimam, Dominam Katerinam prædictam. Ad contrahendum et componendum ad matrimonium prædictum pro parte præfatæ nobilis sororis suæ, præfatum Magistrum Petrum, Archidiaconum, ut præfertur, et non in alia forma destinavit. Qui quidem Magister Petrus facit se fortem sub pœna mortis omnia peracta et concordata in hac parte et

---

[1] There is an erasure here.

tractata [integra] et firma prædictum illustrem Princi- A.D. 1402.
pem Regem Daciæ, etc., necnon [prædictam Dominam]
regnorum prædictorum Daciæ, etc., Reginam, ac etiam
ipsam sororem suam legitimam habituros, et inviolabiliter observaturos.

"Item, præfatus Dominus Rex Daciæ, etc., promittet
bona fide dotare Dominam Philippam uxorem, ut
dignitati convenit reginali, prout præfatus Dominus
Princeps Valliæ dotabit Dominam Katerinam, suam
uxorem, secundum quod convenit suo statui et honori,
et quod præfatus Dominus Rex Daciæ, etc., transmitteret
ad Angliam in expensis suis prædictam Dominam,
sororem suam, ornatam vestibus dotalibus páramentis,
et aliis, prout sibi placet, et honori suo conveniat,
prout idem Dominus, Rex Angliæ, suam filiam ornatam
vestibus et aliis paramentis, prout sibi placet, et suo
convenit honori, ambassiatoribus et procuratoribus dicti
Domini Regis Daciæ, etc., faciat liberari, eamque ad
Daciæ terras mittat suis sumptibus et expensis.

"Item, præfatus Dominus, Rex Daciæ, etc., cujuscumque avaritiæ et ambitionis cæcitate repulsa, licet
magnas et notabiles summas auri pro maritagio suo,
et sororis suæ potuit habuisse, præelegit ex causis
prædictis maritagia prædicta mutuo sine aliquo interventu æris aut monetæ, seu dotis vel donationis,
propter nuptias ex una parte et alia gratis contrahere,
et absque onere pactionali hinc inde partium prædictarum.

"Item, si dictus Rex Daciæ, etc., fuerit congrue
requisitus in auxilium Domini Regis Angliæ, seu filii
sui primogeniti Principis Valliæ, etc., ad expugna-
tionem inimicorum suorum, sive per terram, sive per
mare, cum omni potestate sua faciat Regi Angliæ et
filio suo supradicto prout sibi vult ab eisdem, si opus
fuerit, fieri, et bonus filius dilecto patri, et bonus
frater dilecto fratri, tenetur facere. Et similiter Rex
Angliæ, et filius suus Princeps Valliæ, faciant Regi
Daciæ, etc., vice versa.

A.D. 1402.    " Item, de modis et articulis alligantiæ, inter in-
victissimos Reges prædictos et regna ac Dominia sua
faciendæ, dignetur inclitissimus Rex Angliæ sufficientem
informationem suæ regiæ voluntatis, cum satis ampla
potestate hujusmodi alligantiam faciendi; necnon ante-
dictam Dominam Katerinam, sororem legitimam sæpedicti Regis Daciæ, etc., ex parte nobilissimi Principis
Valliæ, etc., ambassiatoribus suis versus Daciam ituris
conferre.   Qui per Dei gratiam, serenissimum Dominum Regem Daciæ, etc., cum jure suo et consilio
invenient ad omnia media rationabilia pro hujusmodi
alligantia, et ad ipsam spectantibus, sincero cordis
affectu totaliter inclinatum."

## LI.

MARGARET, QUEEN OF DENMARK, ETC., TO HENRY IV.

*Invictissimo Principi ac Domino, Domino Henrico,
Dei gratia Regi Angliæ illustrissimo, et Domino
Hiberniæ, fratri nostro carissimo, Margareta, eadem gratia Waldemari, Danorum Regis, filia, salutem, et votivæ prosperitatis continuum in Domino
augmentum.*

[Invictissime] Princeps.

A letter of
thanks.

Pro multiplicibus vestris benefactis favoris et dilectionis intersigniis, nobis ac nostris multipl[iciter] exhibitis, et specialiter pro eo quod Magistrum Petrum
Lucke, Archidiaconum Roskildensem, dilectum carissimi filii nostri Regis Erici et nostrum servitorem et
[Clericum], dum jam novissime penes vestram præclaram
præsentiam erat, honorifice excepistis, et regali muni-

---

LI.]  MS. Cotton. Nero, B. III.,  | A  considerable  portion of this
fol. 23 (β).—On  paper;  original. | letter has been effaced by damp.

ficentia . . . . . . . . . . . . . . . . . . . . . . -libus, et A.D. 1402.
caritativis litteris vestris et munere nobis jam missis ;
de quibus omnibus nos, vestram [Regiam Celsitudinem
com]mendare non sufficientes, sibi gratiarum intimas
exsolvimus actiones.

Verum, Princeps serenissime, si qua D[ominationi
vestræ] grata et accepta partibus forent in istis, de
quibus sibi poterimus complacere, ea nobis jugiter
de[nunciare velitis] pro summo desiderio et grati-
tudine nostræ mentis.

Ceterum in negotiis et tractatibus per præscriptum
Magistrum [Petrum Lucke, et] Johannem Parant, inter
vos et præscriptum filium nostrum ac regna vestra
utrimque jampridem locutis et habitis [comprehe]n-
dimus ex parte sua vel suorum regnorum nullum
esse defectum ; et ut ipse filius noster regiæ vestræ
Celsitudini de [dictis negotiis et] tractatibus propositum suum et voluntatem per suas litteras fecerat
intimari. Et ideo per nos amplior super . . . . . . . .
. . . . . . . . . . . . de præsenti, prout credimus, non
videtur. Si quid ergo Deo et vobis super præmissis
ipsi filio nostro remandare placeret, [non dubita]mus
quin ipsa regalis Sublimitas satis sagaci industria
perpendere studeat quid super hoc partis utriusque
[fieri deberet. Sin] autem qualitercumque Deus fieri
voluerit ad quævis regiæ vestræ Majestati gratuita
nos semper in cunctis . . . . . . . . . . . . . . . . .
. . . offerimus et para[tas]. Illud insuper, licet modicæ
reputationis et exiguum, atque in conspectu tanti
Pr[incipis] . . . . . . . . . . . . . . , vestræ sinceræ
Fraternitati jam transmittimus gratum nostri intuitu;
quod velitis accipere, cum plus ex sano [animo] . .
. . . . . processerit quam alicujus pretio donativo.

Princeps et frater dilectissime, invictissimam vestram
Fraternitatem et [regnum vestrum bonis] successibus
et jocundis annuat Altissimus continue prosperari!

I

A.D. 1402.   Scriptum in Castro Helsingborgh, . . . . . . . . . . .
. . . . . . . . . . . die[1] mensis Novembris, nostro sub
secreto.

*Endorsed :*—" Serenissimo Principi, Domino Henrico,
D[ei gratia Regi Angliæ] illustrissimo,
et Domino Hiberniæ, Fra[tri nostro
carissimo]."

## LII.

THE BISHOP OF BANGOR AND JOHN PARANT TO THE
PRIVY COUNCIL.

Reverendi Patres, illustres ac magnifici Domini ;

*Stating why they had added the Article alluded to in their previous letter.*

sincera recommendatione præmissa.

Quoniam quæ de novo emergunt, et singularia
maxime quæ spirituali nota sunt digna, non immerito
signantur, sunt appunctuanda ideo certa quæ intelleximus in partibus Daciæ, quæ forte Domino nostro
Regi et vobis ante recessum nostrum de Anglia plene
non claruerunt, in quadam [cedula[2]] præsentibus interclusa pro avisamento duximus annotanda. Nosque
insuper, in quantum Deus nobis monstravit, periculis
in ea contentis volentes obviare, dedimus quemdam
articulum ultra nostram instructionem, pro conditione
partis nostræ melioranda, ad quod tenentur procuratores quicumque, prout alias vobis scripsimus,[3] ad quem[4]
aliquantum intelleximus partem aliam se velle inclinare

---

[1] The day of the month has been
obliterated. It is clear, however,
that this Letter was written on, or
about, the same day as the preceding
Letter, viz., on the 3rd of November.

LII.] MS. Cotton. Nero, B. III.,
fol. 22.—On paper; original.
[2] See below " *in dicta cedula.*"
[3] See Letter XLIX.
[4] Several words have been
erased here.

et etiam condescendere. Cui, si Domino nostro Regi A.D. 1402.
et vobis placuerit, sagaciter, more vestri sacri loci solito,
poteritis insistere, etc.

Ceterum, licet quoad victualia pro tempore more *They re-*
nostro in partibus Daciæ sit nobis honorifice provisum, *quest addi-tional*
cum, ut nostis, multa alia etiam pro expensis nostris *means of*
versus partes, quum Domino nostro Regi et vobis pla- *subsistence.*
cuerit, sunt nobis necessaria; ad quæ et alia quæ-
cumque, ne tanquam mortui a corde[1] dediti simus,
dignemur nos habere recommissos.

Et, quia Domini Willelmus Bourcher, Miles, et
Ricardus de Derham, Domini nostri Regis capellani,
tam de contentis in dicta cedula, quam aliis occasionibus
vivæ vocis oraculo vos noverint plenius informare,
idcirco, hic sistendo ratem, calamum dictis Reverentiis
ac Magnificentiis vestris ulterius non duximus extendendum.

Quas ad reipublicæ regimen et munimen vobis com-
missum conservet Altissimus feliciter ut optamus, etc.

Scriptum in civitate Roskeldensi, in festo Beatæ
Katherinæ Virginis,[2] etc.

Vestri in omnibus, { RICARDUS,[3] Episcopus Bangorensis, et JOHANNES PARAUNT, Domini nostri Regis serviens ad arma.

*Endorsed :*—" Reverendis in Christo Patribus ac magnificis Dominis de Concilio Domini
nostri Regis, Londoniæ existentibus,
Dominis suis præcipuis, etc."

---

[1] *a corde.*] Added above the line.

[2] November 25.
[3] Richard Yonge.

I 2

## LIII.

### HENRY IV. TO HENRY III., KING OF CASTILE.

*Effectus litterarum per illustrissimum Principem Regem Angliæ, etc., serenissimo Principi Regi Castelli, fratri suo carissimo, scribendarum, juxta ea quæ hesterna die in præsentia præfati Serenissimi Domini Regis Anglia apud Eltham fuerint concordata, est iste qui sequitur :—*

The King promises to make a restitution of two thirds in the matters complained of, on condition that the King of Castile.

Primo, cum post diversos tractatus inter Concilium præfati serenissimi Regis Angliæ et Gundesalvum Maure, ambassiatorem dicti Domini, Regis Castelli, habitos, non potuerunt concordare in reformatione hinc inde fienda, cum ambassiator prædictus peteret plenariam restitutionem ante omnia ; nunc, pro bono pacis et concordiæ, necnon consideratione vinculi fraternitatis et amicitiæ inter præfatos Reges feliciter observandæ, idem serenissimus Rex Angliæ præsentialiter mandavit liberare certas naves cum earum affletamentis, ac etiam obtulit se liberare et restitutionem facere duarum par-

---

LIII.] MS. Cotton. Vespas., C. XII., fol. 111.—At Vespas., C. XII., fol. 112, is the following similar document :—

" *Substantialia super quibus illustrissimus Dominus, Rex Angliæ, debet scribere amantissimo fratri suo, Domino Regi Castellæ, reparationem hinc inde per eorum subditos attemptatorum, juxta ea quæ nuper apud Eltham coram eo fuerunt concordata, præsentibus Domino Cancellario et aliis de Concilio suo, sunt hæc :—*

" Primo, cum post longos et varios tractatus inter Concilium ejusdem serenissimi Domini, Regis Angliæ, et ambassiatorem Domini, Regis Castellæ, habitos, super restitution-

ibus fiendis mutuo non poterint esse concordatum, idem ambassiator inter omnia peteret plenariam restitutionem, nolens aliter dictum Dominum, Regem Castellæ, ad restitutionem eorum quæ in regno suo sunt sequestrata vel arrestata aliquatenus obligare, secundum quod in diversis cedulis et appunctamentis, super hoc ordinatis et præsentatis, hinc inde latius continetur.

"Idem serenissimus Dominus, Rex Angliæ, pro bono pacis, et concordiæ contemplatione, etiam fraternitatis et amicitiæ, etc., cum dicta restitutio plenaria, ut per ipsum ambassiatorem patebatur, ad præsens fieri non posset, præcepit statim gratiose aliqua bona et na-

tium omnium navium, mercimoniorum, et aliorum A.D. 1403.
bonorum, per ligeos Angliæ captorum, vel alias quomodolibet ablatorum, subditis præfati Domini, Regis Castelli,
tam per mare quam per terram, habita primo certa et
æqua æstimatione omnium prædictorum bonorum et
navium, secundum ea quæ per præfatum ambassiatorem
fuerunt denuntiata prædicto Concilio quæ quidem
partes restituendæ vel earum æstimationes restituantur
vel solvantur de bonis illis quæ meliori seu breviori
modo restitui seu recuperari possint.

Ita tamen quod præfatus Dominus, Rex Castelli, obli- on his part
gabit se firmiter et sufficienter quod, facta dicta resti- make a full
tutione duarum partium, ut præmittitur, cum effectu restoration,
ipse effectualiter restituet, vel restitui mandabit, Anglicis, aut eorum procuratoribus, omnia bona, naves, et
mercimonia, quæ in regnis et dominiis suis sunt arrestata
aut sub sequestro servata, mandato suo vel suorum
officialium.

Insuper etiam idem Dominus Rex promittet in verbo and that
regio facere ac ministrare, et fieri et ministrari mandare without
complementum justitiæ cum omni celeritate possibili, delay.
omnibus dolo et fraude cessantibus, universis et singulis Anglicis conquerentibus, seu conqueri volentibus,
de cursariis sive piratis regni Castelli, vel de quibus-

vigia cum nautis sibi debitis liberari, unum alium terminum, per dictum
offerens se de residuis liberare ambassiatorem et commissarios præ-
etiam et restituere subditis præfati fingendum, Anglicis, aut eorum
carissimi fratris sui, per Anglicos procuratoribus, omnia bona merci-
damnificatis, aut eorum procura- monia et naves, in regnis et terris
toribus, infra unum terminum con- sibi subditis arrestata aut seques-
decentem, per dictum ambassiatorem trata, facta realiter et de facto
suum cum commissariis ejusdem restitutione dictarum duarum par-
Domini, Regis Angliæ, præffingen- tium, restituere et restitui facere
dum, duas partes integras, habita cum effectu.
primo vera notitia et justa æsti-    "Et quod insuper promittat in
matione omnium bonorum per verbo regio facere, et fieri man-
dictos Anglicos aut subditos An- dare, cum omni celeritate possibili,
gliæ raptorum, captorum, seu alias dolo et fraude cessantibus, com-
quovis modo indebite detentorum. plementum justitiæ quibuscumque
    "Item, tamen, quod ipse frater Anglicis conquerentibus, aut con-
suus, obliget se sufficienter infra queri volentibus, de subditis et

A.D. 1403. cumque gentibus sive terris dicti regni Castelli dictis cursariis sive piratis ad aliquas rapinas vel latrocinia, aut aliqua alia maleficia, contra Anglicos committendum, auxilium sive favorem præstantibus, vel post prædicta maleficia commissa scienter eos receptantibus, occultantibus, seu defendentibus.

*He engages thereafter to restore the remaining third part,*  Item, quod præfatus serenissimus Dominus, Rex Angliæ, sufficienter se obligabit quod, facta dicta restitutione bonorum et navium, ut præfertur, in dicto regno Castelli arrestatorum, necnon facto complemento justitiæ dictis conquerentibus cum effectu, idem Dominus Rex Angliæ faciet restitutionem alterius tertiæ partis residuæ, vel ejus æstimationis, infra certum tempus, sub certis pœnis per ejus commissarios et ambassiatorem prædictum limitandis.

*and stipulates for free and uninterrupted commerce in the meantime.*  Item, quod medio tempore quo prædicta tractantur et ad effectum ducuntur, omnes gentes, cujuscumque status seu conditionis existunt prædictorum regnorum, poterunt ire, venire, transire, morari, salvo et secure, per mare et per terram, cum omnibus suis bonis et mercimoniis, etc., hinc inde.

*Endorsed :*—" Effectus litterarum per Regem Angliæ Regi Castellæ dirigendarum." [1]

---

gentibus suis piratice aut alias quovis modo eosdem Anglicos indebite lædentibus sive damnificantibus, necnon de omnibus aliis personis, terris, aut locis, dictis gentibus auxilium, consilium, sive favorem ad hujusmodi damna præstantibus, aut post illationem scienter receptantibus seu defendentibus.

"Iterum etiam quod idem serenissimus Dominus, Rex Angliæ, sufficienter se obligabit quod, facta realiter dictis Anglicis restitutione bonorum suorum, in dicto regno Castellæ arrestatorum, ac etiam ministrata justitia dictis querelantibus, ut præmittitur, restituet et restitui faciet Castellanis, aut eorum procuratoribus, infra unum alium terminum condecentem, aliam tertiam partem residuam.

"Et quod dictus ambassiator manebit hic, in Anglia, quousque interveniat consensus vel assensus ejusdem fratris sui carissimi ad prædicta omnia peragenda.

"Item quod medio tempore gentes utriusque partis, cujuscumque status vel conditionis fuerint, poterunt ire, redire, morari, et transire, salvo et secure, cum omnibus bonis suis."

[1] See Rymer, VIII., 312, 345.

A.D. 1403.

## LIV.

### HENRY IV. TO THE BISHOP OF COVENTRY AND LICHFIELD.

*Henricus, Dei gratia Rex Angliæ et Franciæ, et Dominus Hiberniæ, venerabili in Christo Patri J.,*[1] *eadem gratia Episcopo Conventrensi et Lichfeldensi, salutem.*

Volentes certis de causis certiorari super tenore cujusdam sententiæ in quadam causa divortii, nuper in Curia Christianitatis coram Magistro Roberto de Appeltre (nuper officiali Rogeri[2] nuper Episcopi loci prædicti), inter Isabellam Perers, nuper filiam Ricardi Perers, Militis, ex una parte, et Robertum de Grendoun, nuper filium Radulphi de Grendoun, Militis, ex parte altera, ut dicitur late; vobis mandamus quod, scrutatis registris de tempore prædicti nuper Episcopi in custodia vestra existentibus, ut dicitur, tenorem sententiæ prædictæ nobis in Cancellariam nostram citra Octavas Sancti Johannis Baptistæ[3] proxime futuras, sub sigillo vestro distincte et aperte mittatis,[4] et hoc Breve.

Teste me ipso, apud Westmonasterium, xviij die Maii, anno regni nostri quarto.

BUBBEWYTH.

*Side notes:* Requiring information as to the divorce of Robert and Isabella Grendon.

---

LIV.] MS. Publ. Rec. Off., Portf. 1.—On vellum ; original.
[1] John Burghill.
[2] Roger de Northburgh.

[3] July 1.
[4] The answer of the Bishop was written on the 30th of June following. See the next Letter.

A.D. 1403.

## LV.

### THE BISHOP OF COVENTRY TO HENRY IV.

*Excellentissimo in Christo Principi et Domino nostro, Domino Henrico, Dei gratia Regi Angliæ et Franciæ, et Domino Hiberniæ, Johannes,[1] permissione divina Coventrensis et Lichfeldensis Episcopus, salutem in Eo per Quem reges regnant et principes dominantur.*

In answer to the foregoing letter.

Breve vestrum, præsentibus interclusum et consutum, nuper recepimus, sub tenore contento in eodem. Virtute cujus Brevis scrutari fecimus Registrum Domini Rogeri,[2] nuper Coventrensis et Lichfeldensis Episcopi, prædecessoris nostri, de et super prolatione cujusdam sententiæ divortii inter Isabellam Perers, nuper filiam Ricardi Perers, Militis, partem actricem, ex parte una; et Robertum de Grendoun, nuper filium cujusdam Radulphi de Grendoun, Militis, partem ream, ex altera. Prout sequitur, invenimus continere quod Magister Willelmus Appeltre, Reverendi in Christo Patris, Domini Rogeri, Episcopi antedicti, Officialis, vj$^{to}$ Id. Junii, anno Domini Millesimo CCC$^{mo}$ quadragesimo quinto, in Ecclesia Cathedrali Lichfeldensi pro tribunali sedens, quandam sententiam in quadam causa divortii inter dictam Isabellam Perers et Robertum de Grendoun mota, et tunc pendente indecisa, partibus sufficienter coram eo comparentibus ad instantiam et petitionem dictæ Isabellæ, partis actricis, tulit et promulgavit in scriptis, sub hac forma verborum :—

"Cum Isabella Perers, filia quondam Ricardi Perers, Militis, de facto matrimonialiter copulata Roberto de

---

LV.] MS. Publ. Rec. Off., portf. l.,—On vellum : original.

[1] John Burghill.—This Letter is stitched to the preceding Letter.
[2] Roger de Northburgh.

Grendoun, filio Domini Radulphi de Grendoun, Militis, A.D. 1403. prætendens dictum Robertum quandam Johannam de Tonford, mulierem dictam Isabellam, in gradu consanguinitatis ad contrahendum matrimonium a jure prohibito attingentem, ante quemcunque contractum matrimonialem inter ipsos Robertum et Isabellam initum cognovisse in causa divortii occasione præmissa agitanda seu movenda, fecerit prædictum Robertum coram nobis, Willelmo Appeltre, Reverendi Patris, Domini Rogeri, Episcopi antedicti, Officiali, ad judicium limine evocari, omnibus partibus coram nobis sufficienter comparentibus, libelloque per partem dictæ Isabellæ in forma juris oblato, lite contestata, juratis partibus hinc inde, testibusque productis et examinatis, et eorum attestationibus publicatis, aliisque terminis et juris solemniis in ea parte de jure requisitis in omnibus observatis ad sententiam diffinitivam processimus in hunc modum,—'In Dei nomine, Amen. Audite per nos, Officialem prædictum, peritis et intellectis dictæ causæ meritis, processuque in eadem habito, inspecto diligenter et rimato, quia invenimus præfatam Isabellam intentiam suam in hac parte probasse, matrimonium inter prædictos Isabellam et Robertum de facto contractum minime substitisse, nec subsistere potuisse, aut posse, seu debere, sed quod inter eosdem actum extitit, ut præfertur, dumtaxat de facto processisse, jurisque effectum minime habuisse, seu habere, pronuntiamus et declaramus, ipsosque quatinus de facto ad invicem contraxerunt ab invicem separamus sententialiter et diffinitive in his scriptis.'"

Super quibus omnibus et singulis vestram regiam Celsitudinem, in Cancellaria vestra, certiorem reddere curavimus per præsentes, dictum Breve remittendo.

Diutissime valeat vestra regia Sublimitas in prosperis et jocundis!

Scriptum apud Eccleshale, ultimo die mensis Junii, anno Domini Millesimo CCCC^mo tertio, et nostræ translationis quinto.

## LVI.

### JOHN FAIREFORD TO THE AUTHORITIES OF HEREFORDSHIRE.

Praying for assistance against the rebels in South Wales.

Honures Sires.

Vous pleise assavoir que Jankyn Hanard,[1] Gardein del Chastell de Dynevour, yceste Mesquerdy a matyn, par un de ses gentz m'as certifiez coment Res ap Griffith, del Countie de Kermerdyn, William ap Phillip, Henry Doun, et son fitz, ovesqes plusours lour adherentes du dit Countie, et d'autres Seignuries, le Lundy darrein traiterousement fuerent levez en le Champagne, encontre le Roy, nostre tressoveraigne Seignur, et son Mageste, et ount assegez le dit Chastell ove graunde poar des rebelles.

Glyndwr at Llandovery.

Et outre al faisance d'ycestes y fuist moy certifiez par Raulyn Monyngton, et autres en le Chastell

---

[TRANSLATION.]

Honoured Sirs.—May it please you to know that Jenkin Hanard, Warden of the Castle of Dynevor, this Wednesday morning, has certified to me by one of his men, that Rees ap Griffith, of the County of Carmarthen, William ap Philip, Henry Donn and his son, with many their adherents of the said County, and of other Lordships, were on Monday last treasonably rising in the plain country, against the King, our most sovereign Lord, and his Majesty, and have laid siege to the said Castle with a great force of rebels.—And, moreover, at the writing of these presents it was certified to me by

---

LVI.] MS. Cotton. Cleopatra F. III. fol. 112 b. — On paper; original.

[1] A letter from Jankyn Hanard to John Faireford (apparently the one brought by the messenger alluded to in this letter) is printed in Ellis (2nd series), i. 14. It is dated "Yn the fest of Seint Thomas the Martyr," by which, it would appear, is meant July 3rd, the translation of S. Thomas, Apostle and Martyr. At least the dates can only be reconciled on this assumption.

de Llamendevery esteantz, coment Oweyn Glynder, A.D. 1403. ove son false poar, le Mardy fuist a Llamendevery; et que les gentz illeoqes forsurprises cieux en le dit Chastell a luy sont assurez et retainez, et CCC de les rebelles ad lesse gisantz entour la sege de mesme le Chastiell et le noet fuist loggez a Landeilo a quelle temps les gentz du dicte countie, et des altres Seignouries la environ, a luy feurent auxi assurez et jurrez.

Et que mesme ceste y Merquedy le dit Oweyn, Brecon et toutz les autres rebellez, sount se taillantz threatened. devers ceste ville de Brechon pur la destruction d'icelle (que Dieu ce defende), et depuis purposont detrecher as autres parties en le March, s'ils ne soient resitez; que pleise par vostre tressage advise en ceste matiere certifier au Roy, nostre tressoveraigne Seignour; a le mesme temps de garnier toutes les Countees vous environs, de eux enforcier, et arraier prest, pur y resister mesme les rebelles en toute la haste possible, pur eschuer le greindre peril en ceste cas.

---

Raulin Monington, and others who were in the Castle of Llandovery, how that Owen Glyndwr with his false troops was at Llandovery on Tuesday; and that the men there being surprised they in the said Castle are assured and secured to him, and three hundred of the rebels were at their ease, lying round the siege of the same Castle, and at night were lodged at Llandeilo; at which time the men of the said county, and of other Lordships around, were also assured and sworn to him.—And that this same Wednesday, the said Owen, and all the other rebels are on their march toward this town of Brecon, for the destruction of the same (which God avert), and, after, they purpose to make a diversion against other parties in the March, if they be not resisted; which may it please you by your most sage counsel in these matters to certify unto the King, our sovereign Lord: at the same time to supply all the Counties around you, to reinforce them, and array them at once for resisting the same rebels, with all the haste possible, for the avoiding of greater peril in

A.D. 1403.
Spread of the rebellion.

Et savoir voulliez que toute la natioun del Walshere, forsurprise poy, a ceste malveyse purpos de rebellite est assentant, et a ycelle assurez, come pleinment de jour en altre pour lour support bien appiert pluis overtement : et prie vous pleise d'ordener le pluis hastif resistence encontre les rebelles que vous pourrez, et, si ascune chivache soit fait vous pleise ce de faire primerement[1] en cestez Seignouries de Brechan et Cantrifselly.

Autres n'estey a vous escriverer mes.

Le Tout-Puissant Dieux vous governe en honour!

Et vous pleise de donner credence al portour du cestez.

Escript a Brechan, yceste Mesquerdy[2] apres none, et ce en grande haste.

Le vostre,
JOHAN FAIREFORD,
Receviour de Brechan.

this case.—And you will know that all the Welsh nation, being taken a little by surprise, is adhering to this evil purpose of rebellion, and they are assured thereunto, how fully, from one day to another by the support they give to it, clearly appears more openly ; and, I pray you, please to ordain the most speedy resistance against the rebels that you can, and if any expedition of cavalry be made, be pleased to do this first in these Lordships of Brecon and Cantref-Sellyf.—I have no other things to write to you at present.—The Almighty God keep you in honour !—And may it please you to give credence to the bearer of these presents.—Written at Brecon, this Wednesday afternoon, and that in great haste.

Yours,
JOHN FAIREFORD,
Receiver of Brecon.

---

[1] *primerement*] Added above the line.

[2] Wednesday, July 4, 1403.

## LVII.

JOHN FAIREFORD TO HENRY IV.

Mon tresnoble et tresredoute Seignur.

A vostre roial Magestie je me humblement recomande.

Et pleise a vostre tresnoble Seignurie assavoir que mesme ceste y Samady, al houre de none, le vij jour de Juyllet, j'ay rescue a Brechon certoigne lettres [1] depar Johan Skydemor a moy adressez, les quelles, deinz ycestes closes, par le portour du cestes jeo presente a vostre haute persone ; que pleise a vostre tresgraciouse Seignurie les mischiefs et periles en ycelles comprises de considerer, et sur ce d'ordener hastif remedie, pur la

*Progress of the rebellion.*

---

[TRANSLATION.]

My most noble and most dread lord.—I humbly commend myself to your royal Majesty.—And may it please your most noble Lordship to know that, this same Saturday, the 7th day of July, at the hour of nine, I have received at Brecon certain letters addressed to me by John Skidmore, the which, enclosed within this letter, I present unto your high person by the bearer of these ; that it may please your most gracious Lordship to consider the mischief and perils comprised in them, and to ordain thereon speedy remedy, for the

---

LVII.] MS. Cotton. Cleopatra, F. III. fol. 116 b.—On paper ; original.

[1] Printed in Ellis (2nd Series), i. 19, Letter VII.

A.D. 1403. resistence et destruction de les rebellours du cestes parties de Southgales encontre vous et vostre Majestie traiterousement levez, que voz Chastelles, et villes, et les foialx gentz en ycelles, ne soient ensy pur defaute d'aide et socour perduz et destruiez.

Dangers in Breck-nockshire. Et outre pleise a vostre tresnoble Seignurie assavoir que les rebelles de ceste vostre Seignurie de Brechon, ovesque lour adherents, sont gisantz joust la ville de Brechon, en faisantz le mal et destructioun q'ils purront a y envirron ; et ceux de Cantrifselley et Bullt, le Vendresdy darrein, conburerons certeines maisons deinz vostre manoir de Brenlis, et proposont ils trestoutes ensemble pur conburer et destruier toute la Englissherie en cestes ditz parties, s'ils ne soient en haste resistez. Entendant auxi, mon tresnoble Seignur, s'il vous pleise, q'ils trestoutes de la Walsshe nation par toutes cestes ditz parties a ceste rebellite sont assurez, et de lour bone volunte en un assentez, come overtement appiert de jour

resistance and destruction of the rebels in these parts of South Wales, who are treacherously raised against you and your Majesty ; so that your Castles and towns, and the faithful men in them, be not thus ruined and destroyed for lack of aid and succour.

And, besides, may it please your most noble Lordship to know that the rebels of this your Lordship of Brecon, together with their adherents, are lying near the town of Brecon, doing all the mischief and destruction that they can to its neighbourhood ; and they of Cantreff-Selyff and Builth on Wednesday last did burn certain houses within your manor of Bryn-Llys, and they purpose all of them together to burn and destroy all pertaining to the English in these same parts, if they be not resisted in haste. Considering also, my most noble Lord, if it please you, that the whole of the Welsh nation are by all these said parties confirmed in this rebellion, and with good will consent together, as openly appears from day to day, by

en altre, par leur governance, et auxi de leur support A.D. 1403.
devers vous et toutz voz foialx, que pleise a vostre
roial Magestie d'ordener un fynel destructioun de toute
la false natioun susditz, ou altrement toutz voz foialx
en cestes parties sont en graunde peril.

Mon tresnoble et tresredoute Seignur, la puissance
de Jhesu, et la beante de Sa graciouse Miere, toute temps
governe vostre Hautesse en honours, et vouz mainteine
en toutz voz pleiscrs, a la governance de vostre poeple,
et destructioun de toutz voz enemis rebelles !

Escrips a Brechon, le vij jour de Juyllet.

Vostre humble Clerc et Oratour,

JOHAN FAIREFORD,
Recevour de Brechon.

their governance, and also of their support against you
and all your faithful ones, may it please your royal
Majesty to ordain a final destruction of all the false nation
aforesaid, or otherwise all your faithful ones in these parts
are in great peril.—My most noble and most dread Lord,
the might of Jesus, and the kindness of His gracious Mother,
at all times keep your Highness in honour, and maintain you
in all your pleasures, to the governance of your people, and
the destruction of all your rebellious enemies !—Written at
Brecon, the 7th day of July.

Your humble Clerk and Orator,

JOHN FAIREFORD,
Receiver of Brecon.

A.D. 1403.

## LVIII.

### JOHN FAIREFORD TO HENRY IV.

Mon tressoveraigne et tresgraciouse Seignur.

Je me recomande humblement a vostre roial Magestie.

Enclosing a letter with news from Dynevor Castle.

Et pleise a vostre tressoveraigne Seignurie assavoir que yceste Samady, a noet, le vij jour de Juyllet, j'ay resceu certeines lettres depar Jenkyn Hanard [1] moy adressez; lesquelles par le portour d'ycestes deinz ycestes closez j'envoie a vostre roial personne, que pleise a vostre trespuissant et tresredoute Seignurie d'ordener remedie, pur y resister et destruier les traitours que de jour en autre se en-

---

### [TRANSLATION.]

My most sovereign and most gracious Lord.—I recommend me humbly to your royal Majesty.—And may it please your most sovereign Lordship to know that on this Saturday, the 7th day of July, at night, I received certain letters addressed to me by Jenkin Hanard, the which, by the bearer of these presents, and enclosed within them, I have sent to your royal person, that it may please your most puissant and most dread Lordship to ordain a remedy, for the resistance and destruction of the traitors, who are daily reinforced,

---

LVIII.] MS. Cotton. Cleopatra, F. III. fol. 121 b.—On paper; original, with marks of the seal.

[1] Printed in Ellis (2nd Series), i. 15, Letter V. This letter concludes thus,—" Ywrytten at Dynevor this Wednesday in hast," i. e. on Wednesday, July 4, the day after the date of the letter alluded to at page 138, note [1].

forceant, et grande mal et destruction a voz foialx A.D. 1403.
de temps en temps faciont, sanz ascune resistence;
considerant, mon tresgraciouse Seignour, si aide en
haste ne veigne, toutz les Chastelles, et villes, et les
foialx en ycelles, sont en grande peril et du poynt
d'estre anientisez, pour defaute de socour et de bone
governance.

Mon tressovereign et tresgraciouse Seignour, luy
Tout-Puissant Dieu vous governe toutdys en vostres
tresjoyeuses honours, et bone prosperite, longe a
durer.

Escript a Brechon, le vij jour de Juyllet, a l'houre
de mid nyȝt.

Le vostre simple Clerc et Oratour,
JOHAN FAIREFORD,
Recieviour de Brechan.

*Endorsed :*—" Au Roy, mon tres[soverain] Seignour."

---

and from time to time cause great evil and destruction
to your faithful subjects, without any resistance; considering, my most gracious Lord, that if assistance come not
speedily, all the Castles and towns, and your loyal subjects
in them, are in great peril, and on the point of being
utterly ruined, for default of succour and of good governance.
—My most sovereign and gracious Lord, the Almighty God
keep you always in your most joyful honours, and in
good prosperity, long to endure. Written at Brecon, the
7th day of July, at the hour of midnight.

Your simple Clerk and Orator,
JOHN FAIREFORD,
Receiver of Brecon.

*Endorsed:*—" To the King, my most sovereign Lord."

K

A.D. 1403.

## LIX.

### THE SHERIFF, &C. OF HEREFORD TO HENRY IV.

In answer to a letter from the King.

Nostre tresredoute et soverein Seignur le Roy.

Nous nous recomandons humblement a vostre roial Mageste, come voz humbles et povres lieges, prestez et apparaillez de vivre et morir pour resister la fause malice de voz enemys.

Et, nostre tresredoute et soverein Seignur le Roy, plaise a vostre roial Magestie d'entendre que nous avons resceux voz honurables lettres du prive seal, chargeantz nous d'aler a vostre ville de Breghennok pour rescower voz Chastiele et ville illeoqes, ove toutz les gentz defensables del countee de Herford.

Success of the royal arms at Brecon.

Please a vostre roial Magestie savoir que Dymenche darrein passe devant que nous avoions resceux vostre honurable lettre desusdicte, estoions a Breghennok, et

---

[TRANSLATION.]

Our most dread and sovereign Lord the King.—We commend ourselves humbly to your royal Majesty, as your humble and poor lieges, ready and prepared to live and to die for resistance to the false malice of your enemies.—And, our most dread and sovereign Lord the King, may it please your royal Majesty to understand that we have received your honourable letters under your privy seal, charging us to go to your town of Brecon, for to rescue your Castle and town there, together with all the defensive force of the county of Hereford. May it please your royal Majesty to know that on the Sunday last past since we received your honourable letter aforesaid, we were at Brecon, and (God

---

LIX.] MS. Cotton. Cleopatra, F. III. fol. 123 b.—On paper ; original.

(Dieux mercy) avons remue la siege ; et illeoqes furent A.D. 1403.
tuez par les gentz de vostre dicte countee la nombre
de XII$^{xx}$ et autres, et sumes prestez d'obeier a vostre
haut comandement contenuz en la dicte lettre, ove
tout nostre poair.

Mais, tresredoute et soverein Seignur, nostre Sei- Renewed
gnur le Roy, le jour de fessaunce d'ycestes nous avons dangers there, in
resceux deux lettres,[1] quelles nous envoions a vostre conse-
roial Magestie ensealez, declarantz le fait en partie quence of a great
entent et purpos de voz ditz faux rebelx, et avons gathering
autrement entenduz q'ils soy purposent en haste, ove of the rebels.
grande multitude, de venir a Breghennok et gainer la
ville (que Dieux defende), et approcher les Marches et
countees adjoynantz, en destructioun d'ycelle, quele
poer ne sumes santz vostre tresbosoignable aide et
socour de poair pur resister, que nous displaist grande-

---

be thanked) have removed the siege; and there were killed
by the men of your said county the number of two hundred
and forty, and upwards ; and we are ready to obey your
high commandments contained in the said letter with all our
power.—But, most dread and sovereign Lord, our Lord the
King, the day of the writing of these presents we have
received two letters, which we have sent unto your royal Majesty, sealed within, declaring the proceedings, intent, and
purpose of your said false rebels, and we have, moreover, considered that they purpose to come in haste, with a great multitude, to Brecon, and to take the town (which God avert),
and to approach to the Marches and counties adjoining, to the
destruction of them ; which force we have no power to resist
without your most earnest aid and succour, and this greatly

---

[1] One of these was, without doubt, the letter written to them by John Faireford on the previous Wednesday (No. LVI.), and the other was either Jenkyn Hanard's letter to Faireford, or a copy of that of Rau- lyn Monington, alluded to in letter LVI., and, it is presumed, forwarded with it. The original of Monington's letter seems to have been sent to Hugh de Waterton (*See* Letter LX.)

K 2

A.D. 1403. ment pur les grevouses coustages et travalx que nous coviendra sustenir.

They entreat the King to come in person to their assistance.

Sur quelles matires, nostre tresredoute et soverein Seignur, vous plaise ordener hastif remedie, que ne poet estre, come nous quydons, santz vostre graciouse venue as parties; car autre espoir ne remanit, come nous supposons vraiement, synon que toute la natioun Galoie est de semblable purpos, come en sount les rebelx desusdicts.

Nostre tresredoute et soverein Seignur le Roy, nous prions a Luy Tout Puissant, q'Il vous ottroie tresbonne vie et longe saute, ove graciouse victoire de voz enemys.

Escript a vostre ville de Herford, le vij$^{me}$ jour de Juylett.

Voz humbles lieges,

LES VISCOUNTES, CHIVALIERS, ESCUIERS, et COMMUNES, de vostre Counte de Herford.

---

displeases us, by reason of the grievous costs and labours which it will be needful for us to sustain.—In reference to which matters, our most dread and sovereign Lord, may it please you to ordain speedy remedy, which cannot be, as we deem, without your gracious arrival in these parts; for no other hope remains, as we truly suppose, unless the whole of the Welch nation is of like purpose, as are the rebels above-mentioned.—Our most dread and sovereign Lord the King, we pray Him who is Almighty, that He grant you a most happy life and long enduring health, with gracious victory over your enemies.—Written at your town of Hereford, the seventh day of July.

Your humble lieges,

THE SHERIFFS, KNIGHTS, ESQUIRES, and COMMONS of your County of Hereford.

A.D. 1403.

## LX.

### Hugh de Waterton to Henry IV.

Treshaut et trespuissant Prince, et mon tresredoute et tressouverain liege Seignur.

Je moy recomancz a vostre tresexcellente Hautesse de si humble entire obeissant cuer come aucun povere liege pluis obeissantement poet faire a son soverain liege Seignure; humblement ensuppliant vostre graciouse Hautesse de moy avoir pur excuse de ce que ne ouse unqore approchier vostre graciouse presence, de vous enformer de plusours matieres busoignables, pur doute de surfaire enprignant froidure, que me purroit legierment grever. Nepourtant, mon tressoverain et tresredoute Seignure, y me semble que ne me puisse devers vous loialment acquiter si vous ne signifiez les novelles que j'ay des parties de Guales. Et pur tant que ma infirmitee ne me voet suffrier

*News from Wales.*

---

### [Translation.]

Most high and most puissant Prince, and my most dread and most sovereign liege Lord.—I recommend me to your most excellent Highness, with as humble and entire and obedient heart as any poor liege can do to his sovereign liege Lord; humbly beseeching your gracious Highness to hold me excused for that I have not dared up to the present time to approach your gracious presence, to inform you of several matters of importance, by reason of doubt of suffering from taking cold in doing so, which would easily crush me. Nevertheless, my most sovereign and most dread Lord, it seems to me that I cannot acquit myself loyally toward you if I do not signify to you the news which I have from the parts of Wales. And, forasmuch as my infirmity

---

LX.] MS. Cotton. Cleopatra, F. III. fol. 111 *b*.—On paper ; original.

A.D. 1403. de y venir pur vostre Hautesse de ce enfourmer par bouche, me fait a vous escrire en signifiant a vostre graciouse Hautesse que un servant du Receyvoir de Brechon m'ad ore apportiez un lettre des novelles de celles parties, directe a son Meistre depar le Lieute-nuant du Sire d'Audeley a Lanyndevery[1]; la quele pur vous meulx enformer ay closee deinz ycestes.

Burning of Llandeilo and New-town.

Le dit portour d'icelle m'ad en outre reporte par bouche que voz rebelx illeoqes ount ore tard com-burez les villes de Landylo et Newtoun, et fait tres-grande destruxioun en celles parties partout jesques a voz Seignuries de Iskenny, et Kedwelly, sanz aucun resistence, et en point d'avoir entre pur destruyer vos ditz Seignuries, mes q'ils furent distourbez par un cretyn de ewe; et auxi ont chacez le Chamber-lein de Kymordin jesq'a la ville, et tue de ses gentz. Parount mon tressoverain Seignur, al honour de

---

will not suffer me to go to inform your Majesty of this by mouth, it has caused me to write to you, to signify to your gracious Highness that a servant of the Receiver of Brecon has now brought to me a letter of news from those parts, directed to his Master by the Lieutenant of the Lord Audley at Llandovery, the which for your better information I have enclosed within these presents.—The said bearer of this letter has further reported to me by mouth, that your rebels in those parts have lately burned the towns of Llandeilo and New-town, and have made a great destruction in those parts in all directions as far as your Lordships of Iskennen and Kidwelly, meeting with no resistance, and were about to have entry to destroy your said Lordships, but that they were impeded by an inundation ; and also they have driven the Cham-berlain of Carmarthen as far as the town, and have killed some of his men. Wherefore, my most sovereign Lord, for

---

[1] See Letter LVI., where men-tion is made of this communication having been sent to Faireford, the Receiver of Brecon, "par Raulyn " Monington, et autres en la Chastell " de Llamendevery esteantz."

Dieux, et pur la sauvation de vostre estate et honour, y plese a vostre Hautesse d'avoir ce en vostre remembrance, et de y faire tost mettre au tiele ordinance de sufficeantz persones, Chevalers, et Escuiers, tielx que voillent mettre lour entiere peyne et dilligence, pur guarder vostre honour en conservation de voz foialx lieges, et punisement de vos rebellx, ou autrement n'a qu'est dit il est semblable de trouver tout en confusion, que Dieux defende!

Treshaut et trespuissant Prince, et mon tresredoute et tressoverain liege Seignur, je pry et requere a Ly Tout-Puissant Dieux de vous toutdis conservier en prosperite et lesse, ove encrese de pleisance et victorie de touz voz enemys.

Escript a Loundres, en haste, y ce Vendirdy [1] devant la Vespire.

Vostre humble obeisant liege,<br>HUGH DE WATERTON.

the honour of God, and for the preservation of your estate and honour, may it please your Highness to have this in your remembrance, and soon to cause to commit it to such an array of sufficient persons, Knights and Esquires, as shall be willing to give their whole trouble and diligence, for the protection of your honour, in the preservation of your faithful lieges, and the punishment of your rebels, or otherwise, the only thing that can be said is, it is likely you will find all in confusion, which God avert!—Most high and most mighty Prince, and my most dread and most sovereign liege Lord, I pray and implore Him, the Almighty God, to preserve you always in prosperity and ease, with increase of happiness and victory over all your enemies.—Written at London, in haste, this Friday, before Vespers.

Your humble obeisant liege,<br>HUGH DE WATERTON.

[1] Probably July 13, being the second Friday, or nine days after the date of the receipt by Faireford of the letter from Lord Audley's Lieutenant at Llandovery. It could not have been sent to Waterton so early as the first Friday after July 4, and it is not likely that, in a matter of such urgent importance, it was delayed beyond the second Friday.

A.D. 1403.

The writer begs the King to send succours.

A.D. 1403.

## LXI.

### WILLIAM DE BEAUCHAMP TO HENRY IV.

On behalf of John de Assheby.

Mon tressoverain et lige Seigneur.

Je me recomans a vostre royalle Mageste et treshaulte et noble Seigneurie en tant et si humblement de tout mon povre cuer come aucun humble et loyal lege se puet et doit recomander a si treshaulte et puissant Prince, et son droit soverain Seigneur.

His misfortunes.

Et please assavoir a vostre royalle Excellence coment je donais et ottroiay congie et licence a vostre royal lege, Jehan de Aissheby, mon soldour, qui m'a bien et loyaunt service a Bergevenny, d'aller d'icelle lieu de Bergevenny jusques a Hereford, pour parler illeoqes avec sa femme, [en retournan]t a Bergevenny lendemain illeuqes prouchainment ensuivant; mais advint alors de sa malvoise fortune . . . . . . . . . . . . . des rebelx et larons de Gales encontroient luy et son guyde, et luy prinstrent malgre le mesme guyde,

---

### [TRANSLATION.]

My most sovereign and liege Lord.—I commend me to your royal Majesty, and most high and noble Lordship, as much and as humbly, with all my poor heart, as any humble and loyal liege can and ought to commend himself to so very high and mighty a Prince and his rightful sovereign Lord.—And may it please your royal Excellency to know how that I gave and granted leave and licence to your royal liege, John de Assheby, a soldier of mine, who has done me good and loyal service at Abergavenny, to go from that place of Abergavenny as far as to Hereford, to have an interview there with his wife, returning to Abergavenny the day after that next following, but he arrived at that time, of his evil fortune, . . . . . . . . . . the rebels and robbers of Wales met him and his guide, and took him in spite of

---

LXI.] MS. Cotton. Vespas. F. XIII. fol. 19.—On paper.

entre lesquels il estoit en point d'estre mort, par A.D. 1403.
maniere come deux autres de mes soldats y furent
prins et mortz, si ce n'eust estre par l'especialle grace
de Dieu, et de sa bone fortune que un des ditz rebelx offroit et proufroit pour luy x marcs pour sauver
de sa vie, a l'entente qu'il devoit quitter son frere,
qui estoit prins prisoner en vostre ville de Breken.

Si vous supply, mon tressoverain Seigneur, qu'il His
vous pleise prendre le dit Aissheby pour vostre royal loyalty.
lege, et pour nul autre, combien que aucun de ses
enemys luy vouldroient enpirer pardevers vous. Car
je vous jure et promet, mon lige Seigneur, par la foy
et ligeance qui je vous dois, et sur tout mon honneur,
il est tout vray ce que j'escripe pardevers vous de luy
a maintenant.

Et par dessus ce, mon tressoverain Seigneur lege, je The writer
vous vouldrois supplier treshumblement . . . mains et also begs
a tresgrante amertume de cuer, qu'il vous plairroit the King
souvener de vostre bone grace, et de grante miseri- for assist-
corde, de ma povre et souffrastouse personne, qui suy a ance, as he
is in much
peril.

---

the same guide, between whom he was on the point of being
put to death, in like manner as two others of my soldiers
were taken and slain, had it not been that by the especial grace
of God and his own good fortune one of the said rebels
offered and proffered for him ten marks to save his life, to
the intent that he should obtain the release of his brother
who was held in captivity in your town of Brecon.—Therefore I beseech you, my most sovereign Lord, that it please
you to take the said Assheby for your royal liege, and
for no other, though some of his enemies may wish to
calumniate him to you. For I swear and promise to you,
my liege Lord, by the faith and allegiance that I owe to
you, and by all my honour, that it is all true which I have
written to you concerning him now.—And over and above
this, my most sovereign liege Lord, I would most humbly
beseech you, and in very great bitterness of heart, that it
would please you of your good grace and great compassion
to remember my poor and suffering person, who am in ex-

A.D. 1403. tresgrante disease et destresse a present, et a moy
estendre bien hastivement vostre socour et aides graciouse en ce cas qui est bien perillous et piteable; ou
autrement je me juge pour destruit a dis maintenant,
que Dieu ne vuille, ne vostre royale Benignitie, qui
m'a estre toutdis socourable en tout mes bousoignes et
affaires.

Mon tressoverain et lige Seigneur, je pry a Dieu
qu'Il vuille maintenir, prosperer, et accroistre vostre
royal estat en tresbone vie et joyeuse permanable-
ment, et vous ottroier victorial honneur de tous voz
enemys. Amen.

Escript en haste, a vostre dite Citee de Hereford,
le xxiij jour de Aout, dessous le signet de mon clerc,
en absence de mien, par mon charge et mandement.

Vostre loyal lige treshumblement recomande,
WILLIAM DE BEAUCHAMP.

Endorsed :—" A nostre honure et tressoverain et lige
Seignour."

---

ceeding great trouble and distress at present, and to extend
to me with all speed your succour and gracious aid in this
case, which is very perilous and pitiable; or otherwise, I hold
myself for destroyed this present day, which may God not
will, nor your royal Benignity, who has always been ready to
assist me in all my business and affairs.—My most sovereign
and liege Lord, I pray God that he will maintain, prosper,
and increase your royal estate with life happy and lastingly
joyous, and give you the honour of victory over all your
enemies. Amen.—Written in haste, at your said city of
Hereford, the 23rd day of August, under the signet of my
clerk, in the absence of my own, by my charge and commandment.

Your loyal liege, most humbly commended to you,
WILLIAM DE BEAUCHAMP.

Endorsed : — " To our honoured and most sovereign and
liege Lord."

## LXII.

RICHARD KINGESTON TO HENRY IV.

[Mon tressouverain, trespu]issant, et mon tresredoute
Seignour.

Jeo moi recomande [a] vostre treshaute Seigneurie He reports
come vostre treshumble oratour, et . . . . . . . . . . . the success
                                                          of the
Mon tressouveraigne et tresredoute Seignour, please a rebels in
vostre tresgraciouse Seignourie entendre que a jour- Hereford-
                                                     shire,
duy, apres noo[ne] . . . . . . . . . . . . . . . q'ils furent
venuz deinz nostre countie pluis de CCCC des les rebelz
de Owyne, Glyn, Talgard, et pluseours autres rebelz
des voz Marches de Galys, et ount prisez et robbez
deinz vostre countie de Hereford pluseours gentz, et
bestaille a graunte nombre, nient contre esteant la nostre trewe, si come mon [ami] et compaignon, et vostre

---

[TRANSLATION.]

My most sovereign, most mighty, and my most dread Lord.—
I commend me to your most high Lordship as your most humble
orator and . . . . . . . . . My most sovereign and most dread
Lord, may it please your most gracious Lordship to consider
that to day, after noon [I was informed that] there were come
into our county more than four hundred of the rebels of Owen,
Glynn, Talgard, and many other rebels besides from the
Marches of Wales, and they have captured and robbed within
your county of Hereford many men, and beasts in great number, our truce notwithstanding, as my friend and companion,

---

LXII.] MS. Cotton. Cleopatra, F. III. fol. 79.—On paper; original. A letter written in a similar strain, and to the same effect, and sent by Kingeston to the King nearly two months earlier, is printed in Ellis (2nd Series), i. 17.

A.D. 1403. Esquier, Miles Walter, portur du cestez, vous dira plus pleinement par bouche que jeo ne puisse escripte a vous a present.[1] A qi vous please, de vostre graciouse Seignourie, donner ferme foi et credence de ceo, q'il vous enformera de part moi pur salvatioun de vostre dit counte et dez toutz les paiis environ.

*and entreats the King's special favour for the bearer of his letter.*

A quelle Esquier vous please faire bone chire, a luy en mercier de son grant labour et bone et loial service, q'il vous ad fait et monstre deinz vostre counte, et a Brechon,—qar, mon tresredoute Seignour, par la foi que jeo doy a Dieux, et a vous, jeo luy tigne un dez lez pluis vaillantz hommez dez armez que vous avez deinz vostre countee ou Marche, si come vous trouverez certeinment a vostre tresgraciouse venue a nous,—et que vous please de a luy prometter bone et graciouse Seignourie et luy comforter, qar il ad perduz tout ceo q'il ad, et ceo a graunte summe.

---

and your Esquire, Miles Walter, the bearer of these presents, will more fully tell you by mouth than I can write to you at present. To whom may it please you, of your gracious Lordship, to give firm faith and credence in that on which he shall inform you on my part, for the preservation of your said county, and of all the country around.—To which Esquire may it please you to give good cheer, thanking him for his great labour, and good and loyal service which he has done and shown you within your county, and at Brecon,—for, my most dread Lord, by the faith which I give to God, and to you, I hold him to be one of the most valiant of the men of arms that you have within your county or March, as you will most certainly find at your most gracious arrival among us,—and that it please you to promise to him good and gracious Lordship, and to comfort him, for he has lost all that he had, and that to a large amount.—Besides this, my most sovereign and

---

[1] *vous dira . . . a present*] Added above the line.

Outre ceo, mon tressoveraigne et tresredoute Seignour, vous please, de vostre graciouse Seignourie, et pur le salvatioun de vostre dicte Countee et tout la March, moi envoire en yceste noet, ou demeyn bien matyn a pluis tarde, mon treshonoure Mestre Beauford ou ascune autre vaillaunt personne, que veot et peot laborer, ove C launcez, et DC archiers,[1] tanque a vostre tres- graciouse venue en salvatioun dez nous trestoutz ; qar autrement, mon tresredoute Seignour, en bone foy jeo tigne tout nostre paiis destruez, qar les coers des toutz vous foialx lieges de nostre pays ove les comyns outre- ment sount perduz, et pur ceo que ils oiont que vous ne vendrez illeoqes en vostre propre persone (que Dieux deffende). Qar, mon tresredoute Seigneur, vous trouverez pour certein que si vous ne venez en vostre propre persone pour attendre [apres] voz rebelx en Galys, vous ne trouverez un gentil que veot attendre deinz vostre dit Countee.

A.D. 1403. He ear- nestly begs the King to come into Wales and mean- while to send succours.

---

most dread Lord, may it please you, of your gracious lordship, and for the preservation of your said county and all the March, to send to me this night, or early to-morrow morning at the latest, my most honoured Master Beaufort, or some other valiant person, who is willing and able to labour, with one hundred lances and six hundred archers, until your most gracious arrival to the salvation of us all; for otherwise, my most dread Lord, in good faith I hold all our country to be destroyed, for the hearts of all your faithful lieges in our country, with the commons, are utterly lost, and for this, that they hear that you are not coming to this place in your own person (which God avert). For, my most dread Lord, you will find for certain that, if you do not come in your own person to await your rebels in Wales, you will not find a single gentleman that will stop in your said county.—Where-

---

[1] *et DC archiers.*] Altered from " et sufficiauntz archiers."

A.D. 1403.　War fore, for Goddesake, thinketh on ʒour beste Frende, God, and thanke Hym as He hath deserved to ʒowe; and leveth nought that ʒe ne come for no man that may counsaille ʒowe the contrarie; for, by the trouthe that I schal be to ʒowe ʒet, this day the Walshmen supposen and trusten that ʒe schulle nought come there, and there fore, for Goddeslove, make them fals men. And that hit plese ʒowe of ʒour hegh Lordeship for to have me excused of my comynge to ʒowe, for, yn god fey, I have nought ylafte with me over two men, that they beon sende oute with Sherref and other gentils of oure Schire, for to with stande the malice of the Rebelles this day.

Tresexcellent, trespuissant, et tresredoute Seignour, autrement say a present nieez.

Jeo prie a la Benoit Trinite que vous ottroie bone vie ove tresentier sauntee a treslonge durre, and sende ʒowe sone to ows in help and prosperitee; for, in god fey, I hope to Al Mighty God that, ʒef ʒe come ʒoure

fore, for God's sake, think on your best friend, God, and thank Him, as He hath deserved of you ; and leave nought that you do not come for no man that may counsel you the contrary : for, by the truth that I shall be to you yet, this day the Welshmen suppose and trust that you shall not come there, and therefore, for God's love, make them false men. And that it please you of your high Lordship to have me excused of my coming to you, for in good faith I have nought here left with me over two men, that they be sent out with sheriffs and other gentlemen of our shire, for to withstand the malice of the rebels this day.—Most excellent, most mighty, and most dread Lord, I know nothing besides at present. —I pray the Blessed Trinity to give you good life, with most complete good health, very long to endure, and send you soon to us in help and prosperity ; for, in good faith, I hope to Almighty God, that, if you come your own

owne persone, ȝe schulle have the victorie of alle ȝoure A.D. 1403. enemyes.

And for salvation of ȝoure Schire and Marches al aboute, treste ȝe nought to no Leutenaunt.

Escript a Hereford, en tresgraunte haste, a trois de la clocke apres noone, le tierce jour de Septembre.

Vostre humble creatoure et continuelle oratour,

RICHARD KYNGESTON,

Deane de Wyndesore.

---

person, you shall have the victory of all your enemies.— And for salvation of your Shire and Marches trust you nought to any lieutenant. — Written at Hereford, in very great haste, at three of the clock after noon, the third day of September.

Your humble creature and continual orator,

RICHARD KINGESTON,

Dean of Windsor.

## 5 HENRY IV.

### 30 September, 1403, to 29 September, 1404.

## LXIII.

### THE CONSTABLE OF KIDWELLY TO HENRY IV.

Treshaute et tresexcellent Seignour.

Nous nous recomaundons a vostre tresroialle Mageste en tanque come nous savons oue puissons.

*On the dangers threatening his Castle.* Et, tresexcellent Seignour, vous pleasse assavoir que, le jour al fesant de cestez, Harry Doun, et touz les rebellez de South Gales, ovec les gentz de Fraunce et Brutayne, fueront venuz verz le Chastiell et la ville de Kedwelly, ovec toute lour ordinaunce, et illeoqes ount

---

[TRANSLATION.]

Most high and most excellent Lord.—We commend us to your most royal Majesty, so far as we know or are able.— And, most excellent Lord, may it please you to know that, on the day of the execution of these presents, Henry Don, and all the rebels of South Wales, with the men from France and Bretagne, were coming towards the Castle and town of Kidwelly, with all their array, and

---

LXIII.] MS. Cotton. Cleopatra, F. III. fol. 119 (a).—On paper; original.

destruer touz les bleez de voz povrez liegez chacun A.D. 1403. partie environ vostre dit Chastiell et la ville ; et que plusours de voz povrez comynerez illeoqes sont alez et venuz en Engleterc, ovec lour femez et enfantez, et les autres sont deynz vostre dit Chastiell, du doute de lour viez.

Sur quoi vous pleasse de vostre tresroialle Mageste, sur ceo ordeigner aide, rescoez, et socour, en sauvation de vostre dit Chastiell, et voz povrez lieges dedeynz, deynz breife, oue autrement vostre dit Chastiell, et touz les liegez illeoges sumes destruez et defaitez a touz jours, come les portours de cestez a vous plenement certifie par bouche.

A quellz vous pleasse de vostre tresexcellent Mageste donner credence de ceste mater, et touz autrez chosez touchant ceste pays.

Treshaute et tresexcellent Seignour, le Seignour de touz seignurs vous ottroie bone vie et longe durre en prosperite !

---

there have destroyed all the grain belonging to your poor lieges, on every side around your said Castle and the town ; and that the greater part of your poor commons there have taken their departure and gone into England, with their wives and young children, and the rest are within your said Castle in uncertainty about their lives.—Concerning which may it please you of your most royal Majesty to ordain in this matter aid, rescue, and succour, for the preservation of your said Castle and your poor lieges within it, in a short time ; or, otherwise, your said Castle and all we your lieges there, are destroyed and undone for ever, as the bearers of these presents will more fully certify to you by mouth. To whom may it please you of your excellent Majesty to give credence in this matter, and all other things touching this land.—Most high and most excellent Lord, the Lord of all lords grant you good life, and long

L

A.D. 1403.    Escript a Kedwelley, en tresgrande haste, le Mes-
curdy[1] prochein apres le feste de Seint Michell l'Arch-
angle.

Par voz povrez liegez,
LE CONESTABLE DE VOSTRE CHASTIELLE
DE KEDWELLY,
et les Comyneres illeoques.

---

continuance in prosperity !—Written at Kidwelly in very
great haste, the Wednesday next after the feast of S. Michael
the Archangel.

By your poor lieges,
THE CONSTABLE OF YOUR CASTLE
OF KIDWELLY,
and the Commons there.

## LXIV.

### THE ENGLISH COUNCIL TO CONRAD DE JUNGINGEN.

*The following introductory matter is prefixed to the
copy of this letter :—*

Anno Domini Millesimo CCCC^mo tertio, in die Sancti
Michaelis Archangeli,[2] venerabiles Domini, Dominus
Episcopus Lincolniensis,[3] Cancellarius Angliæ, et Domi-
nus de Rosa,[4] Thesaurarius Angliæ, et Ambassiatores

---

[1] Wednesday, October 3, 1403.
LXIV.] MS. Cotton. Nero, B. II.,
fol. 25.

[2] September 29, 1403.
[3] Henry Beaufort.
[4] William, twelfth Baron de Ross.

Pruciæ, Johannes Godeke de Danzik, et Henricus A.D. 1403.
Monk de Elvingo, Magistri Civium, tractaverunt in
modum compositionis in Westmonasterio articulos sub-
scriptos inter Reverendissimum Dominum, Dominum
Regem Angliæ, et Reverendum Dominum, Generalem
Magistrum Pruciæ, ut de damnis illatis terris Pruciæ
et Livoniæ in mari ab Anglicis,—

"Primo,[1] quod omnes naves, cum ipsarum perti-
nentiis, et fructubus nautarum pro conductione rerum,
ac omnia alia bona ab eis derobata actu indivisa
debent restitui incontinenti ; et, si in aliquo fuerit
defectus, summa istius defectus debet computari, et
debet referri ad terminum cum aliis damnis bonorum
restitutionis faciendum et persolvendum.

"Item, quod omnes naves damna et bona, ut in
bulla nostra accusationis continentur, quæ nunc incontinenti non restituuntur, illa debent restitui et solvi
in terra Pruciæ, infra hinc et terminum deputatum,
cum debito justitiæ complemento.

"Item, de personis ejectis sive interfectis in mari
hoc manebit ad voluntatem serenissimi Domini, Domini Regis Angliæ, et Reverendi Domini, Magistri
Pruciæ, determinandum.

"Item, infra hinc et terminum bonorum illatorum
restitutionis deputatum, et quousque fiat debitum solutionis damnorum complementum, mercatores Angliæ,
necnon Pruciæ, in prædictis terris non debent iterum
mutuo mercandisando communicare."

Venerabilis ac magnifice Domine.

Accedentes jam dudum ad serenissimi Domini nostri, On the
Angliæ et Franciæ Regis, præsentiam, honorabiles viri restitution
of certain
nuncii, Johannes Godek et Henricus Monk, præsentium ships and
exhibitores, (quos idem Dominus noster vultu recepit merchandise, cap-

---

[1] *Primo*] Corrected from "Item."

L 2

A.D. 1403. hilari et jocundo,) quasdam litteras ex parte vestra
tured by Majestati regiæ, ea qua decuit reverentia, præsentarunt,
the
English. exponentes eidem diversa deprædationes et gravamina
per suos ligeos et subditos nuper vestratibus illata
fuisse super mare, contra pacis et dilectionis fœdera,
quæ hinc inde Dei gratia viguerunt, de quibus quidem
deprædationibus et gravaminibus antedicti vestri nuncii
restitutionem seu recompensam integram damna passis,
aut eorum procuratoribus, sibi petierunt.

Allusion to Nos utique, tunc nuperius Domini nostri Regis
the rebel-
lion in præsentia constituti, qui cum suo exercitu bellicoso
Wales. versus remotas Walliæ partes, ditioni suæ subjectas,
se accinxit ad iter, pro suis partium illarum subditis
justificandis, qui, ausu temerario ducti, erga eum et
suorum ligiantiam rebellionis spiritum assumere præ-
sumpserunt ; intentionem regiam esse percepimus
justitiæ debitum unicuique fideliter impartiri, et præsertim vestratibus etiam cum favore, quos semper ut
incolas suos naturales tractavit utiliter temporibus
retroactis, quosque de cetero proponit amicabiliter
confovere, ita quod inter se et suos ex una, et vos et
vestros subditos ex altera, mutuæ dilectionis vigeat
plenitudo ; et idcirco supradictis nunciis vestris, postquam ipsi talia nobis in specie depredationes et
gravamina demonstrarunt, obtulimus ad transmittenda
mandata regia illis de quibus extitit querelatum, eis
sub pœnis gravibus firmiter injungendo quatinus naves,
mercandisas, res atque bona per eos de vestratibus
capta sive deprædata, damnificatis aut eorum procuratoribus restituant, seu restitui faciant indilate.

The pro- Et, ut sæpefati nuncii vestri partim attingere
perty
found in valeant desiderii¹ sui fines, quædam navigia,² mercan-

---

¹ *desiderii*] desidarii MS.
² Here the following words are
inserted in the margin :—
" Navem Egardi apud Calesiam.

" Naves . . anni Dordewant. Ger-
" manni Vurowen . . et Wett et
" Zepyswyk."

disas, res atque bona, in certis nostris portubus inventa, A.D. 1403.
eis mandavimus liberari.

Quantum vero ad alia bona, quæ dissipationis sive English ports is to be restored; but the restitution of the value of scattered property cannot be made in the King's absence. devastationis forsan incommoda subjecerunt, et pro quibus iidem nuncii vestri solutionem petunt sibi fieri infra certum terminum per nos eis limitandum, scire placeat Reverentiæ vestræ quod, in absentia dicti Domini nostri Regis, adhuc longe agentis, hujusmodi terminum nullo modo poterimus limitare. Nihilominus, in ipsius Domini nostri felici reditu, super hoc communicare disposuimus cum eodem, de cujus cum fuerimus certiorati responso ejus intentionem superinde nostras per litteras vobis intendimus explicare.

Cumque, venerabilis ac magnifice Domine, sæpedicti Meanwhile mutual forbearance is recommended. vestri nuncii de oblatione nostra prædicta contententur ad præsens, sicuti debeant inde merito contentari, maxime cum per hanc viam citius ad suorum effectum propositorum valeant pervenire, ad cujus oblationis executionem celerem et votivam totis viribus anhelabimus, Deo duce; velitis et placeat ut, quemadmodum in regno Angliæ mercatores et subditi vestri commode pertractantur, consimiliter supradicti Domini nostri et sui regni mercatores et ligei partes vestras, mercandisandi causæ, seu alio modo pacifico, frequentantes, amicabiliter inibi valeant pertractari, ac cum mercatoribus et subditis vestris communicare, et mercantiliter insimul conversari, pristinæ gaudiis amicitiæ potiti: per hoc etenim sentietur indubie zelus fervidus, si quem ad splendidam coronam Angliæ congeratis, etiam si inter inclitas domus Angliæ et Pruciæ veræ dilectionis amicitiæ vinculum firmari et continuari contigerit temporibus successivis.

Et utinam, venerabilis ac magnifice Domine, honoris et gaudii vobis adveniant incrementa!

A.D. 1403.   Scriptum Londoniæ, mensis Octobris die quinta.

CANCELLARIUS, THESAURARIUS, ac alii DOMINI, REGIS ANGLIÆ ET FRANCIÆ CONSILIARII, Londoniæ præsentialiter constituti.[1]

[1] The following note follows the letter (fol. 26), and relates to the same matter :—

"Memorandum quod tertio die mensis Octobris, anno Domini Millesimo CCCC$^{mo}$ tertio, et regni serenissimi Principis et Domini, Domini Henrici, Dei gratia Regis Angliæ et Franciæ Quarti, quinto, inter venerabilem Patrem Dominum Henricum, Lincolnensem Episcopum, Cancellarium, ac Magnificum Dominum Willelmum, Dominum de Roos, Thesaurarium Angliæ, Consiliarios ejusdem Domini Regis parte ex una, et venerabiles viros, Johannem Godeke et Henricum Moncke, per sacræ religionis virum, fratrem Conradum de Jungingen, Ordinis Beatæ Mariæ Theutonicorum Magistrum Generalem, in dictum regnum Angliæ nuncios destinatos, ex altera parte, ad ipsorum requisitionem seu instantiam nunciorum appunctuatum extitit et mutuo concordatum quod ipsius Domini Regis ligii et sub-

diti universi hinc usque Festum Paschæ proximo futurum* possint ad terram Pruciæ supradictam libere transire, inibi morari, et exinde cum navigiis, mercandisis, rebus, ac aliis suis bonis quibuscumque, ad propria remeare; quodque prænotati Magistri Generalis omnes subditi valeant interim in dicto regno Angliæ agere consimiliter vice versa; proviso semper quod, infra tempus superius limitatum, nec antedicti regni Angliæ mercatores in præfata terra Pruciæ, nec ejusdem terræ mercatores in dicto regno Angliæ ullatenus mercandizent, nisi per tractatus inter præfatum Regem Angliæ dictumque Magistrum Generalem interim ineundos aliter contigerit ordinari.

"In cujus rei testimonium una pars hujus indenturæ penes antedictos nuncios dinoscitur remanere.

"Datum in Domo Capitulari Ecclesiæ Sancti Pauli, Londoniæ, die et anno supradictis."

* 30 March 1404.

## LXV.

HENRY IV. TO THE PRIVY COUNCIL.

Depar le Roy.

Reverent Piere en Dieu, nostre treschier et tresame frere.

[Nous salvons] vous tressovent, vous esmerciant de voz lettres, a nous apportees par Johan Drax, nostre [message, es quelles enforme]z nous avez entre autres des novelles que vous sont venuz hors de nostre port de Hampton, [coment est en peril si bien pa]r terre come par meer, et coment, pour eschuir le peril que avenir pourroit a nostre navie, q'est . . . . . . . 

*On the passage of the King's galley, and other matters.*

---

[TRANSLATION.]

By the King.

Reverend Father in God, our right dear and most beloved brother.—We greet you full often, thanking you for your letters brought to us by John Drax, our messenger, in the which you have informed us of the news, among others, that have come to you from our town of Southampton, [how it is in danger as well] by land as by sea, and how, in order to avoid the danger which might befal our navy, which is . . . . .

---

LXV.] MS. Cotton. Calig., D. IV., fol. 27. On paper; original.—This letter has been most seriously injured by fire, and considerable difficulty has been experienced in restoring it to an intelligible condition. The emendations are in many instances, as will be seen, wholly conjectural, the original words having been destroyed utterly: it is hoped, however, that the general significance of the letter has been recovered, though it is still somewhat obscure in parts. *See* the Introduction.

A.D. 1403. . . . . . -dage,[1] vous avez fait armer nostre balynger, desous la governance de nostre chier et foial Chivaler, Wi[llaume de Wilford, pour aller v]ers nostre port de Dertemuth, pour y faire demorer la navie vers le West, s'il y soit uncore, et s'il . . . . . . -er, et par force de nostre commission la faire amesner a tiel lieu come nous plerra, selom ce que n[ous ferons env]oier instruction a nostre dit Chivaler a nostre dit port.

Si vous faisons savoir que nous avons en[tenduz que] . . . . -emble a mesme nostre port est passez. Et pour tant il ne fault plus escrire de lour governance, n[e] . . . . . . . . . -ussant pour lour bon passage et gracious exploit. Et puis que par vertue de vostre ordenance nostre dit Chivaler [s'a mis] sur son passage, ovec autres niefs et vesselx assemblez a nostre port de Londres, vers nostre dit port de [Dertemuth] escrit luy avons pour soy bien avisez de son passage, s'il ne soit

---

. . . . . . . . . . . . you have caused our galley to be armed under the command of our dear and faithful Knight, William de Wilford, to proceed towards our port of Dartmouth, for the purpose of causing our navy of the West to remain there, if he be there still, and if he . . . . . , and by force of our commission, to cause it to strike sail at such place as shall please us, according to the instructions which we will cause to be sent to our said Knight at our said port.—Also we would cause you to know that we have heard that . . . . . . . . . . at our said port is passed. And so far there is no need to write more of their governance, nor . . . . . . . . . for their good passage and thankworthy exploit. And since, by virtue of your ordinance, our said Knight has set out on his passage, together with other ships and vessels assembled in our port of London, towards our said port of Dartmouth, we have written to him to be well advised of his passage, if he be not very strong,

---

[1] " [en danger d'abor]dage " (?)

bien fort, en attendant de savoir com[ent on] fait, et A.D. 1403.
attendant auxi la remenant de nostre navie, au fin
qu'ils puissent passer tout enfer[mees que] pourra
par invasion de noz enemys ainsi assemblez come om
suppose. Et nous pensons nient . . . . . nombre des
niefs ordennez par les Brutons, ne ceux de France
comme les novelles pourportent, mais en . . . . . . come
bien avisez.

Et quant a le bon exploit de noz treschiers et foialx
le Conte de Warrewyk et du Sire d'Audel[ey, dont
vous faisez] mention, nous vous mercions d'entier cuer,
et de la bone diligence que mettez entour l'exploit de
[Monsieur le] Duc d'Everwyk.

Si avons par noz autres lettres vous escrit pour
faire envoier paiement a m[oi, a la vil]le de Bristuyt,
contre la Samady prochein, pour le plus brief expedition de luy.

Et touchant [les matieres] dont escrit nous avez, il
nous plest bien, en cas que vous ne pourrez venir
plus en haste dev[ers nous, come e]n charge par noz
autres lettres.

---

while he waits to know how things are going on, and awaits
also the remainder of our fleet, to the end that they may be
able to proceed as well guarded as may be, by invasion of our
enemies so assembled as is supposed. And we think . . . . .
the number of vessels ordained by the Bretons, nor those of
France, as the news purports, but . . . . . as well advised.—
And as for the brave exploit of our very dear and faithful, the
Earl of Warwick, and the Lord Audley, of which you have
made mention, we thank you with all our heart, as well as for
the ready diligence which you use about the exploit of the
Duke of York.—Also we have by our other letters written to
you to cause to send payment to me, at the town of Bristol,
by Saturday next, for his more speedy expedition. — And,
touching the matters of which you have written to us, it
pleases us well, in case that you are not able to come with
more speed to our presence, as charged by our other letters.—

A.D. 1403. Et Nostre Seigneur vous ait tous dys en Sa sainte garde !

Donne [a nostre ville de] Bristuyt, le xxv jour d'Octobre.

*Endorsed :*—" A nostre Conseil, de presen[t esteant a Londres]."

*Also :*—" Touchant le passage du balynger du Roy, et le paiement pur le garnison a Kermerdin, et l'exploit du Conte de Warrewyk."

And Our Lord have you always in His holy keeping !—Given at our town of Bristol, the 25th day of October.

*Endorsed :*—" To our Council, at present being in London."

*Also :*—" Touching the passage of the King's galley, and the payment for the garrison at Carmarthen, and the exploit of the Earl of Warwick."

## LXVI.

HUGH LUTTRELL, ETC. TO THE DUKE OF BURGUNDY.

*Copia litteræ transmissæ Duci Burgundiæ ac Magno Concilio Franciæ :—*

They complain of certain infringe-

Illustris ac excellens Princeps et potentissime Domine, necnon alii Domini ac Nobiles et Fideles de Magno Concilio Franciæ.

LXVI.] MS. Cotton. Calig. D. III. fol. 175.—On paper ; a contemporaneous MS.

Cum,[1] juxta tenorem communis appunctuamenti, ambassiatores utriusque regni, quinto die Septembris ultimo præterito, pro deliberatione et expeditione incarceratorum utriusque partis, in loco consueto tenebantur interesse, ac pro bono communi utriusque regni insimul convenire; præfato vero quinto die Septembris ex tunc adveniente, certi ambassiatores pro parte Franciæ, videlicet honorabiles Domini, A.[2] de Longovillari, Dominus de Engodessent, Miles, ac Philippus d'Aussy, Dominus de Dounperre, ac Allermus de Beucouvroy, Locumtenens Admiralli Franciæ in partibus Stapulæ et Boloniæ, necnon certi ambassiatores nostri pro parte Angliæ apud Lulyngham pro deliberatione incarceratorum, juxta formam dicti appunctuamenti, insimul convenerunt, ac termino dicto diei prout melius poterant satisfecerunt; quodque subsequenter præfati ambassiatores utriusque regni, ex certis causis eos moventibus, dictum terminum pro deliberatione hujusmodi incarceratorum per appunctuamentum expressum, usque ad vicesimum diem mensis Novembris ex tunc proxime futurum, prorogarunt et expresse continuarunt. Et ad satisfaciendum termino prædicto nos ambassiatores infrascripti, de mandato Domini nostri Regis illustrissimi astricti, decimo septimo die mensis Novembris nunc ultimo elapso, in villa Calisii applicuimus, ac in crastino diversas litteras Boloniæ præfato Domino de Engodessent ac aliis suis collegis supranominatis præsentandas, cum copia commissionis et potestatis nostræ in eisdem interclusæ, transmisimus, de quibus nullum responsum hactenus reportavimus; quodque subsequenter, post nostrum introitum in villam Calisii, relatione fidedignorum intelleximus quod Dux Aurelianus ac Comes Sancti Pauli in contrarium treugarum, tanquam destructores ipsarum et infractores, quantum in eis est, et proprii juramenti, prout apparet, violatores,

---

[1] *See* Rymer. viii. 330.    [2] Ancelmus (*Rymer*).

A.D. 1403. Excellentia vestra semper salva, certas litteras inhonestas illustrissimo ac invictissimo Principi, Domino nostro, Regi Angliæ et Franciæ, scripserunt, quorum malicia et calumnia per Dei gratiam reprimetur, ac publicabitur in futurum, et declarabitur per universum.

also of the offensive attitude of the French fleet.
Præmissis etiam non contenti, potentiam non faciliter numerabilem, tam navium quam gentium armigerarum, in diversis portubus Franciæ, prout fertur notorie, contra formam treugarum prout in eis continetur, in præjudicium Domini nostri Regis et regni sui congregarunt, treugas infringendo, ac bonum publicum utriusque regni, quantum in eis est, multipliciter perturbando, ac ipsorum juramenta pro conservatione treugarum præstita, prout apparet cuilibet debite intuenti, multipliciter violando; ac etiam in Francia proclamatum est publice, prout asseritur ex ipsorum suggestione, quod nullus Gallicus cum Anglicis in continctibus seu mercimoniis debet communicare; quæ non sunt treugarum conservativa seu pacis inductiva, quin verius cujuscumque boni utriusque regni radicitus extirpativa, et penitus extinctiva.

De quibus omnibus vehementer admirandum unde, si præmissa processerunt de mandato et auctoritate ipsorum Domini ligei seu Concilii sui, et præsertim vestræ Excellentiæ, ac aliorum Ducum regni Franciæ, quæ pro præsenti credere non valemus, cum ad eos pertineat de jure etiam naturaliter conservare juramentum Domini sui ligei sicut proprii, præsertim tempore infirmitatis suæ, quousque per vestram Excellentiam seu per Magnum Concilium aliud fuerit intimatum, et notorie publicatum, non expediret pro tractatu ulteriori quod ambassiatores utriusque regni debeant, salvo vestro judicio meliori intendere, seu inanibus expensis se vexare.

They demand an explanation,
Rogamus igitur vestram Excellentiam et aliorum Reverentias et Dominationes, necnon ipsas requirimus et exhortamur in Domino, quatinus,—pensata justitia ac

fidelitate quæ hactenus viguerunt in eadem Excellentia A.D. 1403.
vestra pro bono publico utriusque Regni, et pro conservatione treugarum; attento quod Dominus noster,
tanquam Rex Christianissimus, peractus est treugas
generales ac appunctuamenta tenere, et fideliter observare, — placeat per præsentium portitorem,[1] seu
alium, nobis rescribere, si pro deliberatione incarceratorum in præsenti, seu pro ulteriori tractatu, etiam de
mense Martii proximo futuro, inter utrumque regnum,
debeamus intendere, seu si præmissa, per Ducem et
Comitem supradictos attemptata, de ipsorum Domini
ligei seu ipsius Concilii, et præsertim vestræ Excellentiæ,
seu aliorum Ducum regni Franciæ processerint mandato
et auctoritate, ac vestram intentionem in omnibus, si
placeat, vestræ Excellentiæ lucide explanare.

Et revera multi admirantur quod præfati Domini *and report*
sunt tantæ potentiæ infra terminos et limites Franciæ, *the general*
pensata ipsorum fragilitate et calore juvenili, adeo *surprise*
quod carbones inter utrumque regnum valeant re- *that such*
accendere, ac treugas, quantum in eis est, ut præ- *youths*
mittitur, infringere, ac Divinam Majestatem taliter *should be*
offendere, et publicam utilitatem utriusque regni irre- *permitted*
parabiliter intervertere, ac incendia — etiam ecclesia- *wantonly*
rum, et sanguinis Christiani effusionem, et plura alia *to break*
mala non faciliter numerabilia, lamentabiliter et detes- *the peace.*
tabiliter — de quo, proh dolor! procurare, in ipsorum
animarum grave periculum, ac etiam Christianitatis
disturbium et perturbationem, necnon utriusque regni
præjudicium non modicum et gravamen. Absurdum
enim est ac grave et inhonestum, inconveniens necnon
contra omnem rationem, ac mirabiliter in regno Franciæ contra justitiam toleratum, quod Dux et Comes
supradicti valeant guerram universalem contra Dominum nostrum Regem et regnum, per terram et per
mare, propter suas querelas privatas et particulares

---

[1] *portitorem*] Written upon an erasure.

A.D. 1403. prætensas, instituere, ac tantum scandalum commovere, necnon ad sui defensionem et receptaculum totum regnum Franciæ, et ipsius potentiam in pecunia et gentibus assumere, ac per modum castri et bastilli, pro ipsorum clipeo et scuto, regnum Franciæ sibi incastellare, absque eo, prout ipsi prætendent, quod videantur treugas infringere ac juramenta propria violare. Ad quæ Deus pro Sua Pietate in defectu justitiæ advertat et remedium apponat! Cum ipsorum querela privata et prætensa, contra Dominum nostrum, Regem Angliæ illustrissimum, mota, ac ex fragili principio et juvenili fundamento intentata, ipsos ab infractione treugarum, juxta tenorem litterarum suarum, eidem Domino nostro Regi transmissarum, non poterit exemere, nec a proprii juramenti violatione, prout apparet, merito excusare.

Super quibus omnibus et singulis vestra Excellentia, necnon aliorum Dominationes et Reverentiæ dignentur nobis rescribere, ac, prout placeat in præmissis, nos certiores reddere.

Trinitas Increata vestram Excellentiam, aliorum Reverentias et Dominationes, conservet feliciter et votive!

Scriptum Calisii, quarto die Decembris.

> HUGO LUTRELL;
> JOHANNES DE CROFFT,—Milites;
> NICHOLAUS DE RYSSHETOUN, Utriusque Juris
>     Professor; ac
> JOHANNES URBAN,
>     Ambassiatores pro parte Angliæ.

*Endorsement:*—" Illustri ac excellenti et potentissimo Domino, Domino Duci Burgundiæ ac Comiti Flandriæ, necnon aliis Dominis ac Nobilibus et Fidelibus de Magno Concilio Franciæ."

*Also:*—" Presentetur Serenissimo Principi, Domino nostro, Domino Regi Angliæ et Franciæ illustrissimo."

A.D. 1403.

## LXVII.

THE FLEMISH DEPUTIES TO THE ENGLISH
AMBASSADORS.

*Copia litterarum Quatuor Membrorum Flandriæ,
pro loci mutatione extra Calisium, ac pro termini
assignatione, transmissarum Ambassiatoribus Angliæ.*

Nobiles, honorabiles, ac magnifici Domini.

Vestras circumspectionum litteras, xiiij die mensis Decembris Calesii scriptas, nos noveritis recepisse xviij die hujus mensis ultimo præterito: per quas inter cetera nos requirendo hortamini, quatinus, juxta tenorem appunctuamentorum et juramentorum nostrorum prædictorum, ad tractatum vestrum communem in villa Calisii pro reparatione attemptatorum utriusque partis fiendum, nostros ambassiatores, cum sufficiente potestate, absque dilatione curaremus transmittere, prout nostram legalitatem, necnon sigilla nostra juramenta prædicta appetimus defendere, ac facta nostrorum ambassiatorum, qui suffulti erant nostra potestate sufficiente, prout Dominus vester Rex paratus est tenere juramenta per vos in ipsius persona præstita illæsa conservare, prout in dictis litteris vestris plenius continetur: insuper quoddam instrumentum, una cum quodam libello cum eisdem litteris vestris nobis destinato, attente visitasse.

*In reply to their letter fixing on Calais for the meeting of the deputies to discuss the restitution of goods taken from English merchants;*

Super quibus vestræ noverint Magnificentiæ quod, licet vestris allegationibus satis commode responderi posset, ne tamen scintilla discordiæ in tanto negotio, ubi concordiam quærimus et favorem, argumentorum involutione generetur, eisdem pro præsenti respondere supersedimus, loco et tempore quibus principalis quæstio ventilabitur, vestris querelis quibuscumque taliter responsuri quod rationis exigente dictamine

---

LXVII.] MS. Cotton. Calig. D. III. fol. 178 (*a*).—On paper; a contemporaneous MS.

A.D. 1403. debebitis esse contenti. Sed quia neminem sanæ mentis inveniri putamus quin lucide cognoscat parvum prodesse præterita damna, privatas dumtaxat personas respicientia, reparare, futuris injuriis quæ publicam in tantum læderent utilitatem aditum planum relinquendo, non veremur loci mutationem requirere, quem videlicet locum juramento acceptatum non poteritis comprobare, nec in indenturis super hoc confectis reperiri: attento maxime quod, sicut vestræ litteræ circa finem sentire videntur, sine dicta loci mutatione impossibile esset super securitate providere, honore serenissimi Principis et Domini nostri supremi, Regis Franciæ, necnon metuendissimi Domini nostri, Ducis Burgundiæ, Comitis Flandriæ, obstante.

*requesting that some other place be chosen.* Quapropter vestras Dominationes attentius quo valemus hortamur quatinus, nostræ petitioni annuentes, locum medium una cum conveniente termino nostris ambassiatoribus seu deputatis, sine damnosa dilatione, designari eædem vestræ Dominationes procurent; vel, in eorum absentia, per latorem præsentium nobis transcribere; alioquin incolis patriæ et comitatus Flandriæ, necnon aliis mercatoribus extraneis, ad quorum notitiam præsentia pervenient, lucide poterit apparere vestram partem discordiæ potius occasionem quærere quam utilitatem communis mercaturæ inter Angliam et Flandriam affectare.

Dominationes vestras venerabiles conservare dignetur Altissimus per tempora longiora felices!

Scriptum die xxiiij mensis Decembris, sub sigillo dictæ villæ Gandensis pro nobis omnibus.

SCABINI et CONSULES VILLÆ GANDENSIS, necnon DEPUTATI Villarum Brugensis, Yprensis, ac Franci territorii, ad placita Gandensis principaliter congregati.

*Endorsement :*—"Nobilibus, honorabilibus, ac magnificis viris, excellentissimi Regis Angliæ Ambassiatoribus, Calisii præsentialiter existentibus."

A.D. 1403.

## LXVIII.

LUTTRELL, CROFT, ETC. TO THE FLEMISH DEPUTIES.

*Litteræ Ambassiatorum Angliæ transmissæ Quatuor Membris Flandriæ, ipsorum litteris in qualibet particula responsivæ.*

*Et primo recitatur tenor dictarum litterarum Quatuor Membrorum :—*

Honorabiles ac magnifici et circumspecti Domini. Ex parte honorabilium ac magnificorum Dominorum, Scabinorum, Consulum, villæ Gandensis, necnon deputatorum vestrarum villarum Brugensis, Yprensis, ac territorii Franci officii certas litteras, scriptas vicesimo quarto die præsentis mensis Decembris,[1] sigillo villæ Gandensis sigillatas, quibusdam aliis nostris litteris Quatuor Membris Flandriæ alias intitulatis et directis responsivas, recepimus Calesii vicesimo sexto die ejusdem mensis Decembris, inter cetera continentes, quod, licet nostris allegationibus, in memoratis litteris nostris expressatis, satis commode ac faciliter, prout dicitis, poteritis respondere, ne tamen scintilla discordiæ in tanto negotio, ubi concordiam quæritis et favorem, argumentorum involutione generetur, eisdem nihilominus litteris nostris pro præsenti respondere supersedistis et distulistis loco et tempore quibus principaliter quæstio ventilabitur nostris querelis quibuscumque taliter responsuri quod, rationis exigente dictamine, merito debeamus contentari. Sed quia neminem sanæ mentis invenire putatis quin lucide

*In reply to the foregoing;*

---

LXVIII.] MS. Cotton. Calig. D. III. fol. 178 (β). — On paper: a contemporaneous MS.

[1] See Letter LXVII.

M

A.D. 1403. cognoscat parum prodesse præterita damna, privatas personas dumtaxat respicientia, reparare, futuris injuriis quæ publicam in tantum læderent utilitatem aditum planum relinquendo, et sic non deceret, secundum vos, in reparatione attemptatorum privata et particulari primo procedere ac reparationem attemptatorum indiscussam, quæ respicit utilitatem publicam, relinquere, seu alias pro tempore suspendere ac prorogare. Quibus consideratis non veremini loci mutationem requirere ; quem locum, prout asseritis, per vestrum juramentum, nec in indenturis de partium consensu confectis poterimus comprobare ; attento maxime quod hujusmodi litteræ nostræ circa hunc (finem) sentire videantur quod impossibile est super securitate providere absque loci mutatione, honore Domini vestri Regis Francorum, quem pro præsenti denominatis Dominum vestrum supremum, necnon Domini vestri Ducis Burgundiæ Comitis Flandriæ obstante. Concludendo petitis quod vestræ petitioni deberemus annuere, ac in locum medium una cum conveniente termino consentire, ac super hoc vobis rescribere, ac aliis mercatoribus extraneis, ad quorum notitiam præsentia pervenient, in futurum clare poterit apparere nostram partem discordiæ potius occasionem quærere, quam utilitatem communis mercaturæ inter Angliam et Flandriam affectare.

complaining that they of Flanders had broken their oaths, Ad quæ, quantum ad loci mutationem ex continuatione et prorogatione super reparatione attemptatorum de consensu expresso vestrorum ambassiatorum facta, primo, in Anglia apud Westmonasterium, vicesimo septimo die mensis Martii ultimo præterito, usque ad villam Calisii, videlicet ad primum diem mensis Julii ex tunc proxime futurum, prout patet in certo appunctuamento puro et simplici, nulla conditione restricto, de consensu partium indentato, quod appunctuamentum ac etiam treugas generales inter Angliam et Franciam initas, quamvis Gallici eas velint infringere, abstrinxistis

vos per vestrum juramentum servare, ac subsequenter A.D. 1408.
in villa Calisii usque ad decimum diem Novembris
ex tunc proxime futurum in eadem villa Calisii secuta
alia continuatione, prout hæc omnia ex appunctuamentis
et indenturis diversis vobis transmissis, ac ex instru-
mento originali super hujusmodi vestro juramento con-
fecto, alias vobis transmisso, et per vestrum nuncium,
præsentium portitorem, in præsenti vobis remisso, clare
poterimus ostendere, et ex sigillis vestris et instrumentis
publicis merito comprobare, adeo quod eisdem in futurum
de jure et ratione non poteritis contradicere, seu commode respondere. Sed est impossibile ipsa quovis colore
quæsito defensare, quamvis loco et tempore opportunis
quibus tractabitur quæstio principalis vestras Reverentias quibuscumque nostris querelis ut prætenditis velle
respondere ac rationi condescendere, cessante quacumque
subtilitate, adeo quod merito debeamus contentari—quod
Deus concedat! Non enim est dubium, sed notorium
considerando acta nostra communia inter vestros ambassiatores ac nostros gesta,—nunquam servastis, vestris
Reverentiis salvis, vestra juramenta, seu appunctuamenta per vestros ambassiatores sigillata seu inden-
tata, et præsertim quoad bona mercatorum Angliæ in
Sclusa per vestras Reverentias ex certa scientia vestra
arrestata,—

Primo, post et contra dictum appunctuamentum and that
factum per vestros ambassiatores apud Westmonas- the goods
terium, ac vestris juramentis subsequenter, ut præfertur, had been
roboratum, quodque lite pendente super reparatione seized
attemptatorum coram judicibus ac ambassiatoribus (1) after,
utriusque partis dictum arrestum fuit factum, contra lation of,
juris ordinem, et sic tanquam in jure privilegiatum the agree-
ante quamcumque aliam reparationem fiendam, hujus- which they
modi arrestum est revocandum, et in pristinum statum had sworn;
restituendum. and

Secundo, hujusmodi arrestum fuit factum post et (2) after
contra litteras Quatuor Membrorum Flandriæ, litteras their
et sigilla vestra propria violando. the same
effect;

M 2

A.D. 1403.
(3) against the truce and
(4) the privilege, granted by the Duke of Burgundy.
The English Ambassadors insist on the necessity of immediate restitution,

Tertio, contra treugas generales inter Angliam et Franciam initas, vestris juramentis confirmatas:

Quarto, post et contra privilegium Domini vestri, Domini Ducis Burgundiæ, Comitis Flandriæ, de non arrestando concessum, violando etiam ipsius sigillum, ac faciendo illud adulterinum.

Merito igitur hujusmodi attemptatum lite pendente contra juris ordinem, ac contra vestras scripturas proprias et Domini vestri, ac ipsas et vestris sigillis sigillatas, necnon contra treugas prædictas vestris juramentis confirmatas, ac contra dictum appunctuamentum apud Westmonasterium factum, nulla conditione restrictum, vestrisque juramentis subsequentibus approbatum, ante quamcumque aliam reparationem fiendam, est revocandum et restituendum. Unde. quamvis istud attemptatum respiciens privatas personas a jure ac per vestras litteras et appunctuamenta, et per vestra juramenta, ut præfertur, privilegiatum, ante aliam reparationem quamcumque fiendam fuerit, ut præmittitur, executioni mandandum, et in hoc respicit utilitatem publicam propter justitiam cuilibet privato indifferenter ministrandam, ac etiam cum hujusmodi appunctuamentum factum apud Westmonasterium fuerit editum propter utilitatem privatam tam regni Angliæ, quam comitatus Flandriæ, propter pacem firmandam, seu alias propter conservationem treugarum per utramque partem juratarum, per quod appunctuamentum arrestum maxime in bonis certum fuit prohibitum ; et in hoc respublica utitur jure privati, quamvis respublica in pluribus utitur jure speciali, præsertim cum hujusmodi attemptatum privilegiatum respiciens utilitatem privatorum, attemptatum aliorum attemptatorum utilitatem publicam secundum vos respicientium non absorbeat, seu in toto extinguat, sed usque ad tempus suspendat,—videlicet quod fiat plenaria restitutio dictorum bonorum in Sclusa arrestatorum. Et sic non parum, prout scribitis, sed valde prodest præterita damna privatas personas dumtaxat respicientia reparare, etc.

Et revera de vestris litteris in pluribus expressatis A.D. 1403.
nullatenus admirari non poterimus, cum nostras litteras and com-
vobis nuper directas, quarum copias penes nos semper plain that the mean-
retinemus, ad intellectum perniciosum—quia contra verba ing of their
et sensum verborum ipsarum litterarum—nitamini tra- letter had been per-
here, ac propriis vestimentis exuere ac vestimenta nova verted.
et mendicata per inadvertentiam, seu aliter per negli-
gentiam vel calumniam vestrorum clericorum vestras
litteras scribentium, eis attribuere : scribitis enim quod
litteræ nostræ prope finem sentire videntur quod impossibile est super securitate providere absque loci mutatione; salva reverentia illorum clericorum novitiorum
volentium nostras litteras a vero sensu et a propria
significatione vocabili avertere, ac ipsa verba corrumpere,
et intellectum vitiosum vobis imprimere.

Scripsimus enim in fine litterarum nostrarum in They quote
hæc verba :—" Et quamvis super ordinatione treugarum a portion of this
" inter Angliam et Flandriam, quoad terræ et maris letter ;
" securitatem perpetuam in futurum fiendam, expedit
" auctoritatem et consensum Domini Ducis Burgundiæ,
" qui est Comes Flandriæ, intervenire, ac etiam forsan
" Domini sui ligei, ipsorum Domini, ut præmittitur, su-
" premi, intervenire ; non tamen in reparatione attemp-
" tatorum, quæ habet fieri non in bonis prædictorum
" Dominorum, sed de bonis Flandrensium tantum, qui
" damna incolis Angliæ intulerunt. Ideo super hujus-
" modi reparatione attemptatorum non expedit consen-
" sum ipsorum Dominorum per se vel per suos ambas-
" siatores intervenire, sed quod Quatuor Membra Flan-
" driæ velint cautionem sufficientem præstare de stando
" jure et de judicio solvendo."

Ecce ergo quod vere seu interpretative nulla talis and point
clausula in litteris nostris reperitur, videlicet quod out the perversion
impossibile est super securitate providere absque loci of their meaning.
mutatione ; sed istæ duæ dictiones in nostris litteris
sunt expressata *expedit* et *forsan*, quæ sunt verba avi-
satoria et deliberatoria, ac per modum avisamenti et

A.D. 1403. consilii expressata, ad totam clausulam præcedentem vel sequentem de Jure Civili et Canonico extensiva.

*They also affirm that the Flemish Deputies have no right to ask for a change of place,*

Honor enim Domini vestri Regis Francorum, quem vocatis Dominum vestrum supremum, seu etiam Domini vestri immediati, Domini Ducis Burgundiæ, Comitis Flandriæ, non poterit inducere loci mutationem, quantum ad tractatum nostrum communem, per vestrum consensum proprium sub sigillis vestris expressatum ac juramento vallatum. Liberum enim ab initio erat honorem prædictorum Dominorum vestrorum salvum facere, ac locum indifferentem in origine tractatus eligere, ac per vestræ accessionis, quam accessionem originaliter non allegastis, respectum Gallicorum ad tractatum accedere, prout apud Lulyngham inter Angliam et Franciam hactenus est fieri consuetum. Sed inter Angliam et Flandriam, quantum ad locum extra districtum Domini nostri Regis Angliæ mutandum, penitus est mandatum, nec unquam fuit visum. Ideo petere alium locum, maxime post et contra vestrum consensum proprium, denotat magnam inconstantiam ac variationem.

*but that they are ready for the sake of peace to consent to the arrangement.*

Hujusmodi tamen variatione vestra, necnon contradictione inordinata et illegitima, non obstante, parati sumus pro bono pacis, prout aliter vobis scripsimus, locum medium seu indifferentem eligere ; ac justitiam, quantum in nobis est, partibus ministrare, —ponderatis tamen prædictis appunctuamentis, ac vestris juramentis postea secutis, et quod hujusmodi arrestum dictorum bonorum in Sclusa factum per vestras Reverentias contra juris ordinem lite pendente fuit interpositum, ac contra treugas generales per vos juratas, ac contra vestras litteras proprias vestris sigillis sigillatas, necnon contra privilegium a Domino vestro concessum, et contra appunctuamentum commune nulla conditione restrictum, vestris que juramentis vallatum, prout superius per extensum est expressatum ;—considerando etiam quod serenissimus ac

illustrissimus Princeps, Dominus noster Rex, qui hac- A.D. 1403. tenus afficiebatur vestris partibus Flandriæ, ac afficitur, prout de ipsius mandato vobis etiam intimamus in præsenti, ac treugas appetit inire inter regnum suum Angliæ ac patriam Flandriæ, et illas inviolabiliter observandas, et plurium attemptatorum et damnorum illatorum per incolas Angliæ vestris Flandrensibus, prout Johanni Paldyng de Ypris, et aliis, fecit fieri realem restitutionem, ac de aliis mandavit fieri justitiæ comple- mentum ;—pensato insuper quod super relaxatione dicti arresti, ac super restitutione bonorum hujusmodi arres- tatorum, certam responsionem vestram imaginariam, ac penitus inauditam, post diversas dilationes ad plenius respondendum vestris ambassiatoribus concessas, pro parte vestra recepimus ; cujus copiam, cum quadam nostra replicatione ad eandem responsionem, una cum certis articulis relaxationem dicti arresti continentibus, mittimus vobis per præsentium portitorem ad vestram informationem pleniorem ;—attento etiam quod præfatus Dominus noster Rex subditis et ligeis suis quorum bona in Sclusa sunt arrestata, per viam arresti consimilis, aut reprisaliarum, seu marquæ, hactenus recusavit providere, volens rigorem juris omittere, ac affectionem et pacem enutrire et continuare : ad quæ omnia superius expressata non curastis advertere, sed per dilationes frivolas et diffugia restitutionem dictorum bonorum protelare.

Unde, si vultis ad præmissa diligentius solito attendere, ac cum saniori consilio deliberare, potius quæritis occasionem discordiæ quam utilitatem communis mercaturæ affectare.

Quæ omnia et singula tam vestris mercatoribus, ac aliis vestris popularibus Flandriæ, ac etiam auribus mercatorum, tam Stapulæ quam aliorum quorumcumque, procurabimus intimare, ac merito inculcare, et eadem lucide declarare.

Vestras igitur Reverentias et Dominationes rogamus, They demand restitution,

A.D. 1403. ac preciso et peremptorie requirimus et exhortamur in Domino, quatinus juxta tenorem appunctuamentorum ac vestrorum juramentorum prædictorum, necnon omnium aliorum et singulorum superius expressorum, circa xij diem Januarii proxime futurum, arrestum dictorum bonorum faciatis effectualiter relaxari, ac ipsa bona illis quorum sunt, absque diminutione et deterioratione, realiter restitui ; cum idem Dominus noster Rex paratus existat quodcumque arrestum consimile intra regnum suum in bonis Flandrensium, etiam interpositum ante quamcunque aliam reparationem fiendam relaxare, ac hujusmodi bonorum arrestatorum restitutionem finalem facere fieri ; prout vestram honestatem ac legalitatem, necnon vestra sigilla et juramenta vestra prædicta, appetitis defendere, ac pœnam perjurii et infamiæ pro perpetuo evitare.

*and promise it on their own part.*

Super quibus omnibus, circa præfatum xij diem Januarii, placeat nobis per præsentium portitorem rescribere, et, facta restitutione dictorum bonorum, taliter ordinare quod vestri ambassiatores cum potestate sufficiente, qui habent a nobis salvum-conductum sufficientem, eodem die nobiscum velint convenire, ac locum eligere, et vestram voluntatem in omnibus absque dilatione ulteriori nobis declarare, prout vestris Dominationibus et Reverentiis videbitur expedire.

Quas custodiat Altissimus feliciter juxta votum !

Scriptum Calisii, vicesimo nono die Decembris.

*Instructio qualiter Quatuor Membra debent examinare litteras suas nobis transmissas, et litteras nostras eis transmissas :—*

Et, ut plenum intellectum litterarum vestrarum nobis transmissarum, ac etiam nostrarum vobis remissarum, absque sinistra informatione clericorum vestrorum, poteritis clare concipere, placeat nostras litteras pri-

mitus vobis transmissas, cum vestris litteris responsivis A.D. 1403. per præsentium portitorem nobis remissis, una cum præsentibus, insimul conjungere ac easdem insimul visitare.

Supplicamus insuper quod nostras litteras, Domino Duci Burgundiæ ac magno Concilio Franciæ directas,[1] et per præsentium portitorem vobis præsentandis, placeat eisdem Parisius transmittere, ac de eisdem nobis facere responderi, et super iis cum aliis nobis rescribere.

HUGO LUTREL;

JOHANNES DE CROFT,—Milites ;

NICHOLAUS DE RYSSHETOUN, Utriusque Juris Professor ; ac

JOHANNES URBAN,
            Ambassiatores pro parte Angliæ.


*Endorsement* :—"Honorabilibus ac magnificis Dominis, Burgimagistris, Scabinis, et Consulibus Gandensis, Brugensis, Yprensis ac territorii Franciæ officii partium Flandriæ, ac ipsorum deputatis."

---

[1] See Letter LXVI.

A.D. 1403.

## LXIX.

### LUTTRELL, CROFT, ETC., TO HENRY IV.

They report the progress they have made,

Serenissime Princeps, ac illustrissime et invictissime Domine.

Quia Quatuor Membra Flandriæ pro attemptatorum reparatione ad tractatum recusabant accedere, prout recusant in præsenti nisi locum indifferentem velimus eligere, extra vestram villam Calisii : quodque super diversis litteris vestræ Excellentiæ super mutatione loci transmissis, nullum responsum pro tunc reportavimus, scripsimus eis litteras monitorias et requisitorias, quarum copias [1] mittimus vestræ Majestati præsentibus interclusas, quatinus, juxta formam juramentorum suorum ac appunctuamentorum per utramque partem sigillatorum, tractatum in vestra villa Calisii velint continuare. Super quibus dicta Quatuor Membra Flandriæ non curabant hactenus nobis rescribere, nec ipsorum voluntatem declarare. Die Mercurii tamen, decimo nono præsentis mensis Decembris, certas litteras, ex parte Concilii vestri emanatas, una cum quadam instructione nova super mutatione loci recepimus, ad locum alium extra vestram villam Calisii juxta nostram discretionem poterimus eligere, ac super reparatione attemptatorum juxta formam etiam alterius instructionis nobis traditæ, ad ulteriora procedere.

Unde quamvis prædictæ litteræ generaliter quoad loci mutationem declarent vestram voluntatem regiam,

---

LXIX.] MS. Cotton. Calig. D, III. fol. 177.—On paper ; original, with marks of the seals.

[1] See Letter LXVIII.

non tamen specialiter juxta tenorem certarum aliarum A.D. 1403.
litterarum nostrarum, ultimo vestræ Excellentiæ transmissarum, videlicet utrum debeamus consentire in alium
locum, intra tamen districtum vestræ villæ Calisii,
vel extra districtum Calisii,—prout apud Lulyngham,
seu alias apud Gravelyng,—juxta partis adversæ petitionem et intentionem instantem; seu alias uno die
intra districtum Calisii, alio die extra.

Super quo dignetur vestra regia Majestas vestram and re-
intentionem et voluntatem lucidius declarare, ac ipsam quest
nobis absque dilatione remittere, adeo quod ad ulteriora further instructions.
super reparatione attemptatorum poterimus clare procedere, absque offensa et indignatione vestræ Majestatis
excellentissimæ.

Item, excellentissime Domine, remittimus vestræ
Excellentiæ Regiæ quendam salvum-conductum, alias
super facultate piscandi, piscatoribus Franciæ et Flandriæ, usque ad certum terminum quasi in præsenti
elapsum, per vestram regiam Majestatem concessum;
super cujus renovatione usque ad annum, seu aliter
ad certum terminum, prout vestræ Majestati videbitur expediens et opportunum, vestro almo Concilio
quoad hujusmodi salvum-conductum placeat committere, ac vestram voluntatem absque dilatione, cum
hujusmodi salvo-conductu, nobis remittere et penitus
declarare.

Item, de litteris transmissis Domino Duci Burgundiæ,
ac Magno Concilio Franciæ,[1] juxta tenorem aliarum
nostrarum litterarum, in præsenti nobis non extitit
responsum, quamvis quotidie credamus obtinere responsionem, ac ipsorum, prout asseritur, finalem intentionem.

Nova non sunt, nisi quod Comes Sancti Pauli, prout News of
fertur, reversus est Parisius. the Count
of St. Pol.

---

[1] See Letter LXVI.

A.D. 1403.    Vestram Majestatem sanctissimam custodiat Trinitas
Increata, ad felix regimen regni vestri juxta votum !

Vestræ  Majestatis excellentissimæ
commissarii, et nuncii, ac servitores humillimi,
HUGO LUTRELL, Locumtenens Calisii,
JOHANNES CROFFT,—Milites;
NICHOLAUS DE RYSSHETOUN ; ac
JOHANNES URBAN.

*Endorsed :*—"Serenissimo Principi, illustrissimo  et
invictissimo Domino, H., Dei gratia
Regi Angliæ et Franciæ excellentissimo . . . . . . . ." [1]

*Also :*—" Touchant l'instruction a estr[e] . . . . . . .
envoiee as Ambassatours estea[ntz
de present] a Calays."

## LXX.

### HENRY IV. TO HIS PRIVY COUNCIL.

Depar le Roy.

Requesting
them to
attend to
the de-
mands of
the Eng-
lish Am-
bassadors
in Flan-
ders.

Reverent Pere en Dieu, nostre treschier et tresame frere, et noz treschiers et foialx.

[TRANSLATION.]

By the King.

Reverend Father in God, our most dear and well-beloved
brother, and our very dear and trusty.—We have sent unto

---

[1] This letter was probably written
on the 29th of December, when the
preceding letter, a copy of which
was enclosed in it, was written. If
not, it must, at all events, have been
written on the 30th or the 31st, as

it was clearly not written before
No. LXVIII., and mention is made
in it of "the present month of
December."

LXX.] MS. Cotton. Calig. D. III
fol. 176.—On vellum ; original.

Nous vous envoions, closee deinz cestes, une lettre[1] A.D. 1403.
a nous envoiee par noz commissairs et deputies par
nous assignez a traiter ovec les commissairs de
ceux de Flaundres, pour la reformation de les attemp-
tates d'ambe partz, faissante mention d'assignation
par nous a faire d'un lieu en certein, ou si bien noz
ditz commissairs, comme les commissairs d'autre part,
pourront faire lour assemblee pour la traitee avantdit;
et auxi du renouvellement d'une saufconduyt par nous
naguiers grante a les pesceours de Fraunce et de
Flaundres, sicomme par la susdicte lettre il vous pourra
plainement apparoire.

Si voulons et vous mandons que, quant a l'assignation du lieu susdit, vous le fatez ordenner et assigner
la ou par vostre boun avis il semblera plus conve-

---

you, inclosed in these presents, a letter sent unto us by our
commissaries and deputies, assigned by us to treat with the
commissaries of them of Flanders, for the reformation of the
attempts on either side, making mention of the assignation by
us to fix a certain place, where as well our said commissaries, as
the commissaries of the other side, might hold their assembly
for the treaty aforesaid ; and also concerning the renewal of a
safe-conduct by us lately granted to the fishermen of France
and of Flanders, as by the above-mentioned letter it may
appear to you more fully.—We will, therefore, and command
you that, as to the assigning of a place, as aforesaid, you cause
to ordain and assign it wherever by your good counsels it shall

---

[1] This letter is not an answer to
the preceding one, though at first
sight it appears to be ; but it is clear
that they were both written on, or
about, the same day, and that they
crossed each other on the way to
their respective destinations. It is
a reply (through the Council) to a
letter of the same purport written
several days before (which has not
been found), one of the several
letters from the Ambassadors to
Henry IV. which they complain
had not been answered—" *super
diversis* litteris vestræ Excellentiæ
super mutatione loci transmissis,
nullum responsum pro tunc reportavimus." See also Letter LXXIII.

A.D. 1403. nient et expedient pour mesme la traitee, par instruction ent a donnir a noz ditz commissairs par nos lettres a faire dessoubz nostre prive seel en due forme. Et, quant a le renouvellement du dit saufconduyt, nous voulons que, eue de ce d'entre vous bonne communication avecques aucuns des plus souffisans pesceours deinz nostre cite de Londres, en cas qu'il vous semble, par leure information et avis, que la dicte saufconduyt pourra bonnement par nous estre grantee, sainz prejudice ou vraisemblable damage de nous et de noz foiaulx liges, vous le fatez renouveller, a durer par tant de temps que mieulx vous semblera et verrez estre necessaire et expedient en celle partie.

Donne soubz nostre signet, a Abyndon, le xxix jour de Decembre.

*Endorsed :*—" A nostre Conseil . . . . . . . . . . . . . .
                       a Loundres . . . . . . . . . ."

seem more convenient and expedient for the same treaty, by giving instruction in this matter to our said commissaries by our letters under our privy seal in due form. And, as to the renewal of the said safe-conduct, we will that, after good communication had between you with any fishermen of sufficient standing within our city of London, in case that it seem to you, by their information and advice, that the said safe-conduct can be properly granted by you, without prejudice or likely damage to us and our faithful lieges, you cause to renew it, to last for so long a time as shall seem best to you, and you shall deem to be necessary and expedient in this behalf.—Given under our signet, at Abingdon, the 29th day of December.

*Endorsed :*—" To our Council . . . . . . . . . . . . . . . . .
                       at London."

A.D. 1403.

## LXXI.

### JOHN I. KING OF PORTUGAL TO HENRY IV.

*Muitalto, muy nobre, e muy excelente e poderoso Principe, nosso muy amado e muy precado irmaão e amigo, Rey d'Ingraterra, de França, e Senhor d'Irlanda, nos el Rey de Portugal e d'Algarve, vosso irmaão e verdadeiro amigo, de todo curaçom vos envyamos muyto saudar como a irmão e amigo que muy verdadeiramente amamos e preçamos sobre todo los Principes do mundo, e para que queriamos que desse Deus longa vida e saude, com grande exalçamento d'honnra, tanto como vos mesmo deseiades.*

Muy nobre Rey, irmaão, e amigo. Bem sabedes como vos fezemos saber per Joham Gomez da Silva, nosso alferez, e de nosso Consilho, 

On their mutual alliance with the King of Castile.

---

### [TRANSLATION.]

*Most high, most noble, and most excellent and powerful Prince, our most beloved and most esteemed brother and friend, King of England, of France, and Lord of Ireland, we the King of Portugal and of Algarve, your brother and true friend, from all our heart send you much salutation, as to a brother and friend whom we most truly love and esteem above all the Princes of the world, and because we desire that God may give long life and health, with great exaltation of honours, as much as you yourself . may desire.*

Most noble King, brother, and friend.—You know well that we informed you by John Gomez da Silva, our standard-

---

LXXI.] MS. Cotton. Nero., B. I. fol. 28. On paper; original, with marks of the seal.

A.D. 1403. e per o Doutor Martim Dossem, que a vos envyamos com nossa ambaxada, que avyamos feitas e firmadas tregoas por dez annos com el Rey de Castella com condiçom que fossedes vos posto em ellas como nosso aliado que sodes. Par o beerdes : e se vos pruguesse desseer nas dittas tregoas e gonvyr d'ellas as reteficardes e nos envyardes dello vossa carta, par per ella certeficaremos o ditto Rey de Castella segundo se contem nos trautos das dittas tregoas, e o ditto Doutor nos mandou aco duas cartas çarradas[1] que envyasdes andes. Em nas quees se contynha que a vos plazia desseer nas dittas tregoas e gonvenir d'ellas e as retificardes ; das quaas cartas nos logo mandamos huma ao ditto Rey de Castella e vista per ello e per os de seu Consellho diserom que porque veera çarrada a nos e nom era

bearer, and of our Council, and by the Doctor Martin Dossem, whom we have sent to you with our embassy, that we had made and concluded treaties for ten years with the King of Castile, with the condition that you should be put in them as our ally, which you are. By this you will see : and if it should please you to be in the said treaties and agree with them, you should ratify them and send them to us with a letter of yours, by which we would certify to the said King of Castile according to what our draft of the said treaties contains. And the said Doctor sent hither to us two enclosed documents which you had sent previously. In which it is contained that it had pleased you to be in the said treaties, and to agree with them, and which you would ratify ; of which papers we immediately sent one to the said King of Castile, and when seen by him and by those of his Council, they said that because it was enclosed to us, and

---

[1] *çarradas.*] This is a doubtful reading. It is probably an ancient way of spelling " serradas," from an obsolete word, meaning "to enclose," for which in modern Portuguese " fechar " is used.

posta em ella a ora quando fora feita, nem tragia seelo A.D. 1403.
outentico que se podesse conhocer, que por tanto a nom
avyam por aprovado; e que coupera Deos certifica-
remos por outra carta nossa que voosse abreda e
posta em ella a ora e firmada de nosso nome
e seellada de nosso seelo pendente outentico.

E porem, irmaão, amigo, vos rogamos que pois vos
prougue de conssentirdes nas dittas tregoas, e de
gonvyr dellas, e nollo envyastes dizer par as dittas
vossas cartas, que vos plazia de nos envyar huma tal
carta de sobre esto, e seia feita per huma forma que
mandamos ao ditto Doutor Martim Dossem, e aman-
dedes dar ao ditto Doutor para nola envyar, e
faredes em elo cousa que vos muyto gradiceremos.

Muytalto, muy nobre, e muy poderoso Principe,
nosso muy amado e muy preçado irmaão e amigo,
Dios vos aia em Sua guarda e encommenda e acre-
cente vosso stado e honnra!

---

because the date when it was made was not put in it,
nor did it bear any authentic seal which could be known,
they for these reasons did not approve of it; and that
we should certify before God by another document from
our part that it was engraved, and the date put in it and
confirmed by our name, and sealed with our authentic seal
depending. — And, therefore, brother, friend, we request
you, that since it pleases you to consent to the said treaties,
and to agree with them, and you have sent to tell us thereof
by the aforesaid documents, that it may please you to send
us one such paper in addition, and that it may be made
like a form which we send to the said Doctor Martin
Dossem, and cause it to be given to the said Doctor to
send it to us, and you shall do by that a thing for which
we shall be exceedingly obliged to you.—Most high, most
noble, and most powerful Prince, our most beloved and
esteemed brother and friend, may God have you under
His protection, and forward and increase your estate and

N

A.D. 1403.    Scritto na cidade de Lisboa, xxx dies do mez de Deçembro.

Yo El Rey.

*Endorsed :*—" Ao muytalto, muy nobre, e muy excelente e poderoso Principe, nosso muy amado e muy precado irmãao e amigo, Rey d'Ingraterra, de França, e Senor d'Irlanda."

---

honours !—Written in the City of Lisbon, the 30th day of the month of December.

I the King.

*Endorsed :*—" To the most high, most noble, and most excellent and powerful Prince, our most beloved and most esteemed brother and friend, King of England, of France, and Lord of Ireland."

## LXXII.

A.D. 1404.    LUTTRELL, CROFT, AND DE RYSSHETON TO THE MAGISTRATES AT BRUGES.

*Littera ambassiatorum Angliæ, responsiva litteris Brugensium, super restitutione vini transmissa, etc.*

On the restitution of some wine, supposed to belong to

Honorabiles, ac magnifici, et circumspecti Domini.

Ex parte vestra certas litteras vestras, scriptas vicesimo nono Decembris,[1] recepimus Calisii ultimo die ejusdem mensis Decembris, inter cetera continentes,

---

LXXII.] MS. Cotton. Caligula, D. III. fol. 178 (γ).—On paper ; a contemporaneous MS.

qualiter, licet treugæ in singulis portubus Flandriæ
fuerint proclamatæ, ac de mandato Domini vestri, ac
etiam ex parte Quatuor Membrorum Flandriæ, inhibitum publice et expresse, quod nullus Flandrensis
prædam seu inprisam in bonis Anglicorum per terram
seu per mare reciperet, quodque post proclamationem
ac mandatum prædictum pro parte vestra nihil in
contrarium, prout asseritis, extitit attemptatum; his
tamen non obstantibus, quædam navis armata,
" Balengier" vulgariter nuncupata, de portu Calisii
fuit insecuta quamdam navem vestram de Sciedamme
venientem de Rupella cum vinis onustam, ac ipsam
venientem de Rupella in prædam recepit, una cum
viginti una tonnellis vini in eadem navi existentibus,
signatis certo signo in vestris litteris expressatis,
supplicando petitis, pro bono pacis, ac pro incre-
mento communis mercandisæ, quatinus dicta vina seu
eorum valorem velimus facere restitui, prout convenit
rationi.

Respondendo ad præmissa, vobis tenore præsentium
notificamus qualiter in singulis portubus Angliæ, et
in villa Calisii, fuit inhibitum de mandato Domini
nostri Regis, qui pacem vobiscum, prout pridie per
alias litteras nostras vobis declaravimus, voluit enutrire,
quod nullus ligeus suus navigio vestro Flandrensi
revertenti hac vice de Rupella, cum suis vinis et aliis
mercimoniis, violentiam inferret, seu alias quovis modo
molestaret. Et, nisi istud mandatum Domini nostri
Regis sub forma prædicta emanasset, forsan quod
nulla navis vestra evasisset; quidam tamen nautæ
de villa Calisii, informati quod certæ naves de navigio
vestro erant onustæ cum vinis Gallicorum, prædictam
navem invaserunt, ac dicta vina, juxta tenorem
litterarum vestrarum, receperunt; quas, statim prout
intelleximus, viginti unam tonnellas vini fecimus ar-
restari, et sub salva custodia reponi, adeo quod,

A.D. 1404. termino adveniente super reparatione utriusque partis fienda, si vina vere fuit Flandrensium vestrorum, non Gallicorum, faciemus fieri ipsorum vinorum restitutionem, seu aliter, quantum ad valorem secundum omnem rationem.

*They remind them of the misdeeds of their own people,*
Reducere tamen debetis memoriæ vestræ qualiter vestri Flandrenses, non solum de Gravelyng, sed de diversis partibus Flandriæ, nostros Anglicos in mari, diversis vicibus non faciliter numerabilibus, post dictam prætensam vestram proclamationem spoliarunt, ac bona ipsorum in prædam receperunt; ac nostros nautas et piscatores, prout clare novistis, in mari submerserunt; ac nuperime quamdam navem nostram, onustam cum pellibus Anglicorum de Hibernia, etiam ceperunt, ac nautas omnes et singulos in mari submerserunt, ac subsequenter pelles in vestra villa Brugensi vendiderunt, absque eo quod de nullo spolio facto per vestros in bonis Anglicorum in mari hactenus nullam fecistis fieri reparationem seu restitutionem, quod nobis et nostris, pensata affectione quam Dominus noster Rex semper vobis ostendit et exhibuit, est nimis grave et molestum, nisi celerius pro parte vestra apponatur remedium opportunum.

*and request an answer to their letters on that subject.*
Scripsimus enim vobis, ac aliis tribus Membris Partium Flandriæ, certas litteras nostras[1] sub datam xxix die mensis Decembris, vel circiter, per vestrum cursorem Torbot transmissas, aliis vestris litteris responsivas, una cum certis aliis litteris Domino vestro Duci Burgundiæ, ac Magno Concilio Franciæ, per vos, si placeat, transmittendas.[2]

Super quibus placeat, juxta ipsarum continentiam et tenorem, per dictum Torbot, seu aliter per alium cursorem, celeriter nobis respondere, ac vestram vo-

---

[1] See Letter LXVIII.　　　[2] See Letter LXVI.

luntatem in omnibus lucidius declarare, prout vestris A.D. 1404.
Reverentiis et Dominationibus videbiter expedire.

Quas custodiat Altissimus feliciter et votive!

Scriptum Calisii, secundo die Januarii.

> Hugo Lutrell,
> Johannes de Crofft,—Milites;
> Nicholaus de Rysshetoun, Utri-
> usque Juris Professor, ac
> Johannes Urban,
> Ambassiatores pro parte Angliæ.

*Endorsement :*—" Honorabilibus ac magnificis Dominis, Burgimagistris, Scabinis, et
Consulibus villæ Brugensis."

## LXXIII.

Luttrell, Croft, and De Ryssheton to Henry IV.

Serenissime Princeps, ac excellentissime et invictis- On the
sime Domine, votiva ac humillima recommendatione treachery
of the Fle-
præmissa, tanto Domino, nostro ligeo illustrissimo, tam mish.
debita quam devota.

Vestras litteras regias recepimus sub vestro sigillo They acknowledge
privato sigillatas, scriptas apud Westmonasterium the receipt
decimo octavo die mensis Decembris ultime præterito, of the
King's let-
una cum quadam instructione obscura, (prout fuit alia ter,
super eadem materia nobis nuper transmissa), in eisdem
interclusa, necnon certas alias vestras litteras sub vestro si gneto regio consignatas, una cum quadam billa
Johannis Fitz-Richard, Roberti Coventre, ac plurium
aliorum mercatorum Londoniæ in eisdem interclusa,

---

LXXIII.] MS. Cotton. Galba, B. i. fol. 113.—On paper; original, with traces of the seals.

A.D. 1404. inter cetera continentes qualiter certa bona dictorum mercatorum in Sclusa indebite fuerunt, prout sunt arrestata in præsenti; quodque juxta ipsarum litterarum vestrarum formam et continentiam, scripsimus quasdam litteras Burgimagistris, Scabinis, et Consulibus Gandensis, Brugensis, Yprensis, et territorii Franci officii partium Flandriæ, responsivas quibusdam aliis litteris, per ipsos nobis alias directis; ipsos in eisdem nostris litteris monendo et requirendo, quatinus sub diversis pœnis in hujusmodi litteris nostris expressatis arrestum in bonis dictorum mercatorum usque ad valorem notabilem, ad instantiam Flandrensium, ut præfertur, in Sclusa interpositum contra treugas generales inter Angliam et Franciam initas, etiam per jurata dictorum Flandrensium confirmatas, ac etiam contra appunctuamenta communia ipsorum sigillis sigillata, necnon contra litteras, eorum sigillo sigillatas, ac contra privilegium a Domino ipsorum de non arrestando concessum, citra duodecimum diem mensis Januarii proxime futurum procurent relaxare, ac hujusmodi bona, ut præmittitur arrestata, prædictis mercatoribus, ac aliis quorum hujusmodi bona existunt, realiter restituere, prout pœnam perjurii et infamiæ velint evitare.

*and, in reply, relate in detail their own proceedings.*

Quarum litterarum ultro citroque transmissarum tenorem, etiam cum certis responsionibus sophisticatis et calumniatis ipsorum Flandrensium, ad impediendum relaxationem arresti dictorum bonorum, post dilationes diversas ad plenius respondendum eis concessas, coram nobis præsentatis, una cum quibusdam nostris replicationibus, dictorum responsionum extinctivis et penitus expugnativis, mittimus vestræ regiæ Majestati, præsentibus interclusa; adeo quod ex serie omnium promissorum poteritis comprehendere ipsorum Flandrensium manifestam calumniam, ac variationem inexcusabilem, nec non ad ostendendum in præmissis nostram diligentiam aliqualem.

Item, quantum ad litteras nostras, directas Domino

Duci Burgundiæ, ac Magno Concilio Franciæ, super observatione terminorum inter Angliam et Franciam alias præfixorum, ac super aliis diversis in eisdem litteris expressatis — ipsarumque copiam vestræ Excellentiæ alias transmisimus,—in præsenti nullum responsum reportavimus. Fertur tamen in publicum quod in crastino Epiphaniæ Parisius celebrabitur magnum Concilium. Et quousque illud Concilium fuerit finitum non reportabimus, prout creditur, responsionem litterarum nostrarum.

Nova non sunt hic alia nisi quod navigium Flandrensium, cum vinis onustum de Rupella in Flandriam nuper est reversum. Et, quamvis certi vestri marinarii, de vestra villa Calisii, receperunt certa vina de navigio dictorum Flandrensium, credentes illa fore vina Gallicorum, contra quos ex parte Flandrensium de Brugis,[1] super viginti unam tonellis vini tantum loquendo juxta modum ipsorum, fuerunt coram nobis litteraliter querimoniæ depositæ, de aliis vinis captis nulla facta mentione ; quibus rescripsimus juxta tenorem ceterarum litterarum per nos eis transmissarum ; earumque copiam,[2] etiam cum aliis supradictis præsentibus interclusam mittimus eidem Excellentiæ vestræ.

Quam custodiat Trinitas Increata, ad felix regimen regni vestri, juxta votum.

Scriptum Calisii, quarto die Januarii.

Vestræ regiæ Majestatis invictissimæ commissarii ac nuncii,

HUGO LUTRELL,
JOHANNES DE CROFFT,—Milites ;
NICHOLAUS DE RYSSHETOUN, ac
JOHANNES URBAN.

*Endorsed :*—" Serenissimo et excelle[ntissimo Principi, Regi Angliæ] et Franciæ illustrissimo."

*Marginalia:*
A.D. 1404.
A great Council at Paris.

On the seizure of wine from Flemish merchants.

---

[1] *de Brugis.*] Added above the line. | See Letter LXXII.

A.D. 1404.

## LXXIV.

### THE FLEMISH DEPUTIES TO THE ENGLISH AMBASSADORS.

*Copia litterarum Flandrensium Ambassiatoribus Angliæ transmissarum :—*

Nobiles ac magnifici Domini.

Magnificentiarum vestrarum litteras,[1] vicesimo nono die mensis[2] Decembris ultimo præterito Calisii scriptas, una cum certis articulis eisdem interclusis, nos noveritis recepisse ac earum tenorem sane concepisse.

They announce that they have sent deputies to the Duke of Burgundy, Super quibus Honestates seu Amicitias vestras scire desideramus nos, post receptionem præfatarum litterarum vestrarum, pro celeriori expeditione negotii præsentis, quod tamen respicit et concernit tam patriarum Angliæ et Flandriæ utilitatem, quam totius mercandisæ prosperitatem, quam unusquisque tenetur affectare, certos nostros deputatos in notabili numero Parisius, penes metuendissimum Dominum nostrum, Dominum Ducem Burgundiæ, Comitem Flandriæ, transmisisse, eundem per prædictos deputatos nostros humillime deprecando ut indilate certos suos ambassiatores, seu deputatos, juxta ejus promissum, huc destinare velit, qui vobiscum super dicto negotio in loco medio per vos concesso et ad hoc aptando, convenire possent, ac tractatum nostrum communem ad finem congruum deducere; quod toto mentis nostræ conamine desideramus.

---

LXXIV.] MS. Cotton. Caligula, D. III. fol. 179 (δ).—On paper; a contemporaneous MS., being the copy sent to Henry IV., and alluded to in Letter LXXVI.

[1] See Letter LXVIII.

[2] *mensis*] Added above the line.

Sed quia, nobiles ac magnifici Domini, præfatorum A.D. 1404.
ambassiatorum penitus ignoramus adventum, hinc est *and request*
quod Honestates seu Amicitias vestras, affectu quo *that no-thing may*
valemus ampliori, duximus rogitandum quatinus dietam *be done till*
in prædictis litteris vestris denotatam, necnon respon- *they bring back his*
sionem nostram super eisdem, differre seu prorogare *answer.*
curetis, usque ad ipsorum ambassiatorum adventum
celerem ut speramus; scientes pro firmo quod illo tunc
omnibus et singulis querelis vestris taliter responde-
bimus, quod, ratione suadente, debebitis merito contentari, ut super multiplicibus laboribus, sumptibus, et in-
commodis quos in hac materia tulistis, ac semper subire
parati fuistis, vobis quantum possumus regratiamur.

Honestates vestras conservare dignetur Altissimus
prosperas et longæve felices!

Scriptum Gandavi, et sigillatum sub sigillo villæ
ejusdem pro nobis omnibus, die sexto mensis Januarii.

> SCABINI et CONSULES VILLÆ GANDENSIS,
> necnon DEPUTATI villarum Brugensis,
> Yprensis, ac territorii de Franco, præ-
> sentialiter ad placita congregati in dicta
> villa Gandensi.

*Endorsement :*—"Nobilibus et magnificis Dominis, Dominis illustrissimi Regis Angliæ,
in Calesio existentibus."

## LXXV.

### LUTTRELL, CROFT, ETC. TO THE FLEMISH DEPUTIES.

*Copia litteræ responsivæ, transmissæ per Ambassiatores Angliæ Flandrensibus, etc. :—*

Honorabiles, ac magnifici, et circumspecti Domini.

They acknowledge the receipt of the foregoing letter,

Ex parte vestra certas litteras vestras, scriptas Gandavi sexto die Januarii,[1] recepimus Calisii nono die Januarii, circa meridiem, sub sigillo vestro Gandavi sigillatas, inter cetera continentes, qualiter certas litteras nostras, vicesimo nono die mensis Decembris Calisii scriptas,[2] una cum certis articulis in eisdem interclusis, recepistis; super quibus, ac pro hujusmodi litterarum nostrarum expeditione, certos vestros deputatos Parisius ad Dominum vestrum in numero notabili transmisistis, parati ad omnia respondere in litteris nostris expressata pro loco et tempore opportunis occurrentibus: sed quia adventum seu reditum vestrorum ambassiatorum penitus ignoratis, supplicastis quatinus usque ad adventum vestrorum deputatorum celerem ut speratis, velimus dietam nostram præsentem continuare, ac responsionem vestram juxta tenorem litterarum nostrarum differre seu prorogare.

and, in reply, complain of the proposed delay as unusual; and inconvenient,

Ad quæ pro aliquali responsione, vestræ Reverentiæ curent advertere qualiter non decet ambassiatores Regum et Principum quorumcumque, et præsertim excellentissimi ac invictissimi Principis, Domini nostri, Regis Angliæ et Franciæ, vestros ambassiatores Quatuor Membrorum Flandriæ tanto tempore, absque

---

LXXV.] MS. Cotton. Caligula, D. III. fol. 179 (ε).— On paper; a contemporaneous MS., being the

copy sent to Henry IV., alluded to in Letter LXXVI.
[1] See Letter LXXIV.
[2] See Letter LXVIII.

congrua responsione, contra vestra sigilla et juramenta A.D. 1404.
propria, nostris litteris satisfacere, pro bono communis
mercandisæ, sub cujus mercandisæ prætextu obtulimus
nos paratos, contra omnem honestatem alias consuetam,
ac a tempore cujus contrarii non extat memoria
usitatam, prout alias vobis scripsimus, loco indifferenti
extra villam Calisii consentire, in quo pro tractatu
communi debeamus insimul convenire. Quibus non
obstantibus, ac etiam tanto tempore, vestras Reverentias absque effectu expectavimus. Et quod parlia- as they are
mentum regni Angliæ celebrabitur Londoniæ quarto required to
attend the
decimo die Januarii proxime futuro ; in quo parlia- Parliament
mento, juxta mandatum regium, oportet nos interesse, in London.
supplicamus vestris Reverentiis, pro bono communi tam
regni Angliæ, quam patriæ Flandriæ, quatinus peremptorie, ante vicesimum diem mensis Januarii proxime
futurum, placeat vestros ambassiatores transmittere, ac
super contentis in nostris litteris diversis etiam præsentibus, et sub dicto vicesimo nono die, ac etiam secundo
die Januarii ex tunc sequente, vobis nuper transmissis, et in litteris vestris confessatis litteraliter nobis
respondere, ac sub sigillis Quatuor Membrorum Flandriæ vestram responsionem in scriptis quoad inscripta
in hujusmodi nostris litteris expressata, nobis transmittere, sic quod vestri ambassiatores transmittendi a
vestra responsione non poterunt variare, quia alias non
intendimus responsionem hujusmodi ambassiatorum in
præmissis acceptare.

Et in vestra complacentia, ac ad nostram excusationem majorem, mittimus unum de co-ambassiatoribus
nostris in Angliam ad interessendum primo die parliamenti nostri prædicti, et ad allegandum causam quare
concessimus vobis diem ampliorem, ultra terminum in
dictis litteris nostris, sub vicesimo nono die Decembris
vobis præsentatis, assignatum.

Idcirco, consideratis præmissis ac aliis considerandis, They de-
non quæratis dilationem ulteriorem ; sed intra dictum mand an
immediate
terminum remittatis nobis responsionem finalem, et answer.

A.D. 1404. præsertim si bonorum arrestatorum in Sclusa vultis facere restitutionem paratam juxta requestam in dictis litteris vobis factam.

Vestras Dominationes custodiat Altissimus feliciter et votive !

Scriptum Calisii, decimo die Januarii.

HUGO LUTRELLE, et

JOHANNES CROFFT,—Milites ;

NICHOLAUS DE RYSSHETOUN, Utriusque Juris Professor, ac

JOHANNES URBAN,

Ambassiatores pro parte Angliæ.

*Endorsement :*—" Honorabilibus, ac magnificis, et circumspectis Dominis, Burgimagistris, Scabinis, et Consulibus Villæ Gandensis."

## LXXVI.

### LUTTRELL, CROFT, ETC. TO HENRY IV.

Serenissime Princeps, ac excellentissime et invictissime Domine.

They report progress.

Nono die Januarii certas litteras, ex parte Flandrensium nobis præsentatas, recepimus, quarum copias[1] vestræ Majestati transmittimus. Quibus rescripsimus alias litteras responsivas, prout in copiis[2] nostrarum litterarum, præsentibus etiam interclusis, plenius continetur. Juxta quæ vestra Majestas intentionem Flandrensium Partium poterit concipere, ac contra malitias ipsorum in futurum, prout necessitas exigit, de remedio opportuno providere.

LXXVI.] MS. Cotton. Calig., D. III. fol. 182. — On paper ; original, with traces of the seals.

[1] See Letter LXXIV.
[2] See Letter LXV.

De aliis autem, concernentibus tractatum Angliæ et Flandriæ, honorabilis et nobilis Miles, Dominus Willelmus Lyle, præsentium portitor, litteraliter et verbaliter vestram Majestatem poterit instruere, ac lucidius declarare. <sub>A.D. 1404.</sub>

Et dignetur vestra Excellentia nobis rescribere si ad vestrum parliamentum Londoniæ debeamus redire, et quæ gesta sunt inibi declarare; seu aliter Calisii residere, ac responsionem finalem Gallicorum et Flandrensium inibi expectare. <sup>and inquire whether they are expected to attend the Parliament.</sup>

Vestram Majestatem custodiat Altissimus feliciter et votive!

Scriptum Calisii, decimo die Januarii.

       Vestræ Majestatis invictissimæ commissarii

          et nuncii,

             HUGO LUTRELL, et

             JOHANNES CROFFT,—Milites;

             NICHOLAUS DE RYSSHETOUN, ac

             JOHANNES URBAN.

Nova alia non sunt hic, nisi quod in Concilio celebrato Parisius, prout fertur, his diebus, extitit conclusum quod Concilium Parisius, certis diebus elapsis, misit quendam Havart de Chaverbernard ac quendam alium, Ambassiatores in Scotia, ad contrahendum parentelam ex parte Gallicorum cum filio Comitis de Dougleys, qui prætenditur heres apparens in regno Scotiæ successurus; ac duos alios ambassiatores in Lumbardiam, ad contrahendum parentelam cum Duce Mediolani[1]; necnon duos alios ambassiatores in Britanniam, ad præparandum aliquod factum arduum nobis aliis penitus incognitum. <sup>News of the proceedings at the Council in Paris.</sup>

Endorsed:—" Serenissimo Principi ac illustrissimo et
           invictissimo, Dei gratia Regi Angliæ et
           Franciæ excellentissimo, nostro Domino
           ligeo . . . . ."

---

[1] John Mary, who succeeded John Galeas in 1402.

## LXXVII.

### JOHN COPPYL, CONSTABLE OF BAMBOROUGH, TO HENRY IV.

Excellent et tresdulce Seignour Sovereynge.

*Reporting that Bamborough is safe,* Je moy humelment recomande a vous auxi entierment come ascoun houm poet penser, requeraunt a Dieu Omnipotent a moy envoier de vous bones et joyous novalx, com je dissire.

Et outre, tresexcellent et tresdulce Seignour Sovereynge, si vous please d'oyer de lez novalx qels sount en lez partiez de Northumbre; vostre Chastell et Seignourie de Baumburgh estoyent en sauffegarde al *but that the* fesance de cestez, loyes ent soyt Dieu. Et auxi que *Percies* lez Chastell de Berwyk, Alnwyk, et Warkworth sount *threaten a* *stubborn* garde par le mayn force par Monsieur William de *resistance.* Clyfford, Monsieur Henry Percy, et Monsieur Thomas Percy, et voilliount tener lez ditez Chastell encontre vous s'ils pourount. Et auxi que lez ditez Chevalers procurount a eoux graunt pupil de vostres gentez, et

---

[TRANSLATION.]

Excellent and most sweet sovereign Lord.—I recommend me humbly to you, as entirely as any man can think, imploring God Almighty to send to me from you good and joyous news, as I desire.—And, moreover, most excellent and most sweet sovereign Lord, be pleased to hear the news which are in the parts of Northumberland ; your Castle and Lordship of Bamborough were in safety up to the writing of these presents, praised be God for it. And also that the Castles of Berwick, Alnwick, and Werkworth are kept by main force by Master William de Clifford, Master Henry Percy, and Master Thomas Percy ; and they will hold the said Castles against you, if they can. And also that the said Knights have procured to themselves a great multitude of your men, and given them the

---

LXXVII.] MS. Cotton. Vespas. F. VII. fol. 112.—On paper ; original.

donent a eoux le lyveray des cressauntz, et jourrount A.D. 1404.
pour mayn tener eoux encontre vous et touz autres.

Leqel rebelte ne voilliont sesser ne poet estre sesse The neces-
pour vostre honeste, saunz que voes chevachees en propir sity for the King's pre-
person en mesme lez parties; autrement voes averez sence in the
graunt affeir en breef temps. Et cestz, tresexcellent et North.
tresdulce Seignour, voilliez a coer prend en ensessaunt
de graundeour damage en breef temps venaunt.

A Dieu, tresexcellente et tresdulce Scignour Sovereynge, Que vous dona bonne vie, et longement pour
durrer, et encresse vous en honours a touz jours.

Escrite en graunt hast, al Chastell de Baumburgh,
le xiij jour de Januar.

Je vestre,

JOHN COPPYLL,

Constabyll de Chastell de Baumburgh.

*Endorsed :*—" Au tresexcellente et tresdulce Seignour
Sovereyn, le Roy Henry, le Roy
d'Engleterre et de Fraunce."

*Also :*—"Novelx des Marches d'Escoce."

---

livery of the crescents, and have sworn to keep them by force
against you and all others.—The which rebellion they will
not stop, nor can it be made to stop for your dignity, unless you
proceed in your own person through these parts; otherwise you
will have a serious affair in a short time. And these things, most
excellent and most sweet Lord, be pleased to take to heart, for
putting an end to the great mischief which is coming in a short
time.—I commend you to God, most excellent and most sweet
sovereign Lord, and may He give you good life, and long to last,
and increase you in honours at all times.—Written in great
haste, at the Castle of Bamborough, the 13th day of January.

I am yours,

JOHN COPPYLL,

Constable of the Castle of Bamborough.

*Endorsed :*—" To the most excellent and most sweet sovereign
Lord, the King Henry, the King of England
and of France."

*Also :*—"News from the Marches of Scotland."

## LXXVIII.

### THE ALDERMEN, ETC. OF THE HANSE TO HENRY IV.

*Gloriosissimo Principi, serenissimoque Domino, Domino Henrico, Regi Angliæ et Franciæ, Dominoque Hiberniæ, Domino nostro gratiosissimo, littera cum omnimoda reverentia præsentetur, promptitudine nostri humillimi famulatus ad quævis vestra beneplacita continue antemissa.*

Illustrissime Princeps, gratiosissimeque Domine.

Comparuerunt coram nobis honesti et fide digni mercatores de Almania Hansæ Theutonicæ, dolorose conquerentes qualiter nonnullæ gentes de vestræ excellentissimæ Dignitatis subditis quandam navem breviter in partibus Orientalibus venientem in portu, dictam "Camera," hostiliter invaserunt; nauclerum ejusdem, dictum Reynerus Coniissone, cum suis mercatoribus in navi existentibus, secum captivos perducentes; navem cum suis mercandisis in spolium detinentes.

Quæ quidem navis, et mercandisæ antedictæ ad mercatores de dicta Hansa spectabant et spectant, juxta tenorem cedulæ papireæ huic inclusæ, et ad nonnullos alios personaliter jam extra Flandriam existentes.

Pro quibus mercandisis et navi a vestra benignissima Pietate repetendis, prædicti mercatores in Flandria existentes, pro se et aliis absentibus, concorditer elegerunt, constituerunt, et ordinaverunt, in eorum plenipotentem procuratorem, factorem, et nuncium specialem, Nicolaum de Egher præsentium exhibitorem; qui jam existens in vestro regno, nomine ipsorum mercatorum, pro dictis ablatis institit coram vestra illustrissima Majestate,—dantes et concedentes ei omnimodam aucto-

*Marginal note:* Complaining of the seizure of a ship by the English,

---

LXXVIII.] MS. Cotton. Vespas., F. i., fol. 110.—A contemporaneous MS.

ritatem ad prosequendum, rehabendum, et sublevandum A.D. 1404.
omnia et singula supradicta, et generaliter omnia et
singula faciendum quæ in præmissis, et circa præmissa,
necessaria fuerint et opportuna.

Quapropter, illustrissime Princeps ac gratiosissime and beg-
Domine, vestram nobilissimam Dignitatis clementiam ging the
King to
devotis precibus duximus implorandam, quatinus, divinæ order re-
bonitatis intuitu, et ob meræ justitiæ complementum, stitution to
be made.
vestros subditos, hujusmodi damni perpetratores, tales
habere dignemini in effectu, eosdem admonitionibus et
mandatis diris exhortantes ut præfatarum navis et
mercandisarum restitutionem debitam et sufficientem
prædicto Nicolao de Egher, nomine et ex parte prædictorum mercatorum et aliorum hic absentium, faciant
improtractim, exhibentes vestram regalem dignitatem
in præmissis, ut in vestra præpotenti Majestate plenarie sumus confisi.

Quam Altissimus feliciter et longæve regere dignetur
per tempora longiora !

Scriptum nostris sub sigillis, xviij die mensis Januarii.

> Vestræ excellentissimæ Dignitatis humillimi
> servitores,
>
> ALDERMANNI et JURATI COMMUNIUM
> MERCATORUM DE ALMANIA, Sacri Ro-
> mani Imperii Hansæ Theutonicæ, pro
> præsenti Brugis Flandriæ residentes.

O

## LXXIX.

### THE FLEMISH DEPUTIES TO THE ENGLISH AMBASSADORS.

*Copia litterarum ex parte Flandrensium Ambassiatoribus Angliæ transmissarum :—*

Nobiles ac circumspecti Domini.

Alleging that there had been a mistake as to the return of their deputies from Paris.

Ultimas vestras litteras Quatuor Membris Partium Flandriæ directas, scriptas Calisii xiiij° die præsentis mensis recepimus, mentionem inter alia facientes vos nuper audivisse quod deputati prædictorum Quatuor Membrorum Flandriæ pro sollicitatione adventus ambassiatorum metuendi Domini nostri tractatui vobiscum tenendo vacativorum, Parisius legati, tempore scripturæ prædictarum vestrarum litterarum, reversi fuerant, et quod ideo admirabamini vehementer quod in nostris litteris, Reverentiis vestris de Ypris postremo missis, de hoc nulla facta fuerat mentio ; parati nihilominus omni quo placet infra primum diem mensis Martii proximum, cum ambassiatoribus præfati Domini nostri vestrisque convenire, et, prout expediret, super incepto negotio tractare ; in conclusione earundem vestrarum litterarum nos requirentes quatinus super illo, necnon adventu ambassiatorum præfati Domini nostri, vellemus vobis rescribere ac nostram voluntatem in omnibus declarare.

Super quibus, nobiles ac circumspecti Domini, Prudentiæ vestræ velint advertere, quod, salva reverentia illorum qui de reversione [deputatorum] patriæ Flandriæ de Parisius vos informarunt, supradicti deputati non omnes sed solum in parte reversi fuerant, reliquis pro sollicitatione prætacta Parisius remanen-

---

LXXIX.] MS. Cotton. Galba, B. I. fol. 110. — On paper ; a contemporaneous MS.

tibus usque tertium decimum diem præsentis mensis, A.D. 1404. quo per Reverendum in Christo Patrem, Dominum Episcopum Attrebatensem, metuendi Domini nostri Cancellarium, in præsentia nonnullorum de Concilio ipsius præfati Domini nostri, præfatis nostris deputatis responsum fuerat, quod causa quare metuendus Dominus noster præfatos deputatos tantum tardaverat finaliter expedire erat ad sciendum si forsan dieta, jamdiu inter regna Franciæ et Angliæ pro primo die mensis Martii proximi captata, teneretur apud Lulyngham, vel non. Sed quia per ambas partes prædictas and postconclusum est illam teneri debere, quodque vos, vel poning the treaty of saltem vestrum aliqui, ordinati essetis illi tractatui Flanders. generali vacare, et ne forsan unus tractatus per alium obfuscari valeat seu quomodolibet impediri, propter etiam aliquas alias causas quas distinctim scribere nimis esset longum, non videbatur supradicto Domino nostro aut suo Concilio expediens huic nostro tractatui vacare ad præsens, sed potius expectare donec videatur quid in prædicto universali tractatu forsan actum erit; talia etiam ut asseruit in illo concludi poterunt quæ pro nostro prædicto tractatu maximam exhibebunt prosperitatem.

Nobiles et circumspecti Domini, Altissimus vestras conservet Discretiones prospere et votive!

Scriptum sub sigillo ad causas villæ Brugensis, pro omnibus nobis, die xxiij mensis Februarii.

> BURGIMAGISTRI, SCABINI, et CONSULES villæ Brugensis necnon DEPUTATI villarum Gandensis, Yprensis, ac territorii Franci officii partium Flandriæ, præsentialiter in præfata villa Brugensi congregati.

*Endorsement*:—"Nobilibus ac circumspectis Dominis, Dominis ambassiatoribus illustrissimi Principis et Domini, Domini Regis Angliæ, Calisii existentibus."

# LXXX.

### CROFT AND DE RYSSHETON TO HENRY IV.

Serenissime Princeps, ac excellentissime et illustrissime Domine; votiva ac humillima recommendatione præmissa vestræ Excellentiæ debita.

Scire dignetur vestra Majestas regia sacratissima, quod die Martis vicesimo sexto præsentis mensis [1] de sero recepimus certas litteras, ex parte Quatuor Membrorum Flandriæ nobis præsentatas; ipsarumque copias [2] mittimus vestræ Majestati regiæ præsentibus interclusas.

On the deceit practised by the Flemings.

Ex quarum serie intentionem Partium Gallicorum, quamvis in litteris Flandrensium narrativam et velatam, necnon etiam ipsorum Flandrensium voluntati, conclusioni, et determinationi Gallicorum conformem et accessoriam, ac a tractatu et exitu Gallicorum principaliter et penitus dependentem, cum subtilitate verborum in ipsorum litteris declaratam, vestra Serenitas poterit concipere; et quod Gallici primo die Martii, seu prout alias cum celeritate f . . . . . . bile in tractatu volunt nobiscum a l . . . . . . . . . . . . . ac subsequenter ambassiatores Ducis Burgundiæ ac Quatuor Membrorum Flandriæ [tra]ctatum ipsorum juxta [?] . . . . . . . . conclusion . . . . . . . . . . orum nobiscum . . . . . . . . . . . . . . . . . . . . . . . . alias hujusmodi tractatum ipsorum a capite si poterunt

---

LXXX.] MS. Cotton. Calig. D. III. fol. 183.—On paper; original, with marks of the seal. This letter has been considerably torn.

[1] Tuesday, February 26.

[2] See the preceding Letter.

prout fertur ex diversis causis resumere, ac juri nobis
in pluribus ad . . . . . ,—quod non eveniet per Dei
gratiam, præjudicare . . . . . . . . . .

Unde, præmissis consideratis et diligenter attentis,
prout vobis et Concilio vestro fuerit visum, quia
ex parte Gallicorum die confectionis præsentium super
veritate præmissorum nihil nobis extitit intimatum,
pro vestris ambassiatoribus super tractatu Franciæ,
videlicet pro uno prælato ac pro aliis, prout decet et
expedit cum celeritate possibili[1] ; qui in laboribus
et expensis cum aliis poterunt intendere et participare
cum instructione sufficienti pro tractatu Franciæ et
Flandriæ, et præsertim pro excusatione equitaturæ
per stipendiarios vestræ villæ Calisii nuper factæ,
quam non credimus vestram Majestatem ignorare ;
una cum stipendiis nostris ; ac ante omnia—non obstante nostro tractatu pro securitate maris cum forti-
tudine maxima, usque in conclusionem tractatus—pro
defensione et salva custodia maris, non autem pro
derobatione seu partium spoliatione dignemini providere ; necnon oculos vestræ Majestatis ad villam de
Gravelyng pro defensione vestrorum subditorum dirigere, ac de remedio opportuno providere. Capitanei
enim vestrorum Castrorum Pykardiæ, ac etiam Locumtenens Calisii, propter regimen et occupationes quas
habent in præsenti, Castra sua libenter nolunt exire,
nec super vestris ambassiatis se intromittere.

Super quibus omnibus fidem credulam vestris fidelis-
simis servitoribus, Domino Hugoni Lutrell, Militi, ac
Johanni Urban, super veritate præmissorum in hujusmodi tractatibus præexpertis, dignetur adhibere, ac
rescribere[2], vestra Majestas benignissima ac excellentis-
sima.

A.D. 1404.

They ask that further instruc- tions may be sent ;

that their expenses may be paid ; and that the sea may be protected,

and the King's French subjects succoured.

---

[1] *cum celeritate possibili*] Added above the line.

[2] *ac rescribere*] Added above the line.

A.D. 1404.   Quam custodiat Trinitas Increata in longævum, ad vestri regni felix regimen et munimen!

Scriptum Calisii, xxvij die Februarii.

Vestræ regiæ Majestatis sacratissimæ commissarii ac nuncii,

JOHANNES DE CROFFT, Miles, ac
NICHOLAUS DE RYSSHETOUN.

*Endorsed :*—" Serenissimo [ac excell]entissimo Principi . . . . . Regi Angliæ et [Franciæ,] illustrissimo ac . . . . . . ."

*Also :*—" Littera Ambassiatorum pro parte Angliæ, existentium in Calesio."

## LXXXI.

### RICHARD ASTON TO THE DUKE OF BURGUNDY.

*A tresexcellent et tresredoubte, puissant Prince, le Duc de Burgoigne, Conte de Flandres, etc.*

Tresexcellent, treshaut, et redoute, puissant Prince. Je me recommant a vostre Excellence aussi treshumblement comme je scay, en tout honnour.

*He thanks the Duke for at last receiving his letter,*

---

[TRANSLATION.]

*To the most excellent and most dread and mighty Prince, the Duke of Burgundy, Count of Flanders, etc.*

Most excellent, most high and dread and mighty Prince. —I commend me to your Excellency with all the humility that I know, with all honour.—And forasmuch as it has

---

LXXXI.]   MS. Cotton. Galba, B. i. fol. 123.—On paper; original, with traces of the seal.

Et pour ce qu'il m'a este dit que graciousement, et A.D. 1404. en benigne et douce manere, il vous a pleu ore tarde rescepvoir mes humbles lettres, a vous deliverees par un Varlet Escotois, prisonner de John Moltoun, Escuier, maistre porter de Calais, de quoy je regracie tres-humblement vostre excellente Puissance.

Et ore est ainssi que, nonobstant les griefs, oppres- and com-sions, torts, et deffautes de droiture, fais au Roy plains that the nostre Seigneur et ses subges, comme desclare est English en mes dictes lettres, l'Evesque de Chartres, le Sire had been unjustly de Hengueville, et Maistre Johan de Saintes, darreins accused. ambassatours pour vostre partie sur le fait des attemptes aucuns sur les presentes treves, ont a present escript a Reverent Pere en Dieu, l'Evesque de Bathe, Messieur Thomas Rempstoun, Maistre Nichol de Ryssetoun, Doctour en Lois, et a Johan Urban, ambassatours et messages pour nostre coste, que en nostre partie a plus de deffautes que en la vostre, disans nos gens avoir couru, pillears, et proie es parties de la conte de

---

been told to me that graciously and in benign and pleasant manner it has pleased you now lately to receive my humble letters, delivered to you by a certain Scotch varlet, prisoner of John Molton, Esquire, master porter of Calais, on that account I return thanks most humbly to your excellent Highness.—And now it is so that notwithstanding the griefs, oppressions, wrongs, and breaches of justice committed against the King our Lord, and his subjects, as is declared in my said letters, the Bishop of Chartres, the Lord of Hengueville, and Master John de Saints, late ambassadors on your part concerning the making of any attempts upon the present truce, have, at the present time, written to the Reverend Father in God, the Bishop of Bath, Master Thomas Rempston, Master Nicholas de Ryssheton, Doctor in Laws, and to John Urban, ambassadors and envoys on our side, that there is more fault on our side than on your own, alleging that our men have ravaged, pillaged, and robbed in the parts of the county

A.D. 1404. Boulloigne, et aillours en Picardie, et ovesque ce occis et prinse prisonners hommes, femmes, et enfans, et tous autres oevres faites accoustumez au fait de guerre ; par quoy il pouroit semble as vous, et as autres Princes et hauts Seigneurs, que par les dessusditz, ou par aucuns autres pouriez ou pouvez avoir de ce evidemment este inffourmez que trop grande et orrible deffaute deust estre en nous plus avant sans comparison que deservy n'avons.

Plese vostre excellente Hautece entendre que de courses, depredations, d'arsions ne d'aucun autre fait de guerre n'a riens estre fait es dictes parties autrement que contenu est en mes dictes lettres.

He details the outrages committed on the other side,— Mais quant est cremations, courses, et occisions yci devant faites il est voir que nadgaires de temps les ditz ambassiatours des deulx roialmes estans ensemble a Leulingham sur le fait des ditz attemptes Wybert de Freytoun, nonobstant les lettres par vous envoiees a Havart Campbernard come darreinment vous escrips

---

of Boulogne, and elsewhere in Picardy, and withal have killed, and taken prisoners, men, women, and young children, and have done all other works accustomed to be done in making war ; by which it might seem to you, and to the other Princes and high Lords, that by the abovementioned, or by any others, you might or may be able to be clearly informed herein that a very great and horrible fault ought to be in us, incomparably beyond our real demerits. —May it please your excellent Highness to understand that of forays, depredations, arsons, or any other warlike act, nothing has been done in the said parts otherwise than is set down in my said letters.—But as to the burnings, forays, and slaughters committed here previously, it may be seen that lately, what time the said ambassadors of the two realms were assembled together at Leulingham, concerning the fact of the said attempts, Wybert de Freyton, notwithstanding the letters sent by you to Havart Campbernard, as you last wrote, entered the isle of l'Orne, and there

entra l'isle de Orny et illeoques occise hommes, femmes,
et enffans, et aussi ardit mesme l'isle, et prinst tant
de prisonners comme prendre peut, et par appres ce
retourna es parties de Sayne, et aillours ou il luy pleut
la, ou il fut amiablement resceu et conforte, comme
paravant avoit este, appres ses robberies faictes ; de
quoy vous fut parlle par le Conte de Saintpol, sicomme
appert par ses lettres, seallez du seal de ses armes,
portant date du xxvj$^{eme}$ jour de Juyng, l'An de Grace
Mille CCCCO1, et contenant un article qui s'en-
suit,—

" Et que nous savons bien que sur toutes riens
" mon dit Seigneur le Roy, et mes autres Seigneurs
" de son sanc, vouillent les treves entretenir sans les
" enfraindre ne souffrer estre enfrainces aucunement
" de lour partie, nous avons monstre vos dictes lettres
" a mon Seigneur de Burgoigne, que du contenu en
" icelles a en tresgrant displaisance." [1]

---

killed men, women, and children, and also fired the said
isle, and seized as many prisoners as he could take,
and afterwards returned to the parts of the Seine, and
elsewhere, wheresoever it seemed him good, where he
was kindly received and encouraged, as he had been
before, after the commission of his robberies ; concerning
which speech was made to you by the Count of Saint
Pol, as appears by his letters, sealed with the seal of
his arms, bearing date the 25th day of June, the year of
Grace 1401, and containing an article which follows :—
" And forasmuch as we know well that, above all things,
" my said Lord the King, and others my Lords of his blood,
" wish to keep the truce mutually, without infringement of
" it, and without suffering it to be infringed, in any manner
" on their part, we have shown your said letters to my
" Lord of Burgundy, the contents of which he regards with
" supreme displeasure. " — Yet, nevertheless, of the said

---

[1] " *Et que ... displaisance.*"] This quotation is marked off and under-
lined in the MS.

A.D. 1404.  Nientmains unqore du dit Wybert en celle, en droit
which were ne en doit des prises et robberies par luy au devant
permitted
to pass un- faictes et apportez a lour descharge en hable de Crotoy,
punished ; en poair et jurisdiction du dit Seigneur de Hengueville,
radresce ne fut faicte, j'a soit ce que le dit Sire de
Hengueville fut souvent fois requis de y pourvoier de
droiture, a quoy il ne voulut oveques obeier. Mais
furent les dictes prises deschargiez et distribuez par le
dit Sire de Hengueville et le Seneschalle de Pontieu
ainssi comme il lour pleut, sicomme poet apparoir par
ses lettres, seallez de son seal.

and the      Et aussi en icel temps ou bien tost appres les gens
robberies
by the    de Harfleu et autres des divers parties du roialme de
men of    France, soubz umbre et coulour d'un ou deux Escos
Harfleur.
demourantz et enherites entre eulx, se mistrent a la
mer, et prendrent et robberent des marchans et subges
du Roy nostre dit Seignour, plus que C. mylle livres
d'esterlingz, par dessus les rautions des marchans et
maroiners par eulx amesnes au dit lieu de Harfleu

---

Wybert [mentioned] herein, neither in right nor in due of
the seizures and robberies by him before made, and brought
for their discharge into the harbour of le Crotoi, within the
authority and jurisdiction of the said Lord of Hengueville,
has redress been made, although the said Lord of Hengueville has been ofttimes requested to provide restitution hereof,.
whereunto he did not choose to obey. But the said seizures
were discharged and distributed by the said Lord of Hengueville and the Seneschal of Ponthieu just as it seemed fit
to them, as may appear by his letters, sealed under his
seal.—And also at that time, or very shortly after, the
men of Harfleur, and others from divers parts of the realm
of France, under the pretence and colourable pretext of
one or two Scotchmen domiciled and inheriting among
them, put to sea, and seized and plundered from the merchants and subjects of the King our said Lord more than
one hundred thousand pounds sterling, over and above the
allowances of the merchants and mariners, brought by them
to the said place from Harfleur and elsewhere, and there

et aillours, et illeoques penes et mis a destresse, comme A.D. 1404.
en nom et en la guerre du Roy d'Escose, non prinnans
regarde a l'article des dictes treves de quoy mes dictes
lettres font mention ; et ainssi firent bastilles de lour
dictes villes en nom du dit Roy d'Escoce contre le
Roy nostre dit Seignour.

Et quant est de ce que aucun vesselx et gens de
poy de value et de nulle reputation, contre la voulente
du Roy nostre dit Seigneur, et sans son congie, sceue,
ou licence, par appres firent aucun emprise sur aucune
isle entre icy et La Rochelle, il est verite que eulx
furent combatuz, disconfitz, et prins par les gens du
pais, et en fere justice selon lour demeritz, ou autrement prendre d'eulx amendes, on fere ce que lour
eust pleu ; et ce sceit vostre haute Discretion, que par
raison povoit et devoit as ses souffire, sans pour ce
fere ne commencher aucun fait de guerre, et par especial sans sommation fere de ce au Roy nostre dit
Seignour.

*He excuses the reprisals made by the English.*

---

punished them and put them to distress, as in the name
and serving in the war of the King of Scotland, paying no
regard to the article in the said truce, whereof my said
letters made mention ; and so made fortresses of their said
towns, in the name of the said King of Scotland, against
the King our said Lord.—And so far as this that any
vessels and men, of but small value, and of no reputation,
against the will of the King our said Lord, and without
his leave, knowledge, or licence, did afterwards take in
hand any enterprise on any island between this place and
La Rochelle, it is the truth that they were attacked,
discomfited, and taken prisoners by the people of the
country, and in doing justice according to their demerits,
or otherwise taking amends of them, they have done what
they pleased ; and this your high Discretion knows, that
in reason it might and ought to suffice them, without
on that account doing or commencing to do any warlike
act, and especially without causing a citation hereupon to
the same the King, our said Lord. — Notwithstanding,

A.D. 1404.
The burning of
Plymouth by the Bretons;

Non pourtant tantost appres les gens du pays du Bretaign, qui sont purs subges de la courone et de l'obeissance de l'Amiralle de France, a grant poair de vesselx d'armeis passerent en Engleterre et ardirent, pillerent, et robberent la ville de Plommeuth, et les bonnes gens d'icelle mourdrirent, prendrent prisonners, et ovec eulx amisueront, contra l'estat des dicts treves, et la natour des serementz, que vous scavez que de icelles loialment et inviolablement tenir furent fais.

and their ravages in Jersey and Guernsey, are contrary to the terms of the truce.

Et plus oultre arriverent es Isles de Gerresey et Guernesey, et illeques firent combustions de maisons, prendrent prisonners et proie, et par dessus ce rannconnerent les dictes Isles a certains grands et importables sommes; lesquelles choses sont purement et proprement faits de marque, comme en executant les innocens pour le fait des coulpables, en allant contre les ditz serementz, et iceulx enfreignant en tout comme en eulx estoit.

Et ensuant de ce le dit Conte de Saintpol jure as

---

shortly afterwards, the men of the country of Bretagne, who are clearly subjects of the crown, and under the jurisdiction of the Admiral of France, with a great force of armed vessels, passed into England, and burned, pillaged, and plundered the town of Plymouth, and the good people therein they murdered, took prisoners, and carried away with them, contrary to the terms of the said truce, and the nature of the oaths, of which you know that they were made by them to hold loyally and inviolably. And moreover they made their way to the Isles of Jersey and Guernsey, where they set fire to the houses, took prisoners and booty, and, over and beyond this, laid the said islands under a contribution of certain great and intolerable sums of money; the which things are clearly and properly acts of reprisal, as punishing the innocent for the deed of the guilty, going contrary to the said oaths, and infringing them as far as in them lay. — And following upon this the said Count of Saint Pol sworn to the said truce,

dictes treves, ovecque vous et les autres du roial sanc, A.D 1404. continuelment a tenu en vostre Seigneurie de Flandres, en hable de Gravelings, divers vesselx d'armeis, par les quelx il a fait prendre et robber nos marchans et vittaillers a la value de xx mille livres, a ce que l'en tient pardeca, et que plus est a fait sursigler, soubmerger, et effondrer divers vesselx, et les gens fait voier, et tirantement fait occer a lances et a dartes quant aucun s'est pene de soy sauver au nage.

Et semblablement ount fait vos autres propres subges du dit pais de Flandres, tant de Donekerk et Neufport, que d'Osthende, Berflete, et autres de qui la correction et punition appartenit a vostre Seigneurie.

Et en la fin a le dit Conte diffie le Roy nostre Seigneur, et a grant nombre de vesselx, et poair de gens d'armes ennaie le roialme d'Engleterre, et en siglant vers l'Isle de Wight desconfit et prins certains pouvres peschours et lour reis et apparlois, et a sa

*Ravages in the Isle of Wight.*

---

together with you and the others of the blood royal, continually has kept in your Lordship of Flanders, in the harbour of Gravelines, divers armed vessels, by the which he has caused to seize and plunder our merchants and victuallers to the amount of twenty thousand pounds, according to what they maintain here; and further he has caused to give chase to, sink, and upset divers vessels, and caused the crews to fly, and tyrannically caused to kill them with lances and darts, when anyone tried to save himself by swimming.—And in like manner have acted others of your own subjects, of the said country of Flanders, as well belonging to Dunkirk and Newport, as to Ostend, Bieruliet, and other places, the correction and punishment of whom appertains to your Lordship.—And finally the said Count has defied the King our Lord; and with a great number of vessels, and force of armed men, he sails against the realm of England; and proceeding towards the Isle of Wight overcomes and takes prisoners certain poor fishermen with their nets and implements, and

A.D. 1404. descente en la dite Isle prins certains ovailles, de quoy le povre puepple se tient aggreve ; lesquelles choses sont mielx abusives, et merveilleuses, entendu le dit article contenu es dictes treves, puis que le dit Conte est droit subget et lige homme du Roy, et aussi de vous, en droit de ses heritages assises en dit vostre pays de Flandres. Et aussi doit il estre entendu du Duc d'Orliens, de qui la correction et punition appartenir a la dicte courone, et qui est si pres du sanc du Roy que nullement il ne deust par raison fere ne souffrer estre faicte aucune emprise ne motion de guerre contre le serement de son Seigneur.

Et pour ce, tresexcellent, puissant Prince, que a ce que la renommee en courte publiquement parentre nous vous estre si plain de loialte, et tant amez et doubtes Dieu que nulle extortion ne faute de droiture ne vous est plesante ne agreable, le dit Maistre Nichol de Ryssetoun, un des ambassiatours de nostre partie, a

---

on his descent upon the said Isle seizes on certain sheep-folds, on which account the poor people consider themselves aggrieved ; the which things are exceedingly great abuses, and more marvellous, considering the said article contained in the said truce, since the said Count is a rightful subject and liegeman of the King, and also of you by right of his heritages situated in your said country of Flanders. And also it ought to be understood by the Duke of Orleans, of whom the correction and punishment appertains to the said crown, and who is so nearly allied by blood to the King, that on no account ought he in reason to make or to suffer to be made any enterprise or warlike movement contrary to the oath of his Lord.—And on this account, most excellent, mighty Prince, that, as the report is publicly current among us that you are so full of loyalty, and so love and fear God that no extortion nor default of right is pleasant or agreeable to you, the said Master Nicholas de Ryssheton, one of the ambassadors on our part, who is at present stationed in this place, has

present estant pardeca, m'a prie de vous escripre et A.D. 1404.
declarer les choses susdites, pour vous fere clerement
entendre que la deffaute que les diz ambassiatours de
vostre coste ont escript pardeca, ou que aucun autres
qui n'aiment pas as ses paes et charite vous povent
avoir fait entendre estre en nous, n'est pas tielle ne si
grande comme eulx dient. Car ja, se Dieu plest, tant
de enormes defautes, comme dessus est desclarie ne
sera trouve en Roy nostre dit Seigneur, ne en ses
subges. Et aussi affin que par vostre gracious aide et
puissance, les choses soient mises en voie d'amende- He prays
ment pour l'avancement du bien commune et pour for redress,
eschuer a l'effusion du sanc Christien, en fesant cesser
les emprises des ditz Duc et Conte, en gardant l'estat
des ditz serements. As quelles choses le dit Maistre
Nichol et moy, qui aussi vouldroie que tout bien fust
fait et avancie, a la plesance de Dieu, et honour des

---

besought me to write to you, and to declare the matters
aforesaid, for to make you clearly to understand that the
default of which the said ambassadors on your part have
written to us here, or which any others who do not at
all delight in peace and charity may have caused you
to understand to be in us, is not at all such, nor so great
as they say. For now, if it pleases God, such an extent
of enormous defaults, as is declared above, will not be
found in the King our said Lord, nor in his subjects.
And also to the end that, by your gracious aid and might,
these matters might be put in the way of amendment,
for the advancement of the common weal, and for the
avoiding of the shedding of Christian blood, in causing
to cease the enterprises of the said Duke and Count, by
guarding the integrity of the said oaths. To which
matters the said Master Nicholas and myself, who also
desire that the good of all should be secured and advanced,
to the pleasing of God, and the honour of the Kings our

A.D. 1404. Rois nos Seigneurs de chacun coste, vous requirons que vous plese benignement et graciousement entendre et y pourvoier comme vous scavez que besoign en est, en vous remembrans que aunciennement les drois Rois de France, que entre tous autres Rois Christiens porterent le nom de excellence, comme adonques Seigneurs de l'aboundant fontaigne de droiture et justice, ne seullent pas estre desobeis. contredis, ne oppresses par lour subges.

and an answer to his letter, Sur ces choses, tresexcellent et puissant Prince, plese vostre dicte excellente Seigneurie moy mander et fere savoir vostre honourable voulente.

with a safe-conduct for John Cheyney. Et aussi se Monsieur Jehan Cheiney, pour qui je vous escrips ore tarde, pourra avoir saufconduit pour venir par devers le Roy, vous, et les autres Seigneurs du Grant Consseil, sur l'entent contenu en mes lettres, lesqueilles je avide que grandement pourront valoir au bien commun des deux roialmes.

---

Lords on either side, require you that you would please kindly and graciously to consider and provide herein as you know that the business requires, calling to your remembrance that of ancient time the rightful Kings of France, who bore the reputation of excellence among all other Christian Kings, as up to that time Lords of an abundant fountain of equity and justice, were not accustomed at all to be disobeyed, or frustrated, or oppressed by their subjects.— Concerning these matters, most excellent and mighty Prince, may it please your said excellent Lordship to communicate to me, and to cause me to know your honourable will.—And also whether Master John Cheyney, on whose behalf I wrote to you now recently, will be able to have a safe-conduct for to go to the presence of the King, to yourself, and to the other Lords of the Great Council, with a view to the matters contained in my letter, the which I desire that they may greatly avail to the common good of the two realms.

Et je prie a Dieu, etc.

Escript a Calais, le xviij jour de Mars.

RICHARD ASTOUN, Chivaler,
Depute et Lieutenant a Calais.

*Endorsed :*—" Litteræ Ricardi Aston, Locumtenentis
Capitanei Calesii."

—And I pray God, etc.—Written at Calais, the 16th day
of March.

RICHARD ASTON, Knight,
Deputy, and Lieutenant at Calais.

## LXXXII.

### RICHARD ASTON TO HENRY IV.

Mon tresredoubte et souverain Seigneur.

Je me recommant a vostre roiale [Majeste] treshumblement, comme je scay ou plus puis.

A la quille plese entendre que selon ce que ore tart
vous pleut a moy commander par voz roial[les] l[ettres

*On his letter on behalf of John Cheyney.*

[TRANSLATION.]

My most dread and sovereign Lord.—I commend me
to your royal Majesty with all the humility that I know,
or, moreover, am able. — The which may it please to
understand that, according as now lately it pleased you
to give me commandment by your royal letters to send

LXXXII.] MS. Cotton. Calig. D. IV. fol. 47.—On paper; original,
and much injured by fire.

P

A.D. 1404. envoier] pardevers tielx Seignours que je cognois en France, pour avoir saufconduit du Roy pour Monsieur Jehan Cheigny; j'en escrips prestement au D[uc de Burgoigne], Sire d'Angondessent, et as autres Seigneurs unes lettres, les quilles je delivray a Derby, vostre herault, portour de cestes, le quel pu[isque le] Lieutenan[t] de Bouloign ne le voulloit lesser passer, ne plus avant aller vers les dictes parties de France, les delivra au mesme Lieutenan[t] par lettres certifficatoires d'icelluy; le quel les envoia pardevers la Court, ovecque les lettres de vos ambassiatours adreschantes [a les ambassiatours] de France, les quelx ont rescript pardevers vos ditz ambassiatours lour voulente, sicomme vous pourra apparoir par lour dictes lettres, l[es quelles le mesme vostre herault a] vous porte. A qui plese vostre Excellence roialle adjouster foy et credence tant de la response du dit Lieutenant de [Bouloign, quant] des nouvelles qui ore courent pardeca. Et aussi en droit

---

to such Lords as I know in France for to have a safeconduct from the King, for Master John Cheyney, I wrote a letter forthwith to the Duke of Burgundy, the Lord d'Angodessent, and to the other Lords, the which I delivered to Derby, your herald, the bearer of these presents, who, when the Lieutenant of Boulogne would not let him pass, nor proceed further towards the said parts of France, delivered them to the same Lieutenant by letters of certification from this place, who sent them on to the Court, together with the letters from your ambassadors, addressed to the ambassadors of France, who have written back their will to the said your ambassadors, as will appear to you by their said letter, the which the same your herald carries to you. To whom may it please your royal Excellency to award faith and credence, as well of the answer of the said Lieutenant of Boulogne, as of the news which are current over here. And also by right of the said safeconduct, so

du dit saufconduit, en tant que je n'en ay nulle res[ponse A.D. 1404. unquore a mes] nouvelles escript au dit Duc par les messages des ditz ambassiatours de France. Et aussitost que j'auray response, je le . . . . . . . . . . . . . . [Exc]ellence.

Et je prie a Dieu Toutpuissant que Il vous vuille ottroier bonne vie et longe, ovec joieux victore de [touz voz enemis].

Escript a[1] . . . . . , le] xviij^{me} jour de Mars.

*Endorsed :*—" A nostre tresredoubte [et souverain Seignour le Roy]."

*Also :*—" Littera Ricardi Asshton, Militis."

___

far as I have no answer yet to my news written to the said Duke by the commissaries of the said ambassadors of France. And immediately that I receive an answer I [will communicate it to your] Excellency.—And I pray God Almighty that he will grant to you good life and long, with joyous victory over all your enemies. — Written at' . ˉ. . . . . , the 18th day of March.

*Endorsed :*—" To our most dread and sovereign Lord the King."

___

[1] At Calais, probably.

P 2

## LXXXIII.

### JOHN I., KING OF PORTUGAL, TO THE PRIVY COUNCIL OF ENGLAND.

*Johannes, Dei gratia Portugaliæ et Algarvii Rex, Reverendis Patribus ac Spiritualibus Dominis de Concilio serenissimi et illustrissimi Domini, Regis Angliæ et Franciæ, fratris nostri carissimi, salutem pariter et amorem.*

On the truce with the King of Castile.

Unigenitus Dei Filius, Dominus noster naturalis, Jesus Christus, de Quo scribitur in Psalmo *Deus, judicium Tuum Regi da,*[1] pia miseratione disposuit sibi subditos fore pacificos et modestos, pacificos dico, id est, pacem facientes et custodientes ; et alibi 'Beati pacifici, quoniam ipsi filii Dei vocabuntur,'[2] nos solicitat, instruit, evidenter adjiciens 'pacem Meam do vobis, pacem Meam relinquo,'[3] ubi et secundum doctrinam Apostoli prædicavit.   Omnis Christi actio nostra est instructio : propterea universi Christiani et singuli, præsertim Reges ac Principes, et alii in sublimitate positi, debent, juxta possibilitatem ab Eo sibi datam, eis vesti[giis dili]genter inhærere ; et quæ Ipse prædicavit et docuit dum erat in terris, pro viribus custodire.

Hinc est, reverendissimi Patres et Spirituales Domini, quod nos, prædicta doctrina Christi æquanimiter ponderata, . . . . . . . . . . . aliqualiter eruditi, nuperrime pro nobis nostrisque regnis, terris, gentibus, et subditis, ac pro præfato serenissimo Domino Rege Angliæ,

---

LXXXIII.] MS. Cotton. Nero, B. I. fol. 28.—On vellum ; original, with marks of the seal.  A portion of the left-hand side of this letter has been torn away.

[1] Psalm lxxii.

[2] S. Matth. v. 9.

[3] S. John, xiv. 27.

Domino vestro, fratre nostro carissimo, regnis, dominiis, A.D. 1404.
terris suis, gentibus ac popu[lis], cum adversario Castellæ
pro se, suisque gentibus, terris, dominiis, subditis, et
alligatis treugas inivimus, et proprio firmavimus juramento, sub forma, conditionibus, et modis, temporibus,
instrumentis[1] [pub]licis, quæ vestræ Serenitati transmittimus interclusa, ut latius ex inscriptione vel alias
lectione ipsorum vobis liquide poterit apparere, et si
oporteat per relationem prædilecti nostri Fernandi
Gunsalvi in . . . . . . bi licentiati, præsentium portitorem, quem in his omnibus plene informatum transmittimus ad præfati serenissimi Regis Majestatem,
necnon vestras Paternitates et Circumspectiones similiter
informandas.

Quapropter Paternitates et Circumspectiones antedictas attente rogamus, quatinus super prædictis omnibus
et singulis fidem velitis eidem credulam exhibere in iis
quæ nostri ex parte vobis duxerit referenda, necnon
scitius et commodius quo fieri poterit finaliter expedire.

Spiritus Sanctus vos omnes protegat et custodiat ab
adversis!

Scriptum in nostra Coimbriensi civitate, die prima
mensis Aprilis.[2]

EL REY.

Endorsed :—" Reverendis Patribus ac Spiritualibus
Dominis de Concilio serenissimi et illustrissimi Principis, Domini Regis Angliæ
et Franciæ."

---

[1] instrumentis] insturmentis, MS. | [2] See Rymer, viii. 354.

A.D. 1404.

## LXXXIV.

Swynborn, Croft, etc., to the Flemish Deputies.

Acknowledging their letter announcing the death of the Duke of Burgundy, and the readiness of the Countess Margaret to continue the treaty;

Honorabiles ac magnifici et circumspecti Domini.

Litteras vestras, ultimo die Aprilis Brugis scriptas, recepimus, inter cetera continentes qualiter consideratis quod dominium et regnum patriæ ac comitatus Flandriæ pro præsente est revolutum ad manus illustris Principissæ, Dominæ Comitissæ Flandriæ modernæ, filiæ ac heredis bonæ memoriæ Domini Lowisii, quondam Comitis Flandriæ; speratisque in Domino quod eadem Domina vestra, per Dei gratiam, una cum Concilio suo provido et maturo, impedimentum cursus communis mercandisæ, originatum per discordiam ac guerram inter regna Angliæ et Franciæ per quosdam prædones et piratas maris, seminatores zizaniæ ipsius Belial, iniquitatis filios, duobus annis elapsis resuscitatum, studebit infra patriam suam Flandriæ removere, ac pacem et tranquillitatem, et favorem communis mercandisæ ad utilitatem reipublicæ inibi interserere; quod vestris viribus possibilibus quantum in vobis est curabitis sollicite procurare submergendo.

Insuper in eisdem litteris vestris suppediendo nobis exprimitis quod pro parte nostra diligentiam consimilem velimus apponere, adeo quod tractatum inchoatum inter regnum Angliæ ac inter vestram patriam Flandriæ, prout extitit tempore præfati Lowisii ultro citroque poterimus perficere, necnon cursum communis mercandisæ ac reipublicæ stabilire, et, Domino annuente, perpetuare.

---

LXXXIV.] MS. Cotton. Galba, B. 1. fol. 140. — On paper; a contemporaneous MS.

Ad quæ, honorandi Domini, excellentissimus Princeps ac Christianissimus Dominus, noster Rex, volens pacem cum quibuscumque Christianis, et præsertim cum Quatuor Membris Flandriæ, quantum in eo est, enutrire, ac stragem et effusionem sanguinis Christianorum effugere, necnon ipsius almum Concilium, non obstantibus injuriis ac gravaminibus, homicidiis, ac submersionibus, crudeliter factis—non faciliter numerabilibus—per vestros Flandrenses incolis ac subditis regni Angliæ incessanter illatis, sub confidentia quod præmissa omnia volueritis, prout juris fuerit, effectualiter reformare, parati sunt quocumque termino legitimo assignando in tractatu cum ambassatoribus Dominæ vestræ ac vestris convenire, ac prout juris fuerit, sub pari numero et dignitate, in omnibus satisfacere et respondere. Super quibus omnibus cum omni celeritate placeat nobis rescribere; necnon vestram voluntatem ac Quatuor Membrorum Flandriæ, et præsertim præfatæ Dominæ vestræ lucidius declarare, prout vestris ac ipsorum Reverentiis videbitur expedire.

Quas dirigat Altissimus feliciter in longævum!

Scriptum Londoniæ, vij° die Maii.

THOMAS SWYNBOURNE,

JOHANNES CROFFT,—Milites;

NICHOLAUS DE RYSSHETOUN, Utriusque Juris Professor, ac

JOHANNES URBAN, domicellus;—
Ambassatores pro parte Angliæ.

*Endorsement :*—" Honorabilibus, ac magnificis, et circumspectis Dominis, Burgimagistris, Scabinis, et Consulibus villæ Brugensis.

A.D. 1404.

and stating that the English King and his Council are of the same mind.

## LXXXV.

### THE DUCHESS OF BURGUNDY TO THE BAILIFFS OF FLANDERS, ETC.

[La] Duchesse de Burgoigne, Comitesse de Flandres, d'Artois et de Burgoigne Palatine, Dame de Salins et de Malines, a noz soverain Bailliz [de] Flandres et Bailliz de Bruges de l'eaue et de la terre a le Scluse de Nuefport de Bierivlet, et a touz noz aultres officers de nostre dite paiis de F[landres], ou leurs lieutenants, salut.

For the preservation of peace while the treaty with England is pending.

Il est venue a nostre cognoissance par la complainte et doleance de noz ville de Gand, Bruges, Ypre, et de nostre t[erre] de France, lesquelx par leurs deputes envoiez presentement pardevers nous nous ont fait exposer, que pur certain temps en ce, plusers de nostre dictes [villes], tant marriners come aultres pouraens et gernis

---

[TRANSLATION.]

The Duchess of Burgundy, Countess of Flanders, of Artois, and of Burgundy Palatine, Lady of Salins and Malines, to our high Bailiffs of Flanders and Bailiffs of Bruges, of the water and of the land at Sluys, of Newport, and of Bieruliet, and to all other our officers of our said country of Flanders, or their lieutenants, greeting.

It has come to our knowledge, by the complaint and express grievance of our towns of Ghent, Bruges, and Ypres, and of our territory of France, the which by their deputies presently sent before us have laid open to us, that, for a certain time back, several persons of our said towns, as well mariners as others, bearing and provided with armour and other habiliments of

---

LXXXV.] MS. Cotton. Galba, B. i. fol. 115 b.—On paper.

d'armures et autres abillemens pur la guerre se sont par- A.D. 1404.
tis de havens et pors dites . . . paiis de Flandres, et eulx
trais sur meer ou as marchans du pays d'Engleterre,
et d'autres nations et contrees, ils ont faitez et portez
en corps [et] biens beaucoup de tresgrans damages.
Pur la quelle chose le fait de la marchandise, sur le
quele nostre dicte pays est principalement fonde et
sousten[u est] tresfort amenri et . . . . . ; mais les mer-
chans sibien ne si seurement haunter et frequenter
come ils souloient en temps passe pour [peur] meismement de perdre leur biens; ce que tourne a moult
grand prejudice et damage generalment de touz les
habitans et bones gens du dicte nos[tre paiis], et feroit
encores plus; dont grans inconveniens se purroient en-
sieuir, si, qu'ils dient, se par nous n'estoit purveu sur
ce de remede, d[ont] ils nous ont moult humblement
supplie.

Pur quoy nous veuillanz et desirans a nostre povoir
que le dicte fait de la marchandise puisse au [tous]
noz subgez mieulx avoire cours et estre exerce et con-

---

war, have set out from the havens and ports of the said country
of Flanders, and to those met on the sea, and to the merchants
of the country of England, and of other nations and countries,
have caused and carried much of very heavy damage in person
and in goods. For the which matter the state of the merchandise, upon which our country is chiefly built and sustained, is
very seriously prejudiced and . . . . . . ; but the merchants
as well cannot so securely haunt and frequent the seas as they
used to do in time past, for fear at the same time of losing
their goods; a thing which turns to the very great prejudice
and damage generally of all the inhabitants and good people of
our said country, and will do so still more ; from which great
inconveniences will follow, if, as they say, there be not provided for us a remedy herein, for the which they have very
humbly besought us.—Wherefore we, willing and desiring to
the utmost of our power that the said state of the merchandise
may to all our subjects have course and be exercised and

A.D. 1404. tinue en icellui nostre pays, vous mandons et commettons par ces presentes, et a chacun de vo[us comme] droit soy et si come a lui appartiendra, que vous faitez tantost crier et deffendre publiquement depar nous, en tous les ditz havens et pors [de] Flandres, et par tout ailleurs ou busoins serra, que nulx quelz quilz soient se partent d'ores en avant d'iceulx pors ou havens, pur pillier [ou] rober aucuns marchans quelxconques soient du dicte pays d'Engleterre ou d'ailleurs; la quele deffense leur faisons des maintenant par ces meisme [Lettres] sur quanques mesfaire se povent envers nous; et s'aucuns y avoit faisons le contraire oultre et pardesus nostre dit deffense, et que par information [donne] ou autrement devenant il fust ensi trove, nous veullons que vous en faites punitioun viguereusement, sens deport ascun, et tiellement se . . . . apprehender on les peut, que ce soit exemple a tous autres d'eulx engarder, purveu que ceux de la partie d'Engleterre facent, et facent faire, le pareil.

Car ainsi on cas et pur lez considerations dessusditz,

---

continued in this our country, do charge you and commit by these presents, and to each one of you as the right belongs, and so as it shall appertain to him, that you shortly cause to proclaim and to forbid publicly, on our part, in all the said havens and ports of Flanders, and everywhere else where need shall be, that no persons whatsoever set out henceforward from such ports or havens, to pillage or to rob any merchants whatsoever of the said country of England, or of any other; the which prohibition we make to them now by these same letters, wheresoever they may be able to misconduct themselves towards us; and if any there be who do the contrary over and beyond our said prohibition, and that by information given, or otherwise coming, it shall be so found, we will that you inflict punishment vigorously, without any delay, and in such sort, if . . . . they can apprehend them, that this shall be an example to all others to guard themselves, provided that those of the part of England do, and cause to do, the like.—For so, in the

nous plaist il et le voulons estre fait, et vous en donnons A.D. 1404. et a chacun de [vous] es termes de son office, povoir, auctorite, et mandement especial, se mestier est.

Donne en nostre ville d'Arras, le xiiij$^e$ jour de Maii, l'an de [Grace] Mille CCCC et quatre.

Par Ma Dame la Duchesse.

---

case and for the considerations aforesaid, it pleases us, and we will that it be so done, and we give you in charge, and to each one of you, in the terms of his office, power, authority, and commission special, as the custom is.—Given in our town of Arras, the 14th day of May, in the year of Grace 1404.

By my lady the Duchess.

## LXXXVI.

THE DUCHESS OF BURGUNDY TO RICHARD ASTON.

Treschier et bien ame.

Les comon gens de noz villes de Gand, Bruges, Ypres, et de nostre terre du France, par leures deputez envoie[s ore tard a nous], entre autres choses fait exposer coment vous leur avez nadgaire escript du fait de la

---

[TRANSLATION.]

Most dear and well beloved.—The common people of our towns of Ghent, Bruges, Ypres, and of our territory of France, by their deputies lately sent unto us, have declared, among other things, how that you have recently written

---

LXXXVI.] MS. Cotton. Galba, B. ɪ. fol. 115.— On paper ; a contemporaneous MS. The upper right-hand corner of this letter has been torn off.

A.D. 1404. prinse fait sur meer d'ascuns vesseaulx ou ils . . . . . .
. . . . et de leur biens, qui sont encore detenuz en la
ville de Nuefport par ascuns mariners et autres du dit
lieu de Nuefport et d'illeoques environ, pur avoir
[surete q'] adreschement vous serroit fait de et sur
dicte matiere.

Si vuillez savoir que pur en savoront la verite nous
avons ordennez et appointez . . . . . . commander a
ceux de nostre dicte ville de Nuefport et leure com-
pagnons, que le Dymenge proschein venant en x x
jours ils envoient pur ceste cause [devant] nous et
nostre Conseil jusques a huit ou dix des plus princi-
palx et plus suffisans d'eulx tous, afin que par nous la
verite sceue en soit ordenne, et [cela] par la manere
que appartiendra de raison. Et semble, pus que ausi
par raison proceder y voulons, qu'il n'y a point de cause
pur la quelle l'en devroit . . . leissier a entendre pur
entretenir la traite autresfoys encommencie sur le fait
du cours de la marchandise entre Angleterre et Flan-

---

to them of the fact of the capture made on the sea of certain
vessels . . . . . . . . . . . and of their goods, which are still
detained in the town of Newport, by certain mariners and
others belonging to the said place of Newport and the
neighbouring parts, in order that you might have assurance
that redress should be made to you of and upon the said matter.—Be pleased to know that, for the sake of ascertaining
the truth, we have ordained and appointed . . . . . . to charge
them of our said town of Newport, and their associates, that
within twenty days from the Sunday next ensuing they send
for this cause to the presence of us and our Council, to the
number of eight or ten of the principal and more influential
persons among them all, to the end that by us, the truth known,
an ordinance may be made thereon, and that in the manner that
belongs to reason. And it seems that, since we are willing
to proceed herein thus by reason, there is no cause whatever for the which one ought to cease from the understanding to entertain the treaty formerly commenced concerning
the carrying on of the commerce between England and

dres; meismem[ent] attendu que plusieurs de noz subgis, A.D. 1404.
tant du dit lieu de Nuefport, come d'autres de nostre
dit pays, passe a longe temps ont este et sont encorez
dete[nuz] en grande povrete et miserie en Caleys, et
en divers autres lieux de la partie d'Engleterre.

Aussi pur monstrer la bone affection que avons a
ce que le dicte besoingne sur le fait de la marchandise
puisse parvenir a bone conclusioun, nous avons ordenne,
mande, et commande de faire crier et deffendre publiquement depar nous, que nulx quelz quils soient partent
d'ores en avant des portz ou havenes de nostre dicte
pays de Flandres pur robber ne pillier aucuns marchans
quelxconques soient du dicte pays d'Engleterre, ou
d'ailleurs, sur quanques ils se peuent mesfaire envers
nous ; et des transgressours on faisans la contraire,
s'aucuns y avoit, et qu'ilz puissent estre apprehendez,
nous ferons sans deport aucun faire punitioun tiellement que ce serra exemple a tous autres ; mais que de
la partie d'Engleterre l'on face le pareil ; et que depar

---

Flanders; considering likewise that many of our subjects,
as well belonging to the said place of Newport, as others
of our said country, have been for a long time past,
and still are detained, in a state of great destitution and
misery, in Calais, and in divers other places in the territory of England.—Also, to show the good desire that we
have that the said business concerning the carrying out
of the commerce may come to a good conclusion, we have
ordained, charged, and commanded to proclaim and prohibit
publicly, by our authority, that no persons whatsoever depart
in future from the ports or havens of our said country of
Flanders, for the purpose of robbing or plundering any
merchants, whosoever they may be, belonging to the said
country of England or anywhere else, whenever they may
be able to misbehave towards us; and of the transgressors,
or those who act in a contrary manner, if any there be, and
that they may be taken, we will cause without any delay
to inflict punishment upon them in such manner that they
will be an example to all others ; provided that on the
part of England the like be done herein, and that on the

A.D. 1404. ycelle partie d'Engleterre l'on ne tengne mieultz qu'il n'a este fait en temps passe.

Lesquelles choses nous vous signifions, afin que vostre reponse sur ce nous veullez rescripre le plus brief que faire se purra.

Treschier et bien ame, Nostre Seigneur vous ait en Sa seinte garde !

Escript a Arras le xvj jour de May.

---

same part of England they hold to it better than has been done in time past.—The which matters we signify unto you, to the end that you may be willing to write back an answer to us hereupon as quickly as you can possibly do it.—Most dear and well-beloved, Our Lord have you in His holy keeping !—Written at Arras, the 16th day of May.

## LXXXVII.

### THE ALDERMEN OF THE HANSE TO HENRY IV.

*Gloriosissimo Principi ac serenissimo Domino, Domino Henrico, Regi Angliæ et Franciæ, Dominoque Hiberniæ, Domino nobis gratioso, omnimoda reverentia presentetur, humillimi obsequii nostri promptitudine ad quævis vestra beneplacita continue antemissa.*

Gratiosissime Princeps, serenissimeque Domine.

Complaining of losses inflicted on merchants of Hamburgh by English sailors, Significarunt nobis honesti viri mercatores, cives Hamburgenses de Almania Hanzæ Theutonicæ, qualiter nonnulli vestri subditi quantitatem navigiorum breviter de civitate Hamburgensi præfata venientium, cum bonis et mercimoniis eisdem mercatoribus de Hamborch appertinentibus, manu hostili invaserunt, ipsa navigia et mercimonia et bona ad vestræ excellentissimæ Dig-

---

LXXXVII.] MS. Cott. Vesp. F. i. fol. 111.(a). — On paper; a contemporaneous MS.

nitatis portus captiva perducentes, veluti vestram dig- A.D. 1404.
nissimam Majestatem a Ludolpho Cleytzen, præsentium
ostensore, cum suis collegis, prædictorum mercatorum
procuratoribus in hac parte, ore tenus plenius salva
vestra gratia de præmissis speramus informandam.

Cum ergo inter vestram regalem Dignitatem et *and asking*
vestros subditos ex parte una, et mercatores Hambur- *for resti-*
*tution.*
genses prædictos ex parte altera, mutua pacis ac amicitiæ fœdera scimus confoveri, quoniam vestri mercatores infra districtus civitatis Hamburgensis benevolis
promotionibus et honorificis favoribus ubilibet semper
pertractantur, idcirco vestræ illustrissimæ Nobilitatis
Excellentiam devotis affectibus duximus exorandam,
quatinus divini amoris et meræ justitiæ ob respectum,
vestrique exigui famulatus intuitu, vestros subditos,
prædicti facti perpetratores, ad prædictorum navigiorum,
mercimoniorum, et bonorum restitutionem constringan-
tur in effectu, ne prædicti mercatores Hamburgenses,
talibus et tantis bonis et mercimoniis, absque eorum
demeritis, sub spe totius confidentiæ, alienentur et minus
juste; in his vestram favorabilem dignitatem exhibentes
ut vestræ præpotenti regali Majestati sumus plenarie
confisi.

Quam Altissimus felicem et votivam conservet per
tempora longiora!

Scriptum nostris sub sigillis secunda die Mensis
Junii, anno XIIIIcIIII.

> ALDERMANNI, necnon JURATI COMMUNIUM
> MERCATORUM ALMANIÆ HANZÆ THEU-
> TONICÆ, Sacri Romani Imperii, pro
> præsenti Brugis Flandriæ residentes,
> ad vestræ excellentissimæ Dominationis
> famulatum parati.

*Endorsement:* —"Gloriosissimo Principi ac serenissimo
> Domino, Domino Henrico, Regi
> Angliæ et Franciæ, Dominoque
> Hiberniæ, Domino nobis gra-
> tioso, etc."

## LXXXVIII.

### THE SENATE OF HAMBURGH TO HENRY IV.

*Serenissimo Principi et excellentissimo Domino, Domino Henrico, Regi Angliæ etc., dignissimo, Domino nostro, sincere benigno, cum reverentia tam debita quam devota, humillima subjectione cum nostrorum promptitudine servitiorum devote præmissa.*

Complaining of the capture of certain ships by the English,

Serenissime Princeps, et excellentissime Domine.

Cum, teste Scriptura, summum in regibus bonum est justitiam colere, sua unicuique jura servare, a subjectis non sinere quod potestatis est fieri, sed quod æquum est custodiri, vestræ igitur Celsitudini cupimus tenore præsentium enodare nos gemebundis aliquorum nostrorum concivium querelis dolenter percepisse nonnullos vestræ excellentissimæ Majestatis ministros ac subditos nuper de portibus regni vestri Angliæ, cum pluribus magnis navibus ad bellandum paratis, in et ad mare se exposuisse; quodque vestræ Celsitudinis ministri ac subditi præfati postmodum nonnullas naves infrascriptas in mari, cum bonis et mercimoniis inibi existentibus invaserunt, hostiliter vicerunt, et detinuerunt, et nihilominus easdem [1] secum, ut dicitur, ad partes regni vestri Angliæ deduxerunt. Ex quibus nostri concives prædicti, suis demeritis ut asserunt minime exigentibus, sunt graviter damnificati.

Primo quidem capta est navis Arnoldi Zedeken, concivis nostri in portu nostro, onerata cum cervisia Hamburgensi, cupro, lineo panno, et diversis aliis mercimoniis, nostris prædictis concivibus ac aliis mercatoribus de Hansa pertinentibus.

---

LXXXVIII.] MS. Cotton. Vesp. F. I. fol. 110 (β).—On paper ; a contemporaneous MS.

[1] *easdem*] Added above the line.

Item, navis Hæmonis Somez, concivis nostri, cum A.D. 1404. cervisia Hamburgensi per nostros concives onerata.

Item, tres naves Radekun Scroten, civis Lubicensis; Makepiaugh, oppidani in Herdervoiik; et Kerciani Comaussone, oppidani in Campen; quas quidem naves concives nostri cum cervisia Hamburgensi nostro in portu oneraverunt.

Item, duæ naves, videlicet Johannis Vorn Iden, ac Rochgheri Hoppen, concivium nostrorum, de partibus Flandriæ cum diversis mercimoniis et bonis concivium nostrorum ac aliorum mercatorum venientes.

Hinc est, serenissime Princeps et excellentissime and re-
Domine, quod nos, de solitis et benignis vestræ regalis questing
clementiæ favorosis promotionibus devotius confidentes, that resti-tution may
ad vestram præexcellentem Pietatem iterato recurrimus, be made.
humiliter et devotissime supplicantes quatinus mandare et severius injungere dignemini ministris et subditis belligeris vestris supradictis, quatinus præfatis nostris concivibus, tam de navibus, quam cervisia ac bonis et mercimoniis aliis, ad ipsos nostros concives, ut præ-mittitur, spectantes, restitutionem integram et debitam faciant cum effectu, ut vestræ regiæ Majestatis benig-nitas et justitia, ac subditorum vestrorum æquitas et obedientia, ex hoc clarius elucescant. Cum nos semper ad vestræ Celsitudinis mandata, necnon regni et sub-ditorum vestrorum honores et commoda adimplenda multiplicandos et procuranda pro posse nostro sinceris-simis affectibus fuimus, sumus, et diligenter erimus indefessi et promptiores, Teste nobis Altissimo.

Qui vestram excellentissimam Celsitudinem regere conservareque dignetur salubriter et prospere ad tempora longiora!

Scriptum anno Domini Millesimo quadringentesimo quarto, mensis Junii die quinta, nostro majori sub sigillo.

Vestræ regiæ Majestatis { humiles et devotissimi
{ CONSULES HAMBURGENSES.

Q

A.D. 1404.

## LXXXIX.

### HENRY IV. TO CONRAD DE JUNGINGEN.

*Henricus, Dei gratia Rex Angliæ et Franciæ, et Dominus Hiberniæ, nobili ac potenti sacræ religionis viro, Fratri Conrado de Jungingen, Ordinis Beatæ Mariæ Theutonicorum Magistro Generali, amico nostro carissimo, salutem, et antiquæ dilectionis et sinceritatis continuum incrementum.*

On the dangerous state of the seas, in consequence of the outrages committed by pirates.

Non sine gravi querela ligeorum nostrorum facta mercatoria exercentium utrobique, quasi per orbem, nostris est auribus conculcatum quod, propter injurias varias atque damna, quæ tam mercatores nostri quam vestri qui in factis eorum mercatoriis consueverunt mutuo conversari pacifice, unde quam plura commoda provenisse noscuntur, occasione piratarum hinc inde per mare nonnunquam hactenus sunt perpessi, jam dicti mercatores nostrates et vestrates a mercatoria conversatione sueta se abstinent, prout per aliqua tempora retroacta se abstinere curarunt, ac præsertim a tempore quo ad vestrorum instantiam et requisitionem nuntiorum jam dudum apud nostram præsentiam existentium mercatorum nostrorum ad terras et dominia vestra, necnon et vestrorum ad regnum nostrum accessus, fuerat interdictus.

The King promises to do his best to ordain a remedy.

Cum igitur, amice carissime, hujusmodi attemptata contra vestrates, si qua fuerint, nunquam de nostra voluntate processerint, sicuti de vobis hoc idem fore credimus ex adverso, simusque, quatinus ad nos attinet, semper dispositi cuicumque de vestris querelare volentibus plenam exhibere justitiam, cum favore,

---

LXXXIX.]     MS. Cotton. Nero, B. II. fol. 40.

dummodo mercatoribus nostris vobis et vestratibus A.D. 1404.
simili modo gravatis justitia, prout convenit, æque
fiat; nos, habentes in desideriis ut amicitia et dilectio
consuetæ, quæ viguerunt jam diu inter regnum nostrum ac terras et dominia vestra, perseverare valeant
in futurum, ut pacis amœnitas, a cunctis Christicolis
amplexanda, pro pacis Auctoris beneplacito nutriatur,
· eandem amicitiam ex corde requirimus, et hortamur
in Domino, quatinus pro parte vestra consentire ac
etiam ordinare velitis, prout, si idem feceritis, nos ex
parte nostra modo simili consentimus ut hinc ad
festum Paschæ proxime futurum,¹ mercatores et subditi nostri per vestra, et vestri per nostra terras,
dominia, et territoria, pacifice ac amicabiliter incedere,
moreque solito conversari valeant et mercari, cessantibus
gravaminibus et injuriis interim inferendis utrimque.
Quoniam aliquos de ambassatoribus nostris ad vos et
Concilium vestrum medio tempore destinare proponimus super præmissis prætensis injuriis, quatinus vestrates concernere poterit, per viam amicabilem tractaturos. In quorum adventu speratur quod, per
exhibitionem hinc inde justitiæ, de tali via (Domino
concedente) providebitur, quod pax et tranquillitas
pro futuris debeat temporibus mutuo stabiliri. Et ut
in specie mercatores et ligei nostri ad Sconæ partes,
pro allecibus et aliis piscibus inibi providendis, liberius
transire, ibidem morari, et ad propria valeant securius
remeare, ipsos nostros mercatores et ligeos, ob nostræ
considerationis intuitum, habere velitis, quæsumus
specialiter recommissos eosdem, si necesse fuerit, sub
vestræ defensionis clipeo salubriter protegendo, prout
vice versa vestratibus in casu consimili, volueritis nos
facturos.

Quid autem in hac parte duxeritis faciendum, nos
per litteras vestras, per fidelem ligeum nostrum,

---

¹ Easter Day fell on April 19th in the year 1405.

Q 2

A.D. 1404. Johannem Broun, exhibitorem præsentium, Amicitia vestra velit efficere certiores.

In Filio Virginis gloriosæ diu et feliciter, pro mentis vestræ desiderio, valeatis!

Datum sub privato sigillo nostro apud Palatium nostrum Westmonasterii, quinto die Junii, anno regni nostri quinto.

He excuses the prolonged absence in England of Arnald de Dassele. Ceterum, venerabilis vir, amice carissime, etsi dilectus nobis Arnaldus de Dassele, antedictorum vestrorum procurator nuntiorum, volens hac[1] vice vestras ad partes finaliter proficisci, super negotiis pro quibus in regno nostro Angliæ remansit, hucusque votivam expeditionem nequeat obtinere, mirari non debet, nec cordi tenere vestra Sinceritas quovis modo, quoniam, supervenientibus guerrarum turbinibus quæ nobis aliqualiter immittebantur, et præsertim continuis in nos et regnum nostrum Francigenarum et Britonum insultibus, in quorum offensam et nostri defensionem ligei nostri et specialiter ii de quibus damnificati vestri subditi fuerant querelati, armata manu se posuerunt in mari, præfato Arnaldo expeditionem talem qualem votivis habere desideravit affectibus nequivimus impartiri; cui quidem Arnaldo procuratori obtulimus per celeriores processus quibus fieri poterit justitiæ complementum facere cum favore, in eventum quo ex hac causa se in regno nostro Angliæ disponeret permansurum, et nihilominus illud idem in ipsius procuratoris absentia faciemus.

Datum ut supra.[2]

---

[1] hac] ac, MS.

[2] See Letter XCIX., which is in answer to this.

A.D. 1404.

## XC.

### The Duchess of Burgundy to John Urban.

*Copia litteræ Ducissæ Burgundiæ, transmissæ Johanni Urban, uni de vestris[1] commissariis ;—*

Chier et bien ame.

Nous avons receu vos lettres, contenantes que, apres la reception de nos lettres a vous desrain escriptes, avez notifie a vostre Seigneur la publication que avons fait faire es pors et havres estans sur les costes de la mer de nostre pais de Flandres, que aucun n'en ysse pour faire grief ne dommage aux marchans d'Angleterre, ne autres, on cas que de la partie d'Angleterre l'en face deffense pareillement, affin que vostre dit Seigneur face faire depar luy semblable publication, et qu'il donne aussi charge a ses ambassateurs de procedier au

*Acknowledging the receipt of his letter.*

---

[Translation.]

Dear and well-beloved.—We have received your letters, containing how that, after the receipt of our letters last written to you, you have notified to your Lord the proclamation which we have caused to be made in the ports and havens situated along the sea-board of our country of Flanders, that none should come out to do mischief or damage to the merchants of England, or any others, in case that on the part of England a prohibition should be made therein in like manner, to the end that your said Lord should cause to be made by his authority a like proclamation, and that he also give to his ambassadors charge to proceed

---

XC.] MS. Cotton. Galba, B. i. fol. 78. (γ).—On paper ; a contemporaneous MS.

[1] *de vestris*] This copy was sent to the King. See Letter XCVI.

A.D. 1404. traictie autrefoys encommencie, de et sur la seurte de la marchandise, ce qu'il fera comme esperez, mais que nous soions en volente, comme il est, de faire reparer tous attemptas, ce que vous supposés que si et que le plus grant avancement de parvenir a bon traictie et conclusion, si seroit que les marchans d'Angleterre et de nostre dit pais de Flandres, se peussent entre convenir lez uns avec les autres, ce quil a este delaissie par aucun temps, pour les entreprinses que l'en a fait d'un coste et d'aultre ; et que sur ce eussies noz gracieuses lettres de seurte pour les marchans de l'Estaple de Caleys venir en nostre dit pais de Flandres frequenter leur fait de marchandise avec noz subgez d'icelluy, les queilx avroient semblable seurte de venir faire leurs marchandises par de la, avec plusieurs autres choses contenus en vos dictes lettres, que avons veues et bien fait veoir.

and pro-
mising to

Si vueilliez savoir, chier et bien ame, que, pour le

---

with the treaty commenced at a former time, of and concerning the safety of the merchandize, the which he will do, as you hope, provided that we be disposed, as he is, to cause reparation to be made of all the attempts, inasmuch as you suppose that so and so much the greater advancement will be made in coming to a good treaty and conclusion, if it shall be that the merchants of England, and of our said country of Flanders, can agree together, the one with the other, the which has been for some time abandoned by reason of the enterprises which they have made on one side or the other; and that you might have thereupon our gracious letters of security for the merchants of the Staple of Calais to come into our country of Flanders, and carry on their commerce with our subjects therein, who would have like security to come and carry on their commerce over there, together with several other matters contained in your said letters which we have inspected, and caused to be inspected carefully.—You will know, then, dear and well-beloved, that by reason of the great desire that we

tresgrant desir que nous avons que le fait de mar- A.D. 1404.
chandise se puisse faire et continuer en nostre dit pais, expedite
si tost que feu mon Seigneur (dont Dieux ait l'ame) the progress of the
fut trespasse, lequel, comme vous savez, assez avoit treaty to
the utmost
en povoir de mon Seigneur le Roy de faire traictier of her
par ses ambassateurs avec ceulx de la partie d'Angle- power.
terre, de et sur la seurte du fait de la marchandise
dessusdicte, et aussi des attemptas, nous envoiasmes
devers mon dit Seigneur le Roy, affin qu'il luy pleust
nous donner semblable povoir ; ce qu'il a fait, tant
a nous comme aussi a nostre treschier filz le Duc de
Bourgoigne et a chacun de nous ; et ont este les lettres
commandees et seront tost expediees.

Et quant les dis povoirs serront apportez par de ce,
qui sera bien briefment, nous ferons entendre le plus
diligentement que faire se pourra par noz ambassateurs,
avec ceulx du coste d'Angleterre au traictie autrefois
encommencie, qui prenra bonne conclusion, se Dieux

---

have that the commerce may be carried on and continued
within our said land, so soon as my late Lord, (on whom God
have mercy) was dead, who, as you know, was sufficiently
empowered by my Lord the King to cause a treaty to be
made by his ambassadors, with those on the part of England,
of and concerning the security of the commerce above
mentioned, and also concerning the attempts, we sent to
my said Lord the King, to the intent that it should please
him to give us like power : the which he has done, as
well for us as also for our most dear son, the Duke of
Burgundy, and for each and either of us ; and the letters
have been commanded to be drawn up, and will be presently despatched.—And as soon as the said powers shall
be brought hither, which will be very shortly, we will
cause to be considered with all diligence what can be done
by our ambassadors, together with those on the part of
England, as to the treaty heretofore commenced, which
will obtain a good conclusion, if God will, unless it suit not

A.D. 1404. plaist, s'il ne tient a ceulx de vostre coste. Et par ce moien pourra estre pourveu a la seurte dont touchie est en vos dictes lettres.

Si nous vueilliez rescripure, au plus tost et hastivement que vous pourrez, l'entente de vostre dit Seigneur de et sur lez choses avantdictes, meismement de la publication et deffense, qui devoit estre faicte depar luy a ses subges, de non porter dommage aux marchans de nostre dit pais ne a autres frequentans icellui.

Chier et bien ame, Nostre Seigneur soit Garde de vous !

Escript en nostre ville d'Arras, le vij. jour de Juing.

*Endorsement :*—" A nostre treschier et bien ame, Jehan Urban, Lieutenant de l'Estaple a Caleys."

---

them of your side. And by this means provision will be able to be made as to the security to which allusion is made in your said letters.—Please it you, therefore, to write back to us, with all the speed and haste that you shall be able, the intentions of your said Lord of and concerning the aforementioned matters, in like manner of the proclamation and prohibition, which ought to be made by his authority to his subjects, as to the abstaining from doing any damage to the merchants of our said country, or to others frequenting the same.—Dear and well-beloved, Our Lord be your protection !—Written at our town of Arras, the 7th day of June.

*Endorsement :*—" To our very dear and well-beloved, John Urban, Lieutenant of the Staple at Calais."

## XCI.

THE FLEMISH DEPUTIES TO THE ENGLISH
AMBASSADORS.

[Honorabile]s, magnifici, et circumspecti Domini. *Thanking them for their letters,* Ex insinuatione amicabilium litterarum vestrarum, nobis per præsentium gerulum directarum, de dato primo die Junii, sane concepimus bonam ac immensam diligentiam quam in facto nostri tractatus communis adhibuistis, et, Deo dante, in futurum adhibebitur incessanter penes illustrissimum Principem et Dominum vestrum, Regem Angliæ, ac ejus nobile Concilium, ut ille tractatus congruum sortiri `possit effectum: unde Amicitiis vestris ad infinitas gratiarum tenemur actiones;—subjungendo insuper in eisdem qualiter præfatus illustrissimus Princeps Dominus vester, necnon ejus nobile Concilium ad supplicationem mercatorum partium Angliæ parati sunt quocumque termino legitimo assignando, in tractatu cum ambassiatoribus metuendissimæ Dominæ nostræ ac nostris convenire, ac, prout juris fuerit, sub pari numero et dignitate, in omnibus satisfacere et respondere, prout hæc alia in præfatis litteris vestris lucidius enarrantur.

Super quibus, nobiles ac circumspecti Domini, vestras *and announcing that the Countess of Flanders was favourable to the treaty.* Nobilitates cupimus non latere nos super certos nostros deputatos penes metuendissimam Dominam nostram, Dominam Comitissam Flandriæ destinasse, ad cujus manus dominium et regimen communitatis Flandriæ pro præsenti est devolutum; cui de novo, ac ejus filio, Duci Burgundiæ, et cuilibet in solidum, potestas et auctoritas tractandi, aut tractari faciendi, cum ambas-

---

XCI.] MS. Cotton. Galba, B. I. fol. 118.—On paper; a contemporaneous MS.

A.D. 1404. siatoribus partium Angliæ per illustrissimum Principem Regem Franciæ, Dominum nostrum superiorem, est commissa, prout Dominus noster metuendissimus, bonæ memoriæ, Dux Burgundiæ (cui Deus parcat) ab eodem hactenus obtinuit.

Ex quorum nostrorum deputatorum relatione accepimus quod prædicta Domina nostra metuendissima, habitis litteris commissionis a Domino nostro Rege, ut plenius de commissa auctoritate et potestate constare possit, parata est omnibus viis et modis possibilibus per suos deputatos et ambassiatores, una cum ambassiatoribus illustrissimi Principis et Domini vestri, ad continuationem inchoati tractatus possetenus intendere, et feliciter, Deo prævio, pro bono patriæ utriusque partis, utilitateque communis mercaturæ ac reipublicæ, finire; prout hæc et alia plenius Locumtenenti Stapulæ Calesii per suas litteras[1] declaravit.

Nobilitates et Magnificentias vestras Altissimus conservare dignetur per tempora longiora felices !

Scriptum et sigillatum, sub sigillo villæ Gandensis ad causas, in absentia aliorum pro nobis omnibus, die mensis Junii xiij.

> SCABINI et CONSULES villæ Gandensis, necnon DEPUTATI villarum Brugensis, Yprensis, et Franci territorii, præsentialiter in prædicta villa Gandensi ad placita congregati.

*Endorsement :*—"Nobilibus ac magnificis et circumspectis viris, Dominis Thomæ Swynborne, Johanni Crofft, Militibus; Magistris Nicholao de Rysshetoun, Utriusque Juris Professori, ac Johanni Urban, Domicello, Ambassiatoribus pro parte Angliæ."

URBAN.

---

[1] See Letter XC.

## XCII.

### THE ALDERMEN OF THE HANSE TO HENRY IV.

*Gloriosissimo Principi serenissimoque Domino, Domino Henrico, Regi Angliæ et Franciæ, Dominoque Hiberniæ, Domino nobis gratioso, littera omnimoda reverentia præsentetur, recommendatione humillima nostri proni obsequii cum benevolo animo ad quævis et singula vestra beneplacita continue antemissa.*

Gratiosissime Princeps serenissimeque Domine. Comparuerunt coram nobis Henricus Kule, Hermannus Vulff, et Gosschaltus Johanssonne, mercatores de Almania Hanzæ Theutonicæ, de civitate Lubicensi oriundi, voce querelosa referentes qualiter nonnullæ gentes de vestræ Majestatis subditis duas naves, quarum unius magister erat Johannes Vornyden, alterius vero Rotgherus Hoppe, cives Hamburgenses, circa festum Penthecostes[1] ultimo elapsum, portum Flandrensem, videlicet Zwen, ineuntes, invaserunt, habentes intentum versus Hamborch cum onere dicto 'ballast' velificandi; sed tantum navis ejusdem Johannis Vornyden quibusdam mercimoniis et bonis onusta fuerat, ad prænominatos mercatores de Lubeka spectantibus, et ad nonnullos alios de Hamborch et circumvicinis locis de Hansa Theutonica, pro præsenti in Flandria personaliter non residentes; quos quidem nautas prædictos, cum eorum navibus et mercimoniis in eisdem existentibus, iidem vestri subditi ad vestram villam Nuecastell captivos perduxerunt.

*Marginal note:* Complaining that certain ships of Hamburgh had been captured by the English, and taken to Newcastle.

---

XCII.] MS. Cotton. Vesp. F. i. fol. 11. (γ).—On paper; a contemporaneous MS.

[1] Whitsunday fell on the 18th of May in the year 1404.

A.D. 1404.

They request that restitution may be made.

Sed, quoniam inter vestram serenissimam Dignitatem et vestros subditos ex parte una, et mercatores de Lubeka, Hamborch, et aliis civitatibus Hanzæ Theutonicæ ex parte altera, mutua pacis et amicitiæ fœdera continue speramus confoveri, cum vestri mercatores et subditi benevolis conversationibus et honorificis in eisdem civitatibus antedictis semper pertractantur, vestram illustrissimam regalem Majestatem cordintime humillimis precibus duximus implorandam quatinus, ob Dei reverentiam et justitiæ complementum, prædictis nautis, ab eorum captivitate quitis et solutis proclamatis, restitutionem eorum navium, et Marquardo Grelle et Ludolpho Cleyseke, ostensoribus præsentium, bona et mercimonia mercatorum prædictorum de Lubeke, et aliis civitatibus de Hansa antedicta, nomine eorundem fieri permittatis, ne nostrates de Hansa sæpedicta tantis et talibus damnis absque eorum demeritis et innocenter subjiciantur, et minus juste.

In his vestra regalis Majestas se exhibere dignetur.

Quam Altissimus felicem conservet et longævam, veluti in serenissima vestra Dominatione fiduciam gerimus ampliorem nobis præcipiendam.

Scriptum nostris sub sigillis xvij die mensis Junii, Anno XIIIIcIIII.

ALDERMANNI, necnon SENIORES JURATI COMMUNIUM MERCATORUM DE ALMANIA, Sacri Romani Imperii, Hanzæ Theutonicæ, pro præsenti Brugis Flandriæ residentes, vestræ excellentissimæ Dignitatis humillimi servitores.

A.D. 1404.

## XCIII.

### THE FLEMISH DEPUTIES TO THE MAYOR, ETC. OF THE STAPLE AT CALAIS.

Honurables et sages.

Pour ce que diverses merveilleuses nouvelles sont puis quatre ou synk jours en ce venuz nagueres on pays de par deca de [cer]taines entreprinses que, nonobstant les gracionses et amirables lettres, que lez ambassiatours de treshault et excellent Prinche le Roy d'Engleterre, vostre Seigneur, ont nouvellement escriptes par deca, contenans que le dit excellent Prinche et son noble Conseille sont prest et apparaillie d'entendre au traittie de la commune marchandise avoir cours d'entre le royaume d'Engleterre d'une part, et le pays de Flandres d'autre, devroient estre faictes en Engleterre pur enver le pays de Flandres, dont, se ainsi feust ce que pas ne povons croire, nous devroit tresgrant

*Inquiring as to the truth of a report that the English were preparing an expedition against Flanders.*

---

[TRANSLATION.]

Honourable and wise.—Forasmuch as sundry marvellous reports have lately within the past four or five days reached this land concerning certain enterprises which, (notwithstanding the gracious and admirable letters which the ambassadors of the most high and excellent Prince, the King of England, your Lord, have recently written to us here, setting forth that the said excellent Prince and his noble Council are ready and prepared to take into consideration a treaty as to the common interchange of merchandise between the realm of England on the one part and the country of Flanders on the other,) were to be undertaken in England against the land of Flanders, whereat if it were so, as we cannot at all believe, we must needs very greatly wonder, at the same time that, without

---

XCIII.] MS. Cotton. Galba, B. I. fol. 120. — On paper ; a contemporaneous MS.

A.D. 1404. merveille, meismement que, senz la bonne feance que nous avons es dessusditz ambassiatours, avons de nouvell ad certeigne nostre tresredoute Dame du dit traittie de par lez ditz ambassatours, et a elle supplie qu'il lui plaise au dit traittie ordonner et establir sez commissaires au plustost qu'elle purra aucunement, sicome plus a plain en escripvons aux dessusditz ambassiatours d'Engleterre.

Nous vous[1] prions, honurables et sages, tresaffectueusement et de coer, tant pur garder l'onneur des ditz ambassiatours que le nostre, que si aucun tiel entreprinse soit faicte en Engleterre ce que point ne croions, come dit est, il vous plaise tant faire qu'elle ne procede point, a vis que la traittie en commencie entre le dit excellent Prinche et le pays de Flandres puis estre continue. Car si les ambassiatours d'un coste et d'autre puissent venir en journees de traittie sicome ils serront bien briefment si Dieu pleist, nous avons ferme esperance que la chose sortira bone effect.

---

the good affiance that we have in the above-mentioned ambassadors, we have anew certified our most dread Lady of the said treaty made by the said ambassadors, and have besought her that it would please her, as to the said treaty, to ordain and confirm her commissaries as quickly as she can in any manner, as more plainly we have written to the above-mentioned ambassadors of England.— We pray you, honourable and wise, most faithfully and from our heart, as well to protect the honour of the said ambassadors as our own, that if any such enterprise be made in England, which we do not at all believe, as it is reported, it would please you as well to cause that it proceed not at all, with a view that the treaty commenced between the said excellent Prince and the country of Flanders may be continued. For if the ambassadors of the one side and of the other can come on the days of treaty as they shall arrive in a very short time, if it please God, we have firm hope that the matter will attain to a good result.—Also

---

[1] *vous*] Added above the line.

Auxi vous prions, honurables et sages, que lez lettres A.D. 1404.
que sur ce nous escripvons aux dessusditz ambassiatours
vous pleise a eux envoier par le premer seur message.

Et en la matere dessusdicte faire come en vous en
avons la plaine feance; et nous sur ce escripre vostre
bone et amiable response par le portour de cestes.

Honurables et sages, Nostre Seigneur soit garde de
vous!

Escript le xvij. jour de Juyn, souz le seel de la
ville de Bruges, pur nous tous.

> BOURGMAISTRES, ESCHEVINS et CONSEIL
> de la ville de Bruges, et lez DEPUTEZ
> dez Gand, Yprc, et du terroir de France,
> presentement assemblez en la dite ville
> de Bruges.

*Endorsement*:—" A honurables et sages, les Mair ou son
Lieutenant, Conestables, et Com-
paignye dez Marchans de l'Estaple
a Caleis."

---

we pray you, honourable and wise, that the letters which
we have written on this matter to the above-mentioned
ambassadors you would please to send to them by the first
trusty messenger; and to do in the matter above mentioned according as we have full trust in you; and write
to us concerning this matter your good and pleasant answer
by the bearer of these presents.—Honourable and wise,
Our Lord be your protection!

Written the 17th day of June, under the seal of the
town of Bruges, on behalf of us all.

> THE BURGOMASTERS, ASSESSORS, and COUNCIL
> of the town of Bruges, and the Deputies
> of Ghent, Ypres, and of the territory of
> France, at present assembled in the said
> town of Bruges.

*Endorsement*:—" To the honourable and wise the Mayor
or his Lieutenant, the Constables, and
Company of Merchants of the Staple at
Calais."

A.D. 1404.

## XCIV.

### THE FLEMISH DEPUTIES TO THE ENGLISH AMBASSADORS.

Stating that they have no doubt as to the successful result of the treaty,

[Hono]rabiles, magnifici, et circumspecti Domini.

Prout per certas litteras nostras vestris Reverentiis, per quemdam histrionem seu heraldum præpotentis et magnifici Domini, Domini Comitis de Somerset, Capitanei Calesii, ex parte Quatuor Me[mbrorum] Flandriæ prioribus vestris bonis respondendo, pridie scripsimus, nos indubie speramus, . . [et] pro certissimo tenemus, quod metuendissima Domina nostra naturalis, Domina Comitissa Flandriæ tractatui communi super cursu communis mercaturæ inter regnum Angliæ suasque partes Flandriæ solito more exercendæ, per suos ambassiatores, quemadmodum Locumtenenti Stapulæ dicti loci Calesii ipsa pridie litteraliter significavit, . . . . . . in melius vocabit et intendet. Nec formidamus quin, si vos cum prædictis Dominæ nostræ nunciis tractatui hujusmodi convenire contingat, simplici et bono zelo procedendo, quin idem tractatus debitum et utilem sortiatur effectum.

but inquiring as to the truth of the report that the English fleets were preparing to attack the coast of Flanders.

Verum, magnifici et circumspecti Domini, quia, non obstantibus prædictis vestris gratiosis litteris, varia et diversa vagabunda huc delata et publicata sunt nova, nobis tamen immo et omnibus probis proceribus et fidelibus patriæ penitus incredibilia, de insultu videlicet proxime fiendo patriæ Flandriæ per classes Anglicorum; per quem, si contingeret (quod absit), patria Flandriæ non solum damna incurreret, sed et nos penes nostram metuendissimam Dominam prædictam, omnesque suos proximos et cognatos, pro falsis sibique infidelibus

XCIV.] MS. Cotton. Galba, B. i. fol. 121.—On paper; a contemporaneous MS.

forsan teneremur, præsertim quia sub spe vestræ bonæ A.D. 1404. fidei innotuimus eidem Dominæ nostræ serenissimum Dominum, vestrum Regem, ac ipsius almum Concilium tractatui amicabili cum eadem Domina nostra intendere et vacare velle.

Hinc est quod Magnificentias et Circumspectiones vestras affectuose rogamus, quatinus, si qua in detrimentum, præjudicium, vel gravamen supradicti tractatus per Episcopum de Norwicis,[1] seu quosvis alios de parte Angliæ sint attemptata vel attemptanda, tamen facere quod illa effectum non sortiantur; quin immo juxta inceptum et laudabile vestrum propositum procedatur tractatu in prædicto; in hoc quoque, magnifici et circumspecti Domini, facturi prout in vestris Fidelitatibus fiduciam gerimus pleniorem, et de his vestris litteris nos reddere certiores citius quo possitis.

Honorabiles, magnifici, et circumspecti Domini, Altissimus vestras conservet Discretiones prospere et votive!

Scriptum die xvij. mensis Junii, sub sigillo ad causas villæ Brugensis, pro omnibus nobis.

> BURGIMAGISTRI SCABINI et CONSULES villæ Brugensis, necnon DEPUTATI villarum Gandensis, Yprensis, ac territorii Franci officii partium Flandriæ, præsentialiter in præfata villa Brugensi congregati.

*Endorsement*:—"Honorabilibus, magnificis, et circumspectis Dominis, Dominis Ambassiatoribus excellentissimi Principis et Domini, Domini Regis Angliæ, Londoniæ existentibus."

> URBAN.

---

[1] Henry Le Spenser.

R

## XCV.

### THE MAGISTRATES OF STRALSUND TO HENRY IV.

*Illustrissimæ Serenitatis magnifico et præglorioso Principi que Domino, Domino Henrico, Regi Angliæ et Franciæ excellentissimo ac Domino Hiberniæ, quamgratioso Domino et benignissimo promotori nostro, Consules Stralessundenses humillimi totius humilitatis nostræ cum recommendatione reverentialissima ac jugi intendiosissimorum benevolentia nostrorum servientium incessabilem ferventissimamque propertelam.*

Quammagnifice gratiose Domine, Rex serenissime.

Complaining of outrages committed by certain Englishmen, especially by John Brandon, of Lynn,—

Sane quia inter illustrissimos Principes, Dominos Reges Angliæ, vestros prædecessores, et prædecessores nostros, ac utrorumque ipsorum cives et mercatores alternæ dilectionis et bonæ concordantiæ ab olim præviguit sinceritas, qua se benignis favoribus ad alterutrum protractarunt, unde utilitas reipublicæ, cujus corona vestra regia non solum zelatrix, immo revera adauctrix proclamatur præcipua, notabile inter dictos mercatores susceperat incrementum.

Cui utilitati reipublicæ nos, laudifluis prædecessorum nostrorum instructi exemplis, merito intenti, licet hujusmodi sinceritatem alternæ dilectionis et bonæ concordantiæ fovere cordialiter optaverimus, quo non minus adhuc optantes nonnulli tamen vestratum ipsam in multo lacerarunt per damna, gravamina, et violentias plurimas, præsertim et principaliter a Johanne Brandoun, vestro subdito in civitate vestra Lindensi, suosque in hac parte complices, securitate et tranquilla pace utrimque vigentibus, nobis et nostris injuriose pluries illatas; unde alias Majestati vestræ regiæ nostras porreximus

litteras, juxta informationem pro tunc nobis factam A.D. 1404.
super duarum ablatione navium nostrorum concivium
et mercatorum, suorumque bonorum inibi contentorum.

At vero iidem concives nostri, certiori de suis ablatis
habita inquisitione, nos distinctius pro nunc super
eisdem informabant sub modo subsequenti, ut puta
quod Anno Domini $M^oCCC^{mo}XCVII.$, circa festum
Omnium Sanctorum,[1] famuli dicti Johannis Brandoun
cum suis navibus abstulerunt . . . . . . . . . Nicholai
Borins xi. vasa vinorum, de valore lxix. nobilium, et xj.
nobiles promptæ pecuniæ nostris concivibus pertinentes et pertinentia; quæ in dicti Johannis Brandoun
usum pervenerunt.

Insuper eodem anno, ante festum Dominicæ Incar- at Lynn,
nationis,[2] dictus Johannes Brandoun, in portu Lindensi,
personaliter recepit in navi Pauli Stenneld xiij. lastas
et iiij. tunnas allecium, et iiij$^c$ lignorum Voag Henschot,
concivibus et mercatoribus nostris pertinentes; quarum
lastarum allecium quælibet in foro Lindensi xxij. nobiles,
et quælibet centena dictorum lignorum ij. nobiles solve-
bant. Super quibus bonis præmissis sumptus xxvij.
nobilium facti sunt, et expensæ quorum bonorum et
sumptuum præmissorum summa ad ccc. et xviij. nobiles
unus quartus se extendit.

Ceterum anno Domini M.CCCXCVIII., circa festum at Bos-
Paschæ,[3] dictus Johannes Brandoun recepit in portu ton,
Bustensi Petro Vranken, concivi nostro, navem sibi et
Domino Nicolao Veghe, nostro conconsulari, pertinentem,
de valore c. et x. nobilium, et navulum scilicet xc.
nobiles de mercibus ejusdem navis derivatum.

Item in navi Johannis Romer, ex portu Hasloensi
Norvoegiæ velificante, recepit idem Johannes Brandoun
in bonis nostri concivis ad valorem viginti nobilium.

---

[1] November 1.
[2] December 25.

[3] Easter Day fell on April 7 in the year 1398.

R 2

A.D. 1404.

They lament the aggravations attending these outrages,

De quibus omnibus præmissis, navi et bonis nostrorum conconsularis, concivium, et mercatorum, nondum quidquam æquitatis aut rationis eisdem meminimus refluxisse, licet iidem in bonis vestrorum mercatorum, in quantitate et valore notabilibus interim in civitate nostra frequenter existentibus, se dudum potuissent revelasse : quod tamen permittere nolentes præmissa non importuno pertransivimus animo vestræ Majestatis regalis contemplatione ac spe pacis et bonæ concordantiæ adhuc utrimque confovendæ, vestrates nostram civitatem visitantes, non obstantibus præmissis caritative colligentes cum benigna promotionis pertractatione et honore. Ast præcipue vestris regalibus pensatis hortamentis, de quibus litteræ vestræ regiæ, nuper nobis porrectæ, et per nos debita reverentia humiliter susceptæ, in hæc verba cecinere,—et ne cœptis deinceps in nos et nostros hujusmodi benefactis gratuitis desistatis attentius exoramus. Necnon pacis et securitatis concessionibus, in eisdem litteris vestris regiis expressatis, concives et mercatores nostri, hujusmodi cœpta benefacta juxta exhortationem et affectum vestrum regalem frequentare volentes, bona sua super regalibus vestris prætactæ pacis et securitatis concessionibus versus regnum vestrum Angliæ iterato legare assumpserunt ; vestri autem, prætactis damnis et violentiis non contenti, ad præfatas vestras regales pacis securitatis concessiones enervandas, ac sinceritatem dilectionis alternæ et bonæ concordantiæ prædictæ, spirabant, et quantum valebant conabantur extinguendam. Et, quod dolendum est, dolorem super dolorem addentes, vulneribus novissima pejora prioribus reddiderunt, concivesque et mercatores nostros non solum bonis et rebus, sed etiam (proh !) corporibus eorum et personis ; horride namque submersionis acerbitate aliquos eorum inhuman[iter] interimentes, gravius et multiplicius damnificarunt, prout in cedula papyria lucide continetur præsentibus involuta. Quæ non paucas nostro incus-

sabant pectori molestias, concivibus et mercatoribus A.D. 1404. nostris damnificatis adeo provocatis, quod per eos incitati vestrorum mercatorum bona in civitate nostra pro nunc existentia poni fecimus sub arresta, eisdem tamen simultate sana et fida conservantia indispersis, super eo quod vestrates, ad quos hujusmodi arrestata bona spectare noscuntur, vestro regali se presentent conspectui, ac erga Majestatem vestram regiam conentur quantum valeant et procurent; ut, si ipsa clementi mota animadversione dictis concivibus nostris et mercatoribus suorum allatorum decreverit responsionem creare condignam, quam intimis affectamus visceribus, vestratum manibus prætacta arrestata libere et integre reaffluant sua bona. Res enim onerosa, et nimirum intollerabile,[1] nobis existit quod vestrates, securitate et pace pro nobis et nostris gavisi, nostros mercatores de die in diem reddunt non indemnes, damna damnis incessanter accumulantes.

Placeat igitur, gloriose Domine, Rex serenissime, *and entreat the King to interfere.* vestræ regali Clementiæ ad præmissa animo pietatis inclinari, nostram attendendo benevolentiam, qua semper ad vestra regalia beneplacita eramus præsto, cujusmodi adhuc nos fore affectamus gloriæ vestræ regiæ humiliter famulandi, ac vestros quantum possumus honoratos promotosque habendi, vestræ gloriosæ regalis contemplatione Majestatis.

Cui misericorditer intendat ubilibet Rex Æternus diutinæ convalescentiæ et felicitatis cum salute, vestris tanquam humillime benevolis confidenter præcepturæ quid Majestas vestra regia in præmissis facere decrevit; de isto clementem vestram regiam humillime petimus responsivam.

Datum Stralessundiæ, Anno Domini Millesimo quadringentesimo quarto, vicesima tertia die mensis Junii, nostræ civitatis sub secreto.

---

[1] Sic.

A.D. 1404.  *The following is the document referred to in the above letter as being inclosed in it:—*

A list of other robberies committed by Englishmen, besides those by John Brandon.

In hac Cedula nos, Consules Strallesundenses, conscribi fecimus bona per gentem serenissimi et magnifici Principis, Domini Regis Angliæ, nostris concivibus et mercatoribus ablata, de quibus in nostra littera, cui præsens cedula est inclusa, continetur; exceptis bonis quæ Johannes Brandoun nostris concivibus auferebat et mercatoribus.

Unde vestram regiam humillime petimus Majestatem de solutione bonorum præmissorum, tam per dictum Johannem Brandoun, quam alios vestros quoscumque nostris concivibus ablatorum, clementer eisdem providere.

(1) By the servants of the Earl of Northumberland:

In primis namque Anno Domini M°.CCCC°, circa festum Nativitatis Beati Johannis Baptistæ,[1] per gentem Domini Comitis de Northumberlant, suasque bardiese et naves alias, ablata fuit in mari Johanni Bokelman, nostro concivi, nova navis, cum tritico, braseo, farina, cervisia, terebinto, et lignis voag henschot onustata; quæ navis, cum bonis præmissis, de valore iij$^c$ et xxxvj. nobilium, nostris concivibus pertinebat; nauclero dictæ navis, scilicet Johanne prædicto, met duodecimo viro, per dictam gentem Comitis prædicti horribiliter submerso.

(2) By Lord Grey:

Item, Anno Domini M°.CCCCII°, Dominus Greie, pro tunc ex parte Domini Regis prædicti amerarius seu capitaneus maris, in navi Tidemani Kule recepit amigdala, mitras, et caligas, de valore xxxj. nobilium, nostris concivibus pertinentia.

(3) By men of Hull:

Eodem anno receperunt Johannes Tutbard et Willielmus Terry, de Hol, navem quam rexit Hermannus Burovoe, et bona inibi contenta, scilicet siliginem braseum, et hordeum; cujus navis medietas et quarta

---

[1] June 24.

pars dictorum bonorum, de valore iii$^c$ et v. nobilium, A.D. 1404.
nostro concivi pertinebant.

Item, Anno Domini M$^o$ CCCCIII$^o$, circa principium (4) By men of Lynn and
Quadragesimæ,[1] cum duabus navibus bardiesen, quarum
unam rexit Laurentius Mundy, ex parte Johannis Hyde:
Barbran civis Lundensis ipsam expedientis, alteram
vero rexit Voilhelmus Lye de Heyde, ex parte Johannis
Inbrok, in Dovernia morantis, illam expedientis, et cum
alia nave ballinger dicti Laurentius et Voilhelmus
receperunt Hermanno Voernersone suam navem, cum
bonis inibi existentibus, scilicet liiij. lastis et ij. tunnis
allecium, et uno harnesio, de iiij$^{or}$ nobilibus, nostris con-
consularibus concivibus et mercatoribus pertinentibus ;
omnes homines in dicta navi constitutos, præter
dictum Hermannum cum duobus viris, crudeliter
demergentes. Qui Hermannus prædictus, cum hujusmodi navi et bonis, versus Hathin velificasse debuisset,
ubi quælibet dictarum lastarum allecium xxiiij. nobiles
bene solvisset : de quibus præmissis bonis summa ad
xiij$^c$ et xij. nobiles se extendit.

Eodem anno, circa festum Paschæ,[2] auferebantur in (5) From Peter Warre :
navi Petri Voarre v. vasa vinorum, quodlibet de valore
x. nobilium et xvj. florein (seu francones), nostro concivi
pertinentia ; quorum summa lvij. nobiles.

Eodem anno, tempore hyemali, in navi Jacobi Bodiker (6) From James Bodiker :
auferebantur ij. lastæ allecium, nostro conconsulari pertinentes, quælibet lasta in Anglia, ubi pervenerat, xx.
nobiles solvente.

Item, Anno Domini M$^o$ CCCCIIII$^o$, circa festum (7) By men of Blaken-ham :
Paschæ,[3] in navi Symonis Smarte, ablatæ fuerunt per
illos de Blacknam vj. lastæ cum j. tunna Voysmariensis
terinsiæ in eorum portum pervenientes, quæ in civitate
Voysmariensi xxxvj. constabant nobilibus.

---

[1] Ash Wednesday fell on February 28th in the year 1403.

[2] Easter Day fell on April 15th in the year 1403.

[3] Easter Day fell on March 30th in the year 1404.

A.D. 1404.   Eodem anno circa festum Pentecostes,[1] in navi
(8) From   Johannis Deghener, conconsularis nostri, auferebantur
John
Deghener : sua bona de valore x. nobilium.

By        Eisdem anno et tempore Voilhelmus Bighe de Novo
William   Castello, cum navi bardiese Voilhelmi Jonsone, ibidem
Bigh, of
Newcastle; morantis illam expedientis, abstulit Johanni Suteboter
and others. navem, cum sale, sibi ac nostro conconsulari et concivibus
pertinentem, de valore ij$^c$ et xxviij. nobilium, præter
bona salis in eadem navi ad civitatem Grypes Voal-
densem pertinentia.

Eisdem anno et tempore, in classe de Rossele, ablata
fuerunt nostro concivi xiiij. vasa vinorum, quolibet x.
nobiles valente; et in navi Lollenhusen xvj. tunnæ
allecium de valore xx. nobilium. Quæ vina et allecia
in Kaleys fuerunt apportata. Quorum summa c. et
xxxiij. nobiles.

Summa valorum præmissorum bonorum in præsenti
cedula conscriptorum, una cum bonis per Johannem
Brandoun nostris concivibus ablatis, iij$^m$ et lxxxiiij.
nobiles minus quarterium.[2]

## XCVI.

### DE RYSSHETON TO HENRY IV.

Inqu iring   Serenissime Princeps ac excellentissime Domine;
as to the
truth of the votiva humillima recommendatione præmissa, vestræ
reports of
an attack   regiæ Majestati sanctissimæ tam debita quam devota.
onFlanders  Copias quarumdam litterarum etiam sub diversis
being me-
ditated by  datis duplicatas ex parte Quatuor Membrorum Flan-
the En-     driæ vestris commissariis pro ipsius tractatu pro parte
glish Ad-
mirals.

---

[1] Whitsunday fell on May 18th    XCVI.] MS. Cotton. Galba, B
in the year 1404.                  I. fol. 119.—On paper ; original.
    Altered from " iijm et xc. nobiles    [2] See Letters XC., XCI., and
iijm."                             XCIV.

vestra alias deputatis; in quibus litteris, mihi directis, A.D. 1404. eidem vestræ Majestati illustrissimæ transmitto præsentibus interclusas, ex quarum serie lucide poteritis concipere quod Comitissa Flandriæ pro se et filio suo Duce Burgundiæ, prout alias Quatuor Membris Flandriæ scripseram, propter tractatus validitatem firmiorem a Rege Francorum, Domino suo prætenso, ad tractandum cum vestris commissariis pro unitate inter vestrum regnum Angliæ ac communitatem Flandriæ, obtinuit licentiam et commissionem sufficientem, prout bonæ memoriæ Dux Burgundiæ, dum ageret in humanis, ut prætenditur hactenus, obtinuit; quodque Flandrenses timent vestros admirallos, ac ipsorum classem et navigium, et præsertim quod in partibus Flandriæ, prout varia et vagabunda super his delata extiterant intendant applicare, ac damna non faciliter enumerabilia eis inferre; necnon propter tractatum ipsorum Flandrensium penes Dominam ipsorum procuratum eadem Domina ipsos tanquam falsos velit reputare, ac infidelitatem ipsis ascribere, propter prædictum navigium, pendente tractatu, subordinatum.

Vestra Majestas regia illustrissima vestro nobili Concilio, ac mihi, vestro Clerico humillimo, dignetur clare rescribere qualiter præmissa ac alia hujusmodi tractatum concernentia placeat dirigere, ac vestram voluntatem in eisdem juxta tenorem aliarum litterarum nuper eidem vestræ Majestati transmissarum lucidius declarare, prout eidem vestræ Excellentiæ videbitur expedire.

Quam dirigat Altissimus ad regni vestri prosperitatem feliciter et votive!

Scriptum Londoniæ, xxv. die mensis Junii.

Vestræ regiæ Majestati sacratissimæ,

[NICHOLAUS DE RYSSHETOUN.][1]

---

[1] The signature has been torn off.

A.D. 1404.
and re-
questing
that the
arrears of
his stipend
may be
paid.

Quia, ultra omnia bona mea in tractatu Calisii consumpta ac penitus exhausta, sum indebitatus in magnis quantitatibus pecuniarum, dignetur vestra Majestas vestro almo Concilio committere, quod realiter ac integraliter, absque assignationibus,[1] velint mihi satisfacere; quia propter paupertatem ad vestram præsentiam non potero accedere.

*Endorsed :*—" Serenissimo Principi, ac illustrissimo et [invictissimo Domino], Domino H., Dei gratia Regi Angliæ et Franciæ e[xcellentissimo]."

## XCVII.

### THE DUCHESS OF BURGUNDY TO JOHN URBAN.

*La Duchesse de Bourgongne, Contesse de Flandres, d'Artois, et de Bourgongne.*

Having re-
ceived au-
thority
from the
French
King,

Chier et bien ame.

En continuant ce que autresfois par noz lettres[2] de la date de vij<sup>e</sup> jour du mois de Juing darrain passe

---

[TRANSLATION.]

*The Duchess of Burgundy, Countess of Flanders, of Artois, and of Burgundy.*

Dear and well-beloved.—In continuation of that which, on a former occasion, by our letter of the date of the

---

[1] *absque assignationibus*] Added above the line.

XCVII.] MS. Cotton. Galba, B. I. fol. 105.—On paper ; a contemporaneous MS.
[2] See Letter XC.

escript vous avons entre autres choses, veulliez savoir, A.D. 1404. que noz gens que envoiez aviens devers mon Seigneur le Roy, nous ont nagaires a leur retour apporte les Lettres Patentes de mon dit Seigneur le Roy, par lesquelles il a donne povoir semblable a nous, et a nostre treschier filz aisne, le Duc de Bourgongne, et a chascun de nous, sur le fait du traitie de la seurte du cours de la marchandise entre le pays d'Engleterre et le nostre de Flandres, comme paravant avoit eu feu nostre treschier Seigneur et mari, dont Dieux ait l'ame.

Et pour ce que nous desirons que le dit traitie soit entretenu et puisse venir a bon et brief effect, au prouffit commun des deux pays dessusdiz, nous avons desia ordonne noz commis a ce ceulx qui paravant y furent commis et deputez depar nostre dit feu Seigneur et mari ; c'est assavoir le Vidame d'Amiens, Messieur Gulliaume de Halewin, Chevaliers, Maistir Jehan de

*she desires that the treaty may be renewed, and names her deputies ;*

---

7th day of the month of June last past, we wrote to you, among other things, be pleased to know that our people, whom we sent to my Lord the King, have recently on their return brought unto us the Letters Patent of my said Lord the King, by the which he has given like power to us, and to our most dear eldest son, the Duke of Burgundy, and to each and either of us, as to the making of the treaty for the security of mercantile intercourse between the country of England and our own country of Flanders, as was formerly possessed by our late most dear Lord and husband, whose soul God have in keeping.—And forasmuch as we desire that the said treaty be taken in hand, and that it may attain to a good and speedy result, to the common benefit of the two countries above mentioned, we have long since ordained to be our commissaries in the matter those who formerly were commissaries and deputies therein on behalf of our said late Lord and husband ; that is to say, the Vidam[1] of Amiens, Master William de Halewin, Knights,

---

[1] *See* the Glossary.

A.D. 1404. Nyelles, et Maistir Thierry Cherbode, noz conseilleurs, et qu'ilz soient aux hosteulx en nostre ville de Saint Omer, de huy en xv. jours, xx$^e$ jour de ce present mois de Juillet, pour entendre et vaquier au dit traitie, avec les commis ou messages qui a ce sont ou serront commis de la partie d'Engleterre.

and requests that the English commissaries may be sent at once,

Si veulliez pour l'avancement de ceste besoigne, (dont au plaisir de Dieu tant de bien se ensieura d'un coste et d'autre) faire tant que par vostre bonne diligence les dis commis ou messages de vostre coste soient pour la dicte cause prest au dit jour en la ville de Calais pour le lendemain faire savoir les uns aux autres le jour d'estre ensemble au lieu de Rodelinghem empres Campaignes autresfois avise et accorde entre eulz.

and an exchange of safe-conducts made.

Et pour abregier le fait veulliez pour noz dis commis envoier saufconduit en la fourme de cellui que autresfois, par le porteur de cestes ; les noms de ceulx

---

Master John de Nyelles, and Master Thierry Cherbode, our councillors, and that they should be in their houses in our town of S. Omer on this day fifteen days, viz., the 20th day of this present month of July, for to consider and deliberate upon the said treaty, together with the commissaries or envoys who are or shall be commissioned on this matter on the part of England.—So please you, therefore, for the sake of advancing this business, (from which, if it be God's pleasure, as much good will ensue on one side as on the other) to cause, by your good diligence, that the said commissaries or envoys on your side may be, for the said cause, ready on the said day in the town of Calais, that the one set may acquaint the others on the morrow of the day of meeting at the place of Rodelinghem, near Champagne, at a former time arranged and settled between them.—And to cut short the matter, you will be pleased to send for our said commissaries a safe-conduct, in the form of that which was made on the former occasion, by the bearer of these presents ; the names of

qui au dit traitie sont ou seront ordonnez pour la dicte A.D. 1404
partie d'Engleterre, sur aventure se l'en y averoit commis autres que ceulx qui autresfois y ont este nommez
et commis, affin que pour eulz semblable saufconduit
vous soit envoie depar nous, et que l'en puisse senz
delaier entendre et vaquier au dit traitie, et le demener
a bonne fin et conclusion.

Et sur ce nous veulliez rescripre vostre bonne response par le dit porteur de cestes.

Nostre Seignur vous ait en Sa garde!

Escript a Arras, ce Dymence, vje jour de Juillet.

MOERKKEN.

*Endorsement :*—"A nostre chiere et bien ame Jeh[an
Urban], Lieutenant du Maire de
l'Estaple [a Calais]."

*Also :*—"Copia litteræ Ducissæ Burgundiæ."

---

those who are or shall be appointed to effect this treaty
on the said behalf of England, on the chance that she may
have commissioned others than those who on the former
occasion were nominated and commissioned thereunto, to the
end that on their behalf there may be sent to you by us
a like safe-conduct, and that they may be enabled without
delay to consider and deliberate on the said treaty, and
conduct it to a good issue and conclusion.—And hereupon
you will be pleased to write back to us your favourable
answer by the bearer of these presents.—Our Lord have
you in his keeping!—Written at Arras, this Sunday, the
6th day of July.

MOERKKEN.

*Endorsement:*—"To our dear and well-beloved John Urban,
Lieutenant of the Mayor of the Staple at
Calais."

A.D. 1404.

## XCVIII.

### JOHN HAULEY TO HENRY IV.

Tresexcellent, trespuissant, et tresredoute Seigneur.

Excusing himself from appearing before the King,

Humblement jeo me recomande a vostre treshaut et roial Magestie, come vostre poevre liege.

Plese a vostre haut et roial Magestie savoir, que jeo ay rescue vostre treshonourable et tresgracious lettre a moy directe le Samady prochein devant la fessaunce d'icestes, le quel lettre fait mention que jeo devoie estre personalement devant vostre tresexcellent et tresredoute presence, le Lundy prochein apres le feste de Seint Mergarete[1] prochein venant, en quiconque lieu que vous, tresgracious et tresnoble Seigneur, soiez en Engletere.

---

### [TRANSLATION.]

Most excellent, most mighty, and most dread Lord.— Humbly I recommend myself to your most high and royal Majesty, as your poor liege.—May it please your high and royal Majesty to know that I have received your most honourable and most gracious letter, directed to me on the Saturday next before the writing of these presents, the which letter makes mention that I ought to appear personally before your most excellent and most dread presence on the Monday next after the feast of S. Margaret next ensuing, in whatever place in England you, most gracious and most noble Lord, may

---

XCVIII.] MS. Cotton. Cleop. F. III., fol. 60 b.—On paper; original.     [1] July 20.

Qe plese a vostre tresexcellent, trespuissant, et <sub>A.D. 1404.</sub> tresredoute Seigneurie de moy tenir pur excuse que jeo ne veign moy mesmez devant vostre treshaut et tresgracious presence a present : qar, tresexcellent, trespuissant, et tresredoute Seigneur, si plesir soit a vostre treshaut et roial Magestie savoir, que jeo ay este si grantement malade en l'un de mes jambez, plus qu'un mois devant la venu de vostre treshonorable et tresgracious lettre, et unqore je fieu, que jeo ne puisse chevachier, ne bien aller.

Et, si plesir soit a vostre tresexcellent, trespuissant, et tresredoute Seigneurie, un Thomas Hille de Dertemouth, ad fait subgestioun sur moy que je devoie envoier un Richard Leyne, et autre, a Salthasshe, pur prendre un Oliver Arelle, Breton, prisoner ; et, tresexcellent et tresredoute Seigneur, salve la reverence de vostre treshaut et roiale Magestie, jeo ne savoie unqores rien de celle fait, ne un fieu al concent en bon foy de Jhesu Crist, tanque que le dit Richard

*and inquiring what he is to do with certain Breton prisoners.*

---

happen to be.—May it please your most excellent, most mighty, and most dread Lordship to hold me excused, for that I cannot come myself in person before your most high and most gracious presence at this time : for, most excellent, most mighty, and most dread Lord, if it please your most high and royal Majesty, know that I have been suffering from so severe a disorder in one of my legs, for more than a month previously to the arrival of your most honourable and most gracious letter, and still am, that I am not able to ride, and not well able to walk.—And, if it please your most excellent, most mighty, and most dread Lordship, one Thomas Hill, of Dartmouth, has made a suggestion to me, that I ought to send one Richard Leyne, and another, to Saltash, for to take one Oliver Arelle, a Breton, prisoner ; and most excellent and most dread Lord, saving the reverence due to your most high and royal Majesty, I know nothing yet of this matter, nor was at all consenting, by the good faith of Jesus Christ, until the said Richard Leyne came to me, and offered to

A.D. 1404. Leyne venoit a moy, et moy offrast a vendre le moite du dit prisoner, en disant a moy qu'il avoit abatu le dit prisoner en le sconfiture a Blakpolle, et lessast le dit prisoner en le gard du dit Thomas Hille, et ency jeo ay achate le moite du dit prisoner du dit Richard, le quel prisoner, tresexcellent, trespuissant, et tresredoute Seigneur, jeo envoie envers vostre treshaut et tresgracious presence.

Et, tresexcellent, trespuissant, et tresredoute Seigneur, si plesir soit a vostre treshaut et roial Magestie savoir que touchant le moite du dit prisoner, jeo me mette tout en vostre tresnoble et tresgracious ordenance ; et, tresexcellent, trespuissant, et tresredoute Seigneur, si plesir soit a vostre treshaut et tresroialle Magestie savoir, que jeo avoie et ay achate de Antony Johan le moite de Tange Castelle, frere au Seigneur de Castelle, prisoner, le quel Tange est en vostre tresexcellent, trespuissant, et tresredoute commandement, que plese a vostre tresexcellent, trespuissant, et tresredoute Seig-

---

sell the moiety in the said prisoner, telling me that he had knocked down the said prisoner in the discomfiture at Blackpool, and had left the said prisoner in the custody of the said Thomas Hill ; and also I have purchased the moiety in the said prisoner of the said Richard, the which prisoner, most excellent, most mighty, and most dread Lord, I have sent to your most high and most gracious presence. And, most excellent, most mighty, and most dread Lord, if it please your most high and royal Majesty, know that, touching the moiety in the said prisoner, I commit myself entirely to your most noble and most gracious disposal.— And, most excellent, most mighty, and most dread Lord, if it please your most high and most royal Majesty, know that I have and have purchased of Anthony John the moiety in Tange Castell, brother to the Lord of Castell, prisoner, the which Tange is at your most excellent, most mighty, and most dread disposal, that it may please your most excellent, most mighty, and most dread Lordship to

neurie de ordeigner pur moy et pur null autre, ceo A.D. 1404.
que vostre tresgracious volounte est que appartiendra
a le moite du dit prisoner. Qar le dit Antony Johan
fuist a le prendre a le jurons de Blakepolle et fuist
en botyn ovesque un Stephen Modberie.

Et, tresexcellent, trespuissant, et tresredoute Seigneur,
le Tout-Puissant Dieux vous ottroie bon vie et longe
a vostre plesir, et vous encrese en joye et en honours
devant tout autres Seigneurs en monde vivant!

Escript a Dertemouthe, le xiiij. jour de Juillet.

> Vostre povere liege, si plesir soit a vostre
> haut Seigneurie,
>
> JOHAN HAULEY,
> de Dertemouthe.

---

ordain for me, and for no other, that which is your most
gracious will in that which shall appertain to the moiety
in the said prisoner. For the said Anthony John was at
his taking before the jurors of Blackpool, and had a share
of the booty with Stephen Modbury (?).—And, most excellent, most mighty, and most dread Lord, the Almighty
God grant to you good life and long at your pleasure, and
increase you in joy and honours before all other Lords, living
in the world.—Written at Dartmouth, the 14th day of July.

Your poor liege, if it please your high Lordship,

> JOHN HAULEY,
> of Dartmouth.

A.D. 1404.

## XCIX.

### CONRAD DE JUNGINGEN TO HENRY IV.

In reply to a previous Letter.

Humili recommendatione cum votiva nostrarum precum instantia jugiter ad vestræ regiæ beneplic[itum] præaccepta.

Serenissime Rex, Princeps magnifice, Domine gloriose ac nobis sincere dilecte.

Pridem nobis exhibitis litteris[1] dignativis per Johannem Broun, vestræ præclarissimæ Magnificentiæ ligium, quæ sane intellectæ hæc in summa continere videbantur, qualiter a diu inter negotiatores regni vestri et terrarum nostrarum etiam quantum ad pacificos accessus sibi mutuo comparticipando fuerint communia commercia plurimarum utilitatum productiva. Sed nunc præfata et perutilis conversatio, propter quædam damna facta[2] a piratis in mari hinc inde accessus vestratim ad terras nostras eisdem esset penitus interdictus. Insuper reminiscentes[3] veteris et habitæ dilectionis amicitiæ, cum amœnitatis pace, quæ a Christi fidelibus sunt summo opere amplexanda; quarum gratia clementissimam vestram Celsitudinem ad hoc consentaneam plene obtuleritis, quatinus laxato interdicto hinc ad festum Paschæ proxime affuturum[4] mercatores dicti per dominia vestræ Serenitatis ad terras nostras, et e converso nostrates ad vestras possint, quibuslibet gravaminibus cessantibus, sua consueta negotia contractare, præsertim cum medio

---

XCIX.] MS. Cotton. Nero, B. II. fol. 41.
[1] See Letter LXXXIX.
[2] *facta*] fata, MS.

[3] *reminiscentes*] renmiscientes, MS.
[4] Easter Day fell on April 19th in the year 1405.

tempore vestra regalis Providentia disposuit ad nos A.D. 1404. dirigere suos ambassiatores de prætensis injuriis, quatinus vestrates concernere poterit nobiscum per viam amicabilem tractaturos, adjicientes in specie ut, cum vestrates ad Sconiæ partes pervenerint pro allicibus capiendis, vestræ considerationis intuitu, eosdem habeamus recommissos, etc.

Serenissime Domine Rex, ac Princeps gratiose, vestræ gratuitæ ac nobis valde acceptabilis exhibitionis oracula suspenso et desiderato corde amplectimur, quibus læsis complementum justitiæ cultumque pacis et amicitiæ tam diligentissime persuasistis, de persona vestræ Serenitatis sicuti de nostra minime hæsitantes, et quarumlibet de parte nostra quin per omnia æqualia in hoc nostra sint motiva nec transgredi earum terminos de facili vellemus ullo modo sine justa ac rationabili causa, cum dicta revera sint felicissima adjumenta reipublicæ et naturæ.

Ad illud vero quod de laxando interdicto accessus vestratum ad terras nostras subjunxeritis infra hinc et festum Paschæ,[1] etc., respondemus, salvo vestræ Magnificentiæ consilio saniori, magis expedire utrimque ejusmodi interdictum suspensum, quam laxatum, quousque læsis hinc inde non verbis tantum sed executive ac realiter fuerit satisfactum, vel via juris ac amicabilis compositionis. Non enim æque contrahendo consortiuntur depauperatus et locupletatus, justitiæ complementum consecutus et non consecutus, offensor et offensus, quia ii non paribus affectibus stimulantur. Reminiscientia siquidem injuriarum inconsultos iracundiæ calores faciliter evocat. Talis etiam permixtio velut opposita lege plus affert amaritudinis quam dulcedinis, plus livoris quam amoris; e quibus duriores querelæ, tam apud vestram Magni-

---

[1] April 19.

s 2

A.D. 1404. ficientiam, quam nos, possent occasionaliter suboriri. Novit Deus quod adusque importunis et instantibus querelis nostratim nimium sumus fatigati et pulsati, quod dictum interdictum laxare aut dissolvere nequeamus ad præsens bono modo, nisi ab ambassiatoribus Dominationis vestræ fuerimus sufficienter informati de satisfaciendo damnum passis.

Verum, quod vestra Serenitas adjungit de vestratibus cum venerint ad partes Sconiæ, eos habere sub clipeo protectionis, etc., notum sit vestræ Celsitudini quod, ob causas nos rationabiliter moventes, provocati per Dominam Reginam Daciæ ac suam gentem, juncti non benevoli, gratia propulsandæ injuriæ, misimus contra eas exercitum nostrum ; sed ad tempus certum treugæ hinc inde sunt interpositæ, ita quod nostro actu jam ad propria redierunt. Absit etiam ut, frementibus . . . . . . . per nostrates scienter extranei ab eisdem quarumcumque terrarum aut nationum quolibet deberent molestari aut calumniari ; quia hoc esset opprimere innocentes propter nocentes, damnare justos pro injustis, quo nihil crudelius, et ultio impietatis. Revera, Princeps et Domine gloriose, de omni incommodo vestri regiminis cordialiter compatimur, alto desiderio cupientes singula prospere agi ac felicitari circa personam et regimen vestræ illustrissimæ Magnificentiæ, per tempora diuturna.

Cui confidimus de simili nos totumque ordinem nostrum ob precum nostrarum intuitum humillime commendantes.

Datum in Castro nostro Merienburgh, xvi. die mensis Julii, Anno Domini Millesimo CCCC$^{mo}$ quarto.

Frater CONRADUS DE JUNGINGEN,
    Ordinis Beatæ Mariæ Theutonicorum Ierusolymitani Magister Generalis.

A.D. 1404.

## C.

### DE RYSSHETON AND URBAN TO THE FOUR MEMBERS OF FLANDERS.

*Copia litterœ, transmissœ Quatuor Membris Flandriœ per Ambassiatores Angliœ:—*

Honorabiles ac magnifici et circumspecti Domini.

Nuper certas litteras[1] honorabilis ac magnificæ Dominæ, Dominæ Margaretæ, Ducissæ Burgundiæ, etc., ac Comitissæ Flandriæ, Attrebati vj. die præsentis mensis Julii scriptas ac locumtenenti Stapulæ Calisii transmissas, noveritis nos vidisse, inter cetera continentes, quod præfata Domina recepit Litteras Patentes super licentia pro se et primogenito suo a Rege Francorum, quem vos nominatis Dominum vestrum superiorem, ad tractandum cum nostris ambassiatoribus Angliæ, prout Dominus Dux Burgundiæ, bonæ memoriæ, obtinuit dum agebat in humanis, una cum nominibus ambassiatorum suorum ad tractandum expressatis ; necnon quod sub pari forma Dominus noster, Rex Angliæ, ambassiatores suos pro tractatu velit transmittere, ac nomina ipsorum cum salvo conductu declarare.

Ad quæ, honorabiles Domini, tenore præsentium vobis intimamus, quod Magnum Concilium Domini nostri Regis finaliter conclusit duos Milites et duos Clericos, ad tractandum inter regnum Angliæ ac Comitatum Flandriæ, forsan citra festum Assumptionis Beatæ Mariæ[2] proxime futurum, cum omni celeritate

*Announcing that they had seen the Duchess of Burgundy's Letter to John Urban,*

*and replying thereto.*

---

C.] MS. Cotton. Galba, B. I. fol. 97. — On paper ; a contemporaneous MS.

[1] See Letter XCVII.
[2] August 15.

A.D. 1404. transmittere. Idcirco non tædeat præfatam Dominam vestram nec vos interim sustinere, quousque nostri ambassiatores Angliæ in villa Calisii poterunt applicare. Et in ipsorum introitu in Calisium mittent vobis nomina ambassiatorum nostrorum, et pro vestris salvum conductum.

Et, per Dei gratiam, infra breve pro utraque parte reportabimus effectualem ac finalem et perpetuam concordiam, dum tamen opera vestra verbis et litteris inserviant et correspondeant.

Item, ordinetis quod ambassiatores vestri associentur ambassiatoribus præfatæ Dominæ Comitissæ, et quod provideatur etiam, in quantum expedit, de salvo conductu ex parte Regis Francorum ac Comitis Sancti Pauli.

Vestras Reverentias custodiat Altissimus feliciter et votive!

Scriptum Londoniæ, xx. die Julii.

NICHOLAUS DE RYSSHETOUN,
Utriusque Juris Professor, ac

JOHANNES URBAN, Domicellus,
Ambassiatores, etc.

*Endorsement*:—" Honorabilibus ac magnificis et circumspectis Dominis, Burgimagistris, Scabinis, et Consulibus villæ Gandensis, Brugensis, Yprensis, ac territorii Franci officii partium Flandriæ."

It appears from the following that a letter to the same effect was sent to the Duchess of Burgundy :—

*Tenor litteræ Comitissæ Flandriæ transmissæ per Ambassiatores Angliæ*:—

" Illustris ac excellens Domina.

Nuper certas litteras vestras, etc.," juxta tenorem litteræ supradictæ, mutatis tamen mutandis.

The following is written on the back of the letter : A.D. 1404.

" Super tractatum Franciæ per nobilem virum, Dominum Johannem Cheyney, Militem, etc."

Item, quantum ad tractatum Franciæ super responsione Domini de Henguevilla, etc. ; primo nobilis vir, Dominus Johannes Cheyney, Miles, scribat omnia et singula substantialia, quæ communicavit et tractavit cum Domino de Henguevilla, et super quibus punctis debet responderi per eundem, ac etiam de aliis, prout expedit, una cum copiis omnium litterarum suarum. *On the treaty pending with France.*

Et super his fiat plena instructio qualiter ad ulteriora sit procedendum per ambassiatores Domini nostri Regis substituendos in locum præfati Domini Johannis Cheyney, adeo quod culpa eisdem non imputetur in futurum."

## CI.

### DE RYSSHETON TO HENRY IV.

Illustrissime Princeps, ac excellentissime et invictissime Domine mi metuendissime, sincera ac votiva et humillima recommendatione præmissa, vestræ regiæ Majestati sacratissimæ tam debita quam devota. *Complaining of the nonpayment of his stipend.*

Scire dignetur eadem Majestas vestra quod nuper Reverendus Pater, Dominus meus; frater vester, Lincolnensis Episcopus,[1] ac vestri regni Angliæ Cancellarius, vivæ vocis oraculo ex parte vestræ Excellentiæ mihi facto, injunxit pariter et mandavit, quod pro tractatu Flandriæ iter meum versus Calisium celeriter deberem

CI.] MS. Cotton. Galba, B. I. fol. 96.—On paper; probably original,

[1] Henry Beaufort.

A.D. 1404. arripere, ac pro eodem providere ; eidemque Domino meo, fratri vestro, clare respondebam, quod in partem solutionis stipendiorum meorum præteritorum per vestrum almum Concilium fuit mihi assignata summa centum librarum, quam summam a Thesaurariis guerrarum hactenus, quia non habebant, prout asserebant, non poteram obtinere. Et quamvis hujusmodi summa centum librarum esset mihi realiter persoluta, vix debita mea interim contracta, ultra fructus beneficiorum meorum in vestris servitiis consumptos, sufficeret persolvere, nec me ab ære alieno liberare.

Præfatus tamen Dominus meus, Cancellarius, frater vester, mihi respondit quod commissiones pro tractatu Flandriæ necessarias, necnon de dubiis circa hujusmodi tractatum occurrentibus, super quibus fieret instructio, juxta vestram responsionem regiam, et vestri almi Concilii, deberem disponere. Et pro centum libris hujusmodi tractatus non deberet differri nec impediri, ac pro residuo mihi debito faciliter poterit provideri. Ad cujus mandatum tres commissiones in hac parte videre in eo necessarias, formavi, ac easdem eidem Domino meo, fratri vestro exhibui, ac easdem de ipsius mandato Clerico Rotulorum, pro earum ingrossatione et finali expeditione, liberavi. Et subsequenter dubia circa hujusmodi tractatum magis urgentia et prægnantia recollegi ; quæ coram Dominis meis de Concilio feci examinari, et eadem vestræ Clementiæ præsentanda, Domino meo Clerico Privati Sigilli etiam tradidi et liberavi.

His tamen non obstantibus, a xiiij. die Novembris usque in diem confectionis præsentium, pro stipendiis meis præteritis unum denarium nec a Domino meo, vestro Cancellario, nec a Thesaurariis guerrarum, poteram obtinere, nec qualiter in futurum pro stipendiis meis poterit mihi provideri. Vestram Majestatem sacratissimam, flexis genibus, duxi humiliter deprecandam, quatinus caritatis intuitu de stipendiis meis, mihi pro

præterito debitis, et qualiter in futurum debeam me A.D. 1404. dirigere, ac de hujusmodi stipendiis, effectualiter mandare mihi satisfieri, ac super omnibus clarius solito facere responderi. Litteram originalem[1] Comitissæ Flandriæ ultimo pro tractatu transmissam, una cum copiis aliarum litterarum[2], quas ego et Johannes Urban tanquam responsivas eidem Comitissæ ac Quatuor Membris Flandriæ, de mandato vestri Concilii, direximus, vestræ Excellentiæ transmitto, præsentibus interclusam.

Et, si de equis, ac de aliis necessariis, quibus ex defectu sum destitutus in præsenti, potero providere, celerius quo potero visitabo personaliter eandem vestram Excellentiam.

Quam ad felix regimen regni vestri dirigat Altissimus feliciter et votive!

Scriptum Londoniæ, xxiiij$^{to}$ die Julii.

> Vestræ regiæ Majestatis sacratissimæ
> Clericus, ac servitor humillimus,
> NICOLAUS DE RYSSHETOUN.

*Endorsed* :—"Serenissimo Principi, ac illustrissimo et invictissimo Domino, D[omino] H., Dei gratia Regi Angliæ et Franciæ excellentissimo, Domino suo metu[endissimo]."

*Also* :—"Littera ambassiatorum Regis exis[tentium] in Calesio."

## CII.

### THE BISHOP OF BANGOR TO HENRY IV.

Serenissime Princeps; meipso toto cum recommendatione tantæ Celsitudini debite præmissa.

---

[1] See Letter XCVII.
[2] See Letter C.

CII.] MS. Cotton. Galba., B. I. fol. 100.—On paper; probably original.

A.D. 1404.
News of
Isabella,
the late
Queen;

Scire dignetur Celsitudo vestra antedicta gloriosa quod fidelis servitor vester, Angelus Cristofore, et alii mercatores recipiunt litteras ab amicis eorum in Brugga, continentes quod Domina Isabella, quondam Regina Angliæ, debet desponsari primogenito Ducis Aurelianensis, ætatis xj. annorum, cum qua recipiet in dotem totum subsidium jam ultimo concessum Regi prætenso Franciæ.[1]

and of the
preparations for
the invasion of
Wales.

Item quod Magnus Constabularius Franciæ est ordinatus versus Aquitaniam, non designato numero armigerarum in eisdem, et Comes de Marchia versus Walliam cum quingentis bassinettis et ij$^c$ balisteriis, quibus, Domino concedente, adversa fortuna succedet.[2]

Hæc rogavit me scribere idem Angelus ex parte sua Majestati vestræ; cui strictissime se recommendat, qui, ut mihi dixit, propter necessitatem cito recedere intendit a regno vestro Angliæ versus partes exteras.

Alia non occurrunt his scripturis digna, nisi quod mei, vestri assidui oratoris quam sibi et prout videbitur, recordari dignetur dicta vestra Celsitudo gratiosissima. Quam ad dictis adversantibus resistendum, de eis et aliis similibus triumphos reportandum, conservet Altissimus feliciter, prout opto.

Scriptum Londoniæ, ij. die Augusti.

Vester orator assiduus,

RICARDUS, Ecclesiæ Bangorensis[3] humilis minister, sem[per] ad vota paratus.

*Endorsed* : — " Illustrissimo et invictiss[imo Regi] Angliæ et Franciæ, ac D[omino Hiberniæ] "

---

[1] See page 339.
[2] See Nicolas, I. 233.

[3] Richard Yonge.

A.D. 1404.

## CIII.

### HENRY IV. TO THE DOGE OF VENICE.

*Henricus etc. magnifico et præpotenti viro, Duci Venetiarum,[1] amico nostro carissimo, salutem ac votivæ dilectionis continuum incrementum.*

Amice præcarissime.

Scire velitis quod sumus in præparando nobis certas magnas naves, quas munire intendimus fortibus et tutissimis paramentis.

An order for cables, ropes, and hawsers.

Informatique sumus quod meliora cables et cordalia[2] nullibi reperire poterimus quam in civitate vestra Venetiarum.

Quapropter vestram Magnificentiam prædilectam, in qua specialissimam habemus confidentiam, ex toto corde rogamus quatinus, cum omni celeritate qua commode fieri poterit, nobis providere velitis de quatuor viginti millibus librarum de filo, facto in cables et cordeliis,[2] sic videlicet percipiendo sexaginta millia in cables, et viginti millia in hausers, de meliori et securiori filo quod reperiri poterit in vestris partibus ; quodque præfata cables et hausers sint in aliqua quantitate majora quam fieri solebant pro carraccis civitatis Venetiarum. Et quod per proxima navigia partium vestrarum intervenientia in Angliam transmittantur. Quod si omnia ante primum adventum navigii provideri non poterint, transmittantur ea quæ haberi poterint ea vice, et residuum quam cito commode fieri poterit, cum descriptione summarum transmissarum, atque auri pro eisdem debiti ; habentes pro certo quod, cum gratia

---

CIII.] MS. Cotton. Nero, B. VII. No. 16.—On vellum ; a contemporaneous draught.

[1] Michele Steno.
[2] *cordalia—cordeliis.*] Sic MS.

A.D. 1404. Altissimi, mercatoribus vestris præmissa nobis aut nostris liberantibus, talis fiet et tam prompta solutio quod merito reputabunt se contentos : scituri pro firmo, amice præcarissime, quod si onus tantilli negotii pro nobis [ad] præsens subire volueritis, in singulis vestris agendis, etsi majora fuerint, erimus promptiores.

Præcarissime amice, vos diu conservet in prosperis Trinitas Increata !

Datum etc. x. die Augusti, Anno etc. quinto.[1]

## CIV.

### RICHARD ASTON, ETC., TO HENRY IV.

Nostre tresredoubte [et tressouverain liege Seigneur].

*Complaining of the poverty and misery of the garrison of Calais;*

Nous nous recommandons humblement com]me scavons, ou plus pouvons, [a] vostre roialle excellent Hautele [pour ord]ener haut et excellent pussant Seigneur, .  . . Monsieur de Somerset, a estre n[omme de l'assent] de vostre roial Conseil, [que pour la sustenance] de nous seroit paie en main en . . . . . . . es [certains divers

---

[TRANSLATION.]

Our most dread and most sovereign liege Lord. — We commend ourselves humbly as we know how, or at all can, to your royal excellent Highness, for appointing the high and excellent and mighty Lord, Master Somerset, to be named by the assent of your royal Council, that for our sustenance there be paid . . . . . . . . certain divers ports,

---

[1] Another letter to the same purport was written to the Doge of Venice on the 4th of November in the same year.

CIV.] MS. Cott. Calig. D. iv. fol. 52.—On paper; original. The deficiencies in this letter, which was sadly injured by the fire, have to a great extent been supplied by collation with Letter CV.

portz le tiers denier de] la coustume de[s portz icelles A.D. 1404.
pour prest] et seur paiement de noz gages, et [pour
sustenance des chasteaux et autres souldiers de la
Marche], pour seurte [et salvation] de Calais et des
chasteaux environ, [sans estre tourne ne aucunement
mis a autre] usage. Et [par appres] pour ce que [de
ce] . . . . . . effectuel paiement, pour nous et eu[lz
satisfier, nous avons fait supplication enver]s vous
en vostre darrain parlement, en de[sclarant a vostre]
roial Hautele, et as estas du roialme [illeques estans.
et assez, la pov]erte, desaise, et misere, en quoy nous
estoieons [et encor] sumes par deffaute du dit paiement,
afin [que si veuillent en]voier de remede en salvation
des dictes villes [et chasteaux].

Sur quoy, par avis de tous les Seigneurs et . . . . . .
. . . envoier au dit lieu de Calais vos roialles Lettres
[soubz vostre] secret signet, contenantes que des primieres
[monnaies que] serroient receus de ce que par les dis estas
vous serroit ottroye de subside en [dit] parlement, le dit

---

the third money of the custom of the said ports, for the
ready and sure payment of our wages, and for the maintenance
of the garrisons and other soldiers of the Marches, for the
security and preservation of Calais, and of the fortresses in
the neighbourhood, without its being turned or put to any
other use. And further, for that herefrom . . . . . effectual
payment may be made, to satisfy us and them, we made
supplication to you in your last parliament, declaring to your
royal Highness, and to the estates of the realm there present
and in session, the poverty, distress, and misery, in which
we have been and still are, by default of the said payment,
to the end that so they would please to send for a remedy,
for the preservation of the said towns and castles.—Concerning which, by the advice of all the Lords and . . . . .
to send to the said place of Calais your royal letters, under
your privy signet, setting forth that out of the first instal-
ments that should be received of that which by the said estates
should be granted to you by way of subsidy in the said parlia-

A.D. 1404. paiement serroit prestement paie; [sur͵fiance des quilles voz Lett]res les bonnes gens, marchans, et vitaillours ylloeques [nous] ont depuis soustenus et conffortes par [prest de lour biens et vitailles, jus]ques a ore tarde que eulz regardent que par l'une des dictes voies ne par l'autre le dit paiement n'est f[ait, ne lour semble estre taille] estre fait en temps convenable. De quoy ilz sont cho[ez] en tel disespoir que plus avaunt eulz ne veuillent [ne osent a nous aucun cho]se prester en soustenance de noz vies et estas, pour doubte [de] tout perdre, ne aussi vraiement eulz ne sont [pas a pouvoir de guerr]es plus prester.

and be-
seeching
the King to
send them
the means
of paying
their debts.

Et pour ce, nostre tresredoubte et tressouverain liege Seigneur, nous en humblement implorant v[ostre graciouse aide et con]ffort, supplions a vostre tresroyale et souv-eraine Hautele, que a la reverence de Dieu, et de Saint Jorge, et pour sal[vation des dictes ville et] chasteaux, et aussi affin que par necessite meschief et pove[rte] il ne nous convienge pas guerpir la dit ville a [confusion

---

ment, the said payment should be presently made ; relying on which your letters, the good people, merchants, and victuallers there have since maintained and cherished us by the loan of their goods and victuals, until now lately that they consider that neither by one of the said ways nor by the other the said payment is made, nor seems to them likely ever to be made at all within a suitable period. On which account they have fallen into such despair that they no longer are willing nor venture to lend us anything for the maintenance of our lives and estates, for doubt of losing the whole ; and in very truth they have it not at all in their power to lend more.—And on this account, our most dread and most sovereign liege Lord, most humbly imploring your gracious aid and consolation, we beseech your most royal and sovereign Highness, out of reverence to God and to S. George, and for the preservation of the said town and castles, and also to the end that through necessity, mischief, and poverty it may not happen at all that

d'icelle] ; de quoy couardise puisse estre entendue en A.D 1404. nous autrement que desservi n'avons, ne desservir vouillons, ou autrement [fere et ouvrer po]ur la soustenance de noz viez et simples estas en deshonn[este] maniere ; de quoy nous puissons perdre ou estre [amendris de noz] simples noms et honnours chescun en son endroit, dont Dieu nous veuille garder ! il plese vostre Majeste roialle o[rdener que prest] paiement soit envoie au dit lieu de Caleis, de ce que nous est [aderere], qui se montera a la Saint Michelle prochein venant ad [deux ans en]tiers et plus. En quoy la roial et haute discretion de vous [scait] pleinement entendre les perilles et aussi les rem[ediez quy y pu]ent estre conceups.

Nostre tresredoubte et tressouverain Seigneur [liege], autres choses ne scavons escripre a present pardevers v[ostre roial] Hautele, forsque, au plesir de Dieu, se trop importante [matiere] de soustenance de nous, surment nous esperons en Dieu . . service en salvation

---

we have to abandon the said town, to the confusion thereof, for which cowardice might be imputed to us otherwise than we have deserved, or are willing to deserve, or otherwise to act or work for the maintenance of our lives and simple estates in a dishonest manner, for which we might lose or be deprived of our simple names and honours, each in his own regard, from which God will to keep us ! please it your royal Majesty to ordain that ready payment be sent to the said place of Calais, of that which is in arrear to us up to the present time, and which will amount at Michaelmas next to two entire years and more. In which your royal and high discretion knows fully how to understand the perils, and also the remedies which may be therein conceived.—Our most dread and most sovereign liege Lord, we know not of anything else to write at present to your royal Highness, save that, at God's good pleasure, of this very important matter of our maintenance, we have sure trust in God . . . . . . . for the preservation of the town and castles, that if he will direct it to the honour of

A.D. 1404. des dictes ville et chastelx, que se di[riger veuille] a l'onneur de nostre nation, ne sera ja abaisse en nostre [governanc]e.

Tresredoubte et tressouverain liege Seigneur, nous prions a la [Benoit] Trinite, que Elle vous ottroit aussi parfaite victorious [sur voz a]nemis, ovecques honnour, saute, longe vie, et joieux prosp[erite], comme vostre roial et franc couer mieulx vouldre [deviser] ou souhaiter.

Escript a Calais, le xvij$^{me}$ jour d'Aout.

Voz humbles liges et loials subges et obeissans,

RICHART ASTOUN, Lieutenant a Calais,

HUE BLIES, [Mar]chal,

Et tous vos autres souldoiers au dit li[eu].

---

our nation, it will never be abused in our government.— Most dread and most sovereign liege Lord, we pray the Blessed Trinity to grant you also perfect victory over your enemies, with honour, safety, long life, and joyous prosperity, as your royal and free heart would most wish to devise or to desire.

Written at Calais, the 17th day of August.

Your humble lieges and loyal subjects and obeisant,

RICHARD ASTON, Lieutenant at Calais,

HUGH BLIES, Marshal,

And all your other soldiers at the said place.

## CV.

### RICHARD ASTON, ETC., TO THE COUNCIL.

Nos tresreverens, haus, [puissans, honnourables, Seigneurs].

[Nous nous recommandons humblement] et comme plus pouvons a vostrez hautz et puissantz Seigneuries, et pour [informer vostr]es Discretions come appres ce que il eut pleu au Roy, nostre tressouverain lig[e Seigneur ordener Monsieur d]e Somerset, Capitaine de sa ville de Calais, ovesque pouvoir de lieutenancie et g[overnance] de nostre dit Seigneur, de l'assent de son royal Conssel, que pour la sustenance de nous seroit pai[e en main en] . . . . . . . . . . es certains

*On the same subject as the preceding letter to the King.*

---

[TRANSLATION.]

Our most reverend, high, mighty, and honourable Lords.—
We commend ourselves humbly, and as much as we can to your high and mighty Lordships, and inform your Discretions how, after that it pleased the King, our most sovereign Lord, to ordain Master de Somerset, Governour of his town of Calais, with power of lieutenancy and government from our said Lord, by the assent of his royal Council, that for our sustenance there should be paid in hand . . . . . certain divers ports the third

---

CV.] MS. Cott. Calig. D. IV. fol. 53.—On paper ; original. This Letter was written on the same day as the preceding Letter, and relates to the same business. Both are sadly mutilated, but by a comparison of the portions in which they correspond nearly all the *lacunæ* have been filled in.

T

A.D. 1404. divers portz le tiers denier de la coustume de[s ic]elles, pour prest et se[ur paiement de noz gages, et pour sust]enance des chasteaux, et autres souldiers de la Marche, pour seurte et salvation de [Calais et des chasteaux envi]ron, sans estre tourne ne aucunement mis a autre usage. Et par appres pour ce que de ce ...........[effectuel paie]ment pour nous et eulz satisfier, nous eussions fait supplication envers le Roy, nostre dit tre[sredoubte Seigneur, en darr]ein parlement, en desclarant a sa royalle Hautele, et as estas du royalme illeques estans et ass[ez en parliament la poverte, desa]ise, et misere en quoy nous estoieons et encor sumes par deffaute du dit paiement, afin que si [veuillent en]voier de remede en salvation des dictes ville et chasteaux.

Sur quoy, par avis de tous les [Seigneurs et] ...... .. puist pleu envoier au dit lieu de Calais ses roialles Lettres soubz son secret signet, conten[antes que des premieres monnaies que] serroient receus de ce qui par les dis estas luy serroit ottroie de subside en dit

---

part of the customs of the said ports, for the ready and sure payment of our wages, and for the maintenance of the garrisons and other soldiers of the March, for the security and preservation of Calais, and of the fortresses in the neighbourhood, without its being turned or put to any other use. And further, for that herefrom ..... effectual payment may be made, we made supplication to the King our sovereign Lord in the last parliament, declaring to his royal Highness, and to the estates there present and sitting in parliament, the poverty, distress, and misery in which we have been and still are by default of the said payment, to the end that it may please them to send a remedy, for the preservation of the said town and castles.—Concerning which, by the advice of all the Lords and ...... to send to the said place of Calais his royal Letters under his privy seal, setting forth that out of the first monies that should be received from that which by the said estates should be granted to him by way of

parlement, le dit p[aiement serroit prestement paie]; sur A.D. 1404. fiance des quilles ses Lettres les bonnes gens, marchans, et vitaillers illeques nous ont depuis s[oustenus et conffortes] par prest de lour biens et vitailles, jusques a ore tarde que eulx regardent que par l'une des dictes voies ne par [l'autre le dit paiemen]t n'est fait, ne lour semble estre taille estre fait en temps convenable. De quoy ilz sont choez en tel disepoir [que plus avaunt eulz] ne vcuillent ne osent a nous aucun chose prester en soustenance de noz vies et estas, pour doubte de [tout perdre; ne aussi v]raiement eulz ne sont pas a pouvoir de guerres plus prester.

Et pour ce, noz tresreverens, haus, puissans, honno[urabl]es Seigneurs, nous en humblement implorant vostre graciouse aide et conffort, supplions a voz hautes et honnourables [Seigneuries] que a la reverence de Dieu, et de Seint Jorge, et pour salvation des dictes ville et chasteaux, et aussi afin

---

subsidy in the said parliament, the said payment should be presently made ; relying on which his Letters, the good people, merchants, and victuallers there have since maintained and cherished us by the loan of their goods and victuals, until now lately that they consider that neither by one of the said ways, nor by the other, the said payment is made, or seems to them likely ever to be made at all within a suitable period. On which account they have fallen into such despair, that they no longer are willing, nor venture to lend us anything for the maintenance of our lives and estates, for doubt of losing the whole, and in very truth they have it not at all in their power to lend more.—And on this account, our most dread and most reverend, high, mighty, honourable Lords, humbly imploring your gracious aid and consolation, we beseech your high and honourable Lordships, out of reverence to God and to S. George, and for the preservation of the said town and castles, and also to the end that through necessity, mischiefs, and poverty, it

AD. 1404. que par necessi[te, meschief, et] poverte il ne nous convienge pas guerpir la dit ville a confusion d'icelle ; de quoy couardise puisse estre [entendue en] nous autrement que desservi n'avons ne desservir vouillons, ou autrement fere et ouvrer pour la soustenance de noz viez [et simples] estas en deshonneste maniere, de quoy nous puissons perdre ou estre amendris de noz simples noms et ho[nnours chescun] en son endroit ; dont Dieu nous veuille garder ! il plese voz hautz et honnourables puissantz Seigneuries ainssi q[ue plus] prest paiement soit envoie au dit lieu de Calais de ce que nous est aderere, qui se montera a la Saint Michelle [prochein venant ad] deux ans entiers et plus. En quoy les hautz et sages Discretions de vous sceient pleinement ente[ndre les perilles] et aussi les remediez quy y puent estre conceups. Et sur ce vous plese fere et mettre voz sagez et grac[ieuse Seigneuries] en accomplisement de la dit paiement.

---

may not happen at all that we have to abandon the said town, to the confusion thereof ; for which cowardice might be imputed to us otherwise than we have deserved, or are willing to deserve, or otherwise to work or act for the maintenance of our lives and simple estates in a dishonest manner, for which we might lose or be deprived of our simple names and honours, each in his own regard, from which God will to keep us ;— please it your high and honourable, mighty Lordships, that very ready payment be sent to the said place of Calais, of that which is in arrear to us up to the present time, and which will amount at Michaelmas next to two entire years and more. In which your high and sage Discretions know fully how to understand the perils, and also the remedies which may be therein conceived. And herein please you to devote and commit your sage and gracious Lordships to the accomplishment of the said payment.—And we pray the blessed

Et nous prions a la Benoit Trinite du Chiel que A.D. 1404. Elle vous ottroit bone vie.

Escript a Calais le xvij$^{me}$ jour de Aoust.

Voz humblez recomandez,

RICHART ASTOUN, Lieutenant a Calais,

HUE BLIES, Marchal,

Et tous les autres souldours au dit lieu.

*Endorsed* : — " A tresreverent Piere et Seigneur, l'Evesque de Cant[orbille et les autres Seigneurs] du Consseil nostre tressouv[erain liege Seigneur.]"

---

Trinity of Heaven to grant you happy life.—Written at Calais, the 17th day of August.

Yours humbly commended,

RICHARD ASTON, Lieutenant at Calais,

HUGH BLIES, Marshall,

And all the other soldiers at the said place.

*Endorsed:*—" To the most reverend Father and Lord, the Bishop of Canterbury, and the other Lords of the Council of our most sovereign liege Lord."

A.D. 1404.

# CVI.

### SWYNBORN, CROFT, AND DE RYSSHETON TO THE FOUR MEMBERS OF FLANDERS.

*Copia litteræ Ambassiatorum Angliæ, transmissæ Quatuor Membris Flandriæ, etc. :*

Honorabiles ac magnifici et circumspecti Domini.

*Requesting that their letters may be answered,* Juxta tenores quarundam litterarum [1] mei Nicholai, et Johannis Urban,[2] nobili ac illustri Dominæ, Dominæ Ducissæ Burgundiæ, Comitissæ Flandriæ modernæ, etc., necnon Reverentiis vestris, nuper transmissarum, vicesimo primo die præsentis mensis Augusti applicuimus Calisii cum potestate sufficienti, parati tractatum perficere inter regnum Angliæ ac patriam Flandriæ ; dum tamen ambassiatores ejusdem Dominæ vestræ, ac vestrorum Quatuor Membrorum, cum potestate consimili, etiam cum salvo conductu Regis Francorum, ac Comitis Sancti Pauli tanquam Capitanei Pikardiæ et West Flandriæ, seu ipsius locumtenentis, in hujusmodi tractatu absque dilatione nobiscum velint convenire, necnon injurias subditis ac incolis regni Angliæ illatas pro parte vestra, sicut parati sumus pro parte nostra, prout juris et rationis fuerit,[3] reformare ;—vestras Reverentias requirimus, et exhortamur in Domino, quatinus litteras nostras, præfatæ Dominæ vestræ intitulatas, placeat eidem facere præsentari, ac de eisdem litteris, tam sibi

---

CVI.] MS. Cotton. Galba, B. I. fol. 86 (*a*).—On paper ; a contemporaneous MS.

[1] See page 278.

[2] The word " infra-scriptorum " has been here struck out.

[3] *fuerit*] Added above the line.

quam vobis directis, nobis indilate respondere. Et præ-. A.D. 1404.
sertim quod bona mercatorum Angliæ, in Sclusa inde- and that
bite arrestata, quia contra vestra juramenta, et contra English
merchan-
litteras tam Domini vestri bonæ memoriæ, quam vestras, dise cap-
ipsius ac vestris sigillis sigillatas, et contra appunctua- Sluys may
menta communia apud Westmonasterium etiam per be restored
without
vestros ambassiatores sigillata, ac subsequenter vestro- delay.
rum ambassiatorum juramentis vallata, ordinetis ante
omnia, seu ipsorum bonorum æstimationem ac verum
valorem, restituere. Necnon vestros ambassiatores una They fix
the spot for
cum ambassiatoribus Dominæ vestræ ad tractatum meeting,
cum auctoritate et salvo conductu sufficienti destinare;
qui cum ambassiatoribus Angliæ, sexto die mensis
Septembris proximo futuro, tanquam pro termino congruo, necnon in confinio regnorum Angliæ et Franciæ
juxta Santyngfeld, videlicet pars vestra in territorio
Domini vestri superioris, ambassiatores vero nostri in
territorio Domini nostri, Regis Angliæ et Franciæ, in
loco illo quo fines et limites utriusque regni per lapides
finales notorie distinguuntur, ad tractandum super præparatoriis ac decisoriis nostri tractatus communis insimul nobiscum valea[nt] interesse. Fines enim et
termini juxta Eynes non sunt clare distincti pro præsenti, adeo quod absque limitum turbatione inibi non
poterimus pariter convenire. Hactenus enim gentes and complain that
nostras abstinuimus, et navigium nostrum restrinxi- the for-
mus, sub colore treugarum, ne ad partes vestras pro bearance
of the En-
damno inferendo valeant declinare, seu inibi applicare, glish had
quamvis, hujusmodi litteris vestris multiplicatis nobis been rewarded by
directis, ac vestris juramentis et treugis captis non treachery.
obstantibus, subditis et incolis regni Angliæ [1] sustinuistis
vestros Flandrenses ex certa scientia omnia mala inferre.

Item, ordinetis [2] quod ambassiatores deputandi pro

---

[1] The word "latenter" has been here struck out.    [2] *Item, ordinetis, etc*.] See the next Letter.

A.D. 1404. parte Dominæ vestræ, ac etiam pro parte vestra, sint legales ac tractabiles viri, quia forsan Gallici intendunt præsentem tractatum nostrum et vestrum impedire, si a Domina vestra et a vobis potestatem tractandi valeant obtinere ; ad quod merito debetis advertere ; et quod pro parte vestra fiat diligentia amplior solito in nostro tractatu. Super quibus omnibus curetis in Calisium nobis per aliquem discretum et notabilem nuncium vestrum indilate rescribere, ac vestram voluntatem et præsertim Dominæ vestræ in omnibus remittere, prout vestris Reverentiis pro bono publico videbitur expedire.

Quas custodiat Altissimus feliciter et votive!
Scriptum Calisii, xxiij° die mensis Augusti.

THOMAS SWYNBORN, et

JOHANNES CROFFT, Milites, ac

NICHOLAUS DE RYSSHETOUN, Utriusque
Juris Professor,
Ambassiatores pro parte Angliæ.

*Endorsement* : — "Honorabilibus ac magnificis et circumspectis Dominis, Burgimagistris, Scabinis, et Consulibus, Gandensibus, Brugensibus, Yprensibus, ac territorii Franci officii partium Flandriæ."

The names of the English Ambassadors to be inserted in the safe-conduct. Quamvis quatuor ambassiatores pro parte nostra cum vestris ambassiatoribus etiam totidem in tractatu debeant convenire, ordinetis tamen salvos conductus vestros pro nostris ambassiatoribus pro personis infrascriptis omnibus et singulis propter recessum seu infirmitatem aliquorum de eisdem, videlicet pro Thoma Swynford, Johanne Crofft. Willielmo Lyle, juniore, Thoma Swynford, et Radulpho Botriaux, Militibus,

ac Nicholao de Rysshetoun, Utriusque Juris Professore, A.D. 1404. et Johanne Urban, Domicello.

Et licet aliqui prædictorum sint in præsenti in Anglia, erunt tamen Calisii citra terminum supradictum.

## CVII.

SWYNBORN, CROFT, AND DE RYSSHETON TO THE DUCHESS OF BURGUNDY.

*Copia litteræ ambassiatorum Angliæ, transmissæ Dominæ Ducissæ Burgundiæ, etc.*

Illustris, necnon præclaræ nobilitatis ac magnæ potentiæ Domina.

On the same matters as the preceding letter to the Four Members of Flanders.

Consideratis certis litteris missivis vestræ Nobilitati pro parte regni Angliæ transmissis, etiam quibusdam vestris litteris[1] Attrebatj xvj. die mensis Maii ultimo præterito scriptis, ac nobis pro parte vestra præsentatis xxjo die præsentis mensis Augusti, applicuimus Calisii cum potestate sufficienti, parati tractatum perficere inter regnum Angliæ ac vestram patriam Flandriæ. Dum tamen ambassiatores vestri ac vestrorum Quatuor Membrorum cum potestate consimili, etiam cum salvo conductu pro nobis, ex parte vestri Regis Francorum, ac Comitis Sancti Pauli, tanquam Capitanei Pykardiæ et West Flandriæ, seu ipsius locum-tenentis, in hujusmodi tractatu absque dilatione nobiscum velint con-

---

CVII.] MS. Cotton. Galba, B. I. fol. 86 (β).—On paper; a contemporaneous MS.

[1] See Letter LXXXVI.

A.D. 1404. venire; necnon injurias subditis et incolis Angliæ illatis etc., præsenti in littera ex parte altera cedulæ plenius continenti etc., ista clausa — "Item, ordinetis quod Ambassiatores deputandi pro parte Dominæ vestræ etc." dumtaxat cancellata.

THOMAS SWYNBORN, et

JOHANNES CROFFT,—Milites, ac

NICHOLAUS DE RYSSHETOUN, Utriusque Juris Professor, Ambassiatores pro parte Angliæ.

*Endorsement*:—"Illustri, necnon præclaræ nobilitatis ac magnæ potentiæ Dominæ, Do- minæ Margaretæ, Ducissæ Bur- gundiæ, Comitissæ Flandriæ, Ar- thesii, et Burgundiæ, etc."

## CVIII.

### ROBERT III. OF SCOTLAND TO HENRY IV.

*Serenissimo Principi, Domino Henrico, consan- guineo meo Angliæ, Robertus, Dei gratia Rex Scot- torum, salutem et quietis desiderium.*

Serenissime Princeps.

With a message by David Fleming.

Ex relatione dilecti consanguinei nostri, David Flemyng, Militis, latoris præsentium, concepimus ipsum habuisse vobiscum colloquium super quibusdam ma- teriis. Et easdem nobis retulit viva voce; quæ nobis bene placent. Ac sibi mentem nostram communicavi-

---

CVIII.] MS. Cotton. Vesp. F. VII. fol. 72.—On vellum; original.

mus, vestræ Serenitati referendam. Cui in dicendis, A.D. 1404.
vobis si placet, quo ad materias vobis prælocutas, fidem
credulam velitis adhibere.

Valeat Serenitas vestra feliciter juxta votum!

Scriptum sub sigillo nostro secreto apud Lithai [1]
vicesimo sexto die mensis Augusti.

## CIX.

### The Countess of March to Henry IV.

Mon tresexcellent et tresredoute sovereigne Seignour. On behalf
Jeo me recomanke au vous sy entierment come of herself
and her
seigrie creature terrien poet penser ou diviser au Roy husband.
du monde coronne, vous esmerciant humblement as
genoilles de lez hautz graces et beneficez que vous
m'avez faitz devant ces heures, vous supliant piement
de vostre gracieus continuance, et nomement de le
gracieus refresshement que vous m'envoiastes darreyne-

---

[Translation.]

My most excellent and most redoubted sovereign Lord.—
I recommend me to you as entirely as lone earthly creature
can think or devise to the crowned King of the world,
thanking you humbly on my knees for the high favours
and benefits that you have done me before this time, at your
feet supplicating of you your gracious continuance, and especially the gracious refreshment which you sent recently.

---

[1] Leith.

CIX.] MS. Cotton. Vespas F. vii.
fol. 104.—On paper; original, with
traces of a seal.—This letter has no
date either of the year or the day
of the month. It, however, appears
to belong to this period.

A.D. 1404. ment. Dieux vous eurent greez la ou jeo ne puisse
noun pur ceo.

Their
distresses.     Mon tresgracieus Seignour, vous pleis savoir que
mon Seignour mon Baron, et moy avoms este en
taunt duresce et distresce puysque nous fuymes excluz
de nostre paiis, que uncore jeo suy remys en graunt
debt, de quelle sanz vostre gracieus eide et soicour
ne me puysse deliverer. Et ore la pestilence est
taunt fort et dure la ou nous sumes, que jeo suy
molt [paorous] que jeo morra en le graunt debt
que jeo suy encorue. Et pour nulle traitie que nous
poons fair ne poons avoir suffrance de noz enemys,
pour nous treer a nostre fortres de Colbrandespath,
pour illoex attendre tanque la mortalite soit cesse.
Et pour celle cause jeo emprie humblement a vostre haut
Roiall majeste que vous me pleisez avoir en remembrance, quant vous verretz loisir, et me eider que
parmy vostre gracieus re[l]evement jeo puisse estre
eygettez de le debt qi me face tristes.

—————

God have you rewarded there where I have no power for it.—
My most gracious Lord, may it please you to know that my
Lord my Baron, and I have been in such hardship and distress
since we were shut out of our land, that I am still involved
in heavy debt, from which I cannot deliver myself without
your gracious aid and succour. And now the pestilence is
so severe and cruel where we are that I am very much
afraid lest I should die in the great debt which I have
incurred. And by no treaty that we are able to make can we
obtain sufferance from our enemies to withdraw ourselves to
our fortress of Colbrandespath, to remain there till the mor-
tality has ceased. And for this cause I humbly implore
your high royal Majesty that you will be pleased to have
me in remembrance, when you see leisure, and aid me, that
through your gracious relief I may be delivered from the
debt which makes me sorrowful—Besides this, most redoubted

Outre ceo, tresredoubte et mon tresgracieus Seignour, A.D. 1404. nous portons grant enemyte pour la mort de Sir Henry Percy, issint que sovent foiz est graive a mon Baron et ses gentz [tant q'ils] vueillient estre mortz s'ils ne se retrehent hors du paiis: issint[1] lez gentz le dit Sir Henry ne facent rien fors escoutent confortables [nouvelles] de vous, pour alors faire la malice que est f[orme][2] . . . . . . en lour coers.

Et, mon tresgracieus et tressovereigne Seignour, touchant la pars de nos gentz par ceux attendantz au Count de[2] [Douglas] deignetz ent doner credence al porteur d'icestz, et sur ceo que vous pleisez ordener tiell remedy, sicome le dit porteur vous dirra par bouche.

Et prie sovereignement et tresbenoit Dieux de Ciel, q'Il vous ottroie longe vie, ove tout encresment de honoure et joy, ensemble ove victorie de voz ene-

---

and my most gracious Lord, we suffer great enmity for the death of Sir Henry Percy, insomuch that it is often so heavy to my Baron and his men, that they wish to be dead if they may not retire from the land : meanwhile the men of the said Sir Henry do nothing without hearing encouraging news of you, in order then to do the malice which is conceived in their hearts.—And, my most gracious and most sovereign Lord, touching the capture of our people by those who attend on the Earl of Douglas, deign to give credence to the bearer of these, and to ordain such a remedy thereof as you please, according as the said bearer shall tell you by word of mouth.—And I most earnestly pray to the most blessed God of Heaven that he grant you a long life, with all increase of honour and joy, together with victory over

---

[1] *issint*] Altered from "issint q'ils." | [2] A portion of the MS. is here torn away.

A.D. 1404. mys, et apres ceste mortell vie vous rent la regne de gloire.—Amen.

Vostre humble oratrice,

LA COUNTESSE DE LA MARCHE D'ESCOCE.

*Endorsed :*—" A mon tresexcellent et tresredoute Sovereyn Seignour, le Roy d'Engleterre."

*Also :* — " Littera Comitissæ Mar[chiæ] . . . . . Sc[otiæ]."

---

your enemies ; and, after this mortal life, may give you the kingdom of glory. Amen.

Your humble suppliant,

THE COUNTESS OF THE MARCH OF SCOTLAND.

*Endorsed :*—" To my most excellent and most redoubted Lord, the King of England."

CX.

THE FLEMISH DEPUTIES TO THE ENGLISH AMBASSADORS.

*Copia litteræ responsivæ Quatuor Membrorum Flandriæ, transmissæ ambassiatoribus Angliæ etc.*

Nobiles ac circumspecti Domini.

Acknowledging the receipt of their letters, and promising an early reply.

Vestrarum Nobilitatum et Circumspectionum litteras [1] per quendam cursorem, latorem præsentium, Quatuor Membris Flandriæ novissime directas, scriptas die xxiij$^{tia}$ præsentis Mensis, una cum certis aliis litteris [2]

---

CXI.] MS. Cotton. Galba, B. I. fol. 82.—On paper; a contemporaneous MS.

[1] See Letter CVI.
[2] See Letter CVII.

metuendæ Dominæ nostræ, Dominæ Ducissæ Bur- A.D. 1404.
gundiæ, Comitissæ Flandriæ, dirigendis, recepimus,
prædictasque vestras litteras, supradictæ Dominæ nostræ intitulatas, misimus eidem.

Et quam cito voluntatem supradictæ Dominæ nostræ
assertive scire poterimus, illam per discretum nuncium,
prout petitis, vestris Nobilitatibus proponimus, Deo
duce, significare.

Quas conservet Altissimus feliciter et votive!

Scriptum die ultima mensis Augusti, sub sigillo ad
causas villæ Brugensis pro omnibus nobis.

> BURGIMAGISTRI, SCABINI, et CONSULES villæ
> Brugensis, necnon DEPUTATI villarum
> Gandensis, Yprensis, ac territorii Franci
> officii partium Flandriæ præsentialiter in
> præfata villa Brugensi congregati.

*Endorsement:*—"Nobilibus ac circumspectis Dominis,
Dominis Ambassiatoribus excellen-
tissimi Principis et Domini, Domini
Regis Angliæ, Calesii existentibus."

## CXI.

### SWYNBORN, CROFT, AND DE RYSSHETON TO THE PRIVY COUNCIL.

Reverendissimi in Christo Patres, ac magnifici et Requesting
excellentes Domini. that other

Juxta informationem nobis traditam, scripsimus Commis-
litteras[1] Quatuor Membris Flandriæ, ac ipsorum Do- saries be
appointed,
as all ex-

---

CXI.] MS. Cotton. Galba, B. I.    [1] See Letters CVI. and CVII.
fol. 84.—On paper; original, with
traces of the seals.

A.D. 1404.
cept De
Ryssheton
are incapa-
citated for
active ser-
vice. minæ, Comitissæ, pro tractatu perficiendo inter Dominum nostrum, Regem Angliæ, ac patriam Flandriæ; subsequenterque Magno Concilio Franciæ, necnon Domino Johanni de Hangesto Domino de Henguevi[lla, et] Magistro Willielmo Boisratier, commissariis pro parte Franciæ, etiam alias litteras direximus, pro responsione quatuor punctorum etc. reportanda.

Quarum litterarum tenores [mittimus] vobis, præsentibus interclusas.

Item, quantum ad tractatum Flandriæ noverint Dominationes vestræ, qualiter quinque commissarii in hujusmodi commissionibus Flandriæ extiterant no[minati], Thomas Swynborn, qui in proximo revertetur in Angliam; Johannes Crofft, qui non poterit equitare nec castrum suum exire propter ægritudines diversas quas pat[itur] in præsenti, et præsertim tempore guerrarum; Willielmus Lyle, junior, Milites,[1] ac Johannes Urban, etiam commissarii, sunt in Anglia. Idcirco, ne noster collega Nicholaus de Rysshetoun remaneat solus absque consilio, dignemini pro novis commissariis, prout vobis videbitur providere, ac commissiones antiquas reformare. Mittimus enim [vobi]s copiam . . . . . . commissionis nostræ, cum certis nominibus expressatis in eadem, seu etiam pro aliis juxta vestrum beneplacitum exprimendis ac in eadem interserendis.

Item, pro responsione reportanda ex parte Franciæ, Johannes Clerk misit mihi, Nicholao infrascripto, Londoniam, quandam commissionem defectivam, quia clausulam salvi conductus in eadem non inseruit; quam clausulam salvi conductus, cuilibet commissioni accessoriam, et de necessitate requisitam, interserere debuit, quamvis in eadem commissione hujusmodi clausulam prætermisit. Copiam igitur hujusmodi commis-

---

[1] *Milites*] Added above the line.

sionis una cum clausula salvi conductus expressa in A.D. 1404. eadem mittimus vobis etiam præsentibus interclusam.[1] Quam cum omni celeritate reformatam dignemini transmittere, ne frustra videamur laborare.

Vestras Paternitates ac Magnificentias dirigat Altissimus feliciter in longævum!

Scriptum Calisii, ultimo die mensis Augusti.

THOMAS SWYNBORN, et

JOHANNES CROFFT, Milites, ac

NICHOLAUS DE RYSSHETOUN, Utriusque Juris Professor,
Ambassiatores pro parte Angliæ.

Item, post scripturam præsentis litteræ, recepimus litteras responsivas ex parte Quatuor Membrorum Flandriæ, quarum copiam mittimus vobis præsentibus interclusam.[2]

Endorsed :—" Reverendissimis in Christo Patribus, necnon magnificis et excell[entissimis] Dominis de almo Concilio Domini nostri Regis Angliæ."

---

[1] See MS. Cotton. Galba. B. I. fol. 107.

[2] This postscript is written with another ink.

U

A.D. 1404.

## CXII.

### SWYNFORD AND DE RYSSHETON TO THE FRENCH COUNCIL.

*Copia litteræ Ambassiatorum Angliæ, transmissæ Magno Concilio Franciæ, etc.*

Reverendi Patres, necnon excellentes, ac magnifici et potentes Domini.

On the treaty with France.

Vestras Magnificentias credimus non latere qualiter nobilis et strenuus vir, Dominus Johannes Cheynee, Miles, ac ambassiator et consiliarius Domini nostri, Regis Angliæ et Franciæ illustrissimi, ad partes Franciæ ex parte ejusdem Domini nostri Regis ac regni sui, ad requirendum et recipiendum responsionem certarum litterarum, una cum quatuor punctis seu articulis, ex parte ejusdem Domini nostri Regis, ac aliorum Dominorum regni sui, tam spiritualium, quam temporalium, Domino vestro superiori, ac aliis Dominis tam spiritualibus, quam temporalibus regni Franciæ præsentandis, nuper extitit transmissus.

Et quia idem Dominus Johannes Cheynee, Miles, non poterat habere salvum et liberum introitum in Franciam ad Dominum vestrum, ac ad ipsius Magnum et Supremum Concilium, juxta ordinationem ac avisamentum et consilium nobiliorum Dominorum, Domini Johannis de Hangesto Domini de Henguevilla, ac Magistri Willielmi Boisratier, ambassiatorum pro parte vestra, hujusmodi litteras cum dictis quatuor

---

CXII.] MS. Cotton. Galba, B. I. fol. 86 (γ).—On paper; a contemporaneous MS.

punctis seu articulis pro fideli examinatione eorundem A.D. 1404. fienda et responsione litteraliter reportanda,[1] eisdem Domino de Henguevilla ac suo collegæ, in præsentia notarii publici et testium, tradidit et personaliter liberavit. Quodque iidem collegæ promiserunt cum omni celeritate responsionem personaliter per se aut per alios commissarios deputandos reportare, ac de omnibus supradictis ipsum Dominum Johannem Cheyne, Militem ac ambassiatorem etc., seu alios commissarios ex parte Domini nostri nominandos, certiores reddere ; necnon Domini vestri ac aliorum Dominorum regni Franciæ, tam spiritualium quam temporalium, circa præmissa voluntatem ac beneplacita sua declarare, prout hæc et alia in litteris præfati Domini, Johannis Cheynee, Militis, præfatis vestris ambassiatoribus directis expressatis plenius continetur.

Quorum articulorum seu punctorum copiam mittimus vestris Paternitatibus ac Excellentiis, præsentibus interclusam.

Vestras Paternitates ac Magnificentias requirimus ac pro utriusque regni utilitate exhortamur in Domino, quatinus cum celeritate super præmissis omnibus et singulis, per litteras Domini vestri superioris, et per litteras vestras, ac etiam aliorum Dominorum Franciæ, tam spiritualium quam temporalium, ipsorum ac vestris sigillis sigillatas, et præsertim super prædictis quatuor punctis, absque dilatione ad locum consuetum per prædictos vestros commissarios ac ambassiatores, seu per alios pro parte vestra nominandos, placeat respondere, ac super ipsis punctis in Latinis, et non in Gallico, penitus declarare. Pro ista enim responsione expectamus Calisii ad finem et effectum quod hujusmodi responsionem Domino nostro Regi Angliæ et Franciæ illustrissimo poterimus referre ac

---

[1] *reportanda*] reportanta MS.

U 2

A.D. 1404. celeriter reportare. Utinam respondeatur pro parte vestra ad honorem Dei, ac utriusque regni prosperitatem ac utilitatem et pacem!

Quam, temporibus nostris, vobis et nobis concedat Trinitas Increata pro Sua misericordia!

Scriptum Calisii, primo die mensis Septembris.[1]

> THOMAS SWYNFORD, Miles,[2] Custos Castri villæ Calisii, ac
>
> NICHOLAUS DE RYSSHETOUN, Utriusque Juris Professor,
>
> Ambassiatores pro parte Angliæ.

*Endorsement :*—" Reverendis in Christo Patribus, ac magnæ excellentiæ Principibus et Dominis, necnon aliis Dominis et nobilibus de magno Concilio Franciæ."

---

[1] Immediately after this letter occurs the following :—

" *Copia litteræ Ambassiatorum Angliæ, transmissæ Ambassiatoribus Franciæ.*

" Honorabiles ac circumspecti Domini.

" A vestra memoria non credimus recessisse qualiter nobilis vir, Dominus Johannes Cheynee, Miles, Ambassiator et consiliarius Domini nostri, Regis Angliæ et Franciæ illustrissimi, ad partes Franciæ, ex parte ejusdem Domini nostri Regis, et regni Angliæ transmissus ad requirendum et recipiendum responsionem certarum litterarum ;—*ac prout*

*in littera proxime superscripta. ac Magno Concilio Franciæ directa continetur, mutatis mutandis, etc.*

" THOMAS SWYNFORD, Miles, Custos Castri villæ Calisii, ac
" NICHOLAUS DE RYSSHETOUN, Utriusque Juris Professor:— Ambassiatores pro parte Angliæ.

*Endorsement :* — " Honorabilibus ac circumspectis Dominis, Domino Johanni de Hangesto, Domino de Henguevilla, ac Magistro Willelmo Boisratier, Utriusque Juris Doctori, Ambassiatoribus pro parte Franciæ."

[2] *Miles*] Added above the line.

## CXIII.

HENRY IV. TO THE DUCHESS OF BURGUNDY.

*Henri, par la grace de Dieu Roi d'Engleterre et de France, et Seigneur d'Irlande, a haulte et puissante Princesse, la Duchesse de Bourgoyne, Contesse de Flandres, salut et tresentiere dilection.*

Haulte et puissante Princesse.

Savoir veullez qu'il est venuz a nostre notice par relatioun a nous faite par dignes de foy, que vos subgitz de Flandres gisantz en agait sur la meer pour faire le mal qu'ils pourroient a noz liges, pristrent ja tard une nief en la quelle nostre treschier

Complaining of the detention of the Bishop of Hereford,

---

[TRANSLATION.]

*Henry, by the grace of God King of England and of France, and Lord of Ireland, to the high and mighty Princess, the Duchess of Burgundy, Countess of Flanders, greeting and most cordial affection.*

High and mighty Princess.—Be pleased to know that it is come to our notice by a relation made to us by men worthy of credit, that your subjects of Flanders, who are lying in ambush along the sea coast, with a view to committing all the evil that they shall be able upon our lieges, have just recently captured a ship, in the which our most

---

CXIII.] MS. Brit. Mus. Addit. 14,820 B. — On paper ; original, with the seal attached. The device | is much obliterated. but it appears to have been the royal arms of England.

A.D. 1404. en Dieu, Frere Robert Maskall,[1] nadgaires nostre
Confessour, estoit en venant hors de Middelburgh
pardevers nostre roiaume; et apres que voz ditz subgitz avoient gettez touz les serviteurs hors de la nief
en la meer, ils amesnerent le dit Frere Robert a
Donkirk deinz vostre dicte seigneurie; et la ils de-
tiegnent mesme celui Robert come lour prisoner, et
ne lui volont deliverer hors de lour garde sanz lui
mettre a finance et raunceon, a finiale destructioun
de son povre estat, a ce qu'est dit: dont nous avoms
grande cause de nous merveiller, puisque a graunde
instance et desir de les marchantz de vostre dicte
seigneurie, et meisment de les trois villes de vostre
pays de Flaundres, et a l'excitatioun de voz amyables
lettres, nadgaires envoiees tant a nous come a noz
messages lors esteauntz a nostre ville de Calais traitie

dearly beloved in God, Brother Robert Mascall, lately our
Confessor, was proceeding on his way from Middleburgh
towards our realm; and after that your said subjects had
thrust all hands out of the ship into the sea, they sent
away the said Brother Robert to Dunkirk within your said
lordship; and there they detain this same Robert as their
prisoner, and will not deliver him out of their custody
without his paying them a sum of money and a ransom, to the
final destruction of his poor estate, as it is said. Whereof
we have great cause to wonder, since at the urgent instance
and desire of the merchants of your said lordship, and
especially of the three towns of your country of Flanders,
and on the suggestion of your friendly letters, recently sent
as well to us, as to our commissaries at that time residing
at our town of Calais, a treaty was arranged between your

---

[1] The Bishop of Hereford.

se prist d'entre les messages de vous et de nous A.D. 1404.
qu'ore est pendaunt, dont on espoire que Dieu devaunt bonne conclusion se feire, en cas que tieles
mesprisions et attemptatz ne soient en cause de la
countraire et de rumpure d'icel.

Si vous prioms trescherement, et requeroms, haulte and re-
et puissante Princesse, que commander veullez voz ditz quiring his
subgitz de mettre le dit Robert a delivre sanz luy release without
raunceoner, ou autre damage faire, ainsi come vous ransom.
desirez que nous feroms a les voz en cas semblable.
Car vraiement, haulte et puissant Princesse, nous ne
pourroms ne voloms tieles horribles faitz longement
endurer.

Haulte et puissante Princesse, certiffier nous veullez
a plustost que vous pourrez bonnement ce que vous
pensez faire a la reverence de nous en celle partie.

Et Nostre Seigneur vous vueille tousjours avoir en
Sa seinte garde!

---

commissaries and our own, which is still pending, whereof
I hope God may give a good conclusion, in case such
outrages and attempts be not a cause for the contrary and
for the rupture of it.—Therefore we pray you with all
affection, and require you, high and mighty Princess, that
you would command your said subjects that they give the
said Robert his liberty without compelling him to pay his
ransom, or doing to him any other damage, even as you
would desire that we should do to you in a similar case.
For of a truth, high and mighty Princess, we cannot and
will not endure such horrible proceedings any longer.—
High and mighty Princess, be pleased to certify to us, as soon
as you possibly can, that which you deem it right to do
out of regard for us in this behalf.—And may our Lord be
pleased to have you always in his holy keeping.—Given

A.D. 1404. Donne soubz nostre signet, a nostre Chastcl de Tuttebury, le x. jour de Septembre.

*Endorsed :*—"A haulte et puissaunte Princesse, la Duchesse de Bourgoygne, Countesse de Flandres, etc."

*Also (in another hand) :*—"Le Roy d'Angleterre de la prinse de l'Evesque de Herford.[1]"

under our signet, at our Castle of Tutbury, the 10th day of September.

*Endorsed :*—"To the high and mighty Princess, the Duchess of Burgundy, Countess of Flanders, etc."

*Also :*—"The King of England on the capture of the Bishop of Hereford."

## CXIV.

### THE FRENCH TO THE ENGLISH AMBASSADORS.

Declining to enter into particulars in their reply, and reminding the English Ambassadors of the limit appointed for the truce.

Honorabiles et circumspecti Domini.

Litteras vestras datas Calesii xxiij. die Augusti, recepimus, inter cetera concludentes quatinus ad quæsita scripta per Dominum Johannem Cheyny, Militem, per nos aut alios ad locum consuetum per certos modos in dictis litteris vestris declaratos sine dilatione curemus respondere.

---

[1] *Herford*] Altered from "Norwic."

CXIV.] MS. Cotton. Galba,B. 1. fol. 87 (β).—On paper; a contemporaneous MS.

Ad quæ vobis respondemus quod (sicuti vos cre- A.D. 1404. dimus plene scire dum ultimo congregavimus cum parte vestra), abstinentia guerræ in certis confinibus inter nos et dictam partem vestram capta fuit et firmata, usque ad festum Omnium Sanctorum [1] proximo futurum duratura; infra quem terminum nos, vel alii a Domino nostro Rege Franciæ deputandi,[2] secundum condicta debemus cum vestris convenire.

Quapropter, et etiam quia Domini nostri Duces, cum Domino nostro Rege, ex quo sumus regressi, invicem ad tractandum de istis materiis nostris convenerunt, tempusque satis est infra quod ad ea quæ appunctuata fuere poterit provideri, non possumus ad contenta in vestris litteris de præsenti latius respondere. Sed in termino inter nos ab utraque parte convento, vel infra, quæ pro parte nostra fieri debebunt, concedente Domino, complebuntur.

Valete feliciter!

Scriptum Parisius, die xiij. mensis Septembris.

> J. DE HANGESTO, Dominus de HENGUEVILLA, Magister Balisteriorum Franciæ, et
>
> G. BOURRATERN,
>
> Domini nostri Regis Franciæ Consiliarii.

*Endorsement :*—" Honorabilibus et circumspectis Dominis, Domino Thomæ Swynford, Militi, Custodi Castri Calisii, et Nicholao de Rysshetoun, Utriusque Juris Professori, ambassiatoribus pro parte Angliæ."

---

[1] November 1.  |  [2] *deputandi*] depudandi, MS.

A.D. 1404.

## CXV.

### SWINBORN, CROFT, AND DE RYSSHETON TO THE DUCHESS OF BURGUNDY.

Illustris, necnon præclaræ nobilitatis Domina.

Promising to meet her Ambassadors at Santingfield, on condition that the Four Members of Flanders be represented;

Vestras litteras, scriptas Attrebati, xij. die præsentis mensis Septembris, una cum quodam salvo conductu pro ambassiatoribus Domini nostri, Regis Angliæ et Franciæ illustrissimi, quamvis defectivo,[1] recepimus Calesii, xiiij. die ejusdem mensis Septembris, inter cetera continentes, quod vicesimo quinto die ejusdem mensis Septembris, ante meridiem, in loco apud Santyngfeld in nostris litteris assignato, vestri ambassiatores et commissarii, in eisdem litteris vestris nominati, cum ambassiatoribus Domini nostri Regis, pro parte vestra parati sunt convenire pro tractatu communis mercandisiæ; quodque salvum conductum consimilem pro vestris commissariis nominatis debeamus transmittere pro vestrorum ambassiatorum securitate. Et in eventu quo visum et nobis utile ac necesse fuerit alium salvum conductum a Comite Sancti Pauli pro nostra securitate obtinere, vestra Magnificentia offert hujusmodi salvum conductum citra prædictum terminum nobis liberare.

---

CXV.] MS. Brit. Mus. Addit., 14,820, C. (a).—On paper; original, with the seals of the three Ambassadors in a tolerably perfect state. That of Swynborn represents a man's head with a long pointed beard; that of Croft a stag couchant. The third has the mutilated remains of a device surrounded by a motto which is no longer legible.

[1] *quamvis defectivo*] These words have been added above the line. See the safe-conduct appended to this letter, and the notes at pp. 322, 3.

Ad quæ, illustris ac nobilis Domina, dictis die et A.D. 1404.
loco, etiam ante meridiem, cum vestris ambassiatoribus
et commissariis per Dei gratiam conveniemus, parati
perficere quod est honestatis et justitiæ; dum tamen
illi de vestris Quatuor Membris per suos ambassiatores
et commissarios, ad quorum instantiam primo, ac subsequenter ad vestram, Dominus noster Rex consentiit
in hujusmodi tractatu,—quos per diversas litteras
nostras nuper monuimus, ac in Domino exhortati
fuimus, etiam juxta formam juratorum et sigillorum
suorum, cum vestris et nostris commissariis et ambassiatoribus, in hujusmodi tractatu velint interesse, ac
bona mercatorum Angliæ, seu valores eorundem, in
Sclusa arrestata contra ipsorum jurata et sigilla, et
præsertim contra litteras et sigilla claræ memoriæ pro
tunc ipsorum Domini, Domini Ducis Burgundiæ, con-
sortis vestri, (cujus anima requiescat in pace!) ad conservationem juratorum, ac status et famæ eorundem—
pro liberatione etiam animæ ejusdem Domini claræ
memoriæ, primitus velint restituere, ac ad ulteriora in
tractatu successive, juxta formam appunctuatorum et
juratorum, procedere.

Credimus enim, per Dei gratiam, ut ab experto and pro-
novimus, quod vestros cives et burgenses Quatuor testing
Membrorum vestræ patriæ Flandriæ adeo notabiles their being
contra ipsorum jurata et sigilla non intenditis susti- encouraged
nere, nec ipsos in perjurio auctorizare; sed eos ad conservationem juratorum suorum astringere, ne infamiam
juris per mundum ac scandalum perpetuum videantur
incurrere.

Salvum enim conductum pro vestris commissariis They en-
mittimus vobis per præsentem portitorem, parati ipsum close a safe-
salvum conductum, (si expedit) reformare juxta ordina- conduct,
tionem vestram, etiam ante prædictum terminum.

Et quia vester salvus conductus, juxta tenorem po- and return
testatis Domini vestri superioris nobis transmissus, est them by the
insufficiens, præsertim cum in potestate a Domino for alteration.

A.D. 1404. vestro superiori vobis commissa, vestro salvo conductu
interclusa, non attribuitur potestas seu auctoritas vestræ
Nobilitati ad dandum salvum conductum, quantum ad
loca in hujusmodi dictis et tractatibus de consensu
ambassiatorum utriusque partis assignanda, ac etiam
quantum ad alios defectus in copia vestri salvi conductus reformandos expressatos, cujus tenorem pro
reformatione potestatis Domini vestri superioris remittimus vestræ Magnificentiæ præsentibus interclusum.

Et quamvis sub confidentia vestræ Magnificentiæ
in prædicto vicesimo quinto die, si vobis videbitur, cum
vestris commissariis poterimus convenire, ordinetis
tamen auctoritatem et potestatem vobis commissam, ut
præfertur, cum omni celeritate, et, si poterit fieri, ante
prædictum terminum plenius reformari.

They com-
-plain of the
detention
of the
Bishop of
Hereford,
and some
English
fishermen,
and request
that they
may be set
at liberty.

Item, quamvis abstinuimus hactenus gentes nostras
armigeras, ac etiam nostrum navigium, quod non ap-
plicarent ad vestras partes Flandriæ, intuitu vestræ
Magnificentiæ ac litterarum vestrarum, prout alias
scripsimus eidem Reverentiæ vestræ, nihilominus tamen
vestri subditi de Dunkyrk, et de aliis partibus vestræ
patriæ Flandriæ, tanquam piratæ et latrunculatores,
invaserunt quendam Fratrem, Sacræ Paginæ Professorem, Episcopum Herfordensem, in mari, capiendo, vul-
nerando, incarcerando, et ad financiam finaliter expo-
nendo, adeo quod de jure tota terra Flandriæ interdicto
est exposita : ac etiam quosdam pauperes piscatores, in
partibus borialibus Angliæ, ad numerum CLXVJ. capiendo, ac pro financia ipsorum apud Dunkyrk receperunt
ac etiam extorserunt certos plegios et fidejussores,
vestro tractatu communi juxta tenorem litterarum
vestrarum non obstante ; quod est satis vile et inhonestum, et pro effectu tractatus periculosum ; vestram
Magnificentiam rogamus ac exhortamus in Domino,
quatinus prædictos piscatores in Angliam placeat remittere, ac hujusmodi obligationem etiam quoad præfatum Episcopum Herfordensem et alios per plegios
præstitam relaxare.

Ex certis causis nos moventibus placeat salvum A.D. 1404.
conductum Comitis Sancti Pauli, cum insertione tenoris They also
potestatis suæ, seu alium salvum conductum locum- require the
safe-con-
tenentis sui, cum insertione tenoris potestatis suæ ac duct of the
Domini sui, juxta formam litterarum vestrarum, celerius Count of
St. Pol, for
quo poteritis nobis transmittere. themselves,

Item supplicamus vestræ Magnificentiæ et Nobilitati, and safe-
quatinus salvum conductum pro Thoma Holden, cum conducts
for Thomas
tribus sociis de Anglia transituro versus Romam,[1] in Holden and
uno salvo conductu[2] pro quolibet per se et pro uno his companions,
illorum, prout eidem Thomæ expedit; ac etiam pro going to
Roberto Brets de Aquitania, pro Henrico Brenge, et Rome;
also for
Jankyn Bradelier, mercatoribus de Anglia; etiam pro Robert
illis tribus conjunctim et divisim in alio salvo conductu Brets and
other mer-
per vestram patriam Flandriæ placeat cum omni cele- chants of
ritate transmittere, ac super præmissis omnibus prout England.
placuerit nobis rescribere, prout confidimus in vestra
Magnificentia.

Quam custodiat Altissimus feliciter et votive!
Scriptum Calisii, xvj. die mensis Septembris.

Item, quantum ad moram vestri nuncii, præsentium They ex-
portitoris, rogamus vestram Magnificentiam habere eum cuse the
delay of
excusatum, quia revera non est ipsi imputandum. the messenger.

THOMAS SWYNBORN, ET

JOHANNES DE CROFFT, Milites; ac

NICHOLAUS DE RYSSHETOUN, Utriusque Juris Professor,
Ambassiatores pro parte Angliæ.

Endorsed:—" Illustri, necnon præclaræ nobilitatis ac
magnæ potentiæ Dominæ, Dominæ
Margaritæ, Ducissæ Burgundiæ, Comitissæ Flandriæ, Arthesii, et Burgundiæ."

---

[1] *Romam*] Added above the line.    [2] *conductu*] There has been an
erasure here of several words.

A.D. 1404.

### [THE SAFE-CONDUCT.]

*Marguerite, Duchesse de Bourgoigne, Contesse de Flandres, d'Artoys, et de Bourgoigne Palatine, Dame de Salins, et de Malines, a touz ceulz qui ces presentes lettres verront salut.*

Inclosed in the preceding letter, and marked for alteration.

Comme a la supplication des gens d'Eglise, bourgois, et habitans de nostre pais de Flandres, il ait pleu a mon Seigneur le Roy, par ses Lettres Patentes, pour lez causes plus a plain contenues et declarees en ycelles, et pour le bien et la continuation du fait de la marchandise en nostre dit pais de Flandres, de commettre nous et nostre treschier et tresame filz aisnè, le Duc de Bourgoigne, Conte de Nevers, et chescun de nous,

---

### [TRANSLATION.]

*Margaret, Duchess of Burgundy, Countess Palatine of Flanders, of Artois, and of Burgundy, Lady of Salins, and Malines, to all those who shall see these presents, greeting.*

As at the supplication of the Clergy, burgesses, and inhabitants generally of our country of Flanders, it has pleased my Lord the King, by his Letters Patent, for the causes more fully contained and declared therein, and for the benefit and the continuation of the commerce in our said country of Flanders, to commission us and our most dear and most beloved eldest son, the Duke of Burgundy, Count of Nevers, each and either of us, and to give

---

MS. Brit. Mus. Addit., 14,820 C. (β).—On paper ; original. This interesting document is the copy of the safe-conduct sent by the Duchess to the English Ambassadors, and returned by them to her, inclosed in the preceding letter. Their suggestions for its alteration are written at the bottom, and referred by marks to their places in the text. Opposite these suggestions, on the left-hand side of the document, are the following words :—" Defectus signati in vestro salvo conductu, qui reformentur."

et donner licence povoir et auctorite de traictier et A.D. 1404.
accorder nous et nostre dit filz, ou nos commis, ou de
l'un de nous teilz qu'il nous plairoit, avecques les gens,
commis, ou messages de la partie d'Angleterre, aians
povoir a ce souffiesant des manieres seurtez et provisions
par lesqueilles le fait de la marchandise entre les
marchans de Flandres et d'Angleterre, et leurs alliez,
faiteurs, gens, et famille, pourroit avoir cours, et estre
exerce seurement en temps de guerre s'elle estoit entre
mon dit Seigneur le Roy, et son roialme d'une part,
et la dicte partie d'Angletere d'autre. Et pour entendre
au dit traictie, et les dis commis ou messages d'Angleterre assembler seurement avecques nous, ou nostre dit
filz, ou nos dis commis, ou de l'un de nous, es lieux
et aus journees qui sur ce seront permis et accordez
d'un coste et d'autre; et estre asseures de leurs personnes
et biens, mon dit Seigneur le Roy ait semblablement
ottroie et donne a nous, et a nostre dit filz, et chescun

---

licence, power, and authority, to treat and accord, ourselves and our said son, or our commissaries, or of one of
us, such as it shall please us, together with the persons,
commissaries, or ambassadors of the part of England, having
a sufficient power in this matter, concerning safe ways and
means by which the commerce between the merchants of
Flanders and of England, and their allies, factors, servants,
and households, may have free course, and be carried on
safely in time of war, if it should break out between my
said Lord the King and his realm on the one side, and
the said part of England on the other. And for the consideration of the said treaty, and that the said commissaries
or envoys of England may assemble in safety together with
us, or our said son, or our said commissaries, or the commissaries of one of us, in the places and on the days which
shall be consented to and arranged on the one side and on
the other ; and that they may be assured of their persons
and goods, my said Lord the King has in like manner granted
and given to us, and to our said son, and to each and

A.D. 1404. de nous, auctorite et puissance de donner de par luy saufcondit a yceulx commis ou messages d'Angleterre par ses aultres Lettres Patentes, desqueilles la teneur feussint de mot a mot :—

"*Charles, par la grace de Dieu Roy de France, a*
" *touz ceulz qui ces presentes Lettres verront salut.—*
" Comme, a la supplication des gens d'Eglise, bourgois,
" et habitans du conte et pais de Flandres, nous,
" par grant et meure deliberation de Conseil, pour
" plusiours causes et considerations qui a ce nous ont
" meu, aions commis et donne licence, povoir, et auc-
" torite, a nostre treschiere et amee tante, la Duchesse
" de Bourgoigne, Contesse de Flandres, d'Artoys, et de
" Bourgoigne, et a nostre treschier et tresame cousin,
" le Duc de Bourgoigne, Conte de Nevers, son filz
" aisne, et chescun d'eulx, de traictier et accorder par
" eulx, ou leurs commis teil qu'il leur plaira, aveques
" les gens, commis, ou messages de la partie d'Angle-

---

either of us, authority and power to give, as from himself, a safe-conduct to those commissaries or envoys of England, by others his Letters Patent, the tenor of which was as follows, word for word :—

" *Charles, by the grace of God, King of France, to all*
" *those who shall see these present letters, greeting.—*
" As, at the supplication of the Clergy, burgesses, and
" inhabitants generally of the country and land of Flanders,
" we, by the weighty and mature deliberation of our
" Council, for various causes and considerations which have
" moved us hereunto, have commissioned, and have given
" licence, power, and authority to our most dear and be-
" loved aunt, the Duchess of Burgundy, Countess of Flan-
" ders, of Artois, and of Burgundy, and to our most dear
" and most beloved cousin the Duke of Burgundy, Count
" of Nevers, her eldest son, and each and either of them,
" to treat and accord, by themselves, or their commissaries
" such as it shall please them, with the subjects, com-
" missaries, or envoys on the part of England, having

" terre, aians povoir a ce souffiesant des manieres A.D. 1404.
" seurtes et provisions, par lesqueilles le fait de la
" marchandise entre les marchans de Flandres et
" d'Angleterre, et leurs allies, facteurs, gens, et famille
" pourroit avoir cours, et estre exerce seurement en
" temps de guerre, s'elle estoit entre nous et nostre
" roialme d'une part, et la dicte partie d'Angleterre
" d'aultre. Et pour faire et entendre au dit traictie
" convendra lez dis messages ou commis d'Angleterre
" souventeffois assembler avec noz diz tante et cousin,
" ou leurs commis, et passer et frequenter par aucunes
" des parties de nostre roiaume, ou quel par aventure
" ils n'oseroient bonnement converser sans avoir sauf-
" conduit de nous, et estre asseures de leurs personnes
" et biens. Nous, pour la grant affection et singuliere,
" que tousjours ont eu, et encores ont au bien de
" nous et de nostre dit roiaume noz diz tante et cousin,
" ainsi que par experience de fait l'avons trouve,
" confians de leurs prudences, loiautez, et preudommie,

---

" sufficient power thereunto, concerning the safe ways and
" means by the which the carrying on of the commerce
" between the merchants of Flanders and of England, and
" their allies, factors, servants, and households, might have
" free course, and be exercised in security in time of war,
" if it should break out between us and our realm on the
" one side, and the said part of England on the other.
" And for the drawing up and considering of this treaty,
" it will be expedient that the said envoys or commissaries
" from England should oftentimes meet with our said aunt
" and cousin, or their commissaries, and pass through and
" frequent any of the parts of our realm, whereon perchance
" they shall not well dare to hold parley, without having
" a safe-conduct from us, and being assured of their persons
" and goods. We, for the great and singular affection that
" our said aunt and cousin always have had, and still have,
" for the welfare of us and of our said realm, even as by
" actual experience we have found, relying on their pru-

A.D. 1404. " a yceulz nos tante et cousin, et a chescun d'eulx,
" avons donne et donnons povoir et auctorite de donner
" et ottroier de par nous bon et seur sauf-conduit
" aux diz messages ou commis de la partie d'Angleterre,
" pour eux, leurs gens, familliers, et serviteurs, or,
" argent, joyaux, chevaulx, harnois, telx et en tel
" nombre, et jusques a tel temps que l'on leur semblera
" durant, le temps que noz diz tante et cousin, ou
" leurs diz commis, ou de l'un d'eulx vaqueront au
" fait dessusdit, pour venir pardevers noz dis tante
" et cousin, ou l'un d'eulx, assembler avecques eulx,
" ou leurs diz commis, ou de l'un d'eulx,[1] passer et
" repasser par mer et par terre, demourer, sejourner par
" jour et par nuit, la ou mestier leur sera, par nostre

---

" dence, loyalty, and trustworthiness, to them, our aunt and
" cousin, and to each and either of them, have given, and
" give power and authority to give and to grant, as from
" us, good and secure safe-conduct to the said envoys or
" commissaries on the side of England, for them, their
" servants, household officers, and attendants, their gold,
" silver, jewels, horses, harness, such and in such number,
" and extending for so long a period as shall seem good
" to them, what time our said aunt and cousin, or their
" said commissaries, or the commissaries of one of them,
" shall have leisure, for the above purpose, to come to our
" said aunt and cousin or one of them, to meet with them
" or their said commissaries, or the commissaries of one of
" them, [at the places, and on the days, which they shall be
" able to select on this matter,] to pass and repass by sea and
" by land, to abide, to sojourn by day and by night, wher-
" ever their necessity shall require, throughout our said

---

[1] Here a mark refers to the following addition, suggested by the English Ambassadors, and written at the bottom :—" As lieux et jour- " nees qui sur ce se pourront prendre." The note was at first written above the line, but this has been erased.

" dit roialme, villes, chasteaux, forteresses, pons, pors, A.D. 1404.
" passages, jurisdicions, et destrois,[1] senz ce que aucun
" destourbier ou empeschement leur soit ou doit estre
" fait en corps ne en biens au contraire. Si donnons
" en mandement[2] par ces mesmes presentes a nostre
" treschier et feal cousin, le Conte de Lyney et de
" Saint Pol, Capitaine General de par nous en pais
" de Picardie, et on .West pais de Flandres, aux baillis
" de Vermendois et d'Amiens, et a tous capitaines de
" gens d'armes, et aultres a qui il appartendrai, que
" les dis commis ou messages de la partie d'Angleterre,
" aus quelx noz dis tante et cousin, ou l'un d'eulx,
" auront donne sauf-conduit, comme dit est, ils laissent

---

" realm, the towns, castles, fortresses, bridges, harbours,
" passages, jurisdictions, and districts, [and also through
" the sea, and through all the places whither the fortune
" of wind or tempest by sea might bring or drive them,]
" without any obstacle or impediment being offered to them,
" or done against them in their persons or in their goods
" to the contrary. Therefore we give in charge, [to our
" admiral for the better guard of our sea-ports,] by these
" same presents, [and] to our most dear and trusty cousin,
" the Count of Ligni and of Saint Pol, Governour-General
" on our behalf in the country of Picardy, and in the West
" of Flanders, to the bailliff of Vermendois and of Amiens,
" and to all the captains of our forces, and others to whom
" it shall appertain, that the said commissaries or envoys
" on the part of England, to whom our said aunt and
" cousin shall have given safe-conduct, as it is said, they

---

[1] The following passage is here suggested as a necessary insertion : —" Et aussi par la mer, et par tous " les lieux ou fortune de vent, ou " tempeste de mer les purroit con- " dure ou chacier."

[2] Here is suggested for insertion: —" A nos amirral a plus gard de " pors marins."

X 2

A.D. 1404. " passer par leurs povoirs, lieux, juridicions, et destrois
" paisiblement, avecques leurs familliers, et serviteurs,
" senz leur faire ou donner ne souffrir estre fait ou
" donne aucun destourbier ou empeschement au con-
" traire ; aincois s'aucun leur estoit fait le facent
" tantost reparer et remettre au premier estat et deu,
" car ainsi nous plaist il estre fait.—En tesmoing de
" ce nous fait mettre nostre seel a ces presentes
" Lettres.—Donne a Paris le xxiiij$^e$ jour de Juing, l'an
" de Grace Mil quatre cens et quatre, et le xxiiij$^e$
" de nostre regne."

Pour la quelle partie d'Angleterre ont este et sont
ordenez et commis Messire Thomas Swynborn, Messire
Jehan Crofft, Messire Williame Lyle, Messire Thomas
Swynford, et Messire Raoul Botriaux, Chevaliers,
Messire Nicole de Risschetoun, Docteur en Loys et
en Decrez, Jehan Urban, et Pierres le Loharenc,
Escuiers, pour chescune fois, les quatre d'iceulx commis

---

" shall suffer to pass through the places and districts
" subject to their authority and jurisdiction peaceably,
" with their attendants and servants, without causing
" or offering to them, or suffering to be caused or offered,
" any obstacles or impediments to the contrary ; also if any-
" thing have been done to them, they shall cause repara-
" tion and restitution to be made soon to their former state
" and right, for thus it pleases us that it be done.—In
" witness whereof we have caused our seal to be set to
" these present letters. Given at Paris, the 24th day of
" June, in the year of Grace 1404, and the 24th of our
" reign."

For the which part of England there have been and are
appointed and commissioned Master Thomas Swynborn,
Master John Croft, Master William Lysle, Master Thomas
Swynford, and Master Ralph Bottreaux, Knights, Master
Nicholas de Ryssheton, Doctor in Laws and in Decrees,
John Urban, and Peter de Lorraine, Esquires, for every
occasion, four of these commissaries or less, if it shall please

ou mains, s'il leur plaist, entendre et proceder au fait A.D. 1404.
du dit traictie avec les commis qui a ce sont ou
seront ordenez de par nous, selon ce que de par la
dicte partie d'Angleterre nous a este signifie. Savoir
faisons que nous, desirans l'avancement et bon effect
du dit traictie, pour le bien utilite et proufiet de la
chose publique de nostre dit pais de Flandres, et en
usant du povoir obtenu en ceste partie de mon dit
Seignieur le Roy, avons par vertu d'icelluy et aussi
en nostre nom, aux dessus nommes Messire Thomas
Swynborn, Messire Johan Crofft, Messire Guillem Lyle,
Messire Thomas Swynford, et Messire Raol Bottriaux,
Chevaliers, Messire Nichole de Risshetoun, Jehan Urban,
et Pierre Loharenc, come et messages ou commis de
et pour la dicte partie d'Engleterre, et a chascun
d'eulx, donne et donnons par ces presentes, bon et
seur sauf-conduit pour les quatre des huit commis
dessus nommez, telz qu'il leur plaira, ou mains, s'il
leur plais, a chascune fois, et ensemble leurs gens,

---

them, to consider and proceed to the drawing up of the said
treaty with the commissaries who are or shall be thereto appointed by ourselves, according as has been signified to us
on the said part of England. We cause you to know that
we, desiring the advancement and good effect of the said
treaty, for the benefit, advantage, and profit of the public
weal of our country of Flanders, and employing the power
obtained on this behalf of my said Lord the King, by
virtue thereof, and also in our own name, to the above-
named Master Thomas Swynborne, Master John Croft,
Master William Lysle, Master Thomas Swynford, and
Master Ralph Bottreaux, Knights, Master Nicholas de
Ryssheton, John Urban, and Peter Lorraine, as the envoys
or commissaries of and on behalf of the said part of
England, and to each of them, have given and do give by
these presents good and sure safe-conduct for four of the
eight commissaries named above, such as it shall seem
good to them, or less if it please them, on every occasion,

A.D. 1404. familliers, et serviteurs, jusques au nombre de soixante, personnes, et autant de chevaulx, ou au dessoubz, avecques leur or, argent, joyaux, harnois, et autres biens quelxconques, venir pardevers nous, ou assembler avec nos diz commis au lieu, ou aux lieux et journees, qui serront ordonnez, pour entendre et vaquer au dit traictie, toutes les fois et quanteffois que les dictes journees serviront et autres jours, et que aussi autrement besoing sera, pour le fait du dit traictie, et des circumstaunces et dependens d'iceluy ; et que pour yceulx commis de la dite partie d'Engleterre y traire, et autrement aler es diz lieux pour la dite besoigne ilz et chacun d'eulx puissent passer, demourer, et sejourner, de jour et de nuit, par tout la ou mestier leur serra, es Marches des pais d'Artois, de Boulenois, de Tournois, et des Ressors, et lieux enclavez en yceulx, de la conte de Guysnes, et du West pais de Flandres par

---

and together with their men, attendants and servants, to the number of sixty persons, and the like number of horses or upwards, with their gold, silver, jewels, harness, and all other goods whatsoever, to come unto us, or to assemble with our said commissaries, at a place, or at places, and on the days, which shall be appointed for to consider and deliberate on the said treaty, on all and every occasion that the said days shall serve, as well as other days, and also when otherwise there shall be need, for the accomplishment of the said treaty, and of the circumstances and things arising thereout ; and for these commissaries of the said part of England to approach thither, and otherwise to proceed unto the said places on account of the said business, they and each of them might be able to pass through, tarry, and sojourn, by day and by night, everywhere where their occupation shall be, to the Marches of the country of Artois, of Boulogne, of Tournois, and of Resors, and places included within the same, of the country of Guisnes, and of the land of West Flanders, by the bridges,

les pons, pors, passaiges, juridicions, et destrois d'iceulx A.D. 1404. senz estre empeschiez ne destourbez, en corps ne en biens, par les officiers, subgez, allians, aidans, et bien-vueillans, de mon Seigneur le Roy, ou autres quelx-coques de quelque natioun quilz soient tenans la partie d'icelui mon Seigneur le Roy, par voie oblique ne directe, en aucune maniere, durant nostre dit conduit jusques au premier jour du mois de Decembre pranchain venant.

Si donnons en mandement a tous les capitaines, justiciers, officiers, subgez, ailliez, aidans, et bien-vueillans, tant de mon Seigneur le Roy comme de nous, et a chascun d'eulx endroit soit et si comme a lui appertendra, que nostre present sauf-conduit en la maniere, et durant le temps dessusdiz, tiengnent, et gardent, et d'icelui laissent, facent, et sueffrent les dessus nommez commis, ou messaiges de la dicte partie d'Angleterre, et leurs gens, familiers, et serviteurs, jusques au dit nombre de soixante personnes, et autant

---

harbours, passages, jurisdictions, and districts of the same, without being obstructed or impeded, in person or in goods, by the officers, subjects, allies, aiders, and well-wishers of my Lord the King, or any others whatsoever of any nation who shall be holding to the part of this my Lord the King, whe-ther indirectly or directly, in any manner, while our said safe-conduct lasts, viz., till the first day of the month of December next coming.—We give, therefore, in command-ment unto all the governours, justiciaries, officers, subjects, allies, aiders, and well-wishers, as well of my Lord the King, as of ourselves, and to each of them, right of action and in such manner as shall appertain unto them, that our present safe-conduct, in the manner and for the duration of time above specified, they do hold and keep, and henceforth do permit, cause, and suffer the above-named commissaries, or envoys, of the said part of England, and their people, domestics, and servants to the said number of sixty persons, and as many

A.D. 1404. de chevaulx ou au dessoubz, ensemble ou par parties, et chascun d'eulx, jusques au nombre de quinze personnes et chevaulx avec lui, ou mains s'il lui plaist, paisiblement et plainnement joir et user senz enfraindre, ne leur faire ou donner ne suffrir estre fait ou donne aucun destourber ou empeschement quelconque, en corps ne en biens, au contraire, pour[1] cause de marque reprisaille entreprinse, ne soub umbre de guerre particulere que aucuns tenons le partie de mon dit Seigneur le Roy pevent avoir contre la dicte partie d'Angleterre, ne des entreprinses et dommages qui en sont ensieviz ou pourroient ensievre, ne pour autre quelconque cause ou occasion que ce soit. Et s'aucune chose estoit fait en contraire si le reparent, ou facent reparer tantost et senz aucun delay, ne sur ce attendre mandement de mon dit Seigneur le Roy devans, ne d'autre quelconque.

---

horses, or under, together or in parties, and each of them, to the number of five persons, and their horses with them, or less, if it please them, in peace and to the full to enjoy and to use without infringement, not causing or giving to them, nor suffering to be caused or done unto them, any annoyance or hindrance whatsoever, in their person or in their goods to the contrary, on account of reprisals undertaken, or under the pretence of any particular war that any who hold to the part of my said Lord the King may have in hand against the said part of England, or of the attempts and damages that have ensued or may ensue, nor for any other cause or occasion that may arise. And if anything be done to the contrary then they shall repair it, or cause the reparation to be made soon, and without any delay, without waiting first for a commandment from my said Lord the King in the matter, nor from any

---

[1] *pour*] pou, MS.

En testmoing de ce nous avons fait mettre nostre A.D. 1404.
seel a ces Lettres.

Donne en nostre ville d'Arras, le ix. jour de Septembre, l'an de Grace Mil quatre cens et quatre.

---

other whatsoever.—In testimony whereof we have caused our seal to be affixed to these Letters.—Given in our town of Arras, the 9th day of September, the year of Grace 1404.

## CXVI.

### SWINFORD AND DE RYSSHETON TO HENRY IV.

Illustrissime Princeps, ac invictissime et metuendissime Domine.

Quamvis pars Franciæ vestris litteris regiis, ac alio- Announc-
rum Dominorum, spiritualium et temporalium, regni $\frac{\text{ing that}}{\text{the French}}$
vestræ, per nobilem ac vestrum providum Militem, were caus-
Dominum Johannem Cheyny, ambassiatoribus pro parte ing delays,
Franciæ pro responsione reportanda præsentatis, hactenus distulit respondere ; die tamen confectionis præsentium recepimus certas litteras ex parte dictorum ambassiatorum Franciæ, hujusmodi responsionis usque ad festum Omnium Sanctorum[1] proximo futurum dilatorias. Quarum litterarum tenorem vestræ Majestati mittimus præsentibus interclusum.

Et revera consideratis treugis usque ad festum and that it
Omnium Sanctorum[1] supradictum captis, ac ad certa $\frac{\text{was proba-}}{\text{ble that}}$
loca per malitiam Gallicorum subtiliter restrictis, pen- they con-

---

CXVI.] MS. Cotton. Galba, B. i. | [1] November 1.
fol. 90.—On paper ; original.

A.D. 1404.
templated a
diversion
in favour
of the re-
bels in
Wales.

satisque litteris eorundem ambassiatorum Franciæ, Gallici citra festum Omnium Sanctorum,[1] prout veri-similiter speramus, cum suis navigiis armatis suas malitias excogitatas in favorem vestrorum rebellium Walliæ intendunt ostendere, ac etiam vestrum regnum potenter invadere, ac navigium regni (quod absit!) destruere, ac omnia mala possibilia interim vestro regno referre et penitus procurare.

The neces-
sity for
defensive
measures in
England.

Et, si mare interim, præsertim in partibus Walliæ, potenter fuerit munitum pariter et defensatum, credimus quod a Gallicis ex tunc reportabimus responsionem placabilem: alias facient ultimatum potentiæ suæ cum ipsorum adhærentibus ad regni vestri læsionem non modicam et gravamen.

Ad quod Deus advertat, ac Suam Manum Dexteram, de Sua benignitate solita, erigat in favorem vestræ Majestatis!

Quam concedat Altissimus feliciter et votive!

Scriptum Calisii, xix$^{mo}$ die mensis Septembris.

Vestræ regiæ Majestatis sacratissimæ commissarii et nuncii,

THOMAS SWYNFORD, ac

NICHOLAUS DE RYSSHETOUN.

*Endorsed*: — "Serenissi[mo Domino, Henrico, Dei] gratia Regi A[ngliæ et Franciæ]."

---

[1] November 1.

A.D. 1404.

## CXVII.

CROFT AND DE RYSSHETON TO THE PRIVY COUNCIL.

Reverendissimi in Christo Patres, ac magnifici et excellentes Domini.

Nuper vestris Paternitatibus ac Magnificentiis per Ricardum Wandesford, servientem Stapulæ, misimus copias diversarum litterarum pro tractatu Flandriæ, tam Dominæ Ducissæ Burgundiæ, Comitissæ Flandriæ, quam ipsius Quatuor Membris, necnon Magno Concilio Franciæ, ac Domino de Henguevilla et ipsius collegæ, ambassiatoribus pro parte Franciæ, pro responsione certarum litterarum, ex parte Domini nostri Regis et regni, adversario regni Franciæ ac ipsius regni Dominis spiritualibus et temporalibus transmissarum. Quas nobilis vir Dominus Johannes Cheynee, Miles, pro tunc ambassiator, etc., Domino de Henguevilla ac suo collegæ tradidit et liberavit. De quibus litteris in Franciam transmissis in præsenti nullam recepimus responsionem.

*Announcing that they had received no answer from the French Ambassadors,*

Quantum tamen ad tractatum Flandriæ, juxta tenorem dictarum litterarum, Comitissæ Flandriæ ac Quatuor Membris antedictis transmissarum, præfata Domina Comitissa remisit nobis litteras responsivas cum salvo conductu, juxta potestatem et auctoritatem a Domino suo superiore Rege Francorum sibi concessam, in hujusmodi salvo conductu expressatam, ad nostri tractatus soliditatem ac perfectionem ampliorem. Cujus salvi

*and giving an account of their progress in the treaty with Flanders.*

---

CXVII.] MS. Cotton. Galba, B. I. fol. 93.—On paper ; original, with marks of the seals.

A.D. 1404. conductus ac dictæ potestatis interclusæ, ut appareat de ipsius validitate seu invaliditate, copiam eisdem vestris Paternitatibus et Dominationibus mittimus, præsentibus interclusam.

Et sub prætextu hujusmodi salvi conductus vicesimo quinto. die præsentis mensis Septembris, ultra Santyngfeld, in confinio utriusque dominii Angliæ et Franciæ, qua dominia per lapides finales, tanquam limites, inibi sunt distincta, pro præparatoriis tractatus, præsertim quo ad locum indifferentem eligendum, ambassiatores utriusque partis debent insimul convenire, ac pariter interesse, non obstantibus quibusdam defectibus in hujusmodi salvo-conductu assignatis interim reformandis.[1]

Item, pro persecutione dicti tractatus Flandriæ, vestræ Dominationes ordinarunt quinque commissarios, quorum duo, videlicet Dominus Thomas Swynborn, Miles, ac Johannes Urban, sunt in Anglia ; et, ante prædictum terminum, Dominus Willielmus Lyle, Miles etiam revertetur in Angliam ; Dominus Johannes Crofft, Miles, Capitaneus del Mark, quartus commissarius, propter quasdam ægritudines suas castrum suum faciliter non poterit exire, quamvis offerret se paratum exhibere quam commode poterit interesse.

They complain of the non-payment of their stipends,

Et, juxta ordinationem communem, in hujusmodi tractatu quatuor pro parte nostra, prout pro parte adversa, debent pariter convenire ; alias istum tractatum ex defectu commissariorum poteritis faciliter destruere. Commissarii enim in vestris commissionibus nominati absque stipendiis seu remuneratione merito recusant labores suscipere, quia nullus compellitur expensis propriis militare,[2] quodque a xiiij. die mensis Novembris continue citra pro stipendiis meis præteritis et futuris, Ego Nicholaus[3] recepi solummodo lx. libras

---

[1] See pp. 322, 3.
[2] 1 Cor. ix. 7.

[3] Ego Nicholaus] Added above the line.

sterlingorum, computatis quibuscumque computandis, A.D. 1404. et defalcatis defalcandis, prout patet per compotum meum in Thesaurariam redditum, quod est manifestum. Concilium enim Domini nostri Regis commisit Thesaurariis guerrarum ad solvendum mihi centum libras. Subsequenterque Concilium Leycestriæ commisit eisdem ad solvendum mihi centum libras sub litteris privati sigilli et signeti, de quibus ducentis libris solummodo recepi lx. libras, ut præfertur, nec assignationem residui potui obtinere. Idcirco pro Dei misericordia ordinetis ac mandetis Thesaurariis guerrarum, quod de residuo ducentarum librarum, defalcatis lx. libris supradictis, velint realiter mihi et Nicholao[1] satisfacere, quia alias diutius labores propter defectum non potero continuare : alias, infectis negotiis, revertar in Angliam, excusaturus me penes Dominum nostrum Regem et Parliamentum.[2]

Necnon quod dictæ commissiones, una pro tractatu Flandriæ, alia pro responsione dictarum litterarum in Franciam transmissarum, juxta tenorem aliarum litterarum nostrarum vobis nuper transmissarum, reformentur ac cum omni celeritate in Calisium citra præfatum vicesimum quintum diem transmittantur.

Et præsertim quod tales commissarii ponantur in vestris commissionibus qui onus volunt assumere, ac in laboribus participare ; et quod onus ex defectu remunerationis non valeant recusare.

Item, quia notabile ac magnum navigium armatorum in Francia est præparatum, quod de præsenti mense, prout prætenditur, applicabit in partibus Walliæ, seu in aliis partibus Angliæ, ideo pro ampliori securitate expedit quod mare cum omni celeritate sit fortiter munitum, ac in singulis portubus defensatum, quia Gallici disponunt se potius ad gladium quam ad treugarum

*and announce that the French fleet will shortly invade Wales.*

---

[1] *et Nicholao*] Added above the line.

[2] *alias infectis . . . . . Parliamentum*] Added in the margin.

A.D. 1404. observationem, seu ad respondendum articulis seu punctis superius memoratis.

Vestras Paternitates ac Dominationes custodiat Altissimus, ad felix regimen juxta votum !

Scriptum Calisii, xix. die mensis Septembris.

Vestræ servitores humillimi,

JOHANNES CROFFT, Miles, ac

NICHOLAUS DE RYSSHETOUN,

Commissarii, etc.

Et quamvis solus cum duobus clericis continue scribentibus, propter absentiam aliorum commissariorum, in complacentia Domini nostri Regis et regni in quantum sufficio velim labores assumere, ac expensas consuetas non modice factas exponere, locum tamen seu numerum quatuor personarum in tractatu non potero prætendere seu quovis modo repræsentare.

*Endorsed* : — " Reverendissimis in Christo Patribus, necnon excellentibus ac potentibus Dominis, Dominis de almo Concilio Domini nostri Regis Angliæ et Franciæ serenissimi."

*Also in another hand* :—" Tradatur Domino Cancellario Angliæ, ejus clerico privati sigilli tradenda."

It appears that, after the above letter was sealed, a Letter of an alarming character was received from the French Ambassadors, in reference to which the following Postscript was written. It is separated from the Letter in the MS., occurring at fol. 87 ($\alpha$); there can be no doubt, however, that it is now assigned to its proper place. The Letter from the French Ambassadors referred to in it was written on the 13th of September, and will be found at page 312 in its proper chronological order.

THE POSTSCRIPT.

Reverendissimi Patres ac Domini.

Post scripturam et sigillationem præsentis litteræ, quædam litteræ ex parte ambassiatorum Franciæ fuerunt præsentatæ, per quas judicio nostro poterit apparere quod usque ad festum Omnium Sanctorum[1] Gallici disponunt omnia mala nobis præparare et inferre ; ipsarumque litterarum copiam mittimus vobis inferius annotatam et descriptam.[2]

Et revera, nisi apponatur debitum ac consultius regimen solito contra potentiam inimicorum, futurum erit periculum, nisi Deus ex Sua benignitate consueta apponat remedium, et erigat Suam Manum Dexteram ad nostrum favorem.

Item expedit instructionem plenam citra prædictum terminum remittere, si treugas virtute commissionis novæ transmittendas debeamus prorogare, et numquid generaliter seu alias quo ad certa loca, seu qualiter, et distincte.

Item, remittatur commissio, juxta tenorem litterarum nostrarum, pro tractatu Flandriæ.

## CXVIII.

CROFT AND DE RYSSHETON TO THE PRIVY COUNCIL.

Reverendissimi Patres, ac magnifici et excellentes Domini.

Quamvis Ducissa Burgundiæ, Comitissa Flandriæ, per suos ambassiatores, xxv[to] die præsentis mensis Septembris, juxta tenorem aliarum litterarum nostrarum

On the refusal of the Duchess of Burgundy

---

[1] November 1.
[2] See Letter CXIV.

CXVIII.] MS. Cotton. Galba, B. 1. fol. 73.—On paper ; original, with traces of the seals.

A.D. 1404.
to permit
the Four
Members
of Flanders
to enter
the treaty.
vestris Dominationibus transmissarum, in tractatu communi nobiscum in loco assignato distulit convenisse; viso tamen nostro salvo conductu, pro ambassiatoribus suis per nos eidem transmisso, una cum tenore potestatis seu commissionis nostræ in eodem interclusæ, eadem Domina Ducissa et Comitissa nobis rescripsit, ante dictum vicesimum quintum diem, quod cum commissariis et ambassiatoribus suorum subditorum Quatuor Membrorum Flandriæ in nostro[1] tractatu communi in eodem termino non intendebat convenire.

Idcirco eadem Domina misit nobis copiam commissionis pro parte nostra reformandæ, ac de novo fiendæ absque adjunctione Quatuor Membrorum suorum, cujus copiam mittimus vestris Dominationibus reformandam, ac, postquam fuerit reformata, scripta, et sigillata in forma fieri consueta, cessantibus aliis commissionibus, mittatur Calisium cum omni celeritate.

Et in hujusmodi commissione Willelmum Moubray, Armigerum, Constabularium Castri villæ Calisii, quem inter alios reputamus ad hujusmodi onus sufficientem, una cum aliis commissariis alias nominatis, ac etiam cum aliis nominandis juxta vestram ordinationem, præsertim qui voluit onus ambassiatæ suscipere, cum ipsorum debita remuneratione in hujusmodi commissione dignemini interserere, ne ex defectu commissariorum frustra videamur laborare.

Super quibus, ac super sufficientia seu invaliditate potestatis seu commissionis Ducissæ Burgundiæ, Comitissæ Flandriæ, in aliis litteris nostris vestris Reverentiis transmissis, in ipsius salvo conductu interclusæ, dignemini respondere, ac etiam super aliis vestrum beneplacitum nobis rescribere, prout eisdem vestris Paternitatibus et Dominationibus videbitur expedire.

---

[1] *nostro*] Added above the line.

Quas custodiat Altissimus feliciter et votive !  A.D. 1404.
Scriptum Calisii, vicesimo sexto die præfati mensis
Septembris

JOHANNES CROFFT, Miles, et
NICHOLAUS DE RYSSHETOUN,
Ambassiatores pro parte
Angliæ.

Item, nisi de residuo de ducentis libris, per vestrum De Rysshe-
almum Concilium Londoniæ et Leycestriæ pro stipen- ton threatens
diis meis mihi assignatis, per Thesaurarios guerrarum, England if
ultra lx. libras mihi (Nicholao infrascripto[1]) persolutas, his stipend
celeriter ac realiter fuerit satisfactum, ordinetis vobis quickly.
unum alium clericum loco mei ad hujusmodi tracta-
tuum prosecutionem; quia propter penuriam et defectum
non potero ulteriorem sustinere laborem.  Ideo alias
revertar in Angliam ad Parliamentum.

[NICHOLAUS DE RYSSHETON.]

Endorsed :—" Reverendissimis in Christo Patribus,
necnon magnæ excellentiæ singularis-
simis Dominis Consiliariis de Almo
Concilio di[rigatur]."

---

[1] Nicholao infrascripto] Added above the line.

Y

A.D. 1404.

## CXIX.

### SWYNFORD AND DE RYSSHETON TO HENRY IV.

Illustrissime Princeps, ac invictissime et metuendissime Domine.

On the treachery of the French.

Cum pars Franciæ infractionem treugarum vestræ regiæ Majestati sacratissimæ, ac vestro regno Angliæ videatur ascribere, adeo quod illi pro parte Franciæ vestris litteris regiis, seu etiam litteris aliorum Dominorum regni vestri, per vestrum providum Militem, Dominum Johannem Cheyny, ambassiatoribus Franciæ præsentatis, aut etiam nostris litteris tam magno Concilio quam ambassiatoribus Franciæ transmissis, hactenus distulerunt, prout in præsenti differunt, respondere; litteras tamen ipsorum ambassiatorum Franciæ nuper recepimus, quarum tenorem nuper Excellentiæ vestræ per Johannem Budde, famulum nobilis viri Domini Thomæ Erpyngham, vestri Militis, Senescalli hospitii vestri, in aliis litteris nostris misimus interclusum. Ex quarum tenore clare poterit apparere quod, citra festum Omnium Sanctorum,[1] vestris litteris regiis non intendunt respondere, sed interim, per se et suos adhærentes etiam de Ispannia, mala possibilia vobis per eorum navigium, in mari potenter armatum, intendunt inferre, ac culpam et treugarum infractionem vestræ Excellentiæ imponere. Unde ad ostendendum vestram ac regni vestri innocentiam, circa conservationem treugarum, necnon ad declarandum culpam et defectum ac infractionem treugarum quoad partem Franciæ adversam ac etiam sigillorum suorum et

---

CXIX.] MS. Cotton. Galba, B. I. fol. 95.—On paper; original, with marks of the seals.

[1] November 1.

appunctuamentorum communium violationem, et præ- A.D. 1404. sertim quoad ampliorem vestram excusationem et declarationem, sub prætextu resignationis per Dominum Regem Ricardum nuper factæ vestræ Celsitudini, ac vestro regno, per Ducem Aurelianum ac Comitem Sancti Pauli, nequiter ac malitiose impositæ. Necnon quoad ducenta millia francorum ratione dotis ex parte Dominæ Isabellæ nuper Reginæ Angliæ petita indebite, certas litteras Magno Concilio Franciæ pro declaratione præmissorum, ac ad removendum scandalum decrevimus transmittere. Quarum copiam, præsentibus insimul colligatam, cum concernant vestrum statum regium ac regni vestri honorem pariter et commodum, prout in eisdem taliter qualiter est declaratum, eandem vestram Celsitudinem non tædeat easdem [1] perlegere, ipsarum prolixitate propter[2] difficultatem materiæ non obstante.

Item, quamvis vicesimo quinto die elapso præsentis Delays in mensis Septembris ambassiatores Comitissæ Flandriæ the treaty cum vestris, juxta tenorem aliarum litterarum vobis with Flanders. transmissarum, in tractatu communi debuissent interfuisse, præfata tamen Domina Comitissa, viso nostro salvo conductu pro suis ambassiatoribus per nos sibi transmisso, ante dictum vicesimum quintum diem nobis rescripsit, quod cum ambassiatoribus subditorum Quatuor Membrorum suorum in tractatu non intendebat convenire, sed solum per se et suos ambassiatores. Idcirco eadem Comitissa misit nobis copiam commissionis fiendæ absque adjunctione Quatuor Membrorum suorum, cujus unam copiam mittimus vestræ regiæ Majestati ac aliam vestro magno Concilio reformandam. Quatuor tamen Membra Flandriæ, juxta formam juramentorum suorum et sigillorum, post tres requestas solemnes, sub pœna perjurii, infamiæ, et reprehensionis perpetuæ eis factas, rescripserunt nobis per litteras,

---

[1] easdem] Added above the line. | [2] There is an erasure here.

Y 2

A.D. 1404. ipsorum sigillis sigillatas, quod in dicto termino nobiscum in tractatu volebant convenire : unde prædicto xxv. die non poteramus insimul convenire, sed oportet expectare reformationem commissionis vestræ cum omni celeritate nobis in Calisium remittendæ ; et ex tunc per Dei gratiam insimul conveniemus, et tractatum nostrum perficiemus, prout melius poterimus.

Et cum præmissa sunt scripta ad honorem et defensionem status vestræ Majestatis regiæ, quamvis ex quadam grossitie et ruditate absque debita forsan digestione, ipsorum tamen correctionem suppletionem ac determinationem vestra regia Majestas sacratissima dignetur benigne suscipere, ac nostras simplicitates et ignorantias saltim in favorem hujusmodi vestræ materiæ ac intentionis nostræ ad ipsius executionem, quantum in nobis est executæ, gratiose excusare, prout flexis genubus humiliter supplicamus eidem Celsitudini vestræ.

Quam ad regni vestri felix regimen, ac ad reductionem rebellium in brevi per Dei gratiam, ad vestram obedientiam ac ad [1] resistendum victoriose malitiis inimicorum, concedat Altissimus juxta votum !

Scriptum Calisii, vicesimo sexto die dicti mensis Septembris.

Vestræ regiæ Majestatis sacratissimæ
Commissarii vestri
THOMAS SWYNFORD, et
NICHOLAUS DE RYSSHETOUN.


Endorsed :—" Serenissimo Principi, ac illustrissimo et invictissimo Domino, Domino [Henrico, Dei] gratia Regi Angliæ et Franciæ excellentissimo, Domino suo metuendi[ssimo.] "

---

[1] Above the line.

*The following document (MS. Cotton. Galba B. 1. fol. 71,—on paper; a contemporaneous MS.) was inclosed in this Letter:—*

*Copia Commissionis reformandæ pro tractatu Flandriæ, juxta petitionem Ducissæ Burgundiæ absque Quatuor Membrorum adjunctione.[1]*

*Henri, par la grace, etc. a touz ceulz qui ces presentez lettres verront salut.*

Comme a l'onneur de Dieu, et au proufiet commun du fait de la marchandise dont en partie nostre roiaulme est soustenu, et pour aultres causes et considerations qui a ce nous ont meu, nous aions par nos aultres commis et ordene nos amez et feaulz (*tel et tel*), noz ambassateurs et messages a toute plaine puissans pour traictier et accorder avec lez ambassateurs, messages, ou commis de par nostre treschiere cousine, Marguerite Duchesse de Bourgoigne, Contesse de Flandres, d'Artoys, et de Bourgoigne, aians a ce povoir souffiesant, dez manerez seurtez et provisions par lesquelles marchandise pourroit avoir cours et estre exerce seurement,

---

[TRANSLATION.]

*Henry, by the grace of God, etc., to all those who shall see these presents, greeting.*

Whereas for the honour of God, and for the common benefit of the commercial intercourse whereby in part our realm is sustained, and for other causes and considerations moving us hereunto, we have by our other letters commissioned and appointed our beloved and faithful (*such and such*) to be our ambassadors and envoys, with all and full authority for to treat and accord with the ambassadors, envoys, or commissaries of the part of our most dear cousin, Margaret, Duchess of Burgundy, Countess of Flanders, of Artois and of Burgundy, having sufficient powers for that purpose, concerning the ways, securities, and means whereby the commerce may have due course, and be carried on

---

[1] See page 347,

A.D. 1404. entre lez marchans, habitans, et subgies de nostre dit roiaulme et ceulz de la conte et pais de Flandres en temps de guerre, s'elle estoit ouverte (que Diex ne veulle) entre nous et nostre dit roialme d'une part et nostre Adversaire de France d'autre ; et aussi de faire reparer lez dommages, prinses, et exces qui ont este fais d'un coste et d'autre avec lez circumstances et depende.

Et pour entendre au dit traictie, convendra lez dis ambassateurs, commis, ou messages de nostre dit cousine souvent assembler, et autrement besoignier avec nos dis ambassateurs et messages, et passer et frequenter par . aucunes parties de noz terres, povoirs, et juris-dictions, es quilles par aventure ilz n'oseroient converser sans avoir saufcondit de nous et estre asseurez de leurs personnes et biens. Pour ce est il que nous, pour la bonne affection que nous avons a ceste besoigne, et que le dit traictie puisse venir a bon effect, au proufiet et utilite de l'une partie et de l'autre, confians plaine-ment dez sens, loiaultez, et proudommes des dessus

---

safely, between the merchants, inhabitants, and subjects of our said realm, and those of the county and land of Flanders in time of war, in case it should break out (which may God not will) between us and our said realm on the one part, and our adversary of France on the other ; and also to cause reparation to be made of the damages, seizures, and excesses which have been committed on one side and on the other, with the circumstances and things depending.— And for the consideration of the said treaty, it shall be arranged for the said ambassadors, commissaries, or envoys of our said cousin to assemble together often, and otherwise to negotiate with our said ambassadors and envoys, and to pass and go at will by any parts of our lands, powers and jurisdictions, which by chance they might not dare to frequent without having a safeconduct from us, and being assured of their persons and goods. On this account it is that we, for the good affection that we have towards their business, and that the said treaty may be able to arrive at a good result, to the benefit and advantage of the one side and of the other, con-fiding fully in the judgment, loyalty, and prudence of the

nommes (*tel et tel*) a iceulx huit, aux quatre, aux A.D. 1404. trois, aux deux d'iceulx, avons donne et donnons povoir et auctorite par ces presentes de donner et ottroier de par nous bon et seur saufconduit aux dis ambassateurs, messages, et commis, qui seront ordenez au dit traictie de par nostre dicte cousine, pour eux, leurs gens, familles, et serviteurs, ove argent, joiaulx, hernois, teilz et en tel nombre et jusques a tel temps que a nos dis ambassateurs et messages bon semblera, durant le temps en dedens le quel ils ou les aucuns d'eux vaqueront au fait dessusdit, pour venir devers yceulx nos ambassateurs, et assembler avecques eux aux lieux et aux journees qui sur ce se pourront prendre, passer et repasser par mer et par terre, demourer sejourner, par jour et par nuyt, par nos terres, jurisdictions, seignouries, villes, chasteaux, forteresses, pons, pors, passages, et destrois, et ailleurs la ou mestier leur sera, sanz ce que . aucun destourbier ou empeschement leur soit ou doit estre fait en corps ne en biens au contraire.

---

above-named (*such and such*) to these eight, or four, or three, or two of them, we have given and give power and authority by these presents to give and to grant, on our behalf, good and secure safe-conduct to the said ambassadors, envoys, and commissaries, who shall be appointed to the said treaty by the authority of our said cousin, for themselves, their men, their households, and servants, with silver, jewels, harness, such and in such number, and up to such a time as shall seem good to our said ambassadors and envoys, during the time within which they or any of them shall be attending to the business above-mentioned, for to go to these our ambassadors, and to assemble with them at the places and on the days which they shall be able to appoint for the purpose, to pass and repass, by land and by sea, to abide and sojourn, by day and by night, in our lands, jurisdictions, lordships, towns, castles, fortresses, bridges, harbours, passages, and districts and elsewhere, wheresoever their business shall be, without any impediment or obstacle being thrown in their way, or caused to be done to them in person or in goods to the con-

A.D. 1404. Si donnons en mandement au Capitaine de Caleis, et a tous admiraulx, capitaines de gens d'armes et de navire, chastellains, baillifs, sergens, et autres noz officeres quelconques, et leurs lieutenants, et a chacun d'eux sicomme a lui appertendra, que lez ambassateurs, messages, ou commis de nostre dit cousine, aux quilz noz diz ambassateurs auront ainssi donne saufconduit de par nous laissent passer, demourer, et retourner par leurs villes et chasteaux, povoirs, lieux, et jurisdictions et destrois paisiblement avec leurs familliers et serviteurs, sanz leur faire ou donne, ne souffrir estre fait ou donne aucun destourbier ou empeschement en corps ne en biens au contraire.

Aincois s'aucun leur estoit fait si le facent tantost reparier, et mettre au premier estat et deu ; car ainsi nous plaiet il estre fait.

En tesmoing de ce nous avons fait mettre nostre seel a ces presentez.

Donne, etc.

---

trary.—Therefore, we give commandment to the Governour of Calais, and to all admirals and captains of soldiers and of the navy, warders of castles, bailiffs, serjeants, and all other our officers whatsoever, as well as their lieutenants, and to each of them as shall appertain unto him, that they suffer the ambassadors, envoys, or commissaries of our said cousin, to whom our said ambassadors shall have thus given safe conduct from us, to be free to pass, abide, and return by their towns and castles, dominions, places, jurisdictions, and districts, peaceably, with their households and servants, without doing or offering against them, or suffering to be done or offered, any impediments or obstacle, either in their bodies or in their goods, to the contrary.—Meanwhile if any be done to them, that they cause as quickly as possible to make reparation, and to restore it to its first and due estate ; for thus it is our pleasure that it be done.—In witness hereof we have caused our seal to be set to these presents.

Given, &c.

A.D. 1404.

## CXX.

CROFT, LYSLE, AND DE RYSSHETON TO THE DUCHESS OF BURGUNDY.

*Copia litteræ Ambassiatorum Angliæ nuper transmissæ Dominæ Ducissæ Burgundiæ, &c.*

Illustris Principissa, ac magnæ nobilitatis et potentiæ Domina.

Vestram Excellentiam memoriosam credimus non latere qualiter eandem nuper per certas litteras nostras [1] requisivimus et exhortati fuimus in Domino, ad relaxandum financiam ac redemptionem reverendi Patris, Fratris Roberti, Episcopi Herefordensis, necnon C et LXVIII pauperum piscatorum, in partibus borialibus Angliæ per vestros subditos nuper captorum, pro cujus financiæ relaxatione, ac dictorum piscatorum liberatione, seu pro financiæ ipsorum relaxatione, vestra Magnificentia nos non curavit certiores reddere, seu vestram voluntatem in præmissis hactenus declarare: quodque, pro relaxatione financiæ præfati Domini Episcopi, certas litteras [2] Domini nostri Regis illustrissimi ac invictissimi, vestræ Excellentiæ intitulatas, mittimus per præsentium portitorem, quodque idem Dominus noster Rex, per alias litteras suas diversas nobis directas, præcepit et mandavit quod eandem Excellentiam vestram requireremus ac exhortaremur in Domino, juxta requestam alias vobis factam pro dictorum piscatorum restitutione ac plenaria liberatione, et quod cum celeritate possibili vestram responsionem super præmissis eidem Domino nostro de-

On the imprisonment of the Bishop of Hereford;

---

CXX.] MS. Cotton. Galba, B. I. fol. 74 (β).—On paper: a contemporaneous MS.

[1] See Letter CXV.
[2] See Letter CXIII.

A.D. 1404. beamus rescribere ac plenarie reportare; vestram Excellentiam requirimus, ac exhortamur in Domino quatinus financiam præfati Domini Episcopi, ac etiam dictorum piscatorum placeat relaxare, seu ipsos piscatores a carceribus absque financiæ solutione plenarie liberare.

and complaining of the threatening attitude of the Flemings. Reducat enim eadem Excellentia vestra vestræ memoriæ litteras vestras in Calisium nuper transmissas,[1] quas paratas habemus ostendere, qualiter ab omni actu guerrino et a quacumque guerra voluistis desistere, ac treugas publice in patria vestra interim proclamare, dum tamen sub forma consimili velimus eadem pro parte nostra peragere. Et revera sub prætextu vestræ Excellentiæ ac dictarum litterarum vestrarum Dominus noster Rex præcepit ac mandavit suis admirallis, ac subditis suis quibuscumque, quod subditis vestris nullum damnum seu gravamen debeant inferre, nec eosdem molestare; quæ præcepta Domini nostri Regis ac ipsorum publicationem notificavimus per litteras nostras[2] scriptas Calesii xxiij. die Augusti præsentis anni; quas litteras vestra Excellentia recepit; ac quoad quædam in eis contenta per vestras litteras responsivas, quas habemus etiam paratas[3] ostendere, prædictis etiam non obstantibus, vestri subditi de Newport, et de Dunkirk, ac de aliis partibus Flandriæ, de novo congregarunt et congregant in præsenti quoddam navigium ad spoliandum ac nostros subditos capiendum et derobandum; de quibus omnibus vehementer admiramur, cum istud sit præparatorium et inductivum ad gladium et non ad pacem. Super quibus omnibus placeat Domino nostro Regi excellentissimo ac nobis vestram voluntatem clare rescribere et plenarie declarare.

---

[1] See Letter LXXXVI.
[2] See Letter CVI.

[3] There is an erasure here.

In Angliam scripsimus, ac copiam commissionis[1] per A.D. 1404.
vos nobis transmissam in Angliam misimus de novo
reformandam, prout voluit vestra Excellentia.

Quam custodiat Altissimus feliciter et votive!

Scriptum Calisii, xxviij° die Septembris.

JOHANNES CROFFT, et

WILLIELMUS LYLE, Junior, ac

NICHOLAUS DE RISSHETOUN, Utriusque Juris Professor,
Ambassiatores pro parte Angliæ.

*Endorsement :*—" Illustri Principissæ, necnon præclaræ
nobilitatis ac magnæ potentiæ Do-
minæ, Dominæ Margaretæ, Ducissæ
Burgundiæ, Comitissæ Flandriæ,
Arthesii, et Burgundiæ."

---

[1] *commissionis*] Added above the line.—See Letter CXIX., and page 341.

A.D. 1404.

# 6 HENRY IV.

29 September, 1404, to 30 September, 1406.

## CXXI.

### CROFT, LYSLE, AND DE RYSSHETON TO THE DUCHESS OF BURGUNDY.

*Copia litteræ Ambassiatorum Angliæ, nuper transmissæ Dominæ Ducissæ Burgundiæ, etc.*

Illustris Principissa, ac magnæ nobilitatis et potentiæ Domina.

On the seizure of their letters by theLieutenant of Boulogne;

Pridie certas litteras Domini nostri, Regis Angliæ et Franciæ illustrissimi, sub signeto suo regio sigillatas, necnon quasdam alias litteras nostras, tam vestræ Excellentiæ[1] quam Magno Concilio Franciæ, ac etiam ambassiatoribus Franciæ intitulatas, per nostrum cursorem, etiam præsentium portitorem, juxta ipsarum subscriptionem et tenorem præsentandis, transmisimus. Quas litteras Boloniæ Petrus de Seyn Michelle, Locumtenens Boloniæ, eidem cursori nostro violenter abstulit, ac hujusmodi litteras, eidem vestræ Excellentiæ ac Magno Concilio et ambassiatoribus Franciæ directas, juxta ipsarum continentiam et subscriptionem, prout in litteris ipsius Locumtenentis sub signeto suo sigillatis, nobis transmissis, plenius continetur, præsentare promisit. Prædictarum litterarum tenorem per Dominum nostrum Regem serenissimum et invictissimum ac per nos vobis transmissarum, eidem Excel-

---

CXXI.] MS. Cotton. Galba, B. I. fol. 74 (γ).—On paper ; a contemporaneous MS.

[1] See Letter CXX.

lentiæ vestræ, pro celeriori ac pro pleniori responsione obtinenda, mittimus præsentibus interclusum. Vestram Magnificentiam ac nobilitatem requirimus, et exhortamur in Domino, quatinus, pro bono pacis ac pro utilitate communis mercandisæ, responsionem plenariam juxta tenorem tam [nostrarum]¹ dictarum litte- rarum, quam etiam copiæ earundem præsentibus interclusum, Domino nostro Regi excellentissimo ac nobis per præsentium portitorem placeat rescriberc quam responsionem eidem Domino nostro Regi cum celeritate poterimus reportare. Miramur enim vehementius quam in scripturis sufficimus exprimere, quod vestras subditos de Dunkirk, Neuport, Berflete, et de Sclusa toleratis ad spoliandum nostros subditos Angliæ, per terram et per mare ; necnon hujusmodi spolia facitis apportari ad vestram præsentiam, ac prout placet (prout asseritur), facitis distributionem; quod non est honestum, considerata forma diversarum vestrarum litterarum in Calisium transmissarum, nec diu tolerandum, nec præparatorium ad pacem, sed indicium ad gladium pro parte vestræ Excellentiæ.

Quam custodiat Altissimus ad tranquillitatem vestræ patriæ Flandriæ feliciter et votive !

· Scriptum Calisii, ultimo die mensis Septembris.

JOHANNES DE CROFFT, et

WILLELMUS LYLE, junior,—Milites, ac

NICHOLAUS DE RYSSHETOUN, Utriusque
Juris Professor,
Ambassiatores pro parte Angliæ.

*Endorsement :*—" Illustri Principissæ, necnon præclaræ nobilitatis, ac magnæ potentiæ
Dominæ, Dominæ Ducissæ Burgundiæ, Comitissæ Flandriæ, Arthesii,
et Burgundiæ."

A.D. 1404.

They complain bitterly of the injuries inflicted on the English in certain Flemish ports,

---

¹ There is here a small hole in the MS.

A.D. 1404.

## CXXII.

### SWYNBORN, CROFT, AND DE RYSSHETON TO THE FOUR MEMBERS OF FLANDERS.

*Copia litterarum Ambassiatorum Angliæ, transmissarum Quatuor Membris Flandriæ:—*

Honorabiles ac magnifici et circumspecti Domini.

*Acknowledging their letter, and recapitulating*

Vestras litteras, sub sigillo dominorum villæ Gandensis sigillatas, recepimus Calisii ultimo die mensis Septembris, inter cetera continentes, quod, licet vicesimo quinto die ejusdem mensis Septembris ambassiatores vestri, una cum ambassiatoribus Dominæ vestræ, in loco assignato juxta tenorem vestrarum litterarum etiam veniendo, ad tractatum et dietam usque ad Ypras disposuistis pro bono pacis nobiscum insimul convenire ac in tractatu interesse, pensato tamen quod eadem Domina vestra insinuavit vestris nunciis et deputatis, in villa de Yprys insimul congregatis, quod propter certos defectus in nostro salvo conductu pro suis ambassiatoribus per nos sibi transmissis per suum Concilium assignatos, ambassiatores suos ad hujusmodi nostrum tractatum communem eisdem die et loco mittere interim justa ratione, prout asseritis, non decrevit, quousque de alio salvo conductu sufficientiori pro suis ambassiatoribus per partem nostram esset provisum. Unde, quia toto vestræ mentis conamine pacem et tranquillitatem utriusque partis videmini appetere, ad finem quod tractatus diu et sollicite peroptatus congruum sortiri possit effectum, nos rogatis, requiritis,

---

CXXII.] MS. Cotton. Galba, B. I. fol. 74 (*a*). — On paper; a contemporaneous MS.

et exhortamini in Domino, quatinus in favorem com- A.D. 1404.
munis mercandisæ, ac propter utilitatem reipublicæ,
ambassiatoribus præfatæ Dominæ vestræ de salvo
conductu et securo ac sufficiente, juxta materiæ exi-
gentiam velimus providere, ne occasione hujusmodi
causæ expressatæ tam magnum bonum utriusque partis
valeat impediri, ac suo effectu (quod absit) frustrari ;
cum eadem Domina vestra suos ambassiatores ad locum
medium et indifferentem ad aliam dietam ac tractatum
sit parata transmittere, ac hujusmodi tractatum perficere. Quam dietam seu terminum assignandum, et per
utramque partem acceptandum, vobis, qui finem desi-
deratis, per præsentium portitorem celeriter curaremus
intimare.

Ad quæ, honorabiles ac magnifici Domini, pro declara- and reply-
tione materiæ ad ostendendum omnem diligentiam $\begin{smallmatrix} \text{ing to its} \\ \text{contents.} \end{smallmatrix}$
possibilem partis nostræ pro nostri tractatus communis
expeditione, scire velitis quod ordinavimus duas commissiones ex parte Domini nostri Regis serenissimi ;
primo, unam ad tractandum cum Domina vestra ac
cum vestris Quatuor Membris, necnon cum aliis quibuscumque quodcumque prætendentibus interesse, cum
potestate resumendi hujusmodi tractatum, etc.; ac etiam
cum potestate dandi salvum conductum tam ambassiatoribus et commissariis ejusdem Dominæ vestræ, quam
vestris etiam commissariis et deputatis. Secundo, ob-
tinuimus aliam commissionem ad tractandum cum vestris Quatuor Membris Flandriæ, absque adjunctione
Dominæ vestræ. Sed ex privilegio vobis concesso poteritis tractatum inchoatum perficere, dum tamen Domina
vestra recusaverit in hujusmodi tractatu interesse, ac
in eodem nobiscum insimul convenire. Istam secundam
commissionem, prout novistis, vobis seu aliis hactenus
non exhibuimus, nec eadem usi fuimus.

Quarum commissionum tenores ut appareat de diligentia nostra mittimus Reverentiis vestris præsentibus
interclusos ; dictamque commissionem nostram primam

A.D. 1404. ac potestatem, in nostro adventu ad Calisium, per litteras nostras Dominæ vestræ intimavimus. Subsequenterque eadem Domina vestra misit nobis suum salvum conductum, ac tenorem potestatis a Domino suo superiore sibi concessæ in eodem salvo conductu interclusum. Et e converso nos pro ambassiatoribus tam Dominæ vestræ, quam vestris etiam deputatis, misimus salvum conductum nostrum, juxta tenorem nostræ commissionis primæ supradictæ; ac consensimus prædicto xxv. die cum suis commissariis ac vestris in loco indifferenti assignato, ultra Santyngfeld,—in quo fines et dominia utriusque regni notorie distinguuntur,—in tractatu, prout vobis et eidem scripsimus, insimul convenire; certis defectibus in suo salvo conductu ac potestate diversim per nos expressatis[1] non obstantibus. Domina vestra nobis rescripsit per litteras suas, quas recepimus Calisii xxiiij. die Septembris in vesperis, quod hujusmodi tractatum inchoatum cum suis Quatuor Membris noluit resumere, sed de novo tractatum inchoare, etiam absque adjunctione aut mentione vel expressione Quatuor Membrorum, seu aliorum quorumcumque quodcumque prætendentium interesse. Et pro renovatione dictæ commissionis nostræ primæ, qua Domina vestra non contentabatur propter adjunctionem vestrorum Quatuor Membrorum Flandriæ, cum vestros ambassiatores seu commissarios ad hujusmodi tractatum cum ambassiatoribus suis non intendebat adjungere, misit nobis copiam commissionis[2] per Concilium suum factæ, pro parte Domini Regis fiendæ, absque adjunctione seu mentione vestrorum Quatuor Membrorum Flandriæ, una cum copia salvi conductus etiam pro ambassiatoribus suis solummodo absque mentione vestrorum Quatuor Membrorum, per nos sibi remittendi; quodque juxta ipsius salvi conductus tenorem inserendo copiam dictæ nostræ

---

[1] See pp. 322, 323.     |     [2] See page 341.

commissionis primæ in eodem, quia aliam potestatem non A.D. 1404.
habuimus, eidem remisimus, ac in tractatu in dicto loco
indifferenti in festo Sancti Dionisii[1] proximo futuro,
obtulimus in hujusmodi nostro[2] tractatu communi convenire alias, quam cito receperimus novam commissionem
per Concilium Dominæ, ut præmittitur, ordinatam, quam
misimus in Angliam per Dominum nostrum Regem reformandam : cum ambassiatoribus suis tamen parati erimus
tractatum perficere, si vestra Quatuor Membra, contra
formam juramentorum ac suorum sigillorum, in tractatu
recusant aut in hujusmodi tractatu interesse noluerint.
De quibus omnibus, cum receperimus nostram commissionem reformatam, Dominam vestram ac vestras Reverentias reddemus certiores. Per quæ poteritis depre-
hendere nostram diligentiam possibilem, quoad tractatus
nostri per Dei gratiam felicem expeditionem.

Et revera, ultra quam in scripturis poterimus ex- They com-
primere, vehementer admiramur quod subditi et incolæ plain of the
Flandriæ indies congregant navigia sua ad spoliandum committed
quoscumque subditos regni nostri, per terram et per on the English, and
mare, post et contra tenorem litterarum Dominæ vestræ, threaten to
cum Dominus noster Rex restrinxit navigium suum. take serious
measures
et præsertim quoscumque subditos suos, quod juxta if they are
tenorem litterarum Dominæ vestræ in Calisium trans- continued.
missarum, quod in partibus Flandriæ non debeant
applicare, nec incolis Flandriæ qualecumque damnum
inferre. Quibus non obstantibus, quoddam navigium in
Flandria noviter est congregatum, ad spoliandum et derobandum nostros subditos, prout fertur ; necnon latrunculatores et piratæ de Dunkyrk, Newport, Berflet, et de
Sclusa,[3] nuper Episcopum Herfordensem[4] ac CLXVIII.,
quin verius sexcentos aut circiter pauperes piscatores
de Anglia, cum XXVII. aut XXXVII. navibus, ce-

---

[1] October 9.
[2] *nostro*] Added above the line.
[3] *Sclusa*] Sculsa, MS.
[4] Robert Mascall.

Z

A.D. 1404. perunt, ac ipsos ad financiam exposuerunt, quod non est honestum, pensatis præmissis, nec diu tolerandum. Ista et alia non faciliter numerabilia fiunt per subditos Flandriæ, absque reformatione seu emendatione quacumque. Vestras Reverentias requirimus, monemus, ac exhortamur in Domino, etiam sub periculo majoris mali evitandi, quatinus cum Domina vestra, seu per vos Dominos de Quatuor Membris, placeat ordinare quod dicti piratæ maris de Flandria restringantur, et debite pro suis excessibus puniantur; necnon quod fiat relaxatio financiæ tam præfati Domini Episcopi Herfordensis, quam ipsorum piscatorum, et financiæ eorundem absque dilatione, ante omnia; necnon cum bonis et mercimoniis mercatorum Londoniæ alias in Sclusa, aut valore eorundem, contra privilegia tam Domini vestri bonæ memoriæ, quam vestra, ipsius ac vestris sigillis sigillata, juxta formam juramentorum vestrorum, necnon treugarum generalium ac etiam specialium apud Westmonasterium in Anglia captorum, una cum restitutione dictarum navium, prout Dominus noster nuper scripsit Dominæ vestræ,[1] ac etiam nos ad hoc eidem sæpius[2] scripsimus, saltim pro relaxatione financiæ dicti Episcopi, ac ipsorum piscatorum liberatione, præsertim cum prædicta omnia, ac etiam alia non faciliter numerabilia, sunt commissa post et contra tenorem litterarum Dominæ vestræ. Miramur enim supra modum, ultra admirationem prædictam, quod vos, Domini Gandenses, toleratis illos piratas et latrunculatores maris de Dunkyrk, Newport, et de Sclusa, ad derobandum et spoliandum in mare adeo continue nostros subditos, absque restrictione seu punitione. Dicitur enim publice quod vestra Domina facit spolia capta importari ad suam præsentiam, et inibi facit destributionem, et propter talem participationem per Dominam vestram, ac per alios sibi consentientes, hujusmodi derobationes fiunt adeo publice absque

---

[1] See Letter CXIII.    |    [2] See Letters CXV. and CXX.

reformatione. Non enim credimus, sed ex parte novimus A.D. 1404. quod vos, Domini Gandenses, seu Yprenses, de hujusmodi spoliis utilitatem aliquam seu participium hujusmodi spoliorum non percipitis ; ideo apponatis remedium contra præmissa. Post scripturam enim præsentis litteræ intelleximus quod non solum LXVIII. piscatores nostri, sed sexcenti sunt capti in dictis XXVII. navibus, sed secundum alios in XXXVII. navibus captis et vivis, exceptis aliis submersis et in mari projectis, non faciliter numerabilibus, vos enim deberetis formidare Divinam Justitiam, quæ superat omnem malitiam.

Rescribatis ergo celeriter nobis Dominæ vestræ ac vestram voluntatem et responsionem super restitutione et executione præmissorum ; vos enim, Domini Gandenses, habetis bonum forum victualium propter ista spolia ; ideo non curatis, prout fertur, apponere remedium, quod est inhonestum, nec diu tolerandum. Super quibus, ac etiam super aliis vestrum beneplacitum concernentibus, placeat seriatim ac punctatim, et non per saltus nobis celeriter rescribere et respondere, prout vestris Dominationibus videbitur expedire.

Quas custodiat Altissimus feliciter et votive !

Scripta Calisii, primo die Octobris.

THOMAS SWYNBORN, et

JOHANNES CROFFT,— Milites, ac

NICHOLAUS DE RISSHETOUN, Utriusque Juris Professor,

Ambassiatores pro parte Angliæ.

*Endorsement* :—" Honorabilibus ac magnificis et circumspectis Dominis, Burgimagistris, Scabinis et Consulibus Gandensibus, Brugensibus, Yprensibus, ac territorii Franci officii partium Flandriæ."

z 2

## CXXIII.

### SWYNBORN, CROFT, AND DE RYSSHETON TO THE DUCHESS OF BURGUNDY.

*Copia litterœ Ambassiatorum Angliœ transmissœ dictœ Dominœ Ducissœ Burgundiœ, etc.*

Illustris Principissa, necnon præclaræ ac magnæ nobilitatis et potentiæ Domina.

*In reply to her letter on the safe-conduct, and the commission of the English Ambassadors.* Vestras litteras honorabiles, scriptas Attrebati ultimo die mensis Septembris, recepimus secundo die mensis Octobris; inter cetera continentes quod licet noster salvus conductus, pro ambassiatoribus vestræ Excellentiæ ultimo transmissus,[1] sit validus quantum ad sui formam et tenorem, non tantum (prout dicitis) quantum ad potestatis seu nostræ commissionis insertionem in eodem salvo nostro conductu factam; cum salvus conductus recipiat suum vigorem et effectum juxta potestatem et commissionem nostram, quantum ad tractatus resumptionem in eadem interclusam. Idcirco quousque commissiones vestræ et nostræ juxta tenorem aliarum vestrarum fuerint reformatæ, non expedit in tractatu insimul convenire pro securitate communis mercandisæ ac utilitate utriusque partis rei publicæ. Et cum omni celeritate facietis fieri reformationem commissionis vestræ ex parte Domini vestri superioris, ac etiam quantum ad concessionem quoad salvum conductum nepotis vestri, Comitis Sancti Pauli. Et quod sub pari forma faceremus commissionem nostram reformari juxta ipsius copiam, per vestram Ex-

---

CXXIII.] MS. Cotton. Galba, B. I. fol. 74 (γ).—On paper; a contemporaneous MS.

[1] *transmissus*] transmissas, MS.

cellentiam nobis transmissam; ac etiam quod salvum A.D. 1404.
conductum, pro vestris ambassiatoribus transmittendum,
debeamus extendere usque ad primum diem mensis
Januarii.

Ad quæ, illustris Principissa ac honorabillima Domina,
pro utilitate communis cursus communis mercandisæ, ad
complacendum vestræ Excellentiæ, parati sumus tractatum nostrum communem differre quousque commissiones utriusque partis pariter fuerint reformatæ; necnon salvum conductum usque ad primum diem mensis
Januarii, juxta tenorem vestrarum litterarum, extendere. Commissionem enim nostram, in Angliam pro
reformatione per unum de nostris collegis, juxta
formam per vos nobis transmissam, credimus celeriter obtinere. Et cum hujusmodi nostram commissionem reformatam receperimus, juxta ipsius tenorem,
absque dilatione pro vestris ambassiatoribus mittemus
salvum conductum, usque ad primum diem mensis
Januarii duraturum, per Dei gratiam ad nostri tractatus
communis felicem expeditionem.

Quantum autem ad validitatem seu invaliditatem
tractatus inchoati ex parte vestrorum Quatuor Membrorum, illud terminabitur, et videbitur in præsentia
utriusque partis ambassiatorum prout de jure fuerit
faciendum. Novimus enim per experientiam eandem
vestram Excellentiam nolle pati vestros subditos adeo
notabiles violare ipsorum juramentum, ac incurrere per-
jurium et infamiam perpetuam.

Et quamvis treugæ generales inter Angliam et
Franciam per Dominos et Principes temporales, videlicet Duces Laancastriæ, et Eboraci, necnon Buturiæ, ac
Burgundiæ, bonæ memoriæ, qui perfecte non intellexe-
runt Latinum sicut Gallicum, (de consensu eorundem
expresso) in Gallico fuerunt captæ et firmatæ, litteræ
tamen missivæ ultro citroque transmissæ, una cum
appunctuamentis communibus in tractatu inter Angliam
et Franciam continue citra in Latino, tanquam in

*They re-
quest that
all future
corre-
spondence
may be in
Latin, as
they under-
stand not
French so
well, and
Latin is the
common
language of
the Church.*

A.D. 1404. idiomate communi et vulgari extiterant formata; quæ omnia habemus parata ostendere, exemplo Beati Ieronimi, qui omnia Hebræorum Volumina ex Veteri Testamento in Latinam linguam, tanquam intelligibiliorem et vulgarem evertit et transtulit,—ex qua translatione apud Ecclesiam, tam Triumphantem quam Militantem, valde promeruit.

*They complain bitterly of the imprisonment of the Bishop of Hereford, and other outrages committed on the English;*

Item, serenissima Domina, cum dictus noster Rex ac ipsius Concilium, necnon ipsius regni communitas, valde commoventur, ac contra vestros subditos Flandriæ immensum turbentur, ex eo quod quidam vestri subditi et populares Flandriæ de Dunkirk, Neuport, Berflet, de Osten Lumbardi et de Sclusa, reverendum Patrem, Fratrem Robertum, Sacræ Paginæ Professorem, Episcopum Herfordensem,. necnon quingentos nostros pauperes piscatores, secundum relationem aliorum sexcentos piscatores, de nostris, cum XXVIIJ. navibus ipsorum, in partibus borialibus Angliæ, latenter de nocte in ipsorum piscaturis captivarunt, et ad financiam importabilem exposuerunt, plures in mari submerserunt, pro quibusdam tamen certos plegios, quasi quinquaginta sufficientiores receperunt, post et contra formam vestrarum litterarum sub dato vij. Junii anni præsentis Locumtenenti Stapulæ, nostro collegæ, in Calisium transmissarum[1] ; quarum vestrarum litterarum tenorem, ut veritas eorundem melius appareat, vestræ Excellentiæ remittimus eisdem præsentibus interclusum. Novit enim eadem vestra Magnificentia qualiter nuper, in nostro adventu in Calisium, nostras litteras sub xxiij. die Augusti ultimo præterito scriptas[2] eidem direximus, vobis intimando ac notificando quod Dominus noster Rex admirallis navigii sui, de mense Julii, alias aliis quibuscumque subditis regni sui præcepit, ac sub pœna vitæ et membrorum eisdem mandavit, ac publice pro-

---

[1] See Letter XC.    |    [2] See Letter CVII.

clamari fecit, ut nullus ligeus sub confidentia dictarum A.D. 1404.
vestrarum litterarum, et præsertim propter affectionem
quam semper gerebat ad Dominum vestrum bonæ
memoriæ, (cujus anima requiescat in pace !) ac ad
vestram Excellentiam in partibus Flandriæ debeat
applicare, seu inibi aliquod damnum inferre; quod
præceptum regium hactenus fuit servatum, et, prout
novistis, fideliter executioni mandatum.

Vestram Excellentiam prout alias requirimus ac ex- Requiring
hortamur in Domino, quatinus, pensatis præmissis ac redress,
and expect-
aliis considerandis, cum celeritate financiam placeat ing that
relaxare, ac captivos et incarceratos liberare, necnon strong
measures
cum ipsorum navibus et bonis integraliter restituere, to secure it
ante quamcumque aliam reparationem fiendam, una cum will be
taken in
bonis et mercimoniis seu valore eorundem indebite in the ensu-
Sclusa arrestatis, propter ipsorum specialem præeminen- ing Parliament.
tiam ac privilegium in specie, prout sæpius extitit
allegatum, etiam sub prætextu majoris mali evitandi.
Tales enim injuriæ adeo notoriæ, nisi celerius fuerint
reformatæ, ipsum tractatum communem (quod absit)
faciliter possunt intervertere, ac penitus impedire. Die
enim Martis proximo futuro inchoabitur in Anglia
parliamentum; et, nisi celerius super præmissis fuerit
consultius responsum, timendum erit quod communitas
regni apponet remedium (quod absit) nimis rigorosum.
Præfati enim vestri subditi præmissis non contenti in
Sclusa pro præsenti in mari congregarunt quoddam
navigium, ad nostros subditos derobandum, quod non
est diu tolerandum. Non enim est honestum quod
vestri consiliarii, seu alii collaterales qualescumque vobis
assistentes, tales latrunculatores et piratas debeant
defendere, seu ipsorum facta colorare aut de ipsorum
spoliis, prout fertur, participare, sed ipsos ultione ac
pœna condigna coercere adeo quod alii ab hujusmodi
excessibus se valcant retrahere et abstinere, ac pœnas
talibus imponendas merito formidare: alias hujusmodi
malefactores non puniti vestram Nobilitatem et Ex-

A.D. 1404. cellentiam. ac ipsius famam laudabilem, ex defectu justitiæ, faciliter poterint lædere et (quod absit) denigrare.

De his et aliis litteras Domini nostri Regis ac nostras nuper geminatas scripsimus vestræ Excellentiæ. Super quibus omnibus, ac super aliis vestrum beneplacitum concernentibus, placeat vestræ Excellentiæ nobis celeriter rescribere et respondere.

Quam dirigat Altissimus feliciter et votive!

Scriptum Calisii, iij° die Octobris.

THOMAS SWYNBORN, et

JOHANNES CROFFT,—Milites, ac

NICHOLAUS DE RISSHETOUN,
Utriusque Juris Professor,
Ambassiatores pro parte Angliæ.

*Endorsement :*—"Illustri Principissæ, necnon præclaræ nobilitatis ac magnæ potentiæ Dominæ, Dominæ Margaretæ, Ducissæ Burgundiæ, Comitissæ Flandriæ, Arthesii, et Burgundiæ."

*Also :*—"Copia litterarum transmissarum Ducissæ Burgundiæ, quarum responsio in litteris regiis est interclusa."

*And,*—"Detur Domino nostro, Regi Angliæ et Franciæ, [pro] ipsius plenaria informatione."

## CXXIV.

THE DUCHESS OF BURGUNDY TO THE ENGLISH
AMBASSADORS.

*Copia litterœ Ducissœ Burgondiœ, transmissœ Am-
bassiatoribus Angliœ :—*

Honourables et sages.

Nous avons receu les lettres de vostre Seigneur [1] In reply to their Letters; donnes le $x^e$, et les vostres [2] donnes le $xxviij^e$ jour de Septembre, a nous envoiees par le Lieutenant du Caphitaine de Boulouigne, contenans en effect que par vos aultres lettres vous nous avez requis faire delivrer, sans finance, Frere Robert, Evesque de Herford, et certain nombre de pescheurs d'Angleterre, nagueres prins par nos subgies, dont n'avez en aucune response de nous. Et qu'il nous plaise relaxer la finance du dit Evesque, et dez dis pescheurs, ou iceulx pescheurs

---

[TRANSLATION.]

Honourable and wise.—We have received the letters of your Lord, dated the 10th, and yours, dated the 28th day of September, sent to us by the Lieutenant of the Governour of Boulogne, setting forth in effect that by other letters of yours you have required us to cause to be delivered up, without ransom, Brother Robert, Bishop of Hereford, and a certain number of fishermen of England, lately captured by our subjects, concerning which you have received no answer from us. And that it would please us to remit the ransom money of the said Bishop and of the said fishermen, or to de-

---

CXXIV.] MS. Cotton. Galba, B. 1. fol. 78 (a).—On paper; a contemporaneous MS.

[1] See Letter CXIII.
[2] See Letter CXX.

A.D. 1404. delivrer de prison sens paier finance ; et que nous avons en memoire nos lettres envoies a Caleis, par lesquelles nous avons voulu desister de tout fait de guerre, et avons fait publiquement proclamer trieuves en nostre pais, pourveu que semblablement vous voulsissies faire de vostre partie.

Contenoient aussi vos dictes lettres que, soubs umbre de nous et de nos dictes lettres, vostre dit Seigneur a mande a ses admiraulx et subgies, que a noz subgies ne portassent aucun grief, molestation, ou dommage. Et toutevoies ce non obstant noz subgez de Neufport, Dunkirk, et des aultres parties de nostre pais de Flandres, appaireillement de nouvel ung navire pour prure et desrober vos subgez.

Des quelles choses vous avez graunt merveille, et vous semble que ce soit preparatoire a guerre, et non mye a paix.

acknow-
ledging
that a
procla-

Si vueilliez savoir, honourables et sages, que il est vray que nous avons piecea fait deffendre a tous nos

---

liver those fishermen out of prison without payment of money ; also that we should bear in memory our letters sent to Calais, by the which we have declared our will to desist from every warlike act, and have caused proclamation of the truce to be made publicly in our country, provided that you were willing to act in like manner on your part.—Also your said letters set forth that, relying upon us and our said letters, your said Lord has given commandment to his admirals and subjects, that they should not inflict on our subjects any mischief, molestation, or damage. And nevertheless, notwithstanding this, our subjects of Newport, of Dunkirk, and of the other parts of our country of Flanders, had arrayed afresh a fleet for preying upon and robbing your subjects.— Concerning which matters you have great marvel, and it seems to you that this is preparatory for war, and not at all for peace.—Be pleased to know, therefore, honourable and wise, that it is true that we have long since issued a prohibition to all

subgez de noz villes estans sur la coste et frontiere A.D. 1404.
de la mer de Flandres, que aulcun d'iceulx ne feist ou mation had
portast aucun dommage aux Anglois parmi ce que against
vostre dit Seigneur feroit semblable deffense a ses doing in-
subgez, qu'ilz ne portassent aucun dommage a nostre English,
pais de Flandres, ne a nos subgiez, la quelle deffense but that
ne nous semble pas avoir este faicte du coste de vostre glish were
dit Seigneur ; et se faicte a este, il appert cleirement to blame
que ses subgez l'ont mal tenue ; considere que le xiiij. being
jour d'Aoust desrain passe, ou environ, grant nombre disobeyed.
d'Anglois descendrent en ung isle de nostre pais de
Flandres, asses pres de le Scluse, appelle Wlpen, et en
icelle desroberent une Egliese, bouterent le feu en plusours maisons, roberent et pilleirent noz subgez de leur
bestail et autres biens. Et si il est aussi que aucuns
de nos diz subgez, doulans et courouciez de ce dommage
fait a nous et a eulx, dont ilz evidoient estre asseurez
se soient efforciez apres nos deffenses publiees de faire

---

our subjects in our towns situated along the coast and sea-
board of Flanders, that none of them should do or inflict
any damage on the English, on this condition, that your said
Lord should make a like prohibition to his own subjects,
that they should not inflict any damage on our country of
Flanders, nor on our subjects, the which prohibition does
not at all seem to us to have been made on the part of
your said Lord ; and if it has been made it appears clearly
that his subjects have kept it badly, considering that on the
14th day of August last past, or thereabout, a great multitude of English descended upon an island belonging to our
country of Flanders, situated near Sluys, called Wulpen, and
therein dismantled a church, set many of the houses on fire,
and robbed and plundered our subjects of their cattle and
other property. And so it comes to pass also that some of
our said subjects, grieving and irritated at this damage done
against us and against them, of which they have had clear
assurance, were forced, after our public prohibitions, to commit

A.D. 1404. aucune chose sur ceulx de vostre partie, et en ce faisant aient prins le dit Evesque, ceste chose ne vient point de nostre commandement ne volente. Et pour ce que nous ne vouldrions pour riens le traictie sur la seurte de la merchandise d'entre les diz Anglois et nostre pais de Flandres estre, pour le dit fait ne pour aultre, rompu, ou empeschie, nous nous informerons des emprinses que vous ditez estre faictes par nos subgez, pour en estre ordene et appointie, quant nos gens seront avecques vous, ou aultres commis de vostre partie assemblez, pour le fait de la dicte marchandise.

Et quant a l'appareil de navire que vous maintenez que on met sus a Neufport, Dunkirke, et autre part en nostre pais de Flandres, nous n'en saviouns riens a la reception de voz lettres. Et neantmains nous avons tantost mande et fait deffendre, que par le dit navire ne soit porte aucun dommage a ceulx de vostre partie.

Et pour ce que vostre dit Seigneur a volu estre

---

some assault upon those of your side, and in doing so have taken prisoner the said Bishop, this act not springing at all from our desire or will. And forasmuch as we would not for anything that the treaty on the safety of commercial intercourse between the said English and our country of Flanders should be, on account of the said proceedings or on account of any other, broken through or frustrated, we will inform ourselves of the enterprises which you allege to have been made by our subjects, for the ordaining and appointing therein, when our people shall meet with you, or with other commissaries of your part, for the carrying on of the said commerce.—And as to the array of the fleet, which you maintain is established at Newport, Dunkirk, and other parts in our country of Flanders, we knew nothing at the reception of your letter. Nevertheless we have promptly charged, and caused prohibition to be made, that no damage should be done by the said fleet to those of your side.—And forasmuch as your said Lord has willed to be clearly informed of the

acertene de choses dessusdictes—comme il appert par A.D. 1404.
ses lettres—nous vous prions que vous escrisons pre- The King
sentement lui vueilliez signifier, honourables et sages, of England is to be
quant a ce que par voz autres lettres, escriptes le assured of
desrain jour de Septembre,[1] nous avez escript, que her good intentions.
vous avez grant merveille de ce que nous souffrons
noz subgez de Dunkirke, Neufport, Bieruliet, et de l'
Escluse, pillier et desrober vos subgez par terre et par
mer, et que leurs despoilles nous faisons apporter en
nostre presence, et d'icelles, comme l'en dit, faisons
distribution ainssi qu'il nous plaist, la quelle chose
n'est pas honneste consideree la fourme de pluseurs
nos lettres envoiees a Caleis ;—veuilliez savoir que nos
devanciers ne nous n'avions pas accustume de vivre
de pillages ne roberies, ne nous entremetre de telles
choses, ne d'autres deshonnestes ; et nous donnons
grant merveille de ce que vous nous en escrisez par


matters above mentioned—as it appear by his letter—we
pray you that you write presently and signify to him,
honourable and wise, as to that which you wrote to us about
by your other letters, written the last day of September,
viz., that you have great marvel at the fact that we suffer
our subjects of Dunkirk, Newport, Bieruliet, and of Sluys,
to plunder and rob your subjects by land and by sea, and
that we cause their spoils to be brought into our presence,
and make distribution thereof, as it is said, just as it pleases
us, the which thing is not at all honourable, considering
the purport of many of our letters sent to Calais ;—be pleased
to know that neither our predecessors nor we have at all been
accustomed to live by plundering or robberies, nor to mix
ourselves up in such affairs, nor in other dishonest proceedings;
and we are greatly surprised that you should write to us

---

[1] See Letter CXXI.

A.D. 1404. teille maniere, et que on vous a dit qui est contre verite.

Et quant au contenu de voz aultres lettres, de date du tiers jour de ce present mois d'Octobre,[1] nous avons asses respondu sur la plus grant partie par ce que dessus est dit, fors a ce que voz dictes contiennent, que ce n'est une honneste [chose] que nos conseilliers, ou aultres collateraux quexconques assistans avec nous doyent deffendre les larrons et pirates, qui desrobent vos gens ne colorer leurs fais, ou participer a leurs roberies. Surquoy nous vous respondons que nous ne savons mie que nouz aions teilx gens a nostre Conseil, ne teilx collateraux, et ne vouldrions mye avoir gens de teille condition, et pour certain si nous trouvions telx entour nous (que Dieux ne vueille,) nous les pugnirions teillement que ce seroit example a tous autres.

Honnourables et sages, vueilliez savoir que tantost

---

in such a strain, and should have brought a charge against us which is contrary to the truth.—And as to the contents of your other letter, dated the 3rd day of this present month of October, we have sufficiently replied to the greater part by that which has been said above, except as to one thing which your said letter contains, that it is not an honourable thing that our councillors or any of our collaterals whatever, giving us their support, should defend the robbers and pirates who plunder your people, or should colour their deeds, or participate in their robberies. Concerning which we answer you that we are not in the least aware that we have such people in our Council, nor such collaterals, and we would not at all have people of such a description, and for certain if we were to find such among us (which may God forbid) we would punish them in such a manner that it would be an example to all others.—Honourable and wise, you will know that as soon

---

[1] See Letter CXXIII.

que nous aurons nouvelles de la reformation des lettres A.D. 1404. du povoir a nous donne par mon Seigneur le Roy, pour la quille chose nous avons envoie divers luy, et pour autres servans a la matiere, nous le vous ferons savoir.

Le Saint Esprit vous ait en Sa sainte garde!

Escript a nostre ville d'Arras, le vj<sup>e</sup> jour d'Octobre, Mil CCCC et quatre.

---

as we have news of the reformation of the letters of authority given to us by my Lord the King, for the which thing, and for others tending to this matter we have sent unto him, we will let you know.—The Holy Ghost have you in His holy keeping!—Written at our town of Arras, the 6th day of October, 1404.

## CXXV.

### De Ryssheton to the Archbishop of Canterbury.

Reverendissime in Christo Pater ac singularissime Domine mi.

Cum nostri collegæ omnes et singuli pro tractatu Flandriæ in commissionibus nominati, quamvis dum erant præsentes in villa Calisii apposuerunt, ac parati erant omnem diligentiam apponere, asseruerunt tamen quod in futurum hujusmodi onus noluerunt assumere, nisi Domini de Concilio pro laboribus suis partim eis velint satisfacere ; quodque Domina Ducissa Burgundiæ, Comitissa Flandriæ, cum suis Quatuor Membris recusat

*Complaining that no attention had been paid to his frequent letters to the Council.*

---

CXXV.] MS. Cotton. Galba, B. 1. fol. 76.—On paper ; original, with traces of the seal.

A.D. 1404. nobiscum in hujusmodi tractatu interesse, sed solum per se hujusmodi tractatum intendit perficere, ac in eodem nobiscum convenire, adeo quod hujusmodi commissiones factas pro tractatu Flandriæ pro parte nostra pro eadem Comitissa, una cum Quatuor Membris suis in eisdem commissionibus nominatis et adjunctis, juxta processum apud Westmonasterium per Magnum Concilium cum ambassiatoribus Quatuor Membrorum Flandriæ inchoatum, cum celeritate possibili expedit re formare.

Pro quarum commissionum reformatione quatuor vicibus[1] scripsimus litteras Magno Concilio, una cum copia cujusdam commissionis fiendæ pro præfata Domina Comitissa, absque adjunctione seu mentione suorum Quatuor Membrorum Flandriæ, in eisdem litteris nostris interclusæ; quia alias ad tractatum cum præfata Domina Comitissa non poterimus devenire.

Mirum enim est quod vestrum almum Concilium a Festo Assumptionis Beatæ Mariæ[2] etiam citra, fuit adeo vagum et infirmum ac ab invicem separatum, adeo quod de hujusmodi litteris nostris nobis non extitit responsum, consideratis tempestatibus quæ quasi ex omni parte indies fluunt adversus Dominum nostrum Regem, et ipsius regnum,— quem Deus pro Sua pietate preservet et defendat, quamvis refluant incontinenti absque potentia humana, ex gratia Dei, Eodem laudato Altissimo et Benedicto.

**The French and the Flemings prepare for the invasion of Wales.** Scire velitis vestra Paternitas reverendissima inter alia qualiter quoddam navigium apud Harflet, et in aliis partibus Normandiæ est congregatum, ad intrandum in Walliam, seu secundum alios ad applicandum apud Orwelle, vel in aliis partibus regni Angliæ. Ideo expedit quod mare per admirallos,[3] cum in præsenti valeant obtinere resistentiam et contradictionem, esset

---

[1] See page 398.
[2] August 15.

[3] admirollos, MS.

A.D. 1404.

potenter custoditum, ad resistendum malitiis inimicorum. Quædam enim gentes armigeræ Gallicorum etiam in multitudine notabili quæ non poterant intrare navigium prædictum apud Harflet, pridie porrexerunt ad Sclusam ad intrandum mare ad aliquod propositum notabile, prout fertur, exequendum.

Ac etiam Flandrenses congregarunt quoddam navigium de XXXVII. navibus majoribus et minoribus, et intrabant mare ad spoliandum, prout fertur, nostros piscatores in partibus borialibus, seu alias contra Dominum Ducem de Hollandia, vel in favorem Gallicorum, quorum propositum pro præsenti nobis est incognitum.

Super his tamen, et super relaxatione financiæ Reverendi Patris, Domini Episcopi Herfordensis, ac etiam pro liberatione et relaxatione financiæ certorum piscatorum nostrorum nuper per Flandrenses captorum, ut asseritur, in partibus borialibus, ac super aliis, collegæ mei et ego scripsimus[1] litteras requisitorias Ducissæ Burgundiæ Comitissæ Flandriæ, una cum litteris Domini nostri Regis[2] eidem præsentandis, per quendam nostrum nuncium etiam octo diebus elapsis et ultra in præsenti non reversum. Et cum fuerit nobis responsum scribam vestræ Paternitati reverendissimæ.

Quam custodiat Altissimus feliciter et votive!

Scriptum Calisii, vj. die mensis Octobris.

Vester Clericus ac servitor humillimus,

NICOLAUS DE RYSSHETOUN.

*Endorsed* :—Reverendissimo in Christo Patri ac Domino, Domino T., Dei gratia Can[tuariensi] Archiepiscopo, etc., Domino suo singularissimo."

---

[1] See Letter CXX.     [2] See Letter CXIII.

A A

A.D. 1404. *The following Postscript (Galba B. 1. fol. 77) appears to have belonged to this letter:—*

Item, reverendissime Pater, quia abstinentia guerrarum est capta per nobilem virum, Dominum Ricardum Astoun, Militem, Locumtenentem villæ Calisii, per certa confinia ab aqua de Somme ad aquam de Gravelyng, usque ad festum Omnium Sanctorum[1] proximo futurum : unde quia nos alii commissarii Domini nostri Regis in villa Calisii pro præsenti personaliter existentes, nullam habemus potestatem continuandi dictam abstinentiam guerrarum ultra festum Omnium Sanctorum[1] supradictum, quodque præfatus Dominus Locumtenens non intendit petere si Gallici hujusmodi abstinentiam guerrarum ultra dictum festum Omnium Sanctorum[1] velint continuare ; pensato quod nos alii commissarii, cum ambassiatoribus et commissariis 'partis adversæ, citra dictum festum Omnium Sanctorum[1] in tractatu insimul non poterimus convenire, placeat vestræ Paternitati cum Domino nostro Rege ordinare et statuere qualiter hujusmodi abstinentiam guerrarum velit continuare, seu ipsam dirigere pro utilitate Marchiæ villæ Calisii ; quodque super statu et regimine villæ Calisii vestri servitores Willielmus Lyle, junior, Miles, ac Ricardus Gest vestram Paternitatem vivæ vocis oraculo poterint informare. Timemus enim quod præfatus Dominus Locumtenens, cum suis stipendiariis, hujusmodi tractatum quoad Franciam faciliter poterit impedire, nisi celerius apponatur remedium opportunum.

---

[1] November 1

## CXXVI.

THE SENATE OF LUBECK TO HENRY IV.

*Illustrissimo ac serenissimo Principi ac Domino, Domino Henrico, Regi Angliæ et Franciæ ac Domino Hiberniæ excellentissimo, promotori nostro favorabili et benigno, reverentias, humillima servitiorum nostrorum recommendatione cum omni reverentia præoblata.*

Serenissime Princeps, fautor, et Domine.

Ex quorundam veridicorum relatione nobis innotuit, qualiter nonnulli vestræ Majestatis subditi nuper in mari plurimos de Hansa naucleros et mercatores, et præcipue quosdam de civitate Rygensi, hostiliter invaserunt, suasque naves et mercimonia rapuerunt, et—quod humanus detestatur auditus—præscriptis navibus et bonis ablatis, eosdem naucleros et mercatores inhumaniter submergendo interfecerunt, licet iidem naucleri et mercatores, de regalis vestræ Celsitudinis et vestrorum subditorum indubitata securitate confisi, et, prout accepimus, per eosdem vestræ Majestatis subditos singulariter securati, hujusmodi excessus sibi nullatenus accidisse formidabant. Ceterum quidam mercatores qui missi causa prædictorum bonorum rehabitionis vestram Majestatem accesserant, inter cetera, quæ ipsis ibidem occurrerunt, coram nobis affirmabant se de eadem vestra Majestate satis gravia et ingratiosa responsa reportasse, de qualibet tamen responsione minime præsumentes de vestræ Celsitudinis innata benignitate beneviliora et placentiora speramus responsa.

*Complaining of the seizure of certain ships by English sailors;*

---

CXXVI.] MS. Cotton. Vespas. F. I. fol. 111 (δ).—On paper; a contemporaneous MS.

A A 2

A.D. 1404.
and requiring redress.

Quapropter, serenissime Princeps, vestræ regali Majestati ex intimis affectibus humillime supplicamus, quatinus Dominum Deum præ oculis habentes, justitiæ et nostri sermonis intuitu taliter disponere dignemini quatinus prædicta bona, et, ut præfertur, ablata, simul et indivisa permaneant; eosdem vestræ Majestatis subditos ad satisfactionem et condignam emendam prædictorum excessuum, et ne de cetero talia nefanda attemptare præsumant, cum debita cohibitione compulsuri. Alias etenim exinde ulteriores et majores displicentias perniciosioraque mala, (quæ Deus avertat) suboriri formidamus; desiderantes nobis super his benevolum reformare vestræ Celsitudinis responsum.

Quam incolumem et longævam conservet Altissimus!

Scriptum nostro sub sigillo, Anno Domini MCCCCIIII. mensis Octobris die septima.

Vestræ Majestatis humiles et sincere benevoli,

PROCONSULES et CONSULES CIVITATIS LUBICENSIS.

## CXXVII.

### HENRY IV. TO THE SENATE OF LUBECK.[1]

In reply to the preceding letter.

Honorabiles viri, amici sincere dilecti.

Gravem querelam deponitis apud nos per Amicitiæ vestræ litteras, mensis Octobris ultimo præteriti die septima scriptas, asserentes ex quorundam informatione veridica vobis innotuisse qualiter nonnulli de subditis nostris nuper in mari quamplurimos de Hansa naucleros

---

CXXVII.] MS. Cotton. Vespas. F. I. fol. 110 (θ).—On paper; a contemporaneous MS.

[1] This letter has no date, but is clearly in answer to the foregoing.

et mercatores, et præcipue quosdam de civitate Rigensi, A.D. 1404. hostiliter invaserunt, ac naves et mercimonia sua ceperunt, et, hujusmodi navibus et bonis ablatis, eosdem mercatores et naucleros inhumaniter submerserunt, quamvis iidem naucleri et mercatores, de nostra et subditorum nostrorum indubitate securitate confisi, tales excessus eisdem fieri vel accidisse nullatenus formidabant: asserentes quoque, præter ea, quod quidam mercatores, qui, missi causa rehabitionis bonorum hujusmodi, ad nostram præsentiam accesserunt, coram vobis affirmasse debuerant se a nobis multum gravia et ingratiosa responsa super commissis hujusmodi reportasse : vos tamen de talibus responsis vestri gratia minime præsumentes, ut scribitis, magis benevola et placabilia super inde responsa vos confiditis habituros.

Nos itaque, cupientes ut dilectionis et amicitiæ fœdus, quo subditi nostri, necnon et vestrates ab olim exiterant alligati, pro mercatorum utilitate communi pariter et quiete de cetero conservetur irruptum, ac de bono semper in melius augeatur, Amicitiæ vestræ significare censuimus quod quidam J. de W. et B. de L., asserentes se fore de partibus vestris pro hujusmodi prætensis allatis penes nos alias insteterunt; qui cum per nos essent interrogati de signis mercandisarum hujusmodi, et de navium nominibus et apparatibus eorundem illa declarare penitus ignorarunt. Verumtamen diximus eis quod si aliqui per vos missi, sufficientem in hac parte potestatem habentes, ad nos veniant super præmissis justitiam petituri, vellemus esse parati ad faciendum eisdem justitiæ complementum. Et ideo, licet iidem instantes, quos præterea reputabamur in eorum petitione inspectos, responsum a nobis juxta sua desideria nullatenus obtinere valebant, Vestra Dilectio non miretur, nec esset consonum rationi quod, quamvis forsitan unus rem tulerit alienam injuste, alter, ad quem rei venditatio non pertinet, ipsam exigeret vel haberet. Cum autem non omnium spiritui sit creden-

A.D. 1404. dum,[1] ut nostis, non confidentes in illis quos reperimus [2] infideles, quique inter nos et vos dilectionis vinculum infringere moliuntur, aliquos de vestris quorum in his interesse versatur, aut alios in hac parte sufficienti potestate munitos—quibus, si opus fuerit, litteras nostri salvi conductus exhiberi mandabimus—ad nostram præsentiam destinetur; qui de præmissis omnibus et singulis nos plene noverint facere certiores. Scientes, amici sincere dilecti, quod illos de quibus queremoniam in hac parte fieri contigerit, ad vestram mandabimus evocari præsentiam, et si suggesta veritate [3] nitantur conquerentibus illis faciam exhiberi justitiam cum favore; et ut vestra desideria compleamus ulterius faciendum in portibus nostris publice proclamari, districtius inhibentes ne quis subditorum nostrorum vobis aut vestratibus damnum quodcunque, molestiam, vel gravamen inferant, vel inferri faciant ullo sensu, etc.

*Endorsement :*—"Honorabilibus viris Proconsulibus et Consulibus Civitatis Lubicensis, amicis nostris sincere dilectis."

## CXXVIII.

### SWINFORD AND DE RYSSHETON TO THE FRENCH AMBASSADORS.

*Copia litteræ Ambassiatorum Angliæ, transmissæ Ambassiatoribus Franciæ.*

Honorabiles ac magnifici et circumspecti Domini.

Acknowledging the receipt    Vestras litteras, scriptas Parisius vicesima septima die Septembris, recepimus Calesii sexto die Octobris, de

---

[1] 1 S. John, iv. 1.
[2] *reperimus*] reparimus MS.
[3] *veritate*] varitate, MS.

CXXVIII.] MS. Cotton. Galba. B. 1. fol. 78 (δ). — On paper; a contemporaneous MS.

sero nobis per honorabilem scutiferum, W. Mauneville, A.D. 1404.
de Bolonia præsentatas, inter cetera continentes quod of their letter,
penes Dominum vestrum superiorem extitit conclusum
quod ambassiatores, videlicet reverendus Pater, Dominus
Episcopus Carnotensis, vos ambo Domini subscripti,
ac Magister Johannes de Sanctis, deputandi pro parte
Franciæ, xv$^{mo}$ die nunc instantis mensis Octobris
cum ambassiatoribus etiam pro parte Angliæ in tractatu
communi ac loco consueto insimul debebant convenire,
adeo quod pro utraque parte deputandi aliquid communis utilitatis ambarum partium inibi, favente Domino, invicem valeant operari : necnon quod deputandi
pro parte Angliæ fulsiantur potestate tanta ac consimili, prout pro parte vestra deputandi sic quod ob
defectum potestatum seu auctoritatum negotia communia in nostro proximo parliamento, per Dei gratiam, non debeant ulterius protelari. Et quid super
hoc intendimus peragere vobis celeriter debeamus
rescribere.

Ad quæ, honorabiles et circumspecti Domini, pen- and re-
sato quod potestas a serenissimo ac excellentissimo plying thereto.
Principe, Domino nostro, Rege Angliæ et Franciæ,
illustrissimo, nobis commissa primo et principaliter
extenditur ad prosequendum responsionem super litteris et punctis per nobilem virum, Dominum Johannem Cheyne, Militem, vobis præsentatis, vestras
Reverentias requirimus et exhortamur in Domino, quatinus vos, seu alii Domini ambassiatores pro vestra
parte deputandi, super dictis litteris et punctis
dicto xv$^{mo}$ die per vos, in loco consueto, literato placeat respondere, prout Domino vestro superiori ac suo
Concilio videbitur expedire. Vestras enim litteras
supradictas Domino nostro Regi transmisimus, ipsius-
que responsionem et voluntatem remittendam cum
omni celeritate vobis transmittere et significare cura-
bimus. Præfato enim quinto decimo die nostri ambassiatores in gradu et statu consimili, cum hujusmodi

A.D. 1404. amplis potestatibus et auctoritatibus, juxta formam vestrarum litterarum, propter brevitatem termini, et arduitatem materiæ, ac distantiam loci, cum vestris ambassiatoribus non poterint insimul convenire, nec personaliter interesse.

Super quibus, ac super aliis, placeat nobis rescribere, ac vestram voluntatem plenarie declarare.

Vestras Dominationes et Reverentias custodiat Altissimus feliciter et votive !

Scriptum Calesii, octavo die Octobris.

> THOMAS SWYNFORD, Miles, Custos Castri villæ Calesii, ac
>
> NICHOLAUS DE RISSHETOUN, Utriusque Juris Professor;
>
> Ambassiatores pro parte Angliæ.

*Endorsement :*—" Honorabilibus ac magnificis et circumspectis Dominis, Domino Johanni de Hangesto, Magistro Baliesteriorum Franciæ, et G. Bouratern, Ambassiatoribus pro parte Franciæ."

## CXXIX.

### CROFT AND DE RYSSHETON TO HENRY IV.

Serenissime ac excellentissime Princeps, necnon invictissime et metuendissime Domine.

Inclosing the letter of the French Ambassadors.

Cum certæ litteræ, sexto die præsentis mensis Octobris de sero ex parte ambassiatorum Franciæ nobis extiterant præsentatæ, quodque juxta ipsarum

CXXIX.] MS. Cotton. Galba, B. I. fol. 80. — On paper; original, with traces of the seals.

continentiam et tenorem, prout nobis primo videbatur A.D. 1404.
honestum et congruum, formavimus quandam responsionem,[1] ambassiatoribus Franciæ remittendam, cujus
tenorem, una cum copia dictarum litterarum propter
passagium eadem hora versus Dovoriam ad navigandum
absque dilatione præparatum propter celeritatem materiæ transmisimus vestræ regiæ Majestati, in litteris
nostris eidem directis interclusum, quamvis hujusmodi
responsionem taliter qualiter formatam Willelmo Maundeville, nuncio ambassiatorum Franciæ, pro tunc non
liberavimus, subsequenterque dictam responsionem partim reformavimus, ac ipsam reformatam prædicto
Willelmo, nuncio ambassiatorum Franciæ, tradidimus
ac eidem liberavimus.

Item litteras vestras regias Ducissæ Burgundiæ pro Of the im-
relaxatione financiæ reverendi Patris, Domini Episcopi prisonment
Herfordensis,[2] necnon alias litteras nostras diversas Bishop of
tribus vicibus separatis,[3] etiam pro relaxatione plurium Hereford.
piscatorum cum triginta septem navibus eorundem, ut
asseritur, in ipsorum piscaturis per Flandrenses in
partibus borialibus captorum, ac etiam pro pluribus
aliis in hujusmodi nostris litteris expressatis, transmisimus ac per nostrum cursorem eidem Dominæ
Ducissæ præsentari fecimus; nosque dictæ Dominæ
Ducissæ litteras dictis litteris vestris regiis et nostris
responsivas, non vestræ Majestati sed nobis intitulatas,[4]
recepimus Calisii decimo die præsentis mensis Octobris.
Quarum litterarum copias tam per dictum Willelmum
Maundeville ambassiatoribus Franciæ quam præfatæ
Dominæ Ducissæ, una cum copia aliarum litterarum

---

[1] See Letter CXXVIII.
[2] Robert Mascall.—See Letter
CXIII.
[3] See Letters CXV., CXX.,
CXXII., CXXIII.
[4] See Letter CXXIV.

A.D. 1404. suarum Johanni Urban, nostro collegæ, in Calisium transmissarum, ac litterarum suarum pro responsione nobis remissarum, vestræ Celsitudini sacratissimæ, pro plenaria deliberatione præmissorum, et ut appareat de diligentia nostra, mittimus præsentibus interclusas.

*They foresee that the peace will be probably broken,*

Item, cum ambassiatores Franciæ in statu, forma, ac gradu consimili, juxta tenorem prædictarum litterarum suarum nobis transmissarum, tractatum communem inter ambo regna appetunt resumere, ac cum vestris ambassiatoribus in tractatu communi pariter interesse, qui citra festum Omnium Sanctorum,[1] prout verisimiliter creditur, in tractatu resumendo insimul non poterunt convenire; etiam ad renovandum seu continuandum abstinentiam guerrarum, per nobilem virum Ricardum Astoun, Militem, Locumtenentem vestræ villæ Calisii, usque ad festum Omnium Sanctorum[1] proxime futurum captam, ab aq[ua] de Somme usque ad aquam de Gravelyng restrictam.

Unde cum nos alii vestri commissarii non obtineamus potestatem seu auctoritatem ad continuandam dictam abstinentiam guerrarum ultra dictum festum Omnium Sanctorum,[1] quodque, si non continuetur hujusmodi abstinentia guerrarum ultra festum supradictum faciliter poterit impedire tractatum inter ambo regna per Dei gratiam resumendum, ac utriusque regni publicam utilitatem;—item, excellentissime Domine, cum nos duo vestri commissarii pro tractatu Flandriæ, aliis absentibus, solummodo simus præsentes in villa Calisii, in quo quatuor pro parte vestra cum commissariis partis adversæ pariter debent interesse, dignetur vestra Excellentia alios, et utinam illum strenuum et discretum militem, Dominum Willielmum Lyle, juniorem, adjungere, ac inter alios communicare, necnon commissionem pro tractatu Flandriæ, cujus copiam eidem Excellentiæ

---

[1] November 1.

vestræ transmisimus,[1] ac etiam vestro almo Concilio A.D. 1404.
mandare et facere reformari, ac nobis remitti, ne alias,
ex defectu commissariorum et collegarum ac commissionis, in vanum inibi videamur laborare.

Et revera de nostris litteris transmissis in Angliam
post introitum nostrum in Calisium, nunquam poteramus
reportare minimam responsionem, quoad reformationem
commissionum nostrarum etiam duarum usque in diem
confectionis præsentium, nec etiam de validitate seu
invaliditate commissionis partis adversæ eidem Celsitudini
vestræ, ac vestro Concilio transmissæ.

Item, noscat vestra Excellentia, prout eidem sæpius and state
scripsimus, quod quoddam magnum navigium, cum that an
invasion of
gentibus armigeris Gallicorum ac Flandrensium, et Wales is
aliarum nationum diversarum, in Sclusa est congregatum certainly
contem-
et fulsitum ; et—prout noster nuncius, heri de Flandria plated.
reversus, nobis retulit — quod idem navigium in partibus
borialibus vestri regni seu in alia parte ejusdem intendit
applicare, quamvis alii asserant quod velint se dirigere
versus partes Walliæ. Expedit, igitur, vestrum parliamentum, per Dei gratiam, celeriter expedire, ac mare
potenter custodire. Credimus enim verisimiliter, considerato quod patria Flandriæ unanimiter et integraliter
adeo subest vestro adversario Franciæ, sicut aliqua
patria Angliæ subjacet Celsitudini vestræ ; pensato
etiam quod quasi omnes officiales Flandriæ sunt Gallici ;
ideo timendum est quod tractatus cum patria Flandriæ,
seu cum Domina Ducissa Burgundiæ, modicum valebit
absque tractatu Franciæ ; super quibus omnibus expediret deliberare cum magna maturitate. Flandrensium
enim fidelitatem etiam ab olim credimus vestram
Excellentiam non ignorare.

Ad quæ omnia advertere, ac nobis vestræ Majestatis
beneplacitum in præmissis tempestive pro continuatione

---

[1] See page 341.

A.D. 1404. hujusmodi abstinentiæ vestra rescribere dignetur Celsitudo.

Quam custodiat in longævum feliciter et votive Trinitas Sancta !

Scriptum Calisii, xj. die mensis Octobris.

Vestræ regiæ Majestatis sacratissimæ comissarii et nuncii,

JOHANNES DE CROFFT, ac
NICHOLAUS DE RYSSHETOUN.

*Endorsed :—*" Serenissimo Principi ac illustrissimo et Invictissimo Domino, Domino H., Dei gratia Regi Angliæ et Franciæ excellentissimo, Domino nostro metuendissimo."

*The following Postscript evidently belongs to the above Letter. It stands by itself in the MS. Collection, and will be found at fol. 78 (β) :—*

Vestræ regiæ Majestati sacratissimæ.

Warlike preparation in Sluys.

Item, excellentissime Domine, post sigillationem præsentis litteræ venit alter nuncius, die confectionis præsentium, de Sclusa, qui nobis retulit quod inibi intraverunt XVIII. magnæ naves, una cum duabus carectis magnis, fulsitæ cum gentibus armorum, in quibus est magnum fulcimentum et præparamentum tam de fœno minutatim inciso, quam etiam de aliis victualibus pro equis. Fertur enim quod. in Sclusa provisum est pro tribus millibus equorum, et pro totidem juxta Harflet, et ipsius præsentibus circumvicinis, ad applicandum in partibus Walliæ, seu alias infra vestrum regnum Angliæ.

Vestræ Excellentiæ commissarii,

JOHANNES DE CROFFT, ac
NICHOLAUS DE RYSSHETOUN.

## CXXX.

THE FRENCH TO THE ENGLISH AMBASSADORS.

*Copia litteræ Ambassiatorum Franciæ nuper transmissæ Ambassiatoribus Angliæ.*

Honorabiles ac circumspecti Domini.

Hodie litteras vestras,[1] datas Calesii viii° mensis hujus, recepimus, ad alias quas per ante vobis misimus responsivas, inter cetera continentes, quod litteras nostras Domino vestro transmisistis responsum suum super contentis in eis expectantes. Et cum crastina dies sit xv. dicti mensis præsentis qua nos aut alios pro parte Serenissimi nostri Regis deputandos exhortamini per scripturas vestras ad locum consuetum interesse; quod, obstante tardo per vos ad nostras litteras misso responso, non est fieri possibile : tamen, Domino concedente, sic festinabimus gressus nostros, quod die Lunæ vel Martis proximo ad tardius, nos, aut alii per dictum Dominum Regem deputandi, poterimus in dicto loco consueto vobis convenire, sperantes quod interim a dicto Domino vestro responsum habebitis de iis quæ super contentis in dictis aliis litteris nostris per vos scribitis sibi fore scriptum. Quod vobis significamus ut ad hujusmodi congregationem vos, aut alii a dicto Domino vestro deputandi, etiam si vobis visum fuerit, præparetis.

Dominationes vestras conservet Omnipotens feliciter et ad votum !

Scriptum Parisius, die xiij. mensis Octobris.

> J. DE HANGESTON, Dominus de HENGUEVILLA, Magister Balisteriorum Franciæ, et
>
> G. BOUSRATIERN, Domini nostri Regis Francorum Consiliarius.

*Promising to delay their proposed meeting as little as possible.*

---

CXXX.] MS. Cotton., Galba, B. I. fol. 64 *b* (a). — On paper ; a contemporaneous MS.

[1] See Letter CXXVIII.

A.D. 1404.

## CXXXI.

### HENRY IV. TO THE MAGISTRATES OF STRALSUND.

Per Regem Angliæ et Franciæ˙ et Dominum Hiberniæ.

Honorabiles viri, amici carissimi.

On the outrages alleged to to have been committed at sea by John Brandon and others.

Post salutis affectum, non sine quadam amaritudine mentis inspeximus Amicitiæ vestræ litteras, nobis quasi pridie præsentatas, intuentes in eis, et in cedula litteris illis inclusa, nonnullas injurias ac immensa gravamina vestratibus, sicut prætenditur, per subditos nostros illata, et specialiter per Johannem Brandoun[1] villæ nostræ de Lenne, quæ specifice declarantur aliorum nominibus, licet non omnium, expressatis in cedula memorata. Unde, cum sitis amici nostri firmum propositum retinentes (ut scribitis) eandem amicitiam continuandi, de cetero petitis confidenter a nobis, etiam cum sinceræ dilectionis instantia, ut concivibus vestris et mercatoribus, super præmissis damnis et injuriis eis illatis, restitutionem fieri facere mandaremus.

Nos itaque, cupientes ex intimo cordis nostri, veluti qui tantis damnis ac injuriis pia mente compatimur, ut et fœdus amicitiæ, quo regnum nostrum Angliæ et patria vestra progenitorum et antecessorum vestrorum temporibus invicem extiterant alligata, pro utilitate rei publicæ perseveret irruptum, et subditi hinc et inde benignis favoribus alterutrum amodo pertractentur, ut convenit, ac moti quidem propter ea vias illas exquirere per quas Amicitiæ vestræ votis satisfieri poterit in præmissis omni dilatione cessante,

---

CXXXII.] MS Cotton., Vesp., F. I. fol. 111 (e).—On paper; a contemporaneous MS.

[1] See Letter XCV.

mandavimus admirallo nostro versus boream ad cujus A.D. 1404.
officium pertinere dinoscitur injurias et damna quæ-
cumque per nostros subditos supra mare commissa
corrigere, ut partibus in ea parte conqueri volentibus
exhibeat justitiæ complementum; nec habet ipsa vestra
Dilectio dubitare quin eisdem concivibus vestris quatinus de præmissis coram eodem admirallo nostro
plene liquere poterit plena, Deo propitio, fiet justitia
cum favore, et eo favorabilius quod nostræ considerationis intuitu subditos nostros, civitatem vestram
etiam post aliqua præmissorum illata gravamina frequentantes, in caritatis et benignæ promotionis gremio
collegistis. Habemus etenim in desideriis, amici carissimi, ut interim tam nostri subditi quam vestrates,
prout consueverant in tranquillæ pacis pulchritudine,
mutuo conversentur, ne protracta solitæ communi-
cationis abstinentia mutuæ dilectionis ardorem extin-
gui contigeret succedentibus inconvenientiis aliis non
faciliter accendendum. Esset autem immensæ dilectionis
indicium, amici sincere dilecti, si bona mercatorum
nostrorum apud vos quasi per modum reprisaliarum
noviter posita sub arresto duxeritis illico relaxanda,
maxime cum simus libenter expositi vestratibus damna
passis exhiberi facere cum effectu justitiæ complementum. In quo casu præsertim inter amicos reprisaliarum hujusmodi rigor non caderet, ut videtur.

Honorabiles viri, amici carissimi, in pacis et salutis
Auctore prospere valeat vestra Dilectio, nobis cara!

Datum sub signeto nostro apud Civitatem nostram
Coventrensem, mensis Octobris die quarta decima.

*Endorsement* :—" Honorabilibus viris, Consulibus Strallessundensibus, amicis nostris caris-
simis."

A.D. 1404.

## CXXXII.

### DE RYSSHETON TO WILLIAM ASKHAM.

On the hostile preparations in France and Flanders.

Honorabilis ac magnifice et circumspecte Domine, humili ac debita recommendatione præmissa.

Pensatis beneficiis honoribus et gratitudinibus per vestram Magnificentiam, quamvis absque meritis meis mihi vestro gratiose impensis et exhibitis, regratior vestræ Dominationi, offerens me ad vestræ voluntatis beneplacitum per Dei gratiam promptum pariter et paratum.

Item, cum Gallici ac etiam Ispalenses nuper contra nos reaccensi cum ipsorum navigio potenti de Harflet numero XV. millium armatorum ac equitum vel circiter fulciti pro dimidio anno, tam pro se, quam pro equis suis pro præsenti sunt in mari ad invadendum Burdegaliam seu alias ad intrandum in Walliam, ad occupandum et reædificandum castra in Wallia destructa et ad omnia mala ac damna possibilia nobis inferenda, quamquam navigium Flandrensium etiam cum totidem Gallicis et equitibus in Sclusa congregatum pro præsenti est paratum, etiam cum auxilio illorum de Pruscia ad

Calais threatened.

invadendum Sandewicum, seu alias partes Angliæ. Et finaliter intendunt, prout fertur, declinare ad Calisium cum celeritate, et ad ipsius obsidionem.

Unde, cum Dominus meus, Capitaneus Calisii ac stipendiarii sui in certo numero sint absentes, prout vestri mercatores stapulæ; et si omnes stipendiarii essent præsentes inibi villa Calisii non esset sufficienter fulcita, gentibus arma[tis] ac etiam victualibus, et aliis pluribus requisitis, etiam artillariam concernen-

CXXXII.] MS. Cotton. Galba, B. I. fol. 63. — On paper; original, with marks of the seal.

tibus; vestra igitur Magnificentia ad prædicta dignetur A.D. 1404. advertere, et præsertim ad villam Calisii, ac pro ipsius defensione tam in gentibus quam in victualibus, et præsertim in concernentibus artillariam, celeriter providere, necnon pro defensione regni mare debite custodire, ac ad custodiam portuum maris diligenter attendere; et quod naves onustæ cum lanis seu frumento versus Burdegaliam interim non debeant se dirigere.

Vestram Magnificentiam custodiat Altissimus feliciter et votive!

Scriptum Calisii quarto decimo die mensis Octobris.

Vester humilis servitor,

NICHOLAUS DE RYSSHETOUN,

Commissarius, etc.

*Endorsed* :—" Honorabili ac magnifico et circumspecto Domino, Willelmo Askham, Majori Civitatis Londoniæ, magistro suo præcipuo."

## CXXXIII.

SWYNBORN, CROFT, AND DE RYSSHETON TO THE DUCHESS OF BURGUNDY.

Illustris Principissa, ac magnæ nobilitatis et potentiæ Domina.

Vestras litteras,[1] una cum quadam billa querelosa pro Hannequin le Voiturier in eisdem interclusa, sexto

They recapitulate.

---

CXXXIII.] MS. Brit. Mus., Addit. 14,820. D. — On paper; original, with the seals of the three Ambassadors attached. The first in order, that of Swynborn probably, has on it a human head with a long beard. The second, that of Croft, represents a stag couchant The third has a motto around it, which is so mutilated as to be illegible; and the device in the centre is destroyed.

[1] See Letter CXXIV.

B B

A.D. 1404. die præsentis mensis Octobris scriptas, recepimus Calisii,
their inter cetera continentes, qualiter recepistis certas lit-
complaints
against the teras[1] Domini nostri, Regis Angliæ et Franciæ illus-
Flemings; trissimi, ac etiam nostras[2] exhortatorias et requisatorias
super relaxatione financiæ reverendi Patris, Fratris
Roberti,[3] Episcopi Herfordensis, ac aliorum piscatorum
non faciliter numerabilium, in ipsorum piscaturis per
vestros subditos Flandriæ captorum, una cum restitutione xxxvij. navium eorundem : necnon quod vestras
litteras,[4] sub vestro signeto sigillatas, in Calisium transmissas, vestræ memoriæ deberetis reducere ; quibus fuit
cautum quod ab omni actu guerrino volueritis desistere,
ac treugas facere proclamari, dum tamen sub forma
consimili Dominus noster Rex velit desistere, ac pariter
facere proclamari : propter quæ Dominus noster Rex
præcepit suis admirallis quod incolis Flandriæ nullum
damnum debeant inferre. Quibus non obstantibus,
vestri subditi incolas regni Angliæ captivarunt, spoliarunt, ac damna possibilia eis intulerunt. Quodque
vestra Excellentia, respondendo ad præmissa, dicit quod
hujusmodi defensio seu proclamatio pro parte nostra
non fuit servata, considerato quod in quadam insula
vestra de Wlpen nostri subditi ignem exposuerunt,
ac certam ecclesiam et quasdam domos inibi spoliarunt :
unde quamvis captivatas Episcopi Herfordensis, et
aliorum nostrorum piscatorum per vestros subditos captorum, de vestra voluntate seu præcepto non processerit,
subditi vestri Episcopum ac piscatores prædictos captivarunt ad ipsorum defensionem, pro restitutione dictorum damnorum eis illatorum. Asseritis tamen ne
rumpatur tractatus communis—informabitis vestram
Reverentiam de præmissis, etiam cum contigerit vestros
ambassiatores cum nostris ambassiatoribus insimul

---

[1] See Letter CXIII.        [3] Robert Mascall.
[2] See Letter CXV.         [4] See Letter XC.

convenire ac pariter interesse, ordinabitur, ac appunc- A.D. 1404.
tuabitur, et reformabitur ; et consimiliter dicitis quod
navigium in Sclusa contra Anglicos congregatum vobis
est incognitum; nihilominus mandastis inhiberi quod
per hujusmodi navigium nullum damnum nobis esset
inferendum ; et quod hujusmodi spolia, per vestros
subditos capta, nec ad commodum vestrum seu vestrorum familiarium sunt distributa, et quod prædicta
omnia Domino nostro Regi debeamus manifestare.

Ad quæ, illustris ac nobilis Domina,—cum adhærentes
seu inclusi in treugis generalibus, inter Angliam et
Franciam initis, easdem treugas teneantur servare, ac
ipsas nullo modo instringere seu violare; quodque
illustris Princeps, ac claræ memoriæ Dominus, Dux
Burgundiæ, Comes Flandriæ, vester maritus, dum ageret
in humanis, sub sigillo suo—necnon vestra Quatuor
Membra Flandriæ—quoddam privilegium, sub eorum
sigillis etiam sigillatum, mercatoribus Angliæ in Calisium transmiserunt, continens inter cetera quemlibet
mercatorem Angliæ posse libere in Flandriam cum bonis
suis et mercimoniis venire, ac abinde redire, et quod
ipsi in personis suis aut bonis non debeant molestari
infra districtum et fines Flandriæ, occasione guerrarum
seu alterius attemptati cujuscumque, nisi prius facta
denunciatione per xl. dies antea dictis mercatoribus
Angliæ, quod bona et mercimonia sua primitus debeant
removere, prout in dicto privilegio plenius continetur.

Officiales tamen et ministri præfati Domini Ducis
Burgundiæ, Comitis Flandriæ, bonæ memoriæ, prædictis
non obstantibus, — quamvis omnes et singuli subditi
Flandriæ sub treugis generalibus antedictis tanquam
adhærentes seu inclusi notorie sunt comprehensi,—
contra formam dictarum treugarum, et appunctuamentorum communium utriusque regni, ac post et contra
privilegium suum ac ipsius proprium sigillum, ac
etiam sigilla dictorum Quatuor Membrorum, bona ac
mercimonia mercatorum Angliæ in portu Sclusæ

A.D. 1404. arrestata, ad valorem notabilem, etiam post et contra
tractatum inchoatum et pendentem pro tunc Londoniæ,
apud Westmonasterium, inter Dominum nostrum
Regem ex una, ac vestra Quatuor Membra parte ex
altera, juratis ambassiatorum ipsorum Quatuor Membrorum ad dictarum treugarum ac ipsius tractatus
conservationem vallatum, prout patet per instrumenta
publica super hujusmodi juratis confecta, aliquando
eisdem Quatuor Membris transmissa et nobis remissa;
hujusmodique bona et mercimonia, ut præfertur, arrestata dicti officiales et ministri, de mandato ejusdem
Domini vestri, et mariti, prout fertur, non obstantibus
diversis requestis et exhortationibus per nos notorie
factis, venditioni publicæ exposuerunt, ac juxta ipsius
mandatum distribuerunt, prout ista ex relatione plurium et præsertim vestrorum subditorum veraciter
didicimus. Subsequenterque præfatus Dominus vester
hujusmodi processum per dicta Quatuor Membra inchoatum noluit, prout etiam eadem Excellentia vestra
pariter noluit, ratum et gratum habere, sed processum
a capite voluit resumere ac elongare; vestraque
Excellentia, post ejusdem Domini vestri ac mariti,
claræ memoriæ, obitum, scripsit in Calisium diversas
litteras, vestro signeto sigillatas, pro hujusmodi tractatus resumptione ac prosecutione, absque dictorum
vestrorum Quatuor Membrorum adjunctione, et præsertim inter cetera qualiter vestri subditi ab omni
actu guerrino et a quacumque guerra debuerunt desistere,
ac treugas in patria vestra publice interim facere
proclamari; dum tamen sub forma consimili velimus
eadem pro parte vestra nostra peragere.

excuse the    Et revera sub prætextu vestræ Excellentiæ ac
English;     dictarum litterarum vestrarum de mense Julii ultimo
præterito, ac diu ante, Dominus noster Rex præcepit.
ac districte sub diversis pœnis etiam vitæ et membrorum mandavit admirallis navigii sui, ac quibuscumque subditis regni sui, ac etiam in villa Calisii

publice proclamari fecit ut nullus ligeus de regni A.D. 1404.
Angliæ in patria Flandriæ debeat applicare, seu inibi
qualecumque damnum inferre, prout prædicta omnia
in nostro introitu in Calisium per litteras nostras,[1]
sub datum xxiij. Augusti et vestræ Excellentiæ notificavimus. Quod præceptum regium fuit servatum, ac
citra, prout novistis, debitæ executioni mandatum,
salvo quod nonnulli nostri stipendiarii ad associandum
mercatores Angliæ cum suis mercimoniis deputati in
Midilburgh tanquam obsessos per vestros subditos, qui
eisdem mercatoribus intimarunt quod ipsos et eorum
bona voluerunt capere, ac eosdem derobare, nisi
latenter velint recedere et fugere in ipsorum recessu
de Midilburgh, ad notificandum vestris subditis ipsorum
recessum, ignem in vestra insula de Wlpen, contra
voluntatem Domini nostri Regis et Concilii sui, ausu
temerario imposuerunt, et inibi quasdam domos com-
busserunt,—quamvis ad modicum valorem seu damnum respective non centum nobilium,—de quo per
Dei gratiam fiet satisfactio usque ad minimum denarium.
Et hujusmodi malefactores, propter ipsorum excessum,
sustinebunt pœnam condignam merito infligendam.
Et quantum ad billam in vestris litteris interclusam
mittimus vobis responsionem in litteris Locumtenentis
villæ Calisii, per præsentium portitorem vobis præsentandis, interclusam. Et sic per Dei gratiam mandatum Domini nostri Regis antedictum etiam in aliis
fuit servatum ac debitæ executioni mandatum.

His tamen non obstantibus, vestri subditi post et
contra tenorem dictarum litterarum vestrarum, de
mense Septembris ultimo elapso, reverendum Patrem
Fratrem Robertum, Episcopum Herfordensem, in mari,
necnon quingentos piscatores nostros vel circiter, cum
ipsorum XXXVII. navibus, in partibus borialibus Angliæ,

---

[1] See Letter CVI.

A.D. 1404. in ipsorum piscaturis, latenter et de nocte captivarunt, aliquos ad financiam exposuerunt, etiam ad tria millia nobilium et ultra, alios cum suis navibus in mari submerserunt; quamvis interim taceamus de aliis octuaginta navibus nostris, una cum nostris gentibus non faciliter numerabilibus, etiam clericis ac religiosis et aliis indistincte per vestros subditos captis, ac in mari submersis. Item, cum in ultimis vestris litteris nobis præsentatis sit contentum, quod navigium absque vestra voluntate ac scientia, quamvis notorie in vestris portubus de Nuport, Dunkyrk, et de Sclusa, extitit congregatum; quod mandastis, ac illud defendi præcepistis, quod subditis ac incolis regni Angliæ nullum damnum de cetero debeant inferre; hoc tamen non obstante, vestri Flandrenses ac alii subditi, quin verius rebelles ac hujusmodi vestris monitionibus et præceptis non obedientes, certas partes Angliæ, et præsertim apud Orwell, post et contra tenorem dictarum litterarum vestrarum, invaserunt ac ignem inibi immiserunt, nostros subditos derobarunt, ac naves in numero notabili de portubus Angliæ secum abduxerunt, nostros subditos submerserunt, de quo vehementer admiramur.

Unde, cum præmissa omnia et singula sunt adeo notaria ac manifesta quod nulla tergiversatione poterunt celari, quamvis eadem, prout scribitis, vestræ Excellentiæ sunt incognita nec de vestra voluntate perpetrata,—quæ diu non poterunt tolerari nisi vestra Excellentia celerius eadem fecerit reparari ac reformari,—vestram Excellentiam, prout alias, requirimus ac exhortamur in Domino, quatinus, citra festum Omnium Sanctorum [1] proxime futurum, restitutionem aut verum valorem dictorum bonorum et mercimoniorum mercatorum Angliæ in Sclusa arrestatorum, ac publicæ venditioni expositorum, post et contra privilegium præfati Domini vestri ac

---

[1] November 1.

mariti, bonæ memoriæ, ipsius, ac dictorum Quatuor A.D. 1404. Membrorum sigillis sigillatum, et contra ipsorum jurata, ac etiam contra treugas generales antedictas; necnon financiam præfati Domini Episcopi Herfordensis, ac aliorum, tam piscatorum cum ipsorum navibus et bonis, quam aliorum prædictorum, etiam post et contra vestras litteras impressione signeti vestri sigillatas, de quibus interim per Dei gratiam recepistis plenam informationem, juxta tenorem vestrarum litterarum, propter ipsorum privilegium et præeminentiam, specialem faciatis ante quamcumque aliam reparationem fiendam, absque dilatione celeriter relaxari ac mandare realiter fieri et cum effectu.

Et, si poterit apparere quod aliqua capta pro parte nostra de bonis subditorum vestrorum habeant hujusmodi privilegium et præeminentiam specialem, sub forma consimili eadem bona aut ipsorum valorem indilate faciemus restitui, et præsertim in nostrorum et vestrorum ambassiatorum proxima congregatione ac parliamento, dum tamen citra festum supradictum [1]; quodque copiam litterarum vestrarum Domino nostro Regi transmisimus juxta ipsarum continentiam et tenorem ; cujus responsionem ac voluntatem, et ordinationem sui parliamenti pro reparatione præmissorum, indies expectamus.

Et cum hujusmodi responsionem et voluntatem ac *and* parliamenti ordinationem super præmissis receperimus, *threaten to abandon* ipsam, prout expedit, rescribemus; ac vestræ Excellentiæ *the nego-* intimabimus. Super quibus omnibus, ac super aliis ves- *tiations.* trum beneplacitum continentibus, citra dictum festum Omnium Sanctorum [1] placeat celeriter interim nobis rescribere et respondere, cum ultra festum superius memoratum in villa Calisii pro tractatu non intendamus ulterius remanere, nisi benigniorem responsionem super præmissorum restitutione, ac dictæ financiæ

---

[1] November 1.

A.D. 1404. relaxationem, ante quamcumque aliam reparationem fiendam, præter quam in casibus consimilibus a vestra Excellentia poterimus obtinere ; necnon navigium vestrum in portu Sclusæ congregatum, seu quodcunque aliud in mari constitutum, una cum quibuscumque navibus vobis adhærentibus, etiam Pruscensibus, ad invadendum partes Walliæ seu Angliæ præparatum, confestim reducere, ac celeriter facere revocari ; cum hic aliquando circa præsentem tractatum fatigati in nullo videamur proficere, quin verius laboribus et expensis inanibus nos vexare.

Necnon pro securitate villæ de Gravelyng, (in qua fuit, prout est, spelunca latronum), notorie infra palum ac fines vestræ patriæ Flandriæ constitutæ, providere ; necnon prisonarios et captivos nostros,—prout vestros etiam penes nos captivos constitutos offerimus,—liberare absque financiæ solutione placeat vestræ Excellentiæ.

Quam custodiat Trinitas Increata feliciter et longæve ! Scriptum Calisii, xvij. die Octobris.

THOMAS SWYNBORN, et

JOHANNES CROFFT,—Milites ; ac

NICHOLAUS DE RYSSHETOUN, Utriusque Juris Professor ;

Ambassiatores pro parte Angliæ.


Endorsed :—"Illustri Principissæ, necnon præclaræ ac magnæ nobilitatis et potentiæ Dominæ, Dominæ Margaretæ, Ducissæ Burgundiæ, Comitissæ Flandriæ, Arthesii, et Burgundiæ."

A.D. 1404.

## CXXXIV.

SWYNFORD AND DE RYSSHETON TO THE FRENCH
AMBASSADORS.

*Copia litteræ responsivæ Ambassiatorum Angliæ,
nuper transmissæ Ambassiatoribus Franciæ, etc.*

Honorabiles ac magnifici et circumspecti Domini.

Vestras litteras,[1] scriptas Parisius xiij° die Octobris, recepimus Calisii die Lunæ, de mane, $xx^{mo}$ ejusdem mensis Octobris, inter cetera continentes, qualiter litteras nostras,[2] vestris litteris responsivas, viij° die præsentis mensis Octobris recepistis, cum crastina dies ex tunc post receptionem earundem fuit xv. dies, propter hujusmodi termini brevitatem eodem $xv^{mo}$ die non poteritis nobiscum convenire; tamen, Domino concedente, sic festinabitis gressus vestros quod die Lunæ vel Martis proxima ad tardius,[3] vos, vel alii per Dominum vestrum deputandi, in loco consueto poteritis nobiscum pariter convenire, sperantes quod nos interim a Domino nostro responsum reportabimus super contentis in dictis litteris vestris alias nobis præsentatis, quod nobis significatis ut nos, aut alii ex parte Domini nostri deputandi, præparemus nos ad hujusmodi congregationem, si nobis fuerit visum.

*In reply to their letter proposing a meeting.*

Ad quæ, honorabiles Domini, dum dies hodierna sit dies hinc proxima post data litterarum vestrarum, adeo quod eodem die Lunæ præsente, seu etiam in crastino, ex defectu salvi conductus ultro citroque transmittendi, in loco consueto non poterimus insimul convenire, sed quocumque alio termino congruo[4] assignando ad reci-

---

CXXXIV.] MS. Cotton. Galba,
B. I. fol. 64. — On paper; a contemporaneous MS.

   [1] See Letter CXXX.

[2] See Letter CXXVIII.

[3] *tardius*] taridius, MS.

[4] *congruo*] Added above the line.

A.D. 1404. piendum responsionem Domini vestri, ac aliorum Dominorum spiritualium et temporalium vestræ partis
Franciæ, super quatuor punctis ac litteris tam Domini
nostri, Regis Angliæ et Franciæ illustrissimi ac invictissimi, quam aliorum Dominorum suorum spiritualium
et temporalium regni sui, per nobilem virum Dominum
Johannem Cheyny, Militem, vestris Dominationibus
præsentatis, erimus parati recipere ac salvum conductum
vobis transmittere, necnon in hujusmodi termino per
vos assignando et loco consueto pro hujusmodi responsione in scriptis reportanda pariter convenire, ac eandem responsionem, etiam super aliis litteris nostris
Magno Concilio Franciæ transmissis, recipere.  Responsionem enim super contentis in prædictis litteris
vestris, quarum copiam Domino nostro Regi excellentissimo transmisimus, ab eodem hactenus non recepimus,
quamvis ipsius beneplacitum ac ordinationem super eisdem contentis indies expectamus.  Cujus ordinationem ac
responsionem super hujusmodi contentis nobis per
eundem Dominum nostrum Regem transmittendam
celeriter vobis intimabimus.

Vestras Magnificentias et Dominationes custodiat
Altissimus ad unitatem pacis utriusque regni feliciter
et votive !

Scriptum Calisii, die Lunæ, vicesimo ejusdem Octobris.

> THOMAS SWYNFORD, Custos Castri villæ
> Calisii, ac
>
> NICHOLAUS DE RYSSHETOUN, Utriusque
> Juris Professor,
>     Ambassiatores pro parte Angliæ.

*Endorsement :* — "Honorabilibus ac magnificis et circumspectis Dominis, Domino Johanni
de Hangesto, Domino de Henguevilla, Magistro Balestivorum Franciæ, et G. Bourratern, Ambassiatoribus pro parte Franciæ, etc."

A.D. 1404.

## CXXXV.

THE FRENCH TO THE ENGLISH AMBASSADORS.

*Copia litteræ Ambassiatorum Franciæ transmissæ Ambassiatoribus Angliæ :—*

*Honorabilibus et circumspectis Dominis, Domino Thomæ Swynford, Militi, Custodi Castri Calisii, et Nicholao de Rysshetoun, Utriusque Juris Professori, Ambassiatoribus pro parte Angliæ.*

Treshonnore Seignours.

Il a pleu au Roy de France, nostre soverain Seignour, nous envoier pardeca pour assembler aveques vous, ou autres messaiges envoiez de la partie d'Engleterre, pour parler sur aucunes choses touchans le bien publique. Et sommez prests d'assembler aveques vous et autres de vostre partie commis sur icelles choses Mercurdi[1] prochain venant, a heure de tierce, a Marquise. *(margin: Proposing a meeting at Marquise.)*

Et pour ce vous envoions la coppie du saufconduyt que de vostre coste fut envoie l'annes passes a nous autres, affin que en semblable maniere en autre forme valable le nous envoiez.

---

[TRANSLATION.]

Most honoured Lords.—It has pleased the King of France, our sovereign Lord, to send us hither for to assemble with you, or other commissaries sent on the part of England, to discourse on any matters touching the public good. And we are ready to meet with you and other commissaries of your side concerning these matters on Wednesday next coming, at the hour of tierce, at Marquise.—And for this purpose we send to you the copy of the safe-conduct which was sent from your side in years past to others of us, to the end that in like manner you may send it to us in a valid form.—And we

---

CXXXV.] MS. Cotton. Galba, B. I. fol. 64 *b* (*β*). — On paper; a contemporaneous MS.

[1] The 20th of October, on which day this letter was written, fell on a Monday in the year 1404. The day here proposed therefore was Wednesday, October 22nd.

A.D. 1404. Et nous sommez prests vous envoier saufconduit pareillement bon et valable pour les personnes et nonbre de gens que vous nous ferez savoir que besoing vous serra. Sy vueillez sur ce brefment par ung vostre message nous rescripre, et faire savoir voz bons vouloirs; et se c'est vostre ententioun que l'assembler d'entre nous se tiegne au dit jour et lieu.

Le Saint Esprit vous ait en Sa garde !

Escript a Monsterueil, le xx. jour d'Octobre.

> J., EVESQUE DE CHARTRES,
> J. DE HANGEST, Seigneur de Hengueville,
> G. BOISRATIER,
> J. DE SAINS,
> Ambaxadeurs du Roy de France, nostre Seigneur.

*Endorsement :*—" A treshonnore Seignours, Messieur Thomas Swynford, Chivalier, et Messieur Nicole de Rysshetoun, Docteur, Ambassateurs pour la partie d'Angleterre."

---

are ready to send you a safe-conduct similarly good and valid for the persons and number of men which you shall cause us to know that you will have need of. Be pleased to write an answer to us briefly on this matter by one of your messengers, and cause us to know your good pleasures ; and whether it is your intention that the meeting between us should be held at the said day and place.—The Holy Ghost have you in His keeping !—Written at Monstrueil, the 20th day of October.

> J., Bishop of Chartres ;
> J. DE HANGEST, Lord of Hengueville,
> G. BOISRATIER,
> J. DE SAINS,
> Ambassadors of the King of France, our Lord.

*Endorsement.*—" To the most honoured Lords, Master Thomas Swynford, Knight, and Master Nicholas de Ryssheton, Doctor, Ambassadors on the part of England.

## CXXXVI.

### SWYNFORD AND DE RYSSHETON TO THE FRENCH AMBASSADORS.

*Copia litteræ responsivæ Ambassiatorum Angliæ, transmissæ Ambassiatoribus Franciæ :—*

Reverende Pater, necnon honorabiles ac magnifici et circumspecti Domini.

Vestras litteras[1] scriptas in Gallico, nobis indoctis tanquam in idiomate Hebraico, apud Monstreueille $xx^{mo}$ die Octobris, recepimus Calisii eodem $xx^{mo}$ die de sero, inter cetera continentes qualiter Reverentiæ vestræ, de mandato ac pro parte Domini vestri superioris, pro bono publico cum ambassiatoribus partis nostræ die Mercurii[2] proximo futuro, hora tertia, apud Marquise insimul debeant convenire. Idcirco remittitis nobis copiam cujusdam salvi conductus, alias parti vestræ per partem nostram transmissi, juxta cujus formam, seu alias in alia forma valida, debeamus pro vobis et vestris ad eorum numerum personarum salvum conductum transmittere, cum in pari forma offertis vos salvum conductum nobis remittere. Necnon quod per litteras nostras vobis debeamus rescribere, si præfatis die et loco vobiscum intendimus convenire.

Ad quæ, honorabiles Domini, non videtur nobis quod die Mercurii proximo futuro, seu in loco apud Marquise, per vos assignatis, commode poterimus pariter convenire ; cum in crastino non sufficimus salvum conductum vobis transmittere, ac vestrum nobis

*Postponing the proposed meeting, and fixing on Lulingham instead of Marquise.*

---

CXXXVI.] MS. Cotton. Galba, B. I. fol. 65.—On paper; a contemporaneous MS.

[1] See Letter CXXXV.
[2] Wednesday, October 22. See the note to the preceding Letter.

A.D. 1404. remittendum recipere, ac super ipsis eodem die plene deliberare, nec juxta instructionem nobis traditam locum consuetum variare. Idcirco, salvo vestro judicio meliori, die Veneris [1] vel Sabbati [2] proximo futuris prout vobis placuerit, cum die Jovis proximo ex aliis certis causis urgentibus ad talia non valeamus intendere; sed in loco consueto apud Lulyngham, per Dei gratiam, parati erimus vobiscum convenire. Salvum enim conductum vestris Dominationibus mittimus per præsentium portatorem, quæ etiam offerimus reformare, prout expedit vestris Dominationibus, salvum conductum pro parte vestra nobis remittendum expectando.

Super quibus omnibus placeat nobis rescribere prout eisdem Dominationibus vestris videbitur expedire.

Quas custodiat Altissimus ad unitatem et pacem utriusque regni, ac Universalis Militantis Ecclesiæ!

Scriptum Calisii, xxj$^{mo}$ die Octobris, de mane.

> Thomas Swynford, Miles, Custos Castri villæ Calisii, ac
>
> Nicholaus de Rysshetoun, Utriusque Juris Professor,
>
> > Ambassiatores pro parte Angliæ.

*Endorsement*:—"Reverendo in Christo Patri, Domino J., Episcopo Carnotensi, necnon honorabilibus ac circumspectis Dominis, Domino J. de Hanxto, Domino de Henguevilla, ac G. Bourratern, et J. de Sanctis, Ambassiatoribus pro parte Franciæ."

*Also*:—" Nomina illorum per quos scripsimus litteras divisim Domino nostro Regi ac ipsius almo Concilio:—

> " Primo, per Tremayn, de Cornubia.

---

[1] Friday, October 24.          [2] Saturday, October 25.

" Secundo, per Ricardum Wansford, A.D. 1404. Ballivum Stapulæ.

" Tertio, per Johannem Mershe, Scutiferum Domini nostri Regis.

" Quarto, per Robertum Budd, Servientem Domini Thomæ de Herpyngham.

" Quinto, per Johannem Lardiner et Ricardum Geste.

" Sexto, per Willielmum Hasarin, Scutiferum Domini de Mortuo Mari.

" Septimo, per Edmundum Wyse, familiarem Domini Johannis de Crofft.

" Octavo, per Symonem Campp, Ballivum aquæ Calisii.

" Nono, in præsenti per Locumtenentem Stapulæ, nomine Johannis Bakster."[2]

## CXXXVII.

### SWYNFORD AND DE RYSSHETON TO HENRY IV.

Illustrissime ac excellentissime Princeps, necnon invictissime et metuendissime Domine.

Die Lunæ, vicesimo mensis Octobris, de mane quasdam litteras, ac subsequenter eodem die de sero alias litteras,[1] ex parte quatuor ambassiatorum Franciæ, videlicet Episcopi Carnotensis, Domini de Henguevilla, ac aliorum Dominorum, etc., recepimus; litterasque

*Giving an account of their correspondence;*

---

CXXXVII.] MS. Cotton. Galba, B. I. fol. 67.—On paper; original, with marks of the seal.

¹ See Letter CXXXV.

² See the next Letter (in which this Letter and the above List were enclosed), p. 400, l. 26.

A.D. 1404. responsivas,[1] cum salvo conductu Locumtenentis vestræ villæ Calesii, cum potestate ad dandum salvum conductum pro præsenti non obtineamus, prout vestræ Excellentiæ ac vestro Concilio scripsimus, absque responsione quacumque, ipsis transmisimus, adeo quod die Veneris, vel Sabbati proximo futuro, per Dei gratiam, ordinavimus insimul convenire. Necnon responsionem de et super vestris litteris regalibus, ac super litteris aliorum Dominorum spiritualium et temporalium regni vestri, necnon super litteris nostris, Magno Concilio Franciæ transmissis, in loco consueto recipere, ac prout occurrerit, juxta Providentiam Divinam, alias materias interserere, ac responsionem omnium præmissorum vestræ Majestati celeriter reportare, copias litterarum prædictarum ambassiatorum Franciæ, ac nostrarum eis remissarum, mittimus præsentibus interclusas. Ex quibus omnibus eadem vestra Majestas, pro continuatione treugarum generalium seu specialium, ac pro ambassiatoribus et vestris commissariis pro tractatu Franciæ interim poterit providere, ac prout placuerit nobis rescribere.

*and complaining bitterly that their Letters to the King and his Council remain unanswered.*

Quantum ad tractatum Flandriæ dignetur eadem vestra Excellentia commissionem reformatam nobis transmittere, necnon super validitate seu invaliditate potestatis ejusdem Dominæ Ducissæ, a Domino suo superiore obtentæ, nos declarare. Septies enim et ultra nostras litteras pro hujusmodi commissione reformanda vestræ Majestati ac vestro Concilio per vestros certos ligeos, in quadam cedula[2] præsentibus interclusa descriptos, direximus; de quibus nullum responsum reportare potuimus. Idcirco ego,—et Nicholaus, vester clericus ac servitor humillimus,—nisi celerius remittatur commissio, cum absque commissione pro tractatu Flandriæ in vanum laboro ex pluribus causis, revertar absque

---

[1] See Letter CXXXVI. | [2] See pp. 398, 9.

dilatione post festum Omnium Sanctorum [1] ad pedes A.D. 1404.
vestræ Majestatis regiæ!

Quam custodiat Altissimus feliciter et votive!

Scriptum Calisii, vicesimo secundo die mensis
Octobris.

Vestræ regiæ Majestatis sacratissimæ commissarii
et nuncii,

THOMAS SWYNFORD, ac

NICHOLAUS DE RYSSHETOUN.

*Endorsed :*—" Serenissimo Principi ac illustrissimo et
[invictissimo Domino,] Regi Angliæ
et Franciæ excellentissimo."

## CXXXVIII.

HENRY IV. TO THE MAGISTRATES OF STRALSUND.

Per Regem Angliæ et Franciæ, et Dominum Hiberniæ.

Honorabiles viri amici carissimi.

Post sinceræ salutationis affectum, alias litteras For Robert
nostras transmissis nobis jampridem Amicitiæ vestræ Donyngton.
litteris responsivas, de pluribus et immensis injuriis
per subditos nostros vestratibus, ut conqueruntur,
illatis, facientibus mentionem, per dilectum et fidelem
ligeum nostrum, Robertum Donyngton, mercatorem
villæ nostræ de Kyngeston super Hulle, vestræ Dilectioni transmittimus; vos rogantes attente quatinus
ipsum Robertum ad vos propter ea venientem, regiæ

---

[1] November 1.

CXXXVIII.] MS. Cotton. Vesp.
F. I. fol. 110 ($\eta$).

C C

A.D. 1404. considerationis intuitu recommissum habere velitis, ipsumque favorabiliter facere pertractari pro tempore more suo; non sinentes eidem circa personam, aut bona, vel mercandisas ejusdem, quæ deferet modo secum, a quoquam apud vos injuriam, molestiam aliquam, vel arrestum inferri, cum, prætextu nostræ transmissionis hujusmodi cum bonis et mercimoniis ejus confidentiam plenam assumpserit ad partes vestras hac vice personaliter accedendi.

Vestra Dilectio nobis cara semper valeat et crescat in pacifico Rege regum!

Datum sub signeto nostro apud Coventre, mensis Octobris die vicesima quarta.

*Endorsed:* — "Honorabilibus viris Consulibus Strallessundensibus, amicis nostris sincere dilectis."

## CXXXIX.

### DE RYSSHETON TO THE BISHOP OF CHARTRES.

Reverende Pater, necnon honorabiles ac magnifici Domini.

From Coventry, where he had seen the King of England, Juxta ordinationem, in nostro parliamento communi, apud Lulyngham, die Veneris xxiiij. Octobris ultimo præterito factam, die Lunæ[1] extunc proximo sequente iter meum de villa Calisii versus Angliam arripui; subsequenterque, in festo Omnium Sanctorum,[2] ad

---

CXXXIX.] MS. Cotton. Galba, B. i. fol. 68.—On paper.

[1] October 27.
[2] November 1.

præsentiam utriusque Monarchiæ sacratissimæ Angliæ et Franciæ veni et personaliter appropinquavi ; necnon acta omnia et singula, prædicto die ultro citroque actitata, inibi personaliter exposui, et seriosius, prout potui, declaravi ; quodque eadem Monarchia, visis hujusmodi actis et actitatis pariter et intellectis, pensata utilitate publica, disposuit ac [destinavit] absque dilatione ambassiatores suos vobis, pares ac in numero et dignitate æquales, cum amplis potestatibus[1] citra dictum quintum decimum diem, versus mare pro hujusmodi tractatu transmittere, cum omni celeritate possibili.

Unde, quamvis dies Sabbati[2] proximo futuri erit quinta decima post dictum diem Veneris computanda, usque ad quem diem Sabbati inclusive, juxta ordinationem communem ac vestram promissionem, tenemini expectare pro utriusque regni utilitate usque ad[3] . . . . . . . dies eundem diem Sabbati ex tunc proximo sequentes, mutuæ vicissitudinis obtentu placeat Boloniæ favorabiliter remanere et attendere, ac precibus nostrorum ambassiatorum nominatorum benigne condescendere.

Et, per Dei gratiam, ante adventum prædictorum[4] . . . . . . . dierum, celerius quo fuerit possibile, nostri ambassiatores in gradu pares, cum hujusmodi amplis potestatibus, in villa Calisii—nisi tempestas maris impediat—personaliter debent interesse. Considerantes quod nos alii, vestrarum precum interventu, diutius in Calisio aliquando expectavimus adventum vestrarum Reverentiarum, prout parati sumus expectare in futuro easdem vestras Reverentias.

---

[1] Here the following words have been struck out :—"etiam juxta tenorem aliarum litterarum mearum de Calisio vobis transmissarum."

[2] Saturday, November 8.
[3] A blank space occurs here.
[4] Here also is a blank space which has never been filled up.

A.D. 1404.    Quas custodiat Altissimus feliciter et votive!
Scriptum Coventriæ, secundo die mensis Novembris.

NICHOLAUS DE RYSSHETOUN,
Utriusque Juris Professor, ac
causarum Palatii Apostolici auditor, unus Ambassiatorum pro
parte Angliæ.

*Endorsed :*—" Reverendo in Christo Patri, Domino J.,
Episcopo Carnote[nsi], ac magnificis
Dominis J. de Hangesto, Domino de
[Henguevilla,] Magistro Balisteriorum
Franciæ, G. Bourra[tier, et J.] de Sanctis,
Ambassiatoribus pro parte F[ranciæ]."

## CXL.

### DE RYSSHETON TO THE DUCHESS OF BURGUNDY.

*Copia litteræ Magistri Nicholai de Rysshetoun,
unius Ambassiatorum Domini nostri, Regis Angliæ et
Franciæ metuendissimi, nuper transmissæ Dominæ
Ducissæ Burgundiæ, etc.*

Illustris Principissa, necnon præclaræ et magnæ nobilitatis et excellentiæ Domina.

Stating
that he had
met the
King at
Coventry,

Juxta tenorem litterarum in recessu meo de Calisio
eidem Excellentiæ vestræ transmissarum, die Lunæ[1]
extunc proximo sequente iter meum de villa Calisii
versus Angliam arripui, subsequenterque in festo
Omnium Sanctorum[2] veni ad præsentiam utriusque
Monarchiæ sacratissimæ Angliæ et Franciæ, ac personaliter appropinquavi, necnon omnia et singula hujusmodi tractatum communem concernentia personaliter
exposui, ac, prout melius potui, seriosus declaravi;
q[uodque eadem] Monarchia, pro utilitate communis

---

CXL.] MS. Cotton. Galba, B.i. fol. 69.     [1] October 27.
—On paper; a contemporaneous MS.     [2] November 1.

mercandisæ, ambassiatores ac commissarios suos cum A.D. 1404.
auctoritate et potestate sufficienti cum [omni] celeritate
disposuit destinare, ac [hujusmodi] tractatum effectualiter intendere. Vestram Excellentiam requiro ac and renew-
exhortor in Domino, quatinus pro restitutione bonorum ing his demand for
mercatorum Londoniæ in Sclusa arrestatorum, et pub- restitution.
licæ [venditioni] indebite expositorum ; necnon pro
relaxatione financiæ Reverendi Patris R., Episcopi
Herfordensis,[1] cum piscatorum Angliæ, etc. faciliter
innumerabilium proditione latenter de nocte in ipsorum
piscaturis cum XXXVII. navibus captorum, ac aliorum
incarceratorum quorumcumque. Necnon pro remedio
et securitate villæ de Gravelyng, infra vestrum palum
Flandriæ constitutæ, ante quamcumque aliam reparationem fiendam, propter ipsorum præeminentiam specialem, juxta tenorem diversarum litterarum tam vestræ
Excellentiæ, quam vestris Quatuor Membris Flandriæ
transmissarum, placeat providere, prout in casibus consimilibus ambassiatores Domini nostri Regis parati sunt
respondere, ac realiter satisfacere.

Eandem vestram Excellentiam custodiat Altissimus
feliciter et votive !

Scriptum Coventriæ,[2] secundo die mensis Novembris.

NICHOLAUS DE RYSSHETOUN,
Utriusque Juris Professor,
causarumque Sancti Palatii
Apostolici auditor, unus ambassiatorum pro parte Domini
nostri, Regis Angliæ et Franciæ
metuendissimi.

*Endorsement* :—" Illustri Principissæ, necnon præclaræ
ac magnæ nobilitatis et excellentiæ
Dominæ, Dominæ Margaretæ, Ducissæ Burgundiæ, Comitissæ Flandriæ, Anthesii et Burgundiæ."

---

[1] Robert Mascall.

[2] *Coventriæ*] Corrected from Calisii.

A.D. 1404.

## CXLI.

AUGUSTIN, BISHOP OF ANSLOYE,[1] AND OTHERS, TO
HENRY IV.

Invictissime [Princeps] . . . . . .

Humillima nostri recommendatione vestræ regiæ
Majest[ati sig]nificamus nos continue, post jam proxime
præteritum festum Sancti Michaelis,[2] [transire versus
Angli]am paratos, opportuni venti gratiam, quæ nondum se [nobis] obtulit, expectasse.

Præterea ad vestræ Celsitudinis notitiam tenore
præsentium [deducimus quatinus, si v]enti votivi nobis
arriserit opportunitas, omnem, fa[vent]e Altissimo, ap-
ponamus diligentiam quam possumus ad personas nostras
inclitissimæ M[ajestati vestræ quam] celerius præsentandum.

Si vero, propter hiemalis sævitiei inc[lem]entiam,
transitus noster pro præsenti versus Angliam præclusus
nobis[3] fuerit, ex tunc immediate [post futurum mensem
Febr]uarii, cum nobis de vento convenienti providerit
Altissimus, versus vestræ magnæ Dignationis Altitu-
dinem iter arripere sine dubio erimus præparati, pro
[omnium negotiorum vestræ] Serenitatis litteris invictissimo Domino nostro, Domino Erico, Dei gratia
regnorum Daciæ, Sweciæ, Norwegiæ, Slavorum Goto-
rumque Regi, et Duci Pomeraniæ novissime [directis
content]orum votivo complemento.

Præterea præclarissimæ vestræ regiæ Dignitati cordis ex intimo fore censuimus humillime supplicandum,

---

CXLI.] MS. Cotton. Nero, B. III.
fol. 28.—On paper; original, with
traces of the three seals alluded to at
the end of the letter. This letter
has been very much mutilated.

[1] Christiania.

[2] September 29.

[3] *nobis*] Added above the line.

quatinus eadem cum effectu considerare et . . . . . . A. D. 1404.
[dign]etur, ut in jam proximo futuro mense Maii, termino
videlicet per vestram regiam Magnitudinem limitato,
ipsa negotia præconcepta exsecutioni votivæ ve[litis]
mandari.

Altissimus regiam vestram Majestatem conservet,
suisque processibus semper faveat et assistat !

Scriptum, sub sigillis trium nostrorum, videlicet
Episcopi Asloensis, Turo[nis, Benedicti] Militis, et
Petri Lykka, Archidiaconi, immediate subscriptorum, in
villa forensi Junacopensi, Octavis Sancti Martini, videlicet mensis Novembris die decima octava.

Per nos,

AUGUSTINUM, permissione divina Episcopum
Asloensem,

TURONEM, Benedicti Militem ;

AUBERNUM, Præpositum Ecclesiæ XII. Apos-
tolorum Bergensis,

PETRUM LYKKA, Archidiaconum Rodskil-
densem,

ANDREAM Olavi . . . . . Slevonis,—Milites,
Vestræ regiæ Majestatis humiles servitores.


## CXLII.

PETER LUCKE TO HENRY IV.

Invictissime Princeps, regum præclarissime.

Humillima mei recommendatione, cum benevoli famulatus, ut teneor, promptitudine in Domino præmissa,
ad vestræ regiæ Majestatis notitiam tenore præsentium
deduco quod inclitissimus regnorum Daciæ, Sweciæ,
et Norwegiæ, Gottorum Slavorumque Rex, Ericus, de

CXLII.] MS. Cotton. Nero, B. III. fol. 29.—On paper ; original.

A.D. 1404. limitato per vestram Celsitudinem tempore pro transmissione nobilissimæ filiæ vestræ, Dominæ Philippæ, versus suam præsentiam gratanter contentatus; in nullo hæsitans de iis quæ sibi, non solum per vivæ vestræ vocis oraculum mihi factum, verum etiam per scripturæ seriem, vestra mandavit regia Dignitas aperiri.

Ordinatum est igitur de ambassiatoribus suis, versus vestræ Altitudinis præsentiam transituris, sic eis, largiente Domino, fiat quemadmodum tam in ipsius Regis, quam ambassiatorum prædictorum litteris, quas præsentium offert hac vice bajulus, lucide continetur.

Præterea, Princeps nobilissime, impetrata jure de tanta præscriptione mea vestræ regiæ Dignationis venia, eidem in quantum audeo fore [censuimus] humillime supplicandum, quatinus eadem effectualiter mandare dignetur quod antedictæ filiæ vestræ transitus versus amantissimum filium vestrum prædictum, Dominum Regem Ericum, in tempore per vestram Magnitudinem ad hoc statuto, gaudiose valeat, executioni demandari dignemini; etiam eidem filio vestro super præmisso cum latore præsentium, quanto citius fieri potest vestræ regalis Excellentiæ per litterarum continentiam exprimere voluntatem, ad finem quod eo amplioribus jocunditate et provisione in spe certa penitus ejus gaudiosum adventum valeat expectare. Ceterum, Principum metuendissime, aliqua quæ cartis mancipare non præsumo, præsentium porrectori, cui credere non dedignemini, viva voce commiseram, vestræ declaranda regiæ Majestati.

Quam in sospitate votiva manu teneat Benedictus et Gloriosus Ille per Quem reges regnant!

Scriptum in villa Junecopensi, sub sigillo nostro, mensis Novembris die xviij.

Per vestræ regiæ Celsitudinis humillimum
et devotum oratorem,
PETRUM LYKKE, Archidiaconum
Roskildensem.

## CXLIII.

### Eric X. to Henry IV.

*Invictissimo Principi, Henrico, Dei gratia Regi Angliæ et Domino Hiberniæ, fratri nostro, immo patri carissimo, Ericus, eadem gratia regnorum Daciæ, Sweciæ, et Norwegiæ, Slavorum Gothorumque Rex ac Dux Pomeranensis, salutem et inchoatæ dilectionis continuum in Christo Domino incrementum.*

Serenissime Princeps, pater carissime.

Pro amoris plenitudine gratuiti nobis per vestram regiam Celsitudinem, non paucis vicibus, et specialiter in novissime vestris nobis transmissis litteris exhibiti et ostensi, vobis admodum astrictos claro nos cernentes intuitu ad eas quas valemus gratiarum assurgimus actiones; jam dictæ vestræ Celsitudini significantes quod dilectus noster Petrus Lucke, Archidiaconus Roskildensis, impedientibus ipsum in reditu suo de Anglia tam in mari quam in terra guerrarum disturbiis, ac etiam ventorum contrariorum impulsibus, ad nostram præsentiam in regno Sweciæ antequam circa festum Assumptionis Beatæ Virginis,[1] cum litteris et responsione sibi per vestram regiam Magnificentiam traditis, non devenit. Quibus per nos læta manu receptis et sane intellectis, in nulloque a relatione sibi, ut asseruit, per vestram commissa regiam Majestatem discrepantibus, incontinenti pro ambassiatoribus nostris pro facto illo versus Angliam ituris fore mandavimus transmittendum; qui, certis de causis, in

---

CXLIII.] MS. Cotton. Nero, B. III.     [1] August 15.
fol. 27 (*a*).—On vellum; original.

A.D. 1404. nostris et trium regnorum nostrum negotiis hinc inde occupati, antequam circa festum Sancti Michaelis[1] immediate jam transactum convenire nullo modo potuerunt. Quibus in unum congregatis, pro viagioque suo paratis, accessum versus Angliam continue venti contrarietas eatenus ademerat.

Præterea, inclitissimæ vestræ regiæ Majestatis censuimus declarandum quod, si, favente Illo Cui venti obediunt et mare, ipsis nostris ambassiatoribus in brevi ad vota venti arriserit opportunitas, toto se apponant conamine ad vestram Celsitudinem visitandum.

Si vero ipsos arrestans induraverit brumalis sævitia, quanto citius post futurum mensem Februarii dissolvantur glacies, ad præsentandum se vestræ regiæ Magnitudini omnem quam poterint adhibebunt diligentiam pro inchoati inter nos utrimque negotii votivo complemento.

Nec hæsitamus, pater carissime, quin eisdem nostris ambaxiatoribus de salvo conductu pro vestris in mari et in terra, tam in exitu, quam in reditu suo versus nostram præsentiam, mandare velitis secure provideri. Ea propter, pater carissime, Sublimitati vestræ declaramus quod, quemadmodum nobis eadem, tam per litterarum vestrarum seriem, quam per vivæ vestræ vocis oraculi relationem, præfato Archidiacono [Roskildensi] mandastis, sic adventum filiæ vestræ carissimæ Dominæ Philippæ nobis, annuente Domino, in uxorem tradendæ, in jam proximo futuro mense Maii, gratanti animo perscolari velimus. Hinc est quod prælibatam vestram Celsitudinem summa exoramus instantia quatinus eadem cum effectuali exsecutione sic disponere dignetur ut antedicta vestra filia ad nostram præsentiam, in proximo futuro mense Maii, nobis in litteris vestris assignato, transmittatur, nec

---

[1] September 29.

dilationem ulteriorem, pater carissime, interponere A.D. 1404. velitis, quoniam ipsa, prout vestra excellens considerare novit industria, nec nobis nec regnis nostris hincinde quidque proficui poterit importare. In præmissis igitur disponere dignetur vestra regia Sagacitas, prout inde verisimiliter properari poterint honoris Dei accrescentia, regnorumque et amicorum nostrorum utrobique gloria, robur, et lætitia singularis.

Et quamvis nonnulli sunt partis utriusque æmuli, quibus hujusmodi facti complementum summe displiceret, oppositumque placeret, nihilominus tamen in Domino sperandum est quod neuter nostrum hujusmodi invidis æmulisque latentibus mentem sic apponat, quod ipsorum sinistra desideria sui et regnorum suorum profectibus anteponat.

Et quia pro præsenti prædictum Archidiaconum, vestræ Gratiæ dirigi consuetum, non transmittimus, ex eo est quod ipsum in aliorum nostrorum ambaxiatorum comitiva vestræ Dilectioni dirigere proponimus, Altissimo largiente. Nec prætereundum nobis est silentio, pater carissime, quanta benevolentiæ munificentiæque gratia eundem singulis vicibus quibus in Anglia fuerat vestra respexit regia Magnificentia; cui et merito nos exinde ad condigna gratiarum rependia decernimus obligatos; corde ex intimo exorantes Altissimum ut statum vestrum regnorumque vestrorum propere de bono in melius augeat et exaltet.

Datum in villa nostra Junecopensi, Octava Beati Martini, videlicet mensis Novembris die xviijᵃ, nostro sub secreto.

A.D. 1404.

## CXLIV.

### ERIC X. TO HENRY IV.

*Invictissimo Principi Henrico, Dei gratia Regi Angliæ, et Domino Hiberniæ, fratri nostro, immo patri carissimo, Ericus, [eadem gratia regnorum Daciæ, Sweciæ,] Norwegiæ, Slavorum Gothorumque Rex, et Dux Pomeraniæ, salutem et [prosperos] ad vota successus.*

Carissime Princeps, pater carissime.

Vestræ paternæ Celsitudini censuimus declarandum, quod præsentium exhibitores, burgenses nostri de Aleburgh, Olavus Swevonis, et Albertus Neghler, coram Nobis exponi fecerant quod bonis suis in mari per vestros privati sunt.

Præterea vestram paternam et regiam Majestatem instantius exoratam habemus, quatinus mandare dignemini quod, si sic sit, eidem mercatores nostri per gratiæ vestræ adminiculum, ad sibi ablatorum restitutionem admittantur, quod grata vicissitudine remereri cupimus, Altissimo largiente, ad gratiarum condignas actiones pro generoso juvamine mercatori nostro de Ripis aliquando, in restitutione vini et aliorum sibi ablatorum per vestros facta, eidem vestræ regiæ Magnificentiæ et paternæ dilectioni cordis ex intimis assurgentes.

Pater carissime, Altissimum exoramus ut statum vestrum regnorumque vestrorum propere de bono in melius augeat et exaltet.

---

CXLIV.] MS. Cotton. Nero, B. III. fol. 27 (β). — On paper; original, with the remains of a seal.

Datum in villa nostra Junecopensi, Anno Domini A.D. 1404.
MCD. quarto, quarta feria ante festum Beati Cle-
mentis, videlicet mensis Novembris die xix$^a$, nostro
sub secreto.


## CXLV.

THE ARCHBISHOP OF CANTERBURY TO HENRY IV.

Christianissime Princeps et metuendissime Domine. On the
Excellentiæ vestræ litteras jampridem recepi, inter raising of a
subsidy.
cetera continentes, nihil fuisse in ultima prælatorum
et cleri Convocatione effectualiter factum de subsidio
concedendo per capellanos stipendiarios provinciæ Cantuariensis. Verumtamen, testante veritate ac Deo, Qui
est Summa Veritas, Scrutator cordium, et Cognitor
secretorum, feci omnem diligentiam meam in præmissis.
Testibus insuper venerabili fratre meo, Episcopo Lin-
colnensi,[1] ac honorabili viro Comite Somersetiæ,[2] qui
procuratores cleri ad quos pertinebat concessio, fuerant
mediis quibus sciverant allocuti ; necnon et Clerico Rotulorum, qui cum eisdem procuratoribus primo, secundo,
et tertio allocutis interfuit. Iidem procuratores, non obstantibus mediis antedictis et diligentia mea qualicumque,
quotiens fuit petitum, unanimiter contradixerunt penitus
et expresse. Unde nulla via mihi, aut confratribus
meis, superesse videbatur ; prout nec adhuc videtur
saltem per viam Convocationis, qua mediante materia
ipsius subsidii poterit expediri ; præsertim quia de modo
convocandi hujusmodi capellanos nullam viam invenio
hactenus practizatam.

---

CXLV.] MS. Cotton. Cleop. | [1] Henry Beaufort.
E. 11. fol. 252.—On paper. | [2] John Beaufort.

A.D. 1404. Sane, metuendissime Princeps, consideratis præmissis posset vestræ Serenitatis voluntas una cum motivis ad hoc allectivis locorum diœcesanis exprimi et transmitti, sic videlicet quod ipsi diœcesani eosdem capellanos ad subsidium hujusmodi inducerent viis et mediis opportunis. Et, serenissime Princeps, si ipsa via vobis et Concilio vestro videatur expediens ad omnia facienda quæ ad me et diœcesim Cantuariensem pertinere noscuntur, receptis ad hoc mandatis vestris, habebitis me paratum in omnibus, sicut teneor juxta votum.

Insuper, excellentissime Princeps, quia omnia cor meum moventia scripti serie de facili non poterunt explicari, Magistrum Willelmum Milton, unum de clericis meis, Serenitati vestræ satis notum, cui in hac parte fidem si libeat adhibere velitis, transmitto possibiliter informatum.

Celsitudinem vestram regiam, ad ecclesiæ et regni felix regimen et tutamen, diu et feliciter conservet Altissimus, et dirigat in agendis !

Scriptum in manerio meo de Maydeston vij$^{mo}$ die Decembris.

Humilis vestræ Celsitudinis Capellanus et Orator,

T., Cantuariensis Archiepiscopus.[1]

---

[1] Thomas Fitz Alan.

A.D. 1404.

## CXLVI.

### To Pope Innocent VII.

Post devota pedum oscula beatorum, clementissime Pater, etsi jampridem Ecclesia Londoniensi vacante, vestræ Serenitati cordis intimo [1] scripserim pro venerabili et discreto viro, Roberto Hallum,[2] Legum Doctore, ac Cancellario Universitatis Oxoniæ, meo Clerico prædilecto, quatinus ut eundem ad dictam Ecclesiam promovere dignetur, non credens nec habens in mente protunc quod metuendissimus Dominus meus Rex pro aliquo de clericis suis eidem Serenitati vestræ scribere voluisset ; quia tamen citra percepi quod idem Dominus meus Rex personam carissimi Clerici sui, Thomæ Longley, Custodis sui privati sigilli, jamdictæ Sanctitatis gratiæ recommendare curavit ad præfatam Ecclesiam exaltandam ;—attendens quam sinceris ejus promotio regiis votis inhæreat, nedum propter ipsius diuturnum obsequium clarissimo genitori suo Lancastriæ, præfatoque Regi Domino meo, necnon et regno suo fideliter exhibitum hactenus et impensum, verum etiam propter virtutum suarum merita, vitæ sanctitatem, et conversationem honestam ejusdem ; super quibus idem Dominus, meus Rex, Apostolicæ Sedis clementiam clarius informavit : attendens quoque præterea quam accepta [3] erit ejus promotio singulis statibus hujus regni, et specialiter subditis civitatis et diœcesis Londoniensis sicut meis præcordiis ad-

*On the appointment to the vacant see of London.*

CXLVI.] MS. Cotton. Cleop. E. ii. fol. 249.—On paper.

[1] *cordis intimo*] Altered from " cum omni affectione."

[2] Bishop of Salisbury, 1408–1417.

[3] *accepta*] Originally written " accepta ipsum."

A.D. 1404. modum incunctanter habetur, eidem Serenitati vestræ humillimo supplicamus affectu quatinus, litteris meis jamdictæ Sanctitati directis nequaquam obstantibus, ipsum Thomam amicum meum sincere dilectum, etiam contemplatione regia necnon et intentu præmissorum, quibuscumque aliis in promissione hujus præferat Apostolicæ gratiæ plenitudo.

Si vero, beatissime Pater, in hoc vota regia compleantur, ut cupio, sperarem eo propensius aliunde circa condignam ipsius Clerici mei promotionem, cum consensus regalis applausu, desiderii mei fines attingere, opportunitate temporis arridente.

Beatissime Pater, almam personam vestram in prosperitate votiva conservet Altissimus ad [1] Ecclesiæ Suæ regimen salutare.

Scriptum [2] . . .

---

[1] Originally written "ad tutum regimen," &c.

[2] This Letter was written between the 28th of August 1404, when Robert de Braybrooke died, and the 20th of October in the same year, when Longley was elected. The Pope, however, refused to confirm this election, and gave the vacant see to Roger Walden, 10 Dec. 1404.—Godwin, i. 186.

# APPENDIX.

# APPENDIX I.

The following Letters are printed separately because it was found impossible to assign them to any particular year with sufficient certainty. They belong, however, to the beginning of Henry the Fourth's reign, and have been not inaptly termed by Sir Henry Ellis " Specimens of Henry the Fourth's Eastern Correspondence." [1] All are original draughts, and written upon vellum.

One only has been printed hitherto (Ellis, 3rd ser., i. 56). The others are thus described:—

(1) CXLVII.—To the Emperor of Abyssinia "extolling his intention of assisting to rescue the Holy Sepulchre from the hands of the Infidels. It mentions the wish which Henry himself had long entertained, and still encouraged, to visit the Holy Land. It also recommends to the Emperor's kindness, John Archbishop of the East and of Æthiopia." [2]

---

[1] See Original Letters (Third Series), i. 54–58.

[2] " Wadding informs us, that he was an Englishman, a Minorite or Friar Preacher, of the name of John Greenlaw. John, the second of the name, was made Archbishop of Sultania by Pope Boniface, 20 October, 1400 . . . Sultania or Soldania was a fortified city of Armenia, under the dominion of the Turks, anciently known by the name of Tigranocerta. It was erected into an archiepiscopal see by Pope John XXII. in the year 1318." Ellis, p. 55.

(2) [Printed by Ellis]. To Timur Beg.[1]

(3) CXLVIII.—To the King of Cyprus and Armenia, "complimental and seeking intercourse."

(4) CXLIX.—To Michele Steno, Doge of Venice. "In both these Archbishop John is mentioned" with recommendation.[2]

(5) CL.—To Mirassa Amirassa, "that is, to Mirza Mirân Schab, the third son of Timur, thanking him for the kindness as well as for the security which he had afforded to Catholics, and especially to Christian merchants, both as to their persons and their dealings."[3]

---

[1] Acceding "to an offer which Timur had made through Archbishop John of a free commercial intercourse between the subjects of Timur and Henry. It at the same time congratulates Timur upon his victory over Bajazet, which took place in 1402. L'an 804 de l'H., le 29 de Dzoulcaada (30 Juin 1402 de J. C.), suivant les Historiens Arabes; le 28 Juillet 1402, suivant les Grecs, il gagne près d'Angouri, ou Ancyre, sur Bajazet 1., Empereur Ottoman, une célebre bataille, où ce dernier est fait prisonnier avec son fils Musa" (L'Art de Verifier les Dates, i. 493; Gibbon, vi. 349). It would seem that this Letter was written early in 1403.

[2] See Ellis, p. 54.

[3] There is also a sixth document, being "a letter of general recommendation for this Archbishop John, given under the Privy Seal." It is printed by Ellis, page 55, note (b).

## CXLVII.

HENRY IV. TO THE EMPEROR OF ABYSSINIA.

*Henricus, Dei gratia Rex Angliæ et Franciæ, et Dominus Hiberniæ, magnifico et potenti Principi, Regi Abassiæ, sive Presbytero Johanni, amico nostro in Christo dilecto, salutem in omnium Salvatore.*

Magnifice Princeps, amice in Christo dilecte.

Talia nobis nova de vestra Majestate jampridem nunciata fuere, quæ menti nostræ perimmensum gaudium attulerunt, et [præcipue] cum honorem Dei necnon utilitatem Ecclesiæ concernant, et proficuum animarum. Et utinam ipsa nova fuerint pro consolatione Fidelium latius expressata

Nunciatum est namque nobis per venerabilem in Christo Patrem, Johannem, Archiepiscopum Orientis ac Æthiopiæ per Sedem Apostolicam, Petri videlicet, ordinatum, necnon et per alios fidedignos qualiter ex devoto benevolo ac singulari zelo, Dominum nostrum Jesum Christum, Fidemque Catholicam, et Fideles, necnon et sacrosanctam et immaculatam Ecclesiam Beatorum Petri et Pauli, scilicet Ecclesiam Romanam, vestra Magnificentia persequitur gratiose ; et quantam gerit affectionem ipsa Sublimitas circa Sepulchrum Dominicum ab hostili potentia redimendum. Unde revera, magnifice Princeps, gaudemus in Domino, et gratias agimus Jesu Christo, Qui de fideli devotione

CXLVII.] MS. Cotton. Nero, B. xi. fol. 172. — On vellum ; an original draught.

tanti Principis et suorum, ut speramus, Suam dignatus est Ecclesiam ampliare; Ipsumque suppliciter exoramus ut quod incepit in vobis Ipse perficiat, ut caritas vestra magis ac magis abundet in Domino Jesu Christo.[1]

Et scire velitis, magnifice Princeps, quod ob honorem et reverentiam Crucifixi, necnon et devotionem specialem quam ad Suum Sepulchrum a diu gessimus et gerimus, ut tenemur, Illud jamdudum in persona nostra duximus visitandum quod etiam iterato proponimus, vita comite per Dei gratiam, ad impendendum Sibi servitium, personaliter visitare, velut præfatus Archiepiscopus de intentione nostra in hac parte, necnon de affectione quam erga Majestatem vestram gerimus et habemus, experienter instructus, per quem de statu vestro prospero speramus imposterum effici certiores, vestræ Celsitudini noverit lucidius explicare; cui velitis in suis ex parte nostra dicendis sedulam[2] dare fidem, ipsumque tanquam fortem Ecclesiæ pugilem et pastorem, vobis ut asserit multipliciter obligatum, qui pro visitanda Majestate vestra ad ejusdem præsentiam jam decedit, suscipere velitis nostræ considerationis intuitu recommissum; significantes nobis, si placeat, in quibus vestræ Dilectioni poterimus complacentiam exhibere.

Dies vobis adaugeat in prosperitate fecundos ad Sui Nominis gloriam et honoris, Qui pro nobis de sacratissima Virgine dignanter voluit incarnari.

Datum, etc.

---

[1] Philippians, i. 6.          |          [2] Cedulam, MS.

## CXLVIII.

### HENRY IV. TO THE KING OF CYPRUS AND ARMENIA.

*Serenissimo Principi, Cipri, Jerusalem, et Armeniæ
Regi, fratri nostro carissimo, Henricus, Dei gratia
Rex Angliæ et Franciæ, ac Dominus Hiberniæ, salutem
et fraternæ dilectionis continuum incrementum.*

Serenissime Princeps, frater carissime.

Habentes in votis de Serenitatis vestræ statu
prospero frequenter suscipere grata nova, ipsam Serenitatem vestram petimus ex affectu quatinus nos
superinde quotiens opportunitas nunciorum affuerit
velitis reddere certiores. Et quia tenemus indubie
quod nova de nobis audire consimilia corditer affec-
tatis, scire velitis nos in emissione præsentium congrua sanitate potiri regratiato salutis Auctore; quod
etiam de vobis utinam sæpius audiamus!

Serenissime Princeps, frater carissime, attendentes
qualiter prædecessores vestri, longis a retro temporibus,
pro roboratione Fidei orthodoxæ Sedi Apostolicæ
subsidium procurando gratanter adversus Crucis hostes
non modicum profuerunt, Serenitatem vestram petimus
et hortamur in Domino, quatinus, dictorum prædecessorum vestrorum pia gesta continue recordantes,
vosmet eisdem velitis quantum ad Fidei dilatationem
attinet, conformare, sanoque si placet consilio . . . . .
majoribus Armenorum necnon Patriarchia seu Catho-
licen ipsorum prope vestram Majestatem degentibus
ut cum venerabili in Christo Patre Archiepiscopo
Orientis velint pro bono pacis et unitatis Fidei
Catholicæ convenire. Et revera, serenissime Princeps,

---

CXLVIII.] MS. Cotton. Nero, B. xi., fol. 173. — On vellum; a
contemporaneous draught.

non ambigimus vestris in ea parte diligentiis adhibitis posse succedere plura bona.

Vestram præterea, serenissime Princeps, dilectionem affectuose rogamus, quatinus venerabilem in Christo Patrem etc. (ut infra in littera Duci Venetiarum directa).

## CXLIX.

The following is a copy of the letter referred to above :

HENRY IV. TO MICHELE STENO, DOGE OF VENICE.

*Henricus, etc., nobili et potenti Principi, Michaeli Steno, Duce Venetiarum, amico nostro carissimo, salutem et sinceræ dilectionis argumentum.*

De statu (ut supra, et tunc sic) :—

Amicitiam vestram, nobilis Princeps, affectuose rogamus quatinus venerabilem in Christo Patrem Johannem Archiepiscopum Orientis, amicum nostrum sincere dilectum, qui pro bono pacis et augmentatione Fidei seipsum jam a diu non nullis laboribus laudabiliter exponebat, ad partes vestras inpræsentiarum, ut asserit, accessurum, suscipere velitis, cum servitoribus et subditis suis omnibus, tum propter reverentiam Altissimi, tum nostræ considerationis obtentu, specialissime recollectum.

Quicquid autem Amicitia vestra humanitatis aut favoris impendet eidem nobis reputabimus fore factum, vobis ea propter grata vicissitudine responsuri.

Nobilis et potens Princeps, amice carissime, utinam vobis adveniant salutis et votivorum successuum incrementa !

Datum ——.

Item, scribatur Imperatori Trapisundarum, et Regi Gurganiæ, prout Imperatori Constantinopolitano, usque

ad hæc verba "*corditer exorantes*" inclusive ; et tunc sic, "*serenissime Princeps, frater carissime. Qualiter ex devoto benevolo ac singulari zelo Dominum Nostrum Jesum Christum, &c.*," ut in littera Regi Abassiæ directa.

## CL.

### HENRY IV. TO MIRASSA AMIRASSA, SON OF TIMUR.

*Henricus, Dei gratia, etc., magnifico et potenti Principi, Domino Mirassa Amirassa, filio Themurbey, amico nostro in Deo dilecto, salutem in omnium Salvatore.*

Magnifice Princeps, amice in Deo dilecte.

Non tam diversarum serie litterarum, quam relatu venerabilis in Christo Patris, Johannis, Archiepiscopi Orientis, pleno collegimus intellectu quam favorabiliter et benigne, quantisque favoris et dilectionis indiciis, populum Catholicum, nobis in Unitate Fidei cohærentem, et præsertim viros religiosos et Catholicos Francos, indies pertractatis, omnem eis humanitatis gratiam procurando, necnon mercatoribus Christianis securitatem, in personis et rebus, atque lucrorum beneficia tribuendo ; unde Seipsum vobis conferat in mercedem Qui bonorum est omnium Retributor ; Cui gratiarum actiones devote referimus quod tantum Principem Religionis Catholicæ zelatorem dignatus est in Orientalis plagæ partibus dominari. Vestræ Magnificentiæ superinde præterea regratiantes ex intimo cordis nostri ipsum affectuose rogando quatinus ob reverentiam et honorem[1]

*Thanking him for his support of the Christians in the East.*

---

CL.] MS. Cotton. Nero, B. xi. fol. 175 (*a*). — On vellum ; an original draught.

[1] *et honorem*] Added above the line.

Altissimi de tam pio tamque devoto ac felici proposito vestra jam dicta Magnificentia non desistat.

Speramus etenim quod Qui incepit hoc ipsum in vobis Ipse perficiet, ut caritas vestra magis ac magis crescat in Domino Deo nostro.

Ceterum, magnifice Princeps, amice in Christo dilecte, quantum ad illud quod vestra Majestas sui gratia, prout refertur, habet in votis nobiscum, ad honorem Dei, de quibusdam negotiis, rempublicam et statum pacificum hincinde concernentibus, amicabilem inire tractatum, scire velit ipsa Majestas quod eundem tractatum fieri vobiscum, vice et nomine nostris, per dictum Archiepiscopum desiderabiliter affectamus, velut idem Archiepiscopus, nedum de nostro in ea parte beneplacito, verum etiam de modo et gestis nostris circa Divinum Cultum, et alia experienter instructus, vestræ Majestati referare noverit viva voce. Cui velitis in dicendis fidem credulam adhibere, ipsamque nostræ considerationis intuitu propter honorificam personæ suæ gesturam, necnon et omnes ipsius subditos, atque paucos specialiter suscipere recommissos, nobis cum fiducia rescribentes si qua voluerit vestra Dilectio nos facturos.

Et utinam, magnifice Princeps, amice in Deo dilecte, personam vestram semper incolumem ad Ipsius exaltationem Nominis et honoris conservet Filius Virginis gloriosæ.

Datum Hertfordiæ, mensis Februarii . . .

## CLI.

### HENRY IV. TO THE EMPEROR MANUEL II.

*Serenissimo Principi, Manueli, in Christo Deo fideli, Imperatori Romæorum Palæologo semper Augusto, fratri nostro carissimo, Henricus, etc., salutem et sinceræ dilectionis perpetuam fraternitatem.*

Serenissime Princeps, frater carissime.

Ex quorundam fidedigno relatu concepimus qualiter nostros confideles et Catholicos, in partibus vestris degentes, vestræ Serenitatis clementia continua pietate prosequitur et favore, licet, quod dolenter referimus, aliqui Græci, et quasi majores qui dicuntur spirituales, nitantur pro viribus ex adverso nostros concatholicos, et præsertim prædicatores Veritatis, in scandalis et tribulationibus multipliciter molestare.

Pro quo vestram non ambigimus Excellentiam in conspectu Altissimi non modicum promereri, nosque proinde tantæ Dignationi referimus intima gratiarum, ipsam de continuatione felici corditer exorantes.

Serenissime Princeps, carissime frater, habentes in confidentia magna quod amicos et benevolos nostros vestra Celsitudo benigne recipiet, et internæ recommendationis brachiis amplexari curabit, utpote vestris cupimus impertiri, Serenitatem vestram affectuose rogamus quatinus venerabilem in Christo Patrem, Johannem, Archiepiscopum Soltamenensem seu Orientis, amicum nostrum sincere dilectum, qui pro bono pacis et augmentatione Fidei, sese multis laboribus, uti nostis

---

CLI.] MS. Cotton. Nero, B. XI. fol. 175 (β). — On vellum : an original draught.

ut credimus, laudabiliter exponebat, a diu, pro certis negotiis statum suum et honorem tangentibus, ad Majestatis vestræ præsentiam accessurum, suscipere dignetur ipsa Majestas, una cum suis omnibus nostræ considerationis intuitu specialissime recollectum.

Quicquid autem humanitatis aut favoris jam dicta Majestas impendet eidem nobis reputavimus fore factum, volentes ea propter vestræ Celsitudini grata vicissitudine respondere.

Serenissime Princeps,[1] &c.

---

[1] *Serenissime Princeps*] These words, and (after them) the words "grata vicissitudine respondere," have been accidentally repeated in the MS.

# APPENDIX II.

The following Letter, dated "1404?" in the Catalogue, and apparently belonging to that year, was written in 1403. See the Preface.

## CLII.

### DE RYSSHETON TO THE LORD PRIVY SEAL.

Reverendissime Domine mi, ac consanguiniter confidentissime.

Votiva ac humillima recommendatione præmissa, vestræ Reverentiæ tenore præsentium manifesto qualiter, vicesimo nono diemensis Novembris, quatuor deputati pro parte Quatuor Membrorum Flandriæ, in villa Calisii nobiscum convenerunt, et certas litteras credentiæ ex parte dictorum Quatuor Membrorum nobis præsentarunt, ac ipsorum credentiam nobis declararunt, quod ipsi, ac ambassiatores Domini ipsorum Ducis Burgundiæ, parati erant in tractatu nobiscum convenire

CLII.] MS. Cotton. Galba, B. I., fol. 103.—On paper.

et personaliter interesse, dum tamen locum indifferentem, prout apud Lulyngham, seu alium, velimus eligere ac eidem consentire: non tamen in villa Calisii.

Quibus per nos extitit responsum, considerato quod ambassiatores dictorum Quatuor Membrorum, juxta tenorem appunctuamentorum factorum apud Westmonasterium et apud Calisium, pro tractatu villam Calisii elegerunt, ac tractatum inibi continuarunt, et sic hujusmodi locum variare non possunt.

Item, quia nullum est dare æqualitatem quam ipsi prætendunt quantum ad locum indifferentem, quia inter regnum et comitatum.

Item, ut parcatur laboribus et expensis, villa Calisii est aptior utrique parti quam villa de Lulyngham, prout apparet clare cuilibet intuenti.

Item, Dux Burgundiæ venit ad istum tractatum tanquam tertia persona pro jure et interesse suo; ideo locum judicii in villa Calisii electum non poterit variare.

Et præsertim nos commissarii Domini nostri Regis juxta ipsius instructionem regiam aliter loco non poterimus consentire.

Unde quamvis petitio dictorum deputatorum Flandriæ nulla fuerit subnixa ratione seu colore, consideratis tamen guerris diversarum partium quæ patulant adversus Dominum Regem et ipsius regnum, et quod Flandria est adeo propinqua regno Angliæ, per quam et ad quam omnes mercatores faciunt introitus et exitus suos, præsertim pro lanis nostris emendis; et quod hujusmodi tractatus inter Angliam et Flandriam aliquando solet fieri extra Calisium, juxta Castrum de Mark, prout a senioribus villæ Calisii didicimus et veraciter informamur, deceret, salvo vestro saniori judicio et determinatione, propter bonum publicum et ad pacis conservationem, quod nuncii utriusque partis poterunt locum indifferentem eligere prout utrique parti videbitur expedire.

Ex super præmissis dignemini cum regia Majestate conferre ac consulere, et cum omni celeritate ipsius voluntatem ac vestram nobis rescribere, qualiter in præmissis debeamus procedere et istam materiam dirigere.

Item, quantum ad ambassiatores Franciæ, eisdem ante vicesimum diem Novembris, et sic ante terminum statutum, litteras nostras diversas eis direximus, notificando eis adventum nostrum, et quod sumus parati termino satisfacere. Et copiam commissionis et potestatis nostræ in eisdem interclusimus de quibus hactenus nullum responsum reportavimus, nec reportare speramus, quia via versus Gravelyng, ac etiam versus Sanctum Audomarum, et versus partes Boloniæ, de mandato Regis Francorum est obstructa, ac proclamatum publice quod Gallici cum Anglicis in mercimoniis de cetero non debent communicare.

Vestram Reverentiam et Dominationem dirigat Altissimus feliciter in longævum!

Scriptum Calisii, primo die Decembris.

Vester consanguineus ac clericus humillimus,

NICHOLAUS DE RYSSHETOUN, etc.

*Endorsed :*—" Venerabili ac sapientiæ magnæ viro Domino Johanni Langley, Clerico privati sigilli, Domino suo ac consanguineo singularissimo."

*Also :*—" Littera ambassiatorum Angliæ, missa Custodi privati sigilli super instructione de novo eis transmittenda."

# APPENDIX III.

The following Letter is assigned in the Catalogue to the year 1405, but it is more probable that it was written in the preceding year, and nearly at the same time as the Letter (No. CIX.) from Christine, Countess of March. By an accident the evidence in proof of this was not discovered till the sheet in which it should have appeared was printed. It stands, however, in its proper place in the Chronological Catalogue. Henry was at Lichfield on the 23rd of August 1404,[1] and as late as the 29th.[2] The minutes of the Council which was held there on the 29th are printed in Nicholas i. 233.

## CLIII.

### THE EARL OF MARCH TO HENRY IV.

Mon tresexcellent et tresredoute soveraigne Seignour.

Jeo me recomand a trespuissant Magestie royall de trestout la humblesse de mon cuer.

### [TRANSLATION.]

My most excellent and most dread sovereign Lord.—I commend me to your most mighty royal Majesty, and with all

---

[1] See Rymer, viii. 369.
[2] Ibid. p. 370.

CLIII.] MS Cotton. Vespas. F. VII. fol. 108 (β).—On paper; original, with traces of a seal.

A la quel please assavoyr que j'ay entendue vostre honourablesse lettres, a moy darrayn mandez par mon Esquier, Robert de Westrun, ou vous distezi que pour autres treschargeantes bosoingnes que vous surviendrent de temps en temps vous l'avez mis en suspens jusques a l'assemble de vostre grand Conseil, que sera a vostre cite de Lichefeld [1] ; a quel temps vous ferez ainsi devers moy que jeo me tendra Dieu devant pour bien content. Et quant jeo viendra devers vous jeo⁻ sera tresbien venu.

Mais, mon tresredoute Seignour, ne vous desplease de ceo que jeo ne puys venier a vostre honourable presence, pur tiel cause que mon avantdist Esquier a vostre treshaut Mageste ad monstre, de quel jeo suy dolorous et pensyve ; Car jeo say bien q'est grand damage a moy mesmes.

Et, mon tresredoute Seignour, please a vostre treshaut

humbleness of heart. Whereupon may it please you to know that I have considered your honourable Letter recently sent to me by my Esquire, Robert de Westrun, in which you said that on account of other most important business, which will come upon you from time to time, you have put it off until the assembling of your Grand Council, which will be at your city of Lichfield ; at which time you will do so towards me that I shall hold myself before God well content. And, when I shall come to you, I shall be very welcome. — But, my most dread Lord, let it not displease you herein that I cannot come to your honourable presence, for the reason which my aforesaid Esquire hath shown to your most high Majesty ; on which account I am full of grief and sorrow ; for well I know that it is a great loss to myself.—And, my most dread Lord, may it

---

[1] See Nicolas i. 233.

E E

Magestee d'entendre que voz Tresorers de la guerre ditent que vostre honourable garraunt, a eux derect, n'est pas bon suffisaunt, a cause q'il dust aver estee fait desouth le noun de Monsieur Johan, Gardein des Marches d'Escoce[1]; le quel please a vostre treshaut Magestee de commander le Pryve Seal de amendier cest perol, et bailler au portour d'icestz. Et pur tiel cause jeo suy non servyer de touz partiez. Et sur ceo j'ay paroferte mez terres et mez jowell pour mutier en gages pour venier a vostre presence; mais jeo ne puise acquerer un dener pour venier a vostre honourable presence come ore.

Mon tresexcellent et tresredoute soveraigne Seignour, la Benoit Trinitee vous eyt en Sa seintisme garde corps et alme, come vostre tres gentiel cuer saveray meilz penser ou aviser.

---

please your most high . Majesty to understand that your Treasurers of the War say that your honourable warrant, addressed to them, is not at all good and sufficient, by reason that it ought to have been drawn up under the name of Master John, Warden of the Marches of Scotland; the which may it please your most high Majesty to command the Privy Seal to amend in this particular, and to give to the bearer of these presents. And for such cause I am not served by any party. And thereupon I have offered my lands and my jewels to put in pawn, for to come to your presence; but I am not able to raise a single penny to come to your honourable presence as at this time.—My most excellent and most dread sovereign Lord, the Blessed Trinity have you in Its holy keeping, body and soul, as your most gentle heart will know best to

---

[1] See Rymer VIII. p. 370.

Escript a Somertoun, le xviij$^{me}$ jour d'Augst.

Vostre humble servaud,

GEORGE DE DUNBARR.

*Endorsed* :—" A mon tresexcellent et tre[sredoubte Soveraigne] Seignour le Roy."

*Also* :—" Littera Comitis de Dunbarr."

---

think or to suggest.—Written at Somerton, the 18th day of August.

Your humble servant,

GEORGE DE DUNBAR.

*Endorsed*:—" To my most excellent and most dread sovereign Lord the King."

E E 2

# APPENDIX IV.

### LETTERS FROM

## MS. COTTON. CALIGULA, D. IV.

This Volume, containing a large collection of important Original Documents, has been unfortunately so injured by fire that it may almost be said to have been destroyed.

No attempt is made to describe its contents in the Cottonian Catalogue, where it is dismissed with the following brief notice :—

" Fragments of divers papers relating to the affairs of " the English dominions in France ; chiefly in French, " and of the time of Henry IV., King of England. This " MS. consisted originally of 150 leaves, of which only " 70 are now left, and these so much burned and " defaced as hardly to be of any use."

More recently these fragments have been carefully restored,— so far, indeed, as restoration was possible, —inlaid on drawing-paper, and re-bound.

Not one is perfect ; but several are sufficiently so to enable the reader to understand their general purport ; and one or two are only slightly injured. These have been carefully transcribed, and will be printed with all attainable accuracy. Two or three are comprised within the present Volume. The two which follow are sadly defaced.

They apparently belong to the year 1402, and have been reserved for the last sheet in the hope that some additional light might be thrown upon the mutilated portions, a hope which has to some extent been realised.[1]

The Translation of these Letters has been attended with considerable difficulty, and many passages are still obscure and unsatisfactory. A portion of the second Letter, where the fire has burned a large hole in the middle of the paper, is in so fragmentary a state that translation is impossible.[2]

It is certainly lamentable that so fine a collection of original documents should have met with such a fate, and a striking proof of the urgent necessity for committing to type those unique and invaluable monuments of our National History which yet remain to us.

---

[1] Some of the conjectural emendations may appear rather bold ; it is hoped, however, that all are conceived in the spirit of the original, and that they will serve the purpose for which they are intended, viz, to make the text, as far as may be, connected and readable. All of them are contained within brackets, by which the exact state of the remains of the MSS. themselves is clearly indicated.

[2] *See* p. 450.

## CLIV.

### The Archbishop of Bordeaux to Hen. IV.

Tresexcellent trespuissant Prince.

[Je me recommant humb]lement a vostre royal Mageste; a la quelle plaise savoir que jusques a heures [ces presentes tele est la] position de cest vostre pays tant comme ay compris et entendu de verite, et ausi [selon que j'ay ou]y [1] dire dez faitz du Conte de Foixs; et pense que mes lettres soyent pourtees sauvement [au Governeur de Bo]urdeux, au quel je les ay baillees, si m'a dit qu'il les a envoiees par personnes foyals [et capables] de escripre orez de novel especialment: quar Monsire Jehan de Bearn, Capitaine de Lorde [m'a darreinment] escriz aplen de present, selon qu'il m'a dit; et ausi bien le Sire de Duras,[2]

---

### [Translation.]

Most excellent, most mighty Prince.—I recommend myself humbly to your royal Majesty. To whom may it please to know that, up to this present time, such is the position of this your country, as I have understood and heard of a truth; and also according to what I have heard tell of the deeds of the Count de Foix; and I think that my letters were safely delivered to the governor of Bordeaux, to whom I have committed them, as he has told me that he had sent them by trusty persons and capable of writing present news especially. For Master John de Bearn, Governor of Lorde, lately wrote fully to me up to the present time, according as he promised me; and as

---

CLIV.] MS. Cotton. Caligula, D. iv. fol. 2.—On paper; original.
[1] See p. 441, line 6.

[2] Guallard Durefort.—See Rymer viii., 117, 136, 137, 371, 588.

vostre Seneschal d'[Aquitaine, yce]ste, a ce qu'il m'a dit un son Escuier enfourme ausi bien tout aplen. Toutesfoys une chose [est certaine, quant] rois commensent guerre primierement, que autre confourt n'estoit arrive part dessa eulx q'entre . . . . . . . . . . vostre pays; ou au meyns le destruyeront tiellement qu'il ne se pourra reparer d'un grant temps. [Tant qu'ils] onz prestz de povoir fere guerre, quar le Conte d'Arminihac,[1] a orez ensemble mil et $v^c$ homes. . . . . . de jour en autre, mil et $ii^c$ rossins d'autre part. Et a mandement du Conseil de France qu'il teigne . . . . . . . ite ceste gent; et ainsi le m'a notiffie huy le vostre foyal le Sire de Lescun.

Item, mon tresredoubte Seignour, pour ce que vostre dicte royal Mageste [scait] plus avant la disposition de voz subgis part dessa, je di deux choses.

La premiere est que aucuns si sont tant c . . . . es de vostre grande fame et renomee que ne se pensent

---

well the Lord of Duras, your Seneschal of Aquitaine, herein, as a certain Esquire of his told him also fully. Always one thing is certain, when Kings first commence war that other comfort comes not . . . . . . . . . . or, at least, they will destroy it in such a manner that it cannot be repaired under a very long time. (?) In such great haste are they to be able to make war, for the Count of Armagnac has now together one thousand four hundred men, augmenting from day to day, and, besides, one thousand two hundred horsemen from other parts. And he has order of the Council of France to hold in readiness this people ; and thus has your faithful Lord of Lescun just notified it to me.—Also, my most dread Lord, forasmuch as your said royal Majesty knows of long time the disposition of your subjects over here, I tell you of two matters.—The first is that some are so convinced of your great fame and reputation, that they do not

---

[1] Bernard VII.

que les Franceois ousent commenser guerre; et pour cela ont ilz f[aits p]etite proveison a leur defense ne du pays; et soubz ceste confiance pourront ilz recevoir grant domage et fera grant [domag]e.

L'autre chose est que aucuns, selon qu'il ma este repourte, disent que se eulx ne voyent vostre effors en cest pays ne [se m]eteront point a defense contre le grant povoir de France, quar ne seront autre chose forque leur destruction, atte[ndu] leur petit povoir. Et pour cela la vostre treshaulte discretion puet penser se icest vostre pays est en grant peril.

Item, retournanz au fait du Conte de Foixs, plaise a vostre [tresh]aute Seignourie savoir que piessa je l'escriz une lettre pour luy confourter, et ores je entendoye fere li savoir secretement le vostre gra[cieuse] bon vouloir envert luy, selon que vostre foyal Mestre Henry Bowet m'a notiffie par vostre Procureur Fiscal;

---

think that the French will dare to commence a war; and, on this account, they have made little provision for their own defence, or for that of the country. And, under this confidence, they may incur great damage, and will do themselves great damage.—The other matter is, that some, according to the report which has been made to me, say that if they do not themselves see your efforts in this country, they will not set themselves at all on the defensive against the great power of France; because nothing else will happen but their destruction, taking into consideration their little power. And on this account your most high discretion may consider whether this your country is in great peril.— Also, to return to the deed of the Count de Foix, may it please your most high Lordship to know, that long since I wrote a letter to comfort him, and now I intend to cause him to know secretly your gracious good-will towards him, according as your faithful Master Henry Bowet has notified to me by your procurator-fiscal, who arrived here two months (?)

le quel arriva issy ij [mo]is[1] a passes. Et pleust
a Dieu que je eust peut cecy notiffier au dit Conte
devant qu'il eust fait autre conclusion : quar je suy
enfourme que luy esteant a Paris se complenhoit
grandement de ce que ne avoit aucun confourt de
vostre dicte Seignourie. Mais orez je s[uy] enfourme
que de jour en autre il doit arriver a Boteville. Et
touz sez faitz sont passes ; mais je ne say pas si en
ainsi il comme plusiours disent ; mais que quil ait
fait, je vous suppli et recourde a bonne foy, comme
d'autres foys ay fait, que de cela monstres nulle
malenconie envert luy, quar le temps vous donrra
conseil et bon avis.

Item, tresexcellent trespuissant Prince, mon tresredoubte Seignour, j[e suy av]ise du dit Capitaine
de Lorde de deux choses.

La une est que aucuns de Cherborc font assavoir en

---

ago. And it pleased God that I should be able to notify this
to the said Count before that he had made another conclusion :
for I am informed that when he was at Paris he complained
greatly of this, that he had received no comfort from your said
Lordship. But now I am informed that from one day to
another he is expected to arrive at Boteville. And all his
proceedings are over ; but I do not know at all whether he is
as many say, but for that which he has done, I supplicate you
and bring to your remembrance in good faith, as I have done
on other occasions, that on this account you shew towards
him no angry feelings, for time will give you counsel and
good advice.—Also, most excellent, most mighty Prince, my
most dread Lord, I am advised by the Governor of Lorde
of two things.—The one is that some of those at Cherbourgh

---

[1] *mois*] The remaining letters ap-
pear to be " is." They may be " rs," | in which case the word was probably
" jours."

France tout l'estat don[t]¹ . . . . . . . . et pour cela plaise a vostre hautesse garder de qui vous confies.

L'autre chose est que les Franceois ont comence grand . . . . . . . . t le Roy de Navarre,² donant li entendre qu'ilz li restitueront toute sa terre : et plusiours li donnent conseil que pour cela j . . . . . . . . . . . . Pour quoy je vous suppli et recourde a bonne foy que vous ne perdes les amis pour tardite ne autre negligence, [selon] la doctrine d'icel Sage qui dist—

" Tolle moras, nam semper nocuit differre paratis."

Et, selon que j'ay ouy, [la longue] et tarde deliberation dez Englois leur a fait grant mal et domage et aleurs sequases ; pour [le quel doit se] tenir en cela autre maniere que les autres passes ne ont fait.

Item, mon tresredoubte Seignour, je me repute [bien et moult d'icelx] quelx je conoisse estre voz

---

have made known in France the whole estate . . . . . . . and on this account may it please your Highness to take care in whom you trust. — The other matter is, that the French have commenced great . . . . . . . . . . . . the King of Navarre, giving him to understand that they will restore to him all his land ; and many give him counsel that on this account . . . . . . . . Wherefore, I supplicate you and remind you in good faith, that you destroy not your friends through tardiness, or other negligence, according to the teaching of that Sage who saith "*Tolle moras, &c.*"—And, according to what I have heard, the long and late deliberation of the English has done them great harm and injury, and to the consequences thereof ; on which account they ought to be held in another manner than the past ones have been.—Also, my most dread Lord, I bethink me well and often of those

---

¹ *dont*] " don," so apparently in the MS. It may, however, possibly be " den," in which case the missing words are in all probability " d'Engleterre."

² Charles III., The Noble.

bons et foyals serviteurs. Et pour cela je notiffie
a vostre dicte tres[haute Seignourie] que le surdit
Capitaine de Lorde, pour le grant foyalte et affection
al hon[oure vostre Seignourie, merite bien p]our
icelle; et est home de bon a . . . ; . . . . . . . . . . .
. . . . . . . . . . . . . . . . . . . . . . . . . . . . . . . . . . . .
Conte de Foixs, il doit estre delivre de . . . . . . . .
. . . . . . . . . en quelle maniere; quar p[our y]cest
. . . . . . . . . . demourer en prison; comme Englois
que sal . . . . . . . . . . . . . . . . . . . pour la foyalte
d'Engleterre avoit sufferte la mort en prison. Si que
mon tresredoubte [Seignour, pleust avoi]r maniere
envert li qu'il et les autres cognoissent qu'il est en
vostre bonne grace.

Item, mon tresredoubte Seignour, j'ay escript a
vostre dicte [Seignourie] enfin et de novel, pour
cause je vous notiffie, qu'il est un vaillant et solemne
Docteur, et pour ce grant . . . . . en le voiage quil ha
fait a Paris avec le Conte, il li desplesoit fourt; nient-

---

who I know are your good and faithful servants. And on
this account I signify to your said most dread Lordship, that
the above-mentioned Governor of Lorde, for his great fidelity
and affection to your honoured Lordship, has deserved well for
the same ; and he is a man of good . . . . . . . . . . . . . . .
And as to the Count de Foix, he ought to be delivered from
. . . . . . . . . . . . . . in what manner, because for this
. . . . . . to remain in prison, as the English . . . . . . . . .
for his faithfulness to England have suffered death in prison
so, my most dread Lord, may it please you to shew such
manner towards him, that he and the others may know that
he is in your graces.—Also, my most dread Lord, I have
written to your said Lordship finally and anew, because I
notify to you that he is a brave and learned Doctor, and
for this great . . . . . . in the journey which he made to
Paris with the Count he displeased him greatly ; never-

moyens il ha ensuy n[ous enfourme que] Seignour Hughes le Despenser, et Meistre Henri Bowet,[1] fuerent de opinion qu'il allast. Et a la fin il est [certain que les f]aitz du dit Conte ne alloient einsi bien comme il vouloit se parti : et de cecy la vostre tres-haute Seignourie se puet enf[ourmer] . . . . . . . . . .
. . . . . . na li appelle Monsire Richard de Savoye, le quel est bon Englois, et, selon que je pense, touz diz fut d'une opinion au[thoritative des] choses qui touchoient la honoure vostre et de vostre coronne : si vous suppli et recourde a bonne foy qu'il vous plaise [faire commission a Mo]nseur Pelegrin, et charger luy de voz negocez que aurez a faire part dessa.

Item, je vous suppli pour l'estat et honnoure de vous et de [vostre royaulme, q'i]l vous plaise les em-baisseteurs de iceste vostre cite de Bourdeux delivrer senz autre delay, et bien gracieusement. [Nous prions

---

theless he has since informed us that the Lord Hugh le Despenser and Master Henry Bowet were of opinion that he should go. And at the last it is certain that the affairs of the said Count do not go so well as he would have them go : and of this your said Lordship may inform him-self . . . . . . . . . . called Master Richard de Savoye, who is a true Englishman, and, according as I think, has always been a man of authoritative opinion on the matters which concern the honour of yourself and of your crown. Therefore, I beseech you and remind you in good faith that it please you to give a commission to Master Pelegrin, and to charge him with your business which you have to transact in these parts. — Also, I beseech you, for the estate and honour of yourself and of your realm, that it may please you to deliver the Ambassadors from this your city of Bordeaux without any delay, and most graciously,—We pray

---

[1] Bishop of Bath ; *see* Letter CLV.

le] Trinite du Ciel ; et, tresexcellent trespuissant Prince, et mon tresredoubte Seignour, vous donne pour Sa grace treshonne v[ie a treslonge duree]. Amen !

Escript a Bourdeux, le xvij jour d'Avril.
Le vostre humble orateur de Dieu,

F., ARCEVESQUE DE BOURDEUX.[1]

*Endorsed* :—" A tresexcellent, trespuissant Prince et mon tresredoubte Seigneur, le Roy d'Engleterre et de France."

---

the Trinity of Heaven ; and, most exalted, most mighty Prince, and my most dread Lord, may He give you of His grace a very happy life very long to endure. Amen!—Written at Bordeaux, the 17th day of April.

Your humble suppliant of God,

FRANCIS, Archbishop of Bordeaux.

*Endorsed :*—" To the most excellent, most mighty Prince, and my most dread Lord, the King of England and France."

---

[1] Francis II., Archbishop of Bordeaux from A.D. 1389 to 1412.— *See* Rymer VIII. 223.

## CLV.

### John Morhay to the Bishop of Bath.

Treshonnoure Seigneur et tresreverent Pier.

[Treshumblement que je s]ay, ou pluis puis, je me recommant a vostre tresgracieu[se] Seigneurie. A la quelle plaise entendre que v[ous avez delivere] a le Duc d'Orlienx le Chastiel de Boteville, le quelle chose est trop greff et ennuyouse [a nostre Seigneur] le Roy. Et par voir, d'icelle dicte deleverance est doubte que le pluis graunt partie de le duche de Gu[ienne] . . . . . . . . . . . . . inte et perdue; c'est assavoir Bloye, Bourgh, et pluseurs autres bonnes lieux et villes a l'environ, s['il ne soit] aydie par nostre tressouverain Seigneur le Roy et son Conseil.

Et vuelles savoir que le Erchevesque de Bour[deux et les Seigne]urs et Barons de Guienne se doubtent

---

[Translation.]

Most honoured Lord, and most reverend Father.—With all the humility that I know, or at all am able, I commend myself to your most gracious Lordship. Whereupon may it please you to consider that you have delivered over to the Duke of Orleans the Castle of Boteville, the which thing is exceedingly grievous and injurious to our Lord the King. And in truth, of this said deliverance, there is fear lest the greater part of the Duchy of Guienne . . . . . . . . . . . and destroyed; that is to say, Blaye, Bourg, and several other important places and towns in the neighbourhood, unless it be assisted by our most sovereign Lord the King and his Council. —And be pleased to know that the Archbishop of Bordeaux, and the lords and barons of Guienne, are in very great fear,

---

CLV.] MS. Cotton. Caligula, D. IV., fol. 9.—On paper; original.

fortement si pluis hastif secours ne vient part de ca . . . . . . . . . autrez loiaulx nostre dit [subgis du] tressouverain Seignour le Roy, par cause et conseil de Counte de Foixs de la Seigneurie de . . . . . . . . d'Armaignac, et d'autres esteants de la partie Fraunceise, que ils serount tresgraundes destructions sur les ditz loia[ulx subgis du nostre tressouvera]in Seigneur le Roy. Quar expressement est dit que le dit Counte de Foixs ait fait serement de estre avecque le Roy [sur la foy des t]outz Christiantz vivants. Et aucuns evident et doubtent que le dit Counte de Foixs deliverera a la partie Fraunc[eise diverses ch]astieaulx, villes, et forteresses esteieantz en Boudalois ; yssint que gaires de chastieaulx, villes, et forteresses . . . . . . . . . . . . . . demeureround hors des mains de la partie Fraunceise, sinon tant seulement Bourdeux. Et un- quorres est doubte de yce[lle,] . . . . . . . . . seurs, burgeois, et autres habitants et demourantz en ycelle se dient l'un estre de l'ostiel de la Bret, (?) et l'autre du

---

if exceedingly speedy succours do not arrive . . . . . . . . . . . . . . . . . . . . other loyal subjects of our said most sovereign Lord the King, by the instigation and counsel of the Count de Foix, of the Lordship . . . . . . . . Armagnac, and of others who are on the side of France, that there will very great destructions come upon the loyal subjects of our most sovereign Lord the King. For it is expressly reported that the said Count de Foix has made oath to be with the King on the faith of all Christians living. And some persons there are who perceive and fear that the said Count de Foix will deliver over to the French party divers castles, towns, and fortresses situated in Bordelais ; so that but few of the castles, towns, and fortresses . . . . . will continue out of the possession of the French party, save only Bordeaux. And still there is fear concerning it . . . . . . . . . . . . burgesses, and others dwelling and sojourning therein, say . . . . . . . . . . . . . . . . . . . . and the other of the

. . . . . . . . . .  . . Et par tielles matieres en peut sordre grauntz tribulations et destructions de paix; et ce en special pour deffaute de v[itailles].[1]

Et vuelles savoir que les enfauntz du dit Counte de Foixs sount unquores en la garde du Seigneur de Rochefocaud, et auxi [le Roy] Fraunceois sera en breff deleverer a le dit Counte de Foixs castilli . . . . . de Peiregourgh.

Et vuelles savoir que estoit dit q[ue le] Counte de Foixs surdit voiroit avoir deleveres a le dit Roy Fraunceois un chastiel, nomme Chales, de le quelle un Esquier nomme .  . . . [Peyro]at est Capitaine; le quelle suisdit Peyroat ait recuilli et assemble dains le dit chastiel iiij$^{xx}$ bassinets ou pluis; [et auxi que le] dit chastiel est tresbien estouffe et garniz de vitailles, de engingnes graundes et petites debrides, de canons, et [beaucoup de] bonne artelerie.  Et le dit Peyroat dit

---

. . . . . . . . . .  And by reason of such matters there may arrive great tribulations and destructions of the country ; and that especially through the want of victuals.—And be pleased to know that the children of the said Count de Foix are still in the guardianship of the Lord of Rochefoucauld, and also the King of France will shortly deliver to the said Count de Foix the Castle . . . . of Perigueux.—And be pleased to know that it has been reported that the Count de Foix above-mentioned would have delivered up to the said King of France a castle called Chalus, of the which an Esquire named . . . . Peyroat is Warden ; the which above-mentioned Peyrout has collected together and assembled within the said castle eighty helmed men, or more ; and also that the said castle is stuffed and well supplied with victuals, with great and small engines, . . . . . , with cannons, and a great amount of good artillery.  And the said Peyroat has said expressly that the

---

[1] *vitailles*] " v," or, perhaps, " b," in which case the missing words may have been " bon conseil."

expressament que le dit chastiel de Chales ne sera ja rendus a le Roy Fraunceois [surdit], ne a sa partie.

Et, treshonnoure Seigneur et tresreverent Pere en Dieux, quant a ce que en vostre honnorable lettre, la quelle ores tard moy en . . . . [envoy]astes, feistes mention,—que le clerc de le ville de Bourdeux ait dit et depouse que, depuis son departir de Bourdeux, sont devales . . . . jusques a Bourdeux hors des lieux rebelles et ennemis de nostre dit tressouverain Seigneur le Roy, pluis que iij mille toneaux de vins; vuelles savoir que ce est tout au countraire, combien sera promie par devant vostre treshonnourable personne, et devant le Counseil de nostre tressouverain Seigneur le Roy, si bien en Engleterre comme en Guienne, si mestier soit ou vostre plaisir. De la quelle matiere Robbert Martin, [comptro]ulleour de la dicte disme a ce ordennes par nostre tressouverain Seignour le Roy, comme appiert par ses Patentes, vous enfourmera tout a plain. A le quelle Robert vous plaise donner foy et creance en ycelle partie.

---

said castle of Chalus shall not now be surrendered to the King of France above-mentioned, nor to his party.—And, most honoured Lord and most reverend Father in God, as to that of which in your honourable Letter, the which you have now recently sent unto me . . . . , you have made mention,—that the town-clerk of Bordeaux has asserted and deposed, that, since his departure from Bordeaux, there have arrived . . . . . as far as to Bordeaux, out of the places which are in rebellion and hostile to our said most sovereign Lord the King, more than three thousand tuns of wine ; be pleased to know that the fact is quite contrary, as shall be set forth in the presence of your most honourable person, and before the Council of our most sovereign Lord the King, as well in England as in Guienne, if it be necessary or your pleasure. Concerning the which matter, Robert Martin . . . . . . . of the said dîme, thereunto appointed by our most sovereign Lord the King, as appears by his Letters patent, will inform you with all fulness. To the which Robert may it please you to give faith

F F

Et vuelles savoir que le Regidour de Bourdeux, et les jurats, et autres counseilleurs de le dicte cite ount ordenne que toute manere de hommes demeurantz dains la dicte cite ferount serement sur le Corps de Dieux Sacre, que ils serount bons et loiaulx a le Roy, et a le couronne d'Engleterre, et a le citte le Bourdeux; mais l'intente d'icelle serement je ne suy mie enfourmes. Et auxi les ditz burgeois et jurats ount fait et de jour en autre fount faire les fouses entour le ville de Bourdeux.

Et vuelles savoir que unquorres le Counte d'Armaignac tient graunde assemblee de gents d'armes, et ait gaigne trois ou iiij bonnes villes et chastieaulx du Counte de Pardeac, a ce que disount: et tient le siege devant trois chastieaulx du dit Counte de Pardeac. Et[1] en une des ditz chastieaulx il ad grauntmentz de gents d'armes, et fount tresgraundes deffences en criant de tout jour, "*Saint George et Guienne.*"

---

and credence in this behalf.—And be pleased to know that the Governour of Bordeaux, and the jurats, and other councillors of the said city have ordained that all descriptions of persons residing within the said city shall make oath, on the Blessed Body of God, that they will be good and loyal to the King and to the crown of England, and to the city of Bordeaux; but as to the intent of this oath I am not at all informed. And also the said burgesses and jurats have made, and from one day to another have caused to be dug entrenchments around the town of Bordeaux.—And be pleased to know that the Count of Armagnac still keeps a very great company of men-at-arms, and has gained three or four good towns and castles from the Count of Pardeac, according to common report; and they are maintaining a siege before three castles belonging to the Count de Pardeac; and in one of the said castles he has exceeding many soldiers, and has made very great defences, crying out all day long, "*Saint George and Guienne.*"

---

[1] *Et*] Altered from "Et null."

Et vuelles savoir que le Erchevesque de Bourdeux, et tous les clerges, et autres sages diount et ount determene entre eulx, que par cause de ceste deleverance du dit chastiel de Boteville les Fraunceois ount . . . . . . . . . les treves.

Et vuelles savoir que les ditz Fraunceois fount tresgraunde assemblee de gents d'armes, mais de leur [destination et] entente je ne suy mise enfourmes unquores : mais Watt Clyfford, Capitaine de Courbuffin, escreveit une [lettre a] Janekyn Gravenour, Lieutenant du Chastiel de Fronsac, en disuant en ycelle dicte lettre que a ly estoit dit que [les ditz Fr]aunceois voudrent mettre le siege devaunt le Chastiel de Fronsac ; le quelle lettre estoit enseallee du seal d . . . . . . . . . du dit Clyfford. Et en certein le dit chastiel est trop malament envitaille et destoure affaire aucune [service. Des] quelles surdictes matieres vuelles estre bien avises, et d'icelles enfourmer le Counseil de nostre tressouverain Seignour le R[oy.

Et vuelles sa]voir que le Senechal voudroit aller

---

—And be pleased to know that the Archbishop of Bordeaux, and all the clergy, and other wise persons, say and have determined among themselves, that by reason of this giving up of the said castle of Boteville, the French have . . . . . . . . . . the truce.—And be pleased to know that these said French have made a very great assembly of men-at-arms, but as to their destination or intent I have not been at all informed as yet ; but Walter Clifford, Governour of Corbuffin, has written a Letter to Jenkin Gravenour, Lieutenant of the Castle of Fronsac, saying in this said letter that information had been given to him that the said French would lay siege to the castle of Fronsac ; the which letter was sealed with the seal of . . . . . . . . . of the said Clifford. And certainly the said castle is very badly victualled, and disabled from doing any service. Of the which above-mentioned matters be pleased to be well advised, and thereof to inform the Council of our most sovereign Lord the King.—And be pleased to

en la compaignie de Monsieur John de Bearn devers les Laundes . . . . . . . . . . . . . . . poeble par de la; mais le Counseil de nostre tressouverain Seigneur le Roy, ne moy, ne povouns avoir null . . . . . . . . . . . . . . . . . . . . . . . . . [ex]penses; et voire mes avoir empromptes de le dicte ville de Bourdeux viij francs. Est⌐ . . . . . . . . . . . . . . . . . . . . . ster sinon que parasseouns pour viiiᵉ mille.

Et vueilles savoir que les marchants . . . . . . . . . . . . . . . . . . . . . . . . . . . . . . . . . . . . Gascoignes venantz d'Engleterre counte . . . . . . . . novelles en disants que tresgrant . . . . . . . . . . . . . . . . . . . . . . . . . d'Engleterre a cause de la novelle impo[si-tion] . . . . de forte en Engleterre; c'est . . . . . . . . . . . . . . . . . . . . . . . . . . . . . . . Et dient que l'Archevesque [de Bourdeux] . . . . . . . . . . . . . . . . . . . . . . . . . . . . . . . . . . . . . . . de Bourdeux escrive a nostre tressouverain [Seigneur le Roy] . . . . . en]voier la grace que fe . . . . . . . . avoir la grace a moy donner par le . . . . . . . elle de Lincoln, a la quelle mati[ere] . . . . . . . suplie en tant come je puisse que a vous . . . . . . . eant sains offense de nostre dit tressouverain Seigneur le Roy et de sa roial Majeste et vous supplie . . . . . . . . . . . . . . . . . . faire a nostre tressouverain

---

know that the Seneschal was willing to go in the company of Master John de Bearn towards Landes . . . . . . . . . . . people over there; but the Council of our most sovereign Lord the King¹ . . . . . . . . . . . . . . . . . . . . . . . . . . . . . . . . . . .

\* \* \* \* \* \* \* \* \*

---

¹ The MS. is so badly burned in this place that anything like a coherent translation of the remain-ing fragments is impossible, and conjectural emendation of the text would be idle

Seigneur le Roy assavoir le . . . . . . . . . . attentives,
diligeantes, proufitables, et agre[ables . . . . . . . . . .
p]our li ait fait devant ces heures, et unquores fera
. . . . . . . [s'il] a Dieux plaist.

Et vuelles savoir que a cause [que l'Archevesque de]
Bourdeux, le Senechal, et autres Barons et Clerges sont
. . . . . si favorables a le Counte de Foix, que ils ne
le v[ueillent pa]s li desplaire ; et ne vueillent escrire
nulles lettres comfortables a Peyroat, Capitaine de
Chalis, pour [defense de le dit] chastiel : et pour
ce je ay escript une lettre bonne et comfortable
a le dit Peyroat, en li priant que mette bonne et
dilige[nte garde] entour le dit chastiel ; quar en
bref il avera bon secoure d'Engl[eterre] en hors
comme vous m'avez escript, et li ait envoie l'ad . . .
. . . . . Et comme ainsi soit que Roger Brymnor, et
le sergeant de nostre tressouv[erain] Seigneur le Roy,
et ij des compaignions du dit Roger vostres s[er-
viteurs], estoient trop mailament naffres et playes,
et un compaignion du dit Roger vostre serviteur
mourt en la place ; et le dit Roger et le ser-

---

And be pleased to know that because the Archbishop of
Bordeaux, the Seneschal, and the other Barons and Clergy are
. . . . . so favourable to the Count de Foix that they are not
willing to displease him in the least ; and they will not write
any comforting letters to Peyroat, the Governor of Chalus,
for the defence of the said castle. And on this account I have
written a good and comforting letter to the said Peyroat, and
praying him to keep good and diligent guard within around
the said castle ; for that in a short time he will have good
succour out of England, as you have written to me, and
I have sent to him . . . . . . . . And forasmuch as it is so,
Roger Brymnor, and the serjeant of our most sovereign Lord
the King, and two of the companions of the said Roger your
servants, have been exceedingly badly wounded and bruised,
and a companion of the said Roger, your servant, died on
the spot ; and the said Roger, and the serjeant, and others

geant, et des autres compaignons, vostres serviteurs, estoient pillies et roubbes si bien de harnes comme d'armes (?),[1] par les gents et serviteurs du Sire[2] de la Launde, et puis emprisonnes et menes dains le chastiel du Seigneur de la Launde ; et illeoques le dit Roger estoit pilles et roubbes autrefoiz : et ce feisant le service de nostre dit Seigneur le Roy et le vostre. Et ce par commission et mandament du Senechal et Counseil de nostre tressouverain Seigneur le Roy ; le quelle suisdit fait est repute et counte par de cea, que ce est le pluis graunt et le pluis hidouse offense que fuisse fait a nostre tressouverain Seigneur le Roy, cestes xl ans a et pluis passes ; et est commune fame par de cea que le dit Sire de la Launde, et ses gents en fercount leur pees,[3] et averount pardonnance de leur trespas du Roy nostre tressouverain Seigneur, et de vous, pour vj pipes de vin ; et

---

his companions, your servants, have been plundered and robbed as well of their harness as of their arms by the men and servants of the Lord of Lande, and have since been imprisoned and illtreated within the castle of the Lord of Lande ; and there, on other occasions, the said Roger has been plundered and robbed ; and that while doing the service of our said Lord the King and your own. And that, too, by the commission and commandment of the Seneschal and Council of our most sovereign Lord the King ; the which above-mentioned deed is reported and accounted over here to be a by far greater and more hideous offence than any that has been committed against our most sovereign Lord the King these forty years past and more ; and there is a common rumour over here that the said Lord of Lande, and his men, will make their peace, and will have pardon of their trespass from the King our most sovereign Lord and from you

---

[1] *d'armes*] "*dar*" MS.
[2] *du Sire*] Altered from "du dit Seigneur."

[3] *pees*] Altered from "peys."

ce serroit trop tresgraunt hounte et tresgraunt esclaindre a nostre dit tressouverain Seigneur le Roy, et a vous. Mais toutes foiz vous prie et supplie que vous plaise de ordenner bonnes et gracieuses Lettres de nostre tressouverain Seigneur le Roy, adroissees a le Seneschal, et son tressage Counseil par de cea, que[1] ils facent compliment et justice de les tresgraundes offences et trespas surdictes. Et que vous de vostre partie escrives a le Senechal et Counseil suisdit, et a Mestre Guilliem Boven, et a le Procureour Fiscal, au quel la cause appartient pour nostre tressouverain Seigneur le Roy.

Treshonnoure Seigneur et tresreverent Pere en Dieux, le Trestout-Puissant vous ait tout diz en Sa sainte garde, en corps et arme, et a vous ottroye joie et honnour, bonne vie et longe a treslonge duree!

Script a Bourdeux, le darrein jour d'April.

Le tout vostre humble Chappellein et serviteur,

JOHN MORHAY.

---

for six pipes of wine ; and this will be a most exceeding great disgrace, and a very great scandal against our most sovereign Lord the King, and against you. But even I pray and supplicate you that it would please you to ordain good and gracious Letters of our most Lord the King, addressed to the Seneschal, and to his most wise Council over here, that they cause satisfaction and justice to be done for these exceeding great offences and trespass above-mentioned. And that you, on your part, would write to the Seneschal and Council above-mentioned, and to Master William Boven, and to the Procurator-Fiscal, to whom the case appertains on the behalf of our most sovereign Lord the King.—Most honoured Lord and most reverend Father in God, the Most Almighty One have you always in His holy keeping, both in body and soul, and grant unto you joy and honour, good life and long, exceeding long to last!—Written at Bordeaux, the last day of April.

Your most humble chaplain and servant,

JOHN MORHAY.

---

[1] que] Altered from "que les sa."

Et, treshonnoure Seigneur et tresreverent Pere en Dieux, vueilles savoir que, le jour de la feisance d'icestes, est venues a Bourdeux Frere William Baynard, demourant a Courbuffin, le quel dist qu'il sount assembles en Lemoysin plus que mille basinets des Fraunceois, et count[e aussi] qu'ils mettrount le siege devant Courbuffin, et le vuellent avoir pour fourte de siege maugree de eulx ; quar plusours fois les Fraunceois ount requestis les capitaines et compaignons de Courbuffin qu'ils leur vendisent le dit chastiel, et a leur gree ce ne vuellent ils unquores faire.

Et vuelles savoir que est dit par le dit Frere William que les Fraunceois Mardi prochein venant mettrount siege devant le Chastiel de Chales, et ce a cause qu'ils ne vuellent deleverer le dit Chastiel de Chales au Counte de Foix affin que le Counte le poira deleverer au Duc d'Ourlieanx.

Et vuelles en oultre savoir en certein que, si ceste pais ne est pluis hastivement secoures de gents d'armes hors d'Engleterre avecque autres secours, il est

---

And most honoured Lord and most reverend Father in God, be pleased to know, that the day of the making of these presents, there is come to Bordeaux Brother William Baynard, a resident of Corbuffin, who says that there are assembled in Limousin more than a thousand helmets of the French, and he considers also that they will lay siege to Corbuffin and they will have it by strong siege in spite of them. Because oft-times the French have requested the keepers and comrades of Corbuffin to sell them the said castle, and thanks to them, they will not do it yet.—And be pleased to know that it has been said by the said Brother William, that the French, on the Tuesday next ensuing, will lay siege to the castle of Chalus, and that because they are not willing to deliver up the said castle of Chalus to the Count de Foix to the end that the Count may be able to deliver it up to the Duke of Orleans.—And be pleased, moreover, to know for certain, that, if this country be not more speedily succoured by armed men out of England, together

doubte que en breff tout sera perduz, que Dieux deffende ! Quar jamays en nostre temps ne fuit si semblable de estre perduz comme est de present. Et ce a cause du Counte de Foix s'il soit de la partie Fraunceoise, et par le Counte d'Armaignac et par le Sire de la Bret.

*Endorsed :* —" A mon treshonnoure Seignour et tresreverent Pere en Dieux, le Evesque
de Bath[1] . . : . . . . . . . . . . . . . de
Bourdeux."

with other succours, there is fear that in a short time it will be altogether lost, which God avert ! For never at all before in our time has it been so like to be lost as it is at present. And this because of the Count de Foix, if he be on the French side, and by the Count of Armagnac, and by the Lord of La Bret.

*Endorsed* : — " To my most honoured Lord and most reverend
Father in God, the Bishop of Bath . . .
, . . . . . . . . . . . of Bordeaux."

---

[1] Henry Bowet.

G G

# ADDENDA ET CORRIGENDA.

Page 15, *note*[1], *for* 18 . . . 1400, *read* 3 . . . 1401.

Page 56, l. 3 ; 58, l. 4 : Edybredschellis, (*see* Registr. Magn. Sigill. Scot. 157, 16 ; 176, 35.)

Page 56, l. 12. Galway, i. e. Galloway.

Page 56, l. 19. *for* Paleologus (MS.) *read* Palæologus.

Page 76, l. 15. " Janico," i. e. Janico Dartasso. Admiral of Ireland, (*see* Rymer VIII. 113 ; Rot. Pat. 5 Hen. IV. M. 10.)

Page 86, l. 17. "joioys" very indistinct, ( ? Irroys, i. e. Irish).

Page 87, l. 4. "dartus" (? Dartasso, or Dartassus; *see* above p. 76).

Page 121 (and elsewhere) *for* Eric X. *read* Eric IX.

Page 174, l. 14. *for* exemere (MS.) *read* eximere.

Page 184, l. 1. *for* preciso (MS.) *read* præciso.

Page 186, l. 21. *for* ad *read* et.

Page 229, l. 10. in . . . . . — Mauri (?).

Page 296, l. 32. *for* Swynford *read* Swynborn.

Page 339, l. 6. *for* impositæ.   Necnon *read* impositæ ; necnon

Page 354, l. 33. *for* destributionem *read* distributionem.

Page 448, l. 32. debrides, ? dismounted, dismantled.   *Or,* " de brides." *See* Glossary, Vol. II.

LONDON:
Printed by George E. Eyre and William Spottiswoode,
Printers to the Queen's most Excellent Majesty.
For Her Majesty's Stationery Office.

LaVergne, TN USA
28 January 2010
171417LV00003B/21/A